S. Senex

Old Glasgow and its Environs

Historical and Topographical

S. Senex

Old Glasgow and its Environs
Historical and Topographical

ISBN/EAN: 9783743414990

Manufactured in Europe, USA, Canada, Australia, Japa

Cover: Foto ©Andreas Hilbeck / pixelio.de

Manufactured and distributed by brebook publishing software (www.brebook.com)

S. Senex

Old Glasgow and its Environs

OLD GLASGOW

AND

ITS ENVIRONS,

HISTORICAL AND TOPOGRAPHICAL.

BY

S E N E X.

GLASGOW: DAVID ROBERTSON.
LONDON: LONGMAN & CO.

MDCCCLXIV.

ERRATA.

At page 3, line 3, read "*favore*" for "*favone.*"
At page 3, line 9, read "*ecclesiae*" for "*ecclisae.*"
At page 3, line 28, read "*fossa*" for "*fassa.*"
At page 3, line 35, read "*adeo*" for "*a deo.*"
At page 4, line 2, read "*orationum*" for "*ovationum*"
At page 349, 8th line from the bottom, read "1794" for "1194."

TO THE

Glasgow Archæological Society,

THE FOLLOWING LOOSE JOTTINGS,

RELATING TO

GLASGOW AND ITS ENVIRONS,

ARE RESPECTFULLY DEDICATED

BY

"SENEX."

PREFACE.

It was altogether a chance circumstance which suggested to me the idea of noting down the following loose and desultory jottings regarding Glasgow and its Environs, and particularly respecting the Low Green and its neighbourhood. I possessed little information on the subject of the early history of this our first public park, except what had been taken notice of by our different Glasgow historians; but being in the 92nd year of my age, and remembering the state of the locality in question, shortly after the date when the Plan annexed to this pamphlet was drawn up, and seeing that no part of our city has undergone greater changes than this portion of it, I have thought that a few notices regarding the said locality may perhaps be acceptable to many of our citizens, especially to those who take delight in lingering over stories of olden time.

I eschew all claim to any original information of importance as to the early history of this district of our city, and now come forward merely as a gleaner from the works of others, interspersed with a few of my own memoranda, loosely thrown together.

As I have before stated, it was an accidental circumstance

which turned my attention towards writing a few notanda
regarding the Low Green of Glasgow, viz.:—the following letter,
addressed to me as "Senex," from a stranger:—

"To SENEX,—SIR,—Many friends here, and elsewhere, would
" be highly gratified were you to be good enough to write any
" reminiscences of St Andrew's Episcopal Chapel here. It is
" now the oldest of the Episcopal communion in Scotland, and
" for many years was the sole chapel in the west, and was
" frequented by the Dukes of Hamilton, the Lords of Douglas,
" the Cathcart family, the Pollocs, and the *elite* of Glasgow
" and vicinity. You might have materials for a few articles,
" which would take well.—Yours truly,

"A. B."

To this request I answered as follows :—

" To A. B.,—SIR,—Although it is not in my power to give a
" satisfactory account of the early history of the first Glasgow
" Episcopal Chapel, nevertheless, as I possess a plan of the
" grounds on which the said Chapel and St Andrew's Church
" were erected during the course of last century, I think it may
" be interesting to many of our citizens to look back to the
" days when the lands in question were lying waste, and open
" to the public, as if they had been a mere common in connec-
" tion with the Old Green of Glasgow.

" Perhaps no part of Glasgow has undergone so great a
" change within the memory of our octogenarian citizens as the
" Old Green and its environs, in consequence of the Camlachie
" and Molendinar burns having been arched over, and formed

" into a tunnel ; from the opening up of the south part of the
" Gallowgate, by the formation of London Street and St An-
" drew's Square ; by the erection of the splendid mansions of
" Charlotte Street upon the ancient lands of Merkdailly ; and,
" in short, by the whole of the Saltmarket, and the lands in the
" vicinity of the Green, having been pulled down and rebuilt,
" so that the entire space in question has put on quite a new
" face, and would scarcely be recognised by our forefathers, had
" they returned to us on furlough.—Yours truly,

" SENEX."

Such, then, was the origin of the following sheets.

CONTENTS.

CONTENTS OF THE ADDITAMENTA.

ILLUSTRATIONS.

PLAN
of the
LOW GREEN
of
Glasgow,
AND ITS ENVIRONS
1760

GALLOWGATE
ROAD TO EDINBURGH

BOWLING
GREEN

BRIDGES ST

Calton's
Ground

Garden's
Ground

Bleach Ground

NEW CHURCH

MERE DAILY
LANDS.

PART OF THE
GALLOWGATE
GREEN

Bleach
Ground

Dr Wardrop's
Garden

MERE DAILY
LANDS.

BRIGGATE

CASTLE BOUND

Clerk's Lodge

LOW   GREEN

SCALE OF 300 YARDS.

FOOT RID

WASHING HOUSE

PART
OF THE
HIGH GREEN

RIVER   CLYDE

THE POINT ISLE

OLD GLASGOW AND ITS ENVIRONS.

CHAPTER I.

The Old Green of Glasgow—Charter to Bishop Turnbull in 1450—King's Isles—The Bishop's Forest—Weaponschawings, and penalties for non-attendance—Petition of Hugh Tennent to the Court of Session—Bridgeton in 1725—Walkinshaw of Barrowfield—Orr of Barrowfield—Advertisements of Sale of Barrowfield.

WITH the exception of its ancient Cathedral, no part of Glasgow is so highly endeared to and venerated by our citizens as their splendid public Green of olden time, with its beautiful margin, the river Clyde flowing along through the whole extent of its southern boundary, and its fine circuitous drive around its verdant lawn and graceful slopes. Notwithstanding its formidable rivals, the West-end Pleasance, and South-side Park, the Green of Glasgow still stands conspicuous in the eyes and in the memories of all ranks, like an aged oak or sturdy veteran, recalling to remembrance many thrilling events and youthful sports which there took place during the primitive era of our city. There are few individuals who have not felt a sensation of delight arising from a retrospective view of the scenes and doings of the early period of their lives; and where is the octogenarian citizen of St Mungo who does not remember with rapture the many merry sports, stirring scenes, and military displays which took place on the Green of Glasgow, during his juvenile years, to say nothing of this having been once the favourite mall of the golfer, and the fashionable parade of the Glasgow belles of olden time. Referring back, however, to the Low Green of Glasgow and its environs, as the same stood a century ago, in the immediate neighbourhood of nauseous manufactures, we must not look with too critical an eye at its then objectionable drawbacks, which would now be considered fatal to it as a place of healthful recreation and amusement: but we must take into account that times are changed —*et nos matamur in illis.* Our grandsires were then happy, and con-

B

tented to live in thatched houses, crowded flats and lowly dwellings, and even our Virginia lords to congregate in the polluted atmosphere of the Briggate. But are the Crescenters, Circusers, and Royal Terracers of the present day more happy than those old Fiddler's Closers, Saltmarketers, or Briggaters ?—I doubt it very much ; for, notwithstanding all the cleaning measures of our Deans of Guild, our Police Captains, and our City Superintendents, I believe that there is little or no difference as to the duration of human life, between the two periods, however great the difference may be as to comfort. On the other hand, be it remembered that there were, of old, no Police Assessments, Water Charges, Gas Levies, or Poors' Rates to grumble about, so that our grandsires could live happy and contented, keeping their household establishments alone on what is now paid in taxes by their present descendants. It is wonderful how easily a person can complacently support a little inconveniency, when his pocket is not touched ; and I verily believe that there are many now in our city who would prefer the old state of things with all its drawbacks, to the present polished position of city matters with its heavy assessments.

I shall now, without more ado, proceed to jot down a few loose gleanings regarding the old Green of Glasgow, and its environs, &c., premising, however, that I make no pretensions of giving a regular history of the district in question as of old, or of its modern state of embellishment, but only transcribing of a few extracts from the works of our Glasgow historians and others, along with some of the reminiscences of my early days, by way of help to a future more able Glasgow historiographer. I lay no claim to the disquisition and skill of an antiquary.

Our Glasgow historians have given us no information regarding the state of the Low Green of Glasgow and its environs, previous to the year 560, when St Kentigern founded a religious establishment in Glasgow, and even during the period when the See of the City was held by the Roman Catholic Bishops, no mention has been made in any public record when this Park became the property of the community. It is said, however, to have been included in the grant made to William Turnbull, Lord of Provan and Bishop of Glasgow, on the 20th of April, 1450, by the following charter :—

" CHARTER BY JAMES II., 1450."

Jacobus, Dei gratia Rex Scotorum, omnibus probis hominibus totius terræ suæ, clericis, et laicis, salutem. Sciatis nos, in honorem

et laudem Dei omnipotentis, et gloriosæ Virginis Mariæ, ac beati
Kentigerni confessoris, patroni Ecclesiae Glasguensis, in qua canonicus
existemus, et omnium sanctorum, nec non pro singulari favone, zelo,
et delectione, quos erga reverendum in Christo patrem Willehelmum,
praelatum ejustem ecclesiae, modernum nostrum conciliarum intime
dilectum gerimus propter sua merita servitia, grata atque fidelia nobis
longo tempore impensa, dedisse, concessisse, et hac prasente carta
nostra, confirmasse praefato reverendo in Christo patri Willelmo
Episcopo Glasguensi, et suis successoribus, Glasguensis ecclisae
episcopis, pro perpetuo, quod habeant, teneant, et possideant, per-
petuis futuris temporibus, civitatem Glasguensem, Baroniam de
Glasgu, et terras vulgariter vocatas Bichopforest, in liberam, puram,
et meram Regalitatem, tenendas et habendas praefatas civitatem
Baroniam et terras vocates Bichopforest, dicto Willelmo, et suis
successoribus, Episcopis ecclesiae Glasguensis, de nobis successoribus
nostris, in meram, puram liberam Regalitatem, seu regaliam in feodo
et hereditate in perpetuum, cum universis commoditatibus et pro-
ficuis, dictis civitati et terris pertinentibus, in boscis, planis, moris,
moressiis, viis, semitis, aquis, stagnis, rivolis, pratis, pascuis, et
pasturis, molendinis, multuris, et eorum sequelis, aucupationibus,
venationibus, piscationibus, aquarum decursibus, petariis, turbariis,
carbonariis, lapicidiis, lapide et calce, fabrilibus, bracinis, brueriis, et
genestis, cum homagiis, curiis, et earum exitibus, eschaetis, libero
introitu et exita, bludewits, heryeld, et marchetis mulierum, cum
libera foresta et warrenna, cum forisfacturis, justiciis, antequisque con-
suetudinibus, customis, ac cum iteneribus justitiariae, et camerariae,
et earum exitibus portubus et passagiis, cum capella, in liberam,
puram, et integram Regalitatem, seu regaliam, cum furca et fassa,
sok, sak, thol, them, infangandtheif, outfangandtheif, handsoki, cum
tenandiis et tenandriis, et libere tenentium servitus : nec non cum
piscationibus, antiquis usibus, et advocationibus ecclesiarum, aliisque
omnibus et singulis libertatibus, commoditatibus, et asiamentis, ac
justis pertinentiis quibuscumque, tam non nominatis quam nominatis
ad Regalitatem, seu regaliam, spectantibus, seu quovis modo juste
spectare volentibus, in futurum, et a deo libere, quiete, plenarie,
integre, honorifice, bene et in pace, in omnibus et per omnia,
sicut aliqua regalitas, seu regalia cuicumque ecclesiae, aut personis
ecclesiasticis quibuscumque, in regno nostro liberius, quietius, aut
hononorificentius, concedetur aut donatur : reddendo annuatim
inde dictus Willelmus, et successores sui, Glasguensis ecclesiae
Episcopi, nobis haeredibus et successoribus nostris, unam rosam

rubeam, ad festum nativitatis beati Johannis Baptistæc, apud Glasgu, nomine albae firmae, si petatur : et ovationum suffragia devotorum tantum, pro omni alio onere, exactione, questione, demanda, seu servitio sacculari, quæ de dictis civitate, baronia, et terris vocatis Bischopforest, cum pertinentiis, per quoscumque juste exegi poterunt quomodo libet, seu requiri.   In cujas rei testimonium, præsenti cartae nostrae magnum Sigillum nostrum apponi praecepimus.   Testibus, Reverendo in Christo patre Jacobo, Episcopo Sancti Andreae, Willo dno. Creighton, nostro Cancellario, et consanguineo praedelecto : carissimo consanguineo nostro Willelmo, Comite de Douglas et de Avendale, dno. Galwidiae : venerabile in Christo patre Andrea Abbote de Melros nostro confessore et thesaurio : dilectis consanguineis nostris Patricio, dno. Glamis, magistro hospitii nostri : Willo : dno. Sommervil ; Andrea dno. Le Gray : magistris Joanni Arous, aregediocono Glasguensi, et Georgio de Schoriswod, Rectore de Cultre.   Apud Edinburgh 20 die mensis Aprilis Anno Domini 1450, et regni nostri 14°.

TRANSLATION.

James, by the grace of God, King of Scots, to all our faithful subjects of the land, as well clergy as laity, greeting.   Know ye, that we, for the honour and praise of Almighty God, and the glorious Virgin Mary, and the blessed Kentigern, confessor, patron of the church of Glasgow, wherein we are esteemed a Canon, and of all the saints, and for the singular favour, zeal, and affection which we bear to the Reverend Father in Christ, William,* present Bishop of the said church, our well-beloved counsellor, and for his good deeds and faithful services done to us for time past, to have given and granted, and by this our charter confirmed, to the said Reverend Father in Christ, William, Bishop of Glasgow, and his successors, Bishops of the church of Glasgow, to be for ever held, possessed, and enjoyed by them in all time coming, the city of Glasgow, barony of Glasgow, and lands commonly called Bishop's Forest, in pure and mere regality, to be holden and held, the said city, barony, and lands called Bishop's Forest, by the said William and his successors, Bishops of the church of Glasgow, of us and our successors, in free, pure, and mere regality, in fee and heritage for ever, with the whole commodities and property of the said city and lands, with their pertinents,

---

* William Turnbull, elected bishop in 1448.   He took a journey to Rome, and died there in 1454.   (Keath's Bishops, p. 251.)

in woods, plains, moors, marshes, ways, paths, waters, lakes, rivulets, meadows, pastures, and pasturages, mills, multures, and sequels of the same, hawkings, huntings, fishings, water courses, peats, turfs, coal pits, quarries, stone and lime, smithies, kilns, breweries, and brooms, with vassalages, courts and their issues, escheets, free ish and entry, bloodwits, herelds, and marchetis mulierum, with free forest and warren, with the fee of the forfeitures of courts and ancient usages, together with the customs of the chamberlain, and itinerant courts and their issues, ports and passages, with the chapel, into a free, pure, and entire regality, or royalty, with pit and gallows, sok, sak, thol, them, infangandtheif, outfangandtheif, hamisukkin, with tenants and tenandries, and services of free tenants, together with fishings, ancient usages and advocations of churches, and all and singular other liberties, commodities and easements, and just pertinents whatsoever, as well not named as named, belonging to a regality or royalty, any manner of way in time coming, and that freely, quietly, fully, wholly, honourably, well, and in peace in all things, as any other regality or royalty, given or granted to any other church or ecclesiastical person whatsoever, in our kingdom, paying therefore, yearly, the said William and his successors, Bishops of the church of Glasgow, to us, our heirs and successors, a red rose upon the feast of the nativity of the blessed John the Baptist, at Glasgow, in name of blanch-farm, if asked only, and the assistance of their prayers, and that for all other further exaction, question, demand, or secular service, that can be any way exacted or demanded, for or furth of the said city, barony, and lands called Bishop's Forest, and pertinents. In testimony whereof, we have ordered our great seal to be appended to this our present charter, in presence of the Reverend Father in Christ, James, Bishop of St Andrew's, William, Lord Crichton, our chancellor, and beloved cousin, our dear cousin William, Earl of Douglas and Avondale, Lord of Galloway, the venerable Father in Christ, Andrew, Abbot of Melrose, our confessor and treasurer, our beloved cousin, Patrick Lord Glamis, master of our household, William, Lord Sommervile, Andrew, Lord Gray, Messrs John Arous, Archdeacon of Glasgow, and George Schoriswood, rector of Coulter. At Edinburgh, the 20th day of the month of April, in the year of our Lord 1450, and 14th year of our reign.

In the copy of the chartulary, in the library of the University of Glasgow, there is a copy of the above charter, said to have been

taken "Ex autographo in archivis ecclesiae Glasguensis apud
" ———— in pyxide lignea sub litera ——— huic cartae appensum
" est sigillum magnum Scotiae et cera alba integrum."

The foregoing grant is very extensive, and appears to have
included almost every right of value which could have arisen out of
the lands within the bounds of the Bishop's Forest; which forest
extended several miles around Glasgow, but its exact boundaries are
not known.

It may be remarked, however, that there is no direct gift of the
river Clyde, nor of any part of it which flowed through the lands of
the Bishop's Forest. The word *rivolis* can refer only to rivulets, or
small brooks, such as the Molendinar and Camlachie burns, and not
to a large river like the Clyde. There is nothing said in the charter
regarding, "Fluvii, Rivii, Amnes, or Flumina," neither is any
mention made of Islands, (Insulae or Inches), of which there were
then several in the Clyde, near Glasgow. About the close of the
14th century Robert III. granted the King's Isles, below Rutherglen,
to Robert Hall. (Origines Parochiales, p. 64.) The charter in
question is drawn up quite in general terms, but it is sufficient to
include the Camlachie and Molendinar burns, under the word *rivolis*,
and the Green of Glasgow, under the words *pratis, pascuis, et
pasturis.* The ancient surface of the parish, unless near the river,
was, with very few exceptions, a forest of wood and bush land.
(Origines Parochiales, p. 11.) And the Gorbals lands were not
included as being within the bounds of the said parish. (Page 1.)

From the above circumstances it may be inferred that the north
bank of the river Clyde then formed the south boundary of the
Bishop's Forest.

1632. "In the Testament and Inventur of the guidis geir, debtis,
" and sowmes of money, pertaint to umquhile, James, Archbishop
" of Glasgow, there was owing, 'the fewaries, farmaris, tennants,
" occupiers, and possessiors of the lands and baronie of Bishopis-
" fforrister, xxxiij. li. vj. s. viij. d., as the few duties, landis, the
" crope and yeir of God, above written." (Hamilton's Lanarkshire,
page 149.)

The above shows very clearly that the Bishop's Forest was then
lying in a state of nature, and consisted almost entirely of waste and
uncultivated lands, overgrown with forest trees and bush wood, the
rental of the whole forest, extending to many miles round Glasgow,
being only £2 15s 6½d., sterling—(£33 6s 8d, Scots.)

The Bishop's Forest most probably embraced the whole of our

Eastern and Western Commons, reaching from about Parkhead, on the east, to Hamiltonhill on the west, and bounded on the south by the river Clyde; this, of course, included the Green and the lower parts of the City of Glasgow. As the early inhabitants of our city were then congregated on the high-lands, in the immediate neighbourhood of the Bishop's Palace, they naturally resorted to the commons, in their near vicinity, for pasturing their cattle, or for their public displays and pastimes, in preference to descending to the more distant, low, and marshy lands of the Green of Glasgow. Accordingly, we find that the Green was not then generally used for public exhibitions, or military displays, such as the Weaponschawings, which were held upon the Eastern Common principally, at a place thereon called the *Butts*, near to the present Infantry Barracks, Gallowgate Street; the latter name showing that this Common was also the locality where criminals were executed.

The great meetings for Weaponschawings were held quarterly, by Act of Parliament, and no French conscription could have been more strictly enforced, than was our ancient call of Weaponschawing, as the following Act shows.

" Act Third Parliament, James I., xj. of March, 1425.—*Item.*
" It is ordaned in the second Parliament of our Sovereign Lord the
" King, that ilke Schireffe of the Realme soulde gar Weaponschawings
" be maid foure times ilke zeire, in als monie places as were speedefull,
" within his Bailliarie, bot the maner how Weaponschawings sulde
" be received was not appoynted. Herefor, Our Lorde the King
" throw the haill ordinance of his Parliament statutis, that ilke
" Gentleman hauand ten pounds woorth of land or mair, be suffi-
" cientlic harnished and armed with Basret, haill legge, Harnes,
" sworde, speare, and dagger; and gentleman hauand lesse extentes,
" of landes, nor na landes, salbe armed at their gudlie power, after the
" discretion of the Schireffes, bot all other zeamen of the realme betwixt
" xvj. and sextie zeir, salbe sufficientlic bowed and schafted with
" sworde and buckler, and knife. And that al the burgesses and
" indwellers within the Burrow townes of the realme, in like maner be
" anarmed and harnished and make weaponschawings within the
" Burrowis foure times in the zier, and that be the Aldermen and
" Baillies, vpon the quhilk, the Chamerlane and his Deputes sall
" know and execute the said things. And that all men, Seculares of
" the Realme, be weil purvayed of the said harness and weapons, be
" the feast of the Nativitie of our Lord Jesus Christ next to cum,
" under the pains follow, and : That is to say, of ilk gentilman that

" defaltis at the first weaponschawing fourtie schillinges, and at the
" other default fourtie schillings, and at the third default ten
" punds, and as meikle als oft times as he defaultis afterward.
" And of ilk bow-man at the first faulte ten schillinges, at the
" other default ten schillinges, and at the third fourtie schillinges.
" And swa furth als oft-times as he beis funden faultise afterward."
Burgh Records, 11th October, 1575.—" The quhilk daye Johne
" Wilsone, and James Anderson, flesche^{rs} burgessis of Glasgw, ar
" fund in ye amchia! and unlawis for absenting yame frae ye generall
" wapinschawing, haldin on ye grein, on ye x daye of October,
" instant.   Their being w! in ye toune ye said daye and esteptuslie,
" abydand, yairfra, and drame gevin y! upon."

It appears from another entry in the Burgh Records, dated 21st
March, 1578, that the fines levied for non-attendance at the
Weaponschawings, were appropriated towards causewaying the public
streets of the city.

" 1578, Wapinschawing.—The quhilk day the prouest, baillies,
" and counsale, witht dekynis, pntlie convenit, hes appoyntet yain
" wapinshchawing according to ye statute to be on ye daye of ye
" Symerhill nixt, yet yae be as yae are comandit, ilk persown vnder
" ye pane of xxs., to be tane be ye discretioun of ye puest, baillies,
" and counsale, and to be bestowit on ye calsaye making." (For
an account of the battle of the " Butts," in 1543, in which the
citizens were defeated, see Pagan's Glasgow, p. 16, and Glasgow
Pillaged.)

It may be here remarked that " Butts," (where our Weaponschawings took place) is not a Scotch word, but is derived from the
French, thus, " But, Bute, Butte, (Marque á quoi l'on vise.)"   " A
" mark at which a person aims."   Jamieson says, " Our sense of the
" word may be from the French ' Butte,' an open or void space
" appropriated for archery;" but he might have added, that when a
man is made an object of ridicule, he is said to have been made a
" Butt" of.

The Eastern Common where our Weaponschawings took place, appears at a more recent date to have been a large open waste, with roads
running through it in all directions, which Common the public seem
to have used with all manner of freedom, and without restraint, not
only by traversing it, *ad libitum*, but also by digging up, and
carrying off, stones, clay, turfs, and peats from it, and for so
interfering, they apparently were never challenged by the Magistrates or other public authorities.

I have in my possession a Court of Session Paper, dated 10th February, 1772, being the Petition of Hugh Tennent, the grand-father* of Hugh Tennent, Esq., of Wellpark, to the Lords of Session, requesting power to enclose his lands, then part of the said Eastern Common.

Mr Tennent in his Petition to the Court,

" Humbly sheweth,

" That to the North-east of the Town of Glasgow, there is a " considerable extent of ground, which originally belonged to the " Town, and was possessed *pro indiviso*, as a commonty by the " different inhabitants of the borough. At the East-end of this " commonty at that corner of it furthest removed from the town, " there is a stone quarry, called the Sheep-quarry, belonging to the " borough. A number of years ago, the Magistrates and Town " Council of Glasgow, considering that this ground, so long as it " remained a commonty, or undivided waste, was of little advantage " to the borough, resolved to divide and parcel it out among " individuals, who might cultivate and enclose it, and who would " be willing to pay a price for the same. The Magistrates, did, " therefore, first grant leases to persons willing to take tacks of " certain parts of the commonty; and afterwards they granted " feus thereof to different persons, who agreed to become pur-" chasers, with this reservation only, that the Town should still have " right to the stone and coal within the ground, and the necessary " roads to and from the same. The Petitioner purchased the lands " of Easter Commonty, being part of the foresaid commonty, from " the Magistrates of Glasgow; the same having been exposed " to public roup, in the year 1755, and he obtained a feu " contract from them in the year 1763. The quarry above-" mentioned, the right to which the Magistrates had reserved, and " to a road to and from the town thereto, lies at the east-end of the " petitioner's property, and at the time of the purchase, the road " from the town to the quarry went through the middle of his " property. Nay, it appears from the proof which has been led in " this process, that persons going to and from the quarry did not " observe one uniform road, but sometimes followed one track, " sometimes another, across the ground, now the Petitioner's pro-" perty, as humour or inclination directed. The Petitioner's property " was much lessened in value by these roads running through the

---

* Mr Hugh Tennent, Senr., was born in 1695, and died in 1776.

" middle of it; they not only encroached upon a great part of his
" ground, but put it out of his power to enclose it."

Proof in this case having been led, David Kirkland depones,
" That there were roads every airth through the said Easter
" Common, till the same was feued and enclosed."

James Henderson depones, "That during the time deponed on, (viz.,
" twelve or thirteen years prior to the year 1769,) there were many
" roads passing through the same from east to west." John Scott
(being interrogated) " If there were many different roads through
" the common from the east to the west, and from the north to
" the south, and whether he has known clay and stones digged forth
" of that moor, and feal and divot cut thereon, which were carried
" to different places by the different roads ? depones affirmative.
" James Miller depones, That the lands called Easter Common,
" till such time as they were enclosed, were all used as a
" commonty, and for casting feal, and digging clay by the
" Burgesses of Glasgow; and that he never knew any body
" quarrelled for so using thereof."

Dr Cleland in his Annals (p. 30,) says, that about the end of the
17th century the ground adjoining the east side of the City,
denominated the Gallow-muir, Borough Roads, or Blackfaulds,
were used as a grazing common for the cattle belonging to the
citizens. In 1705, Mr John Walkinshaw, of Renfrewshire, purchased a great part of those lands, and began to feu out ground
for a village which he called Barrowfield, since known by the
name of Bridgeton. The progress of this village was very slow,
for in the year 1724 he had only feued nineteen small lots. At this
period the Town, in conjunction with the Trades' House, became
proprietors of the whole, and it remained in their hands till 1731,
when they conveyed it to Mr John Orr, a merchant in Glasgow, who
was more successful in disposing of the ground than his predecessors.

It appears, however, that the lands above mentioned had received the name of " Barrowfield" before the time of Mr Walkinshaw's purchase, as is shown by the following extract from the
Burgh Records of Council, 25th August, 1643.

"That George Duncan of Barrowfield gave 6000 merks to be
" wait upon a bell to be hung in the steeple of the Blackfriar's
" Kirk, to be rung every morning at Five."* When Rutherglen

* " 4th February, 1657.—John Duncan, of Barrowfield, heir of George Duncan, of
" Barrowfield, his Father brother sone,—in a piece of land callit Deufield," E. 4s.—
(Retours).

Bridge came to be built in 1775, the lands next the bridge received the appellation of " Bridgeton," in honour of the bridge. This bridge was said to have cost only £1800 sterling, of which sum there was about £1000 sterling contributed by the Burgesses of Rutherglen, and the bridge was made free of toll. It is curious to contrast the small expense of building the Rutherglen Bridge across the Clyde, with the enormous outlay for erecting the Broomielaw and Stockwell Bridges of modern times ; one year's interest of the respective costs of the latter bridges would amount to more than the whole cost of the Rutherglen Bridge.

John Orr, mentioned by Cleland, was the grandfather of John Orr, late Town-Clerk of Glasgow, and was Bailie of the City in 1719. He was elected Rector of the University in 1734, and made a present of £500 sterling in aid of its library.

With regard to Mr Walkinshaw, the following notice is taken of him in Crawfurd's Renfrewshire, page 91,—" Gavin Walkinshaw, " of that ilk, thought fit, in the year 1683, to alienate his estate of " Walkinshaw to James Walkinshaw, merchant in Glasgow, second " son of John Walkinshaw of Barrowfield, a cadet of his family who " died in the year 1708 ; his estate devolved upon John Walkin- " shaw, now of Walkinshaw, his son and heir." So far as I have seen none of our Glasgow historians have informed us of Mr Walkinshaw's purchases of the lands known as the Eastern Common : but the following extract will throw some light on the subject, and show that Mr Walkinshaw purchased Barrowfield before the year 1693, and not in 1705, as Cleland states,—

" March 10th, 1693.

" Joannes Walkinshaw de Barrowfield, haeres Joannes Walkin- " shaw de Barrowfield, patris,—in 4 libratis terris antiqui extensus " terrarum de Barrowfield, comprehendentibus terras nuncupatus " Nicalhouse, Litle Park, et Broomward cum decimi, de Broom- " ward inclusis, et mancriei loco de Barrowfield :—33½ acris tanquam " parte aliarum 40 soliditarum terrarum de Barrowfield, omnibus " infra parochiam et regalitatem de Glasgow : E.£5 16s 5d, &c., " feudi Firmae—terris nuncupatis Cumlachie, comprehendentibus 1½ " acram aliquando spectantem ad Jacobem Bredwoodet Gulielmum " Andersone, infra territorium burgi de Glasgow :—posteriori " tenemento cum horto in dicto burgo ex occidentali lattere viac de " de Saltmercat—E. servitium burgi. xiiii. 292."—(Retours.)

TRANSLATION.

" John Walkinshaw, of Barrowfield, heir of John Walkinshaw of
" Barrowfield, his Father, in the four pound land of old extent of
" the lands of Barrowfield, comprehending the lands called Nical-
" house, Little Park, and Broomward, with the teinds of Broom-
" ward included, and the Manor Place of Barrowfield—33½ acres
" part of the other forty shilling land of Barrowfield, all lying
" within the Parish and Regality of Glasgow. E., £5 16s 5d, &c.,
" in feu — the lands called Camlachie comprehending 1½ acres
" formerly portioning to James Bredwood and William Andersone,
" within the territory of the said Burgh of Glasgow :—the back
" tenement with the Garden in the said Burgh on the west side of
" the street of Saltmarket, to be held Burgage."—10th March, 1693.
—(Retours).

Mr Walkinshaw was eldest merchant bailie of Glasgow in 1660, 1665,
and 1673; and it is unfortunate that we have not learned from any of
our historians what was the price which he paid for the above
mentioned lands. Mr Walkinshaw belonged to the clique of the
Blythswoods, Bells, Andersons, and Hamiltons, who then ruled the
City at their pleasure, and who appear to have shared the greatest
part of our great Eastern and Western Commons among themselves. Price paid by them unknown.

Cromwell, by letter dated 30th September, 1657, ordered the
election of the Magistrates of Glasgow to be indefinitely deferred ;
in consequence of which, and the death of Cromwell the ensuing
year, (3rd September 1658,) followed by the troubled times of the
Restoration, the said clique and their party continued to vote
themselves into office, and became supreme in Glasgow till the close
of that century. Hence the loss of the largest portion of our
Eastern and Western Commons, then parcelled out among the
leaders of the clique.

The death of Mrs Walkinshaw is thus announced in the *Glasgow
Mercury* of 23rd Nov., 1780 :—" Edinburgh, 28th Nov., 1780.—On
" Saturday last, (21st Nov.,) died here, aged 97, Mrs Walkinshaw
" of Barrowfield."

For an interesting account of the Walkinshaw family I must
refer to an article in "Glasgow, Past and Present," vol. 3, page 714, and
following, by our learned antiquarian fellow-citizen, J. B., who has
thrown more light upon the former state of the eastern parts of our
City, than all the other Glasgow historians put together. See also
Crawfurd's Renfrewshire, page 90. But to return to the subject,

there were several other feuars of the Western Common before Mr Walkinshaw made the above purchase.

" Sept. 16, 1691.

" Jacobus Parland haeres Joannis Parland, mercatoris burgensis
" de Glasgow, patris,—in 4½ acris terrarum jacentibus in illa parte
" vocata 'Fauld,' infra baronium et regalitatem de Glasgow,—E.
" 23rd." (This was part of the lands of Blackfaulds, Caltonmouth.)

" Sept. 16, 1691.

" Jacobus Parland haeres Elizabathae Stewart conjugis Joannis
" Parland mercatoris in Glasgow, matris—in 4 acris tanquam
" dimidio 8 acrarum terrarum arabilium de Barrowfield, et com-
" prehendentibus duo lie muire riggs, infra baroniam et regalitatem
" de Glasgow,—cum prato nuncupato Reidclothglott.—E. 2s, &c."
(Retours.) The Reidclothglott was the Camlachie Burn.

" October 24, 1676.

" Mariota Hamiltoune haeres magistri Thomas Hamiltoune
" doctoris medicinae in burgo de Glasgow, patris,—in botho
" mercatoria in dicto burgo ex orientali latere viae regiae nuncu-
" patae Saltmercat ; 3 acris terrae infra territorium dicti
" uburgi—4 acris terrarum infra territorium dicti burgi in
" parte vocata 'the Newgallowmour :'—2 terris jacentibus dis-
" contigue in illa parte vocata Newgallowmour :—2 terris cum horto
" infra territorium dicti burgi propa croftam vocatum Egleshawes
" Croft,—E. firma burogalis—xxxiii. 64." (Retours.)

On the 9th of August, 1786, the lands and Barony of Barrowfield were exposed to Sale, by Public Roup, John Orr of Barrowfield
having settled his affairs, which had been in a very embarrassed
state for a considerable time.

" *Glasgow Journal*, 26th December, 1776."

" The Trustees of John Orr of Barrowfield, and Matthew Orr of
" Stobcross, have now settled their affairs in such a manner as will
" enable them to relinquish the trust-right, and have already paid
" off the greatest part of the debts—their creditors who have not
" already been paid, are desired to call for payment ; on which the
" Trustees propose to divest themselves of the trust and reinvest J.
" and M. Orr."

" *Glasgow Mercury*, 20th July, 1786."

" To be Sold, by Public Roup, on Wednesday, the 9th day of
" August next, within the Tontine Tavern, Glasgow, between the
" hours of One and Three afternoon,

" The lands and barony of Barrowfield, with the lands of Cam-
" lachie, Gateside, Selkrigs acres, and some Borough lands
" adjoining to them, all lying contiguous in the immediate vicinity
" of the City of Glasgow, and Barony Parish of Glasgow and
" County of Lanark. The gross rent of this estate for 1786,
" (including £110 per annum of coal lordship,) is,   £1215   1   8½
" Deduct public burdens, including land tax, ...   58 17   8

                   " Nett Rent, ...   £1156   4   0½

" The upset price of the whole, if set up in one
   " Lot, will be £20,000   0   0
" The barony of Barrowfield holds of the crown, and is valued in
" the cess-books of the county at £975, Scots.

" There is upon the estate a good mansion house, with proper
" offices, and a large garden enclosed with a high stone wall, and
" well stocked with fruit trees, of which a purchaser can get posses-
" sion at Whitsunday, 1787, and of 20 acres of land adjoining the
" house, at Martinmas next. If no purchaser appear for the whole
" estate, it will be set up in the following lots, viz :—

" Lot 1. The house, garden, and sundry fields round them,   ... £222 15   0
           which will be set up at £5,100.
" Lot 2. Camlachie parks, Gateside mill, and mill lands, and feus
         of Camlachie, ...   177   0   0
           which will be set up at £3,700.
" Lot 3. Crown-point houses and garden, Mountain blue, Ford Neuk,
         and Stabtree, ...   107 10   0
           which will be set up at £2,160.
" Lot 4. Clyde-side, Goosefauld, and feus of Bridgeton, ... 244   9   0
           which will be set up at £5,760.
" Lot 5. Broomward, and part of new feus of Calton,   ... 195   7   0
           which will be set up at £4,000.
" Lot 6. Old feus of Calton, and remainder of new feus of ditto, ... 158   0   8¾
           which will be set up at £324.
" Lot 7. Coal Lordship, ... 110   0   0
           which will be set up at £550.

" The public burdens will be divided and proportioned upon the
" different Lots, according to their different rents.

" The rental of this estate is yearly increasing by feuing out the
" lands nearest to Glasgow for building upon, for which there is at
" present a great demand.

" The lots will be altered, enlarged, or diminished, as persons in-
" tending to purchase may desire.

" For particulars, apply to the proprietor at Glasgow, in whose
" hands the rental, progress of writs, and a plan of the estate are to
" be seen ; or to Mr Lawrence Hill, writer to the Signet, Edinburgh ;
" or Mr Alexander Robertson, writer in Glasgow ; any of whom will
" also show the rental."

John Orr appears to have become bankrupt soon after this time.

" *Scots Magazine*, September, 1790."

" Bankrupts,—September 1st, John Orr, of Barrowfield, the only
" solvent partner of Colquhoun, Shields & Co., merchants in Glasgow."

" In December, 1723, the Trades' House united to the extent of
" one-fourth of the price in purchasing the estate of Barrowfield,
" then sold by John Walkinshaw, on 3d August, 1730. The House
" concurred in selling those lands to Mr John Orr for £10,000, and
" received £2,553 15s as their share of the price."—(Crawfurd's
Trades' House, p. 157.)

CHAPTER II.

The Andersons of Stobcross—The Bells of Cowcaddens, and Bell's Park—Incorporation
of Tailors—Bailie Ronald, Breeches Maker to H.R.H. the Prince of Wales, and
Provost M'Dowall—Feu-duties in Anderston and Finnieston—Lady Barrowfield—
Story of the Marriage of John Orr of Barrowfield—Anecdote—The Green 80 years
ago—Craig's Park—The Golf Fields Lands in 1758—Provost Mackenzie—Sketch of
Alexander, Richard, and James Oswald—Extracts from " The Glasgow Mercury."

JOHN ORR, Senior, in 1735, purchased the lands of Stobcross, consisting of 62 acres, and formerly the property of the Andersons of
Dowhill, of clique notoriety. These lands anciently formed part of
the Bishop's Forest, and afterwards of the Great Western Common.
John Anderson was bailie of Glasgow in 1631-2-7-9, 1641-2-4-6-8—
1652-3-4—provost in 1655 ; (his son John, bailie in 1655), Provost
in 1656-7-8 ; William Anderson, provost in 1664-5-6 ; (John
Anderson, jun., bailie, 1666); John Anderson, provost, 1667-8 ;
William Anderson, provost, 1670-1-2-3 ; John Anderson, jun.,
bailie, 1674 ; N. Anderson, bailie, 1675-8-9 ; John Anderson, jun.,
bailie, 1683-6; John Anderson, provost, 1689-90-95-96-99, 1700-3-4.
So that the Anderson family formed one of the ruling clique of
Glasgow magistrates for upwards of seventy years, during which
time the Stobcross estates appear to have been acquired by them.*
Those estates consisted of Anderston, Finnieston, Cranstonhill,
Parson's Haugh, and others in that vicinity. Our Glasgow historians
have given us no particulars how, or for what price, the Andersons
came into possession of so large a share of the Great Western
Common, belonging to the community of the city.

The Bells of Cowcaddens, and of Bell's Parks, &c., (another of
the said magisterial clique of the seventeenth century), besides the
above estates of Cowcaddens, &c., had also acquired a part of the
Stobcross lands, as the following advertisement shows :—

" *Glasgow Journal*, 16th August, 1756."

" 'That all and hail, these four acres of land, or thereby, being a

* " 4th December, 1692.—Jacobus Anderson, haeres Jacobi Andersone de Stobcross
" Patris—in 40 solidatis terrarum antiqui extensus de Stobcrosse infra Parochiam
" Baroniam et Regalitatem de Glasgow—E. 12 bollae farinae avenaticae, &c., et 12d.
" in augmentationem feudifirmae, xliii. 128."—(Retours.)

" part of these lands called Parson's Haugh, or Rankin's Haugh,
" lying upon the eastmost part or side of the lands of Stobcross ; as
" also a rood of land upon the east side of Stobcross, in that part
" thereof called the lands of Drouth, with the hail houses, well, and
" green, lying in the Barony parish of Glasgow, belonging to John
" Bell, heir of the deceased Richard Bell, merchant in Glasgow, are to
" be exposed to public roup, within the house of Andrew Armour, late
" Bailie of Glasgow, in different lots or parcels, upon Thursday the
" ninth day of September, 1756 years, between the hours of eleven
" in the forenoon, and two afternoon, said day.

" The conditions of roup and progress of writs in the hands of
" John Wardrop, writer in Glasgow."

In 1605, part of the lands of Parson's Haugh, or Rankin's
Haugh, appears to have been possessed by a Mr Alexand. Andro.

" Maii 17th, 1605."

" Magister Alexander Andro, haeres Jacobi Andro fratris—in terris
" subscriptis prebendae de Glasgow vocatis, Prependarium de
" Glasgow-primo, viz :—13 acris terrarum vulgo nuncupato, ' The
" Parsone's Croft,' ex parte boreali civitatis Glasguensis, prope lie
" Stabillgrene :—terris jacentibus prope Brumelaw ex occidentali
" parte dictae civitatis :—terris vulgo vocatis, the Parsone's Hauch,
" alias Rankynni's Hauch, jacentibus prope Stobcross ex parte
" occidentali civitatis Glasguensis, infra baroniam et regalitatem de
" Glasgow :—E. £20—pomario ac diversis tenementis cum parvo
" horto infra territorium dictae civitatis, E. £8."

The 13 acres of the Parson's Croft first mentioned appear to have
been acquired by the Incorporation of Tailors at a later time, and in
the *Glasgow Mercury*, of date 9th March, 1780, we find the following advertisement :—

" VALUATION IN LANARKSHIRE."

" The Corporation of Tailors in Glasgow have about £120 valua-
" tion holding of the Crown in the county of Lanark to dispose of.

" For particulars, apply to Mr Robert M'Callum, deacon ; or
" Claud Marshall, writer in Glasgow."

In 1857 the Incorporation of Tailors, besides their Gorbals lands,
valued at £895, were possessed of feu-duties and ground rents to
the extent of £529 13s.

The Tailors are the richest of the fourteen incorporated crafts in
Glasgow, their stock in 1857 amounting to £57,961 18s 3d.

(Crawfurd's Trades, page 164.) The greatest part of this capital has arisen from their lands of Parson's Croft, situated at the north-east part of the City. The principal feuar was Mr Basil Ronald, glover. Mr Ronald was the proprietor of the Estate of Broomloan, near Govan, which he sold, and invested the proceeds of it in feuing and improving a large part of the lands of Parson's Croft. It however turned out an unfortunate speculation for Mr Ronald, as the rage for feuing building grounds about Glasgow came to be directed almost entirely towards the west part of the City, so that Parson's Croft lands lay long neglected, or nearly so. Mr Basil Ronald was bailie of Glasgow in 1805-6, and Convener of the Trades in 1811-12. When in London about the end of last century, Mr Ronald had the honour of personally taking the measure of the Prince of Wales,* (afterwards George IV.) for a pair of buckskin breeches, and on this occasion he obtained the privilege from his Royal Highness of being appointed " Breeches maker to his Royal Highness the Prince " of Wales." This title he got conspicuously painted in front of his premises in the Trongate, and for his sign he hung up above his shop door a veritable and true pair of buckskin breeches, surmounted by the Prince of Wales's armorial bearings, and by his Highness's crest of three ostrich feathers. Amongst others I had the pleasure of getting a pair of buckskin breeches made by the Prince of Wales's breeches-maker, which fitted me to a " hair,"— (*i.e.* to the 48th part of an inch.) Mr Ronald was a member of the Royal Glasgow Volunteer Light Horse, and was a man of high spirit, for having received what he considered a gross affront from provost James M'Dowall, he immediately made his will, posted up his books, and then sent a challenge to provost M'Dowall. The provost having been accustomed to associate much with military gentlemen was at a loss what to do, as the matter in any point of view was a serious one for him : he therefore consulted some of his friends, who, having met with the friends of Mr Ronald, these gentlemen, interfered, and after having investigated the matter, they declared their opinion that the provost had been in the wrong, and accordingly recommended him to make an apology to Mr Ronald, which having been done to Mr Ronald's satisfaction, the matter ended *tuto.*

The business of a glover at this time in Glasgow was a more

---

* The Prince of Wales was excessively fond of finery.—" *Mercury*, 27th April, 1790. —The Prince of Wales has a superb brilliant Epaulet now forming at Jeffries, valued at £20,000. The loop-stone is estimated at 5000 guineas."

lucrative one than it is at present, for besides the manufacture of buckskin and doeskin breeches and pantaloons, there was the fashion at that time of making presents of white kid gloves to all the members of a family to whom the notification of a marriage had been given; and it was quite understood by the receivers that the glover who furnished the articles, exchanged any of them if they did not fit. Some of the richer citizens also at family funerals laid down on a table in the lobby of the house where funeral service took place a lot of black mourning gloves for the selection of those who came to the funeral.

The following notice is a curious instance of the practice of making presents in olden time,—

" Glasgow Journal, 31st October, 1758."

" The partners of the old and new silk shops, here, having been " in use for some time past of giving ' *compliments* ' of silk shoes to " their customers, find it a very great expense upon them, and now " the advance in the price of articles, together with the extra- " ordinary charge of land carriage, put it out of their power any " longer to continue the same : they therefore take this method of " making intimation to their customers of this their resolution to " prevent future ' *solicitations.*' "

From the concluding passage of the above notice it appears that the ladies of Glasgow at this time were in the practice of "soliciting" a yearly present of a pair of silk shoes from their silk mercers, nearly as a matter of right. Johnson says that " compli- ment" means something *less* than it declares : but the ladies then considered it to mean something *more* than it declared.

The Bells appear to have acquired the Cowcaddens shortly before the year 1692. Patrick Bell was bailie in 1676, and John Bell, provost, in 1674-5-8-9, 1680-1.

" Nov. 17, 1697.—Patricius Bell, haeres Magistrii Patricii Bell, " mercatoris, nuper unius Ballivorum burgi de Glasgow patris, in 6 " solidatis 8 denariatis terris antiqui extensus de litle Cowcaddens, " infra Baroniam et Regalitatem de Glasgow, E. 6.s. 8.d., &c. " Feudifirmae et 16.d. in augmentationem. xlvi. 905."

" Glasgow Journal, 5th June, 1777."

" Notice.—These eleven acres of ground, or thereby, belonging to " the City, lying on the east side of the road belonging to Mr Peter " Bell, of Cowcaddens, leading from the road to Wishat's House, to

" Bell's Haugh, is to be set on tack for 19 years, by public roup,
" within the Clerk's Chamber,'on the 11th day of June, current.
" The purchaser's entry to commence immediately after the roup,
" and the articles of the roup to be seen in the hands of the Town
" Clerks. N.B.—Some dung belonging to the City, lying near to
" the place where the Gallowgate Toll Bar lately stood, is to be sold
" by roup, at the above time and place."

The City, therefore, appears at this time, to have had a public
depot for dung in the Gallowgate.

It has already been stated that John Orr, Senr., purchased
Stobcross in 1735, which estate having descended to his son William,
appears to have been bequeathed, *pro indiviso*, between the sons of
the said William, viz. : John Orr, Town Clerk, and Matthew Orr, coal
master. John Orr, Sen., died in 1744, and his son, William, in 1755.
" Died at Barrowfield, near Glasgow, William Orr, of Barrowfield,
Esq., 4th May, 1755." (Scots Magazine, 1755, page 210.)

The affairs of John and Matthew Orr,* coal masters, having
become embarrassed, were placed under the management of Trustees,
who, in 1775, thus advertised the lands of Stobcross, for sale.

" *Glasgow Journal,* 11th May, 1775."

" To be Sold—The lands of Stobcross, Cranstonhill, and Rankin's
" Haugh, situated on the River Clyde, a mile west from the City of
" Glasgow. The clear rent, including the superiority of the villages
" of Anderston and Finnieston, amounts to £287 2s 7½d, besides
" the casualties of entry from the heirs and singular successors of
" Feuars. These lands hold of the crown, and are valued in the
" cess-books at £250 Scots."

In December, 1776, John and Matthew Orr, having got a settlement with their Trustees, advertised as follows.

" *Glasgow Journal,* 3d October, 1776."

" To be Sold—The superiority, feu-duties and casualties of the
" Estate of Stobcross, in the Barony Parish of Glasgow, and Shire of
" Lanark, within a mile west from Glasgow, comprehending the
" villages of Anderston and Finnieston, and sundry villas and fields
" adjacent. The lands of Stobcross, which are holden of the crown,
" are valued in the cess-roll at £250. The Feu-duties, which from
" the nature of the right, are perfectly secure, are easily collected,

---

* Matthew Orr died at Kings Bay Estate, in Tobago, on the 1st of August, 1790.

" the vassals not being numerous, and as most of the feu-rights
" contain prohibition to sub-feu or dispose to be holden of the
" vassals, or to allow the lands to be in non-entry, under an irritancy,
" so the casualties (which are doubling the feu-duties at the entry
" of heirs, and in part of the feu-rights doubling the feu-duty, in
" others, tripling it, and in some paying a year's rent at the entry of
" singular successors) will be regularly paid.

" Yearly Feu Duties.

" Hugh Niven pays yearly, ...	£23	8 5
" William Baird's heirs, ...	24	6 4¼
" James Young, ...	15	13 1½
" Matthew Crawford, ...	12	4 5
" Andrew Cochrane, ...	12	0 0
" Ninian Glen and others, ...	10	0 0
" John Smith, ...	8	0 7½
" William Robertson, ...	7	10 0
" John Neilson, ...	5	5 7½
" John Johnston, ...	3	1 1½
" Adam Thomson, ...	2	10 0
" John Govan, ...	1	15 10½
" James Miller, ...	1	9 5½
" Mrs Woodrow's heirs, ...	1	2 2½
" David Watson, ...	1	0 0
" And seventeen other Feuars whose yearly Feu-duties are, ...	6	5 5¼
" Together amounting to, ...	£135	12 8¾

" And this £135 12s 8¾d, is clear rent, the proprietor of the
" Mansion House and property lands being burdened with the feu
" and teind duties and public burdens. The feu-duties and
" casualties will be sold off in lots before the day of the roup, if
" purchasers offer, and if any of the feuars incline their own feu-
" duties, the Superior will be ready to treat with them on reasonable
" terms. The progress of writs, with duplicates of the original Feu
" Contract, and other articles of roup, will be seen in custody of
" Thomas and Archibald Grahame, writers, in Glasgow, to whom
" any willing to treat for whole or part may apply."

" *Glasgow Journal*, 8th August, 1757."

" To be set in tack for a term of years as can be agreed upon,
" the Inn or Public House at the White Hart, in Gallowgate, Glasgow;
" with Bowling Green, and Garden, and whole Offices belonging

" thereto, as presently possessed by James Buchanan, Vintner.
" Entry thereto at Whitsunday next ; these to be set jointly or
" separately.

" Also, the House of Barrowfield, and Offices, with or without
" the Garden, and with or without a Park of four acres, arable,
" besides the grass of the avenues.

" Apply to the Lady Barrowfield, at Barrowfield, or to Robert
" Barclay, writer, in Glasgow."

This Lady was the grandmother of John Orr, Town-clerk, and
belonged to the Stewart family, of Castlemilk.   I think that she was
the sister of Sir Archibald Stewart, of Castlemilk, and of the Barony
of Gourock, who died in 1763, and hence, from courtesy, she came
to be called Lady Barrowfield.

" *Glasgow Journal,* 1st July, 1794."

" On Saturday last, (28th June) died at Jordanhill, in the 88th
" year of her age, Mrs Margaret Stewart. This lady was first
" married to Mr Peter Murdoch, Jr., merchant in Glasgow, and
" after his death, to John Orr, Esq., of Barrowfield."

It is singular enough that Peter Murdoch, merchant, and John
Orr, of Barrowfield, were joint bailies of Glasgow, in 1719, when
their future wife was just commencing her teens.

" William Orr (son of the above-mentioned Margaret Stewart)
" had two sons, John and Matthew, and four daughters, Esther,
" Helen, Martha, and Janet : all were unmarried except the last,
" who became the wife of Mr Kennedy of Auchtyfardle. Mr Gilbert
" Kennedy, who died 4th January, 1855, was the son of this mar-
" riage, with whom the line of this old Glasgow family of Orr became
" extinct. The first John Orr and all his descendants are interred
" in the crypt of the Glasgow Cathedral."—(" Glasgow Past and
Present," page 726, by J. B.)

Mr Kennedy of Auchtyfardle was an advocate in Edinburgh, and
was twice married as follows :—

" *Scots Magazine,* 1771.   May 1st.   Married at Glasgow, ——
" Kennedy, Esq. of Auchterfardle, to Miss Peggy Craig, daughter of
" Dr Andrew Craig, Physician in that City."—(Her uncle was Lord
Craig, of the Court of Session.)

A daughter of this marriage married Mr Archibald Bogle, who
left issue, some of whom, I believe, took the name of Kennedy
Bogle.

"*Weekly Magazine*, 1773."

"14th August. Married at Edinburgh, James Kennedy of " Auchtefardle, Esq., to Miss Jessy Orr, sister of John Orr, Esq. of " Barrowfield,"—(and on the same day,) 14th August, 1773. " Married at Glasgow, Thomas Donald of Geilston, Esq., to Miss " Jeany Dunlop, eldest daughter of Colin Dunlop of Carmyle, Esq." —(Issue, from this marriage, was C. D. Donald, Esq.)

Mr James Kennedy, unfortunately, was a partner in the Ayr Bank, (a concern nearly as ruinous to its shareholders as the Western Bank was in later times) in consequence of which, he was obliged to sell his estate of Auchtyfardle, which estate was purchased by Mr Mossman.

The Ayr Bank commenced business in 1774, and in the short space of two years. viz., in 1776, its partners had not only lost their whole capital, but also had incurred debts to nearly a like extent.

The history of the marriage of John Orr of Barrowfield, late Town-clerk of Glasgow, is rather romantic, and I believe that it is little known to the present generation of our citizens, the circumstance having taken place, more than fourscore years and ten ago, when Mr Orr was quite a young man. It happened thus—

There was a very handsome and well-educated young lady at that time, in Glasgow, who was the bosom-friend and intimate companion of Mr Orr's sisters, Esther, Helen, Martha, and Janet, and was frequently invited by those ladies to pay them family visits, during the course of which Mr Orr fell deeply in love, and came under an obligation to marry her, but the transaction, in the meantime, was to be kept secret. So matters stood for some time; but a lengthened correspondence by letters took place, between the parties; Mr Orr, however, having changed his mind, slackened in his addresses, and delayed in performing his obligation, which ended in his endeavouring to get quit of it altogether, by denying its validity.

In those trying circumstances, the poor young lady, as might have been expected, was distressed beyond measure, and totally at a loss what to do. Being of a mild and gentle disposition, she hesitated to take any legal steps against Mr Orr ; knowing his energy of character, and influence in society, she doubted of being able to obtain redress by applying to a court of law. Here, however, fortunately for herself, she met with a warm and devoted friend in Mr Thomas Buchanan, of Ardoch, a gentleman as energetic and as influential in society as Mr Orr himself. Mr Buchanan took the greatest interest in the young lady's case, as much so as if he himself had been interested in the issue ; and he strongly advised this lady to commence an action of declarator of marriage against Mr Orr. She accordingly put herself entirely in the hands of Mr Buchanan, who thereon immediately, on the part of the young lady, raised an action of declarator before the Court of Session, which action was strenuously opposed by Mr Orr. The action had proceeded some length, with the usual delays of the law, when Mr Buchanan one day happened to ask the young lady to show him the *whole* of the letters, without exception, which she had received from Mr Orr during the time of their correspondence. This at first she expressed her unwillingness to do, as it hurt her feelings to show some of those letters to a third party : she however consented to Mr Buchanan's request, and placed in his hands the entire correspondence which had taken place between Mr Orr and herself.

Mr Buchanan having scanned over a great file of correspondence to no suitable purpose, at length hit upon a letter from Mr Orr, to the lady, in which he concluded by signing himself, "Your affectionate husband, John Orr." No sooner did Mr Buchanan see this signature, than he quickly thrust the letter into his pocket, exultingly exclaiming, "This will do—this will do;" and so in fact it did, for, on its production in court, their lordships found John Orr and the young lady to be lawfully married persons.

Mr Orr did not appeal to the House of Lords against the judgment of the Court of Session, but being greatly chagrined and disappointed at this forced marriage, he obstinately refused to cohabit with his wife, or to have any intercourse whatever with her, so that Mrs Orr remained a number of years a sort of forlorn widow : she, however, conducted herself towards Mr Orr in those trying circumstances with such prudence and propriety as to command the sympathy and regard of all classes in Glasgow.

A considerable number of years having elapsed without Mr Orr having paid any attention to his wife, but, on the contrary, having wilfully neglected her, she, by the advice of her friends, raised an action of divorce in the Court of Session, against Mr Orr, for wilful desertion. Mr Orr made little opposition to this action, except such as the forms of court required, for he was as anxious to obtain a divorce as Mrs Orr herself, in consequence of which Mrs Orr readily succeeded in divorcing Mr John Orr, who never afterwards married. By statute 1573, c. 55, it is enacted that where any of the spouses shall divert from the other without sufficient grounds for four years, the party injured may sue for a divorce. Mrs Orr was married a second time, and lived happily, greatly regarded. She died on the 7th of April, 1790; Mr Orr died on the 16th of December, 1803; and Mr Thomas Buchanan on the 10th of December, 1789.

Although Mr Orr's conduct towards this lady cannot be justified, nevertheless it ought to be kept in view that he was then a young, thoughtless man, whose companions were all dashing country gentlemen, horse racers, and fox hunters, who were not very rigid as to morals. Mr Orr's future conduct, however, was such as to command the highest respect from all classes in Glasgow as a gentleman of strict honour and integrity, discharging all his duties, public and private, without reproach.

In 1794 Mr Orr was elected captain-commandant of the Glasgow Volunteer Light Horse, by the votes of the troop; on which occasion I had the pleasure of giving him my vote, and can vouch for his general affability and gentlemanly manners during the time that he was our captain-commandant. He was a first-rate horseman in his early days; but in 1794 the gout prevented his being very agile at a rapid charge of the troop, or at the Austrian sword exercise.

On the 20th of June, 1781, Mr Orr was elected by the Magistrates and Town Council of Glasgow one of the clerks of the City, in place of Archibald M'Gilchrist, deceased, being at that time an advocate at the bar in Edinburgh.

In 1804, a monument was erected, at the public expense, in the Choir of the Cathedral, to the memory of John Orr, Advocate and Town Clerk of Glasgow, on which there is the following inscription:—

"This Monument,
Erected
By the Lord Provost, Magistrates, and Council,
In Honour of the Memory of
J O H N   O R R,   OF   BARROWFIELD,
Advocate,
Principal Town-Clerk of Glasgow,
Records
The Sense Entertained by
A Grateful Community,
Of the Zeal, Talents, and Integrity
Displayed by him, during a period of 22 years,
In discharging the various duties of
A most important Office.
Died the 16th December, MDCCCIII. Aged 58 years."

The following gossiping little anecdote is perhaps somewhat out of place, nevertheless, as characteristic of the merry mode of conducting dinner parties in Glasgow, during last century, its rehearsal may be pardoned.

Our elderly citizens must remember that, on the occasion of a dinner party being given, it was customary, immediately after the ladies had retired, to place the great punch-bowl upon the table, and the landlord to proceed in calling for a round of toasts of young ladies.

On one of those occasions, the landlord commenced by toasting, in full bumper, " Miss Esther Orr," which was drunk with applause.

The next gentleman being called for his toast, gave " Miss Esther Crawfurd," which was received with like honour.

The third gentleman being requested to name a lady for his toast, gave "Miss Esther Gray," which was also honoured by the usual applause.

It now came to the turn of an Irish gentleman to give a lady for his toast ; but he not being acquainted with our Glasgow customs, on being called to name a lady, thus addressed the landlord :—
" Sir, I am sorry that I cannot give you ' my sister,' as I have never
" ' a sister ' to give you ; but I will give you ' my mother.' "—which toast was received with thunders of applause and merriment. Such little stories in olden times soon passed from mouth to mouth through the whole city, then a small place, and formed the tittle tattle of most social parties.

From this digression I must now proceed to take notice of the Low Green of Glasgow and its environs, and to give a few extracts from various writers who have handed down to us sundry scattered details of the former state of the district in question.

In the Origines Parochiales, page 15, it is stated that the first notice we have of the " Common Green," was in the year 1487, and of the Gallowmuir and Barrowfield in 1529.—(Lib. Coll. N.D. 200 ; and Reg. Glasg. 500.)

M'Ure, in his history of Glasgow, published in 1736, thus writes :—" This City hath acquired three parks, one lying at the
" east corner, which is inclosed with a strong wall, and which now
" belongs to the merchants, commonly called the ' Craig's Park,'
" nobly beautified with a stately grove of trees, which is a beautiful
" view to all resorting to the High Church and the burials within the
" church-yard thereof.   This great planting was set by order of the
" worthy Adam Montgomery, merchant, then dean of gild." (1715-16.)

" The second park is commonly called the ' New Green,' adorned
" with pleasant galleries of elm trees, and situated upon the south-
" east corner of the City, and is enclosed with a stately stone wall
" 2500 ells in length, and fenced on the south with the river Clyde,
" it hath all the summer time betwixt two and three hundred
" women bleaching of linen cloth and washing linen cloths of all
" sorts in the river Clyde, and in the midst of this inclosure there is
" an useful well for cleansing the cloths after they are washed in
" the river ; likewise there is a lodge built of freestone in the midst
" of it, for a shelter to the herd who waits upon the horse and cows
" that are grazed therein. The third inclosure is the old green
" lying closs to the south-west corner of the City, and is much less
" than any of the other two. It is only fenced round with palisadoes,
" and no stone wall, but that loss is made up by one hundred and
" fifty trees growing round the green pretty large. Within this
" green is the rope work, which keeps constantly about twenty men
" at work, and the proprietors thereof can furnish as good tarr'd
" cable ropes, and white ropes untarr'd, as any in Britain. On the
" west end of this green is the Glass Work."

I remember the three Parks mentioned by M'Ure, more than
fourscore years ago, when they stood in pretty much the same state
as described by that historian. Craig's Park, now the Necropolis,
was then a piece of bleak hilly ground, on which grew a clump of
skranky fir trees. This Park could not with propriety have been
called a beautiful stately grove, as M'Ure calls it, but the view from
it was certainly very grand. Besides the grounds of the present
Necropolis, " Craig's Parks" included all the Golf-Hill lands ; both
of these appear originally to have formed part of the Bishop's Forest,
and afterwards of the great Eastern Common, where the golf, no
doubt, was played, long before the time when that game came to be
fashionable last century in the Green of Glasgow. In 1758, the
Golf-field lands, then belonging to the Merchants' House, were let
for Four Pounds Sterling of annual rent. When provost James
M'Kenzie purchased the Golf-Hill property it was lying quite open
to the public, who rambled through it at their pleasure ; but Mr
M'Kenzie put a stop to this state of matters by erecting fences, and
by turning off his grounds all persons who made their appearance
thereon. This he did without ceremony, and in what was then
considered a very rough and rude manner, causing much ill-will to
himself. He, however, had previously stuck up notices at several
places of the grounds giving intimation that trespassers on them

would be prosecuted, as the grounds were private property. Provost James M'Kenzie was the first person in Glasgow who openly and avowedly changed the pronunciation of the name of "M'Kenzie." Provost M'Kenzie and his brothers, Daniel and Matthew, and his sisters, Jess and Mary, were known in Glasgow in my early days only by the surname, pronounced "M'Kingie, or M'Keengie;" indeed the whole clan were so named at that time. As English pronunciation gradually came to be fashionable in Glasgow the change from "M'Kingie or M'Keengie," to "M'Kenzie," soon became general. The above M'Kenzie family resided in the corner tenement of Bell Street and Candleriggs, where the *Herald* Newspaper was afterwards printed. I remember about eighty years ago of having been sent a message to one of this family, and checked by the maid-servant for using the name "M'Keengie," saying that she supposed I meant "M'Kenzie."

With regard to the second park, mentioned by M'Ure, it is shown on the Plan annexed to these jottings; the Saw Mill however did not exist till after M'Ure's time. It may be remarked that this park was called by M'Ure "the New Green," from which it may be inferred that the great Eastern and Western Commons were anterior to the Low Green of Glasgow as Commons. Of this park more will be said in the sequel.

As to the third enclosure, called by M'Ure "the Old Green," I remember it very well in the exact state as described by our said Glasgow historian, only the 150 growing trees had disappeared, and the space on which they flourished was purchased in my time by Mr Alexander Oswald of Shieldhall, the father of the late James Oswald, Esq., M.P., for 10s per square yard; which ground he held for many years till he got a profit thereon. Mr Oswald was a great speculator, and generally succeeded in his land purchases, as he was a stiff holder : but he almost always failed in his produce speculations, as his system of steadily holding out for a rise of price very frequently ended in a heavy loss. He did not seem disposed to adopt the plan of selling quickly on the occasions of a falling market. Mr Alexander Oswald, Jun., appears in the books of the Merchants' House to have become a member 26th January, 1786, as the son of the Reverend Jas. Oswald, Perthshire.

The Custom House in Great Clyde Street is built upon the west boundary of Mr Oswald's purchase in the Old Green.

Richard and Alexander Oswald, the early members of the Glasgow Oswald family, were rather remarkable persons. In 1742 they built a large four storey tenement and offices, also an extensive court of store houses and cellars shut up by a gate, having stone vaults and arched premises that would hold upwards of 700 hogsheads of tobacco, besides brew-house, shades, and stabling, all entering by a paved cartway from the street, and the whole shut up with an outer gate. This property stood on the eastern boundary of the Old Green of Glasgow, and now forms the Rope Work Court, 108 Stockwell Street. In the year 1778, the above mentioned premises, or a great part of them were occupied by Gilbert Hamilton as Agent for the Carron Company.

" *Glasgow Mercury*, 17th September, 1778."

" London Porter

" of the best quality, either for home sale or exportation

" in hds. or in bottles.

' Sold by Gilbert Hamilton and Co., at their cellars, in Mr Oswald's " Close, Stockwell, Glasgow.

" At the same place may be had Bath-Stove Grates of the newest " patterns, and of all sizes. Likewise,

" Boilers,	Tea Kettles,
" Bars and Bearers,	Tea Boilers,
" Pots,	Sad and Box irons,
" Pans,	Adjusted Weights,
" Bushes,	Ship Hearths,
" Girdles,	Cabin Stoves,
" Cylinder Ovens,	Wheels and Pinions,

" And all other goods manufactured at Carron.

" Also, Oil of Vitriol of the very best quality from the works of " Preston Pans."

Mr Hamilton afterwards occupied premises now the south part of Exchange Square, where he acted as Agent for the Carron Company and the Bank of Scotland. He was dean of guild in 1790-91, and provost of Glasgow in 1792-93.

" *Glasgow Journal*, 19th April, 1756."

" They write from London that Mr Richard Oswald, merchant, " there, is appointed Commissary of Provisions and Stores for the " Camp on Burham Downs, consisting, it is said, of 25,000 men."

This appointment led to others of a like lucrative character, and ended in Mr Richard Oswald being promoted to the situation of head commissary to the English Army, during the time when

Britain was engaged in war with France and Spain in Europe, and Canada in America. Mr Oswald's contracts for supplying our troops with necessaries, were renewed from time to time, as the war continued ; in the course of these transactions Mr Oswald acquired an immense fortune. Peace was concluded on the 10th Feb. 1763.

In 1783, the country having become tired of the American war of independence, and the House of Commons having expressed a strong opinion against its continuance, Government employed Mr Richard Oswald, Jun., privately to negotiate for a peace, for it was not the wish of the ministry to appear on the stage at the outset of these negotiations. The preliminaries of the peace of 1783, there- fore, came to be arranged principally through the agency of Mr Richard Oswald, Jun. About the time when these matters were going on, a great disaster had taken place in our Scotch mercantile affairs, by the bankruptcy of the Ayr Bank, in which a large number of landed proprietors, in Ayrshire, held shares. The result of this failure brought a great many estates in that county into the market, and Mr Oswald, taking advantage of the opportunity, made large purchases of lands, in various parts of Ayrshire, amongst which was the estate of Auchincruive. It was reported that he had laid out half a million sterling, in land, before his death, which brought him in a rental of £20,000 per annum.

These lands came by inheritance to James Oswald, Esq., M.P. who died in 1853, but before succeeding to them, Mr James Oswald, had, unfortunately, lost his all, by an unluckly cotton speculation, the lands in question, however, being strictly entailed, still remain in the Oswald family.

Mr James Oswald opened up Maxwell Street, to Great Clyde Street, through that portion of the Old Green of Glasgow which had been purchased by his father. He likewise subscribed £100 towards defraying the expense of widening the said street ten feet on the north part. Before this time Maxwell Street was a narrow lane, shut up on the south by the extensive works of Stephen Maxwell, Coppersmith. Owing to the state of the different properties on the line of Maxwell Street, it became necessary to give the street a slant at Howard Street. East Howard Street was also formed by the energy of Mr Oswald, the greatest part of its ground (being the old ropework mentioned by M'Ure) then belonging to Mr Oswald. This ropework within my memory was a tiled shed extending from Rope Work Court to the corner of the now St Enoch Square, and from thence continued as an open ropework to Jamaica Street, so that a cable could have been spun there, reaching from Stockwell to Jamaica Street.

A considerable portion of the front line of East Howard Street belonged to the City of Glasgow, being the north boundary of the Town's Hospital, and here, I remember, were placed the cells for lunatics, having small iron-grated windows looking into the hospital burying ground. These cells were most wretched holes, on the ground floor, in which the unhappy sufferers for the most part had to sustain the additional affliction of solitary confinement, and the violent ones to pine on a bed of straw. Regarding the change which has taken place in our city, in this respect, we have only to cast our eyes upon the splendid establishment at Gartnavel.

The property next to the Town's Hospital was Bogle and Scott's timber yard, on which the Roman Catholic Chapel has been built. Howard Street was so named, by Mr Oswald, in honour of the celebrated philanthropist, John Howard.

" Glasgow Journal, 27th January, 1763."

"On Monday last, (24th) Died at Scotstown, Alexander Oswald, " Esq., a gentleman of great probity, honour, and knowledge in " trade, by which he acquired a handsome fortune. For some years " past he lived retired from public business, employing himself in " acts of friendship, generosity, and hospitality."

" Glasgow Journal, 14th August, 1766."

"On Tuesday last, (12th August), Died at Scotstown, Richard " Oswald, Esq., late merchant in Glasgow."—(Old Statistical Account of Scotland, vol. 20, page 533.)

" Town and Parish of Thurso, 1798."

"The Oswalds of Glasgow, who have long been eminent " merchants, derived their origin from Thurso. Their ancestor " was one of the bailies of Thurso, in the last century. Richard " Oswald, late merchant in London, and one of the plenipoten- " tiaries from the court of Great Britain, at settling the peace of " 1783, was, in his younger days, an unsuccessful candidate upon " a comparative trial for the office of Master of the Parochial " School of Thurso, whereof the salary was £100—Scotch (£8 6s " 8d,) and took his disappointment so much to heart that he " left the country, and never more returned to it. But for that

" circumstance, it is probable he would have lived and died in
" obscurity." *

Oswald is not a Glasgow name ; we look in vain for the name in
the pages of M'Ure, and other early Glasgow historians, or in the
primitive Annals of Cleland.   Even in the present Glasgow Directory
there are only two individuals of the name of Oswald, neither of
whom are related to the families of Scotstown and Auchincruive.

" *Glasgow Journal*, 11th November, 1784."—" On the 5th
" current, died, at the House of Achincruive, Richard Oswald,
" Esq."

" 18th November, 1784."—" The late Richard Oswald, Esq., was
" formerly an eminent merchant in London, and lately employed at
" Paris as Minister Plenipotentiary from Great Britain, to settle a
" treaty of peace with the commissioners of the United States of
" America.   Perhaps there are few men whose loss will be more
" generally felt or more sincerely regretted than that of Mr Oswald,
" for few men possessed a finer understanding, more liberal senti-
" ments, or more extensive information.   Blessed with affluence, his
" principal study seemed to be to employ it in acts of kindness and
" generosity."

From Crawfurd's "Renfrewshire," page 347, we learn—"That
" Scotstoun was purchased in the year 1748 from Mr Walkinshaw's
" creditors, by Messrs Richard and Alexander Oswald, brothers,
" merchants in Glasgow. They were never married, but conveyed
" the estate of Scotstoun, with their contiguous lands of Balshagrie,
" to George Oswald, merchant in Glasgow, eldest son of their cousin
" the Rev. Dr James Oswald, late minister of Methven, in Perth-
" shire, whose second son, Alexander Oswald, Esq. of Shieldhall,
" died in 1813, and his brother, Richard Oswald, Esq. of Auchin-
" cruive, died in 1784."   " George Oswald succeeded to the estate
" of Scotstoun in 1766. He married, in 1764, Margaret Smyth,
" second daughter of David Smyth, Esq., of Methven.   She died in
" 1792, leaving four sons and seven daughters."

" *Glasgow Journal*, 26th January, 1764."—"Edinburgh, 18th
" January, 1764.—Last night (Tuesday, 17th January), Mr George
" Oswald, merchant in Glasgow, was married here to Miss Peggy
" Smith, second daughter to David Smyth, of Methven, Esq."

Of this marriage there remains here yet alive, Miss Oswald of
Scotstoun, who was born on the 6th of July, 1767, consequently in

---

* I think this anecdote must refer to Richard Oswald, Senr., who died in 1766.

the 97th year of her age, and unquestionably the matron of the city. Miss Oswald is well known over all Glasgow; and it may be truly said of her what was said of the founder of the family, "Blessed with affluence, her principal study seems to be to employ " it in acts of kindness and generosity."

Crawfurd, in his "Renfrewshire," page 347, says that Richard Alexander Oswald was the eldest son of George Oswald of Scotstoun; but I cannot reconcile this with an entry in the books of the Merchants' House, viz.—" Merchant House Records, 1814."— " Richard Alexander Oswald, son of Alexander Oswald of Shield- " hall, entered the Merchants' House on the 26th of August, 1814." This entry must have been made by Mr R. A. Oswald himself.

"*Scots Magazine*, 1750, page 549."—"The Commission of " General Assembly, on the 14th of November, appointing a " committee of their own number, three of whom to be a quorum, " to admit Mr James Oswald to be minister of Dunnet, to the " ministry at Methven, on the 12th of December, or if hindered by " the rigour of the season, on any other day the committee shall " appoint, before the Commissioners' meeting in March next : and " nominate Mr Alexander M'Laggan, moderator. As the Presby- " tery of Perth had been ordained by the last Assembly to admit " Mr Oswald on or before the 10th of July last, the Commission " issued a warrant for summoning them to appear at their bar in " March next, to answer for their disobedience." (Page 590, Mr Oswald was admitted 12th December, 1750, without opposition.)

N.B.—James Oswald, Esq., M.P., was named "James" after his grandfather, the Rev. James Oswald.

Before the Bottle Work, at the Broomielaw, was built in 1730, the ground on which it was erected formed part of the Old Green, which Green included at that time, the whole of St Enoch Square, and Jamaica Street. We find by the following notice, that in 1766, being two years before the Broomielaw Bridge was built, that there had been a ropework in Argyle Street, and Anderston Walk, at the head of Jamaica Street.

" Glasgow Journal, 12th June, 1766."

" This is to give notice, that whosoever has got ropes or twine " from Adam Paterson, ropemaker, at the head of Jamaica Street, " Glasgow, from and after the first of May, 1765, and which may be " unpaid, are hereby desired not to pay the price thereof to the said " Adam Paterson, as he has no right thereto. And whoever has

"got ropes or twine from the said Adam Paterson, and is owing
"money for them since the time above mentioned, are desired, as
"soon as convenient, to pay the same to James Graham at the said
"ropework."

The above appears to have been an open ropework, extending
from Jamaica Street westwards upon the Anderston Road, opposite
Grahamstone, and to have been taken possession of by the Dumbarton Road Trustees, shortly before the foregoing date.

"*Glasgow Journal*, 19th July, 1764."

"The Trustees appointed by Act of Parliament, on the toll roads
"betwixt Glasgow and Dumbarton, having of late, at a great ex-
"pense, caused make a path for persons travelling on foot, to and
"from Anderston and Grahamstone, and for preventing horses and
"carriages going thereon, have erected cross-bars at proper dis-
"tances; some malicious and ill-disposed persons have broken down
"some of those cross-bars; and within these eight days past have
"also broke down sundry gates of the fences about Anderston, par-
"ticularly of those possessed by the proprietors of the brewerie and
"delphhouse, Hugh Niven, John Brown, and James Graham.
"Whoever shall discover the perpetrators, so as they may be con-
"victed of all or any of the forenamed crimes, shall receive ten
"pounds sterling of reward from the Trustees. And the Trustees
"hereby discharge all persons whatever from travelling on the said
"footpath, with horses, or any manner of carriages for the future,
"with certification to the contraveners that they will be prosecuted
"therefor in terms of law. Proper persons are appointed by the
"Trustees to notice and inform of such as offend in this respect."

The proprietors of the ground on the south side of Anderston
Walk at this time appear to have been the above James Graham,
owner of the ropework, Matthew Reid, Hugh Niven, for the Delft-
house Company, Bailie John Brown, for Brown, Carrick & Company's
Bleachfield, and the Anderston Brewery Company. I remember the
cross-bars standing upon the footpath of the Anderston Walk.
They were constructed so as to admit a free passage to a traveller
on foot, but prevented all regular or continuous intercourse by horses
or carriages. In 1756 there seems to have been a toll bar at
Grahamstone. "*Glasgow Journal*, 29th March, 1756." "By order
"of the Trustees, there is to be set in tack, for one year, by public
"roup, the tolls of the bar at Grahamstone and Broomielaw, on
"Dumbarton Road," &c. Besides the Road Trustees, Mr James

Monteith, (father of the late Henry Monteith, Esq., M.P.,) seems to have taken a special charge of the Anderston footpath, as the following extract from the *Glasgow Journal* shows:—

"Glasgow, 16th August, 1781. Gravel walk betwixt Glasgow " and Anderston. That the gravel walk betwixt Glasgow and " Anderston is to be repaired immediately. Any persons willing to " undertake it are desired to apply to James Monteith, manufacturer " in Anderston, who will show the plan, and receive estimates."

The value of ground at this time upon the line of the Anderston Walk may be seen by the following advertisement:—

" *Glasgow Mercury*, 24th February, 1785."

" To be sold, by public roup, &c., all and whole that piece of " garden ground, in Broomielaw Croft, consisting of three acres and a " half, or thereby, lying immediately to the east of the Delft-house " grounds, and presently possessed by John M'Aulay, gardener.

" For the encouragement of bidders, this piece of ground will be " exposed at the upset price of £400 sterling."

Here there is nothing said about square yards, or the one half of the street to be included in the measurement; but half acres, or *thereby*, are set forth in a fine slumpy manner.

In 1775, the greatest part of Jamaica Street, on the west, was waste ground, on which the magistrates of Glasgow had erected a depot for dung.

" Brown's, Glasgow, 113—Brownfield, a part of the Broomielaw " Croft in the burgh roods of Glasgow, consisting of not more than " ten acres, was feued off in 1791, at a ground annual amounting " to upwards of £300 per annum. About 1766, this plot of ground " was feued from the College of Glasgow by Brown, Carrick & Co., " and was used by them as a bleachfield."

" *Glasgow Journal*, 20th April, 1775."

" The grass for this season of the plot of ground on this north side " of the new breast, as railed in, to be set for a cutting only this " season. Also the dung on the west side of Jamaica Street. " Likewise the grass of the old Green, adjoining the ropework ; the " square thereof from Mr Bogle's (timber yard) to the glasswork " dyke only, being upwards of two acres, are to be let for three " years."

The two acres last mentioned were purchased afterwards by Mr Alexander Oswald, as before stated, and descended to his son, James Oswald, M.P., who opened Maxwell Street through them.

" Glasgow Mercury, 10th April, 1777."

" Notice, that the Magistrates of and Council of Glasgow have " resolved to sell the ground for building on the old Green of " Glasgow, St Enoch's Square, on the west of Jamaica Street, " fronting to Argyll Street, and the steadings on the east and west " sides of Jamaica Street. Any person inclining to purchase may " apply to the town clerks of Glasgow."

" Mercury, 13th March, 1777. Notice.—The Cowcaddens Hill " Park, and the three acres of the Laigh Cowcaddens Park, will be " rouped for a 19 year tack."

" Glasgow Journal, 3d April, 1777."—" A new street to be opened."

" To be sold in lots, for the purpose of building upon, That park " or inclosure in the Broomielaw Croft, fronting the lower Quay at " the Broomielaw. In this inclosure there is to be laid open a street " 70 feet wide, leading from the Anderston Road to the river Clyde, " parallel with Jamaica Street. Apply to Mr William Martine, at " the Delft-house."

" 8th August, 1776."—" On Tuesday, a fine field of oats was cut " down at St Enoch's Croft, in the neighbourhood of this city."

" Glasgow Journal, 20th February, 1777."

" The College of Glasgow propose to sell immediately their 3½ " acres, more or less, of land, lying near the Broomielaw. Their " terms are £15 yearly of feu duty or ground annual in the option " of the College, and a sum of money in cash. Offers will be " received by Principal Leachman, till Monday, the 3d of March " next, and the highest offer made on or before that day will be " preferred without delay."

On these lands a short cross street has been formed called College Street, which runs from M'Alpine Street to Brown Street.

It appears that the said property had been originally a gift to a monastic establishment, which at the Reformation was bestowed by the Crown upon the College of Glasgow. The College, being exempted from the payment of certain local taxes, claimed relief from the said taxes which had been charged upon the lands in question, alleging that as these lands formed a part of the College estates, they came within the right of exemption enjoyed by the College itself. This claim, however, was disputed, and failed of success, so that College street lands are held in a like manner with the contiguous properties.

"*Glasgow Journal*, 2d November, 1775."—"Notice."

" The inhabitants of Finnieston request of those gentlemen who
" send their horses to the fields for exercise, that they will desire
" their servants not to ride through the village in such crowds, and
" at such speed, as has been done for some time past. The bleach-
" fields, from the quantities of dust dispersed by the horses, are
" almost ruined, and the lives of the inhabitants, from the number
" and fury of the riders, have been often in danger. They request
" also that no person after this will carry away sand from the High
" Street, as they propose at their own expense to form that street in
" such a manner as to be convenient for those who have occasion
" necessarily to pass along it."

"*Glasgow Journal*, 18th July, 1776."—"To be sold or set
"immediately,

" Three acres of garden ground in St Enoch's Croft, on the north
" side of Argyle Street of Glasgow, as presently possessed by John
" Kennedy and John Colquhoun, gardeners, with several dwelling
" houses and byres, together with the growing crop of garden stuffs,
" cattle, and fruits on the premises. The said three acres are lying
" together between Queen Street and Mr Andrew Buchanan's lands,
" running straight north to the rising grounds, and will admit of
" laying out an elegant square or street thereon. The entry from
" Argyle Street thereto by Bailie King's, now Bailie Buchanan's,
" Close.—Apply to John Kennedy, the proprietor."
These lands now form part of Buchanan Street on the west.

"*Glasgow Journal*, 3d April, 1777."

" A street to be opened directly opposite to St Enoch's Square."
" Andrew Buchanan, Esq, merchant, proposes to enlarge his entry
" in Argyle Street, opposite to St Enoch's Square, to 40 feet, free of
" every incumberance, such as stairs, or other projections. This
" entry will lead into a street running to the northward, opening
" equally on each side, so as to make a street of 70 feet in breadth.
" The ground abounds in fine pit water in digging 10 or 12 feet.
" Access also may be had at small expense to good running water,
" (viz., St Enoch's Burn). It is proposed that purchasers should
" subject themselves to some regulations for the ornament of the
" street. For sight of the ground and plan of the street, please
" apply to the proprietor."
The above notice accounts for the narrow entrance to Buchanan

Street from Argyle Street, which at the time in question was a
narrow close.

"*Glasgow Journal*, 10th October, 1776."

"To be sold, by private bargain, that large kiln and brewery
" lying on the north side of Argyle Street, next to St Enoch's Burn.
" It will make a fine steading of houses, being 84 feet in front.—
" Apply to Alexander Gordon, the proprietor."

(N.B.—Now part of Stewart & M'Donald's warehouse.)

"*Glasgow Journal*, 28th May, 1759."

" The mansion house at Hyde Park, near Anderston, lately built,
" and consisting of eight fine rooms, kitchen, and closets, with
" cellars, offices, houses, barn, a large beautiful garden, with great
" variety of thriving fruit trees of the best kinds, with the ground
" above the said house, and park immediately below, and on the
" south side of the garden and water side, grass of the exact breadth
" of the said park, all consisting of eight acres of land or thereby;
" as also the tann yard, lofts, cellars, several convenient dwelling
" houses, barn, miln, pump well, which is provided with good water,
" and ground below, or on the south side of tann house, and under-
" side grass of the precise breadth of the last grounds, consisting of
" about four acres of land, are jointly, or in two separate lots, to
" be sold by public roup, on the 13th June, 1759.—Apply to John
" Wardrop, writer in Glasgow."

"*Journal*, 1st August, 1757."

" To be let, or sold, by way of public roup, on the first Wednesday
" of September next, within the house of Andrew Armour, Vintner,
" in Glasgow, The whole houses and utensils belonging to St
" Enoch's Factory, at Grahamstone, consisting of a large dwelling
" house, with office houses, and working shops. A large garden,
" stables, and houses, and working shops, a large garden, stables
" and other conveniences, with a pump well in the court; large
" entry from the street; the working shops, looms, and utensils, to
" be entered into at Martinmas next, and the dwelling house and
" garden, at Whitsunday thereafter. Apply to Alexander Gordon,
" the possessor."

"*Mercury*, 17th August, 1780."

" To be Sold, or let, as may be agreed upon, that large and
" commodious brewerie, at Grahamstone, which consists of steeps,

" maltbarn, kill, loft, cellars, vaults, &c., sufficient for carrying on
" an extensive business in brewing strong ale, small beer, two penny
" and whisky, with proper utensils for the same, and at a small
" expense, may likewise be rendered fit for making porter. Also,
" a good dwelling house contained in the same square; together
" with servants' houses, stable, hay loft, &c., with a large garden
" behind the brewerie, and an excellent well in the close, remarkable
" good water for brewing. Free of Multure to the town of Glasgow,
" and all other public burthens whatever, excepting a feu of seven
" pounds sterling, to Mr Graham of Dougalston.

"For particulars, apply to Sir John Stuart of Castlemilk, by a
" letter put into the post house at Glasgow."

(N.B. Grahamstone was named for John Graham of Dougalston,
who died in 1749. " *Scots Magazine*, 11th September, 1749. Died
at his country seat, John Graham of Dougalston, Esquire.")

" *Mercury*, 19th October, 1780."

" To be exposed to sale by public roup, &c., the following subjects
" belonging to the trustees, for the creditors of Messrs Buchanan,
" Hastie, & Co., merchants in Glasgow, and the partners of that
" company."

" 1st, That shop lying on the West side of the High Street
" above the Cross of Glasgow, and at present possessed by Walter
" Grahame.

" 2d, One third part, *pro indiviso*, of the ground storey of the
" eastmost of two tenements, built by John Robertson, Wright in
" Glasgow, on the North side of Argyle Street, as the said ground
" storey is possessed by Messrs William Cunningham and Company,
" and William Rose, Grocer—(corner of Virginia Street.)

" 3d, One-half, *pro indiviso*, of the Westmost of the foresaid
" tenements as possessed by Mrs M'Lae, (widow of William M'Lae
" of Cathkin), and Mrs Henderson, (mother of Richard Henderson,
" Town-clerk).

" Also, an acre and a half, or thereby, of ground, lying in
" Blythswood Holm, to the West of Buchanan Street, as possessed
" by James Young, &c."

" *Mercury*, 7th October, 1788."

" To be sold, by auction, on the 4th November, that large and
" substantial range of grain lofts built about eighteen months ago,

" on the stance of the old theatre at Grahamstone, without the
" territory of the burgh of Glasgow.

" These premises consist of three lofts or storeys, besides garrets,
" and are divided towards the centre by a thick stone partition,
" whereby each division has a distinct front entry. Each of the
" lofts on the north division, are forty feet square within the walls,
" and the upper one or garret is forty by thirty-six. The lofts again
" on the southmost division measure each forty by thirty-six, and
" the upper one forty by thirty-three feet, and adjoining to this last
" division there is a convenient writing office, consisting of two
" well-lighted apartments, each of which has a vent or fire-place.

" The granary is capable of containing with the greatest safety
" near 3000 bolls of grain, and from its particular situation has the
" privilege of exemption from the Town's Custom, or duty of Ladle
" on importation, which is very considerable.

" Also, a tack whereof 67 years are to run, after next Whitsunday,
" of ground, called Bankhead, delightfully situated on the water of
" Kelvin, near Clayslap. The proprietor, a few years ago, erected a
" large house on this property. Apply to James Mathie, writer."

" *Journal*, 23d May, 1782."

" 'To be sold, by public roup, on the 4th of June next, that field
" at present occupied as garden ground, but well situated for
" building, consisting of three acres and a half, or thereby, within
" the territory of Glasgow, adjacent to and east of the Delft-field
" ground, on the South side of the street leading to Dumbarton."

" *Mercury*, 8th May, 1783."

" To be sold, by public roup, on the 21st May, the lands of
" Enoch Bank, Mansion House, offices and garden, lying within ten
" minutes' walk of the Cross of Glasgow. The house consists of 13
" fire rooms, with light and dark closets. In the kitchen there is a
" remarkably fine well, the water greatly superior to any in the
" neighbourhood. There is a stable neatly fitted up, byre, laundry,
" Gardener's room, and washing house, completely finished; Chaise
" house; house for poultry, and several other necessary con-
" veniences. A little Dovecot, stocked. The garden consists of near
" an acre of ground, well inclosed, and having a brick wall on the
" west and east sides, the walls covered with fruit trees of the very
" best kinds, all in flourish, and in the most complete order. The
" garden and walls contain 103 fruit trees, besides a great number

" of gean and plum trees planted in the pleasure grounds, to which
" there is a canal well-stocked with fish, the banks of which are
" covered with an hundred different kinds of shrubs. The park to
" the north of the house* is enclosed with double hedging, and
" verges of various kinds of wood. The garden is sown with all kinds
" of vegetables for a family, and the whole may be entered on the
" day of sale. Apply to James Hill, writer."

" *Mercury*, 6th January, 1789."—"Lands and a Printfield for Sale."

" To be sold, by public roup, on the 4th of February next, &c.,
" all and whole the lands of that hill called Gilmourshill, being a
" part of the thirty-three shilling fourpenny land of old extent,
" lying on the east side of the village of Partick, in the parish of
" Govan and sheriffdom of Lanark. These lands consist of about
" thirty acres, and are within a mile and one half of the town of
" Glasgow, and are all inclosed and sub-divided into six inclosures,
" with thriving hedges, belts of .planting, and a stone dike. The
" situation is most delightful, and commands a most extensive and
" pleasant prospect.—A very eligible situation for setting down a
" house, the avenues to which are already formed, and the planting
" on each side thereof in great forwardness. The water of Kelvin
" runs alongside of the lands on the east and south, and from near
" the summit of the hill a long stretch of the river of Clyde to the
" west is in view, and also the towns of Glasgow and Paisley and
" country adjacent. About 24 acres of the land are at present in
" labour, the tack whereof, which was for 19 years, expires at
" Martinmas, 1791, and the remaining part of the lands, which
" consists of near seven acres, is occupied as a printfield, and
" whereon there are every necessary and convenient house for
" carrying on that business to great extent, besides several dwelling
" houses, the tack whereof, which was also for 19 years, expires at
" Martinmas, 1789, and from the houses and yards at Candlemas
" and first of May, 1790. The lands are full of coal, and which can
" be wrought at an easy and cheap rate.—Apply to Benjamin
" Barton, commissary clerk of Glasgow."

" *Journal*, 5th June, 1758."—" To be sold,

" The lands and estate of Northwoodside, with the Barley mill,
" lying within two miles of Glasgow, and all well inclosed, with stone

---

'* N.B. The park above mentioned was bounded on the north by the present
Sauchiehall Road.)

" dykes and hedges; upon which lands there is a very convenient
" dwelling house and proper office houses, pleasantly situate upon
" the water of Kelvin; and there is also upon the said lands a
" considerable number of trees of different kinds, regularly planted,
" besides a wood which sells every nineteen years at two thousand
" merks and upwards. The purchaser's entry to the lands may
" commence at Martinmas next, and to the houses at Whitsunday
" thereafter.—Apply to Hugh Stuart, the proprietor ; or Alexander
" Stevenson, commissary clerk of Glasgow."

" Journal, 17th January, 1765."—" Notice."

" That John Gibson of Hillhead, having sett in tack to James
" Gibson, late deacon of the weavers in Glasgow, and his assigns,
" for the space of 55 years from Martinmas, 1759, for three pounds
" sterling of yearly rent, a piece of his ground, consisting of about
" one acre, lying on the side of the water of Kelvin, near opposite
" to Woodside-muir, which has since been made a good bleaching
" field, and commodious dwelling house, work house, and boiling
" house, built by the said James Gibson thereon. The benefit of
" the said field, houses, and tack thereof, for the whole years thereof
" yet to run hereafter, to be sold by public roup, within the dwelling
" house of William Muir, vintner, opposite to the Tron Church of
" Glasgow, upon Thursday, the 31st day of January, 1765, betwixt
" the hours of 12 and 2 mid-day. Any person wanting to make a
" private bargain about the aforesaid subject, may apply to William
" Marshall or Robert M'Lintock, senior, merchants in Glasgow,
" trustees for James Gibson's creditors."

" Glasgow Journal, 26th June, 1777."

" For Sale, by public roup, within the Exchange Coffee House,
" in Glasgow, on Thursday the 7th day of August next, to begin
" precisely at 12 o'clock, and to continue till all is sold off,

" The lands of Overnewton, adjoining the village of Clayslap,
" with Sundry acres in Kelvinhaugh, the property of Messrs
" Barclay & Bogle, acquired from the late William Cathcart, and
" others, consisting of about sixty acres of land, in the near neigh-
" bourhood of Glasgow, and beautifully situated upon the rivers
" Clyde and Kelvin. The lands will be sold together, or in parcels,
" as may best suit purchasers. If in parcels, the following lots are
' proposed :—

" I. The houses and yards at Clayslap, and grass plot before the
     " door, about two acres in all.

" II. The park of Blackfauld, adjoining thereto, as now set off
" and inclosed, about eight acres.

" III. The Phœnix Park, lately set off and inclosed, about ten acres.

" IV. The Yorkhill Park, about twenty-two acres.

" V. The west division of Kelvinhaugh, about nine acres.

" VI. The east division of   ditto,   about nine acres.

" These may be also joined, if desired, and the several lots pro-
" posed will be further varied at or before the roup, so as to fit the
" views and convenience of purchasers. For further particulars,
" apply to the proprietors ; or to Maxwell & Graham, writers, &c."

CHAPTER III.

Kelvinbank in 1781, and Kelvingrove in 1790—Coal Quay at Windmillcroft—First Railway in Glasgow—The Windmill in 1780, and Salmon Fishing—Deepening and Embanking the Clyde in 1780—Patrick Reid, possessor by "Wadset" of Washington Street—Henry Monteith's attempted purchase of Washington Street for Clyde Trust in 1814—Washington Street, whence named.

THE following notices, relating to the lands of Kelvin Bank, now the property of the Trades' House, and Kelvingrove, now the West End Park, may prove interesting.

" *Glasgow Mercury,* 22d February, 1781."

" Notice.—To be sold, by private sale, the lands of Kelvinbank, " consisting of about twelve acres of ground, lying between Ander- " ston and Partick, in the Barony parish of Glasgow. The lands " are pleasantly situated, and are within one mile and a half of " Glasgow. They command an agreeable prospect ; are properly " inclosed and subdivided by ditch and hedge in fine order ; and " there is plenty of free stone quarry in the lands which can easily be " wrought. The house, offices, and garden on the lands are in good " order; supplied with water from a spring well, the water excellent " and quantity large. There are also a washing house and washing " field on the lands adjoining the water of Kelvin. Apply to " Archibald Govan, writer, &c."

Kelvin Bank was purchased about 1792 by John Wilson, jun., town clerk, for £1000, and was sold to the Trades' House of Glasgow, by Dr W. Rae Wilson, the nephew of Mr Wilson. George Crawfurd, Esq., in his interesting sketch of the Trades' House of Glasgow, page 207, informs us that, on the 4th of April, 1846, the said Incorporation purchased the lands of Kelvin Bank, " stated as " containing 70,588 square yards of unchecqued measurement, into " the centre of the river Kelvin, at £19,640 3s 9d." Also, " the " adjoining part of the lands of Sandyford, said to contain 18,531 " square yards of unchecqued and uninvestigated measurement, at " £10,250."

" *Glasgow Mercury,* 12th January, 1790."

" Sale of land in Lanarkshire."

" To be sold, by auction, in the Tontine Tavern, on Wednesday,
" 27th January, 1790, between the hours of two and three o'clock
" afternoon.

" The villa and lands of Kelvingrove, beautifully situated upon
" the banks of the river Kelvin, and perfectly retired, although
" within one mile of the city of Glasgow.

" The house, which overlooks the river, is built upon a very com-
" fortable plan, containing a dining room, drawing room, eight bed
" rooms, two lumber rooms, a kitchen, larder, and three cellars
" under ground.   The offices consist of a stable, with stalls for four
" horses, a cow house, milk house, chaise and cart house, a hay loft,
" pigeon house, poultry houses, all in the most complete order.
" There are also a pump-well in the yard, a convenient wash house
" with a pipe from the river, and a large and commodious cold bath.
" The garden, (which, as well as the offices, is hid from the dwelling
" house by trees and shrubbery), is well stocked with fruit trees and
" small fruit, and is surrounded by a brick wall, part of which has
" flues, and the whole of it is at present covered on both sides with
" a great variety of fruit trees of the best kinds.   There is also
" upon the ground a great variety of flowering shrubs, and a consid-
" erable quantity of barren timber, part old, and part lately planted,
" all in the most thriving condition, and the whole disposed in such
" a manner as to add greatly to the beauty of the place.

" The lands of Kelvingrove consist of about sixteen English acres:
" the public burdens are very moderate, and no claim can be made
" by the superior in consequence of the property being transferred.

" Also, to be sold, the benefit of a long lease of the farm of Woodside,
" consisting of about seventeen acres, which lie adjacent to the lands
" of Kelvingrove.   The lands of Kelvingrove and the grounds under
" lease for near half-a-mile are bounded by the river Kelvin, and
" being surrounded on all hands by beautiful landscapes, form such
" a situation as is rarely to be met with.

" Apply to William Blair, W.S., Edinburgh ; or John Maxwell,
" of Dargavel, writer, Glasgow, &c."

" *Glasgow Mercury,* 27th May, 1784."—" To be sold,

" That square piece of ground, being the east side of Kelvin-
" haugh, consisting of twelve Scots acres or thereby, inclosed by a

" bank on the east side and hedge on the west. Apply to Robert
" M'Lintock."

" *Glasgow Mercury*, 1st May, 1792."

" The Provost-Haugh, about 24 acres, has been purchased at
" private sale for no less than four thousand pounds. This added
" to the other pleasure ground along the river belonging to the city,
" is a valuable acquisition. The philanthropic Mr Howard, when
" surveying this tract of ground, declared it to be of inestimable
" value for preserving the health of the inhabitants.

" An acre of ground down the river, where the Coal Key stood,
" and bounded by the Kinning House burn, was sold by public
" roup for £350 sterling. It was let for five pounds yearly for
" sixteen years past."

I remember the Coal Quay, which stood at the present ferry, west
end of Windmillcroft. It was built by the Dumbarton Glass Work
Company to convey coals from the lands of Little Govan to their
works at Dumbarton. The river was then deeper at the Coal Quay
than at the Broomielaw. There was a timber tramway from the
Little Govan coal works to the said Quay, which ran through the
lands of Kingston, and by the road on the east side of Springfield.
I have walked upon this tramroad, which I believe was the first of
our Glasgow railways. The Dumbarton Glass Work Company also
possessed a tramroad on the north side of the Clyde, from the coal
works in the neighbourhood of Gartnavel ; but I do not recollect
the exact place in the river where the coals were shipped.

The footpath along the south bank of the river from the bridge
westward, crossed the south end of the Coal Quay, and when the
traveller came to the Kinning House burn, he was obliged to find
his way over it by a narrow wooden plank, without any protective
railing. I have often crossed the Kinning House burn by this
primitive bridge.

At this time there was a small wood on the lands of Windmillcroft, within a hedge on the south of the footpath which ran along
the banks of the river. This wood stood nearly on the place now
occupied as the north extremity of West Street.

When a little boy I went a fishing one Saturday with some of my
companions, in the river between the Kinning House burn and the
Mile burn (at the west end of the general terminus).

Among my associates was Archibald M'Guffie, of Greenock
(afterwards agent for the Bank of Scotland there).

We had all duly set our fishing lines in the river, and were waiting for a short time to give the fish time to swallow our baits, when Archy M'Guflie said that he would not draw his lines till the gabbert which appeared at the Broomielaw (coming right down the river with a large square sail and fair wind) had passed his lines. We laughed at Archie's speech, but for the fun of the thing said nothing; so we all proceeded to draw our lines, while Archie had his eyes always directed towards the gabbert, which appeared coming down the river at full sail with a fair wind and ebb tide, yet nevertheless did not seem to move out of the spot. Archie now got tired of waiting for the arrival of the gabbert, and so began to draw his lines, when all of us in great glee informed him that the gabbert he was so long looking for was just the windmill near the bridge, which, seen from the lands of the now general terminus, certainly had quite the appearance of a gabbert in full sail.

The site where the windmill stood is now near the centre of the river, a little below the bridge. At this time the windmill was without a roof, and its ground floor subjected to all manner of nuisances, so that a visit to it was rather trying to those who had delicate olfactory nerves. On this piscatory excursion our fishing was pretty successful, as each of us had caught a number of flounders and a few eels, but the great prize came to me of a very fine large salmon fry. I was delighted at my good luck, but in great terror, lest the Sheriff, who lived close at hand, in Park House, or some of the tacksmen of the Salmon fishery should get hold of me, and clap me up in prison for destroying salmon fry, the Sheriff having just issued the following notice:—

" *Glasgow Mercury*, 27th April, 1780."

" By the Sheriff of Lanarkshire."

" Whereas, notwithstanding the public promonitions that have
" been given, and the public examples which have been made, the
" illegal practice of *killing* salmon fry still prevails in this country,
" to the great prejudice of the salmon fishing, a reward of Half a
" Guinea is hereby offered for each information upon that head left
" at the Sheriff Clerk's office in Glasgow, mentioning the names and
" designations of the offenders, and the names and designation of the
" witnesses by whom the offences can be proved, to be paid by the
" Sheriff Clerk upon their conviction. The names of the informers
" shall be carefully concealed."

Having this Notice in view, I carefully hid my salmon-fry under the hedge at Greenlaw till our departure, when I ventured to carry it home, in tribulation, but rejoicing.

The salmon fishing on this part of the Clyde was then of some value, for in 14 years afterwards it appears to have been let for £104 per annum.

"Glasgow Mercury, 21st January, 1794."

" A few days ago the salmon fishing in the river Clyde, belonging " to certain proprietors of the parish of Govan, was let for three " years at £104 per annum."

The fishermen erected a hut on Greenlaw lands, near the Mileburn. It was built of wattles and turf. I have often seen gentlemen there purchasing on speculation for 1s or 1s 6d the draught of a fisherman's net, but in general the speculators only got a few small flounders. I had a strong suspicion that on those occasions, when the fishermen felt, by handling their nets that they had a salmon enclosed in them, they purposely allowed the salmon to escape, in the hopes of securing it to themselves in the next cast of the nets. As the saying goes, there are tricks in all trades.

It was fortunate for Glasgow that the salmon fishing on the river Clyde was not of very great value, for if it had been as lucrative to the proprietors of the lands on its banks as that of the Tay, and some other rivers on the east coast, the magistrates of Glasgow would have met with very strong opposition to all their navigation Bills. It is curious that none of the proprietors of the lands on the banks of the river Clyde, have ever made application to the Clyde Trust, or to the Glasgow magistrates for indemnification for the loss of the salmon fishery, occasioned by the operations of deepening and embanking the navigation.

In 1759, an Act of Parliament was obtained for rendering the river Clyde navigable to Glasgow, for large vessels, by means of locks, and from the following advertisement it will be seen that the magistrates of Glasgow were the first who set the example of gaining ground from the river by means of placing stobs on its margin, and then filling the space so stobbed in, with furze and rubbish.

"Glasgow Journal, 26th April, 1764."

" Any person who is willing to undertake for the delivery of a " considerable quantity of new hoed whins, to be laid down on each " side of the river Clyde below the Broomielaw, may apply to Robert

" Finlay, master of work.   And any person who can provide a large
" quantity of stobs, six feet and a half long, may also apply as above."

The proprietors of the lands on the banks of the river were not
long in discovering that they would derive more benefit from the
channel of the river being narrowed, than from the salmon fishery,
as the ground gained to them by the navigation operations came to
be added to their lands facing the river, and this done without their
bearing any share of the expense.

I remember many of the proprietors of lands next the river filling
up the vacancies between the jetties with the cuttings of hedges and
all kinds of rubbish, so as to form firm land by the deposits of floods.
Mr David Todd, at Springfield, and Mr Francis Reid, at Greenlaw,
each gained above an acre of river side ground by such operations,
which ground came afterwards to be purchased back by the river
Trustees, at £2 2s per square yard, or thereby.

In 1780, the Point House and Ferry appear to have been private
property.

" *Glasgow Mercury*, 9th March, 1780."

" To be sold, privately, the Pointhouse, with the ferry and boats,
" and some lands adjoining the same.   Apply to William Robert-
" son, at Smithfield.   22d November, 1781.—To be sold, jointly, or
" separately, the Smithfield houses and lands on the Broomielaw
" Croft, near the Key of Glasgow, with the lands and houses at
" Point House, and the slitting, rolling, and grinding mills and
" houses on Kelvin, with smith's tools and materials.   Progress of
" writs and inventories of the whole to be seen in the hands of
" William Robertson, Smithfield."

The above Smithfield property not being sold at the time, was
again advertised for sale on 15th February, 1786, at the upset price
of £2200, there being a street 60 feet wide delineated on the plan.

" *Glasgow Mercury*, 29th December, 1786."

" To be sold, the lands of Greenlaw, with the salmon fishing
" effeiring thereto.   The lands of Greenlaw consist of fifteen acres
" or thereby, very rich arable ground, delightfully situated upon the
" river Clyde, and roads leading to Paisley and Greenock, well inclosed
" and sub-divided, lying opposite to Lancefield, within one mile of
" Glasgow.   Apply to Alexander M'Culloch, writer in Glasgow."

Greenlaw was purchased by Francis Reid, Esq., for £1000, and
was sold by the trustees of his widow for £3800.   About three
acres, lying between the Greenock and Paisley roads, were sold by

E

Mr Reid's widow, to Mr Mair, of the Plantion, for £300, and the remainder now forms the General Terminus.

"*Mercury*, 31st January, 1787.—To be sold, the house and lands " of Mavis Bank, about one mile west of the new bridge. The " lands consist of about six acres, of excellent quality, and divided " into several small enclosures. Apply to George Smith, writer."

"*Mercury*, 23d May, 1787.—To be sold, the Bottle House and " other buildings, at Verreville, together with the ground adjoining " it, consisting of about three acres. Apply to John Geddes."

"*Mercury*, 25th July, 1787.—To be sold, six roods of land, or " thereby, in the Broomielaw Croft of Glasgow, whereof three roods " lie from east to west upon Clyde, and the other three roods run " from south to north, and lie upon the south-side of the road lead- " ing to Anderston. Apply to Gilbert Hamilton."

"*Mercury*, 1st December, 1789.—To be sold, feued, or let, that " bleachfield called Brownfield, near to the Broomielaw. As the " field is an extensive square piece of ground, containing more than " ten acres, and runs from Anderston road to the Clyde, few places " are so well adapted for the purpose of building squares or streets " upon. Apply to Brown, Carrick & Company."

"*Mercury*, 1st December, 1789.—Lands to be let.—The com- " mittee appointed by the Magistrates and Town Council of Glasgow, " for setting those parts of the barony of Gorbals, which now belongs " to the City, do hereby intimate that they will set, for one year, " from and after Martinmas last, 1789, the sundry plots of ground, " as after mentioned, viz :—

	Acres.	Roods.	Falls.
" Part of Windmill Croft, ...	13	1	30
" Waterside, west of the Coal Quay, ...	1	1	35
" Part of Trades' Croft and Croft Andrew, ...	19	3	18
	34	3	3

" The above lands are situate upon the side of the river Clyde, a " little below the windmill.

	Acres.	Roods.	Falls.
" Gushet Fauld, ...	8	2	30
" Bryce Land, ...	8	0	34
" Gallow Know, ...	3	0	19
" Bryce Land, ...	6	3	34
" Coply Hill Park, ...	9	1	38
" Coply Hill, ...	3	1	18
" Sceve-wright and Cameron's Eye, ...	16	3	3
	56	3	16

"The last-mentioned lands are situate south from the Gorbals,
" upon each side of the road, leading from thence to Pollokshaws.
" Apply to Bailie M'Lehose, Mr John Lowrie, or the Master of
" Work."

" *Mercury*, 1st December, 1789.—Lands in Gorbals to be let.—The
" Trades' House of Glasgow, and the Incorporations of Hammermen,
" Tailors, Cordiners, Maltmen, Weavers, Fleshers, Bakers, Skinners,
" Wrights, Coopers, and Masons, who are proprietors of a fourth-
" part of the lands and barony of Gorbals, having appointed a
" delegate from each body to act as a general committee in the
" management of the fourth-part of the barony, which has been
" awarded to them by the Arbiters in the submission with the
" magistrates and council, and the patrons of Hutchesons' Hospital,
" the proprietors of the residue of the barony : the committee do
" now intimate that they are willing to give a set of their fourth-
" part of the lands, either in whole or in parcels, and for one year
" or a longer term. Apply to Mr John M'Aslan, convener ; or to
" James Mathie, writer."

" *Mercury*, 6th April, 1790."

"Gorbals ground, belonging to Hutchesons' Hospital, to be
" fened. That large inclosure on the south west of Gorbals, called
" Stirling Fold and Well Croft, measuring 29 acres, 3 roods, 23 falls,
" and that strip of ground opposite to the road leading to the new
" bridge, and of the same breadth with that road, measuring 3 roods,
" and 8 falls. The upset yearly feu-duty of the said Grounds is to
" be £257 16s 6d, or eight guineas per acre. The coal and minerals
" are to be reserved to the proprietors. Apply to James Hill,
" writer in Glasgow."

" *Mercury*, 11th September, 1792."

" Building ground in Gorbals Barony, (Tradeston). To be sold,
" a great variety of Steadings belonging to the Trades' House and
" Incorporations, partly fronting the public road leading to Paisley,
" at the west end of the Toll Bar, and in other respects fronting
" public streets sixty feet wide in parallel lines with the streets of
" the town, which is going on briskly at the end of the new
" bridge. The price to be converted into a feu-duty. Apply to
" convener M'Lehose, or J. T. Mathie, writer." (The town of
Tradeston was laid off by John Gardner, Senr., optician).

Mr Crawfurd, in his sketch of the Trades' House, (page 186), thus

writes:—" The price originally paid by the Trades' House and
" Incorporations, for the Gorbals Lands, as their one-fourth share of
" the whole price paid to Sir Robert Douglas, in 1860, was thirty-one
" thousand merks, equal to £1743 13s sterling.

"The Trades' House and Incorporations received £1692 12s 6d
" from the proprietors of the Glasgow, Paisley, and Ardrossan Canal,
" in 1814, for 2 acres, 1 rood, and 36 falls of the lands taken for the
" purpose of making the canal, and £732 10s further, in 1823, for
" 3257 square yards taken for increasing the company's accommoda-
" tion.   For those sums the Trades' House and Incorporations took
" payment in shares of the stock of the Canal Company, and those
" shares are now worthless through the total failure of that enter-
" prise.   In 1829, however, the Trades' House and Incorporations
" received £10,000 from the trustees for improving the navigation
" of the Clyde, for the ground which lay between Clyde Street on ˙
" the south, the river on the north, the bridge on the east, and West
" Street on the west.   This ground is now chiefly excavated for the
" Harbour of Glasgow, and is partly occupied by the south wharf.

" In 1831, the steadings which had been feued yielded feu-duties
" to the amount of £1769 11s 9d, the highest price obtained having
" been 3s 6d a square yard.   Between 1831 and 1856, the whole of
" unfeued ground was feued, the last feus effected being ten shillings.
" The lowest price taken during this period being 8s, and the highest
" obtained 25s a square yard.   These amounted to £64,127 1s 8d,
" converted into feu-duties amounting to £3,206 7s 1d.   These
" feu-duties, added to the amount payable in 1831, makes
" £4,975 18s 10d of feu-duties now payable.   Every yard of the 78
" acres, 3 roods, and 14 falls, conveyed to the Trades' House, as
" their one-fourth part, is now sold or feued.   The purchase and
" the fortunate management of these lands are the chief source of
" the wealth of the Trades' House and Incorporations."

The following account relative to the lands, now of Washington
Street, is taken from a private MS. in my possession:—Patrick
Reid, maltman in Glasgow, in early life had lent a few hundred
merks to the proprietor of the lands which now form Washington
Street, upon the terms of *Wadset*, by which the lands are absolutely
disponed to, and enjoyed by the lender, and the borrower pays no
interest upon the loan; liberty of redemption, however, is reserved
to the borrower within a certain time agreed upon, but which time,
if allowed to elapse without repayment of the loan, the lands become
the absolute and irredeemable property of the lender.

Under the provisions of the said contract of *Wadset*, Patrick Reid continued to enjoy the use and usufruct of the said lands of Washington Street, till the term of redemption agreed upon had passed over without payment of the loan, consequently the said lands became irredeemably invested in Patrick Reid as absolute proprietor of the same. Patrick Reid was succeeded by his eldest son John, who dying intestate, was succeeded by his uncle, Matthew Reid, merchant in Leicester, as heir at law to the said lands of Washington Street, and he dying, bequeathed, by his will, his estates heritable and moveable, to his wife, Mary Aitcheson, as his universal legatee.

In the meantime a grand-daughter of the original proprietor of the lands of Washington Street having married a writer in Edinburgh, that gentleman conceived that there was a flaw in the deed of *Wadset*, and that Patrick Reid had not taken the usual legal steps to invest himself in the said lands at the expiration of the term of redemption; consequently that the property in question was still redeemable upon payment of the original loan by Wadset. Accordingly he made a judicial offer of repayment of the loan, and demanded a re-conveyance of the lands of Washington Street. This demand, of course, brought on a law suit before the Court of Session, which, having been litigated there for upwards of eighteen years, Mrs Matthew Reid, the defender, became so disgusted with the delay of the proceedings, and harassed in her mind by the various technical objections brought forward against the validity of the Wadset, that she offered to make over her rights, in the subjects in question, to her eldest son Matthew, merchant in Leicester, if he would relieve her of the law suit. Her son accepted his mother's offer, and immediately thereafter set on foot an arrangement for a compromise with the Edinburgh writer, which he fortunately accomplished by the payment to him of £1000 sterling, thereby becoming the unquestionable proprietor of the lands of Washington Street. On the death of Matthew Reid, jun., (the son) intestate, the lands of Washington Street fell by inheritance to his brother, Dr John Reid, physician in London, who, not long after, dying without issue, his sister Mary succeeded to the said lands. This Miss Mary Reid being on very intimate terms with her cousin, Miss Aitcheson, the two young ladies entered into a mutual contract, by which the longest liver of them was to inherit the estates of the one who should first die. Accordingly, on the death of Miss Aitcheson, Miss Reid succeeded to that lady's fortune, which was pretty considerable. Miss Mary Reid was a literary lady, and was spoken of as a blue stocking in my early days. She was a keen politician, of the Foxite school, and, accordingly, employed Robert Grahame, Esq., writer, as her Glasgow agent, that gentleman's political opinions being in unison with her own. Mr Grahame took the entire management of the Washington Street property, for behoof of Miss Reid, who then resided in Leicester. About the year 1814, when Henry Monteith was lord provost of Glasgow, the River Trustees, having thought of excavating docks at the Broomielaw, to accommodate the increasing shipping of the harbour, authorised Mr Monteith to treat with Mr Grahame for the purchase of the said lands of Washington Street, then vacant ground. Mr Monteith, accordingly, waited on Mr Grahame, to know the price which Miss Reid would take for the said lands, fully expecting to acquire them at a very moderate price, seeing that they were waste grounds . bringing in no return. In reply to Mr Monteith's inquiry as to the price which Miss Reid would take for the said property, Mr Grahame at once said that the very lowest price would be £10,000. Mr Monteith, who, in his younger days, had remembered the trifling value of ground in the immediate neighbourhood of Anderston, at the mention of £10,000, held up his two hands in amazement, at what he considered its absolute absurdity, exclaiming that the price demanded was so utterly extravagant and ridiculous, that it was quite unnecessary to say a word more on the subject, and so forthwith left Mr Grahame's office. Provost Monteith reported so strongly against the whole project, that the River Trustees hesitated about making any further attempt to acquire Miss Reid's lands; but about a year afterwards, the said trustees having again taken the matter into their consideration, came to be of opinion that the lands in question, being so favourably situated for a dock, should be purchased by the Trust, notwithstanding of the price being likely to be rather extravagant; they therefore, again, requested Mr Monteith to wait on Mr Grahame with an offer of £8000 for the said lands. When Mr Monteith again waited on Mr Grahame he commenced his address to him by saying that the River Trustees, contrary to his opinion, had now agreed to make Miss Reid an offer of £8000 for the Washington Street lands, and he added, that he was confident that no such offer would ever again be made for these vacant grounds. But Mr Grahame, in reply to this offer, repeated what he had before said, that the very lowest price would be £10,000. In consequence of this answer the treaty for the purchase of the lands in question was finally broken off, and thus the River Trustees lost a most convenient site for a dock, in the very heart of the harbour, and of the city. Mr Grahame shortly afterwards laid off Washington Street for feuing, and ultimately the feus realized a price equal to £30,000.

Miss Mary Reid, in accordance with her political principles, named the new street "Washington Street," in honour of the founder of American independence.

Miss Mary Reid died on the 14th of August, 1839, aged seventy, and was succeeded by her nephews and nieces, the Pearces, of Leicester.

By looking at Fleming's large map of Glasgow, published in 1815, it will be seen that the lands now of Washington Street then consisted of a large oblong piece of ground, stated to be the property of Matthew Reid. On the west it formed the western boundary of the city, lying between Clyde Street and M'Alpine Street. It stood north and south from Anderston Walk to the margin of the river Clyde—a glorious situation for a dock, which our city authorities unfortunately allowed to slip through their hands.

CHAPTER IV.

Cleland's Sketch of the Green—Improvements in the Green, 1638-1664—Fleshers'
Haugh in 1792—The Green as it stood in 1816—Coal under the Green, and proposal
to work it in 1858—Discussion in the City Council—Proposed Improvements in 1813
—Subsidence of the Green in 1754—The Point Isle in 1760—Dowcot Green Island
—The Horse Ford—Battle of the Bell of the Brae.

DR CLELAND in his Annals, Vol. II., p. 457, has given us a more
detailed statement of the history of the Green of Glasgow than our
other Glasgow historians, and in particular has narrated the improvements made on it during the time that he held the municipal
office of superintendent of public works. He says that although it
is by no means certain at what period the Green became the property of the community, it is more than probable that it was included in the grant which James II. made to William Turnbull,
bishop of Glasgow, on 20th April, 1450. The original grant,
whether it emanated from King James or any other having power to
confer it, was of very small extent when compared with what the
Green is at present, being wholly comprehended in what is now
known by the name of the Laigh Green, bounded on the west by
what was termed the Skinners' Green, now the site of the gaol and
public offices, on the north by the Molendinar burn and Camlachie
burn, on the south by the river Clyde, and on the east by the lands
of Kinclaith, at the west end of the High Green where the Washing
House is placed. It would appear that this gift was of very little
use for a long period after it became the property of the community,
as the principal part of the inhabitants resided at the upper part of
the town ; and when, in process of time, they came gradually to reside in the lower part of the town, the Laigh Green lay so low as to
be affected by every spring-tide, so that pools and islands were
formed in it, which have only been removed since the year 1635.

From the year 1638 till 1661, during the provostships of Patrick
Bell of Cowcaddens, John Anderson of Dowhill, and John Campbell
of Blythswood,* the Laigh Green was greatly improved.

* Query.—Was it at this time that those three active provosts acquired among themselves such large slices of our Great Western Common ?

In 1664, during the provostship of John Bell, the magistracy and council, in consideration of the great increase of inhabitants, and the want of a suitable park or green, resolved to purchase such parts of the lands of Kinclaith and Daffiegreen, now called the High Green, as should, from time to time, be brought into the market.* Accordingly, in the course of thirty years, the magistrates and council had purchased, from a great number of individuals, the whole of the High Green, bounded on the west by the east end of the Laigh Green, on the north by the Reidclothglott or Camlachie burn, on the south partly by the river Clyde, and partly by Provost Haugh, and on the east by the boundary of the Royalty, as it was anciently, and is now set off by landmarks.

In the year 1686, immediately before the Revolution, and during the provostship of John Barnes, Esq., the magistrates and council resolved to purchase the run-riggs of Craignestock, now known by the name of the Calton Green. These purchases, which had been begun by Provost Barnes, were completed by Provost Anderson, in 1699.

The lands of Craignestock were bounded on the west by a road on the east of Markdaily lands, now the continuation of St Mungo's Lane, on the north by the loan leading to Rutherglen, on the south by the Reidcloth burn, and on the east by other lands of Craignestock.

In a few years after this purchase was completed, the magistrates and council built a stone-wall along the north boundary of the Green, commencing at Skinners' Green, and terminating at the east extremity.

It does not appear that there was any other addition made to the Green till the year 1773, when the magistrates and council purchased upwards of 28 acres from Colin Rae, Esq., of Little Govan,†

---

* Was the High Green purchased for the community as a Bonne Bouche to stop complaints for the loss of so valuable a part of the Western Common, which had been previously so disposed of?

† *Glasgow Journal*, 28th Nov., 1776—"Notice, that these 11 acres, 1 rood, and 12 " falls of land, belonging to the city of Glasgow, lately acquired from Colin Rae, of Little " Govan, lying beyond the head of the Green of Glasgow, and on the east side of the " road belonging to Peter Bell, of the Cowcaddens, leading from his haugh on the north " side of the river Clyde to the high road leading from the Green to Wishart's House. " As also the lands called St Enoch's Croft, presently possessed by William Horn, " wright, belonging to the said city, are to be let in tack for the space of seven years, " after Martinmas last, 1776, by public roup, within the Council Chambers, on the " 16th curt. Also that part of St Enoch's Croft, on the west side of Jamaica Street, " now used as a timber yard, to be let in tack for seven years after Martinmas.

and several smaller lots of the lands of Kinclaith from other persons, which have since continued to form a part of the Green at the east end ; and that the park might be as extensive and complete as the special localities would possibly permit, the magistrates and council, in 1792, purchased from the late Patrick Bell, of Cowcaddens, the lineal descendant of the respectable provosts of that name, the lands of Provost Haugh, &c., or Fleshers' Haugh, so called from the pasturage being let out to certain members of that incorporation.

The lands of Kinclaith being thus partially acquired at different periods from a number of individuals who all exercised their own mode of improving their property, some by erecting small houses, others by letting out runnings for cropping, or for the purpose of trade, as might best suit their respective interest or views, it is not surprising that the surface was irregular, rendered more so, in consequence of the Camlachie burn which separates the Calton from the High Green, lying considerably under the surface of either. The greater part of the trees in the Green were planted during the time that Robert Roger, John Aird, Peter Murdoch, Andrew Ayton, Archibald Ingram and Arthur Connell held the office of chief magistrate.

In 1730, during the time that Peter Murdoch was provost, the Public Washing House was erected; a lead or water course was afterwards taken from the Camlachie burn for driving the machinery, by which water was forced from the river into the Washing House.

In 1756, Provost George Murdoch commenced the formation of walks in the Green, which has been continued by several of his successors. The serpentine walks, which were formed with shrubbery, came to be so much abused by idle and dissolute persons that it became necessary to root out a considerable part of them.*

" N.B. The old dyke at the head of the Green is to be removed and re-built in the " march of the town's ground, on the west side of the said Patrick Bell's foresaid road. " The new dyke to be five quarters high, twenty inches thick at bottom, and ten inches " thick at top, and to be coped with the cope stones on the said old dyke. Any person " willing to contract for executing the above work may apply to the town-clerk of " Glasgow."

　　　* *Glasgow Journal*, 15th March, 1756.—" By order of the Magistrates."

　　" The Magistrates having directed a further improvement to be made upon the Town's " Park or New Green, by forming a walk and planting trees, do hereby give public " notice, that in case any of these trees shall be cut, peeled, or any way destroyed, they " are determined to take recourse upon the inhabitants of Calton as lying nearest to the " new plantation, in terms of the Act after-mentioned : and they likewise offer a reward

In 1777, the Arns Well or Reservoir was opened, during the provostship of Robert Donald, Esq.

In the year 1744, during the time that Andrew Cochran was provost, the magistrates and council would have sold a part of the Laigh Green, but for the general voice of the public being raised against it.

In 1810, the Gaol and public offices were erected on the west side of the continuation of Saltmarket Street, at the bottom of the Laigh Green, chiefly on the ground which was formerly the Skinners' Green. The ground on the east side of the street, although authorized to be sold, still forms, and is intended to remain, a part of the Laigh Green. Before the stripe of ground in the Calton Green was brought into the market, the magistrates, with concurrence of the trustees on the Muirkirk Road, effected a very important improvement in the formation of Great Hamilton Street, by widening the old road leading to Rutherglen from the stripe of ground authorized to be sold.*

During the currency of the last twenty-five years, the High Green has been increased nearly one third. In 1791, there were

" of five guineas to those who will discover the persons guilty of destroying the trees,
" fences, or walks, so as they can be brought to punishment, in terms of the Act passed
" in the first Parliament of King George the First."

"*Mercury*, 5th April, 1756."

" Whereas, the City of Glasgow hath made new improvements upon their New Green,
" by making of walks and planting of young trees, and that the Magistrates hath adver-
" tised in the public papers that if any of these their new improvements be damaged any
" manner of way, that they are resolved to take recourse upon the inhabitants of tho
" Calton for the same. Bailie Miller, in the Calton, does hereby give notice to the
" inhabitants of the Calton of Glasgow, and others, that they resolve to be so neigh-
" bourly to the City of Glasgow, as to be at all due pains to be watchful of their interest
" to make discovery of any who shall damage the said walks, fencing, or planting ; and
" that he, with the concurrence of some of the principal inhabitants of Calton, will give
" two guineas, over and above what the Magistrates of Glasgow hath offered, to any
" who shall make such discoveries as they may bring the offenders to light. And like-
" wise, that whereas upon the night between the 2d and 3d instant, one of the young
" trees was pulled up by the root by some malicious person, they promise to give one
" guinea over and above the £5 5s that the Magistrates hath offered, for the discovery
" for pulling up the said tree."

* This stripe of ground formed part of the public walks of the Green. It was enclosed on the north by a stone wall, and there was a double row of fine trees upon its whole extent. Its gravel walk joined the serpentine walks at the Camlachie burn, over which there was a bridge. In my time it was a public parade for the citizens.

It is singular that Dr Cleland makes no mention of the large portion of the Calton Green which the magistrates of that time feued off to form Monteith Row ; but it must be remembered that the Doctor himself, as superintendent of public works, had a large share in the act of thus curtailing our Public Park. He was bailie in 1806.

houses and places of business on what is now the public Green, and walls bounding a cart road leading to Provost Haugh. In 1806, the water course connected with the Washing House was often so stagnant during the summer months, as to become offensive to the citizens. The banks contiguous to Peat Bog were so rugged and wasted down by springs, that they were not only offensive to the eye, but completely useless. The Laigh Green lay so low, and was so irregular in its surface, that a slight swell on the river or a smart shower laid it under water, which had to be carried off to the Camlachie burn by an open drain. The entries to the Laigh Green by the Saltmarket Street, Cow Lane, and the Old Bridge, were so narrow, irregular, and dirty, from their vicinity to the Slaughter House, that with the exception to the first they were chiefly used by cattle and fleshers' dogs.

The Molendinar and Camlachie burns ran through the streets in an uncovered state, crossing the Skinners' Green and Saw Mill, in an oblique direction. The Skinners' Green was insulated by the burn and Slaughter House, and the bottom of the Laigh Green was surrounded by offensive pits, used by skinners and tanners. The Slaughter House spread over a large and irregular surface on the bank of the river, and was bounded by crooked lanes on the north and north-east parts, than which there was no other entry to the Green from the west.

The dung of the Slaughter House, and the intestines of slaughtered animals, were collected in heaps, and allowed to remain for months together, till putrefaction took place, to the great annoyance of the neighbourhood. A glue work, and a work in which tharm was manufactured from the intestines of animals in a recent state, was erected at the bottom of the Laigh Green; and to complete the nuisance, the adjoining houses were occupied for cleaning tripe; and rees were fitted up for the retail of coal and coal-culm. The space on the bank of the river at the east side of the old bridge, which had been enclosed for a live cattle market, came now to be used by the police as a receptacle for filth from the streets. The improvements on the Green and the adjoining properties, were so far completed in 1814 that the following may be taken as a description of them since that period.

The Green, as it now stands, (1816) contains upwards of 108 acres. The circuit of the gravel walks has been completed, and the houses and intermediate walls on the High Green removed ; the water course connected with the Washing House has been rendered

unnecessary by a plentiful supply of water from the Water Companies. The banks adjoining Peat Bog have been drained and
turfed, so as to render them at once useful and ornamental. The
Laigh Green is in progress of improvement; a street in connection
with the gravel walks has been formed in front of the range of the
intended Calton Green buildings, to be bounded on the side next
the Green by a parapet wall and rail. The course of a considerable
part of the Molendinar and Camlachie burns, from their junction,
has been completely altered and arched, and streets formed over it.
A breast work at the river supporting an iron railing has been
built from the timber to the old bridge; the enteries to the Laigh
Green by the Saltmarket and East Clyde Street are rendered
spacious by the removal of houses and nuisances, and the thoroughfare has been greatly increased by the Market Lane. The lime and
tan pits, saw mill, tharm work, tripe houses and coal-rees, at the
Skinners' Green, have been removed, and the public offices and gaol
erected on or near their site ; the spacious street, 120 feet, in front
of the portico of the public offices, has been raised so as to protect
it from the highest flood ; the side next the green is to be bounded
by a low parapet wall and railing. The Slaughter Houses have
been removed from the bank of the river, and East Clyde Street, 80
feet wide, formed on part of their site. These buildings which, under
existing circumstances,[*] could not possibly be removed to a greater
distance from the river than where they are now placed, are perhaps
the largest in the Island for the purpose of slaughtering animals.
These operations have cost little short of Fifty Thousand Pounds.

In 1858 the magistrates and council of Glasgow, having expended
large sums in the purchase of the West End Park, the M'Lellan
Property and South Side Park, found themselves short of cash ; it,
therefore, occurred to a number of the council, that by sinking of
shafts and by working of coal in the Green, the funds necessary for
clearing off the debt in question, could easily be obtained. To this
scheme very serious objections were made, such as, that it would
destroy the walks of the Green as a parade, would create a public
nuisance, and would seriously damage the land by causing a subsidence to take place on its surface ; in short, that it would alto-

---

* These circumstances were, that the Incorporation of Fleshers possessed certain
rights and privileges, which they maintained were infringed upon by the magistrates ;
in consequence thereof a law suit took place before the Court of Session on the subject,
when, after a long course of litigation, the Court decided against the magistrates, thereby
establishing the claims of the Incorporation of Fleshers.

gether destroy the amenity of the Green as a public place of recreation.

At a meeting of the town council, on the 1st of April, 1858, Mr M'Dowall, councillor, made the following motion, "That the magistrates and council should remit to the Committee on Finance to make the necessary arrangements for letting the coal in the Green by public roup."

To this scheme, in any shape whatever, Councillor Moir most strenuously objected. He said, "I have not spoken to one working man who would not willingly pay a tax of one penny per pound on his rental, rather than have the Green so destroyed." Mr Moir then gave the following excellent epitome of the history of the Green :—

" I have looked at the different records and documents on the
" subject, and although the details of the origin of the Park are not
" very distinct, they certainly show that the Corporation have been
" the means of the acquisition of the place. It is supposed from all
" that I can gather on the matter, that the first portion of the Green
" was a grant from James II. to William Turnbull, Lord of Provan
" and Bishop of Glasgow. The portion thus granted would seem to
" be that near our present Court House, and named at the period
" (1450) the 'Laigh Green,' or the 'Skinners' Green.'
" In the year 1664, and under the provostship of John Bell,
" another portion of land called the 'High Green,' bounded on the
" north by Camlachie burn, on the west by the east end of the Laigh
" Green, on the south by the Clyde and Provost Haugh, and on the
" east by the boundary of the Royalty, was added to the other.
" In the year 1686, before the Revolution, and during the
" provostship of John Barns, the Corporation commenced the
" purchase of the run-riggs of Craignestock, now called the Calton
" Green, near Monteith Row. In 1780, the whole Green contained
" 59 acres 1 rood and 7 falls; and at that period there was an
" island in the river containing an acre and 30 falls, and situated
" near where the Washing House now stands, and forming one of
" the principal salmon shots. During the provostship of Andrew
" Cochrane, in 1744, the Corporation tried to sell a portion of the
" Laigh Green, in consequence of their being laid under contribution
" through the rebellion of 1715; but public indignation was so
" great, and so strongly expressed against their doing so, that they
" had to abandon the attempt.
" The first walks in the Green were made in 1756; and in the
" year 1783, more than 28 acres were purchased from Colin Rae of

" Little Govan, and several smaller lots of the lands of Kinclaith
" were also bought from other parties. In 1792, the Corporation
" purchased from Patrick Bell of Cowcaddens, the portion of the
" Green called Fleshers' Haugh and Provost Haugh ; and this was
" the last purchase that I know of being made for the purpose of
" forming what is now known as the Green." Mr Moir concludes
his statement by saying, " I think some deference ought to be shown
" to the present hostile attitude of the working classes, especially
" when the people at the east end would pay a tax of a penny a
" pound to avoid the Green being ruined."

In consequence of the public having expressed a strong feeling
against the scheme of working coal on the Green, the magistrates
and council have allowed the matter to drop in the meantime.

The community are much indebted indeed to Mr Moir for the
very great attention which he has paid to improve and ornament
the Green of Glasgow, and to render it not only useful to the public,
but also to make it a place of healthful amusement and recreation
to all classes of our citizens; this he has done without fee or
reward.

In reference to certain operations which were made to meliorate
various portions of the Green, Mr Moir, on a subsequent occasion
thus informs us :

" In the year 1813, the magistrates and council having directed
" a design and specification for improving the Green to be drawn
" up, and a plan thereof to be made, the same was accordingly done
" and approved of. The design comprehended the following par-
" ticulars :—

" 1st. Raising the Laigh Green in some places four, and in others
" five feet.

" 2d. Embanking the Fleshers' Haugh.

" 3d. Forming a tunnel from the head of the Green to the
" Episcopal Chapel, for containing the Camlachie burn.

" 4th. Slope levelling the Calton Green, so as to make it
" assimilate with the High Green.

" 5th. Levelling the other parts of the Green.

" 6th. Converting the road from St Mungo's Lane to Craignestock
" into a street.

" 7th. Laying out the Calton Green in building lots, and forming
" a street between them and the Green.

" 8th. Forming a street from the bottom of the Saltmarket to the
" Calton Green, in front of the English Chapel, in a line with the

" south front of the wing of the southmost house in Charlotte
" Street.

" 9th. Planting trees in various places of the Green, and lastly,
" the removal of the Washing House. After the rise of the surface
" of the Laigh Green above alluded to had been effected, it was still
" common for the Laigh Green to be flooded in the winter season.
" Subsequent to this, but previous to my connection with the
" Corporation in 1848, it was again raised from three to four feet
" all over, since which period I think it has never been again
" flooded. During the time that I have been connected with the
" Corporation the embankment of the river has been completed from
" the Fleshers' Haugh to Hutchesons' Bridge ; numerous new foot-
" paths have been made ; the drainage of the Green has been com-
" pleted ; various corners have been planted with trees, ornamental
" shrubs and flowers, and surrounded with a neat malleable iron ·
" railing, as has also a belt running along the whole length of
" Monteith Row, also enclosed with a neat malleable iron railing ;
" and now, though everything has not been done that may yet be
" done, I look upon Glasgow Green to be one of the noblest recrea-
" tion grounds in the three kingdoms."

At the time when the subject of working the coal in the Green
was under discussion at our Council Board, I addressed the following letter to the *Glasgow Herald* of 22d January, 1858 :—

" Subsidence of the Green of Glasgow."

" There is a curious instance of the subsidence of the Green of
" Glasgow that took place in the year 1754, which has not been taken
" notice of by any of our Glasgow historians ; but on the subject—
" that danger might arise from a similar subsidence, in the event of
" the working of the coal in the Green being proceeded with, per-
" perhaps the following notice may prove interesting to our citizens.
" It may, however, be as well, in the first place, to recapitulate the
" observations of different councillors on the subject, made at the
" last meeting of our Council Board, as I have some doubts of the
" correctness of their views as to the cause of sinkings on the Green
" at different times."

The following is taken from the *Glasgow Herald* :—

" Mr M'Adam asked what kind of roof was over this coal-field ?

" Mr Murray said it was that usually belonging to the Glasgow
" coal-field.

" Mr M'Adam said that his question had reference to the keeping

" up of the ground, for it had been very much sunk from the effects
" of similar works.

" Mr Murray—The coal in the Green lies very deep, and there is
" little fear of the level of ground being much interfered with.
" Where the ground has sunk much the roof has been partly com-
" posed of sand.

" Mr Dreghorn recommended, as* this was a very important
" matter, that it be delayed, and that meanwhile the report be
" circulated amongst the members.

" Mr M'Dowall said it was contemplated by Mr Johnstone that
" there would be subsidence of from two to three feet ; but he said
" that this might easily be filled up by deposits obtained from the
" public, and long before the coal was worked out of the ground
" might be made as good as ever it was.

" Mr Gray—It is very desirable that we should know a little more
" of the subsidence than we do now. The subsidence on the south
" side, in similar cases, is even more than four or five feet.

" Mr Bain said the question of subsidence was an important one.
" On Rutherglen Green, for instance, the subsidence had been so
" great as to form a loch, upon which people skated in winter
" time. At Mr Wilson's coal-fields in the north it was also very
" great. On the Rutherglen Road the subsidence was very great—
" so much so as to have torn some of the houses to shivers. At Mr
" Reid's workings, near Rutherglen, the walls were so much opened
" that any one might put his hands into the crevices.

" Mr Moir stated that on the south side houses were held together
" by iron rods and connecting plates fixed on the walls.

" Mr Binnie said the subsidence would not be of any moment."

From the above extract it appears that all the said councillors
were of opinion that the sinking in the Green had been caused by
certain mining operations which had taken place in the adjacent
lands. But I cannot reconcile this with the undermentioned circumstance of the Green having sunk above ten feet in 1754—and
this upon the highest or strongest ground of the Green, while the
lowest or weakest part remained unaffected, and while the coal in
the Green had not been worked at all.

" Extract—*Scots Magazine*, 1754—page 154."

" Letters from Glasgow, of 6th March, bear that people were
" greatly surprised with the sinking of the walk along the river side,
" near the head of the Green, in breadth in some parts near twenty,

F

" and in length about eighty yards. The sinking, which appeared
" at first to be about five feet, continued gradually for some days,
" and then it was above ten.

" It is remarkable that though the distance from the walk to the
" river is about fifty or sixty yards, with a considerable descent, yet
" it is only the highest ground that is sunk. No alteration appears
" near the water edge, excepting a few small chinks or openings."

" Various are the conjectures about the cause. Some will have it
" that there are springs below ground which communicate with the
" river, and (as the soil is sandy) have formed a cavity by washing
" away the sand, and there being nothing to support the weight
" above, the earth has fallen in. Others suspect that the river—
" which, at this part, forms a curve or crook, and is very deep, has,
" by degrees, washed away the foundation, etc.—by the openings
" that appear at the greatest distance from it, and the way they
" point, they apprehend that if proper care is not speedily taken
" the river will cut out a new channel for itself."

In the year 1754, when the above-mentioned subsidence took
place on the Green of Glasgow the whole of Europe, and likewise America, and the West Indies, suffered from a succession
of earthquakes, which continued till 1775, when Lisbon was
overwhelmed by one of them. In 1754 we learn from the *Scots
Magazine*, that the shocks of an earthquake were felt all over
Yorkshire. That in Sicily two villages were swallowed up, and that
40,000 persons perished at Grand Cairo, and two-thirds of that city
laid in ruins by like convulsions of the earth. Under these circumstances, I think it is probable that the sinking of the walk on the
High Green of Glasgow, in March, 1754, was caused by repeated
small shocks of an earthquake, which, although so slight as not to
alarm the citizens, were quite sufficient to affect the subsidence
mentioned. It may be remarked, however, that the walk which had
thus sunk ten feet, lay on the high ground immediately on the north
of the Arns Well, and might have been soft sandy ground, full of
springs. From the name of " Peat-Bog," which the place still bears,
we may presume that the lands on this portion of the Green had at
one time been a marsh, or peat moss.

It appears from the *Scots Magazine* of 1755, (page 594), and of
1756, (page 40), that there were continued shocks of earthquakes
felt all over the world during the said years, and that these shocks
also affected Glasgow, and the lands in its neighbourhood.

" 1756, 6th January. On Wednesday last, betwixt one and two

" o'clock in the morning, a small shock of an earthquake was felt at
" Greenock, and several places in that neighbourhood, as well as at
" Dumbarton, Inchinnan and Glasgow. A writer from Kilmalcolm,
" about 10 miles from Glasgow, says:—'Yesterday, 1st January,
" I felt about seven or eight shocks of an earthquake all succeeding
" one another—the whole shocks were over in the space of half a
" minute. The second shock was the greatest, and so violent, that
" it fairly lifted me off the bed, jolted me to the head of it, and in a
" moment down again to where I lay before. I believe three or four
" such shocks would have laid this house in ruins.'—(*Edinburgh*
" *Courant.*)"

Those convulsions of the earth which, though slight, nevertheless
having been frequently repeated, may have tended to diminish the
size of the Point Isle, then situated a little below the Arns Well,
and near the place where the subsidence had occurred.

In 1760, as shown in the annexed Plan of the Green, the Point Isle
was quite a conspicuous object, as forming a part of our public park,
but how it came so quickly after this date to have been swept away
has never been satisfactorily accounted for.

From the following quotation it appears that the Point Isle had
become of much smaller extent in 1776, than formerly, as it is there
called merely "a sort of an island," whereas in 1730, during the
provostship of Peter Murdoch, James Moor, land surveyor, having
made a sketch of the Green, reported that the island in question then
contained one acre and 30 falls of ground, and that it had been one
of the principal salmon shots of the river:—

"*Constitutional*, 1776, (page 351), We hear from Glasgow that
" during the late swell on the river Clyde, four women, who were
" attending clothes on the Green, were several times in the most
" imminent danger, from the rapidity of the flood, and at last two
" of them lost their lives; the other two having saved themselves by
" getting on a sort of an island, till the water subsided. A woman
" was also drowned in Clyde a little below the Broomielaw."

Although this accident happened in my day, yet I was then too
young to have remembered any particulars of the circumstance, or
of the Point Isle; and notwithstanding of having been accustomed
very early in life to resort to this part of the river for the purpose of
bathing, I cannot call to my recollection having observed any
vestiges of the Point Isle; it, therefore, must have disappeared very
soon after the above unfortunate calamity had occurred.

Being a good swimmer for a boy, I wished to ascertain what kind of bottom the river had at Peat Bog; accordingly at the bend of the river, near the Arns Well, which place was then considered the deepest part of the stream, I there dived to the bottom of the river and brought up a handful of fine sand, the depth being fully 18 feet. Having then swam a short distance down the stream, I was surprised to find that it suddenly became quite shallow, and that I could touch the bottom of the river with my feet without having been out of my depth. This appeared to me at the time to have been an extraordinary circumstance; but now I am of opinion that the shallow part of the river in question had formerly been the bed of the Point Isle, and that in fact it then was the debris of the said Isle. I further remember that at this period there was a range of old decayed stobs inserted in the bank of the river, between the Arns Well and the Old Bridge, which no doubt had been so placed for the purpose of preventing any part of the Green from being washed away by floods. The plan of thus confining the flow of the river, and the more important measures of building jetties to narrow the Clyde for navigation purposes, just then commenced by Mr Gouldburn, may perhaps sufficiently account for the sudden disappearance of the Point Isle shortly after 1776, without the supposed intervention of earthquakes—at any rate there is no record, so far as I have seen, of the Point Isle having been removed from the channel of the upper navigation by dredging, or by any other operation of manual labour, and therefore it must be presumed to have been wasted away by natural tidal or fluvial operations.

There also existed at this time another island in the river, immediately below the Old Bridge, which, before the breast between the bridges was built in 1772, formed a sort of peninsula that joined the Old Green, or Dowcot Green, at low water, but at other times became an island of considerable size.

In one of Slezer's Views of Glasgow, drawn up in the reign of Charles II., there appears to be three hay stacks upon this island, so that it must have been considerably elevated above the level of the river itself. It appears from the Burgh Accounts, that in 1578 there was a pigeon house or dowcot on the Old Green of Glasgow, and hence came the name of the "Dowcot Green."

"Burgh Records, discharge: Compt. of Patrick Glen, Theasurer " of the Burgh, 3d May, 1578."

"Item for ye dowcatt on ye Grene ———— vi. s. viij. d."

In my infantile days, Bailie Craig of the Water Port, Stockwell Street, used to discharge his cargoes of timber upon the Dowcot

Green island. The channel of the river for sailing vessels was then upon the south side of the river, and was navigable up to Ruther-glen. My mother, who was born in 1734 and died in 1816, informed me that in her young days the Dowcot Green Isle was generally resorted to by the inhabitants of the western district for the purpose of washing and bleaching their clothes, while the inhabitants of the eastern parts of the city usually went to the Low Green of Glasgow for like purposes.

This isle, like the Point Isle, has also gradually passed away, without any efforts having been made by our magistrates to remove it by manual labour; but its disappearance can be readily accounted for in consequence of Gouldburn's operations to deepen the channel of the river, and by the general liberty which was either given to the public, or winked at, to take sand from the river at this spot, there being a direct road from what is now Great Clyde Street to the river, for the purpose of watering horses, and otherwise for giving a free and easy access to the Clyde below the bridge.

Although the city authorities do not seem to have made much objection to individuals taking sand from the river below the bridge, nevertheless they appear to have been careful to preserve the integrity of the Horse Ford (see Plan) immediately above the bridge, as the following quotation shows :—

"Council Records, July 27, 1639."—"The Council granted licence " to Sir Robert Douglas to gett ane hundredth kairtis of the tounes " guarvell to help to build out the dyk of his zaird nearest Clyde " bezound the Bridge."—(This must have been from the Horse Ford.)

I have often waded across this ford without undressing more than my under garments, so that a horse and cart could then readily pass at that point from one side of the river to the other.

I remember that the bottom of the river at the Horse Ford consisted of moderate sized gravel, which rendered the passage of cattle and carriages over this part of the river to have been then easy and free from danger.

Dr Clelland, in the first chapter of his Annals, has given us a romantic account of a battle which was said to have taken place on the streets of Glasgow, near the College, between Sir William Wallace and the English, in the course of which battle Wallace, (as the Doctor says) " rushed forward to the spot where Percy was, and with one stroke of his broad sword cleft Percy's head in two."[*]

---

[*] Query. Could this feat have been done by Wallace, (then on horseback), with the famous Dumbarton two-handed broad sword ?

In opposition to the learned Doctor, however, Mr Pagan, in his Sketches of Glasgow, (at page 6), thus writes:—" The metrical " romance of Wallace, written in the 15th century, by Blind Harry, " gives a long and minute account of a conflict which that hero is " said to have fought with the English, on the streets of Glasgow, " about the year 1300. The silence of all history on the event " compels us to reject the affair as a fable, like nine-tenths of the " same minstrel's works."

Neither the English historian Holinsheid, who wrote the Chronicles of Scotland in 1577, nor our own historians, Buchanan, Lindsay, or Robertson, have said a word on the subject of this so-called battle of the Bell of the Brae ; nevertheless, as Wallace at this time was actively engaged in expelling the English from all their strongholds in Scotland, it is probable that a skirmish of some kind did actually take place in Glasgow, about the year 1300, between Wallace and the English garrison, then occupying the Bishop's Castle.* Chapman's account of this battle is not improbable ; he says (at page 6), " Wallace, leaving Ayr with 300 cavalry, hastened " to Glasgow, which was occupied by an English garrison, consisting " of about 1000 men, under Percy their general. He arrived about " 9 o'clock A M., and drew up his men on the ground, now the north " end of the Old Bridge (Bridgegate). In a spirited action which " now commenced, the superior numbers of the English, for some " time, seemed to promise them success, when the column under " Auchinleck, amounting to about 140 men, marching by St " Mungo's Lane and the Drygate, made a furious assault on the " flank of the enemy. The English instantly broke, and were " pursued, with considerable slaughter, to Bothwell Castle, about 8 " miles distant from the city. In the action and pursuit Percy and " several hundreds of his men are said to have fallen."

There is here a narrative of circumstantial particulars which cannot be altogether overlooked, as they clearly show that the narrator must have been well acquainted with the localities of Glasgow. It is stated by several historians that Wallace drew up his men on the lands of the Bridgegate, but not a word is said of his having crossed the river by the bridge, in fact the bridge at that time was impassable for cavalry. Mr Pagan, in his Sketches, (page 169), thus writes:—" Tradition states that prior to 1340 a wooden

---

* Buchanan writing regarding this period, at (page 254), merely says:—" Scoti omnes Eduardi praefectos, ex omnibus urbibus et arcibus exigunt, hic status rerum prope biennium durasset, &c."

" bridge spanned the Clyde, somewhere west of Saltmarket Street.
" This, however, had fallen into decay, and in consequence, a stone
" bridge was built over the Clyde, about 1345, by the liberality of
" Bishop Rae. It was originally only 12 feet in width, and would,
" of course, offer a roadway where ' two wheel barrows tremble when
" they meet.'" It is, therefore, evident, that in 1300, the usual
passage across the Clyde to Glasgow, for cattle and carriages, was by
the Horse Ford, and that Wallace and his cavalry must have
entered the Bridgegate lands at the north termination of the ford,
near our present Slaughter House, (see small Plan), the wooden
bridge being then only used by foot passengers.

We have reason to believe, from authentic history, that Edward I.
had an English garrison, at this time, in Glasgow, but it most
probably consisted only of about 200 men, which, in number, were
quite sufficient to have kept the peaceable citizens of Glasgow in due
subjection to the tyrant, and more than the Bishop's Castle could
have accommodated. That the garrison then amounted to 1000
men at arms appears a gross exaggeration, for the very next year,
1301, Edward I. peaceably resided three days in Glasgow, and went
regularly to mass, unaccompanied by body guards or military escorts;
no mention is made of there having been a garrison in the Bishop's
Castle when Edward resided in Glasgow.

Mr Pagan (at page 6), in his Sketches thus writes:—"It is certain
" that in the autumn of the year 1301, King Edward I. of England,
" spent three days within the city, taking up his abode in the
" spacious monastery of the Friars Preachers. From the account
" of his expenses, which are still preserved, we learn that he was
" constant in his attendance at mass, in the Cathedral, and that he
" made offerings both at the High Altar and at the Shrine of St
" Mungo." There was no occasion for Edward keeping so large a
garrison in Glasgow, as 1000 men at arms, in order to check any
outbreak of its citizens, or of those in its immediate vicinity, for
the city was not a fortified place. (Robertson I., page 274).

At this time, according to Cleland, Glasgow did not contain even
1500 inhabitants, and the Bell of the Brae was then the south
boundary of the city, few houses being erected beyond the bounds of
the burgh. On the occasion of the battle in question, the English
appear to have taken their stand upon the high grounds of the Bell
of the Brae, and to have successfully resisted the first attack of
Wallace, but to have been broken by the flank movement of
Auchinleck, and to have fled through open lands to Bothwell, where

there was an English garrison. Taking a view of the whole incidents, and the circumstantial manner in which various points are related by different authors, it appears probable that a skirmish between Wallace and the English did really take place at the Bell of the Brae about the year 1300, and that Wallace succeeded in expelling the English garrison from Glasgow.

It must be here remarked that the Green of Glasgow, and the whole lands in its environs, including all the low parts of Glasgow, were at that time vacant grounds or brushwood forests belonging to the Crown, which in 1450 were bestowed by James II. on Bishop Turnbull, and afterwards called the Bishop's Forest; so that the battle of the Bell of the Brae, and the pursuit to Bothwell, must have taken place in the open country in the neighbourhood of the city, and the battle itself to have been fought not in the heart or · streets of Glasgow, as stated by Cleland, but beyond the south boundary of old St Mungo, in the fields.

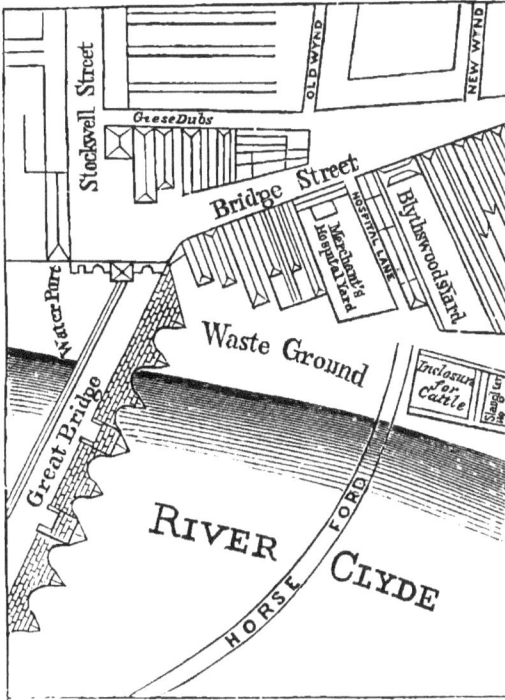

CHAPTER V.

Regent Murray's Approach to Glasgow and Hamilton, after Langside, 1568, by the Horse Ford— Erection of the Stone Dyke across the Clyde—Rutherglen Quay and Traffic—Stoppage of the Fords by Act of Parliament, 1768—Gouldburn and Clyde deepening in 1773—The Broomielaw in 1760—The Old Bottle Work—The Bottle Work Company—Gorbals Church—Hutchesontown in 1794.

By the following extract from Buchanan, page 678, it appears that in 1568, immediately before the battle of Langside, the Regent Murray occupied nearly the same position as Wallace did in 1300, viz., in the open fields (campis patentibus) at the north end of the Old Bridge, and that his cavalry crossed the river by the Horse Ford, and his infantry by the bridge. From the words, "æstu maris tum " libera," we learn that the tide flowed above the bridge, and that the Horse Ford was probably not fordable at high water and spring tides. Buchanan, page 676, says—"Ille (Pro-rex) vero, ut qui " ultro hostes provocare ad certamen statuerat, cum primum suos " educere potuit, ante oppidum in campis patentibus, qua hostes " venturos existimabat, acie instructa, aliquot horas stetit. Sed " cum agmen eorum ulteriore fluminis ripa agi videret, eorum " consilio statim intellecto, et ipse suos pedites per pontem, equites " per vada, æstu maris tum libera transmissos, Lansidium petere " jussit." As the Regent crossed the ford in the summer season (viz., on the 13th of May, 1568), it is probable that the passage was easily made, the waters of the river having then most likely been low.

From Slezer's View of Glasgow, drawn up in the reign of Charles II., it will be seen that the banks of the Clyde immediately above the Old Bridge were then lying in a state of nature, with a gradual slope on each side towards the river, and that the Horse Ford on the north terminated directly opposite the Bridgegate steeple, there being an elevated ridge or mount from thence to the mouth of the Molendinar burn, where the Jail and public offices afterwards came to be erected.

Cattle and carriages crossing the ford entered the Bridgegate by the lane now on the east side of the Merchants' House, and as being the nearest route into the heart of the city, they proceeded into the Trongate by the Old Wynd, the entry by the Stockwell being shut at the bridge, (see small Plan), and King Street not having been opened till 1724. It thus appears that in former times the Horse Ford was the common high-road into Glasgow from the south, and, in fact, that it afforded an easier access to the city, for cattle and carriages, than the narrow Old Bridge itself.

According to Robertson, i., page 276, and Keith, 477, the Regent Murray, after the battle of Langside, " marched back to Glasgow, " and returned public thanks to God, for this great, and, on his " side, almost bloodless victory." Holinsheid, the English historian, thus writes :—" The morrow after the battle, being the xiiij of May, " the Regent sent to somon Hamilton Castle, but the answear was " respited till the next day, and then he that had the charge came . " to Glasquho and offered the keyes to the Regent." In opposition to what is said on this subject by the above historian, Buchanan, page 678, says :—" Prorex reliquum diei quo pugnatum est in " recensendis captivis consumpsit. Postridie quingenties equitibus " tantum comitatus, in vallem glottianam profectus, omnia plena " fugae vestigiis et vastitatis invenit."

We are, therefore, left in uncertainty whether the Regent re-crossed the Clyde with his army, and came to Glasgow, or marched to the east by way of the vale of Clydesdale direct from Langside, the recent scene of the battle. Buchanan's account appears to be the most probable one, as the 500 cavalry mentioned, most likely were sent to Hamilton to demand the surrender of the Castle there. Supposing that the Regent with his army re-crossed the Horse Ford, and came to Glasgow, there would have been no difficulty as to their again crossing the Clyde in their march to Edinburgh, if they took advantage of the Dalmarnock Ford to pass the river. This ford led directly into the lands belonging to the Hamiltons, a family supporting the cause of Queen Mary, and, of course, hostile to the views of the Regent. The point in question is one of historical doubt. The following extract was written by me, and published in the *Glasgow Herald* of 26th July, 1858.

"Your correspondent D. says that the Clyde was fordable for children at the Kinning House burn, in the year before the Broomielaw Bridge was built; but even after that time I myself, when a boy, have waded, only breast high, across the Clyde at the deepest part of the Harbour."

"I cannot recollect the exact year, but I remember that on the occasion of there being a spate in the river, an alarm arose that the New Bridge was in danger of falling. This was upon a Sunday, and on that day I saw a number of carters, employed by the magistrates, throwing stones by cart-loads over the bridge, into the river, in order to strengthen the foundations of the piers. Subsequently, a stone dyke was erected quite across the river, and at low water a person could scramble on this dyke from one side of the river to the other, merely wading through a ripple.* This dyke destroyed the ancient navigation to Rutherglen. At this time the community of Rutherglen was torn into local factions, by disputes between the magistrates, crafts, and inhabitants, as to certain rights of voting, in consequence of which the operations of the Glasgow magistrates at the Jamaica Street Bridge were neglected, and so the upper navigation came to be closed."

"The Rutherglen folks (unlike the Dumbarton folks) never appeared in the Court of Session, or in Parliament, to dispute the schemes of the Clyde Trustees."

"Your correspondent D. is wrong in stating that coals passing through Gorbals to Glasgow, or the neighbourhood, were, at the time in question, generally carried on horseback. Old Mr Dixon had a wooden tram-road running from his Govan Coal Works through the present lands of Kingston to the Coal Quay, then situated at the west end of Windmillcroft, where the river was deeper than at the Broomielaw. I have walked along this tram-road, and have seen old Dixon's waggons passing along it."

I crossed the Old Bridge of Gorbals in the year 1778, when it was receiving an addition of ten feet to its former width of twelve feet, and this improvement shows that the cartage across it was considerable at that time, and the bridge too narrow for the traffic passing over it.

Before the Broomielaw Bridge was built, herring boats and small gabberts plied regularly to Rutherglen, and sometimes there were more vessels lying at Rutherglen Quay than at the Broomielaw Harbour. I remember on one occasion that there was but one large vessel (a gabbert), lying at the Broomielaw. The late Mr Alex. Norris, who was born in 1751, informed me that, in his younger days, there was a regular traffic by sailing vessels up to Rutherglen Quay, from Greenock and the Highlands; and that this traffic was of old date, may be presumed, when we see the Arms of the Burgh

---

* See this dyke represented in Stuart's Views of Glasgow, page 109.

of Rutherglen to be a boat under sail, with two men navigating her.

The following advertisement will show that the upper navigation was open in the year 1781.

"*Glasgow Mercury*, 29th November, 1781."

" That there is a Ferry-boat, or Lighter, lying in a park adjacent " to the Green of Glasgow (Fleshers' Haugh,) possessed at present " by John King, late Deacon of the Fleshers, supposed to have been " cast in by a flood more than twelve months bygone, and as no " person has made inquiry anent her, this is to give notice to any " person who can claim the same between and the 12th of January " next, may call for Thomas Ronald, overseer of the said park, at " the foot of the Old Wynd of Glasgow, who will show the boat, and · " upon making their property good, shall be returned upon defray- " ing charges."

It certainly must appear very wonderful in the eyes of the present generation, when parliamentary contests are so frequent, to see the apathy of the Burgh of Rutherglen, at this time, 1768, and to behold its denizens standing still with folded arms and calmly allowing the magistrates of Glasgow to shut up the old " use and wont" access by the river Clyde to Rutherglen, the most ancient Royal Burgh of the two.

Again, it is curious to observe how modestly the magistrates of Glasgow took parliamentary powers to prohibit all carriage and · cattle traffic, on the Old Bridge, at their pleasure and good-will, notwithstanding of the Rutherglen lieges having possessed a pre-scriptive right, by use and wont, to cross the Clyde, with carriages and cattle, from the days of Bishop Rae, in 1345.

In fact it was of the greatest importance to the Burgh of Ruther-glen to see that the communication between the two burghs, by the Old Bridge, should then have been kept open for the passage of carriages and cattle, as it was the direct highway from Rutherglen to Glasgow, and the north, the present Rutherglen Bridge not having been built till 1776. The magistrates of Glasgow, however, have never exercised their power of shutting up the Old Bridge, from general carriage and cattle traffic, but, on the contrary, have erected a new and more splendid structure, with full liberty of passage of all kinds, and are now zealously endeavouring, by prudent management, to render it a free bridge in all time coming.

"1768."
" Act, Anno Octavo, Geo. III., Regis."

Sec. XXII. " Be it therefore enacted by the authority aforesaid,
" that the said magistrates and council of Glasgow shall have full
" power and authority, and are hereby empowered and authorised, as
" soon as the said New Bridge shall be made passable, to cause all
" fords through the said river Clyde, and from thence to that part
" of the river opposite to the House of Stobcross, (the distance
" between these two places measuring one mile, and a quarter of a
" mile), to be stopt up, and the channel of the said river to be
" dug and made deeper; and the banks of the said river to be cut,
" and posts, and rails, or other fences to be erected thereon, to
" prevent any person evading the payment of the tolls and pontages
" given and granted by the said Act."

Sec. XXIII. " And be it enacted, that in case the magistrates
" and city council, and their successors in office, shall think fit to
" keep up the Old Bridge, after the new intended bridge shall be
" built, they shall have full power and authority, and they are
" hereby empowered and authorised, as soon as the said intended
" New Bridge shall be made passable, to prohibit, and stop the pas-
" sage of all wheel carriages, sledges, or other carriages, or of any
" horses, cattle, sheep, swine, or any sort of cattle or beasts, over the
" said Old Bridge, but to keep the same entirely as a free bridge, for
" the use of foot passengers only; any law or custom to the
" contrary notwithstanding."

Nothing is said in this Act about giving the proprietors of the
lands fronting the Clyde any compensation for damages which might
be sustained by them, in consequence of their respective properties
on the banks of the river becoming injured, and "cut, and posts
" and rails or other fences erected thereon," at the pleasure of the
magistrates : neither is there a word said in the Act about granting
the said river-side proprietors adequate recompense for the loss of
the salmon fishery—but, in truth, the proprietors in question were
too wise to make any objections on the subject, as the Act had
omitted to say that the ground acquired by the operations of the
magistrates from the old channel of the river, should nevertheless
still remain as part and portion of the said river channel, in case of
need. By this omission in the Act, the river-side proprietors have
gained much river-side ground, which the River Trustees lately have
been (in the course of their operations) obliged to buy back at high
prices from the said proprietors.

Within my remembrance, Mr David Todd of Springfield, and Mr Francis Reid of Greenlaw, gained, each of them, about an acre of water side ground, in consequence of the channel of the Clyde having become greatly narrowed by the erection of jetties on both sides of the river immediately after the New Bridge had become passable.*

In 1829 the Trades' House received £10,000 from the Clyde Trustees for the ground which lay between Clyde Street, and the river. A great part of this ground formed part of the channel of the river, as may be seen in Stuart's Views, page 109, where it will be seen that the two southmost arches of the bridge, stood on dry land, but formed part of the bed of the river at floods and spring tides. The ox eyes in the bridge were intended to carry off in part, the extra flow of water in the event of great floods. I have often amused myself when a boy, in climbing up the piers of the bridge into these ox eyes, and walking along the dyke which then crossed the river from side to side, immediately below the arches of the bridge. (See Stuart's Views, page 109.)

In 1768, Mr Gouldburn, civil engineer, having made a survey of the river, reported to the magistrates of Glasgow that the Clyde was then lying in a state of nature, and that as far down from Glasgow as Kilpatrick, the river was navigable only for vessels drawing less than two feet of water. That at low water, upon one of the hirsts the depth was merely 15 inches, and upon the other five hirsts, 18 inches. That at high water the depth on the first hirst was only 39 inches, and on the others, upon an average, ranging rather above 4 feet at full tide.

"Glasgow Weekly Magazine, 20th March, 1773."

"It is with pleasure that we acquaint our readers that Mr Gould-

---

* It will be seen from the following advertisement that those jetties protruded considerably into the channel of the river, and had perches affixed to their extremities there, in order to prevent vessels striking against them at high water.

Glasgow Mercury, 17th June, 1779.

" By the Magistrates of Glasgow :—These are prohibiting and discharging all boat-" men, ferrymen, and others, from fixing and landing their boats, at or upon any of the " jetties, dykes, or other works for improving the navigation of the river Clyde, betwixt " the lower end of Dumbuck ford and the Bridge of Glasgow, and from landing any pas-" sengers or goods upon the same jetties, and from removing or carrying away the " perches fixed on the ends thereof; certifying all who shall transgress, that they will be " prosecuted for the penalties inflicted by the Act of Parliament for improving the navi-" gation of the said river, upon all those who shall hurt or destroy the works made for " deepening thereof." N.B.—The space between the jetties, gradually came to be filled up with rubbish and the wreck of floods, to the great gain of the proprietors of the banks.

" burn is still successfully carrying on his operations in deepening
" the river Clyde ; and that three coasting vessels arrived at the
" Broomielaw, *directly* from Ireland, with oatmeal, without stopping
" at Greenock, as formerly, to unload their cargoes."

" *Scots Magazine*, December, 1775, p. 693."

" From a sounding of the river Clyde, from the lower end of
" Dumbuck Ford to the Broomielaw of Glasgow, taken on the 8th
" of December, by Colin Dunlop, Esq., of Carmyle, Messrs Hugh
" Wylie and John Douglas, merchants in Glasgow, in consequence
" of a warrant directed to them by the Sheriff Depute, of the
" County of Lanark, it appears that the said river, within the
" bounds above mentioned, is more than seven feet water at an
" ordinary neap tide, and that Mr Gouldburn, engineer, has fully
" implemented his contract with the city of Glasgow."

The breast-work between the bridges was built about the year
1772, immediately after the New Bridge had become passable, and
this part of Glasgow then became the fashionable promenade of our
citizens, the route being along Great Clyde Street, from the east to
the New Bridge, and from thence by the parapet of the bridge to the
breast-work fronting the river, and thereafter along the said breast-
work eastward to the Old Bridge—the whole making a circuitous
pleasure-walk of limited extent. I must say, however, that the
stroll was not very inviting when the tide was out. This walk
along the breast was not without danger to careless persons, as there
were three or four gaps in it, from which stairs descended to the
bed of the river, and these gaps and stairs were totally without
fences. There was a free passage or entry across the breast, sloping
from Clyde Street to the river, for the purpose of enabling horses
and cattle to be watered. This access path stood nearly opposite to
the present Roman Catholic Chapel, over which there was a neat
wooden bridge, by which the walk along the breast-work was not
interrupted. It was fenced on both sides. The grass plot between
the bridges was railed in on all sides by a palisade of Scots fir
stobs ; but no attention was paid to having the grass cropped, or
weeds eradicated, nature being allowed its full scope. I have
seen sheep feeding in this enclosure, but no other beasts of
pasture.

It appears that in the year 1775, Mr Gouldburn's operations having
deepened the river so as to admit of vessels drawing seven feet of
water to come up to the Broomielaw, these operations had under-

mined the foundations of the breast-work between the bridges, as the following notice shows :—

"*Glasgow Journal,* 21st August, 1777."

" Notice, that the magistrates of Glasgow being resolved to re-
" build that part of the breast, a little below the Old Bridge of Glas-
" gow, which lately fell down. Any person willing to re-build the
" same are desired to give in their proposals to the town clerks of
" Glasgow."

Mr Gouldburn's deepening operations may further have tended towards the annihilation of the Dowcot Green,* and Point House Isles before mentioned.

The danger of having had open and unfenced stairs from the breast to the river Clyde is seen by the subjoined notice :—

"*Glasgow Journal,* 28th July, 1763."

" On Sunday last (24th) a young boy, wading along the edge
" of the quay, overflowed by the great rains which had fallen the
" day before, coming to one of the stairs that go down from the
" quay to the river, unfortunately fell in ; his sister, somewhat older
" than himself, endeavouring to catch hold of him, fell in likewise.
" The body was carried down by the stream, and his corpse found
" on Tuesday, about twelve miles below. The girl was, by some
" people in boats lying alongside, taken out alive, but died soon
" after, to the inexpressible grief of the poor parents."

There is a plate of the Broomielaw, executed in 1760, to be seen in Stuart's Views of Glasgow, at page 34, which must be regarded as a very curious and interesting antiquarian document.

Mr Stuart, at page 41, thus writes regarding it—

" The View appears to have been executed about the year 1760,
" (date of the annexed Plan), and affords a curious picture of the
" aspect of our harbour in that early stage of its existence, when,
" as yet, it was only visited by the fisherman's wherry, or by the
" humble trading vessels, which now and then made their appearance,
" freighted with domestic produce from the coast of Ireland or the
" Western Isles. The original drawing has been taken from a point
" not very distant from where the Glasgow Bridge now opens into
" Eglinton Street, the ground in that locality being, till within the

---

* In 1770, the magistrates of Glasgow, (as appears from the City Records) hesitated about laying out £100 to remove the shoal, or remains of the Dowcot Green Isle, and hinted to the Merchant House that they should assist them in this great work.

" last forty or fifty years, a rough uncultivated waste—broken,
" where it approached the river, into numerous hollows and indenta-
" tions, which had been formed by the winter currents along the
" soft and crumbling banks. To the right of the Plate, may be seen
" the remains of an ancient tower, said to have been part of a wind-
" mill erected by Sir George Elphingston about the beginning of
" the seventeenth century, for the accommodation of his tenantry
" upon the neighbouring lands, and from which the adjoining
" common received the name of the Windmill Croft.—On the left,
" appear a few detached houses, some of which were removed to
" allow of the formation of Jamaica Street, and prominent above
" all, rises the old Bottle Work cone, a building erected in 1730,
" and the predecessor of that which was removed from the spot
" about fifteen years ago.

" The formation of the original Quay in 1662, with its ' weigh-
" house, fountain, and cran,' was probably the first innovation
" 'which materially changed the old rustic appearance of the
" Broomielaw. The subsequent erection of the Bottle Work made,
" no doubt, another alteration of some consequence ; but the
" greatest change of all took place between the years 1767 and
" 1773, when the first Jamaica Street Bridge was carried across the
" stream."

Having passed my early boyhood at Greenlaw House, upwards of
fourscore years ago, and having then had frequent occasion to
ramble from the now General Terminus into Glasgow by the river-
side footpath, the state of the grounds in that quarter has been so
fully impressed on my memory as still to appear quite fresh, and
almost present to my mind's eye. Mr Stuart correctly describes
this road as having been " a rough uncultivated waste, broken, where
" it approached the river, into numerous hollows and indentations"—
in fact, down to my time, it was lying in a complete state of
nature, except at the Windmill and at the Coal Quay, where the
hand of man appeared to have made some change. Tradeston,
Kingston, and Windmillcroft, were fields in cultivation, having
quick-set hedges separating them from the adjacent public roads
and footpaths. Below the Coal Quay, the Kinning House burn was
crossed by a single plank of rough timber, without fences; and the
lands of Tradeston, Windmillcroft, Springfield, Parkhouse, Greenlaw, and Mavisbank, were inclosed within thorn hedges from the
river footpath. There was a small wood at West Street. The footpath may be said to have included the whole banks of the river,

G

from the Bridge to Govan, it then being completely open, and free
to the public, who made roads through the same at their pleasure.
The narrow lane, from the Paisley Road to the Coal Quay, at
Springfield, was then principally used by the Dumbarton Glass
Work Company, and by Old Dixon, for shipping coals at the Coal
Quay, there having been a wooden tram-road, from Mr Dixon's
works at Little Govan, through the lands of Kingston, and along
the said lane itself, direct to the Coal Quay. The toll-bar on the
Paisley Road was then placed nearly opposite to Clarence Street, off
Kingston. Although the river was deeper at the Coal Quay than
at the Broomielaw, it was not in general use as a place of export
and import.

In Stuart's View, it will be seen that the Broomielaw Harbour
then reached eastwards as far as the mouth of St Enoch's burn,
(a little beyond the site of our present Custom House), and that
there was a breast-work along its whole extent ; but the grounds from
St Enoch's burn to the Old Bridge formed the Dowcot Green and
the Dowcot Isle, on which space there was no breast-work. In
Stuart's said View (at page 34), there appears on the extreme left, a
small house of one storey; this house seems to have been taken down
in 1768, in order to open up Jamaica Street to the New Bridge. I
remember the other houses next the Bottle Work, which remained
entire after the bridge was built, and formed the south-east corner
of Jamaica Street for many years.

In Stuart's View, the cone of the Bottle Work appears a conspicuous object, and as Stuart says:—"Prominent above all rises the old
" Bottle Work cone, which was erected in 1730, and the predecessor
" of that which was removed from the same spot, about fifteen years
" ago." Bailey, in describing a cone, says that it "may be conceived
" to be formed by a revolution of a right-angled triangle round the
" perpendicular leg." Now none of Bailey's angles and triangles
were to be found in the geometrical construction of the old Bottle
Work cone, for it had a most respectable protuberant belly, like a
pear, or, as the joke goes, like a London Alderman's well-fed paunch.
This cone, after having stood the winter blasts of more than half a
century, at last, from the ravages of time, tumbled down by the
bursting of its belly, the top-weight having overcome the adhesion of
its lower members.

" *Glasgow Mercury*, 14th February, 1792., page 54."

" The cone of the first glass-work erected at the Broomielaw upwards

" of fifty years ago, and which had given indication of its decayed
" state, occasioned the company to give up working in it for some
" months past, and prepare for its downfall : that event took place
" on Tuesday, the 7th instant, about nine in the morning. And
" from the precautions taken, we are happy to observe that no
" accident befell any of the workmen, which was to be apprehended
" from the falling of so stupendous a building, and such a mass of
" rubbish."

Immediately after this disaster had occurred, a new cone came to
be erected on the site of the old one, of strict geometrical proportions,
which, as Stuarts says, was taken down about thirty years ago. I think
the ground was feued for two guineas per square yard, and on it now stands
our Custom House. There was a small parapet wall with an iron railing
above it, placed immediately in front of the old Bottle Work, (see
Stuart's Plate) and as the windows of the work fronting the street were
kept open for the admission of fresh air, any person standing on the
public street could readily see the whole process of bottle making,
as the same was going on in the bosom of the cone. The taking of
the melted metal out of the glowing furnace, was the first process to
be seen ; then came the act of blowing the said metal into a bottle
mould through the exertions of the operative's lungs, by means of a
long iron pipe. . It was a beautiful sight to see the red hot bottle
blown up with as much ease as a child blows up its soap bells. The
outward form of the bottle was finished by affixing a little protuberance of metal to the neck of it, and then depositing it in a situation
of the furnace of gentle heat, so as to allow of its gradually cooling.
The men at work were generally dressed in their shirts, and seemed
to have been much oppressed by the extreme heat of the place. I
have often stood in Clyde Street in admiration of the whole process
of bottle blowing.

From the following advertisement, it will be seen that the original
Bottle Work Company did not prove a very lucrative concern.

" *Glasgow Journal*, 27th December, 1756."

" As the contract of co-partnership betwixt Richard Alexander
" Oswald and Company, of the Glass-work at Glasgow, dissolved
" November last, it is expected their customers will make immediate
" payment of the debts due by them to Andrew Scott, the Company's
" clerk, or settle the same by bills, otherwise they will be obliged to
" take the disagreeable method of constituting them by decreet.
" Gentlemen wanting bottles may, by applying to George Buchanan,

" senior, merchant in Glasgow, or to the said Andrew Scott, at the
" Glass-house, be supplied with common quart bottles at 25s per
" groce, champagne quarts at 27s, for ready money only."
The successors of Richard Alexander Oswald & Co., in the Bottle
Work, appear to have also found bottle blowing unprofitable.

" Glasgow Mercury, 21st January, 1779."

"Glasgow Bottle Work.—The Glasgow Bottle Work Company,
" carried on under the firm of Robert Scott, jun., & Co., being now
" dissolved, their whole heritable subject at the foot of Jamaica
" Street, with all their utensils, materials, and stock on hand, are to
" be exposed to public sale in the Exchange Tavern here on Wednes-
" day, the 24th of February next. Part of the property fronting
" Jamaica Street, and measuring from north to south 193 feet, might
" be set off for building, and leave sufficient room for carrying on the
" manufacturing business."

My father, who at this time was engaged in building the large
tenement in Jamaica Street, the third on the north west side of the
Street, urged the magistrates of Glasgow very strongly to purchase
the Bottle Work, seeing how much its removal would benefit the
city property in Jamaica Street, and besides, being in all likelihood a
profitable purchase, would take away the most intolerable nuisance
of its volumes of smoke, covering with its black films the town's
feuing property in St Enoch's Square, and deteriorating all the
heritage in its neighbourhood. The magistrates, however, after
having taken the subject into their consideration, did not think it
prudent to make the purchase. In consequence of the Bottle Work
having been purchased by a new company, and the works continued
in a still more aggravated form, Jamaica Street remained for about
half a century quite a neglected street, but as soon as the said works
were abandoned, and the cone taken down, Jamaica Street rapidly
improved, and is now one of the very first leading streets of our city.

In M'Vean's M'Ure, page 231, there is a plate of the Broomielaw
said to have been drawn in 1768, but it appears to me to be an em-
bellished plan of the locality, and in the minutiae differs in several
respects from that of Stuart, at page 34. The Bottle Work cone
is there represented in an improved shape, with little or no belly ;
and there are rough stobs in front of the cone in place of a neat
parapet stone wall, with iron railings above it. The houses on each side
of the cone differ from those represented in Stuart's Views, and the
Ropework grounds, (or Old Green) are shown as a dense forest, while

in Stuart's Plate there are only a small clump of trees next the Bottle Work to be seen. In my early days these grounds were quite bare of planting, and I have frequently crossed them in going from the city to the Broomielaw, although this was trespassing upon the Ropework lands, which liberty, however, was seldom objected to by the rope spinners. In M'Vean's Broomielaw, the breast-work is represented as a fence of wooden stobs, but in Stuart's View it is drawn as a stone erection, with a stair in it, descending to the river, such as was noticed by me when quoting the case of a boy being drowned by falling into the river over the stair.

As far as my recollection goes I think that Stuart's View, at page 34, is an accurate representation of the Broomielaw locality in 1760, little alteration having taken place in it for many years after the New Bridge was opened in 1772.

In M'Vean's View, the lands where Carlton Place buildings are erected, appear as waste ground, but the first, or original Gorbals Church, (of Buchan Street) is seen in it, standing amidst a few huts or houses of little value. As the present Gorbals Church has been the source of much public interest, and of long and irritating litigation between numerous parties, both civil and ecclesiastical, the following notices regarding its site, fourscore years ago, may prove interesting to many of our citizens.

In June, 1855, I addressed a letter as under to the editor of the *Glasgow Herald:—*

" Sir, as your readers, no doubt, feel interested in the question " at issue, regarding the Gorbals Church, I beg leave to annex an " old advertisement announcing the sale of the site of the present " church in Clyde Terrace. The property was afterwards let for a " dyework, and there being then a cart entry to the river, opposite " the dyework, the goods and yarns which were dyed were subse- " quently washed in the stream. There was a similar cart entry to " the river on the north side, and carts passed to and fro across the " Clyde, a little below the present Victoria Bridge. Towards the " west of the dyework, in the line of Carlton Place, there was a " ropewalk which I remember. I further annex an old advertise- " ment, having reference to the site of the first or old Gorbals " Church. This church was sold by the Gorbals feuars, but in what " manner the titles were made up, or what became of the money, I " cannot say."

" *Glasgow Mercury,* 19th April, 1781." " 'To be sold, by public " roup, on Friday, the 28th curt., within the Exchange Coffee

" House, Glasgow, between the hours of eleven and twelve o'clock,
" that pottery adjoining the Gorbals Church, which belonged to the
" deceased Mr John Holden, and presently possessed by Mr Andrew
" Boag.   If any person incline to make a private bargain, they will
" please apply to Mrs Holden, at Burrel Hall, any time before the
" roup."

" 19th April, 1781."   " To be sold, by public roup, within the
" house of James Pollok, vintner in Gorbals, upon Friday the 11th
" of May next, between the hours of twelve, mid-day, and three
" o'clock afternoon, the two just and equal third-part of that Kill,
" barn, and yard, or piece of waste ground at the back thereof, lying
" in the village of Gorbals, on the south side of the river Clyde, be-
" tween the old and new bridges.   As the same are presently in the
" possession of Arthur Watson, maltman in Gorbals, the proprietor.·
" The articles of roup and progress of writs are in the hands of John
" Sheels, writer in Glasgow, to whom, at the sheriff clerk's office, or
" to the said James Pollok, or Arthur Watson, any person inclining
" to purchase privately may apply betwixt and the day of Sale."

" *Glasgow Mercury*, 3rd July, 1792."—" To be sold, by public
" roup, on Thursday, the 5th of July instant, The whole buildings
" and vacant ground of Joseph Rogers & Sons, cotton spinners in
" Gorbals, on the west side of the road leading from the river Clyde
" to the Church of Gorbals.   The houses are built in the form of a
" square, and inclosed ; and, besides the cotton work, there is a
" good dwelling house and warehouse on the premises.   Apply to
" Wilson & M'Farlane, writers."

" *Glasgow Mercury*, 20th November, 1783."—" To be sold, by
" public roup, on the 11th of December next, That piece of ground
" on the side of the river Clyde, and south side thereof, next
" adjacent to the village of Gorbals, and on the west side of the
" highway or street leading from the town of Glasgow's Bridge on
" the south end thereof, with the whole houses built thereon.
" Apply to John M'Ewen, writer."

" *Glasgow Journal*, 21st November, 1782."—" To be set, for one
" or more years, as can be agreed on, That piece of ground lying
" at the east side of the Gorbals, and extending from the river,
" upwards, to near Rutherglen Loan, consisting of about two acres."
(Muirhead Street was formed on this ground.)

At the south-east end of the old Bridge there was a retaining
wall which stretched up the Main Street of Gorbals by a gradual
slope, but the surface of this wall was upon the level with the street.

Immediately to the east of this wall there was a narrow lane descending from the south extremity of the retaining wall to the river, which was used as a passage to the Horse Ford in former times; but, in my day, was principally taken advantage of for the purpose of watering horses and cattle at the said ford.

From the above-mentioned lane, eastwards to the Blind burn, the banks of our river, within my remembrance, were lying in a state of nature. The Blind burn of old formed the eastern boundary of the Gorbals lands, which lands, according to M'Ure, page 62, at one time belonged to Lady Marjory Stewart, Lady Lochow, grand daughter of Robert II. It was this lady who named those lands "St Ninian's Croft."

At the division of the lands of Gorbals in 1790, the level track of ground on the east of the village named St Ninian's Croft, became the property of Hutchesons' Hospital, and was feued out by the directors of that Institution, and called Hutchesontown. The village was begun in 1794.

On the 24th of June, 1794, the foundation stone of the first Hutchesons' Bridge over the Clyde was laid by Gilbert Hamilton, Esq., lord provost, attended by the magistrates, and a number of respectable gentlemen. This bridge had five arches, was 410 feet long, and 26 feet broad, within the parapets. On the 18th of November, 1795, during a great flood of the river, it unfortunately was swept away; but it has been replaced by the present more elegant structure.

The substance of the following article was published in the *Glasgow Herald* of 10th September, 1859, and is now repeated, with some alterations and amendments :—

"The Old Bridge of Glasgow — Water Port — Bridgegate — Anecdotes, &c."

"Editor of the *Herald*—." ——"Most of your readers are familiar with the principal events which have occurred of old in the north quarter of Glasgow, embracing the bypast history of our noble Cathedral, of the Archiepiscopal Palace, of the Prebendal Manses, of the storming of the Bishop's Castle by Wallace, of the house in which Queen Mary visited Darnley, of the plundering of Archbishop Beaton's Palace, of its household plenishing by John Mure, of Caldwell, and of the rise and progress of our preceptorial College—first as the 'Auld Pedagogue' in the 'Ratten Raw,'* and then as the

* " De terris tenementi et loci muncupati ' Auld Pedagog ' jacentibus in via Ratonum,

erudite University of the City of Glasgow, with its spacious courts and garden, to say nothing of the more ignoble doings of the How-gate head and Castle yard hangings. There are few of your readers, however, who are equally well acquainted with the former state of the south quarter of our city, when it formed the fashionable place of residence of a great part of our aristocratic citizens, and the seat of modish elegance for holding our dancing assemblies and great public meetings." *

" ex Australi inter tenementum Magistri Johannis Reid ex parte occidentale, et terris " Roberti Reid orientale."—(" Book of our Lady College.")

     * " I believe that I was at the last dancing assembly which was held in the large hall of the Merchants' House, shortly before the Assembly Rooms at the Tontine were erected in 1782. I was carried there through the Bridgegate, in a neatly cushioned sedan chair, by two chairmen, the fare of which was sixpence, certainly as comfortable a conveyance as either our modern cabs or omnibuses."

CHAPTER VI.

Residenters in the Briggate—Bailie Craig's House in 1736—The Old Custom House—
The Water Port—The Plague in 1574—The Old Bridge and a walk over it in 1778—
Attempt by the Magistrates to shut it up—Provost George Murdoch.

AMONG the higher class of our citizens, who of old had the
domicile in the Bridgegate, Goosedubs, and upon the banks of the
Molendinar burn, we find the names of the Campbells of Blythswood,
of Douglas of Mains, including her Grace the Duchess of Douglas,
(who died in 1774,) of the Campbells of Silvercraigs, (in whose
house Oliver Cromwell lodged,) of Crawford of Crawfordsburn, of
Provost Sir John Bell of Hamilton Farm, of Campbell of Woodside,
of the Honourable John Aird, (who was ten times lord provost of
Glasgow, and who, in 1720, projected the opening of the Candleriggs,
and of King Street to the Bridgegate,) of Bailies Robert and George
Bogle, of the Reverend Dr Wodrow, of the Reverend Dr John Gillies,
of Provost Cochrane and of Provost Christie, of Bailies Dickie, Gil-
more, Craig, Dreghorn, Clark, and Robertson; of Conveners Findlay
and Crawfurd, of Dean of Guild Bogle, and also of Sir Robert Pollok
of Pollok.   In this quarter were likewise situated the original Ship
Bank and the Glasgow Arms Bank.   M'Ure mentions two of my
great-great-grandfathers having their places of residence in the
Bridgegate—the one situated next to Campbell of Blythswood's
house, and the other the second house east of the bridge ; so that,
perhaps, I may be excused for feeling some interest in this old
locality.   John Craig, who was bailie of Glasgow in 1734, and
Robert Dreghorn, who died in 1760—the grandfather of the well-
known " Bob "—resided, early in life, in the Bridgegate, a little to
the east of Blythswood's house ; but Bailie Craig, like other great
folks of our own day, took a start to the west, and built a large
house in Clyde Street, which was lately taken down.   M'Ure, page
322, thus describes it :—" Bailie John Craig has built, and is yet
" building (1736), a stately house, of curious workmanship, beauti-
" fully inclosed with several workhouses, shades, and storehouses,
" with a garden and summer parlour, of hewen stone, so that no

"carpenter or joyner in the kingdom has its parallell." Mr Robert
Dreghorn's son, Allan Dreghorn, bailie in 1741, (the father of
"Bob,") soon after followed the example of Bailie Craig, and built
the large house in Clyde Street, (still to the fore,) which is now the
furniture warehouse of Mr Thomas Smith, cabinetmaker and uphol-
sterer.

"*Glasgow Journal*, 25th Oct., 1764."—"On Friday last (19th),
"died at his seat in the country, Allan Dreghorn, Esq., an eminent
"merchant of this city." Mr Dreghorn's seat in the country was
Ruchill, purchased by the late James Davidson, Esq.

In the *Glasgow Mercury* of 20th October, 1785, there is the
following notification :—"On Thursday the 13th instant, was mar-
"ried in this city, by the Rev. Mr Taylor of St Enoch's, James
"Denniston, younger, of Colgrain, Esq., to Miss Margaret Dreghorn.
"(Bob's sister), daughter of the late Robert Dreghorn of Blochairn,
"Esq." In consequence of this marriage, the Denniston family
succeeded to the large property of Robert Dreghorn of Ruchill,
best known in Glasgow by the name of "Bob Dragon."

There was a curious old tenement which stood at the south-west
corner of Stockwell Street, at the west extremity of the old Water
Port wall, or dyke, as it was called. This property was purchased
some years ago by the late James M'Hardy, Esq., upon speculation,
and was taken down to form the present Victoria Buildings. This
old building has been the source of various mistakes, and of much
controversy among some of our Glasgow savans and antiquaries,
who have generally concluded that in ancient times it was the
Custom House of Glasgow, rented by the Crown, where all Clyde
entries, by the skippers of our Broomielaw small craft, were wont to
be made, and where the Crown dues of customs were paid. In an
article published in the *Glasgow Herald*, I expressed my doubts of
the Crown ever having had a Custom House at the foot of the Stockwell ; but from the following information, received from Mr Ross of
the Customs, through Andrew Scott, Esq., our distinguished Custom
House historian, I see that I was so far mistaken on this subject, in
doubting of the Crown EVER having had a Custom House at this
spot, as it appears pretty evident that, in 1757, the Crown Custom
House had been removed from some other part of the city, and
located at the foot of Stockwell Street.

From Andrew Scott, Esq.   "Glasgow, 27th May, 1862.

"Dear Sir,—Mr Ross has sent me to-day a copy of the letter

" alluded to in my last; it is from the collector and comp-
" troller at Port-Glasgow, dated 17th Nov., 1757, to the Board
" of Customs then at Edinburgh, defining the situation of the
" premises proposed for, and which were subsequently rented
" as the Custom House, which I am sure you will join with me in
" the conclusion that it is that referred to in 'Stuart's Ancient
" Glasgow,' as being situated at the foot of the Stockwell Street.   I
" annex copy of a letter Mr Ross has sent me.   I am led to the
" belief that the Custom House referred to in the chronological chap-
" ter in Cleland's publication in 1832, of the Statistics, &c., con-
" nected with the city, was not in that building, but probably
" formed a small hut, or other erection, at the north-west side of the
" Stockwell Bridge, and I am now the more inclined on this view,
" from the recollection of reading in Dr Smith's Memorabilia of the
" city, a minute of the town council anent slating and other repairs
" thereon, the expense of which was very trifling; and if my memory
" serves me correctly, I think that the plan of the north side of the
" bridge, which you gave us in the *Herald*, exhibits the spot where
" this hut, or Custom House, as it might be called, stood, for the
" collection of the toll-dues, and other local customs, as the ladle-
" dues, &c., were called; and I also think that said council minutes
" imposed on the toll collector the duty of preventing lepers from
" coming into town."

Copy from Mr Ross to Andrew Scott, Esq.

" Custom House, Port-Glasgow, 17th November, 1757.—Hon.
" Sirs, ... We beg also leave to acquaint your Honours,
" that there is a house now to be lett, and to be entered into at the
" above-mentioned term of Whitsunday next, which is every way
" convenient, and well situated for answering the purpose of a
" Custom House, with a sufficient warehouse belonging to it.   That
" this house is situated nigh to the Broomielaw, being where the
" two streets meet at the end of the bridge, and faces to each of
" them.   That upon inquiry, we find it to be the only one in that
" corner of the town proper for a Custom House, and that the yearly
" rent of it is £12.   Signed—Josiah Coutherie, A. Kinloch."

In 1757, the Broomielaw harbour extended eastwards to St
Enoch's burn, as may be seen in Stuart's View, at page 34, drawn
in 1760, consequently, the house mentioned in Mr Ross's letter was
situated nigh to the Broomielaw.   But in the year 1736, M'Ure, at
page 285, thus writes on the subject :—" Bremmy-Law—The next

" great building is the Bremmylaw harbour and cran, with the lodge
" for his Majesty's weights, beams, and triangles, with a fine foun-
" tain, which furnishes all boats, barges, and lighters' crews that
" arrive at this harbour, from Port-Glasgow, with water, and all
" other vessels which come from the Highlands and far off isles of
" Scotland, besides other places. There is not such a fresh water
" harbour to be seen in any place in Britain ; it is strangely fenced
" with beams of oak, fastened with iron batts within the wall thereof,
" that the great boards of ice, in time of thaw, may not offend it ;
" and it is so large that a regiment of horse may be exercised there-
" upon."

From the above it appears to me that the Custom House was then
situated at the Broomielaw, and was removed from it in 1757, and
located at the foot of the Stockwell, as stated in Mr Ross's letter. ·
I think that Mr Scott is correct in his opinion, that the Custom
House in question was not situated in the old building itself, but
most probably in its wing or office, on the west side of it. This
wing is shown in Stuart's View, and is two storeys in height, being
sufficient for a warehouse, which, from Mr Ross's letter, was required ; and the back court could give ample accommodation for his
Majesty's " weights, beams, and triangles." £12 appears a fair rent
for such premises a century ago.

The old building itself consisted of three storeys and attics, (there
being two windows in the roof,) with fifteen windows fronting Stockwell Street ; such a building, therefore, was of much greater value
than one of merely £12 of rent. Further, the Custom House could
not have been the small hut at the end of the bridge, (marked X in
the Plan,) for it had no warehouse room, nor space for weights and
triangles, &c. ; neither could it have obtained a rent of £12, seeing
that in 1574 the dues of the bridge were let by the magistrates of
Glasgow for the sum of 80 merks, or £4 8s 10¾d sterling. This
likewise shows that it could not then have been a Crown Custom
House, as such a trifling revenue could not have paid even the
salary of a government collector.

The small hut at the bridge, marked in the Plan X, was evidently
used merely for collecting the city dues exigible upon goods entering
Glasgow, either landwards or by the river ; and I think that there
never was a government Custom House at the foot of the Stockwell
before the year 1757.

" Council Records, 1st of June, 1574." " Gift of the Brig."
" The quhilk daye ya new gift gevin to ye brig and small casualties

" grantit yrto ar sett to Nicol Snodgers, for ye somm of four scour
" mks., money to be payit at the terms and the sit and wont, viz.,
" at Michaelmas, Candilmes, and Beltane."

The following advertisement will show what these customs were—

" *Glasgow Mercury*, 24th April, 1783."

" Notice—That the ladle dues, multures, dues of the tron, and
" weigh-house, flesh-market, wash-house, fish and potato market,
" and other common good belonging to the City of Glasgow, as also
" the pontage tolls and duties leviable on the Old and New Bridges
" at Glasgow, are to be set by public roup, within the Court Hall of
" the said City, upon Wednesday, the 14th day of May next, be-
" twixt the hours of twelve and two of that day, for the space of
" one year. The articles of roup are to be seen in the hands of the
" town-clerk of Glasgow."

Mr Stuart, in his Views, (page 55) has given us a pretty accurate
drawing of the tenement in question, which he calls the " Old
Custom House," and he further says:—" This is an edifice of no
" trifling pretensions, and seems to have been reared with more than
" ordinary care and expense, as the appearance of its walls, both
" towards the street, and at the back, sufficiently testify : we have
" heard that this was anciently known as the Custom House, and it
" may not improbably be that which is mentioned in the Burgh
" Records as standing near the bridge in 1643." Mr Stuart also in
a Note says:—" The site of the old Custom House seems to have
" been occupied in 1487 by a building, the property of Roberti
" Stewarde, prepositi, Glasguensis, and which we are informed stood
" adjoining to the Barres Yeth, (south port) on the west side of the
" street (vide ' Registratum Episcopatus Glasguensis.' Maitland
" Club, page 453.) We are not confident, however, (adds Mr
" Stuart) as to the site of the Barres Yeth." At one time, like Mr
Stuart, I thought the Barres Yeth was situated at the Old Bridge,
but from the following quotation, it will be seen that it stood at the
foot of Saltmarket, and appears to have been the principal entry
to the Green.

" *Burgh Records*, 5th October, 1574."

" It is statute and ordanit yat yir persones underwritten euery
" ane w⸴ in ye gayts quhair yai duell pass ouklie thro⸴ ye samyn
" and taist ye aill browin w⸴ in ye boundis limatit to yaim to se gif
" ye saymin be sufficient, accordyng to ye price taxt yairupon, and

" quha brewis yat arc unfrc, and to report ye saymin ouklic to ye
" Baillies—
 " For ye Rattonraw and Drygate :
  "Johne Dalrumpill—Johne Spreull.
 " Frae ye Wyndheid to ye Blackfrers :
  " Cuthbert Herbertson—Williame Rowat.
 " Frae ye Blackfriers to ye Croce :
  " Archibald Mure—Johne Taylor.
 " Frae ye Gallogate and Troyngate :
  Johne Woddrop—Johne Bell.
 " Frae ye Cross to ye Nether Baraszett :
  Matthew Wilsoun—James Craig.
 " Frae ye Baraszett to ye Brig and Stockwell :
  Johne Arbuckle—Johne Gilmor.
 " Item :—It is statute yat all owtintownes burgessis not dwelland
 " w. in ye towne, sall pay custumes usit and wont of auld in ye
 " towne except in tyme of fayris."
 The house of Provost Stewart, mentioned in Stuart's Views, must
have been situated in the Saltmarket, and not in Stockwell Street,
seeing that it stood adjoining to the Barres Yeth. I remember a
summer house standing in a garden at the south-west corner of
Saltmarket Street, which may have been in the site of Provost
Stewart's house and garden. The Molendinar burn, then a limpid
stream, most probably formed the south boundary of the property.
 Our Glasgow historians have given us little information when the
Water Dyke was built, in addition to the gate at the bridge, nor
have they stated the date when the name of "Water Port" first
came to be applied generally to the Port leading to the Broomielaw.
The gate at the bridge is not called the Water Port, in the early
history of Glasgow ; its site, in fact, was originally a part of the old
Green or Great Western Common, and the site of the house alluded
to by Mr Stuart, as standing at the foot of the Stockwell in 1528,
was probably occupied at that time by three small cottages with
their kail-yards, situated beyond the bounds of the city. At page
55, Mr Stuart informs us as follows :—
 " The earliest information we have been able to meet with in
 " connection with this old house is contained in a legal document
 " drawn up in 1599, from which it appears that the spot it occupies
 " formed at that period a portion of the site of three small tene-
 " ments, with adjacent inclosures, commonly known by the name of
 " 'yeards.' These tenements having previously become ruinous, were,

" in the year 1668, disposed of to a Mr John Caldwell, who had
" them demolished, and their places supplied by two edifices of
" better appearance and more respectable pretensions, which stood in
" juxtaposition upon the line of the street. The one to the south
" was many years ago removed to make way for a modern erection :
" the other still braves the adverse assaults of time, and is the house
" which forms the subject of this View."

Mr Stuart, in his Views of Glasgow, page 3, says that in 1639, the
Covenanters who opposed King Charles, directed amongst other
matters, that " a wall should be built between the '*Light House*,'
" and the '*Custom House*,' and that a *Port* should be erected
" BETWIXT the BRIDGE, and John Holme's house." Now it appears
to me that Mr Stuart has made some mistakes in this passage, and
has drawn erroneous conclusions from the words of the original document, which are as follows :—

" *Council Records*, 11th October, 1639."

" Ordanit that ane dyke be built at Stockwall-heid, and ane
" PONT put therein, and to build ane dyke from the LIT HOUSE to
" the CUSTOME HOUSE, in ane cumlie and decent forme, and with
" convenient diligence."

Mr Stuart has concluded that the words, " ANE PONT " meant
" A PORT," but I think that these words meant a bridge with an
arch in it, (derived from the French " un Pont.")* Again, Mr
Stuart construes the words " LIT HOUSE " to mean a " LIGHT
HOUSE," whereas I am of opinion that they are intended to signify
a " DYE-HOUSE." Jamieson, in his Scottish Dictionary, defines the
word " LIT," as meaning " A DYE OR COLOUR," and in the Scotch
Act of Parliament, James II., 6th March, 1457, we find as follows,
" That na ' LITSTER ' by claith to sell." Item—" It is seen speedful
" that ' LIT ' be cryed and vsed, as it was wont to be, and that na
" LITSTER be draper, nor bye claith to sell againe, nor zit thoiled
" thereto vnder the paine of escheit."

In the Burgh Records, 22nd January, 1573, David Howe, "*litster*,"
is stated to have become cautioner for John Campbell. From the
above quotations, I conjecture that the " LIT HOUSE " mentioned in
the Council Records of 1639, was a dye-work, occupied as such by
John Holmes in 1599, and sold to John Caldwell in 1668. The
three small houses, with their kail-yards, most likely being the dwell-

---

* Neither Jamieson, Johnson, nor Bailey, have the word " pont" in their Dictionaries.

ing and dye-works of the above-mentioned John Holmes; these premises standing conveniently situated adjacent to the river, and to the Dowcot Green, commonly used by the public as a washing and bleaching place.

There is no evidence of there ever having been a Light-house at the bridge in former times. If such a building had really existed, we would have found some notice taken of it in our old City Records. It may be further observed that the instructions in the Burgh Records of 1639, are " to build ane dyke at Stockwall-heid, from the Lit-house " to the Custome House," consequently, it is evident that the " Lit-house" and the Custom House were two separate buildings, and that the Lit-house mentioned by Mr Stuart could not have been the Custom House of old. I do not think that a Crown Custom House was ever situated near the Old Bridge before the year 1757, when one appears to have been rented there as stated by Mr Ross. The error in supposing that a Crown Custom House had anciently occupied this spot, seems to have arisen from the circumstance of the city dues for goods coming into Glasgow by way of the bridge, and by water, having generally passed under the name of Customs, as the following notice shows :—

" *Burgh Records,* 21st August, 1574."

" Item—Ye Prouest, Baillies, and Counsale, at my Lord of Glas- " gow's (Bishop's) requist hes supsedit ye small custom of ye brig, " and dischargit ye saymn to be taen frae ye barronie men of Glasgw " beyond ye quhile yai be feryer advysit." It will be seen in the small Plan of the bridge that there was a hut marked by a cross (×) placed at at the north-west corner of the bridge, for receiving payment of these customs. This small house seems to have formed part of the west parapet wall of the bridge itself, and is joined to the Water Port wall, which, along with the wall across the bridge, and at the corner of the Bridgegate, closed the street from east to west except through the ports.

I cannot reconcile the instructions of 1639, " to build ane dyke at Stockwall-heid from the Lit-house to the Custome-house." except by supposing that the Custom House here alluded to, was the small house at the bridge, where the city customs or common good were collected. (See Plan.)

It appears from the following quotation that the Water Port did not exist in 1574, and it is probable that the three small tenements and their kail-yards mentioned by Stuart, as having been sold to

Caldwell in 1668, formerly formed a barrier to any entrance to the city, by way of the Broomielaw, except the passage was made through the port at the bridge.

In the year 1574, the plague, or pest, as it was called, raged in the eastern parts of Scotland, and on the 29th of October of that year there is the following entry in the Burgh Records:—

"In ye first, it is statute and expressly inhibit and forbidden, " yat na maner of persons, indvellars or yat comes furth of Leyt, " Kircaldy, Dysart, Bruoonteland, quilkis ar ellis infectit and " suspect of ye said pest, nor zit of ony wyer townes or places yat " heireftir sal be suspect or fylit, presume to resont and travell to " yis towne, or use trafficque with ye inhabitantes yeirof: And yat " nane of ye inhabitantes of yis towne travell towart ony of ye saidis " placis, or use ony kynd trafficque witht yame under ye pain of " deid.

"Item. It is statute and ordanit yat na maner of persones " induellaris in this towne ressait in their houss ony maner stranger " reparand yairto, except yat yai cum first to ye prouest and " baillies, or yair deputtis, and put yair testimoniales, yat it may " be knawin quhairfra yai cum. And that nane win yis towne " ressaue ony person yat cumis about ye towne, or at yair backzardis; " and yat na induellar of yis towne enter bot at ye port and foirgate " under ye paine of X^{lib} ilk falt, and yat ilk p'sone cloiss his awne " zardend, as he will ans' on his lyf; and gif ony beis apprehendit " cumand about ye towne ye saymin to be tane and presonit and " handlit as suspect persones."

It is well-known that Glasgow was never a fortified town, or surrounded by defensive walls; but we see from the latter part of the above quotation that its inhabitants were required, at the peril of their lives, to keep their backyards constantly closed with some sufficient barrier, or fence, so as to prevent ingress to the city, except through one of its ports. It, therefore, appears to me that previous to the year 1639, when the Covenanting parties in Glasgow ordered a wall or dyke to be built across the foot of the Stockwell, in order to defend the city from the Royalists, that John Holme's back yards (or lit house grounds before mentioned) being barricaded at their south extremity, there was then no access to the city from the present Clyde Street, except by way of the port at the bridge; but when this dyke came to be built there were placed in it two ports or archways, one for carriages, and one for foot passengers, by which travellers could pass and repass without going through the

H

port at the bridge. As this entry led directly from the city to the river, and to the Broomielaw at St Enoch's burn, it came to be known as the " Water Port."

No mention is made in our city annals of there having been any port at the foot of Stockwell Street, called " The Water Port," before the year 1639, when the said dyke was built. The small Plan of the bridge shows the dyke above referred to closing the street from east to west. Although of old all access to the city was closed except by the ports, nevertheless the passage along the banks of the river, from the Broomielaw to the Green of Glasgow, was perfectly open to the public, there being an arch of the bridge founded on dry land (commonly called a dry arch) through which carriages and cattle, crossing the river by the Horse Ford, could freely pass along the present East Clyde Street to the Broomielaw.

It will be seen from the Plan that the Old Bridge was not built in a line with Stockwell Street, but at an angle, and evidently was originally constructed to suit the traffic passing by way of the Bridgegate, and not for the accommodation of that by the line of Stockwell Street.

Bishop William Rae, who built the Old Bridge in 1345, came into the see in 1335, and died in 1367. There was a timber bridge over the Clyde, nearly on the same spot, in 1340, which appears to have gone into decay.

Mr Pagan, in "Glasgow, Past and Present," Vol. I., page 150, has given us an extremely interesting account of the Old Bridge of Glasgow, on the occasion of its being demolished in 1850, and has stated some curious details of its early aspect and revolutions (to which work I refer the readers); but notwithstanding that gentleman's general accuracy, he appears to have hastily taken for granted that the old house at the corner of the Stockwell was the Crown Custom House of ancient times, where government dues used to be collected. At page 155, he says, " The ' Port,' or Custom House, is universally " represented as having been on the north side, and the queer old " house standing at the bottom of Stockwell Street is said to have " been the identical fabric used for that purpose." Mr Pagan, in his " Sketches of Glasgow," at page 152, has given us a plate of the Old Bridge, including a representation of the queer old house in question, with its garden to the west. This plate also shows the horse road descending by a gradual slope from the said queer old house to the river; and here I have frequently seen carters with their carts and horses, and grooms with their hunters, standing knee deep in the water, giving the poor animals their fill of the then limpid stream of the Clyde, and cooling their weary limbs in the purling waters of the place. This watering path was subsequently removed a little to the west, nearly opposite to the old town's hospital, and a timber bridge was erected over it across the wall of the breast, so as that there might be no interruption to passengers going along the said breast in their way to and from the Broomielaw.

Mr Pagan, at Page 154 of "Glasgow, Past and Present," informs us that "At the period of 1776 the original arches (of the "Old Bridge) were all entire (see Plan) with the exception of the 8th, "or the arch next the Gorbals, which fell on the 7th of July, 1671, "one of the days of the Glasgow Fair. The two north arches and "the pier on the Glasgow side were altogether removed, and the "ground filled up; they seem to have been what is termed 'dry "arches,' and in all likelihood were only scoured by the Clyde when "floods invaded the Bridgegate.

"The third arch of the old structure, or the first arch as known "to the present generation, was taken away and lowered four feet "at the centre, the second, third, and fourth arches remained un- "touched, the fifth arch was taken down and lowered three feet six "inches, and the sixth and last arch (that which had been previ- "ously rebuilt) was also taken down and lowered five feet in the "centre—at the same time this arch was taken in or lessened in the "span to the extent of eleven feet. By all these operations the road- "way of the Old Bridge was greatly lowered and vastly improved— "the then summit level of the bridge-causeway above the old low "water mark was forty feet six inches. The bridge went up by a "rapid slope from north to south, and at the Gorbals end the rise "or gradient to be surmounted on coming upon the bridge was at "the rate of 1 in 6½. That this terrible ascent existed there is not "matter of doubt."

We have no dates given here when these operations were executed, and not a word is said regarding the demolition of the ancient port at the bridge, nor of the small hut where of old the city dues were collected—neither is there any notice taken of the removal of the wall or dyke which formed the Water Port. These structures, however, are objects almost as interesting as the Old Bridge itself. I think, however, that these last operations were principally made about the year 1778, as the following extract seems to indicate :—

"*Glasgow Mercury*, 4th June, 1778.—Yesterday the workmen "began to remove the centres from below the additional part of the

" last arch of the Old Bridge. They proceeded in rather too preci-
" pitate a manner, by loosing the wedges on one side, so that the
" weight of those centres not slackened preponderating, tumbled the
" whole over. A mason got one of his legs sorely crushed, but
" happily no other accident happened."

It was during the time that these operations were proceeding, and
while the bridge was receiving an addition of ten feet to its breadth
on the east, that I crossed it from the Gorbals side in the spring of
the year 1778. The east side of the bridge was then encumbered
with stones, and scaffolding; but the west side of it was kept open
and free for foot passengers, so that I walked along it with great
ease and pleasure; my little hand being then held by Miss Grizel
Anderson, daughter of the Rev. William Anderson, the first minister
of Gorbals, and the father of the late eminent Dr William Anderson,
physician in Glasgow.

I distinctly remember the then state of the bridge itself, but I
have no recollection of seeing any operations going on at the place
where the port at the bridge and Water Port stood, the street
appearing to me to be then free of buildings; I therefore conclude
that the above-mentioned ancient ports of the city had been
demolished before the spring of 1778. Further, I do not remember
of then seeing the small hut or house, at the north west corner of
the bridge, where the city customs or dues were wont to be paid in
former times. I think that it must have been demolished between
the years 1776 and 1778, at the time when the two north arches of
the bridge were removed, and when the street leading to the bridge
came to be cleared of the port at the bridge and the Water Port
dyke, and properly levelled to suit the altered gradients of the
bridge. By referring to the small Plan of the bridge, it will be seen
that one of the above-mentioned arches was a blind arch, and the
other partly so.

I think it is probable that the different alterations and improvements which are stated to have been made upon the bridge shortly
after the year 1776 were in the course of execution during the year
1777, being the year before I crossed the Old Bridge of Bishop Rae.
The demolition of the ports, and the removal of the Water Port
dyke, along with the levelling of the lower part of Stockwell Street,
must have made a total change to the appearance of this part of
Glasgow, more especially to the south part of Stockwell Street, and
to the corner of the Bridgegate, by the said alterations giving an
improved access to the bridge and to the river.

The Old Bridge seems originally to have been built with due regard to the lives of passengers, for it will be seen from the Sketch annexed to the present sheet, that there were two recesses in it, on the east side, where, in case of need, a passenger could take shelter from the caperings of skittish horses, or from the crush of two carts or carriages hastily crossing each other while going along the bridge. It must be remembered that the bridge was then only twelve feet wide, and had no trottoirs or side footpaths, such as grace the noble fabrics that now span our river. The Sketch above mentioned was taken in the year 1775, and it would appear from the following quotation, that the bridge at that time must have been in a state of great disrepair, otherwise the passage of carriages along it would not have been so strictly limited and discouraged.

" *Glasgow Journal*, 4th April, 1765."

" By order of the magistrates of the City of Glasgow:—The " magistrates hereby intimate that for further preventing carts " loaden or unloaden to pass the Bridge of Glasgow, they have " caused put up a folding pole upon the said bridge, at the north " end thereof; but in order to accommodate gentlemen and others " passing along the said bridge in coaches and chaises, they have " engaged a servant who is to lodge in the little house on the east " side of, and immediately without the bridge, and on the north end " thereof, and to be ready at all times, from five o'clock in the " morning till eleven o'clock at night, to open the said folding pole. " It is therefore expected that all gentlemen and others, having " occasion to pass along the said bridge in coaches or chaises, will " endeavour to make their time of passing the same betwixt the " said hours of five o'clock of the morning and eleven at night; but " if necessity requires them to pass betwixt eleven at night, and five " in the morning, they will order their servants to call at the said " little house, on the east side of, and immediately without the bridge, " and on the north end thereof, where they will find the said ser- " vant who will open the pole to them."

One is rather curious to know the names of the magistrates who were so careful to exclude common carters and country farmers with their vehicles from passing the bridge, but, nevertheless, were so condescending as to keep a servant for the express purpose of open-ing the pole at all times, and at all hours, to gentlemen and the other great folks, travelling in their coaches and chaises. Here then are their names:—John Bowman, lord provost; John Alston,

Robert Donald, and George Buchanan, bailies; Francis Crawfurd, convener, (of whom more afterwards), Arthur Connell, dean of guild; Robert Finlay, master of works; Archibald M'Gilchrist and John Wilson, town clerks.

The shutting up of the Old Bridge, in the above mentioned manner, gave great offence to the Rutherglen folks, as it prevented all access to Glasgow, with common carts, from their ancient burgh, by the common highway, except the said carts took the route of crossing the river by the Dalmarnock Ford, or by the Horse Ford at the bridge.

It must be remarked here that Rutherglen Bridge was not built till the year 1776. Thus, while Rutherglen was excluded from making use of the Bridge Port to enter Glasgow, the neighbouring burghs of Dumbarton and Renfrew, and the town of Paisley, had free access to the city, both by the Water Port and by the West Port in Argyle Street. In this state of matters, the magistrates of Rutherglen commenced an action of damages against the magistrates of Glasgow, for having shut up the bridge in the manner above stated, and in this action they were joined by several parties connected with the lands on the south and west of the river; but it does not appear that either the folks of Port-Glasgow or Greenock became parties to the suit. Perhaps the influence of the Glasgow magistrates was then paramount in those towns. The Lord Ordinary, in 1766, gave judgment in favour of the magistrates of Rutherglen, by which the passage to Glasgow, by the bridge, was again laid open to the public; but the magistrates of Glasgow reclaimed against this sentence of the Ordinary, and were about to bring the case before the Inner House, when, seeing the opposition so strong against them, they thought it best to acquiesce in the sentence of the Lord Ordinary, and to make the passage along the bridge free, to all description of carriages, as it previously had been.

It was, probably, this unsuccessful contest with the magistrates of Rutherglen, and the general dissatisfaction of the public at the transaction, that induced the magistrates of Glasgow, elected for the ensuing term of 1766-7, to set about building the New Bridge at the foot of Jamaica Street. (The foundation of that bridge was laid on the 29th of September, 1768, by Provost George Murdoch,* Bailies

---

* Provost George Murdoch, while in office, was presented to King George III., in London. His Majesty remarked that the Provost of Glasgow was the handsomest Scotchman he had ever seen. Among the preferments of the *Scots Magazine* of Oct.,

James Buchanan, Peter Murdoch and James Clarke, but the bridge was not passable, for carriages, till 1772.) It is curious to see what a complete overturn had taken place, with regard to our city officials, by the new election, at the above mentioned term. The whole of the old authorities seem to have been set aside, and quite a new and liberal ministry formed to carry on our civic affairs. It was during the time that the above gentlemen held office, that the north-west burying ground was formed.

1771, we find as follows:—" George Murdoch, Esq., and late provost of Glasgow, comptroller of the Customs at Port-Glasgow and Greenock."

CHAPTER VII.

Water Port Dyke and Extension of the Bridge—Ben Barton's House—The First Printer in Glasgow temp. 1638—Removal of Spikes for exhibition of Heads of Traitors— General Assembly in Glasgow in 1638—The Crawfurds—The Mansion of the Campbells of Blythswood—Dillon's law suit with John Campbell of Blythswood—James Campbell and his Creditors—James Rankin, Tobacconist—Speculation in Tobacco in 1776—Curious Story of James Maxwell, Esquire—Flood in Briggate in 1782— Laughable story of David Dales' dinner party in 1795.

In the View of Glasgow, drawn by Captain John Slezer of the Artillery Company, during the reign of Charles II., there is no appearance of the dyke or port ordered to be built by the Covenanters in 1639. Slezer's Views were published at the latter end of the 17th century, but we do not know the date when they were sketched by him. We see, however, by the View in question, that the port of the bridge extended quite across the public street, and must have been about 25 feet in height, as it reaches above the second storeys of the conterminous houses, and if the Water Port dyke had been only half of that height (which was quite sufficient for the purpose), it would have been concealed in the view by the intervening high wall of the Bridge Port. Judging by Slezer's View, and by the Sketch attached to the present sheets, I would be inclined to think that the Bridge Port, or carriage entry, by way of the Bridgegate, was then about six feet in width, or about one half of that of the bridge, which was quite adequate to the passage of ordinary carriages. As to the height of the said carriage entry, judging again from Slezer's View, I would conclude that it must have been at least 15 feet from the causeway to the crown of the arch. There still remains one house in East Clyde Street, depicted by Slezer, with its Dutch front and corby steps.

After the alterations made upon the bridge, in 1778, had been finished, it appears that the tenement immediately joining the bridge on the north-east, was converted into an inn for the accommodation of travellers, as the following notice, taken from a Glasgow newspaper, shows.

"*Glasgow Mercury*, 19th August, 1784."

" Peremptorily to be sold, upon Friday the 20th of August
" current, All and Haill, that tenement of land lying on the south
" side of the Bridgegate, and immediataly to the east of the bridge,
" with the stables, cellars, and other offices, belonging to the
" deceast William Lorimer, stabler in Glasgow.   Articles of roup,
" &c., to be seen."

The Sketch of the bridge herewith given, unfortunately, does not
reach the termination of the roadway at the Main Street of Gorbals,
but I have a distinct recollection of its appearance in 1778, also
subsequently to that time.   The alterations then made upon the
roadway were not very extensive, as may be seen from the Map of
Glasgow, of 1783, in Mr Stuart's Views.   The bridge extended
about seventy feet southwards along the Main Street of Gorbals,
but it was merely a dead wall without arches.   On the west side of
it there was a pretty large tenement which fronted the river on the
north, joined the bridge on the east, and on the south it faced a
public footpath, leading towards the New Bridge, so that it excluded
all direct passage from the bridge along the margin of the river.
This tenement is very clearly laid down on the Map of 1783, in
Stuart's Views, and is there exhibited with a court in the centre.
It seems to have been let as an inn at the time when the alterations
on the bridge were in progress, as the following notice shows.

" *Glasgow Mercury*, 14th May, 1778."

" To be let, and to be entered at the term of Whitsunday, that
" large inn, stable, and others in the suburbs of Glasgow, fronting
" the river Clyde, at the end of the Old Bridge, as presently pos-
" sessed by George Paton at the Spread Eagle.   Apply to Ben.
" Barton, writer in Glasgow."

It appears that this building if it had again been let as a place of
entertainment for travellers, had not met as such, with much success, for we find that soon afterwards it had been turned into a shop
or shops, and even then the same want of success seems to have
attended its course, as the advertisement following shows.

" *Glasgow Mercury*, 17th July, 1783."

" Notice, that the well frequented shop, lying at the end of the
" Old Bridge, Gorbals of Glasgow, lately possessed by Mr James
" Stevenson, is to be let.   Entrance may be had immediately thereto.

"And about £70 of hardware and grocery goods, laid in from the
"best markets are to be disposed of. The shop is well finished, and
"will be very suitable for a young man beginning business. Any
"person inclining to make a purchase of the goods, as an induce-
"ment thereto, upon finding security, a reasonable credit will be
"given. For further particulars inquire at the publishers."

The property in question appears at this time to have passed
from the hands of our old commissary clerk, Ben. Barton, and its
site ultimately to have been occupied by the toll house.

In 1821 there was a second addition made to the width of the
bridge by the erection of ornamental iron footpaths, one on each
side of the bridge ; while the whole extent of twelve feet, as formerly, was appropriated for carriages in the centre of the roadway.

In "Glasgow, Past and Present," Vol. I., page 150, there will be
found an interesting account of the demolition of the Old Bridge
of Glasgow, in 1850, and of the appearances of its original foundations in the river, which truly verify the sagacious and recondite
remark of Dr Cleland, when commencing to elucidate the history of
our bridges, in his Rise and Progress of Glasgow, page 53. The
learned Doctor thus begins : "Bridges are a sort of edifices very
"difficult to execute, on account of the inconvenience of laying
"foundations and walling under water." Mr Pagan, however,
informs us, at page 151, that "the foundations of the old structure
"have been laid in a very simple manner. Instead of driving down
"piles, as would be done in the present day, the ancient masons,
"from the remains still visible, seem to have thrust in a quantity of
"green paling stobs, to give cohesion to the sand, and afford a
"regular bed."

With regard to the remains of Ben. Barton's house, before
alluded to, it is stated that "Mr York has just excavated the wall
"of an old house which stands within three or four feet to the
"westward of the bridge on the Gorbals side. There is a little
"window 2ft. 2in. in width, by 2ft. 10in. in height, by which those
"in the interior could scan the passengers who descended from the
"bridge. There are still remaining the jambs of the large fireplace,
"constructed, as in old times, with four courses of stone on the one
"side and three on the other, instead of being done up on each side
"with one large slab, as is the custom at the present day. The
"wall is 2ft. 4in. in thickness, and 24ft. in length, showing that
"the house of which it formed a part must have been of consider-
"able dimensions. The rubble has been partly removed from the

" outer side of the wall, but in the inner part of the house the " plaster still firmly adheres. What manner of dwelling this was, " no man can tell."

There, however, seems to be a mistake in this last remark regarding the said structure, as our old commissary clerk, Ben. Barton, has left us an advertisement, as before quoted, which shows the purposes for which it had been erected, viz., The Spread Eagle Inn.

My authority thus continues : "This Gorbals concern we take " therefore to have been a public or a change house. It was well " situated for the purpose, being among the first that country people " from the south would reach on approaching the city, and the last " at which they could be entertained, or treat their friends, on leav- " ing it. These old walls doubtless have seen many a merry scene " of jollity, love making, bargaining, polemics, and perhaps strife."

At the south-east or opposite corner of the bridge there was a retaining wall upon the level of the street, which by a gradual slope from the main street descended to the river, and formed the west boundary of a lane leading to the Horse Ford, which ford is represented in the Sketch of the bridge. This retaining wall was merely a breast, and had no parapet; consequently it was very dangerous at night to passengers. In my juvenile days, I have frequently jumped from it to the lane below, as a short cut to the Blind burn, then a favourite place for bathing. On the east side of the said lane were situated the dwelling house and workshop of Mr Mann, a celebrated gunsmith of Glasgow ; but there were no buildings between Mr Mann's house and the Blind burn, the whole of Hutchesontown being then arable lands. The Blind burn formed the east boundary of the Gorbals grounds.

Mr Stuart, in his Views of Glasgow, page 3, does not seem to have been aware that the port at the bridge and the Water Port were two separate and distinct ports ; and appears to have thought that the wall or dyke ordered to be built at the "Stockwell heid" by the adherents to the second "Covenant," in order to strengthen themselves against the soldiers of King Charles I., was the sole south port to the city in 1639 : whereas it was only an addition to the ancient port at the bridge, as before mentioned.

Dr Cleland, in his Annals of Glasgow, has given us no account when the Water Port was constructed ; and he, as well as our other Glasgow historians, appears to have considered the port at the bridge and the Water Port to have been one and the same port : but by looking at the Sketch of the bridge hereto annexed, it will be seen that there were two distinct ports at the foot of Stockwell Street in 1760, being before the Water Port with its two entries was taken down. This dyke and port, as already mentioned, having been erected by the Covenanting party of the General Assembly in 1638, the state of parties at that time ran so high that little notice has been handed down to us of matters regarding our city affairs of that date except what had reference to Covenanting doings.

From a history of the art of printing in Glasgow, we learn that previous to the year 1638 there had been no printer in Glasgow; but in that year a person of the name of George Anderson was induced to commence printing in Glasgow, in consequence, it was said, of receiving a salary from the magistrates. His publications, however, appear to have been confined to pamphlets relating to the troubles before the commencement of the Civil War, and to Covenanting meetings, and not to matters especially connected with Glasgow statistics. The following is believed to have been the first work published in Glasgow :—

" The Protestation of the Generall Assemblie of the Church of " Scotland, and of the Noblemen, barons, gentlemen, borrowes, " ministers and commons : subscribers of the covenant, lately " renewed, made in the high kirk, and at the mercate crosse of " Glasgow, the 28. and 29. of November 1638."

" Printed at Glasgow by George Anderson in the year of grace " 1638."

George Anderson appears to have died in the year 1648, and for ten years after his death there does not seem to have been any printer in Glasgow. In 1655, Principal Baillie, wishing to get one of George Anderson's pamphlets republished, found it necessary to resort to London for a printer ; but in 1658, Andrew Anderson, the son of the said George Anderson, began printing in Glasgow, but he left Glasgow in 1661, and became printer in Edinburgh.

It is curious here to observe to what lengths religious bigotry will sometimes carry even well-disposed persons, and cause them to sanction as a duty many things which appear quite barbarous and shocking to the feelings of the generality of mankind. It will be seen by the following extract that the Covenanters then ruling our city, as alluded to by Mr Stuart, had directed a wall at the cross to be taken down, and translated to the Stockwell, and a "heid" thereon to be put on the "said new wall on Stockwell gait." " Council Records, 11th August, 1638."—"The Council ordains 50

" pounds to be paid to John Boyd, for translating of the Stockwall
" of the Hie Street (Trongate) and setting the sawyer down in ane
" uther plaice, and for taking down ane wall at the Croce, covering
" the same in, and for translaiting the 'heid' that was thereon, and
" setting it on the said new wall on the Stockwall gait."

I remember very well of the iron spikes which were inserted in
the present Cross steeple, for the purpose of exhibiting the ghastly
heads of unfortunate traitors and papists. These spikes were placed
on the north wall of the steeple, so as that the said heads might be
seen to the greatest advantage from the High Street, then the leading thoroughfare of the city.

The head which was translated to the Stockwell from the Cross,
in 1638, was probably that of some unhappy Papist or Jesuit, whom
the Covenanters regarded with the utmost horror as imps of Satan.
In revenge for this and for the like barbarities perpetrated by the
Covenanters, the Royalists, when they became masters, ordered the
head of the godly and reverend James Guthrie to be put on the
Nether Bow Port of Edinburgh, in 1661 ; and the head of Lord
Warriston, another Covenanting leader, to be placed on the wall of
the same port. (See Woodrow, 1st, 57, 1741.)

It was probably by orders of the celebrated General Assembly of
Scotland which met in Glasgow on the 21st of November, 1638,
that the Water Port dyke was ordered to be constructed. This
Assembly consisted of a vast concourse of influential people, almost
all the nobility and gentry of Scotland being present either as elders
or assessors. They declared the whole Acts of the Assembly passed
since the accession of James to the throne of England to be null
and void, all the bishops were deposed and excommunicated, Episcopacy and the Liturgy abolished, and every person ordered to
subscribe the Covenant under the pain of excommunication. These
resolutions were confirmed when the Parliament met in 1639, and
war was then declared by the Covenanters against the adherents of
Charles. There seems to be little doubt, therefore, but the Water
Port dyke was built in that year, as a defence to the city in case of
an attack being made on it by the Royal forces.

Although it appears by the letter of Mr Ross, before quoted, that
the Crown rented part of the queer old tenement at the foot of
Stockwell Street as a Custom House, in 1757, nevertheless, it seems
to have been situated in the wing of the said old house, and not in
the ancient building itself, as at this date the premises in question
formed the mansion house and property of Francis Crawfurd, Esq.,

an extensive timber merchant in Glasgow, whose offices and garden extended westward to the property of Bailie Craig of the Water Port, as may be seen in the first plate of Denholm's History of Glasgow. Shortly before this building was taken down to make room for the Victoria erections, the west part of it was occupied by Mr William M'Cue, as a poultry and provision store. It was in this ancient fabric that Mr Francis Crawfurd's son, the late George Crawfurd, Esq., writer, was born, in the year 1756, being the year before the Crown rented any part of the said premises. Mr Francis Crawfurd was convener of the Trades in 1765, and died in that year while in office, as the following notice shows.

"*Glasgow Journal,* 5th December, 1765."

" On Saturday, Mr Francis Crawfurd, Convener of the Trades of " Glasgow, was interred in the High Church yard. On this occa- " sion all the different corporations walked in procession, each trade " by itself, attended by their officers."

There is a singular circumstance attending Convener Crawfurd's family. Mr Crawfurd had no less than twenty-two children, of whom, I believe, the late George Crawfurd, Esq., writer, was the youngest. Of all that numerous progeny, not one of them is known to be now alive, and none of them have left any descendants, except the said late George Crawfurd, Esq., writer, whose only son, the present George Crawfurd Esq., Justice of Peace Clerk, now repre- sents this old Glasgow family. Mr Robert M'Lintock, the maternal grandfather of the present George Crawfurd, was the founder of the Merchant Bank of Glasgow, and signed the notes of that bank when first issued.

The next house to Convener Crawfurd's, was that of Bailie John Craig, whose son, Bailie William Craig of the Water Port, (who died in 1804), was well-known to most of our Glasgow octogenarians. Bailie William Craig served his apprenticeship with Mr Francis Crawfurd, and afterwards became his partner, the firm being Craw- furd and Craig. Their timber yard was situated in the Bridgegate, being the large yard attached to the Merchants' House. It is thus described in an old paper, which I have seen, dated 1766. " The " yard in the Bridgegate, belonging to the Merchants' House, was " set by tack to Francis Crawfurd and William Craig, for ten years, " after Whitsunday, 1761, at the yearly rent of £6 6s sterling. " The said yard has two entries, the one next the Clyde being a " cart entry, and the other next to the Bridgegate a narrow passage,

" and not fit for a cart. The said yard is well enclosed with a stone " dyke, and contains 1600⅔ yards, superficial measure." (See the Sketch.)

In 1817, the Merchant House sold this yard, and their other property in this part of the Bridgegate, to William and James Carswell, for £7500, who erected thereon the present buildings called Guildry Court. The steeple, however, was reserved. After the expiry of the lease of 1761, Bailie William Craig removed his timber yard and joiner workshops to Great Clyde Street, behind his dwelling house, and in 1790 he again changed the site of his yard and works, to Jackson Street, which street had shortly before been opened by Mr Jackson of the Theatre Royal.

The most remarkable old tenement (which still remains) in the Bridgegate, is the mansion house of the Campbells of Blythswood, with what was once its large garden extending southwards towards the river, as is shown in the annexed Sketch.

This ancient building was, probably, erected about two centuries ago, and originally consisted of two houses, which afterwards came to be united so as to form a single dwelling house. On the 13th of December, 1739, Colin Campbell, Esq., of Blythswood, executed a a strict entail of all his heritable properties, including the said Bridgegate mansion house and garden.

The last of the Blythswood Campbells who resided in the Bridgegate, was James Campbell, Esq., the father of our late member of Parliament, Major Archibald Campbell. Mr James Campbell being rather short of cash, let his large garden to David Lillie, wright, as a timber yard, at the yearly rent of £5; but thinking that he could get a little more of the needful by dividing the garden into lots, he, in 1770, parcelled it out into three parts, granting leases of nineteen years, with breaks at seven years, first to Mr John Robertson, a cooper; second, to Mr William Martin, a wright, and third, to Mr Linn Dillon, a plasterer. In the leases granted to those tenants (whose descendants, I believe, are still in Glasgow) he designed himself *heritable proprietor of the yard after mentioned*, and the stipulated rent, in all, was £20. None of the above tenants were aware that Mr James Campbell was only a life renter of the subjects, but believing him to have had an absolute right therein as *heritable proprietor*, they proceeded to make erections on their respective lots, under the faith of the following clauses, in their leases. " And with " liberty to erect shades or other buildings thereupon, and the land- " lord, at the end of this tack, to pay the value of the said shades

" and buildings, as the same shall be ascertained by two persons, to be
" mutually chosen by the parties." Mr Robertson erected a dwelling house with offices and workshops, on his lot, in value about
£300; and Mr Dillon did the same on his lot also, of like value;
but Mr Martin, in his lease, having taken part of Mr Campbell's
house, had no occasion to erect expensive buildings on his lot, but
only shades and workshops. All these erections were executed with
the consent, and under the eye of Mr Campbell himself.

James Campbell of Blythswood, after a lingering illness of nine
months, died on the 8th January, 1773, leaving little or no real or
personal estate, after sick bed and funeral expenses were defrayed.
His eldest son, John, afterwards Colonel Campbell, succeeded to the
Blythswood entailed estates, to whom the above mentioned tenants
regularly paid the rents of the subjects, in conformity with the terms
of their respective leases. In 1776, Mr Dillon having entered into
another line of business gave regular intimation to Colonel Campbell, that he was going to quit the subjects, and give up the tack,
at the break of seven years, and again did the same, in proper legal
form, at Whitsunday, 1777, when the first seven years of the tack
had expired; at the same time, requesting a proper person to be
named, in order to ascertain the value of the buildings, so that the
amount thereof might be paid to him as especially provided by the
terms of the tack.

Colonel Campbell having returned no answer to Mr Dillon, the
latter raised an action, in the Court of Session, upon the tack, concluding against Colonel Campbell for £300, as the value of the
buildings erected on Blythswood grounds, under the faith of the
said tack. The result of this action was unfortunate to poor Dillon,
the Court, after long litigation, having found that Colonel John
Campbell, being merely heir of entail in the said estate, " does not
" represent the late Blythswood in any other manner." Dillon's
case, of course, decided the two others, and thus Colonel John
Campbell got all the back erections on his Bridgegate garden for
nothing, contrary to the boasted legal apophthegm, " nemo debet
" locuplateri aliena jactura." (For the particulars of Dillon's case,
see Glasgow Past and Present, Vol. II., page 43.) Colonel John
Campbell was a remarkably handsome man. I remember him very
well, walking the Trongate of Glasgow, with a fine military step;
but he was careless about his dress, for his white silk stockings used
to be dangling loose about his ankles in all weathers. He was killed
in Martinico, in 1794, and was succeeded by his brother, Archibald,

our late M.P., then Captain Campbell, and a prisoner at Toulon, where the news reached him of his having succeeded to the large entailed estates of Blythswood.

About sixty years ago Archibald Campbell, M.P., obtained powers to purchase the annexation lands of Blythswood Holm, now in the heart of Glasgow, and also the Bridgegate family mansion and garden, at a valued price, under trustees, who were taken bound to lay out the said price in other lands, to be substituted for the annexation lands, and family burgage property, to be entailed in strict conformity with the terms of the original deed of 1739. In the year 1802, Archibald Campbell, M.P., (then Major Campbell) sold the Bridgegate mansion house, with all the back buildings before mentioned, which had been erected in the garden or yard, by Robertson, Martin and Dillon, under the terms of their leases.

James Campbell of Blythswood, the father of Colonel John and Major Archibald Campbell, was married to Henrietta, daughter of James Dunlop of Garnkirk, (she died in 1788), by whom he had three sons and five daughters, viz:—1st, Colonel John; 2d, Major Archibald, our late M.P.; 3d, James, who died a lieutenant in the 55th regiment, while in Antigua; 4th, Henrietta; 5th, Agnes, 6th, Grace; 7th, Janet, and 8th, Mary. With the exception of John, who succeeded to the entailed estates of Blythswood, this large family were left totally unprovided for, James Campbell, the father, having died involved in debt, and quite insolvent, as the following advertisements show.

"*Glasgow Journal*, 16th November, 1775."—"Notice—To the
" creditors of the deceased James Campbell of Blythswood, Esq.
" Such creditors of Mr Campbell as have lately obtained a Decree of
" Constitution of their debts before the Commissary of Hamilton
" and Campsie are requested to meet by themselves, or agents pro-
" perly authorised, within the house of William Thompson, vintner,
" at the Cross of Glasgow, on Wednesday the 29th November inst.,
" between the hours of one and two o'clock, mid-day, in order to
" concert measures for recovering payment of their several debts,
" certifying such creditors who shall not then attend, or pay the
" charge necessary for prosecuting these measures, that they will
" not be entitled to any benefit that may arise from prosecution."

"*Glasgow Mercury*, 1st January, 1784."—"Notice—To the
" creditors of the deceased James Campbell of Blythswood, Esq.
" That in the process of Ranking and Sale depending before the
" Lords of Council and Session, at the instance of James Hepburn

I

" of Humbie, and James Somerville, apparent heirs of line of the said
" James Campbell, a commission has been granted to John Wilson,
" junior, writer in Glasgow, for the creditors, deponing to the verity
" of their debts. This intimation, therefore, is given to such of the
" said creditors, and to the representatives of such of them as are
" deceased, who obtained a decree of constitution of their debts
" before the Commissary of Hamilton and Campsie in the month of
" August, 1774, to appear before the said John Wilson, with whom
" the above decree lyes, and to depone to the verity of their debts
" as soon as possible."

" *Glasgow Mercury*, 28th September, 1790."—" Notice—To the
" creditors of the late James Campbell of Blythswood, Esq. John
" Jaffrey, late watchmaker in Glasgow, now in Stirling, to whom
" certain creditors of the said James Campbell indorsed for behoof
" of their claims, having now recovered a dividend from the price of
" the unentailed lands of the said James Campbell, those creditors
" or their representatives will call on John Wilson, one of the Town
" Clerks of Glasgow, to receive their dividends and sign a discharge.
" The dividends will be paid at Mr Wilson's Writing Office, foot of
" Saltmarket, on Fridays and Wednesdays, from eleven o'clock
" forenoon till one o'clock afternoon, from Friday the first of October
" next. And as several of Mr Jaffrey's constituents were cut off by
" the Court of Session from a dividend, by reason of their having
" neglected to depone to the verity of their debts, in order to save
" unnecessary trouble, and to give notice to those who are entitled
" to receive dividends, there is hereunto annexed a list of the
" creditors, his constituents, now entitled to receive dividends, viz.,—
" Alexander Bannatyne, seedsman, Glasgow ; William Purdon,
" tenant, Woodside; Robert M'Lintock, senior, merchant, Glasgow;
" Will. Swan, smith and ferrier, Renfrew ; James Park, shoemaker,
" there; Robert Brand, vintner, there; George Paterson, smith, there;
" Thomas Brown, mason, there ; Matthew Burn, at Blackhall ;
" John Ritchie, wright, Renfrew ; William Balcanquhal, corkcutter,
" Glasgow ; Edward Collins & Co., bleachers, Dalmuir ; Andrew
" Ramsay, merchant, Glasgow; Casper Clawson, South Sugar House,
" there ; A. and H. Blackburns, merchants, there ; William Bore-
" land, weaver, Paisley ; William Tassie, glover in Glasgow ; James
" Watson, staymaker, there; Archibald Campbell of Succoth, Esq. ;
" John Brown, cooper, Renfrew; William Campbell, butcher, Paisley;
" Alexander Nasmith, wright, there ; John Christie, merchant,
" there ; Thomas Crichton, there ; Hamilton and M'Farlane, mer-

" chants, Glasgow; Shortridge and Martin, merchants, there; John
" M'Aslan, gardener, there; James Clerk and Arthur Robertson,
" merchants, there; John Mitchell, nurseryman, Renfrew; Patrick
" Croo, slater, Paisley; Michael Bogl and Scott, merchants, Glasgow;
" James Philips & Co., manufacturers, Paisley; Thomas Manfod,
" wright, there; John Robertson, mason, Renfrew; Janet Hume,
" milliner, Glasgow; Buchanan and Crawfords, merchants, there;
" Alexander Spiers, merchant, there; John Brock, mason, Cow-
" caddens; Hugh Niven, merchant, Glasgow; Robert King, hosier,
" Port-Glasgow; Elizabeth Graham, residenter in Glasgow; Carre,
" Ibetson & Co,, merchants, London; John Anderson in Blewarthill;
" Home and Cleghorn, coachmakers, Edinburgh; Walter Macfar-
" lane, wine merchant, there; John Wilson, late town clerk of
" Glasgow; and Mrs Lionell Walkinshaw, relict of William Walkin-
" shaw, late ship master in Port-Glasgow.
" Not to be repeated."

From the foregoing notices it appears that several of Mr Campbell's creditors had made no claims against his estate. These were,
probably, creditors who had supplied the family with furnishings
either for the person, or for the table, which description of furnishings being generally paid in full by the persons succeeding to large
entailed estates, the said creditors might have expected that Colonel
John Campbell, having succeeded to an entailed estate of two thousand per annum, would have paid such family debts in full according
to use and wont.

Among the list of creditors we do not see a tailor. This trades-
man, probably, rendered Colonel John and his two brothers separate
accounts for their respective habiliments, and so may have got paid;
but we find an unhappy milliner on the list, whose account against
so many ladies must have been pretty heavy. There also shine
among the family furnishing creditors a staymaker, hosier, shoemaker, and glover.

With regard to the creditors supplying the family with vivers, we
do not see any grocer in the list; but several of those enumerated
in it called " merchants there" were, in fact, tea dealers, grocers,
and general merchants. Sugar seems to have been supplied by
Casper Clawson of the South Sugar House; and we have the coach-
maker, also wrights, masons, coopers, smiths, and ferriers for job-
bings, besides a poor Paisley weaver, no doubt a creditor for weaving
some house-made shirtings or sheetings, and Collins of Dalmuir for
bleaching the same. Mr James Campbell appears to have got his

wines from Edinburgh but his corks in Glasgow; perhaps he paid ready money for his bottles. There is a gardener in the list for vegetables and garden-seeds, viz., Bailie John M'Aslan, and as for milk, butter, and cheese, these farm productions were most likely supplied from the dairies of Mr Purdon of Woodside, and of Mr Burn of Blackhall. There is also in the list that very necessary furnisher of family wants "a butcher;" but what has become of " the baker," the most important personage of them all, as to vivers, hot rolls to breakfast, quartern loaves to dinner, cookies, short-bread, and " Bell Gordons"* to tea, to say nothing of piping hot penny pies to supper, for such a large family as that of Mr Campbell, would form no small item of household expenditure. The late James Rankin, Esq., tobacconist, however, explained to me how there came to be no baker among the creditors of Mr Campbell in the foregoing published list of them. Mr Rankin said that he was appointed Executor upon the estate of a deceased baker, in whose book there stood an account of upwards of £100 against the Blyths-wood family for bread furnished to them during· the lifetime of James Campbell. The said baker alleged that Colonel John, his two brothers and five sisters, having all intromitted, art and part in the act of consuming his bread, he therefore considered that they were all and each of them liable to him for the debt, "singuli in solidum," as the lawyers say. The baker's demand on the family, however, was repudiated by them, and shortly after the baker died, in consequence of which the matter lay over. Mr Rankin told me that he several times attempted to get payment of this debt from the Blythswood family, but without success. It was thought, however, that Major Archibald, on succeeding to the Blythswood estates, would have discharged the debt if he had been applied to in a gentle and courteous manner, but that he considered the demand had been made upon him in a bullying and threatening style, which he was resolved to resist.

Mr James Rankin's dwelling house, shop, and tobacco manufac-tory were situated in the Bridgegate, immediately opposite to the Blythswood mansion house. His father, John Rankin, is taken notice of by M'Ure as being the proprietor of these premises in 1736, and then carrying on the business of a tobacconist. There was a large garden behind the tobacco manufactory, lying between

---

* "Bell Gordon" is short-bread with large sweeties baked upon its upper surface. The term is a corruption of the French phrase " Belle Guerdonne"—" A handsome reward."

the Old and the New Wynds, at the north end of which there stood
a neat summer house, where tea entertainments were occasionally
given during the summer season by the Rankin family, even down
to my day.

In the annexed Sketch there is a large vacant space of ground
shown between the two wynds; but I think that this space was not
wholly Mr Rankin's property, but that it included Mr Urie's
cooperage. The Irish have now got possession of this once rural
spot, and of late it has become a place of some notoriety, in consequence of Mr James Fleming, of the celebrated M'Lachlan case,
having been accustomed to resort there every week, for the purpose
of collecting the rents due by the tenants to the Rankin family.
This duty Mr Fleming performed in a manner most satisfactory to
Mr Rankin's heirs. Mr James Rankin mentioned rather a singular
circumstance to me regarding his father's family. He said that if
his eldest brother had been then alive, that he would have been 120
years of age, there being upwards of 60 years of difference between
the ages of the brothers. Of course they were by different mothers.
At the death of Mr Rankin's father, his widow (Mr James Rankin's
mother) continued to carry on the tobacco business for behoof of
the family, which she did to their great advantage. When the
American War of Independence broke out, about 1776, tobacco, from
threepence per pound, suddenly rose to sixpence per pound. On
this occasion, Mr William Cunningham (who built the original
house of the Royal Exchange) called on Mrs Rankin, as a friend and
an old acquaintance of the family, and strongly advised her to lay
in a stock of tobacco forthwith, as he was sure that there would be
a still greater rise of the tobacco market. Mrs Rankin, however,
hesitated to speculate upon an article which had already risen to
double of the ordinary price. Mr Cunningham, notwithstanding of
her objections, still urged her to purchase a few hogsheads, when
she at last rather unwillingly agreed to buy one hogshead, but she
refused to venture on any greater purchase, considering the risk to
be too great. She had scarcely concluded the bargain when tobacco
rose to 9d per pound, then to 1s, and thus continued to rise step by
step, till at length it reached the extraordinary price of 3s 6d per
pound; so that ultimately, by manufacturing this single hogshead
of tobacco, Mrs Rankin cleared £1500. Mrs Rankin's eldest
daughter, Janet, (sister-german of Mr James Rankin) was married
to Humphrey Ewing, Esq., the brother of Walter Ewing Maclae,
Esq., of Cathkin, and uncle to James Ewing, Esq., of Strathleven.

Since I have got amongst those old gossiping stories of Bridgegate matters, I shall mention another that was current in my younger days, the truth of which, however, I cannot vouch for, as it occurred before my time : I can only say that it was commonly received as a fact by the folks of Glasgow some seventy or eighty years ago. I have already stated that James Campbell, of Blythswood, had let his garden or yard in the Bridgegate to David Lillie, a wright, who was deacon of the craft in 1772. Mr Lillie was also an extensive builder. About this time, or shortly after, James Maxwell, Esq., the grandfather of the present Sir John Maxwell of Pollok, being then a young man, and having no expectation of succeeding to the Pollok estates, resolved to go out to St Christopher, and settle in that island as a planter. Preparatory, however, to going there, he thought it would be of great service to him to get lessons as a joiner, so that he might be able to show the slaves upon any estate that he might acquire how to handle the saw and the plane. Accordingly, he applied to David Lillie to be admitted to his shop as one of his operatives, and there he sedulously worked at the bench for a considerable time among Mr Lillie's journeymen, till he became an expert joiner, and was familiarly addressed by his fellow-workmen as " Jemmy Maxwell."

At the time when Mr Maxwell was thus working at the bench in Mr Lillie's shop, there were two individuals between him and the Pollok estates, viz., Sir Walter Maxwell of Pollok and his son John, so that Mr James Maxwell felt that he must depend upon his own exertions for rising in the world ; but providence interfered in his favour, and ordered matters otherwise. Sir Walter Pollok died in 1761, and in nine short weeks thereafter Sir John, his only son, followed his father to that place from whence none return : and so Mr Maxwell, as next heir, succeeded to the estates of Pollok, and became Sir James Maxwell of Nether Pollok. Sir James Maxwell, after succeeding to the Pollok estates, took a great interest in the affairs of the city of Glasgow, and was a leading man in all public measures tending to benefit its citizens. In 1782, he became the head partner of the Thistle Bank, the firm being " James Maxwell, James Ritchie and Company." Such, then, was the gossiping story of my younger days regarding Sir James Maxwell of Pollok.

In an article published in the *Glasgow Herald* some years ago, I stated that I was present in the year 1782 when the great flood of Clyde overflowed the whole of the lower parts of the city, and that I beheld boats navigating the Bridgegate, and ascending King

Street above the markets, to the great wonder and terror of the inhabitants.* On the 18th of November, 1795, a similar flood occurred, of nearly an equal magnitude, and quite as destructive as to property. The Bridgegate in this case was also completely inundated, and boats plied along its waters to supply with food the inmates of houses who were detained prisoners in the upper portions of their dwellings. All the arches of the fine new bridge across the river, opposite the Saltmarket, which had been passable on foot, fell in, one after another ; and cows, sheep, and much agricultural produce were carried away by the rapidity of the torrent, and lost.

Amidst all these distressing occurrences there happened one so comic, that its recital by the tittle-tattlers of the day made people almost to forget the general calamity caused by the flood. It seems that David Dale, Esq., whose house was situated at the foot of Charlotte Street, had invited a large party to dinner on the said 18th day of November, 1795, and expected William Simpson, cashier of the Royal Bank, the great millionaire Gilbert Innes, of Stowe, and the whole posse of the Royal Bank directory, to come from Edinburgh to meet Scott Moncrieff, George M'Intosh, and a few others of our Glasgow magnates at dinner on the said day. On the memorable morning of the said 18th, all was bustle and hurry-burry in Mr Dale's house, preparing a sumptuous feast for this

* The following account of this great flood is taken from the *Scots Magazine* of 14th March, 1782 :—

"Glasgow, 14th March, 1782."—"On Tuesday last (12th), the river Clyde rose to a
" greater height than the oldest people in the city remembered. It has sometimes
" overflowed that part of the town which lies very low, but upon this occasion it rose
" about 20 feet of perpendicular height above the usual course of the river. This re-
" markable inundation was occasioned by a very heavy fall of rain and snow, which
" began on Sunday last, about three afternoon, without intermission all that night and
" next day. Upon Monday night, about ten o'clock, some parts of the Bridgegate were
" under water, and the flood continued to increase. It was at the greatest height upon
" Tuesday morning, about seven o'clock. At that time the Bridgegate, the lower part
" of the Saltmarket, Stockwell, Maxwell Street, Jamaica Street, and the populous village
" of Gorbals, were all under water. The inundation was sudden and unexpected.
" Hundreds of families were obliged to leave their beds and their houses. A particular
" account of the damage which individuals have sustained cannot be ascertained, but the
" loss in tobacco, sugar, and other merchandise carried away by the river or spoiled by
" water will amount to a very large sum. A young woman in the Gorbals was drowned;
" and a woman in Partick, thinking herself in safety, refused to leave her house, and
" being afterwards removed from it by her neighbours, expired in half an hour. A great
" number of horses and cows, which could not be removed from the stables or byres,
" were drowned. The river on this occasion was about 18 inches higher than in the
" memorable flood in 1712. Yesterday morning, to the great joy of the inhabitants, the
" river was confined to its usual channel."

distinguished party. The kitchen fires were in full blaze, prompt
to roast the jolly joints of meat already skewered on the spits, to
boil the well-stuffed turkeys, and to stew the other tit-bits of the
table ; while the puddings and the custards stood ready on the
dresser for immediate application to the bars of the grate : when,
lo and behold, the waters of the Clyde began gently to ooze through
the chinks of the kitchen floor, and by and by gradually to increase,
so that in a short time the servants came to be going through their
work with the water above their ankles.   At this critical moment
the Monkland canal burst its banks, and like an avalanche, the
waters came thundering down by the Molendinar burn, carrying all
before it, and filling the low houses of the Gallowgate, Saltmarket,
Bridgegate, and under portions of St Andrew's Square, with a
muddy stream, and the wrecks of many a poor man's dwelling.   In
consequence of the regorgement of water caused by this sad mishap,
and the continued increase of the flood, the Camlachie burn, which
ran close by Mr Dale's house, was raised to an unusual height, and
at once, with a confused crash, broke into Mr Dale's kitchen, putting
out all the fires there, and making the servants to run for their
lives, they having scarcely had time to save the half-dressed dinner.
Then came the great question, What was now to be done ?   The dinner hour was fast approaching, and the great Edinburgh visitors were
already whirling rapidly towards Glasgow in their carriages ; while
the fires of the kitchen being completely extinguished, the kitchen
itself was thereby rendered totally useless.   In this calamitous
dilemma, Mr Dale applied to his opposite neighbour in Charlotte
Street, William Wardlaw, Esq., (Dr W.'s father) for the loan of his
kitchen, and also to another of his neighbours, Mr Archibald Paterson, for a like accommodation, both of whom not only readily
granted the use of their kitchens, but also the aid of their servants
to cook Mr Dale's dinner.   But still the question remained, How
were the wines, spirits, and ales to be gotten from the cellar, which
now stood four feet deep of water ?   After much cogitation, a porter
was hired, who, being suitably dressed for the occasion, was to
descend to the abyss and bring up the said articles.   It however
occurred to Mr Dale that the porter would not be able to distinguish
the bings that contained the port, sherry, and Madeira (Mr Dale
did not sport French wines) from those of the rum, brandy, porter,
and ale.   In this emergency, Miss Dale, then sixteen years of age,
was mounted on the porter's back, and both having descended to
the cellar, Miss Dale, amidst the waters of the deep, pointed out to

her chevalier where he was to find the different articles required for
the table. After having received instructions, the porter brought
up his fair charge to the lobby of the house, where Miss Dale dis-
mounted from the shoulders of her bearer in safety ; and the porter
having again descended to the cellar, readily found the wines and
ales that were wanted, which he delivered to Mr Dale in good order.
All things now went on in a satisfactory manner. The Edinburgh
visitors and Glasgow magnates arrived in due time, the dinner was
cooked and placed on the table in the best style, and the whole
party passed the evening in mirth and jocularity at the odd circumstances which had attended this merry meeting.

It was the waters of the Camlachie burn which inundated Mr
Dale's kitchen, these having been regorged by the sudden rise of the
Molendinar burn, when the two burns met near the Episcopal
Chapel. The arch of the bridge, at that place, was not large enough
to allow a sufficient vent for the accumulated waters of both burns,
which, consequently, caused a flow of back water. There were
three other bridges upon the Molendinar burn before it joined the
river Clyde. All these bridges, upon the occasion in question, were
also overflowed, the top of their arches being only about $4\frac{1}{2}$ feet
above the ordinary surface of the rivulet.

In the year 1764, a very important action of damages, against
the magistrates of Glasgow, was raised in the Court of Session, on
account of their having irregularly demolished a saw mill, upon the
Molendinar burn. On the 3d December, 1859, I published the
following statement of this case, in the *Glasgow Herald*, which I
now repeat.

" In my early days (speaking, however, only from memory) the
" Molendinar burn was an open rivulet from its source, which arose
" from some small lochs lying to the north of the city. After sup-
" plying the Town's Mill with water, it ran through a considerable
" part of the city, receiving, in its course, all the filth and impuri-
" ties of that part of Glasgow through which it flowed. From the
" College Garden to its junction with the river Clyde, there were
" 18 bridges which crossed the Molendinar burn; the Gallowgate
" Bridge and the bridge at the south extremity of the Saltmarket
" being the principal ones. Within my time, this burn from the
" New Vennel to the river Clyde, has been covered in, or arched, in
" various portions, and at various times, so that it would be difficult
" now to say exactly where and when these alterations first took
" place, in the course of their construction."

In ancient times the original level of the Gallowgate Street at the bridge has evidently been the banks of the said burn, which then, most probably, was crossed by stepping stones, being, at the time in question, a limpid stream, crossing the country road to the Gallow Muir and Eastern Common.

When a boy, I remember that there were some small houses situated to the north-east of the bridge, which stood about eight feet back from the line of the carriage road of the Gallowgate, having a passage gradually sloping towards the Molendinar burn. This passage was closed at its eastern extremity, by the retaining wall of the burn. The Gallowgate then was considerably higher at the bridge than the lower parts of the said passage, and there was no parapet on the roadway to protect passengers from falling into the passage from the street. In short, the Gallowgate Street, from the bridge westward to St Andrew's Open, (then called Kirk Loan) appeared like a continuation of the bridge itself, and it is extremely probable that the passage in question, originally, was generally used as a lane to the burn, for the purpose of watering horses. The passage commenced nearly opposite St Andrew's Open, where the street was of its present breadth, but from that spot to the Molendinar burn it became narrowed to the extent of the space occupied by the lane. The line of houses on the north of the passage were built in the old Dutch or Flemish style, with corby steps and gables, fronting the lane or passage.

I remember two of the small shops fronting this alley or passage, in both of which a respectable small business was carried on. One by Mr Watson, a stay maker, and the other by a Mr Richardson, for the sale of worsted articles. The opposite property to the east of the burn belonged to the Old Tannery Company, rather an extensive establishment.* Mr John Sym, writer, resided on the first floor of the tenement, at the south west corner of the bridge, and the Molendinar burn flowed alongside of his dwelling. He was

---

* The Tan Work consisted of 15 large tan pits, 15 smaller do; 7 large handlers, 12 smaller, do.; 12 scours, large latches, 9 lime pits, 2 bait do.; a currying shop, 3 large sheds for holding bark, and drying leather; a stove and beam shode; a writing room, bark mill, with a stone and cast iron ring; a dwelling house of 3 rooms, kitchen, 2 garret rooms and two cellars, &c., &c. The partners, in 1786, were John Bowman, John Campbell, Robert Boyle, William Couts, Robert Marshall, Archibald Spiers and Peter Spiers, who advertised that they had, "men and women's shoes, &c., saddles and saddlery, which they are selling on very moderate terms, and carry on the tanning business in all its branches." Robert Marshall, the father of Captain William Marshall of Rothesay, was the managing partner of the Tan Work.

the great-grandfather of the celebrated professor, John Wilson, of Edinburgh, (Christopher North.) (" 12th February, 1787, Married " at Edinburgh, Mr John Wilson, merchant in Paisley, to Margaret Sym, daughter of Mr Andrew Sym, merchant in Glasgow.") John Sym was the father of Andrew Sym above mentioned.

The under part of the tenement in which John Sym resided, was occupied, by the late Mr Robert Maxwell of Maxwelltown Place, as a place of business. To the south of the said tenement, a person of the name of John or James Findlay, had a dwelling house built over the Molendinar burn itself, there being a space of about six feet and a half between the floor of his house and the ordinary level of the burn, which space was considered sufficient to allow free vent to the water in case of floods. (See this house in the Plan.). Dr Woodrow's garden on the west was bounded by the Molendinar, and it then formed a pleasant rural retreat, being situated in the heart of open grounds, lying between the English Chapel and St Andrew's Square, not a stone of the square at that time having been laid.

From an article published in the *Glasgow Herald* of 27th November, 1861, we learn that in 1773 the Tanwork Company employed 300 shoemakers, for the home and export trade; that they had a shop on the north side of the Trongate, close to what is now Glassford Street, for the sale of shoes, under the charge of Mr George M'Intosh, one of the partners at that time, and father of the late Mr Charles M'Intosh of Dunchattan.

The following is a curious accompt of money received in loan by the Tannery Company, about the year 1765 :—*

" Accompt of Cash borrowed on Bonds and Bills.

Ledger Folios.		£	s.	D.	Rate of Interest.
5	John Shaw, in Glasgow,	300	0	0	4½
	James Shaw, in Slamannan (Bill),	160	0	0	4½
	George Leckie, in Calton of Glasgow (Bill),	100	0	0	
	Girzall Hamilton, in Glasgow,	330	0	0	5
	Borough of Ayr,	1000	0	0	5
	Thomas Hamilton, Minister of Holywood,	230	0	0	5
6	Agnes Lockhart, in Ayr,	300	0	0	5
	James Yeamen, in Dundee,	555	0	0	5
	Jannett Luke (deceased),	300	0	0	5
	Glasgow Merchants' House,	900	0	0	5
	James Waddell, of Hothouseburn (Bill),	140	0	0	4½
	Lillias Grahame, in Glasgow,	700	0	0	5
7	Alexander Cuninghame, for Parish of Symington,	100	0	0	4¾
	Francis Kennedy, of Dunure,	800	0		5

* This concern received money on loan, and had £40,000 lent to them, at 5 per cent. interest, by various individuals.

Ledger Folios.		£	s.	D.	Rate of interest.
7	William Flint (deceased), ...	770	0	0	5
	Andrew Cochrane, for Hutchesons' Hospital, .	300	0	0	5
	Alexander Hogg, in Edinburgh, . . .	1000	0	0	5
	Katherine Wood, in Glasgow, . . .	540	0	0	5
8	Girzall Curry, in Glasgow, ...	200	0	0	5
	John Russell, in Drumduff (Bill), . . .	50	0	0	4½
	John Belches, of Invermay, ...	900	0	0	5
	John Shanks, New Monkland Parish (Bill), .	60	0	0	4½
	John Murray, of Blackbarrony, . . .	900	0	0	5
9	Donald Campbell, of Aird, ...	50	0	0	5
	William Addie of Drumilzie, ...	470	0	0	4½
	John Kingan, Minister at Crawford, . .	200	0	0	5
	James Holme, of Gamlishiels, . . .	500	0	0	5
	John Shaw, in Edinburgh.	500	0	0	5
	Christian Govan, in Glasgow, . . .	500	0	0	5
10	Mrs Dick, in Glasgow, ...	200	0	0	5
	John Boyd, of Burleyside (Bill), . . .	45	0	0	4½
	Margaret and Girzal Sprewls, Glasgow, .	300	0	0	5
	Provost John Alexander, in Peebles, . .	400	0	0	5
	Robert Baillie, of Mayvile, ...	500	0	0	5
	William Wemyss, of Cuttlehill, . . .	1200	0	0	5
11	Michael Luke, in Dundee, ...	1000	0	0	5
	William Duke, of Montrose, ...	1000	0	0	5
	James Hunter, in Ayr, ...	500	0	0	5
	Dr John Erskine, of Carnock, ...	1400	0	0	5
	William Stewart, in Edinburgh, . . .	200	0	0	5
12	Gavin Ralstone, of Ralstone, ...	200	0	0	5
	John Barker, at Kirkaldie, ...	300	0	0	5
	Dame Ann Kennedy, of Dunskay, . . .	500	0	0	5
	William Fullerton. of Carstairs, . . .	1000	0	0	5
	George Earl, of North Esk, ...	700	0	0	5
	Thomas Rigg, of Morton, ...	500	0	0	5
	Margaret, Countess of Stair, ...	1000	0	0	5
	William Cuninghame, of Achanskeith, . .	300	0	0	5
	Robert Hunter, of Thurstone, ...	1000	0	0	5
14	John Bryce, in Cairmuirs (Bill), . . .	610	0	0	4½
	William Wood of Gallowhill, ...	1500	0	0	5
	Isabell Jamieson, in Glasgow, . . .	500	0	0	5
	Robert Buchanan, of Drumakill, . . .	450	0	0	5
15	Barbara and Eliza Scotts, in Glasgow (Bill), .	417	9	4	5
	John Thomson, in Edinburgh, . . .	1000	0	0	5
	Heirs of Thomas Peters, ...	1913	8	4	5
16	Alexander Speirs, Trustee for James Dunlop's Creditors, ...	3000	0	0	5
	Creditors of Robert M'Murich, . . .	11	7	7½	4
	James Coulter in Glasgow, ...	1000	0	0	5
	James Coats, of Blantyre Farm (Bill), . .	417	9	4	4½
	Hew Stewart, East Indies, ...	900	0	0	5
	William Bogle, James M'Dowall, and Robert Marshall, ...	254	16	10	4
	John Young, in Calderside (Bill), . . .	120	0	0	4¾
17	John Kincaid, in Cairnmuirs (Bill), . .	100	0	0	4½
	John Campbell and others, in Edinburgh, .	1300	0	0	5
	Richard Somner, in Haddington, . . .	500	0	0	5
	Lord Stair, ...	220	0	0	5
		40,192	2	7½	

The Trades' House, on the 30th of June, 1693, prohibited the cordiners of Gorbals from bringing shoes and other work into

Glasgow, which was ratified by the magistrates and council on 30th September of that year, under reservation of the right of the inhabitants to go to Gorbals to have their measure taken there, and to bring into Glasgow any shoemaker work for themselves, on any day of the week except Sunday.—(Crawfurd's Trades' House, 24.)

The following is a curious original shoemaker's account :—

Madam Ellisbeth Moor,
Dr to S. Wotton, 3d June, 1819.

	£	s.	d.
closing up Madm Moor, ...	0	0	11
mending Miss Plowden, ...	0	0	2
tapping and bindg Miss hambleton, ...	0	0	11
turning up, closing up, and corking Madam Moor, .	0	0	9
turn hover plase. — brought up,	0	2	9
Welting a pes into Madam Moor, ...	0	0	2
stitching a bust into ditto, ...	0	0	1
heeling Miss Plowden, ...	0	0	6
repairing Madam Moor's soul, ...	0	0	4
pesing and bottoming Miss Plowden, ...	0	0	11
Brought up,	0	4	9
heeling and corking Madam Moor, ...	0	2	11
stitching and making water tight ditto, . . .	0	0	6
tupping Madam Moor, ...	0	0	2
lining, binding, and laying a pece into do., . . .	0	0	4
	0	8	8

horned Madam,
i beg pardon in sendg. you this here.   i be much pressed
and do hop you'll send the muny —

CHAPTER VIII.

Fleming's Saw Mill on the Molendinar—Its demolition by the Magistrates in 1764—
Fleming's Lawsuit against the Magistrates—Depositions of Witnesses, containing many
interesting notices—First introduction of Scots Crown Fir—Sawmillfield—Commencement of Forth and Clyde Canal.

IN the year 1751, Mr William Fleming, an extensive timber merchant, (grandfather of Dr J. G. Fleming and William Fleming, Esq.,
writer), erected a saw mill on the Molendinar burn, about ninety
three yards from the river Clyde. (See the Plan.) It was situated
immediately north of the present Court House, about the angle
where the Molendinar burn turns suddenly to the south from its
western course, but which is now all arched over. This mill was
built under a contract and agreement made between the magistrates
and town council of Glasgow on the one part, and Mr Fleming and
his partner on the other part, and the deed was drawn out by Mr
M'Gilchrist, town clerk of the city. Under the faith of the said
contract Mr Fleming had successfully carried on, for upwards of
twelve years, the business of sawing foreign and home grown timber,
to the great benefit of the city and its neighbourhood, when the
magistrates of Glasgow, having become dissatisfied with their contract, resolved to expel Mr Fleming from his premises, under the
impression that he was merely a tenant at will. Accordingly, on
the 23d of June, 1764, without having given Mr Fleming any
intimation, they sent twelve men under the orders of Robert Findlay,
the master of works, who immediately proceeded, *brevi manu*, to
demolish Mr Fleming's saw mill, and to scatter its debris into the
waters of the Molendinar burn; for which violent and arbitrary
proceeding Mr Fleming immediately commenced an action of
damages against them, before the Court of Session, and after a
keen and protracted litigation, he succeeded in obtaining a final
judgment in his favour, on the 9th of July, 1768, by which the
magistrates and town council of Glasgow were compelled to pay to him
(18th November, 1768), the sum of £610 1s 1d, by way of damages,
and likewise about £100 as dues of extract. The following

were the magistrates, councillors and officials of the City of Glasgow, on the 23d of June, 1764.

Archibald Ingram, re-chosen, lord provost.
Walter Brock, merchant, bailie.
Alexander M'Kie, do.   do.
Duncan Niven, barber, trades' bailie, (Roderick Random's Strap.)

MERCHANT COUNCILLORS.

Alexander Spiers,	George Murdoch,
John Alstone,	John Pagan,
Colin Dunlop,	William Lang,
John Jamieson,	John Gray, new Councillor,
John Bowman,	James M'Call, do.
Robert Donald,	William Coats, do.

TRADES' COUNCILLORS.

James Buchanan, tailor,	James Lindsay, founder,
James Robertson, cooper,	John Fleming, copper smith,
John Lawson, mason,	Robert Martin, watch maker,
John Wilson, wright,	John Miller, maltman, new councillor,
John Jamieson, skinner,	John Jeffrey, watch maker, do.
Daniel Munro, tailor,	

George Brown, re-chosen dean of guild, councillor ex officio.
James Clark, deacon convener,   do.   do.
Peter Murdoch, treasurer,   do.   do.
Robert Findlay, master of works,   do.   do.
John Pagan, bailie of Gorbals.
Hugh Turner, water bailie.
George Hamilton, Provan bailie.
John Martin, bailie of Port-Glasgow.
John Wardrop, procurator fiscal.
William Meiklehouse, visitor of the maltmen,
Robert Colquhoun and Thomas Miller, town clerks, (Mr Miller afterwards
      became lord president of the Court of Session.)
Archibald M'Gilchrist, depute town clerk.

It is curious to see how few of the descendants of the above-named gentlemen now occupy official situations in Glasgow, or even appear in the list of our toping merchants; indeed, many of their names have become strange to us as leading men of our city now a days.

In the course of the law suit which took place between Mr Fleming and the magistrates of Glasgow upon the occasion in question, a great number of witnesses were examined *pro* and *con*, many of whose depositions throw considerable light upon the state of the Low Green of Glasgow and the Molendinar burn, as they stood a century ago, but it would go much beyond the limits allowed for the present jottings to extract these depositions in full, therefore only a selection from them will now be given.

James Duncan, senior,* bookseller in Glasgow, aged 80 years, born about the year 1685, *inter alia*, depones—There is a dam called the Skinners' dam, which the deponent has known for twenty years and upwards, on the Molendinar burn, a little above the pursuer's mill, and that he has often seen the skinners steep and wash their skins in the said dam, and he has also often seen girs steeped in the said burn, both below and above the said bridge.

John Robertson, bookseller in Glasgow, aged 60 years, born about 1704, depones—That the foot of Stockwell Street lies lower than the opposite side of the Bridgegate Street, and that there is a large syver, which runs down the Stockwellgate Street, near to the Goose-dubs, and empties into Clyde. That the skinners of Glasgow have a green for washing and drying their skins on the said green.

James Inglis, hatter, aged 43 years, depones—That he has known and observed the Molendinar burn for these many years past, and has particularly observed that the burn from a little below the chapel (English Chapel) down to the pursuer's saw mill is considerably filled with dirt, and nastiness, and rubbish ; and that where he was in use to see the channel and clean bed of the burn for the distance above mentioned, there is nothing now but glare, rubbish, and nastiness. Depones : about 32 years ago, say 1730, he knows the water in the said burn was clear and fresh, and was used for washing of clothes and other purposes.

Adam Wylie, tanner in Glasgow, aged 45 years, depones—That he was born in the town of Glasgow, say about 1720, where he has resided all his lifetime. That the tannery dam over the Molendinar burn, which is situate on part of the east side of the town, next the Gallowgate Bridge, was erected some years before the pursuer built his saw mill ; that the said dam was built with stones, and had timber sluices both in and above the dam. That the Tannery Company have also another dam a little above the said dam first deponed on, and the said upmost dam was made for keeping the rubbish in the burn from running down to the first mentioned dam, on which the Tannery Company have a bark mill. Depones : that he believes there are more hides manufactured by the said Tannery Company, and more business carried on by them in the

---

* Mr Duncan introduced the art of type making into Glasgow in the year 1718, and M'Ure's History of Glasgow is printed by types from Mr Duncan's manufactory.

tanning way than by all the other tanners in Glasgow. That the
most of the hides manufactured by the said Tan Work Company are
washed and steeped in the Molendinar burn, above the Tannery
Company's bark mill dam, and in the dam; and that in the summer
season, in time of drought, very little water runs in the burn below
the bark mill dam. Depones—That before the said bark mill dam
was built, he has seen the water in the burn, in time of speats, over-
flow its banks, and run into the houses on both sides of the burn,
and also since the bark mill was built ; and at these times he has
seen the water of the burn rise so high so to run into the spring
wells, called the Four Sisters. Depones—That before the said bark
mill dams were erected there were three steps of a stair at several
places opposite to the said wells for people to go down and take
water out of the burn. And depones—That before the bark mills
were built, the said wells were made lock-fast either on Saturday
night or early on Sunday morning, and kept lock-fast all Sunday ;*
and at these times there was a conveyance below ground from the
said wells to the burn, wherein the water of the wells ran, and there
was a spout of stone upon the edge of the burn, whereby any person
wanting water of the wells on Sundays supplied themselves with the
water which ran by the same conveyance to the burn, and those
who wanted water on Sundays used to go down two steps of a stair
that was made upon the east wall of the burn before they could
come at the foresaid spout to get water. (N.B.—Hence came the
name of the Street " the Spoutmouth.") Depones—That by the
stones and rubbish which came down the burn, and bark which is
brought from the Tannery Company tan yard and laid on the
vacant ground opposite to the said wells, the channel of the burn is
filled up so high as the uppermost of the foresaid steps of the stairs
before mentioned opposite the wells. Depones—That the wheel of
the tannery bark mill occupies, with the axletree, three feet of the
channel of the said Molendinar burn. That he has measured this
day the breadth of the said burn betwixt wall and wall opposite the
said bark mill, and found the same measured eight feet and eleven

* *Burgh Records*, 22d September, 1575.—" Item, ye provest and counsale ordanis ye
new comone well in ye Gallogate to be opponit daylie in ye morning, and lockit at ewin,
and deputis Michael Pudzean or sum other to attend y.t to, and keep ye said well and
key yairof, and to haif xl. s. of feall y.r four for ye space of ane zeir nextocum."

Item.—" Paid for Irne work to ye quhelis of ye comone well to stope ye cordis to cum
furthe of ye quhelis at ye maister of works comand."

N.B.—From the above notice it appears that there were no pump wells in Glasgow
in 1575, but only draw wells, with the common machinery of wheel and pinion.

inches or thereby; that he also measured the sluices in the tan work down opposite to the said bark mill, being two in number, one thereof measured three feet nine inches in breadth, and the other two feet eight inches in breadth. That the said sluices are fixed above a stone dam which he computes to be about three or four feet high. Depones—That since the building the said bark mill dam the Tan Work Company have been in use to clean the Molendinar burn below their dam in order to get a fall to their mill water, and by that means the channel or bottom of the burn below the mill has been made lower than it was before the said bark mill was erected. Depones—That there is a common passage from the Gallowgate Street of Glasgow, by the Spoutmouth, on the west side of the said wells, to the foot of the Old Vennel, and from thence to the High Street, leading from the Cross of Glasgow to the High Church, and that in time of speats he has often seen the said passage stopped by its being overflowed with water opposite the foresaid wells and above them for some space. Depones—For these forty years past he has seen two dams on the Molendinar burn above the pursuer's saw mill, the one of these dams called the Tanners' dam, and the other the Skinners' dam, and they are both still extant. Depones—That he knows the town of Glasgow's Slaughter House is situated a little to westward of the said saw mill, and that the cattle which the butchers sell in Glasgow are slaughtered in that place ; and the deponent has seen heaps of dung, composed of tripes, blood, and shearn, which proceeded from the cattle which had been slaughtered in the said slaughter house, lying near to the wells thereof, which is situated on the south side of, and near to the road leading from the foot of the Saltmarket Street, through one of the arches of the bridge to the Broomielaw, and to which road there is access by carts and carriages by a lane that leads from the Bridgegate Street along the side of the Merchants' Hospital and dyke thereof.

Depones—That there are houses on both sides of the Molendinar burn near to the foresaid bark mill dam, and that these houses are nearer the burn than any houses about the foresaid saw mill, and that some of the gavels and walls of the houses near the said bark mill bound the Molendinar burn. Depones—That the Gallowgate Street, through which the said Molendinar burn runs, from the bridge in the said Gallowgate Street to the toll bar (then near Kent Street), is double the length of the Gallowgate Street from the Cross to the said Gallowgate Bridge,* and he judges the foresaid

* Mr Stuart, in his Views of Glasgow, has given us a plate at page 99, showing the

bark mill to be about forty paces above the said Gallowgate Bridge; and he is of opinion that the bark mill dam might drown people, or is as dangerous as the saw mill dam if they fall into it. And on the defender's interrogatory, depones—That the said bark mill is built on the ground lying on the west side of the said burn, and that the east gavel of the mill is the west boundary of the burn. Depones— That the pursuer's saw mill is the west boundary of the burn. Depones—That the pursuer's saw mill is built over the channel of the burn, and that he has seen the road leading by the Spoutmouth, before described, often flooded, and passage by it stopped in time of flood, before the bark mill was erected, and since the erection of the said dam, in the night time, when the sluices were kept shut. When speats happened he has known the water rise in houses of the neighbourhood as high as the people's beds, and has seen people carried out in their shifts from their beds; but so soon as the sluices of the said bark mill dam were drawn the water immediately ebbed.

Robert Glen, dyer, in Glasgow, (deacon in 1765 and 1771,) aged 48 years, depones—That he is proprietor of a house and yard upon the east side of the Molendinar burn, a little way above the bark mill of the Tannery Company of Glasgow, and that he carries on a dyerie factory there, and has twenty-five blue vats and four boilers at present using in the said factory. Depones—That he knew seven or eight speats in the Molendinar burn, in one year, since he came to possess the houses and grounds where he now lives. That upon a particular occasion he had gone out of his house, been absent about an hour, and when he came to return he found the road to his house covered with water of the Molendinar burn, a speat or flood having come down about that time. That he got a horse and rode through the water which covered the causeway leading into his house, and he stepped on the stair leading up to his own house. That he then found Mrs Hunter, his tenant, in his house upon the ground, below his dwelling house, attempting to keep out the water from her

town residence of the late Kirkman Finlay, Esq. The following notice regarding the house in which Mr Finlay was born may, perhaps, be interesting to many of our Glasgow citizens. This house to the best of my recollection was situated a little to the east of the Gallowgate Bridge, and on the south side of the street.

" *Glasgow Mercury*, 26th March, 1778."—" Notice "—" To be sold, and entered into " at Whitsunday next, that tenement of land in the Gallowgate, consisting of seven " rooms, kitchen, and two cellars, stable, hay loft, byre, with a large lead cistern, all " presently possessed by James Finlay, merchant in Glasgow, the proprietor. The " premises are in exceeding good order, and very commodious. Apply to Archibald " Givan, writer in Glasgow." (N.B.—Mr Kirkman Finlay was born in 1772.)

house by claes, which she was putting behind the door; but, as he
observed the speat still increasing, he persuaded her to come out,
and she having said to the deponent she was afraid of being drowned,
he reached over his own stair a cloth, which she took hold of, and
in this manner he pulled her out of her own house, over the half
door thereof, up to where he was standing, and she went into his
house, and slept there all night.   Depones—That the water was so
high as that it was going out and in at the window of the said Mrs
Hunter, her house; and the sole of the said window is, as the
deponent judges, about thirty inches high above the ground.
Depones—That the river Clyde had no influence upon the speats in
the burn above the bark mill, before deponed upon, nor did not raise
the same ; and he does not think that the water of Clyde ever
crossed the bark mill dam, or raised the water in the Molendinar
burn so high as to stagnate the water on the said burn in time of
floods, above the said mill dam, and of this last he is sure.
Depones—That there is a *little-house* (*Forica*) built upon the side of
the burn, Molendinar, in the yard belonging to the Tannery Company, a little below their bark mill, and that the said *little-house*
empties itself into the said burn, upon the west side thereof; and he
has seen the wall, on the west side thereof, immediately below the
said *little-house,* bespattered with ordure ; and the back of the said
little-house is seen from the Gallowgate Bridge, and when the
deponent looked thereto, he observed it in the condition above
deponed upon ; and the deponent has observed the foresaid *little-
house* at different times, for ten or twelve years past. Depones—That
the said Tannery Company are in use to lay the bark which they
take out of the tan holes, upon the ground at the east side of the
burn, betwixt the burn and the Spout well, and that when floods
came down the said burn that bark (being useless) is washed into the
channel thereof.*   Depones—That in the summer time, in time of
drought and warm weather, he has seen the water in the Molendinar burn, above the bark mill dam, stagnate and black, and
belling up, and throwing forth a stench and rotten smell therefrom.
Depones—That the foresaid bark mill and dam thereof is situated a
little above the Gallowgate Bridge, and that he judges the said

* This refuse, or exhausted bark, used frequently (down to my time) to be spread upon
the streets of Glasgow, before the dwellings of persons who were sick, in order, as was
alleged, to prevent their being disturbed by the noise of carts and carriages passing
along. I believe, however, that this was done by the better classes of citizens, more
from sheer vanity and effect, than from any fear of the patients being disturbed by the
rattling of carriages.

bridge lies about two hundred yards from the Cross of Glasgow. Depones—That the deponent complained to Robert Marshall, one of the partners of the Tannery Company, that the dams of the said company did him, the deponent, hurt, but that he got no redress in consequence of the said complaint. Depones—That he, the deponent, and several of his neighbours presented a petition to the magistrates and town council of Glasgow, complaining of the dams belonging to the said Tannery Company, across the Molendinar burn, and of the burn's being choked up thereby, and of their long having lain under that grievance, and asking redress, but to which the town council have not yet given any answer; and the said petition was presented about six months ago. And depones—That the presenters of the said petition employed Mr William Sommervell, writer in Glasgow, who, at their desire, wrote a letter to each of John Bowman, Esq. and Andrew Cochrane, Esq., both partners of the said Tannery Company, informing them that they had presented the above mentioned petition to the town council, and if they did not get redress thereby, they would be obliged to take another method.*

Depones—That he had observed the servants of the said Tannery Company cleaning and carrying away the rubbish out of the channel of the burn every year, from the Gallowgate Bridge, and for a considerable way downwards, and which rubbish they dug up with mattocks. Further depones—That he knows of another *little-house* upon the east side of the burn, Molendinar, a little below the Gallowgate Bridge.

Alexander Dalmahoy, bridle cutter in Glasgow, aged 30, depones— That the house in which the deponent lives, and a tan work which the deponent also possesses, both lie opposite the Slaughter House and below the saw mill, and that when there are floods in the Clyde, water comes in both to deponent's house and tan work. Depones— That he saw the water in the tanners' and skinners' dam, last summer, as black and thick as ever he saw it before. Depones—That he never saw a sluice in either the skinner or tanners' dam, during the time the pursuer's saw mill stood.

William Parlane, indweller in Glasgow, aged 83 (born about 1680), depones—That he knows the deceased William Telfer, upwards of forty years ago, had a saw mill on the Green of Glasgow, at which the

* John Bowman, Andrew Cochrane, and William Coats, partners of the Tannery Company, were lord provosts of Glasgow. Alexander Spiers, and one or two more members of the said tannery concern, were town councillors, so that the Tannery Company possessed great influence at the council chamber.

deponent, at the employment of the said William Telfer (deacon of hammermen in 1705-6, and 1722-3), wrought six weeks; that about forty years ago (say about 1724), Arthur Robertson, (treasurer of Glasgow in 1747, and bailie of Gorbals in 1754; he was the first cashier of the Ship Bank in 1750, then situated at the east end, on the south side of the Bridgegate), merchant in Glasgow, took the said saw mill which was built on the Green, and on the east side of the burn, Molendinar, from the said William Telfer, and also a *wind-mill*, which was erected above the saw mill; and the deponent had the charge of the said mills, from the said Arthur Robertson, for about nine months, or thereby, at the end whereof, the said Arthur Robertson got a new servant to take the deponent's charge of his mills off his hands, and so on. After the new servant came, Mr Robertson gave up the possession of the said mill to the said William Telfer, whose son, Peter, took possession of the mills, and he, being a smith to his trade, took the iron work of the mills and converted it to other purposes, and also sold the stones wherewith the mill was built. That this sale and conversion happened when the said William Telfer was at London, and the deponent knows that he was absent, for some time, when the mill was demolished. That the dam which served the said mill was a laigh timber dam, or a thing fit to set in gang water to a little mill, and did no sort of harm, and the wheel of the said mill was only three feet in diameter: and being interrogated, for the defenders, depones—That while William Telfer had the foresaid saw mill, he caused clean the Molendinar burn, from the mill up to the chapel, once every two years; and that so far as he remembers, at this time, tanners and skinners had no dam in the burn, neither was bark mill dam belonging to the Tan Work Company then erected, and there was no house or building of any kind above the foresaid timber dam which served Telfer's mill.

Alexander Rae, hammerman, St Enoch's burn, aged 68 years, depones—That some complaint having been made to Hugh Roger, then provost of Glasgow (provost in 1732-3), that William Telfer's mill dam caused the water wash off the lime from off the stones of the bridge, a visit of council of Glasgow was called upon the said dam, as the deponent was informed, at which John Telfer was present, and said he would have nothing to do with the dam; whereon the council ordered the dam to be taken down, which was accordingly done; and at this time the saw mill was standing, and a wind mill, which was erected on the said saw mill, was kept going for

some time; but afterwards some differences having happened betwixt the said John Telfer and Peter Telfer his brother, concerning
the said saw and wind-mills, they were both allowed to go to ruin.

Archibald Ingram, late provost of Glasgow (he was provost in
1762-3, and died 22nd July, 1770, Ingram Street was named for
him), aged 60 years and upwards, depones—That to the best of his
remembrance, after Whitsunday, 1764, and when the deponent was
provost of Glasgow, an Act of Council was passed ordering the dam
of the pursuer's saw mill to be taken down, and a committee of the
council were named to see the said Act put in execution.

Depones—That the next day, or a day or two after the foresaid Act
of Council passed and was minuted, the dam of the pursuer's saw
mill was taken down. Depones—The foresaid orders of council to
the committee to take down the pursuer's dam was openly given in
council, and was agreed to by a majority of council.

William Lang (deacon of the hammermen in 1741, and bailie of
Glasgow in 1767), merchant in Glasgow, aged 50 years, depones—
That he has lived in a house built on the west side of the Molendinar burn, immediately below the Gallowgate Bridge, for some
years past; and in the summer seasons he observed the water in the
said burn to be as black as ink almost, except when there was fresh
water in the burn. Depones—That he knows the Molendinar burn
for some space above and below the Gallowgate Bridge is bounded
with houses on both sides thereof, and that the Tannery Company
have a *house of office*, the nastiness of which falls into the burn a
little above the Gallowgate Bridge; and that the nastiness of the
said *house of office* is open to the view of every person who passes
the Gallowgate Bridge, which is but a small distance from the Cross
of Glasgow, and the Gallowgate in which the bridge is, is one of the
four principal streets of Glasgow.

John Woodburn, merchant in Glasgow, aged 55 years, depones—
That in June, 1764, he was desired by Robert Findlay, master of
works, to provide some men, which he did to the number of ten or
twelve; and Duncan Niven, then one of the bailies of Glasgow, the
said Robert Findlay, the deponent, and the said ten or twelve men,
went to the pursuer's saw mill about six o'clock in the morning, and
there the said ten or twelve men, at the order of the said Duncan
Niven and Robert Findlay, entered the pend at the south end of
the pursuer's saw mill, and took down all the wood they found
betwixt the said south pend and the north pend of the said mill,
and also the timber sluices which were fixed on the north end of

the said mill, and removed also some stones, some whereof were
long, that were placed below the pend of the mill, and laid the
stones on the ground at the side of the mill, where the timber was
also laid, and removed every thing that obstructed the course of the
water in the pend; and that the work before deponed to was performed by porters, not by tradesmen.

(Deacon William Fram, mason in Glasgow, and others, deponed
in similar terms as to the demolition of Mr Fleming's saw mill.)

John Wilson, wright in Glasgow, aged 50 years, or thereby, depones—That he is well acquainted with the pursuer's saw mill,
which is built in the channel of the Molendinar burn; also with the
dale yard belonging to the said mill, which is a part of the west end
of the Green of Glasgow, and is situated a little to the north-east of
the Slaughter House of the town of Glasgow, and the said burn and
Skinners' green only intervene betwixt the said dale yard and
Slaughter House.   Depones—That he was a member of the town
council of Glasgow when the magistrates and council passed an
Act in council for taking down the dam of the pursuer's saw mill,
which act was gone openly about, and minuted down by the town
clerk, according to the appointment of the magistrates and council;
but according to uniform custom, the Act was not recorded or
engrossed in the Council books upon the day whereon it passed, nor
was it subscribed until the next meeting of council; before which
time came, the deponent saw the saw mill dam taken down.

William Miller, millwright in Gorbals, aged 50 years, depones—
That at the desire of the pursuer, he took a level of the Molendinar
burn, from the north gavel of the pursuer's saw mill to the tanners'
dam, and from that to the skinners' dam; that he found the
tanners' dam to be two inches higher than the saw mill dam, and
the top of the skinners' store dam was two feet higher than the top
of the saw mill dam; that in measuring he found the distances
betwixt the saw mill dam and the skinners' dam to be seventy-three
yards, and the distance betwixt the saw mill dam and the tanners'
dam to be twenty-eight yards and six inches.   Depones—That on
measuring, he also found the distance from the skinners' dam to the
place where the Molendinar and Camlachie burns join, to be ninety-
one yards; and on measuring the breadth of the Molendinar burn
a little below where it and the Camlachie burn joins, he found it to
be twelve feet: that the breadth of the burn at the skinners' dam
is sixteen feet six inches: that on measuring further, he found the
east sluice in the pursuer's mill was two feet eleven inches broad,

and two feet four and a half inches in depth : that the westmost sluice measured two feet eight and a half inches in breadth, and two feet four and a half in depth : that the distance from the south gavel of the saw mill to Clyde, at low water, is ninety-three yards.

Patrick Maxwell, cordiner in Glasgow, aged 56 years, depones— That since the saw mill dam was built, and before it was taken down, he has frequently observed that the water above the dam was black and thick, and like as if it had been boiling or bubbling up in summer time, or in the drought of summer, and a nauseous smell or stink arising out of that black water, which the deponent has smelt himself; and has heard the skinners when they were washing their skins in the burn say there were vermin therein, which bit their legs, and the deponent has seen the marks thereof, and seen the blood appearing out of the wound. Depones—That during the time the saw mill dam stood, the bottom of the burn was seldom seen, except sometimes on Saturday evenings, when the sluices of the saw mill dam were drawn up ; and then the bottom of the burn was a frightful sight, being covered over with glar, and stinking meat, thrown into it by the butchers when they had been too long kept, dead dogs and cats.

John Fleming, dyer in Glasgow, aged 70 years, depones—That during the standing of the saw mill dam, he, in times of drought in summer, has observed the water above the mill in a great fermentation, which raised such a thick scum upon the top of the water as he thinks would have carried a partridge ; and he has actually seen the bird water-wagtail standing thereon without sinking. Depones —That he remembers that before the tan work and bark mill thereof in the Gallowgate was built, the water in the burn Molendinar was so good, that people in the Bridgegate took the water thereof for the brewing of their ale. Depones—He was informed by several of the skinners that the time of the standing of the said saw mill dam, there was some kind of vermin in the burn that bit their legs, and raised lumps upon them, while they were standing in the burn barelegged, washing their sheep skins ; and that since the saw mill was removed, the skinners have informed the deponent that there were no such vermin in the burn. Depones—He has heard it reported that one child was drowned in the burn, and two or three more got lying dead in the burn ; and also that several children had fallen into the burn, and would have been drowned if persons who had seen them fall in had not come and taken them out. Depones —That the tanners' dam and skinners' dam, from the time the deponent first knew them, were placed across the burn in the same places where they now stand, and that the skinners' dam is at present not above eight inches high above the rubbish in the channel of the burn : That the tanners' dam is situated immediately under the bridge over the said burn at the south end of the Butchers' Street (now Market Street), which is the second bridge over the burn above the saw mill : That the skinners' dam is situated betwixt the tanners' dam and the bridge over the said burn, at the south end of the Saltmarket Street. Depones—The Green of Glasgow is a large enclosure, and the deponent measured the circumference thereof, and found it to measure a mile and a half, and a little more. Depones—That within these twenty years last he remembers to have heard it reported that the magistrates and city council had agreed to feu or set in tack to a company of merchants in the city about two acres at the west end of the Green, including the ground whereon the saw mill stands, in order to build a manufactory for weaving woollen broadcloth : That the company made an entry through the wall that surrounded the Green, and put a gate on the entry : That the gate was thrown down the very first night after it was put up, and thrown into the said burn : There was great grumbling amongst the inhabitants on account of the said feu or set, and the deacon convener and members of the Trades' House took the matter into their consideration, and a stop was put to the further procedure of the said feu or set, and the Green was allowed to continue in its former state.

John Brodie, saddletree maker in Glasgow, depones—That all the floods that ever he saw in the Bridgegate, first began near opposite to Blythswood's house ; but the water from Clyde first runs up a syver at the Merchants' house, and crosses the Bridgegate, and stands on the north side thereof, at the foot of the Old Wynd, and betwixt it and John Rankin's (father of the late James Rankin) house ; and next the water runs in at the mouth of a syver below the Water Port, and from thence runs up the foot of Stockwell-gate and along the Goose-dubs, and all the places lie below and to the westward of the saw mill.

Mr Fleming was the first timber merchant who introduced into Glasgow the general use of Scots grown timber for coarse and common purposes, such as for making coffins, packing boxes, house lathing, coal heugh gearing, cleading of carts, and such like ordinary uses. In fact, the erection of his saw mill effected a great change in various departments of the timber trade, and lowered the prices

of both workmanship and materials of various articles connected
with the trade in question, as the following deposition shows.

John Wilson, wright in Glasgow, aged 50 years, or thereby,
depones—That he knows the pursuer was bred a wright, and that
after he built the saw mill in dispute, he began to purchase different
parcels of Scotch fir, which wood has been used chiefly for making
lath for plaister, boxes for packing goods, bars for coal heughs, and
cleading of carts. That the first time, so far as the deponent knows,
that Scotch fir was used in Glasgow for making boxes, and lath for
plaister, was some time after the pursuer's saw mill was erected, and
the pursuer having lowered the price of boxes, the wrights of Glasgow put an advertisement in the newspapers, that it was improper
to make boxes of Scotch fir; but that, notwithstanding, the demand
for Scotch fir boxes increased. Depones—That Scotch fir has now
become a staple commodity for the purposes before deponed to.
Depones—That so far as he remembers, the price of boxes made of
foreign fir, before the pursuer's mill was erected, was from 5s to 6s
each, and that after the building of said mill, boxes of the same
sizes, made of Scotch fir, were sold at 4s 6d and 5s each. Depones
—That the pursuer furnished the deponent with different parcels
of lathing of Scotch fir, and also nailed the same on the house, and
made it fit for plaister, for all which he charged the deponent only
sixpence per square yard, and the deponent could not have provided
himself with the same quantity of lathing of foreign fir and workmanship under eightpence per yard. Depones—That in his opinion
the saw mill was erected both for the interest of the pursuer and
the public.

John Herbertson, late deacon of the wrights in Glasgow, depones
—That before the pursuer's saw mill was erected, he paid to whip
sawers for sawing a hundred feet of big fir trees into lathing at the
rate of 2s 6d, which was the lowest price, and sometimes he paid 2d
more for sawing the like quantity of wood ; that he also paid the
whip sawers at the rate of 3s for sawing one hundred feet of joisting,
and that he paid at the mill for a like sawing at the rate of 2s 1d
for each hundred feet. Depones—That in his opinion any wood that
he got sawn at the saw mill was better done than that which he got
done by the whip sawers.

John Muirhead, wright in Gorbals, (father of Robert Muirhead,
bailie of Glasgow in 1798, for whom Muirhead Street, Gorbals, was
named,) depones—That Robert Campbell of Finab, about ten or twelve
years ago, informed the deponent that the pursuer had bought from

him Scots fir to the value of £500 or £600 ; and he also knows that
he bought several other considerable quantities of fir from other
persons. Depones—That the expense of carriage of fir by water to
Glasgow from any part of the country below or about Greenock, or
from Lochlomond, or any of the Highland lochs, does generally far
exceed the original price. Depones—That he is of opinion that fir
can be brought from North America to Greenock cheaper than
Scotch fir can be brought from Lochaber to that place. Depones—
That Scotch fir sells about a third part cheaper than either North
America or Norway fir sells for.

A great number of witnesses were examined in the course of this
law suit, regarding the different floods of the river Clyde, and how
far Mr Fleming's saw mill and dam, by interrupting the free passage
of the waters of the Molendinar burn had tended to increase the
damage done by the overflowing of the Clyde to the Bridgegate, and
to the lower parts of the city ; but as none of those old speats
deponed to were at all equal in magnitude to the great inundation
of the 12th of March, 1782, to that of 1795, or even to the one of
1808, I have omitted the depositions of the witnesses thereto.

In articles published in the *Glasgow Herald*, I have taken notice
of those mighty floods last mentioned, having seen them when at
their greatest height, and was personally interested in that of 1808,
being obliged to leave my country dwelling, then situated between
Springfield and Greenlaw, in my shirt, and to wade to dry land
with only my head above the torrent of the Clyde, which was then
running like a mill dam lade. The Paisley road, next to Tradeston,
was then flooded. I may here mention that towards the close of
last century the Philosophical Society of Glasgow issued a proposal
to make the Molendinar burn navigable up to the Gallowgate
Bridge, and if the mania for Joint Stock Companies, with limited
liability, had then been as rife as we have seen them of late, we
might, perhaps, have beheld a little Broomielaw in the Gallowgate,
with its upper and lower navigation. But from this digression I
return to Mr Fleming who, shortly after having received from the
city the sum of £610 1s 1d of damages for the loss of his saw mill
(with £100 for dues of extract), purchased a part of the lands of
Hamilton Hill, and in honour of his victory over the magistrates
and town council of Glasgow, he named his newly acquired lands
"Sawmillfield." It was in or about 1767 that Mr Fleming purchased from John Young of Youngfield, late deacon of the tailors in
Glasgow, for the price of £1200 stg., two pieces of ground which were

part of the Great Western Common of Glasgow. To the first piece, consisting of 21 acres or thereby, Mr Young had acquired right immediately from the magistrates of Glasgow by a feu charter. To the other piece, consisting of 19 acres, Mr Young acquired right from Robert Hamilton, of Hamilton Hill, whose author had acquired right thereto by a feu contract from the magistrates of Glasgow. Mr Fleming appears to have kept the culture of these lands in his own hands during his lifetime, but after his death (for behoof of his family) they came under the management of his widow, who was a Miss Tarbet, the sister of the well known Mrs Dr Balmanno, for whom Balmanno Street was named. In the *Glasgow Journal* of 1st July, 1779, Mrs Fleming advertised the Sawmillfield lands to be let, as follows :—

" To be set by public roup, for such a number of years as may be " agreed on, the lands and farm of Sawmillfield, lying within a mile " of the City of Glasgow, with the farm houses and offices thereon, " which are mostly new, and very commodious. The above lands " lie along the east side of the high road leading from the City of " Glasgow to the basin at the west end of the Great canal, and by " their vicinity to the canal, being within 160 yards of it, may be of " great advantage to an active tenant. For particulars, apply to " Archibald Smith, writer in Glasgow."

Immediately after Mr Fleming* had purchased the lands above mentioned, the Forth and Clyde Canal was projected, which ultimately came through the heart of his lands. On the 10th of June, 1768, the first spadeful of earth for the formation of the said canal was dug out. The navigation was filled with water on 3d September, 1773, and to Stockingfield on 10th November, 1775. On the 10th November, 1777, the collateral cut to Hamilton Hill was finished, where a large basin was made for the reception of vessels and rafts of timber. On the 6th of July, 1786, the operations commenced for extending the navigation from Stockingfield to the Clyde, which was completely finished, and the canal opened from sea to sea on the 28th of July, 1790. The basin at Hamilton Hill having been found too distant from the City of Glasgow, and inconvenient for the trade, the canal company purchased eight acres of ground within half a mile of Glasgow, and on the 11th of November, 1790, finished

---

* Mr Fleming left a family of four sons, all of whom were well known in Glasgow, and I have no doubt are remembered by all our elderly citizens, their names were William, Matthew, John, and Hugh. John was an eminent writer, and the other three were merchants of high standing.

a basin on a larger scale, where they have erected granaries and store house, with all other necessary accommodation for an extensive inland traffic.

Mrs Fleming, like her sister, Mrs Balmanno, was a very clever and acute old lady, and at first was in a mighty passion when she learned that the Forth and Clyde Canal was to be cut through the very middle of the family lands, thereby cutting the family farms in halves, and forcing the tenants to cross the canal on every occasion when they required to plough, or dress the respective detached parts ; but the old lady lived to change her opinion on this subject, when she found that so far from the canal having injured the value of the family lands, it had tended to increase the same to an extent quite beyond all expectation.

CHAPTER IX.

Port-Dundas as a Harbour *versus* the Broomielaw—Cow Milking on the Green—Rates
for Grazing—Dell in the Green—The Washing House, and Scotch mode of cleansing
clothes—Castle Boins—The Big Tree—The Green the scene of Military Punishments
—A Soldier Shot, 1750—Dispute between the Magistrates and the Officers of Colonel
Herbert's regiment.

AT this time Mr Gouldburn had erected 117 jetties on the Clyde
between Glasgow and Greenock, and had deepened the channel of
the river, so that vessels drawing seven feet of water could navigate
up to the harbour at the Broomielaw, but the canal being eight feet
deep, immediately upon its having been made open for traffic,
became a more important port than the Broomielaw.

It is curious to see the numerous arrivals announced by the
newspapers, of vessels discharging their cargoes, at the Canal basin,
in 1778, being only one year after the formation of the basin at
Hamilton Hill, while not a single arrival, at the Broomielaw, during
the same space of time, is taken notice of in the public lists of
arrivals.

"*Glasgow Mercury,* 5th February, 1778."

"Canal, February 4th, 1778.—Arrived, the Borrowstonness,
" Thompson, from Borrowstonness, with merchant goods ; the
" Success, Begg, from Leith, with bark and goods; the Netherwood,
" Baine, with grain and goods; the Bell, Neilson, with wheat and
" barley; the Eagle, Mennon, with wheat; the Industry, Hodge,
" with iron deals and wheat; the Evan, Shaw, with barley; the
" Clyde, Anderson, with iron and tallow; the Industry, Johnston,
" with barley; the Dolphin, Ronald, with beans and malt; the
" Dispatch, Burgess, with goods and grain; the Catherine, Keller,
" with bear and iron; the Janet, Dewar, with goods and grain; the
" Martha, Walker, with grain and iron; the Nelly, Wachop, with
" barley and wheat.   All from the Sea Lock."

" Canal Basin, 18th February, 1778.—Arrived since our last.—
" The Carron Packet, Calder, Carron, merchant goods; Lighter, No.
" 1, Dewar, goods or guns; Dispatch, Burgess, Borrowstonness,
" lintseed and ashes; Borrowstonness, Thomson, do., lintseed and

" wood; the Glasgow, Shaw, do., goods and meal; the Free Mason,
" Easton, barley; Dolphin, Ronald, wheat; the Eagle, Mennon,
" meal; the Glasgow Packet, Aikman, grain; the Martha, Walker,
" grain; the Nelly, Wachop, grain; the Bell, Hodge, meal. All
" from the Sea Lock."

The committee of management at this time appointed Mr Nicol
Baird (the grandfather of the Messrs Baird of the canal), to be
the surveyor on the canal. Mr Baird then lived at Westertown,
near Falkirk.

It may easily be seen that the formation of the canal, through
the lands of Sawmillfield, added greatly to the value of the said
lands, and the prolongation of it, to Port-Dundas, added still further
towards their enhancement.

The following advertisement shows where the dwelling house and
workshops of Mr William Fleming, were situated in Glasgow.

" *Glasgow Mercury*, 11th December, 1792.—To be sold, the
" property in Gibson's Close, Saltmarket, belonging to the heirs of
" the late William Fleming, Sawmillfield, consisting of a back house
" of two storeys, and cellars, with a work house in the close leading
" from the Trongate to Prince's Street, and a stable underneath,
" together with the whole dung of Gibson's Close. The yearly rent
" is at present £30 5s. Henry Barton, one of the the tenants, will
" show the premises. Apply to William Fleming, (father of Dr
" Fleming), opposite the Exchange, Glasgow."

It thus appears that the sweepings of Gibson's Close were held
out as an inducement for purchasers to come forward.

The following notification, regarding this old Glasgow family,
appeared in the *North British Daily Mail*, of 26th February, 1863.

" Glasgow Cathedral.—We noticed in Monday's impression, the
" erection of two windows in the chapter house of the Cathedral,
" designed and executed by Mr Hughes, glass painter of London;
" the set has been completed by the placing of other two. As we
" formerly indicated, a unity of subject connects the four, which are
" representative of charity, or acts of mercy, a thoughtful and un-
" questionably judicious arrangement, for which, we are indebted to
" Mr Charles Heath Wilson. One of the last erected windows is
" dedicated to the memory of their ancestors, merchant burgesses in
" Glasgow, since 1643, and of their parents, William Fleming of
" Sawmillfield, and Janet Gibson, his wife, by William Fleming,
" John Gibson Fleming, and David Gibson Fleming. The texts
" which form the subject of illustration are, ' I was a stranger, and

" ye took me in; I was naked, and ye clothed me.'" The three last named gentlemen were the grandchildren of William Fleming, sen., of Sawmillfield, and his wife, Miss Tarbet.

It will be seen from the Plans herewith annexed that the entry to Mr Fleming's saw mill and wood yard, was by the Bridgegate and along the Slaughter House lane, from which lane there was a narrow crooked passage leading directly to the Slaughter House, and to the enclosure for cattle intended for slaughter. There was no other entry to the Low Green of Glasgow from the west, except by crossing this passage, which passage formed the most intollerable nuisance of the city, for the putrid refuse of the Slaughter House lay there in heaps, and the passage itself was quite a quagmire by dirt, and the dung of the cattle left there by them when passing into the enclosure and shambles. In fact no attention was then paid by the fleshers or by the public authorities to keep the neighbourhood of the Slaughter House clean, in consequence of which the miasmatic effluvia and nauseous smell at or near the place was quite overpowering to all who had delicate olfactory nerves.* I never saw a lady venture to enter the Green from the west by the route of the Slaughter House lane, for if she had made the attempt she would have required to have done so, armed with pattens† on her feet, to

---

* " Glasgow, 1st March, 1764.—By order of the Magistrates of Glasgow."

" Whereas, there are several middens or quantities of dung laid down, and presently " lying on the streets and avenues leading into the city of Glasgow, to the great nuisance " of all persons coming in, or going out of the city, or taking the benefit of the air around " the city. These are, therefore, requiring all persons interested in said dung, that they " carry the same from off the streets and avenues, leading into the city, be- " twixt and the 15th day of March next to come. Certifying all and every person who " shall refuse or delay so to do, that the magistrates will confiscate all dung lying on the " streets, avenues, or lanes, leading into the said city after the said day, and grant a war- " rant for carrying away and applying the same to other uses, and fine the persons who " laid down the same, in ten pounds Scots, each; and these are strictly prohibiting and " discharging all and every person or persons whomever, from laying down any dung on " any of the streets, avenues, or lanes leading into the city, under the penalty of ten " pounds Scots, for each transgression."

† At this time there were no side pavements in Glasgow, for the benefit of pedestrians, in consequence of which pattens were in universal use by all ranks of females, during wet weather. From the following advertisement it appears that pattens could be purchased at a very low rate, which, no doubt, tended to make their use quite common in Glasgow.

" *Glasgow Journal*, 17th July, 1766."

" Reignald Tucker, makes and sells for ready money only, women's pattens, from 7s to " 12s per dozen." (This was the wholesale price.) Some few fashionable ladies wore clogs, but this piece of female dress was not only more cumbersome, but also much dearer, and less serviceable for encountering *clarty* streets than pattens.

L

prevent her shoes being submersed in liquid mud and the ordure of cattle. The usual route to the Low Green from the west, was by the Bridgegate to the foot of the Saltmarket. The main entry into the Green was by a large gate of timber, which was under the charge of the herd of the Green; it was generally kept shut, but always thrown open on public occasions, such as reviews and military spectacles, &c. The entry into the Green, for pedestrians, on ordinary occasions, was by a small turnstile in the form of a cross ✕, which moved upon a pivot, thus preventing access to equestrians.

At nine o'clock in the morning, and at six o'clock in the evening, the cows which pastured on the Green were brought to this place of the common to be milked. And I have seen our gentlemen golfers, after finishing their morning's sport, stopping short here, and with great gusto swigging off a tinful of milk reeking warm from the cow, to give them an appetite for their breakfasts. In the evenings the scene was very lively, for, in all directions, there were seen well-dressed nursery maids, with their little charges, striving who should first get their japanned tinnies filled with the warm reaming milk, and ever and anon looking sharply around them, lest the great bull* (which the magistrates kept in the Green), should be edging towards them.

---

* " State of accounts of John Brown, master of work of Glasgow, for October,
November and December, 1777."

1777	Paid Ninian Hill for selling a bull, - - -	£0	2	6
,, ,,	24th March, James Thomson for spreading mole hills, &c., in the green, - - - - -	1	0	0
,, ,,	9th June, for a bull for the green, - - - -	3	13	0
,, ,,	26th June, paid .or making a gravel walk in the green, being 240 yards long and 17 feet broad, -	4	5	1

"Council Records, 24th June, 1576.—Item, It is statute by the baillies, counsall and " commountie that thair be an calf hird, conducit to keip the calfes upon the grein furthe " of scaythe, wtherwayis gif yai be fundin in scaythe to be pundit, and also ordanis yame " yat hes ye freir land in ye brumilaw, to bige ye weir for halding furthe of ye beistis."

" Council Records, 9th May, 1578.—The quhilk daye Archibald Jobnestoun is made, " and constitute calf birde, for keiping of the calfis vpone ye greyne, for yis instant zeir, " and he to halve meit and drink daylie about of yame yat hes ye calfis, togidner with " vi.d. frae ilk ane yat hes ye samyne, and siclyk frae yame yat hes land besid ye greyne, " for keiping of yair cornes, and yat no hors be fund thairupone unlangalit, (Langletite, " having the fore and hind legs tied together to prevent running,—Jamieson), and entir " to service ye morne, witht power to ye said Archibald to poynd for key or great " stirkies. Souertie for his seruice and guid reull, James Ritchie, cowper."

" Council Records, 26th May, 1579.—Matho Wilsoun is maid and constitut calf hird " quha hes fund Patrik Bell cautione for administratioun in his office, and is ordanit to " have vi.d. for ilk calf, and his meit daylie about, or ellis xii.d. for ilk melte ᵗ, (Melteth " 1st, a meal, 2d, the quantity of milk yielded by a cow at one time.—Jamieson), gif yai " failze and to be poyndit yʳ for."

Since the time when Mr Fleming's saw mill was demolished, the Glasgow Green eastwards has undergone several alterations, particularly by the erection of Monteith Row, of the Camlachie burn at the Calton Green being arched over, and of our old serpentine walks being nearly all grubbed up.

At the eastern extremity of the Green, the late Mr Alexander Allan attempted to throw an arch over the public footpath which leads to Rutherglen Bridge, so as to connect his grounds with the river, thereby making a dark tunnel of this public footpath. This innovation, however, was successfully opposed by the people of Rutherglen, and the footpath kept open.

Brown, in his History of Glasgow, at page 188, thus writes regarding the Green of Glasgow : "The traveller may here see 100 milk " cows giving milk to upwards of 500 old men, women, and children. " Here the aged, the sick, and the young receive uncontaminated " that natural nourishment, the milk from the cow. This beautiful " Green affords grass for about 120 cows, of a large size, and of a " mixed breed, from the Alderney kind, yielding on an average " upwards of 12 Scots pints of milk per day, in the summer " time."

Denholm, in his history, at page 141, informs us that "the " revenue arising from the pasturage of cows on the Green fluctuates " according to their number, the proprietor of each paying £2 for " five months' grazing." Chapman, who published his history in 1812, states : "Another source of revenue from the Green proceeds " from the pasturage of cows, for the grazing of each of which during " about six months the proprietors pay £3 3s, and 2s to the keeper, " per annum." In a report published by Dr Cleland in 1813, he mentions that "in the present situation of the Green, the average

---

"Council Records, 1st October, 1577.—Item, It is statut yat it sall nocht be leful to " nowther fre or unfre to hald by hirsalis, (Hirsell, hyrsale, a flock of sheep—a great " number. 'Jock, man, ye're just telling a hirsel o' e'n down lees, (lies)—Jamie- " son.')"

" Item, It is statut and ordanit yat yer be na swyn nor geis haldin nor pasturat within " the burroruds about the towne, but haldin in houss, vnder ye pane of escheting there- " of."

"Council Records, 7th May, 1574.—The quhilk day William Kyle is fund in ye " wrang, for ye taking and intrometting w.t. at his awin hand, but ordour, ane cow gevin " be him at Alhallovmes last, to Janet Baxtare as tyde,' (Tydie, pregnant, when applied " to a cow; also to a woman, as a " tidy bride," one who goes home enceinte to the bride- " groom's house.—Jamieson), for ye first calf and milk, and being in her possessione " sensyne, and y^r fore is decernit to delyuer to her ane tyde cow, and to satisfe hir for " ye proffett of calf and milk y ^{r} of incontinct and dwme gevin yairon."

"number of cows for the last three years which have paid a grass "fee of £3 3s per head is 127."*

" Notice.—1st July, 1794.—Cows will be admitted into the Green " at the Fair of Glasgow, to graze the remainder of the season, on " payment of 25s grass mail, and 1s 6d fee for the herd, for each " cow, the day before the Fair."—(*Glasgow Advertiser*, 4th July, 1794.)

The following advertisement, showing the rates at which cattle were taken in to graze in muir lands and pasture lands, is curious, when compared with the rates charged for grazing cattle in the Green of Glasgow.

" *Glasgow Journal*, 19th March, 1759."

"Cattle for grazing will be taken into the Parks of Glanderston on the following terms, viz. :—

	Scots.			Sterling.		
Into the Moor Park of Walton, for a Cow or Quey,	£4	0	0	...£0	6	8
For a Stirk,	2	0	0	... 0	3	4
For a Horse,	6	0	0	... 0	10	0
For a Colt of one year old,	4	0	0	... 0	6	8
Into the lower Park of Walton, for a Cow or Quey,	6	0	0	... 0	10	0
For a Stirk,	3	0	0	... 0	5	0
For a Horse,	9	0	0	... 0	15	0
For a Colt of one year old,	6	0	0	... 0	10	0
Into either of the two Parks near the House, for a Cow or Quey,	12	0	0	... 1	0	0
For a Horse,	18	0	0	... 1	10	0
For a Colt of one year old,	12	0	0	... 1	0	0

The two last Parks being the best for making Beef.

The above prices are all Scots money.

None to be admitted into any of the Parks before the 10th of May, and to be taken out some time in the month of October thereafter. When put in, must acquaint whether for the upper or lower Park of Walton."

In 1816, when the working classes could not all find employment, about 200 weavers were occupied in levelling the upper part of the High Green ; and in August, 1819, 324 weavers out of work were engaged in slope levelling the High Green and the Calton Green, some parts of which required an excavation of from six to seven feet, and others a filling up of from eight to ten feet.

These levelling operations made a considerable change in the appearance of some parts of the High Green, more particularly on

* In 1816, the grass mail was raised to £4 4s, and 2s 6d to the keeper. There were two bulls in the Green in 1816.

that part of it through which the Camlachie burn flowed, immediately to the north-east of the Washing House and Fountain. Here there was a beautiful and romantic dell, with hills on each side of it, and the Camlachie burn, uncontaminated with the city filth, greatly purling through its centre. It was quite a retired spot, and hid from the view of the golfers or strollers on the walks of the Green by the rising ground on the south.

In my early days, this was a favourite place of resort of boys to amuse themselves with all the juvenile sports and games of school-day times ; and here was the chosen field when a pitched battle took place between the youthful combatants, either *" in kairs,"* or *" over the napkin."* Many a happy evening have I spent in this pretty secluded spot with my companions, playing at the *"penny stanee,"* at *" hop, stap, and jump,"* at *" leap the garter,"* at *" leap-frog,"* at *" putting the stane,"* and other like sports and games of youthful days. Amongst other youngsters who took pleasure in spending an evening in this retired dell at such exciting pastimes, I remember that our eminent townsman, the late Sir Neil Douglas, stood conspicuous for his dexterity in all the athletic and gymnastic performances which might have been going on at the place, and was considered as one of the leaders in every game which required strength of body and agility of limb.

By the above-mentioned levelling operations, this romantic dell has now passed away, its bosom filled up with filthy rubbish, the purling Camlachie burn arched over, and the Glasgow Green thereby connected with the Calton Green ; which operations, however useful and necessary, have altogether destroyed the primitive amenity of the valley in question as a secluded place of amusement.

This dell has not been generally exhibited in a lucid manner in the different maps of Glasgow, the space it occupied being represented in them merely as vacant undulated ground ; but in the map attached to Stuart's Views of Glasgow, it is there laid down in a conspicuous manner, as a romantic valley, with hills or elevated grounds for its north and south boundaries, and the Camlachie burn flowing through its centre. The said dell is seen to extend from the Washing House on the west to the east end of the Calton Green, and so far as my remembrance goes, it is there very clearly and correctly shown.

I am not sure of the exact date when the Washing House was first erected, but I think that it existed in the year 1741. M'Ure, who published his history in 1736, does not mention the public

Washing House on the Green. He says that the second Park (or Green) " hath all the summer time between two and three hundred " women bleaching of linen cloth, and washing linen cloths of all " sorts in the river Clyde ; and in the midst of this enclosure there " is an useful well for cleansing the cloths after they are washed in " the river : likewise there is a lodge, built of freestone, in the " midst of it, for a shelter to the herd who waits upon the horse and " cows that are grazed therein." * It appears from the above extract that the process of washing and bleaching cloths by the inhabitants of Glasgow was generally performed at that time upon the banks of the river itself, but that there was a well in the midst of the enclosure for cleansing the cloths after they were washed. This well, I presume, was the Fountain delineated on the Plan, situated immediately to the east of the Washing House, which, from its low-lying position and proximity to the Camlachie burn, must have been a fine spring well, with an abundant flow of water.

By referring to the Plan of the Green, there will be seen a building erected upon the bank of the Camlachie burn, a little to the east of the English chapel, and called " Castle Boins." This building was said to have been in old times used as a washing house, and received the name of " Castle Boins" from the number of boynes or washing tubs which were then to have been seen in and around it, during the washing process, which process was mainly performed in the waters of the Camlachie burn, at the time in question a pure and limpid stream.†

* The Herd's house is shown in the annexed Plan.

† The late Dr Strang, in his amusing work of Glasgow and its Clubs, has made two trifling mistakes as to the Washing House on the Green. At page 169 he says: " This " important public establishment was then situated near the spot where Nelson's monu- " ment now stands." Now, Nelson's monument stands on the High Green, close to the spot where the Herd's house is shown in the Plan ; but the Washing House was situated in the Low Green, within 15 feet of the Camlachie burn, as may be seen in the said Plan. At page 170, the Doctor says: " Then along the side of the river might be seen, in fine " weather, the smoke of a hundred black pots, placed in interstices of a wall that ran " along the margin of the river Clyde," etc. This appears to have been merely a little slip of the Doctor's pen, for he was old enough to have remembered that there were no vestiges of a wall having once ran along the south boundary of the Low Green. In my younger days, the bank of the river at this place was fenced in merely by a few scattered portions of rotten fir stobs, which afforded little or no protection to the Green from speats. Besides, " Castle Boins" shows that in ancient times the washings took place on the bank of the Camlachie burn, which then was a clear and limpid stream. Mr Pagan informs us, in his Glasgow, Past and Present, at page 10, that " the title deeds of " property on the east side of the Saltmarket, written 200 years ago, bear that the " owners shall have '*free ish and Entry*' by the closes leading to the burn, and that " they shall also have the privilege of '*Fishing therein*.' " In my boyish days, I have

Ray, in his Itinerary, published in 1661, informs us that the customary mode of washing linens at that time in Glasgow was for the washerwomen to tuck up their petticoats, and tread the linens with their feet in tubs. I have been in the Washing House of the Green of Glasgow, and have there seen more than a score of women all at one time tramping their linens in their boynes, with uptucked petticoats; and so little did they regard my presence, that I was allowed to make the circuit of the Washing House without a single woman lowering the folds of her petticoats. This did not arise from want of modesty, but was caused by long use and wont, whereby the process was considered of so little importance, that no one was understood to pay any notice to it, as at all indecent or unbecoming.

From the following extract, it will be seen that the foregoing mentioned practice of women washing their foul clothes by tramping them with their feet in boynes, was usually done openly in the streets of Glasgow, and required the notice of our magistrates to put a stop to it.

" Council Records, 11th October, 1623.—Washeriss on the Fore-
" gate.—It is statut and ordanit that na manner of persone stramp
" or wesche ony claythis, plading, yarne, or ony uther thing in the
" foregait, or backsyde, quhare they may be sene, but onlie in housis
" and private plassis, ilk persone under the pane of xi.s. toties
" quoties."

It appears from the following advertisement that " Castle Boins," and the lands connected with it, came to be resorted to by the citizens of Glasgow as a place of amusement and entertainment, where a tavern had been erected for the sale of herb ale, and other change house potables, the place being then quite in the country, and a rural retreat. These lands afterwards were occupied as an extensive tannery.

" Glasgow Mercury, 26th March, 1778.—To be sold, the follow-
" ing Lands :—1st Lot. That well constructed Tannery lately
" erected on the east side of the Episcopal Chapel, adjoining to
" Camlachie burn, consisting of steep holes, lime pits, tan pits, bark
" lofts, drying lofts, currying room, bark mill, cellars, and other
" conveniences; together with a good Dwelling House, being the
" most complete work of the kind extant in Glasgow. 2d Lot.

fished for silver eels in the Camlachie burn, near the serpentine walks; and up to the close of last century, the fishing for eels in the Camlachie burn, to the east of Bridgeton, was quite common amongst young anglers.

" That fine piece of ground, presently a Gardener's yard, on the
" side of the Tan-work, fronting the Green of Glasgow (commonly
" called Moodie's yard), with the pleasant Rural Tavern or Change
" house and offices upon it, which has always been much frequented,
" and remarkable for Herb Ale. Apply to Claud Marshall, writer
" in Glasgow."

A portion of the above-mentioned lands was acquired by David
Dale, and formed a part of his garden. When Greendyke Street
came to be widened, a small slice of the said garden was purchased
by the city of Glasgow, for improving this locality. This is seen by
the published Report of Dr Cleland on the intended city improvements, of date 1813. The Report states as follow : " The approach
" from the bottom of the Saltmarket to the Calton Green is to be
" by a street sixty feet wide, the north side of which will be formed
" by running nearly a straight line from the south side of the brick
" wall which is formed a little to the west of the Episcopal chapel
" to the south-east corner of the Rev. Dr Lockhart's property in
" Charlotte Street, touching the south side of the south wing of the
" Misses Dales' house in that street. This street is then to be con-
" nected with Great Hamilton Street by another one of fifty feet
" wide, forming an obtuse angle with it, the west side of which will
" be described by the east wall of the Charlotte Street gardens. A
" street of fifty feet wide is then to be formed in front of the build-
" ing lots on the Calton Green, and the sides of all the streets which
" are next the Green are to be formed with parapet walls and iron
" railings. Exclusive of these approaches, the other entries into the
" Green are to be kept open, particularly that from St Andrew's
" Square, down by the Episcopal chapel, and from Charlotte Street,
" William Street, John Street, from openings in the intended Calton
" Green buildings, and from the head of the Green leading to
" Rutherglen Bridge."

The above intended improvements, with some alterations for the
better, were shortly afterwards carried into effect.

About the year 1861, the land where Castle Boins stood was purchased by John Henderson, Esq. of Park, and on it he built a church
or chapel for the accommodation of that district of the city. The
property is thus described in the disposition granted by Mr Robert
Young to Mr Henderson in the year 1861, viz. : " All and whole,
" that piece of ground near the Episcopal chapel, and also near
" where formerly stood a house called ' Castle Boynes,' through
" which piece of ground the Molendinar burn did at one time run,

" containing 263 square yards and 18 square feet, or thereby,
" bounded on the east by the property sometime of David Dale,
" Esq.; on the west by the stone bridge or arch over the said burn,
" leading to the said chapel ; on the north to the property formerly
" of the said John Burns, above described ; on the south by the
" house called 'Castle Boynes,' and by the street or road leading
" from the Old Bridge to St Mungo's Lane, or ' Burnt Barns,' at the
" back of the Green dyke ; which piece of ground is now included,
" and forms part of the tan-work lying within the Burgh of Glas-
" gow."

With regard to the Washing House on the Green of Glasgow, it is
said that a small building was erected close to the Camlachie burn
for a washing establishment about the year 1732, and that water
was pumped into it from the said burn by means of a wind-mill, but
no machinery was required to supply " Castle Boins" with water, as
its whole northern front joined the Camlachie burn itself, whereby
direct covered access to the said burn was obtained from the washing
premises.

The original public Washing House appears to have received
various additions at different times; in particular, in the year 1807,
its extent was more than doubled, so that the annexed Plan refers
only to its state a century ago. It was before these additions were
made that I visited the said Washing House ; on which occasion the
whole of the four sides of the inside area were occupied by above
100 washerwomen doing their work comfortably under cover, while
a large circular stone reservoir of water stood in the centre of the
building, with ready access to it on all sides, and numerous fires
blazed under cover, on which boilers were placed all around, the
tacksman being obliged to provide hot and cold water to the
washers. The Washing House did not join the Camlachie burn, but
stood a little to the south of it. The inhabitants of the Calton had
easy access to the said Washing House by means of a bridge across
the Camlachie burn, situated immediately to the north of the
washerie.

Many very respectable females, of *bein means*, took the advantage
of using the public Washing House for their domestic washings, and
personally *tramped the tub* along with the throng of the place. I
have known females, even in the rank of ladies, who *duffed their
braws*, and dressing themselves, "*comme Blanchisseuses*," took their
stand at the washing boyne *cheek by Jole* with the ordinary washerwomen.

It appears from Chapmam, page 67, that at this time the Washing
House produced a considerable revenue to the city. He says—" It
" has been let for £600 per annum, but since the introduction of
" water by pipes into the town the rent has been much reduced.
" It is let from 1811 to 1812 at £284." This defalcation seems to
have arisen from the citizens being enabled to perform their washing operations at home, seeing that they possessed an abundant
supply of water within their respective dwellings, from the Glasgow
Water Works, established in 1806, and the Cranston Hill Water
Works, set a going in 1808. To which may be added the extension
of the city to the west, and the general change in residence of the
better classes of the community to the western districts. The dues
of the Washing House were collected in the clerk's lodge, situated
near the Burnt Barns, east end of Greendyke Street, at the entrance
into the Low Green, opposite the Big Tree, which lodge stood within
the boundaries of the Low Green.

The dues payable at the said Washing House were—

For hot and cold water of one day's washing, without the use of tubs and stools, ...	4d.
For use of a washing tub and washing stool for one day, ...	1½d.
Watching through the night a day's washing of clothes, ...	3d.
Boiling clothes in a large boiler, ...	8d.
Three pailfuls of warm water for rinsing, ...	1d.

Any citizen might have bleached clothes on the Green which had
been washed at home without charges, and might have kindled a
fire to warm water in pots for the washings, and might also have
washed at the side of the river without paying any dues to the
tacksman.

A little to the west of the Washing House there stood on the
green (see the Plan) the celebrated "Big Tree" so often mentioned
by our Glasgow historians, under whose umbrageous shelter tradition says that the ladies of Glasgow assembled to view the grand
muster of the wild Highland host of Prince Charles in January,
1746.

Our learned fellow-townsman, Dr Mathie Hamilton, thus describes
the Green of Glasgow and its "Big Tree," as the same appeared in
the year 1800 :—" At that period the Low Green was often inun-
" dated, and presented various inequalities of surface, but in most
" parts of it was seen a fine coat of verdure, the grass being long
" and well adapted for grazing; also, many stately trees were there

" all along and inside the wall above noted. These trees extended
" from the gate which was opposite Saltmarket to the commence-
" ment of what was called the 'Serpentine' walks at the south end
" of Charlotte Street. These walks went over the ground on which
" Monteith Row is now built, and on towards the eastern limits of
" the Green, and were much used as a promenade, giving a romantic
" and sylvan aspect to this favourite place of resort. One very
" large elm-tree deserves notice here, as in a plan of the Green,
" published in the *Glasgow Magazine* in 1783, the site of that once
" celebrated tree is omitted. It stood quite alone on the Laigh
" Green, in front of the old Washing House, and at the bend of the
" ancient gravel walk, which was between the Washing House and
" the tree, the latter being west and south from the entrance
" through the Greendyke from Charlotte Street. That tree was
" distinguished from all others by its insular position, its size, and
" its being so well adapted to give shelter from a sudden shower, or
" the solar rays. It was called the 'Big Tree,' and about the year
" 1800 it was an ornament pleasing to behold, when, during the
" summer months, its wide spread branches were covered with dark
" green foliage. This once famous tree afforded cover for a few
" minutes to General Lord Moira, his numerous staff, and a Guard
" of Honour, on the day of the grand review in 1804. It has been
" asserted that the said ancient tree was the original represented in
" the city arms, but this, of course, is quite apocryphal. This tree
" being in a state of decay, and being in the way of modern improve-
" ment, was removed, along with various other relics of bygone ages."

The Low Green of Glasgow was not only the usual place for
holding military displays and reviews but was also the locality
where the guilty soldier received martial punishment for his trans-
gressions, either by whipping, or by his being drummed out of the
regiment as a rogue and a vagabond, unworthy to associate with his
fellow soldiers. When soldiers were punished in the Green for their
misdeeds by whipping, the executioner was generally one of the
drummers of the regiment, and the punishment was usually pretty
severe; more so than the whippings of the Glasgow hangman
inflicted upon those condemned at our Circuit Courts for theft or
robbery.

As spectacles of military floggings caused great crowds to assemble
in the Green to behold the delinquents punished, the said spectacles
often ended in riot and disturbance to the public, in consequence of
which it became necessary and usual to have military whippings

inflicted privately in the Guard-house, situated at the corner of the Candleriggs.

In August, 1750, a serious dispute arose between the magistrates and citizens of Glasgow on the one part, and the military then quartered in Glasgow on the other part, regarding the death of a soldier who was found dead in a corn field near the New Vennel. On the 20th of August, 1750, a Highland soldier was shot in the Green of Glasgow for desertion. On this occasion, the populace of the city appear to have taken the part of the deserter, and to have been on bad terms with both the officers and privates of the regiment to which the deserter belonged. The following account of this affair is taken from the *Scots Magazine* of August, 1750, at pages 395 and 449.

On the 20th of August, 1750, John M'Leod, a soldier, was shot at Glasgow, for desertion. Two others, under sentence for the same crime, were first reprieved, and afterwards transported. On this occasion some ill humour arose between the people and the soldiers. A threatening letter, unsigned, was sent to the Colonel; some soldiers were knocked down in the streets, under night, and one was found dead in a corn field near the town, on the 23d. On notice of the above anonymous letter, the magistrates, by a proclamation, offered £10 sterling to any person who should discover the author of it; requiring the inhabitants to behave discreetly to the soldiers, and promising £10 sterling for discovering any person that should contravene this order. An advertisement was published in the *Glasgow Journal* of August 27th, by the officers, bearing, that there was great reason to believe that Joseph Kinnelly, the soldier found dead as above, was murdered by persons unknown, and offering fifty guineas for discovering the murderer or murderers; ten guineas for discovering the author of the anonymous letter above mentioned, and five guineas for discovering any person that had been or should be guilty of knocking down or wounding any soldier. P.S.—In the next Journal, that of September 3d, was inserted, by order of the magistrates, the following report, signed by Messrs James Stewart, surgeon's mate of the regiment, and James Muir and John Crawford,* surgeons in Glasgow, dated August 23d, and addressed " To Mr William Weir, Sheriff-substitute for the Shire of Lanark,"

---

* This gentleman appears to have been fortunate in a lottery speculation. " *Glasgow* " *Journal*, 3d November, 1755. Last week, Mr John Crawford, Surgeon in Glasgow, " had a prize of £500, in the present lottery."

viz:—" Sir, According to your order we have inspected the corpse of Joseph Kinnelly, soldier, and found no marks of violence, or any reason to say he hath been murdered."

This produced another advertisement in the papers of September 10th, signed by Col. Will. Herbert, Lt.-Col. Jo. Gray, Capt. Mark Ranton and Rich. Russell, and Lieut. and Adj. Robert Gordon, viz:—" Lest the world may imagine from the report of the surgeons " (above inserted), that the Officers of the Hon. Col. Herbert's " regiment had no reasons for their advertisement (above mentioned), " they, therefore, publish the following circumstances, which they " hope the impartial world will think were sufficient grounds for " said advertisement," viz:—" It is notorious that a most unjust resentment was expressed by several persons in Glasgow, on the occasion of the execution of John M'Leod, late a soldier in the aforesaid regiment, and who was shot the 20th of August last, for desertion to the rebels in January 1745-6, which resentment has manifestly appeared; 1st, by a letter directed to the commanding officer of said regiment, filled with scandalous aspersions and threats, for murdering M'Leod, as the writer termed it; 2d, by several soldiers of the regiment being knocked down in the streets with bludgeons, the evenings preceding and succeeding the day on which Kinnelly was found dead in a corn field near to the town; 3d, by people said to be lying in wait for officers of the regiment, and their lives threatened to be taken away, all which has appeared by the oaths of several persons; 4th, by two persons that fled or absconded upon information being given in against them and summonses issued for their appearance before a civil magistrate; lastly, the surgeons, upon being asked, on oath, if the same appearances might have been on the body of the deceased if he had been murdered?—declared that they might. And though none of these appearances determined them in the least to think the man was murdered, it was not impossible but he might have been murdered notwithstanding. All which makes the officers continue to think that there is great reason to believe that Joseph Kinnelly was murdered; therefore they repeat the reward of fifty guineas, as expressed in the *Glasgow Journal* of date the 27th August last."

" Glasgow, September 17th, 1750."

The magistrates of Glasgow caused insert in the Glasgow and Edinburgh papers the following answer to the advertisement published by the officers of Colonel Herbert's regiment :—

" The magistrates* are extremely concerned that the officers of the Hon. Col. Herbert's regiment seemed to be impressed with a belief that Joseph Kinnelly, late soldier, was murdered, and this upon evidence which, with submission, has no manner of weight. The inhabitants of Glasgow have been so much distinguished for their attachment to the present happy Government under his Majesty, (Geo. II.,) and have showed such respect to the gentlemen of the army, that they see with amazement the necessity they are under of justifying themselves in a public manner, having been accused in a printed advertisement.

" There rarely happens in any place an execution of criminals, but some people are wicked enough to censure the justice of it; but that the people of Glasgow should express any resentment that a deserter to the rebels should be executed, is what the world will not easily believe. They appeal to the honour and consciences of their accusers, and to their own conduct when they lay at the mercy of the rebel army with the Pretender at its head. This desertion was a fact hardly known to any of the inhabitants before the advertisement published by the officers. They believe this is the first time that ever an anonymous letter was produced as an evidence. It is in the power of every person living to write such a letter; and, consequently, at that rate, in the power of any wicked or malicious person to accuse the most innocent. Who is there that can be protected by the laws of the land, if an anonymous letter can rob him of his innocence and convict him of the basest crimes? The magistrates have offered a reward of £50 to any who shall discover the author or accomplices of this infamous piece of malice.

" That there was a crowd both from town and country gathered as usual at the place of execution, is true; some of whom from a foolish curiosity, and the narrowness of the ground, pressing too near the soldiers, were punished on the spot, by being very severely beat by the adjutant, and some of them not of the lower rank of people. It is also true, that there have been squabbles between the soldiers and the inhabitants, which in populous places all over the kingdom of Great Britain, has often happened ; and if the magistrates had at that time had notice given them when the inquiry was made before the sheriff, the particulars might have appeared with greater clear-

---

* John Murdoch, provost; Geo. Black, Wm. Dunlop, Thos. Scott, bailies; George Murdoch, dean of guild; Robert Finlay, convener; the latter was partner of the Old Tannery Co., and when master of work, superintended the demolition of Mr Fleming's saw mill.

ness and impartiality. But they cannot but remark an affectation of using the word *bludgeon*,* an instrument never heard of by the inhabitants of Glasgow, which may be better known to the common soldiers, yet is not once mentioned in the precognition before the sheriffs. If the magistrates had any inclination to recriminate, they could easily bring proofs of many insults and acts of violence with clubs and otherwise, committed by soldiers, whose names are unknown, against the inhabitants and even the constables, whose duty it is to make their rounds at night to preserve the peace ; but they choose rather to draw a veil over all circumstances that may tend to inflame these unhappy disputes.

"The magistrates are at a loss to know the foundation of the assertion, ' That persons were lying in wait against officers.' This does not appear in the precognition, though taken *ex parte*.

" It is with the utmost regret the magistrates observe that one Hamilton, said to be living in the country, had uttered some foolish threatening expressions with regard to Col. Herbert, a gentleman of great honour and worth, and for whom they have the highest respect. They never heard of it till they saw the officers' advertisement, and wish they had been acquainted with it sooner. They immediately called the persons said to be present, and found it was one Robert Hamilton, living in a neighbouring parish in the country, said to be very drunk at the time. The provost, as justice of the peace for the shire, instantly issued a warrant for apprehending and imprisoning him. They are told he left the country about three weeks ago. The strictest inquiry is making for him, and it is hoped he will be found, and punished for his most wicked expressions; and the magistrates have, by a public edict through the whole streets of the city, offered a reward of £50 to any who shall bring proof of threatening expressions, or acts of violence against the Colonel or any of his officers. This Hamilton is the only person who has fled or absconded, and he is not an inhabitant of the city.

" As to the supposed murder of the soldier, the magistrates refer to the annexed affidavits, and they cannot but observe that if the report of the surgeons, viz :—' That it was not impossible but that he might have been murdered,' is an evidence of his having been

---

* Johnson defines the word "bludgeon, a short stick with one end loaded." Jamieson, in his Scottish Dictionary, has not the word bludgeon. The nearest Scotch word to bludgeon is " cud "—" a strong staff "—a " club "—but a club is not a stick *loaded* at one end, but *crooked* at one end, for playing at the shinty or golf. The Scotch " cud " is the English " cudgel."

actually murdered, every man or woman that ever died or shall die of a natural death, may by this method of evidence be proved to have died of a violent one.

"The magistrates must again repeat the concern they are under on being obliged to publish their opinion of this whole affair. They had rather choose merely to lay the case before his Majesty's servants; but since the officers have thought fit to appeal to the public in print, the magistrates could not be answerable to the inhabitants, to the public, or to themselves, but by stating these facts and observations in the manner they have done : and they beg leave to express as great a detestation of disturbing his Majesty's Government as those can do under whose bad opinion they have had the misfortune to fall. They hope they have given no offence—at least none but what the laws of God and man have vested in innocence. They are so fully sensible of the late favour and justice they obtained from his Majesty,* as to be very uneasy under any circumstances tending to lessen the reputation of loyalty and zeal for all the branches of his Majesty's authority, which they flatter themselves they had acquired, and which they will ever endeavour to deserve.

"*Agnes Weir's Affidavit, Sept. 5th*, 1750.

"' Agnes Weir, brewer in Glasgow, examined, declares—That on Thursday the 23d of August last, about four in the morning, she saw Joseph Kinnelly, soldier, in the street called New Vennel, and saw him knock oftener than once at the door of John M'Kean's house, where she was told he lodged, as if he wanted to get in ; and afterwards saw him walk down the Vennel towards the Dovehill, where she heard his corpse was afterwards found. Declares—She saw no person along with Kinnelly, and knows not, nor did she observe if he was in liquor or not : but declares—About five of the clock said morning, a soldier, who then lodged in Robert Ewing's, and who was going to make brick, told her he had found Kinnelly among the corn, and that he was dead ; and another soldier, who lodged in the same house with Kinnelly, upon her asking what had been the cause of Kinnelly's death, he answered that Kinnelly always tied his stock too strait, and that he had not been in his quarters for two nights, from which he apprehended he (Kinnelly)

---

* In 1745-6, the rebels under Prince Charles occupied Glasgow for ten days, and their exactions in money and goods cost the city upwards of £15,000. On the 14th of June, 1749, on application of the magistrates to Parliament, they received £10,000 as remuneration for the losses they had sustained during the Rebellion.

had been in liquor. And this she declares to be truth, as she shall answer to God; and depones she cannot write.'

" *The Surgeons' Report, affirmed upon oath.*

" ' At Glasgow, the 6th day of September, 1750 years. In consequence of a petition presented to the Sheriff of Lanark upon the 31st of August last, by James Stewart, surgeon to the Hon. Col. Herbert's regiment of foot, presently quartered in Glasgow, craving to the effect under written : In presence of William Weir, sheriff-substitute of the said shire, the said James Stewart, James Muir, and John Crawfurd, surgeons in Glasgow, being interrogated upon oath, they each of them depone *affirmative* to a report made and signed by them, and directed to the said sheriff-substitute, upon 23d of August last, in consequence of an order directed to them for inspecting the corpse of Joseph Kinnelly, soldier in the forementioned regiment, deceased ; and being interrogate, at the desire of Captain Russell, of the forementioned regiment, If they found any blotching about Kinnelly's neck, or under any of his ears ? they depone— They found his neck, shoulders, and sides of a thickish livid colour, and more remarkably upon the one side of his face and neck than on the other, which they imagined proceeded from that being the most depending part of his body at the time of or soon after his death. And depones—That before they inspected the corpse, the body had been moved out of the posture in which the defunct was at the time of his death : but depone—They were told by a soldier at the time they inspected the corpse that he had found the corpse with his head inclining aside, and rather lower than the rest of his body ; and being interrogate, at the desire of the lord provost of Glasgow (John Murdoch, Jun., Esq.), Whether in the course of their practice they have not seen dead bodies of a livid colour, such as Kinnelly's was at the time of their inspection, when the person deceased had neither been strangled nor murdered ? depone *affirmative;* and that it is common for the body to be most livid on the part most depending at the person's expiring, or soon after. And being interrogate by Adj. Gordon, Whether the same appearances might not have been on Kinnelly's body if he had been murdered ? and whether they can say he was not ? they depone—That the same appearances might have been upon the body of Kinnelly had he been murdered, but that none of these appearances in the least determined them to think that he was murdered ; and it is not impossible but he might have been murdered notwithstanding : for

M

from the inspection of any corpse whatsoever, they cannot say it is impossible that they were murdered. And being further interrogate by the lord provost, Whether in their opinion Kinnelly's death did not proceed from some other cause than his being either strangled or murdered? the said James Muir and John Crawfurd severally depone—That in their opinion Kinnelly's death proceeded from some other cause than his being strangled or murdered : and the said James Stewart depones—That when he first saw the body of Kinnelly, it had the appearance of a person that had been strangled; but that he cannot say but the appearance might proceed from another cause. And the premises they depone to be truth, as they shall answer to God.' "

(N.B.—An order was soon after issued for this regiment's marching to England.)

CHAPTER X.

Four Orphans in 1741—M'Call's Black House—Prince Charlie in Glasgow in 1745—His appearance described—Review of his host—The Glasgow Royal Volunteers in 1778 —Mutiny at Leith—Collision between Magistrates and J.P.'s—Recruiting as prac- tised in 1778—Population and Mortality Bill of Glasgow in 1777.

It is extremely unpleasant, in loose jottings of the present descrip- tion, to make any allusion to family matters; but as the following anecdotes have reference to the ancestors of several individuals to whom the citizens of Glasgow are greatly indebted, not only for their public services, but also for the liberal use of their purses on every occasion when pecuniary assistance has been needed, I hope that my apology for introducing the subject will be forgiven.

When Prince Charles, with his rebel host, arrived in Glasgow in 1745, and when the foregoing dispute between the magistrates of Glasgow and the military took place in 1750, there lived by them- selves four young misses in their paternal mansion at the corner of the Cow Loan and the Westergate. This dwelling was an old- fashioned house of two storeys and offices, with an extensive back garden, stretching a considerable way up the Cow Loan, now Queen Street, and embracing a large portion of Miller Street. It was then a rural spot, being separated from the city by the West Port, and only a few thatch houses and malt kilns lay scattered along the Westergate, many of which remained there to my day.

The mother of those four misses died in 1739, immediately after having given birth to the youngest of them, and their father died in 1741.

The eldest of those four misses, at the time of their father's death, was only in the 13th year of her age, and the youngest an infant of two years old. Many of our citizens remember well the site of the dwelling of those four misses at the south corner of Queen Street. The trustees of the said four misses sold the property to Samuel M'Call, (bailie in 1723,) who built his large mansion on it, com- monly known as "M'Call's Black House"—one of the finest speci- mens in Glasgow of the old Virginia Lord's dwellings. The stones of which it was built were dug from the Black Quarry, which stones turn black on exposure to the action of the atmosphere. A very accurate representation of Mr M'Call's Black House, with its forty windows, and projecting double stair, as the same stood in 1794, is seen in Stuart's Views of Glasgow, at page 104. Mr M'Call's house was purchased by a Mr Glen, who demolished it to make room for the present south-east corner tenement of Queen Street, and again this corner tenement, having been found insecure by the Dean of Guild Court, has just undergone a curious and scientific alteration, by which the sunk and ground floors have been taken down and rebuilt, while the three upper flats remained intact during the whole process of re-building the lower ones, thus exhibiting a fine specimen of masonic skill.

The property in the Westergate, at the north-west corner of Dunlop Street, extending westward to Turner's Court, also belonged to those four sisters, and was let to Mr Miller of Westerton for his extensive malting establishment. The trustees of the said four sisters sold the corner stance to Bailie John Shortridge, about the middle of last century, on which stance Mr Shortridge erected the large corner tenement of Dunlop Street, now known as " Shortridge's Land."

I remember about seventy years ago the west part of this property, which had been let to Mr Miller of Westerton for malt kilns and barns, still standing between Shortridge's Land and the now Turner's Court. A century ago it formed part of my maternal grandfather's estate, which had descended to his four daughters above mentioned.

Our learned antiquarian citizen, John Buchanan, Esquire, in " Glasgow, Past and Present," pages 192-3, has given us an interesting account of this property, in the course of explaining how the north entry to Dunlop Street came to be formed in so narrow and unsightly a manner. The property, now 87 Stockwell, was also the inheritance of those four misses. It consisted of 14 dwelling houses, all of which were burnt down in one night, and not insured. They stood opposite Stockwell Place.

But to return to the four misses who, after the death of their father in 1741, continued to keep house together, under the able management of their eldest sister, then little more than 12 years of age.

When Prince Charles and his Highland host came to Glasgow in 1745, the eldest sister, Agnes, was then 16 years of age, the second, Isabella, 14, the third, Elizabeth, 12, and the youngest, Janet, 7 years of age. On the arrival of the rebels in 1745, two Highland soldiers were quartered upon those four defenceless misses, living together with a servant, out of the bounds of the city, and without a male protector residing in their dwelling to whose support they could have applied in case of insult or wanton rudeness. The soldiers so quartered on the said misses were two poor ragged creatures without shoes or stockings, who could not speak a word of English; but, fortunately, they were very civil, and gave little trouble to the misses, who, on their part, treated them kindly. All that these soldiers required was a bed, and liberty to dress their meals at the kitchen fire, which meals consisted almost wholly of oat meal porridge and barley bannocks. Many of the Highland soldiers, however, at this time, plundered the citizens of their effects, without the lieges being able to obtain any redress. As an instance of military violence in Glasgow at this time, it may be stated that a Highland soldier, having met a joiner on the public street going to his work with his hammer in his hand, took a fancy to the joiner's glittering shoe buckles, and insolently proceeded to take possession of them by force; but while the soldier was stooping down and unloosing the buckles from the joiner's shoes, the latter resisted the attempt, and with a sudden blow on the plunderer's head with his hammer, knocked him down, and then instantly fled, without waiting to see whether the blow had been fatal or not. Such robberies were common by the Highlanders when not in presence of their officers.

As to the four misses, Agnes, the eldest of them, and the house manager, became the grandmother of our late lord provost, Sir Andrew Orr, and his immediate agnates, also of Mrs Bell, wife of David Bell, Esq., &c.

Isabella, the second of them, became the grandmother of James Smith, Esq., of Jordanhill, of Lord Provost William Smith, of Dean of Guild William Brown, and of William Euing, Esq., and the great-grandmother of Sheriff Smith, &c. Elizabeth, the third of the said sisters, was my mother, who has left a numerous race of descendants now alive, upwards of 50 in number. Janet, the youngest, became proprietor of Greenlaw, now the General Terminus. She married her cousin, Francis Reid of Greenlaw, but left no issue.

All these four sisters, respectively, lived in Glasgow till they became matrons of 83 to 85 years of age, and one of their daughters reached the great age of 101 years. The rebels entered Glasgow on the 25th December, and my mother informed me that she had had a good opportunity of seeing the different Highland regiments while they lay in Glasgow during the rebellion of 1745, as her place of

residence was then situated at the south-east corner of the Cow
Loan (now Queen Street), and as detachments of those regiments
marched daily along the Westergate, and turned up the Cow Loan,
immediately before the door of the above-mentioned four sisters,
and then proceeded eastwards by the Back Cow Loan (now Ingram
Street), thereby making a circuit through the centre parts of the
city. My mother further mentioned to me, that one day when
Prince Charles was marching at the head of one of those detachments, she stood so close to him that she could have touched him
with her hand. She also stated that he was a handsome good-
looking man, but that his countenance appeared rather sombre and
melancholy. I remember when a boy that we had a bust of Prince
Charles standing in our lobby, but it, having received some damage,
was laid aside, and I never could learn what became of it..

While in Glasgow Charles lived in the house of John Glassford of
Dougalston, situated in the Trongate, fronting Stockwell Street,
which splendid seat had formerly been the celebrated Shawfield
mansion. The large garden (now Glassford Street) connected with
it on the north, had an entry into the Back Cow Loan, which
remained entire down to my day. The Chevalier having extorted
from the citizens a heavy levy of shirts, shoes, hose, waistcoats, and
bonnets, and having new clothed his ragged troops with them, he
treated the inhabitants of Glasgow with a grand review, on the
Green of the city, of his newly clothed ragamuffins, who marched to
the Green by way of the Saltmarket, in splendid military array, with
colours flying, drums beating, and the skirling notes of the Highland
piobaireachd resounding from the pipes of every clan. On the next
day, being the 3d of January, 1746, the Prince, with his motley crew,
evacuated Glasgow, to the great joy of its inhabitants who, almost to
a man, were hostile to them.*

On the 1st of July, 1778, there was another grand review on the
Green of Glasgow of the "Glasgow Royal Volunteers;" a military
display most gratifying to all ranks of the inhabitants of the city, who
took the greatest interest in the welfare of those voluntary militants.

---

* The Glasgow Volunteers fought against the rebels at the battle of Falkirk, on the
17th January, 1745, and suffered greatly that day, the Highlanders being inveterately
hostile to them upon old scores. Francis Crawfurd, Esq., afterwards deacon convener,
the grandfather of George Crawford, Esq., carried the colours of the volunteers at this
memorable battle, and Henry Monteith, a country gardener, the grandfather of the late
Provost Henry Monteith of Carstairs, M.P., joined the Glasgow regiment, and was
present at the battle of Falkirk, where he, along with every member of that loyal regiment, behaved most valiantly, though unsuccessfully.

"*Glasgow Mercury*, 2d July, 1778."—"On Tuesday evening
" Major-General Skene arrived in town, and yesterday, (1st July),
" he reviewed in the Green the Glasgow Royal Volunteers. The
" General was highly pleased with the appearance of the regiment,
" and expressed his warmest acknowledgments to Lieut.-Col.
" Fotheringham and the other officers for their having brought such
" a number of men in so short a time so forward in their exercise as
" to be nothing short of veteran troops. The exactness with which
" they performed their different manœuvres received the General's
" high approbation, and gave great satisfaction to a vast crowd of
" spectators. The corps was about 900 strong, and only one or two
" rejected. After the review the General gave an elegant entertain-
" ment to the magistrates of the city, and many other gentlemen."

When we see the present lamentable state of starvation of the
hand-loom weavers of Glasgow, it is curious to look back to the old
times, when those industrious operatives, in place of receiving public
assistance, liberally subscribed, of their own accord, a handsome
contribution towards the fund for raising the regiment of the " Glasgow Royal Volunteers."

" Glasgow, January 8th, 1778. The subscription for raising
troops in support of Government goes on with great alacrity,
and the following letter, addressed to the lord provost, from
a few journeymen weavers, will show the ardent loyalty of this
place.

' At Glasgow, January 5th, 1778, present,

James Ewing, preses, David Jack, collector,

Robert Miller, John Aitken, James Aitken, James Marshall, John
Robertson, Alexander Brown, William Boyle, William Esson, Wm.
Hunter, Alexander Provan, James Bell, Thomas Buchanan, Daniel
M'Farlane, and George Shaw, of the " Old North Quarter Society"
of journeymen weavers in Glasgow, offer their compliments to your
lordship, the lord provost of Glasgow, and hope you will accept of
the small sum of fifty pounds sterling, in name of our society, as a
testimony of loyalty to Government, and a hearty concurrence with
your lordship's laudable proposal to raise a regiment by the city of
Glasgow, to serve his Majesty as the exigency of the affairs shall
require. We beg to know of your lordship when the money will be
called for, and in what manner; and we will give it for the above
purpose, but for none other whatever.—My lord, we are your lordship's
humble and obedient servants, James Ewing, preses.'"

The subscription to raise the regiment of the Royal Glasgow

Volunteers, commenced early in January, 1778, and we find that in
less than a week upwards of £5000 had been subscribed for that
purpose.

"*Glasgow Mercury*, 8th January, 1778. Besides the generous
and ample subscriptions from many private gentlemen, for raising
the Glasgow regiment, public bodies have subscribed the sums
following—

The City of Glasgow,	£1000
The Trades' House,	500
Hammermen,	200
Tailors,	400
Cordiners,	300
Maltmen,	300
Bakers,	200
Wrights,	200
Coopers,	100
Weavers,	200
Skinners,	100
Barbers,	100
Gardeners,	100
Masons,	100
Bonnet Makers and Dyers,	20
Fleshers,	350
	£4,170."

The Faculty of Physicians and Surgeons, 100 guineas, and the
Faculty of Procurators, 100 guineas; Lord Frederick Campbell,
member for the district of boroughs, £500; and by the 21st of
January the sums subscribed amounted to £9,600.

"*Glasgow Mercury*, 29th January, 1778. The Honourable
Major General Alexander Leslie, now in America, Lieut.-Col. of the
64th regiment, and brother to the Earl of Leven, is appointed
Colonel of the Glasgow regiment. Alexander Fotheringham Ogilvie,
Esq.. Lieut.-Col. by brevet from the 25th regiment, is appointed
Lieut.-Col.; and Mr James Butters, Sergeant-Major of the 25th, is
appointed Adjutant."

"On Friday evening last (23d January, 1778), about eleven o'clock,
the adjutant of the Glasgow Volunteers arrived here, and brought
recruiting orders; in consequence of which, the magistrates and
inhabitants, actuated by that zeal for the honour and prosperity of
their country, which has on many former occasions distinguished
this loyal city, eminently exerted themselves in promoting the present business. On Monday, at noon, the bells were set a ringing;

the magistrates and town council, the deacons of the fourteen incorporated trades, and a great number of gentlemen, convened in the council chamber, from whence the following procession began.

1. The city sergeants to clear the way.
2. The magistrates.
3. The adjutant of the regiment.
4. The colours, borne by two young gentlemen, supported by other two with guns and fixed bayonets.
5. The sergeants of tho regiment.
6. Two young gentlemen playing on fifes.
7. Two young gentlemen beating drums, (one of whom was John Wardrop, Esq., the uncle of William Ewing, Esq.)
8. A gentleman playing on the bagpipes, (James Finlay, tho father of Kirkman Finlay, Esq.)
9. The members of the town council, the late deacon convener (John Craig), the present convener (Hugh Niven, being at London), and the deacons of the fourteen corporations, three and three.
10. The sovereign of the Cape Club, supported by two of the members.
11. A great number of gentlemen with cocades in their hats.

" When the procession reached the guard house (corner of Candleriggs) where the first proclamation for volunteers was made, the party of the 2d battalion of Royal Scots, who were on guard, turned out and presented their arms during the time of the proclamation, and while the procession passed. After they had paraded through the lower part of the town, they went up the High Street as far as the College, and returned and continued the procession to the Saracen's Head Inn, in the Gallowgate, where an elegant entertainment was prepared for them. After regaling themselves for some time, and having ordered several casks of porter to be given to the populace, who were assembled about a large bonfire, kindled upon the occasion, the procession again began with torch light, and an additional band of music. The whole windows of the city were immediately lighted, the great bells set a ringing, and thousands of loyal people enjoyed the military parade with great satisfaction. A considerable number of recruits were enlisted for the regiment that evening. Miss Mary Ann Leslie, only child of General Leslie, (Col. of the volunteers), has ordered £200 stg. to be subscribed in her name towards completing of that regiment. Above £10,000 are subscribed, and the subscription is still going forward.

CONTRIBUTIONS FROM INDIVIDUALS.

Lord Fred. Campbell, M.P.,	£500	0	0	Robert Donald, lord provost, £105	0	0
Hon. Miss Leslie, . . .	200	0	0	Peter Murdoch, ... 105	0	0

CONTRIBUTIONS FROM INDIVIDUALS—*Continued.*

Robert Find!ay, jr.,	.	£105	0	0	Ronald Crawford, ...	£50	0	0
James Brown, sen.,.	. .	105	0	0	William Donald, ...	50	0	0
George Crawford,	. . .	100	0	0	Jonathan Anderson, . . .	50	0	0
William French, .	. . .	100	0	0	James Jackson, ...	50	0	0
Patrick Colquhoun,	. .	100	0	0	Peter Blackburn, ...	50	0	0
George Miln,	. . . .	100	0	0	John Robertson, ...	50	0	0
John Clark, .	. . . .	100	0	0	John Laurie, ...	50	0	0
George Miller, sen.,	. .	100	0	0	John Duguid, ...	50	0	0
John Orr, .	. . . . .	52	10	0	Andrew and John Stirling,	50	0	0
James Findlay, & Co.,	. .	52	10	0	James M'Dowall, ...	50	0	0
Andrew Houston,	. . .	52	10	0	Dugald Thomson, . . .	50	0	0
William Clark, .	. . .	52	10	0	John Wardrop, ...	50	0	0
Richard Marshall,	. . .	50	0	0	James M'Gregor, ...	50	0	0

The others under £50. Total sums subscribed, £10,212 15s."

The regiment was fully equipped in the spring of 1778, and in April, 1779, they were ordered on foreign service. Upon the occasion of a mutiny of the Fraser Fencibles, the Glasgow regiment volunteered to march to Leith to suppress this mutiny by force, although they knew that they would have to contend against a well disciplined Highland regiment, and that the Glasgow regiment had received only a year's drill. Their services, fortunately, were not required, as the following extracts show.

" Glasgow, April, 1779. The first division of the Glasgow regiment marched from Dundee on Monday, and the last division on Tuesday, for Bruntisland, in order to embark on board the transports lying there ready to receive them."

" *Ruddiman's Weekly Mercury*, Edinburgh, 21st April, 1779."

" Friday, arrived in Leith Road, his Majesty's ship, Hydra, of 20 guns, Captain Lloyd, with five transports, for the Glasgow regiment.

" A most tragical affair happened, yesterday, at Leith. In the forenoon, about 50 Highlanders, enlisted as recruits for the 42d and 71st regiments, now in America, arrived at Leith in order to be put on board one of the transports lying in the road. Being impressed with an opinion that they were destined for Minorca, along with the Glasgow regiment, and that they were not obliged to serve in any other corps, than those for which they were enlisted, they refused to go on board. Notwithstanding every attempt was made to convince them of their mistake, they persisted. It was then thought necessary to apply force in place of expostulations, and, accordingly, five companies of the Duke of Buccleuch's Fencibles marched down to Leith, a little before five o'clock, headed by their proper officers.

The Highlanders were formed in a line along the houses opposite to the ferry-boat stairs, and the Fencibles very cautiously divided into three parties. One marched by the sands and came to the pier to the northward of the windmill ; another entered the street by the timber bush, and the third marched along the pier opposite to the Highlanders. Seeing themselves thus hemmed in, they presented their pieces with fixed bayonets. Captain Mansfield advanced to them, and taking one of them by the shoulder, began to expostulate with him, drawing him a little out of the line, when the rascal stabbed him ; another fired immediately, and the ball lodging in his head, he instantly dropped down dead. Upon seeing Captain Mansfield fall, the Fencibles were enraged, and immediately fired on the mutineers, on which a dismal carnage ensued. About 23 of the Highlanders fell, of which 8 were killed outright, and the wounded were brought up in carts and sent to the infirmary, two of whom died by the way, four have died since, and most of the wounded are despaired of. Of the Fencibles, one sergeant and two private men of the granadiers were killed, and several desperately wounded. The remainder of the mutineers were directly brought up to the Castle, under a guard. The worthy Captain Mansfield is greatly regretted, especially as he has left an amiable widow, and five or six children. (He was the son of Mansfield the banker.)"

The Highlanders were intended to be incorporated with the Glasgow regiment, which regiment afterwards became the 83d of the line.

At the time when the magistrates of Glasgow were using their utmost endeavours to raise recruits for the Glasgow regiment, the following curious case of disputed jurisdiction between them and the justices of the peace for Lanarkshire occurred, which ended in the discomfiture of the city authorities.

"*Glasgow Mercury*, 2d July, 1778.—Edinburgh, June 30th.— Thursday last, came to be determined before the Court of Session a cause at the instance of William M'Indoe, barber and hair-dresser in Glasgow, against Major William Cowley and Ensign Hugh Wallace, of the 22d regiment of foot. As every cause regarding the recruiting service is at all times interesting, and as it must appear peculiarly so at a period like the present, we shall endeavour to collect all the particulars with respect to this, and lay them before our readers, with as much brevity as possible.

"Upon the 21st of February, 1777, M'Indoe, being much intoxicated with liquor, met with Ensign Wallace at a puppet show in

Glasgow, where he asked him the loan of a shilling. This Mr Wallace refused. From the puppet show, Mr Wallace, with some of his companions, went to a mason lodge ; and M'Indoe followed them through the streets, still insisting for the loan of a shilling. He even followed them into the mason lodge, though not a mason, and persisted in his demand. Mr Wallace, being thus teazed with him, said that if he would take the shilling in the King's name, he should have it. This at first M'Indoe refused ; but at last told him he would take it in the King and Queen's name, and took the shilling. It appears he was at this time so very drunk, that those who were appointed to examine him in another room could not discover whether he was a mason or not. He soon, however, became so very riotous and offensive, that he was by force, and with a good deal of indignity, turned out of doors. From this time M'Indoe continued going every day about his business as usual, without receiving any trouble or molestation, till Wednesday the 19th of March, that he was apprehended by a sergeant and a party of soldiers, who, alleging that he had some weeks before enlisted with Ensign Wallace, immediately carried him before one of the bailies of Glasgow. Having been brought there, and asked the usual questions with regard to enlisting and attesting, he denied that he ever had done the one, and would never do the other. He was, notwithstanding, immediately committed to prison. In this situation he remained till the 21st, when he was brought from prison to the council chamber, before another of the bailies, Ensign Wallace being also present. The same questions were put to him upon this occasion as the former, and the same answers returned. The taking the shilling at the mason lodge was then mentioned ; but he answered that he was drunk at the time, that he took it in a joke, and that he did not expect any gentleman would put a bite on him. The bailie observed, he would answer very well for a soldier, and immediately ordered him back to prison. Here he lay till about nine at night, when the ensign, with a sergeant and corporal, came and desired the jailer to deliver him over to them ; but the jailer refused, until he should have a warrant from a magistrate for that purpose. Upon this Mr Wallace went to the bailie, who sent for the jailer, and ordered him to deliver over M'Indoe ; but having desired a written warrant, the bailie answered, that he having been verbally imprisoned, he ordered him verbally to be delivered over to the ensign. The jailer returned and communicated the bailie's order to M'Indoe, who refused to go ; upon which the sergeant and corporal having seized him, carried him forcibly out of prison, the ensign having given a receipt for him to the jailer. He was accordingly carried from the prison to the military guard house (corner of Candleriggs), where he was kept in close confinement till next morning, and carried off by the same kind of violence to the town of Hamilton, in order to be passed by Colonel Hugonine, a field-officer. Next day he was carried back to Glasgow, set at liberty, and allowed to return to his own house.

" Upon the morning of the 24th, M'Indoe applied by petition to the justices of the peace of the county of Lanark, praying for redress; which having been presented to James Ritchie, Esq. of Craigton,* one of their number, he granted warrant for bringing before him the sergeant and corporal complained upon, in order to be examined; and appointed the petition to be intimated to Ensign Wallace, requiring him to give answers thereto within twenty-four hours of the service: and in the meantime prohibited and discharged Ensign Wallace and all other officers, civil and military, from confining the person of M'Indoe, or any way molesting him on account of the pretended enlistment, until the issue of the cause.

" A great deal of procedure was had before the justice of the peace, after which a proof was allowed, and taken for both parties; and upon advising the whole, Mr Ritchie pronounced a most distinct and pointed interlocutor, finding M'Indoe was not an enlisted soldier, and prohibiting and discharging all officers, civil and military, from molesting or troubling him on account of the pretended enlistment alleged against him. Upon the 15th of April, however, while the parties were assembled before the justice to hear his sentence pronounced, the house was surrounded by town officers and soldiers; and no sooner had M'Indoe been discharged, and come out to go to his own house, than he was seized by a party of *town officers*, in virtue, as they said, of a warrant or order granted by Bailie French,† upon a petition or application of Capt. Cowley, setting forth M'Indoe to be a deserter. He was immediately carried to the town clerks'‡ chamber of Glasgow, where he was told he must remain till further orders. While in this situation, he formally required the town officers, in presence of a notary and witnesses, to acquaint him by what autho-

---

* In 1775, Mr Ritchie built the large mansion in Queen Street which was purchased for £5000 by Mr Kirkman Finlay, for his town residence; and its site is now occupied by the National Bank.

† William French was provost of Glasgow in 1778 and 1779. He was ruined by the American War of Independence, and his estates sequestrated in 1787.

‡ The town clerks were Archibald M'Gilchrist and John Wilson, senior.

rity he was a prisoner; and they having thereupon produced Capt. Cowley's petition, with the order or warrant thereon by Bailie French, he required them to give him a copy thereof. This the officers refused to do. M'Indoe then required them to imprison him in terms of the warrant; but they likewise refused: and notwithstanding every effort to the contrary, he was forcibly carried to the Castle of Stirling, where he was committed as a prisoner. Thus deprived of liberty, and confined by military force in a fortress, M'Indoe applied for redress to the Court of Session, by bill of suspension and liberation. The bill, with answers, came to be advised by two of the Lords on the 6th of May, 1777, who passed the same, upon M'Indoe finding caution to the extent of £50 sterling to sist himself in court at any time during the dependence of discussing the suspension; and of consent of Major-General Skene, for Captain Cowley and Ensign Wallace, appointed M'Indoe to be set at liberty. He was accordingly set at liberty upon the 9th of that month, caution having been found.

"M'Indoe likewise brought an action before the Court of Session concluding against Ensign Hugh Wallace, Captain William Cowley, Bailie George Crawford,* and Bailie William French, conjunctly and severally, for damages and expenses.

"Both actions came before Lord Gardenston, as Ordinary, in July last, who, upon the 5th of August following, conjoined them. His lordship at the same time found that there was no sufficient evidence that M'Indoe was either fairly enlisted or duly attested, and therefore suspended the letters *simpliciter*, and decerned: but with respect to M'Indoe's claim of damages, made avisandum therewith to the whole Lords, in order to be reported: and appointed informations to be given in to the Lords by the respective parties.

"Two representations were offered on the part of Captain Cowley and Ensign Wallace to the Lord Ordinary, both of which were refused without answers; after which a reclaiming petition was preferred to the whole Lords, and it was upon this petition and answers for M'Indoe that the Lords came to pronounce judgment on Thursday last.

"Few of their Lordships delivered any opinion upon the matter, but those who did, coincided entirely with the sentiments of the Lord Ordinary, and expressed a proper detestation of the idea of

---

* Mr George Crawford built the large mansion at the head of Queen Street, which was purchased by James Ewing of Strathleven for £5000. It is now the site of the Edinburgh and Glasgow Railway depot.

enlisting of a man who was totally deprived of his senses, which it plainly came out in proof was the case of this pursuer. They did not enter into the question whether the twenty-four hours mentioned in the Mutiny Act, in which a man was to declare his dissent and lodge the smart money, commenced from the time within the four days in which they are to be carried before a justice of peace or magistrate. There was no occasion for such a disquisition in the present case. The law requires that the person enlisted shall be *carried* before the justice or magistrate, unless he *absconds*. M'Indoe, it was evident from the proof, did not abscond : he every day went about his ordinary business ; and he was so far from having been *carried* before a justice, that he never received the smallest intimation to the purpose till the afternoon of the *fourth* day, when a most indistinct message was left with his apprentice boy, and he never heard more about the matter for the space of three weeks thereafter. They were unanimous in affirming the interlocutor of the Lord Ordinary, and likewise in allowing M'Indoe expenses, an account of which they allowed him to give in.

" (The action of damages has not yet come before the court.)"

I have not been able to learn anything further regarding this action of damages, and therefore suppose that it had been compromised ; but had it taken place in modern times, it would have afforded a fine opportunity of showing the workings of jury trial.

In 1777, Glasgow contained a population of 38,000 inhabitants ; and if we calculate by the returns of the mortality bills of the times, it had been gradually decreasing during the previous five years. This decrease was probably caused by the dispute with our American colonies, which contest at this period had nearly annihilated the foreign commerce of the city, and ruined a great portion of her enterprising merchants.

BILL OF MORTALITY FOR THE CITY OF GLASGOW AND SUBURBS FOR THE YEAR 1777.

Men, . .	202		Males,	548	
Women,	297	in all, 1124.	and		Decrease this year, 37.
Youths, .	44		Females,	576	
Children,	581				

Interred in the year 1772,		.	1579.				
"	"	1773,	. .	1319.—Decreased,	.	.	260
"	"	1774,	. .	1200.—	"	. .	119
"	"	1775,	. .	1173.—	"	. .	27
"	"	1776,	.	1161.—	"	. .	12
"	"	1777,	. .	1124.—	"	. .	37

Last five years decreased, . . 455

Gorbals—Males, 81 ; Females, 83 ; in all, 164
Anderston— " 29 ; " 45 ; " 88
In Glasgow, 1124

Total of Glasgow and Suburbs, . . 1376

In these calamitous circumstances, the magistrates of Glasgow, on the 17th of January, 1778, forwarded a loyal address to his Majesty, in which they state that "the constitutional liberty and the rights of mankind being still trampled upon by your rebellious subjects in America, we beg leave in the most humble manner to represent to your Majesty, that we think vigorous and speedy efforts ought to be made in order to restore peace to your American colonies ; and that for this end, we are ready to raise a regiment of men, to be employed in such a manner as your Majesty shall be pleased to direct," &c.

The magistrates of Glasgow at this time seem to have been very touchy about the constitutional liberty and rights of man having been trampled upon by the Americans, but they appear to have lost sight of such high-flown phrases when they themselves wished to secure a good recruit in the person of M'Indoe the barber.

There can be little doubt but the magistrates and citizens of Glasgow were induced to raise the Glasgow regiment for the express purpose of its being sent to America to assist in quelling the revolt of the colonists, whose mutiny had caused such disastrous consequences to the commercial and manufacturing interests of the city.

CHAPTER XI.

Injury to the Trade of Glasgow by the American War—Sale of Merkdailly Lands—
Opening of Charlotte Street—St James' Square—Barrowfield—Bowling Green and
the Archer's Butts—Struthers' Brewery—First Brewing of Porter in Glasgow—
Lawsuit in regard to it—List of Brewers summoned before the Justices in 1777—
Printfield at Fleshers' Haugh—Favourite Bathing Place—First Person Baptized by
Immersion in Clyde.

AT this time some important changes occurred in the history of
Glasgow, which, as they took place in my day, may be briefly alluded
to. Denholm, at page 407, thus writes : " The American War was
" a dreadful stroke to Glasgow. All commercial intercourse was
" put a stop to betwixt it and that country; and as the fortunes of
" many of the merchants were embarked in that trade, and America
" deeply indebted to them, it proved the ruin of great numbers who
" before reckoned themselves possessed of independent fortunes."
At page 423 he adds, " From the American War, which for a time
" diminished, and it was feared would ruin the trade of Glasgow,
" the most solid advantages have arisen to its inhabitants, by their
" industry being more especially directed than before to the prose-
" cution of manufactures."

Kincaid, who published his history in 1787, alluding to the
Popery riots of 1779 and 1780, says : " The year 1779 must be for
" ever remarked in the annals of Scotland, on account of disturb-
" ances the most extraordinary that could be imagined to have
" taken place in this country at such a period," &c.

As I have taken notice of these riots in Glasgow, in Glasgow,
Past and Present, Vol. III., p. 497, I need not here repeat them.

It was also at this time that the lands of Merkdailly and St
Andrew's Square, in the environs of the Low Green of Glasgow,
came into the market for sale, which was followed by the magistrates and town council of Glasgow feuing the grounds of the Ramshorn for a new town. These progressive steps soon made the city
to put on quite a new face.

When the Plan which accompanies the present jottings was
drawn up, in 1760, the lands of Merkdailly were garden grounds, for

N

the sale of vegetable produce, and let at the rent of 365 merks
Scots, (£20 5s 5d, stg.) per annum; hence arose the name of Merkdailly. These lands came into the market for sale, in the year 1777.

" Glasgow Journal, 14th August, 1777."

" Merkdailly Yard building ground.—To be sold, in lots, for house
" steadings, the grounds lying on the south side of the Gallowgate
" of Glasgow, known by the name of " Merkdailly." As this ground
" fronts the Green, and lyes so near the Cross of Glasgow, it is a
" most convenient as well as pleasant situation for houses. The
" purchase money will be converted into a ground annual rent, if
" any of the purchasers find it inconvenient to pay the price. For
" further particulars, apply to Patrick Robertson, writer in Glasgow."

No sale appears to have taken place at this time, as we find the
said lands again advertised for sale in 1780.

" Glasgow Mercury, 17th February, 1780."

" Ground for building to be sold."—" That, upon Wednesday, 1st
" of March, 1780, there is to be sold, by public roup, within the
" house of Mr Buchanan, vintner, Saracen's Head, Glasgow, that
" piece of ground in Merkdailly, in the Gallowgate of Glasgow, which
" belonged to the deceased Robert Cullen, Esq., of Parkhead, and
" now to William Cullen, Esq., his son. The progress of writs and
" conditions of sale will be seen in the hands of Thomas Buchanan
" of Boquhan, writer in Glasgow."

Mr Archibald Paterson, then a partner with David Dale, became
the purchaser of the Merkdailly lands, and immediately proceeded to
open a street through their whole extent, from the Gallowgate to
the Low Green of Glasgow, which street he named " Charlotte
Street," in honour of her then majesty, Queen Charlotte.

Our learned antiquarian citizen, John Buchanan, Esq., has given
us the following interesting particulars regarding the former state
of the said Merkdailly lands :—

" In a curious old MS. plan, dated 1771, Merkdailly is there
stated to measure 4 acres, 2 roods, and 7 ells, and represented as
covered with trees. On its westmost boundary there were three
small properties, belonging respectively to Mr Moodie, Miss Wallace,
and Mr Hutcheson, all lying at the back of what was then St
Andrew's Kirk-yard. (These may be seen in the Plan now annexed.)
A substantial stone wall enclosed the orchard on the east and south,
but on the west and north, hedges separated it from several small

adjoining subjects. One of the properties bounding Merkdailly on the north was the back yard of the East Sugar House ;* another, the garden behind the tenement of Mr Peter of Crossbasket, which faced Gallowgate, and had a large brass knocker on the street door; and a third was the green at the back of the town house of Mr Aitcheson of Roughsolloch. What is now called Green Street was then an old lone running outside the orchard dyke, and is marked on the map as " the back of the dykes road." This old road passed the Episcopal Chapel of St Andrew's, facing the Green, the first edifice of that kind erected in Glasgow (in Scotland) after the Revolution, and long known by the somewhat contemptuous epithet of the " Whistlin' Kirk."

It seems worth while to note some further particulars about the property of Merkdailly. In ancient times it formed part of an almost forgotten croft, the name of which is rarely seen in old papers. It was called " Eaglesholm Croft," and extended from the Salt-market eastward to Burnt Barns, and from the Gallowgate south to the Green, including, of course, the area of what is now St Andrew's Square.

---

* This building still exists, and exhibits a curious relic of Glasgow architecture in olden time. There is a representation of it in Stuart's Views of Glasgow at page 98, and its delineation on the Plan herewith annexed is shown as bounding the Merkdailly lands on the north. M'Ure, at page 282, informs us that the Easter Sugar Work was built about the year 1669, and the business successfully carried on by Provost Peddie, Bailie George Bogle, Bailie John Luke, goldsmith, John Graham, Esq., of Dougalston, and Robert Cross, treasurer of the burgh. All the great manufactories of Glasgow at this time were carried on by Joint Stock Companies, consisting of the wealthiest merchants of the city. Robert M'Nair, a grocer in King Street, in order to be on a par with those great aristocratic concerns, assumed his wife as his partner, and transacted his business under the firm of Robert M'Nair, Jean Holmes and Co. (M'Ure, 210.)

The Easter Sugar House having come into the market for sale, it was with no little astonishment that the public heard of plain Robert M'Nair, Jean Holmes and Co. buying up the great concern of the Easter Sugar House, which had required the joint stock of five of our wealthiest merchants to carry on. On the occasion of Mr M'Nair making the purchase, some satirical saws and ludicrous songs were composed, and freely circulated about amongst all ranks of the city, such as—

> " Wha would have thocht it,
> That M'Nair could have bocht it?"

> " You're welcome to the Sugar House,
> Robin M'Nair,
> You're welcome to the Sugar House,
> Robin M'Nair.
> How is your sister, Bell?
> And how is Jean Holmes hersel?
> Robin M'Nair," &c.

Robert M'Nair died at Glasgow in June, 1779, aged 76.

As far back as the reign of Charles II., Merkdailly belonged to John Luke of Claythorn, goldsmith, and at the union was the property of his son, who, in old deeds, is described by the soubriquet of "Bristol John."

After passing through a variety of intermediate owners, it became vested, about 1780, in the person of Archibald Paterson, merchant. Some years previous to his purchase an attempt had been made to open up a street from the Gallowgate to the Low Green of Glasgow, by agreements among the small proprietors on the north side of Merkdailly, as well as the owners of that large space of ground, whereby each proprietor should contribute a certain breadth of ground for the said purpose. It was then intended to have formed a square on the Merkdailly lands, with a street leading to it from the Gallowgate ; the former was to have been named "St James' Square," after the King's palace in London. The plan of this projected improvement is shown in the old map appended to "Gibson's History of Glasgow," but the scheme was not successful ; some of the parties indeed went the length of commencing to build houses at certain points on the line, but had to abandon them on account of pecuniary difficulties and otherwise. After Mr Paterson purchased the Merkdailly lands, he entered into arrangements with proprietors to the north for the proper formation of the new street, to be called Charlotte Street, but in order to complete his plan he was obliged to purchase two properties at the Gallowgate Mouth.

Had Mr Paterson laid off his purchase in a manner the most suitable for his own pecuniary advantage, he might have made a fortune by parcelling out the Merkdailly lands, into various streets, leading from the north to the south, and from the east to the west, and crossing each other with as little loss of building ground as possible. On the contrary, however, to such an arrangement, every house at the south end of Charlotte Street was laid off with an extensive garden attached to it, by which a large portion of the said lands became back ground of little value for building purposes. Besides which, Mr Paterson had introduced into the conveyances of the building stances, a variety of very stringent rules and conditions, relating to the shape, size, and position of the houses, and even to the style of their external ornaments. The gardens also were guarded, for preservation, by a variety of strictly prohibitive clauses.

I remember of having gone into the garden of Mr Paterson's own house, situated next to that of Mr David Dale, and was amused to find that Mr Paterson had formed a number of recesses in his garden wall, for the purpose of enticing birds to build their nests in them, and in one of these recesses I saw the nest of a robin redbreast, with eggs in it; and the old gentleman was more proud of the robin's nest than of all the fine aristocratic houses which adorned his lands.

In consequence of the great loss of building ground, caused by the annexation of such large gardens to the houses at the south portion of Charlotte Street, Mr Paterson derived little or no profit from his purchase of the Merkdailly lands. This, however, gave him no concern, as it was not the expectation of realizing large gains that had induced him to enter into the speculation; but an earnest desire to improve the eastern district of Glasgow, which so greatly required amelioration. Mr Paterson consulted his then partner, Mr David Dale, regarding the purchase and laying out of the Merkdailly lands, and had the approval of that gentleman to all the measures which he adopted on the occasion in question.*

The lands lying to the north-east of Merkdailly appear anciently to have been a croft consisting of about 2½ acres, and came to form part of the Barrowfield estate, possessed formerly by the Walkinshaws of that ilk. On the east of this croft there was a narrow road called "St Mungo's Lone" or the "Burnt Barns," which led into the Low Green of Glasgow. (See Plan.)

The Barrowfield estate having been purchased by the first John Orr (grandfather of Town Clerk John Orr), he formed a bowling green as an appendage to his dwelling, situated in the immediate neighbourhood.

M'Ure, at page 323, thus describes Mr Orr's mansion and his bowling green.

* Mr Archibald Paterson was a modest unassuming man, of primitive manners, and of great piety. He held strict orthodox views in religious matters, and, along with Mr David Dale, and a few others, was the founder in Glasgow of the congregation called "The Old Independents." Mr Paterson, at his own expense, built, in the Grammar School Wynd, a church for this associated body of dissenters, and charged them only £20 of rent for the said church, which contained 500 seats. This rent barely paid for the necessary annual repairs of the building.

Mr Paterson occasionally spoke in this church, by way of exhortation, to his brethren and hearers; but Mr David Dale was the original pastor or minister of the congregation.

The Rev. Mr Smith of Newburn, and the Rev. Mr Ferrier of Largo, in Fifeshire, secessionists from the Established Church of Scotland, having come to Glasgow on a visit, preached for several Sundays, while in Glasgow, in the above mentioned church of Old Independents, on which occasions some wag posted a placard on the church door—

"Preaching here, by David Dale, Smith and Ferrier!!!"

"Barrowfield Bowling Green and Butts for Archers. There is a
"beautiful lodging and pertinents thereof, and a curious bowling
"green at the back thereof, for the the diversion of gamsters at
"bowling hereintill, and a stately pair of butts for accommodating
"the archers of our city thereat, and other gentlemen adjacent;
"all well fenced and inclosed by John Orr of Barrowfield, Esq.,
"lying betwixt his village of Calton and the east part of Glasgow."

The Barrowfield estates having descended to John Orr, the town
clerk, on the death of his father, William Orr, on the 4th of May,
1755,* and the affairs of the former, having become embarrassed,
were placed under the management of trustees, in consequence of
which the property in the neighbourhood of the bowling green came
into the market for sale.

"*Glasgow Journal*, 8th December, 1763. To be sold, by voluntary
"roup, all and whole that slated tenement in Calton of Glasgow,
"with yeard, waste ground, malt kiln, barn, and other houses at
"the back thereof, together with a brewerie and sundry dwelling
"houses to the south of said yeard, some of which houses front the
"new street of Calton; and the said subjects and waste ground
"reach all the way from the old toll house, southward to the said
"new street, and may be profitably converted into a lane, from the
"toll-bar to the new street aforesaid, with buildings on either side
"of the same. As also, three tenements of dwelling houses in the
"wide closs, in the Calton, lying near to the above subjects in
"the east, with the half of the foulzie of that closs, and the whole
"of the other. N.B.—Almost all the said subjects are held by old
"feu charters, subject to no burdens excepting a small feu-duty, and
"being free from all cess, ladles, multers, two pennies on the pint
"duty, and all other taxations and burdens whatever; sundry kinds
"of business may be undertaken on the premises with uncommon
"advantage.

"Apply to William Wilson, writer to the signet, or to Js.
"Buchanan, jr., writer."

"*Glasgow Journal*, 30th October, 1766. To be sold, by public
"roup, within the house of John Barron, vintner in Glasgow, on
"the 4th of November next, The Inn, with stables and pertinents,
"possest by said John Barron, lying upon the south side of the
"Gallowgate Street in Glasgow, with a brewerie and malt loft

---

* The first John Orr died in 1744, and was succeeded by his son, William Orr, whose
death is thus noticed.—"*Scots Magazine*, 1755. 4th May, Died at Barrowfield, near
Glasgow, William Orr of Barrowfield, Esq."

" adjoining thereto, and a tenement of houses adjoining to the said
" Inn, upon the east side thereof. Together with a large garden
" and bowling green at the back of the same, containing about two
" acres of ground, or thereby, very fit for steadings of houses front-
" ing to the west, south, and north. The rental, progress, and a
" plan of the grounds to be seen in the hands of Robert Barclay, or
" James Graham, writers in Glasgow, with whom or with the
" proprietor proposals may be made for bargains by private sale."

The mansion house of Barrowfield, situated in this neighbourhood,
consisted of a large tenement, having a garden attached to it of an
acre and a half, and three acres of pasture ground. Besides, there
were above twenty acres of lands, in tillage, around the mansion
and connected therewith.

The property advertised for sale, as above, (30th October, 1766).
was purchased in June, 1767, by Mr John Struthers, who was
visitor of the maltmen in 1764 and 1765. He greatly enlarged the
brew house works and pertinents, on the south parts of his purchase,
and occupied the tenement which fronted the Gallowgate, as his
dwelling house. It was here that Mrs Kirkman Finlay, and Mrs
M'Ilquham or Meiklem, his daughters, were born. Alexander
Struthers Finlay, Esq., M.P., for Argyleshire, is the grandson of Mr
Struthers, and was named for his uncle, Alexander Struthers, visitor
of the maltmen in 1803 and 1804, whose brewery (now in dwelling
houses) was situated near to Anderston.

After the death of Mr Struthers,* his eldest son, John, succeeded
to the brewery and its pertinents ; but he, having fallen into bad
health, left this country, under the medical charge of Dr James
Alexander, to try the effect of a residence in a warmer climate, but,
unfortunately, died soon after leaving Scotland.

The late Robert Struthers, Esq., succeeded to the brewery and
its pertinents, on the death of his brother John, and immediately
thereafter, made extensive alterations and new erections on the
premises, with all the modern improvements of the times, so that
the Gallowgate brewery soon became one of the largest breweries in
Scotland.

When Mr John Struthers purchased the Gallowgate brewery, in
1767, he had not as yet attempted to brew porter; but Murdoch,

* " Glasgow Mercury, 4th January, 1781. As John Struthers, late brewer in Glasgow, is now deceased, the business continues to be carried on as formerly, in all its
branches, by his son. All orders addressed to his son, John Struthers, brewer, shall be
carefully attended to."

Warroch, & Co., of the Anderston brewery, having, just at this time, successfully introduced the brewing of porter into Glasgow, Mr Struthers, being less skilled in porter brewing than in ale and beer brewing, engaged one of Murdoch, Warroch, & Co.'s workmen into his service, by whose instructions he was enabled to brew porter of a like quality with the porter brewed by the Anderston Company. All the porter, however, which was brewed in Glasgow at this time, was of a very inferior quality, being extremely dark in its colour and coarse in its flavour. It contained a strong infusion of brown liquorice, or "sugar-allie," which renderd it saccharine and muddy; the consequence of these imperfections was that Glasgow ale and beer, being of first-rate quality, was preferred by all classes in the city to Scotch porter, and the sale of Glasgow porter came to be confined almost entirely to the export trade. It was at a considerable later date than this that Messrs John and Robert Tennent, of Wellpark, commenced the brewing of porter.

Murdoch, Warroch, & Co., being conscious of the great inferiority of their porter, both as to taste and flavour, when compared with the porter brewed in London, or even in Dublin, engaged a Mr Chivers, who had been bred to porter brewing in London, to come to Glasgow to instruct them in the London method of brewing porter, for which services the company were to pay to him one hundred guineas, and also all his travelling expenses coming and returning. As Mr Chivers was kept longer than was expected, in the employment of Murdoch, Warroch, & Co., he ultimately received about £300 in all, from the said company. In the original contract or agreement which the Anderston Brewery Company made with Mr Chivers, it was expressly stipulated that Mr Chivers should not communicate his art of brewing to any other brewers in Glasgow or its neighbourhood; but the Anderston Company forgot to bind him not to commence or carry on the brewing of porter, in Glasgow, for his own behoof. In consequence of this oversight in the contract of the parties, Mr Chivers, considering himself at full liberty to brew porter in Glasgow on his own private account, engaged part of Mr Struthers' brewery, for brewing of porter agreeably to the London method, and Mr Struthers, being a sharp clever man, soon got hold of the whole arcana of brewing porter as practised in the capital. This state of matters immediately led to a long law suit, in which the Anderston Company alleged that the whole matter in question resolved itself into a concerted scheme between Mr Chivers and Mr Struthers, to get the better of the prohibitive clause in the contract made with Mr Chivers, by the said Anderston Company. The Court of Session interdicted Mr Chivers from teaching Mr Struthers the art of brewing London porter ; but in the meantime Mr Struthers had acquired a sufficient knowledge of the whole London process, so as successfully to compete with the Anderston Brewery Company in the manufacture of Glasgow London porter. The late Robert Struthers, Esq., the second son of Mr John Struthers, continued to carry on the brewing business in the Gallowgate, for a number of years after the death of his father ; but finding the Gallowgate premises too small for his increasing trade, he removed his establishment, including his dwelling house, to the Greenhead, where he erected a larger and more suitable brewery.* Both old Mr Struthers and Mr Robert Struthers, let the bowling green in the Gallowgate to tacksmen, and took no other charge of it but as landlords of the same. I have played at bowls in this green; the butts, for archers, however, had then disappeared, and it had become unfashionable as a place of amusement, being eclipsed by its opponent in the west, viz., the bowling green in the Candleriggs, now converted into the Bazaar or public market. I have also had my game at bowls in the Candleriggs bowling green. The admittance to each of these bowling greens was one penny per visit to non-subscribers. About the beginning of the present century Mr Robert Struthers commenced to lay off the grounds for building on which the Calton brewery and bowling green stood, and accordingly opened up the present Kent Street, and Suffolk Street, &c., &c., through said lands.

"15th June, 1693.—(Fourth session, first parliament of William and Mary.)—This year an act of parliament was obtained in favour of the city of Glasgow, disponing to the magistrates and council, for their behoof, an imposition of two pennies Scots (a Scots penny is one-eleventh of an English penny) upon the pint of all ale and beer to be either brewed or inbrought and vended, hopped, or sold within the said town, suburbs, and liberties thereof, for any space their majesties shall please, not exceeding thirteen years, for the purpose of paying the town's debt ; excepting ale and beer brewed by heritors in the country, and consumed by them and their families in town ; also excepting ale and beer brewed and vended in Gorbals."

This Act was several times renewed, but the tax is now abolished. From the above quotation, it is evident that at this time porter had

* When the Calton was erected into a burgh of barony, Mr Robert Struthers was elected chief magistrate of it.

not been brewed in Glasgow, and that the Calton was then considered a country or rural district, and not even mentioned in the Act.

Referring to the N.B. at the conclusion of the advertisement quoted, 8th December, 1763, we find that property in the Calton was then free from all cess, ladles, multers, two pennies on the pint duty, and all taxations and burdens whatever, chargeable upon the inhabitants of the city of Glasgow as borough dues. In consequence of this exemption, a great number of petty breweries came to be erected in the Calton district, where a flourishing trade in malt liquor arose; and breweries, malt kilns, and malt barns might then have been seen in every quarter of the said district. But amongst the revenue laws which were made applicable to Scotland, the following one proved a great check to the flourishing trade of ale and beer brewing in the Calton.

Act 12th, Charles II., chap. 23d, enacts—"That all common " brewers of beer and ale shall once in every week ; and all inn- " keepers, alehouse keepers, victuallers, and other retailers of beer, " ale, cyder, perry, metheglin or strong water,* brewing, making, or " retailing the same, shall once in every week make true and par- " ticular entries at the office of excise within the limits of which the " said commodities and manufactures are made." And it is further declared by the said Act, that those "who do not once a week make " due and particular entries at the office of excise, shall forfeit £5."

There is no mention made in this Act of porter, which was not manufactured in London in the days of Charles II.

On the 8th of April, 1777, Alexander Stuart, collector of excise, exhibited an information to two justices of the peace for the county of Lanark, setting forth that various persons in Glasgow and its neighbourhood had, betwixt the 8th of January and 2d of April last, made, brewed, or distilled several great quantities of low wines and strong waters, and have not paid duties for the same, as by the law and statutes of excise they were required and appointed to do : judgment, therefore, was prayed against various persons after-named for forfeiture of double duty, and expenses, etc.

List of brewers† and distillers in the Calton district who were pursued before the justices of the peace on the 8th of April, 1777 :—

---

    * " Metheglin—Drink made of honey, boiled with water, and fermented."—*Johnson.*
      " Metheglin—Drink made of water, herbs, honey, spice, etc."—*Bailey.*

    † On the 1st of January, 1784, the brewers advertised as follows : " Notice.—The " brewers in and about Glasgow having hitherto found much inconvenience from the

	Single Duty.				Double Duty.		
Archibald Graham, Calton,	£19	5	7½	...	£38	11	3
William Kidd,	15	17	6	...	31	15	0
William Innes,	26	1	10½	...	52	3	9
William M'Nair,	5	11	3	...	11	2	6
James Bachop,	12	16	10½	...	25	13	9
Alexander Granger,	13	0	0	...	26	0	0
John Dunn,	23	18	1½	...	47	16	3
William Lang,	6	5	0	...	12	10	0
Robert Murray,	26	1	10½	...	52	3	9
Robert Buchanan,	13	3	1½	...	26	6	3
William M'Ilquham,	21	3	1½	...	42	6	3
William Bayle,	25	1	10½	...	50	3	9
Archibald Jamieson,	27	5	7½	...	54	11	3
Duncan Murray,	25	19	4½	...	51	18	9
Mary Stuart,	11	19	4½	...	23	18	9
Andrew Miller,	12	5	7½	...	24	11	3
Thomas M'Ilquham,	8	9	4½	...	16	18	9
Matthew Steven,	16	6	10½	...	32	13	9
Moses Drew,	19	13	9	...	39	7	6
Thomas Smith,	5	8	1½	...	10	16	3
John Arrol,	4	16	3	...	9	12	6
John Harvey,	20	5	7½	...	40	11	3
James Hamilton,	16	18	9	...	33	17	6
Katherine Simpson,	13	11	3	...	27	2	6
John M'Innes,	18	13	1½	...	37	6	3
Margaret Ferguson,	13	11	3	...	27	2	6
Christian Aitken,	25	10	7½	...	51	1	3
Ann Nielson,	11	4	4½	...	22	8	9
Duncan M'Arthur, White Houses,	17	6	10½	...	34	13	9
Henry M'Indoe, Fleshers' Haugh,	4	13	9	...	9	7	6
John Clyde, Craignestock,	15	8	9	...	30	17	6

To this information defences were given in for the whole persons complained on, stating some objections to the form of the citation, which defences the justices repelled, and allowed the collector to prove his information; thereafter, upon advising the proof, they pronounced the following judgment: Having considered the information and oaths of parties, " the justices find the information relevant, and proved against the whole defenders, and decern against each of them for the forfeiture of double duty respectively charged against them in the information, conditionally, for thirty days; but if the defenders pay to the informant, Mr Alexander Stuart, the

" practice of giving presents to their customers at New-year's day, are therefore resolved
" to discontinue that practice in future.—25th December, 1783."

single duties, with sixpence sterling per pound of charges, within the said thirty days from the date hereof, then the justices assoilzie from the double duties, and decern accordingly, and ordain execution to pass hereon, in terms of the laws of excise."

This judgment having been brought before the Court of Session, by bill of advocation, the bill was refused by Lord Kaimes Ordinary.

The advocate for the collector of excise was Henry Dundas, then Lord Advocate, and afterwards the celebrated Lord Melville.

Amongst those who were prosecuted as above, by the collector of excise, for double duties, we see the name of John M'Indoe, residing in the "Fleshers' Haugh." It was in consequence of the "Provost Haugh" having been rented for some time by several members of the incorporation of fleshers, for pasturing cattle, that the name came to be changed from "Provost Haugh" to "Fleshers' Haugh;" and by the following advertisement it will be seen that the inhabitants of the city were in the practice of freely walking on it, and of making roads through it at their pleasure.

"*Glasgow Mercury*, 30th March, 1780."—"Notice. Whereas "several persons take the liberty to walk and make roads through "John King's grass in the High Green of Glasgow, to his hurt and "prejudice, the said John King begs of the inhabitants and others "that they will refrain that practice, seeing there is a sufficient "road and very pleasant walks without injuring his property, for "which he pays a high rent. And (in order to prevent his grass "being treaded and abused in time coming) he hereby certifies all "trespassers, that they will be prosecuted as law directs; and "further offers a handsome reward to any person who will inform "upon trespassers, so as he or they may be convicted."

John King, above mentioned, was the deacon of the fleshers in the years 1768, 1769, and 1775.

It appears, from the annexed advertisement, that Robert Dalglish, Esq., the father of our active M.P., Robert Dalglish, Esq., had his printfield on the Fleshers' Haugh shortly before the city of Glasgow purchased the said haugh.

"*Glasgow Mercury*, 16th November, 1790."—"To be set, for one "year, that piece of ground and houses lying at the head of the "Green of Glasgow, commonly called "Fleshers' Haugh," which "has been occupied for some years past by Dalglish and Hutcheson "as a printfield. Any person wishing to take the same may apply "as above."

I remember the above printfield, situated at the east end of the Fleshers' Haugh, which I think was subsequently rented by Mrs Currie, of the Black Boy tavern in the Gallowgate (afterwards Mrs Jardine, of the Buck's Head inn), for washing and bleaching purposes. Mrs Currie attended her washings herself, amidst groups of bathers, with whom she delighted to give and take jokes. She paid little attention to the nudity of the bathers, who paid as little attention to the modesty of Mrs Currie.

The Fleshers' Haugh at this time was the favourite bathing place for the citizens of Glasgow, as at its eastern extremity the river was sufficiently deep on its north bank to permit a good swimmer to plunge headlong into the stream without danger; while towards the west, the river gradually deepened from its shore to its centre, thereby giving a learner or a timid person an opportunity to select a place of the depth most agreeable to his wishes. There were, however, one or two places in this part of Clyde which went by the name of *plumbs* or *holes*, where several accidents have occurred. I remember when a boy of diving down into one of those plumbs, and bringing up the body of a poor man who had just then been drowned. After the unfortunate individual's corpse had been brought on shore, the persons who took the charge of it, in place of quickly taking it into an adjacent house, or into Messrs Dalglish and Hutcheson's printfield works, and there endeavouring by the usual means to resuscitate it, they hurried away to the Calton, where the poor man had resided, and deposited the body with the members of his family. So much time was thereby lost, that all attempts to revive animality proved unsuccessful. I afterwards learned that he was an operative shoemaker. One of the plumbs was known by the name of the *Dominie's Hole.*

Towards the close of the 17th century, the Fleshers' Haugh appears to have been the property of Sir John Bell, who was lord provost of Glasgow in 1681; and it came to be called Provost Haugh in honour of his lordship the provost. This haugh was purchased by the magistrates and town council of Glasgow in 1792, from Patrick Bell, Esq. of Cowcaddens, and was then added to the Green of the city.

" *Glasgow Journal,* 1st May, 1792."—" The Provost Haugh has just been purchased at private sale for no less than *four thousand pounds.* It consists of about twenty-four acres.

" This, added to the other pleasure ground along the river, belonging to the city, is a valuable acquisition. The philanthropic Mr

Howard, when surveying this tract of ground, declared it to be of inestimable value for preserving the health of the inhabitants.

" An acre of ground down the river, where the coal key stood, and bounded by the Kinning House burn, was sold by public roup, last week, for £350 sterling. It was let for £5 yearly for sixteen years past."

In the year 1770, Mr M'Lean, a Baptist elder or minister, came to Glasgow, and baptized Mary Monro, wife of Neil Stewart, a wright, in the river Clyde, at the Fleshers' Haugh. She was the first person in Glasgow who received baptism by immersion in the river Clyde.

In 1776 a small congregation of Baptists was formed in Glasgow, the entrants to which religious society were also usually baptized in the river, at the west end of the Fleshers' Haugh, where there was a fine shallow sandy shore gradually deepening to the centre of the stream. This place was very seldom used by bathers, who preferred the east end of the haugh as more suitable for natation ; they never disturbed or gave offence to the Baptists during the performance of their religious rites in the river Clyde.

At this time the eastern portion of the Green or King's Park was bounded by a stone wall, along the west side of which there ran a carriage road leading from Bridgeton and Barrowfield to the Fleshers' Haugh ; this road, however, was merely a country highway, and was little used.

CHAPTER XII.

Opening up of Duke Street—Glasgow Police in 1788, and measures of the Magistrates for regulation of the City—Improvements in the City—St Andrew's Church—Eaglesholm Croft—Dispute about electing a Seventh Minister for Glasgow—Dr Porteous—The "Long Stairs"—The "hanging stair" in the Tontine—Weavers' Riots—The Town Herds.

In the year 1792, when the magistrates and town council of Glasgow purchased the Fleshers' Haugh, they also, in the same year, projected a great improvement to the eastern parts of Glasgow, by issuing proposals for opening up and constructing a splendid approach to the city from the east, which came to be called "Duke Street," in honour of his Royal Highness the Duke of York, then commander-in-chief of the British army.

" *Glasgow Mercury*, 6th November, 1792."—" By authority of the Sheriff of Lanarkshire, the magistrates and town council of Glasgow having, in virtue of an Act passed in the last session of Parliament for opening and making certain streets in and near the City of Glasgow, preferred a petition to the said sheriff against the persons after-named, viz.—William Anderson, tanner and merchant in Glasgow ; David Perston, manufacturer, there ; James Brown, merchant, there, trustee on the sequestrated estate of the late William Brown, glover, there ; Miss Janet Boreland, residing in Charlotte Street, there; Misses Janet and Grizel Pettigrews, in High Street, there ; —— Murray, widow of the late Mr Hercules Lindsay, professor of law in the College of Glasgow ; James Kerr, son and heir of the deceased Mr John Kerr, late minister of the gospel at Belziehill ; the Rev. Mr —— Jameson, minister of the Associated congregation in Havannah Street, as representing the said congregation, and residing in Anderston, and tenant of the said James Kerr's property ; William Dunn, wheel-wright in Glasgow ; George Woodburn, wright in High Street, there ; Marion Miller, widow of John Freeland, late huntsman, there ; John Taylor, son of the deceased William Taylor, residing at Barrowfield Bridge ; John Colquhoun, son of the deceased John Colquhoun, residing in St Enoch's Wynd of Glasgow ; Alexander Stewart, son and heir of the deceased

William Stewart, gardener in Glasgow—proprietors or reputed proprietors or occupiers of certain lands and tenements, the areas of which will be occupied by an intended street mentioned in the said Act, to run from the road which leads from Carntyne road to the Drygate Bridge, at or near the house belonging to the late John Anderson, butcher, till it join the High Street of the said city, at or near the tenement on the east side belonging to or reputed to belong to William Robertson, farmer and meal dealer, and Robert Kay of Glins, or at or near the tenement belonging to Alexander Baird, farmer ; and also by another intended street from the west side of the said High Street, at or near the tenement belonging to the heirs of James Millar, late visitor of the maltmen in Glasgow, or at or near the tenement formerly belonging to John Maitland, now in the possession of Michael Bogle and Alexander Gardner, to run in a straight line till it join Duke Street in the said city, on account of the said persons having refused or neglected to treat, or contract for the purchase of the said lands after previous due requisition as prescribed by the said Act ; and, therefore, praying his lordship to fix and ascertain the just amount and value of the said lands by a jury in terms of the statute. His Lordship, the sheriff-substitute, upon receiving the said petition upon the 29th day of October last, ordered notice thereof to be given by proper advertisements in all the Glasgow newspapers, which is now accordingly given, and to which all parties having interest are hereby required to attend.— Glasgow, 1st November, 1792."

At this time (1792) the affairs of police, including the forming and causewaying of the public streets of the city, were under the sole management of the magistrates and council, and supported from the funds of the corporation.

In 1788, the magistrates and council, being anxious to have an established police in Glasgow, but at the same time being unwilling to relinquish any portion of their control or power of management of city affairs, appointed Richard Marshall, one of their own clique, to the office of intendent of police, with a large salary, and then applied for an Act of Parliament to assess the inhabitants to defray the necessary expenses of the establishment ; but as the public were to have had no voice in the election of the police master, or in the choice of the ward commissioners, a general outcry of the citizens arose against the scheme, and a powerful opposition was formed to defeat the measure in Parliament, in consequence of which the bill was lost. The general watch-word then passed from mouth to mouth in Glasgow was that the whole affair in reality was merely a sly scheme of the magistrates to provide a snug situation for their friend, " Dickie Marshall," as he was called. Although Richard Marshall thus lost the situation of police master, he was soon after comforted as to dignity, by being elected a bailie of Glasgow, and when the barracks were built in 1795, he found a pecuniary compensation for his disappointment by obtaining the situation of barrack master, which office the public generally believed was gotten through city influence.

There can be no doubt, however, that, from the great increase of the city, a regular police establishment had then become necessary to preserve the safety and comfort of the inhabitants. This is shown by the following advertisement of the magistrates and town council, which clearly exhibits the loose manner in which the town regulations and government of the city were then kept; a few red coat officers acting as the only police guardians of the city, which, at that time, contained a population of upwards of 60,000 inhabitants.

" *Glasgow Mercury*, 22d March, 1781."—" By the magistrates of Glasgow."—" Whereas it is of great consequence that every regulation calculated to improve the police of the city should be adopted, and that at the same time every irregularity injurious to the inhabitants should be suppressed and prevented. The magistrates hereby give notice, recommend, and enjoin what follows, viz :—

" That all proprietors of houses in this city shall, as soon as the season will admit, remove all water-barges, and fix and erect rones and pipes for the purpose of conveying the water from the eaves of their respective buildings, so constructed as to prevent loose slates from falling upon the streets; and it is recommended to those of the inhabitants who have already conveyed down their water in this manner that they will cause their pipes to be lengthened so as to prevent inconvenience to the public in rainy weather.

" That all proprietors of houses or lands do give strict orders that the flags opposite to their respective properties be regularly cleaned every morning, that so this valuable improvement may not be rendered useless to the inhabitants.*

" That all persons using ladders for repairing houses shall remove

---

* In 1778, Mr John Wilsone, who kept an ironmonger's shop under Hutchesons' Hospital in the Trongate, laid a flagstone pavement in front of his shop, which was the first improvement of the kind in the Trongate. (Mr Wilsone was a brother of Dr Charles Wilsone.)

the same every evening before sunset, and no mason or slater, or any person working on the roofs of the houses in this city, shall throw over rubbish of any kind without keeping a person as a watch to prevent danger to the inhabitants.

" That the person or persons having property in dunghills in the closes opposite to which the dung of the street is laid down, shall remove the same in twelve hours after it is collected by the scavengers, and no dung going to the country will be suffered to remain on the street after sunset on any pretence whatever.

" That all boys shall be discharged by their parents and masters from playing tops, shinty, or using any diversion whatever upon the flags that may be incommodious to the inhabitants; they are likewise discharged from playing shinty in the Green.

" That no person shall shake carpets, or throw water or nastiness over any of the windows of this city.

" That all boys, or others, who shall be detected, at any time, throwing stones, making bonfires, crying for illuminations, or attempting to make any disturbance on the streets of this city, calculated to endanger the public peace, shall be punished with the utmost severity. On all such occasions parents and masters are to be accountable for their children or apprentices, and a reward is hereby offered of Five Pounds sterling to any person who shall detect or discover boys, or others, guilty of these practices, to be paid on conviction of the offenders.

" That all parents and masters shall do their utmost to prevent their children and apprentices from going about in an idle manner on Sunday, and particularly from appearing in the streets or closes during Divine service, the magistrates being determined to punish all such offenders in the most exemplary manner.

" That as the poor who have a right to the charity of the city are amply provided for, it is earnestly recommended to the inhabitants to give their assistance in suppressing and discouraging vagrant and public beggars.

" That no carter shall, on any pretence, presume to ride upon his cart, or to drive hard through the avenues or streets of this city. And as many accidents have happened through the carelessness of carters, particularly on the road leading from the canal, the magistrates hereby order and direct all carters to lead their horses short by the head, and it is earnestly recommended to the inhabitants to give information of the names of all who shall offend in this particular; that practices so dangerous to the public may be prevented, by punishing the guilty in an exemplary manner.

"That all carters employed in carrying goods to and from the canal* shall not load above one ton weight of grain, or any other goods upon the cart, unless the wheels are six inches broad ; and the magistrates recommend it to the inhabitants to pay only according to this regulation, and to inform against all offenders.

" That all horses going to water shall on no pretence be rode hard, nor shall any person be permitted to gallop through the streets or avenues of this city.

" That no persons having charge of buildings shall lay down stones upon the pavement at the side of the street allotted for the inhabitants, nor shall any person be permitted to slack lime upon any of the streets of this city.

" That in all time coming, the practice of selling salmon by the hand shall be discontinued, and no person shall be permitted to sell in any other manner than by weight.

" Notice is hereby given, that there is lodged in the clerk's chamber, a quantity of stolen goods not yet claimed. If no person or persons appear to claim their property, on or before the first day of April, the whole will be sold for the use of the poor of the Town's Hospital."

In May, 1785, the magistrates advertised that " They had got an " offer made to them for keeping the streets of the city clean, and " to gather, and carry off the whole dung and rubbish lying upon " the said streets, provided the offerer should have the property of " the dung." The magistrates accordingly advertised that they were ready to make an agreement of the kind, and " will prefer the " person who shall undertake to perform the work upon the most " reasonable terms, and find security for performing his part of " the agreement."

In the year 1768, the magistrates and town council of Glasgow obtained an Act of Parliament to make certain improvements in the city, the preamble to which states as follows:—

" Anno Octavo, Geo. III. Regis."—" Whereas, by the great increase of inhabitants in the city of Glasgow, an additional church became necessary, which the magistrates and council of the said city have, at a considerable expense, erected and built accordingly,

---

* It is curious to observe that no mention is here made of any traffic being carried on from the Broomielaw to the city, now the most extensive carriage way of Glasgow.

and it is called, or known by the name of St Andrew's Church. And whereas, it is further necessary, for the use and benefit of the inhabitants of the said city, and of others resorting to the said church, that there should not only be a proper and commodious passage to the same, by and from the street called the Saltmarket Street, but also that the area or church-yard, of the said church, should be free and open. And, whereas, the said magistrates and city council, have also, at a considerable expense, erected and built a Town Hall, on the west side of the Tolbooth, near the Cross of Glasgow, and it would be of great advantage to the said city to have an Exchange or Square, near the said Town Hall, for the use and resort of merchants and others. For which purpose the said magistrates have purchased several old houses and areas, on the north side of the said Town Hall and Tolbooth ; but the premises so purchased are not sufficient for building the said exchange or square. And, whereas, those works so necessary for the conveniency and advantage of the said city, and of all persons resorting thereto, cannot be carried out into execution without the aid of Parliament. Therefore, upon the petition of the magistrates and council of the said city of Glasgow, on behalf of themselves and the community of the said city, Be it enacted, by the King's most excellent Majesty, by and with the advice and consent of the Lords Spiritual and Temporal, and Commons in this present Parliament assembled, and by the authority of the same, that it shall and may be lawful for the magistrates and city council of Glasgow, and their successors, by themselves, their deputies, agents, workmen and servants, and they are hereby empowered and authorised to make and complete a convenient passage or street, from the said street called the Salt-market Street, to the said new church called St Andrew's Church, not exceeding seventy feet in breadth, as also to open and complete the area or church-yard of the said church ; and likewise to make, erect, build and complete a commodious Exchange or Square upon the north side of the said Town Hall and Tolbooth."

" And be it further enacted, that the said magistrates and council, and their successors, shall also have full power and authority to treat and agree with the owners and occupiers of the small slip of land belonging to, or reported to belong to Janet Smith, daughter of the deceased Thomas Smith, late writer in Edinburgh, containing 3 roods, 24 falls, and 16 yards of ground or thereabout, in measure, on the south side of the said St Andrew's Church, and bounded by the town of Glasgow's ground on the north, of the said Janet

Smith on the south and east, and by the Molendinar burn on the west parts; as also that little yard belonging to, or reported to belong to Alexander Spiers, Peter Murdoch, Thomas Buchanan, James Dougal, and partners of the hat factory in Glasgow, and to John Blair, merchant there, —— Alexander, widow of George Blackwell, late minister of Bathgate, measuring 16 falls, and 24 yards, or thereabout, bounded by the ground belonging to the town of Glasgow on the south and east, and by the Molendinar burn on the north and west parts; and after payment of such sum or sums of money, as shall be agreed on between the said magistrates and city council, and the owners or occupiers respectively, for the purchase of the said respective premises, to lay out and include the same or so much thereof as shall be thought necessary, into the said area or church-yard, in such manner as they shall think fit."

By referring to the Plan annexed to the present jottings, the different properties adjoining St Andrew's Church, which the magistrates sought to obtain, by the above Act of Parliament, will be seen. The Plan was drawn up in 1760, and the Act was passed in 1768. From the following notices it appears that an alteration had taken place in the entry from Saltmarket Street to St Andrew's Church, shortly before the above dates, by the demolishment of several old houses, which appear to have stood upon the vacant space (shown in the Plan) in the " Weel Close."

" *Glasgow Journal*, 28th February, 1757.—To be sold, a parcel of stones, timber, and slates, being the materials of some old houses, belonging to the heirs of the deceased Bailie James Glen, as they lie in the new street leading to the new church in Saltmarket. Any who inclines to purchase them, may apply to George Anderson, merchant in Glasgow."*

It appears from the Plan that the ancient entry to the land around St Andrew's Square was called the " *Weel Closs*." At the eastern extremity of this close there was a bridge over the Molen-

---

* " *Glasgow Journal*, 11th October, 1756.—Notice—That the stone, timber, lead, glasswork, iron, and whole other materials of the old guard house, and of the old houses and lands, or Well Close, on the east side of the Saltmarket, belonging to the town of Glasgow, upon the last Wednesday of October, inst., between the hours of 12 and 2 afternoon. As also the whole small yearly feu duties, within and belonging to the town, under forty shillings steg., are to be sold, by public roup, within the said time and place. Those who incline to purchase may inquire at William Weir, writer, or Arthur Robertson, chamberlain."

dinar burn, apparently wider than the Gallowgate Bridge; so that
this place was probably at one time resorted to by the citizens for
the purpose of drawing water from the Molendinar burn, or for
washings—the waste ground in front of St Andrew's Church being
very suitable for bleaching and drying clothes, and, judging from
the Plan, quite open to the public.

I must leave it to our antiquarian denizens to give us the derivation of the word "*weel.*" Jamieson and Bailey say : "Weel, wele,
wiel—a small whirlpool or eddy ;" and it is probable that there was
a small whirlpool or eddy at the spot where the bridge crossed the
Molendinar.

The following advertisement, I presume, refers to the oblong (or
long square) tenement shown in the Plan, as situated near the
bottom of the present Charlotte Street ; but I can give no account
of the extent of Eaglesholm Croft.

"*Glasgow Mercury*, 3d May, 1781."—"To be sold, that large
" garden, and house and byre built thereupon, lying in the territory
" of the burgh of Glasgow, in that part thereof called Eaglesholm
" Croft, containing about an acre and three roods of ground, as
" presently possessed by Duncan M'Arthur, gardener. The above
" garden adjoins the St Andrew's Church and Merkdailly grounds,
" fronts the Green of Glasgow, and is pleasantly situated for build-
" ing upon. To accommodate purchasers, the price will be allowed
" to remain in their hands for some time. For further particulars,
" apply to Patrick Robertson, writer in Glasgow, who will show a
" plan of the ground."

I am inclined to think that the garden of the late David
Dale, Esq., formed part of Eaglesholm Croft above alluded
to, but I cannot speak on the subject with any degree of
certainty.

"*Glasgow Mercury*, 24th February, 1780."—"To be sold, a
" house lying at the head of the first close east from the Gallowgate
" Bridge, on the south side of the street, consisting of two storeys
" and a garret, with a cellar, and a large fruit garden on the south
" side of the said house ; with two small brick houses adjacent
" thereto, and a piece of waste ground on both sides of the same,
" as the said subjects were lately possessed by the deceased Alex-
" ander Hutcheson and his sub-tenants. This lot is pleasantly
" situated between Merkdailly's yard and St Andrew's church-yard.
" Also, another house lying near to the said house, with a bakehouse
" and oven thereto belonging, as at present possessed by William

" Fleming, baker, and others, Apply to Charles Hutcheson, book-
" seller in Glasgow." *

The building of St Andrew's Square was commenced in 1787, as
is shown in the following notice, and in a short space of time thereafter it was completed.

"*Glasgow Mercury*, 14th February, 1787."—"To be sold, sundry
" steadings for houses in St Andrew's Square. The plan of the
" Square and the regulations for building are to be seen in the
" hands of the town clerks of Glasgow, to whom persons intending
" to purchase are desired to apply."

On the 23d of April, 1739, the magistrates and town council of
Glasgow agreed to build St Andrew's Church upon the yeard purchased from Patrick Bell and others, which yeard is represented as
having been a church yeard; but I doubt if it ever was used as a
public cemetery, although it may have been a yeard attached to
some religious institution.

I am not aware of there having been discovered any graves or
relics of the dead whilst the foundations of the church or of those
of the buildings which now form the Square were excavating.

There formerly stood a religious institution in the Gallowgate,
and the said yeard possibly might have been the property of that
institution; but I can give no authority on the subject.†

The erection of St Andrew's Church was begun in the year 1740,
but was not finished till 1762. This long delay in executing the
completion of the church was said to have been caused by the want
of funds; and I have heard it said in my younger days that it ultimately became necessary for the city of Glasgow to sell the feus of

* At this time the ground around St Andrew's Church had been shut up from public
access by the erection of a high iron gate across the whole breadth of the Weel Close,
at its eastern extremity, next the bridge; and the Weel Close then received the name
of St Andrew's Street. When divine service came to be performed in St Andrew's
Church on Sundays and other public occasions, this gate was allowed to remain open;
but it was carefully kept locked on ordinary week days. When St Andrew's Square
was advertised to be formed, the iron gate was removed; and about the year 1800, the
post office was brought to St Andrew's Street. (M'Ure, in 1736, calls the Weel Close
Bakers' Wynd, at page 155.)

† I have seen no written authority of there ever having been any church in St
Andrew's Square before the present church was built. The ground there formed part
of the Eaglesholm (or Eagleshoam)* Croft, and was called of old "Luke's Ayle," and
then "Bell's Park," the magistrates having purchased the said ground from Patrick
Bell. Had this "church-yard," as it was called, been formerly occupied as a cemetery,
some remains of the dead would certainly have been found in the course of erecting the
houses of the Square.

    * "Holm, or Hoam—the level low ground on the banks of a river."—*Jamieson.*

the Barony of Provan, and the superiority thereof, in order to liqui-
date the debts incurred for building the said church.* The public
have never been informed of the exact cost of building St Andrew's
Church, but it has been generally estimated to have been upwards of
£20,000; and some allege that it has caused an expense to the city
of £30,000.

On the 23d of March, 1762, "the magistrates and town council
of Glasgow having thought proper to build a new church, which is
now finished, whereby there are now seven churches and only six
ministers in the city, and consequently a seventh minister is wanted
for one or other of the churches; and further considering that the
settling of a seventh minister, and endowing him with a suitable
stipend out of the town's revenue, will be a public benefit, they
resolve accordingly." (Council Records.)

This resolution of the magistrates and council caused a great
ferment among the city clergymen, who claimed a right to have a
voice in the election of the seventh minister, according to what they
said was use and wont; and for gaining their end, they agitated
among all ranks of the citizens to oppose the alleged prerogative of
the city authorities.

The following pretty sharp notice appeared in the *Glasgow Journal*
of 17th February, 1763:

"Glasgow. The General Session being met and constitute; the
moderator having informed the general session that he had called
them together at the desire of their committee, who had prepared a
report to be laid before them : the session approve of their being
called for this purpose, and the committee gave in their report in
writing. The tenor whereof follows :—

"We understand that our business as a committee to transact
with the council committee is now at an end, therefore think it our
duty without delay to report to the general session that there has
been a meeting of the town council the 10th current, at which were
produced the opinions of a numerous subscription of trades and
burgesses and inhabitants of this place, as also the opinion of ten of
the incorporations, relating to the two plans published by order of

* "*Glasgow Journal*, 25th December, 1766.—To be sold, the feu-duties and superi-
"orities of the twenty pound land, of old extent, of Provan, lying in the Barronry parish
"of Glasgow and sheriffdom of Lanark, held feu by the magistrates and town council of
"Glasgow off the Crown. Four of the lots are each of them above £400 of valuation,
"as now divided in the cess books. Progress of writs, rental, and condition of roup to
"be seen in the hands of the town clerks. 25th Dec., 1766."

the council on the one hand and of the general session on the other,
for the information of the inhabitants, which papers by the ten incorporations were not suffered to be read, although no other cause can
be assigned why the council published their plan, and allowed ten
days to intervene, but that the sentiments of the inhabitants might
be gathered and laid before them ; and we are sorry that we can
also report, that at said meeting of council the following two votes
were carried—

" 1st. That they approve of the aforesaid plan, which entirely
excludes the general session from any share in the election and calling of ministers to this city, and ordered it to be inserted in their books
as the rule for calling ministers, in room of the model 1721 years.

" 2d. They ordered the process to be insisted in for obtaining a
declarator of patronage for the seventh kirk, and that the clerk
should write the town's agent at Edinburgh first post to that effect,
even before any plan for settling it is agreed upon.

" And we have further to report, that a prevailing party in the
council urged the above precipitate and arbitrary steps in opposition
to the chief magistrate (Provost Ingram), who protested against
them, and was adhered to by another of the present magistrates,
and five more of the town council.

" The general session having heard with great concern the above
report, cannot help expressing their surprise at such unprecedented
and arbitrary measures, by which an attempt is made wholly to
deprive the session of this burgh of the right which they have in
the calling of ministers, which is confirmed to them by the law of
the land, and which they have hitherto enjoyed without molestation
ever since presbytery was established in Scotland ; by which also
the religious liberties of the inhabitants have been trampled upon,
their ancient model for settling ministers abolished, and an utter
contempt shown to their judgment in the whole matter of calling
their ministers.

" The session do not choose to enlarge upon the provocation
which they and the inhabitants in general have received from the
imprudence and violence of a certain party in the council ; at the
same time, they have a most grateful sense of the noble stand which
has been made for the liberty and peace of this city by the chief
magistrate and those who adhered to him.

" The general session having done what they could to preserve
peace, and having made many concessions for that purpose in vain,
find they are now obliged to defend themselves at law.

" And the general session hereby retract all the concessions which they have made formerly for peace sake, by themselves or their committee, and declare their adherence to the model 1721.

" They also appoint that extracts of this resolution be transmitted to the Merchants' House, and to the several incorporations of the city, and to be inserted in the newspapers.

" Extracted out of the General Session books by

" Matthew Bogle, session clerk."

Shortly after this pithy remonstrance had issued from the press, viz., on the 16th of March, 1763, the magistrates and town council elected Dr William Craig (father of Lord Craig), then officiating as minister in the Wynd Church of Glasgow, to be minister of St Andrew's Church. At this time Dr Craig had been pastor of the congregation of the Wynd Church for twenty-five years, having been admitted to that charge in 1738. Most of Dr Craig's congregation followed him to St Andrew's Church.

The Wynd Church appears to have stood vacant for some time after the translation of Dr Craig to St Andrew's Church, and again a contest arose between the Glasgow Session and the city authorities, when the election of a minister for the charge of the Wynd Church came to be made by the magistrates and town council, as the following extract shows :—

" *Glasgow Journal*, 2d February, 1764.—Yesterday (1st February), the Presbytery of Glasgow met here, and had under consideration the settlement of the Wynd Church, when, after long reasonings, the question was put—' Sustain the magistrates and council of Glasgow's presentation or not ;' it carried not; on which the magistrates entered an appeal to next Synod."

It was not till 1766 that the Reverend George Bannatyne, the nominee of the magistrates and council, was admitted to the pastoral charge of the Wynd Church.

The next minister of the Wynd Church was the celebrated Dr William Porteous. He was ordained at Whitburn, 10th of June, 1760, and admitted in Glasgow, 28th June, 1770 ; for 40 years he was the great clerical leader of the west. The Wynd Church congregation was translated to St George's Church in 1807, and the church which was built in 1687, was then abandoned. (Dr Porteous lived in Moodie's Wynd, in a house of ten apartments.)

The architrave in front of St Andrew's Church has been spoken of as one of the wonders of architecture, and has been represented as a long flat arch spanning the whole breadth of the church; but this architrave consists of five separate flat arches, with a key stone in the centre of each. These arches are placed between the columns, and, in fact, make a stronger support than one formed from a single stone. A fine specimen of this style of building may be seen in the lintels of the shop windows of the tenement at the corner of the Cross, which are so formed as to be quite explanatory of the mystery of the so-called flat arch. Mr David Hamilton was the architect of this tenement, which was built by Dr Cleland on the site of the Jail.

There was a curious old building in the Gallowgate, near the Cross, which stood as next tenement to the Trades' Land, head of the Saltmarket; it was called the "Long Stairs," on account of its having two outside stairs to the floor above the street, one of them on the east, and the other on the west, with a wooden platform or open gallery between the said stairs. From this gallery there were entrances to the upper flats of the tenement.

It was a favourite frolic for boys to make this place a sort of race-course or play-ground by chasing one another up one stair then along the gallery, and down the other stair. There were no police officers in those days to interrupt these amusements, and the place itself was the lounging resort of all idle blackguards. Behind the said "Long Stairs" there was an extensive close, running directly down to the Molendinar burn. (See the Plan.) This close was the Tontine Close of olden time, and was the den of thieves and prosti-tutes; luckily for the public it was accidentally consumed by fire, although many persons believed that the fire was occasioned by an act of wanton mischief.

"*Glasgow Mercury*, 30th October, 1792.—Yesterday (29th) evening, about six o'clock, an alarming fire broke out in that land near the Cross, called the "Long Stairs." It raged with alarming rapidity, and threatened destruction to the Trades' Land and a number of houses backwards. The fire for some time baffled every effort used for extinguishing it, and spread terror and dismay among the people who inhabited the houses adjoining; but by a steady perseverance of the people who had the direction of the water engines it was got under by ten o'clock at night, but the rubbish continued burning, and the engines, with a proper guard, remained all night. About seven this morning it appeared to be gaining head, and the alarm was given, but no bad consequences ensued. This alarming fire was occasioned by one of the bravoes, who frequent

houses of bad fame, throwing a bottle of rum into the chimney of a
bawdy-house, which set fire to some linens that were drying at the
fire. The tenement is rendered untenantable, with an adjoining
back land. Little of the furniture was saved. The premises were
insured in the Sun Fire Office."

In 1768 the magistrates of Glasgow obtained an Act of Parliament
(8th Geo. III.) in which they state—"That it would be of great
" advantage to the city to have an Exchange or Square near the
" Town Hall, for which purpose the magistrates have purchased
" several old houses and areas on the north side of the said hall and
" Tolbooth, but the premises are not sufficient for building the said
" Exchange or Square." They, therefore, sought Parliamentary
powers to make additional purchases, and the following property
appears to have been one of them :—

" *Glasgow Mercury*, 17th March, 1785."—" Sale of houses."—
" To be sold, by public roup, &c., these two back tenements of land,
" lying behind the Tontine Coffee House of Glasgow, and upon the
" common passage between the Trongate Street and Bell's Wynd to
" the east of the Exchange, to which there is also an entry from the
" High Street above the Cross, as the said subjects are possessed by
" Mrs Reid, change keeper, James Cullen, silversmith, and others.
" Apply to John Wilson, jun., writer, Glasgow."

To which, shortly afterwards, was added, as follows :—
" *Glasgow Mercury*, 26th September, 1787."—*Notice.*"
" That the stones, timber, and slates, and whole other materials
of that tenement of land called ' Legat's Back Tenement,' lying at
the back of the clerk's chamber of Glasgow, and on the east side of
the Tontine, are to be sold by public roup, within the Laigh Council
Chamber of Glasgow, upon Wednesday, the 3d of October next,
between the hours of 1 and 2 of that day. Apply to the town
clerks of Glasgow."

These properties came to form a principal part of the back court
behind the Tontine Hotel, and likewise on their site were built the
Sugar sample room, and the large back tenement at present occupied
by the Messrs Cross and others. The back tenement was originally
built for the greater accommodation and extension of the Tontine
Hotel, and was used by the late Mr Smart as a suite of bed rooms
in addition to those of the hotel itself.

In the *Glasgow Mercury* of 12th September, 1787, we find the
following passage regarding the Tontine—" About two o'clock on
Wednesday morning the upper flight of steps of the *hanging stairs*

leading to the Assembly room in the Tontine Buildings fell and
broke the under flight. The goodness of providence was very conspicuous on that occasion. One of the patroles was just returned
from going their round, and about taking the stair to go up to the
hall where the citizens of the guard staid, when the captain of
patrole ordered the roll to be called, during which the stair fell, and
struck them with astonishment, and with gratitude to their omnipotent
preserver; for had they been on the stair they could not have escaped
being crushed to death." It was at this time that a riot had taken
place in Glasgow among the weavers, in consequence of the prices of
weaving having been lowered, and three men had been shot by the
military in the course of quelling the said riot, on the Monday before
the stairs fell. A company of the 56th regiment had arrived from
Ayr to assist the 39th regiment in preserving the peace of the city,
and there happening to be a want of bed accommodation at the
time in Glasgow for the military party so suddenly arrived, temporary bedding had been laid underneath the hanging stair two
nights before the accident happened, and some of the soldiers of the
56th regiment had slept there on the Monday night unconscious of
the danger which had been pending over them. The hanging stair
which fell was a remarkably fine structure, and was greatly admired
for its architectural beauty ; it was immediately replaced by the
present stair which leads up to the Tontine Hotel from the court
under the piazzas.

The herd's house shown on the Plan, was situated near the site of
the present Nelson's Monument ; but in my early days it was not
in the occupation or under the charge of a herd; but was used
by the golfers, as a depot for holding their clubs and balls, when no
play was going on. There was an attendant, however, who took
charge of the said golfers' clubs and balls, and received a per-
quisite from them for his care and attention in so doing; a great
proportion of the players, nevertheless, preferred carrying their
clubs and balls to their own homes, after having finished their
sport, thereby saving the payment of a fee to the attendant of the
place.

Of old the fees of the herds of the Green appear to have been
very trifling, as the following notice shows.

" Burgh Records, 14th October, 1578. Item, eodem gevin to
" Thomas Tempilltoun and Petir Aikin, hirdis, for pouertie and
" almous because yai gat na fee, xl.."

The herds of the Green must have been old decrepit men, quite unfit for ordinary manual labour, as the fees of the office amounted to no more than the pittance of a mere charitable offering.

" Burgh Records, 26th May, 1579. Matho Wilson is maid and constitut calfhird, quha hes fund Patrik Bell cautione for administratioun in his office, and is ordanit to have vi.ᵈ for ilk calf, and his meit daylie about or ellis xii.ᵈ for ilk melte ᵗ.* gif yai failye and to be poyndit y.ᵣfor." It may be here remarked that a Scotch penny is one-eleventh of an English penny, so that the herd received only about one halfpenny English, for each calf, and about one penny for each *melte ᵗ*. Supposing the word melte ᵗ. above used, to mean a meal, we learn by it that in the reign of James VI., (1579) a meal for a working man was valued at or about one penny English.

* Jamieson says, " Melteth," 1st, "The quantity of milk yielded by a cow at one time;" 2d, " A meal."

CHAPTER XIII.

Humane Society House founded in 1790—Nelson's Monument—The Great Storm of 1810—Arns Well—The Slaughter House and Regulations thereanent—Markets in 1744—Queen Mary in Glasgow with Darnley—Lamplighting in 1792—The Glasgow Streets in 1560—Saracen's Head Inn—Causewaying in Glasgow in 1578.

THE Humane Society House is situated in the High Green, a little to the east of the Arns Well. It was founded in 1790. Mr Coulter, a merchant in Glasgow, commenced this institution by a donation of £500, and the residue of the funds was raised by subscription. The following is a notice of the first meeting of its members.

" *Glasgow Mercury*, 17th August, 1790. The Humane Society of Glasgow met yesterday, (16th) in the Tontine Tavern, for the first time, and elected the following gentlmen, viz., Gilbert Hamilton, Esq., president, Dr Robert Cleghorn, secretary, Mr Robert Simpson, treasurer, Dr Thomas Reid, Messrs William Craig, David Dale, and Gilbert Shearer, annual directors, and Mr Lawrence Coulter, (to whose brother the society owes its origin) extraordinary director. The society adopted a number of regulations calculated to ensure success to their exertions, and agreed to meet four times a year. Although out of fifty subscription papers, only eight were returned, yet the sums subscribed in these eight amounted to £83 12s 6d. That much more will be procured we have no doubt."

Nelson's Monument, situated in the High Green of Glasgow, was erected in 1806, by public subscription, at an expense of upwards of £2000. The foundations of this towering obelisk were laid on the 1st of August, 1806, being the anniversary of the battle of Aboukir. It is 144 feet in height, including the pedestal, and is fenced in by a handsome iron railing, to protect it from the mischievous depredations of boys and idlers.

This elegant structure is, unfortunately, situated too near the numerous smoking brick stalks of our wide spread factories, which, from their near resemblance of form to an obelisk, tends greatly to lessen the effect of this graceful cenotaph, erected by our citizens to the greatest naval hero of Britain.

In 1810, Glasgow was visited with one of the most tremendous storms of lightning, thunder and rain, that ever was known to have taken place there, in the memory of its oldest inhabitants. I remember this storm very well, and remained at home on the Sunday when it occurred, watching with great interest the effects of every vivid flash of lightning, and the instant thunder peal, which succeeded each electric stream of light; in particular, just before sitting down to dinner, a little after four o'clock, while I was standing with my face to the window, observing the scene, there occurred the most vivid flash and instant tremendous thunder clap of the storm. It was this thunder bolt which struck Nelson's Monument and rent it nearly from top to bottom, as the following account shows.

" Scots Magazine, 1810, August,—page 633."

" Glasgow 6th August, 1810."—" On Sunday afternoon (5th) we had a most violent storm of thunder and lightning, accompanied by excessively heavy rain. About a quarter past four the lightning struck the top of Lord Nelson's Monument, and we regret to say that it has most materially injured that elegant structure. On the north side, the column is torn open for more than twenty feet from the top, and several of the stones have been thrown down. On the west side the effects of the destructive fluid are visible in more than one place; and on the south side there is a rent in the column, as far down as the head of the pedestal. A number of the stones are hanging in such a threatening posture that a military guard has very properly been placed around the monument to keep, at a distance, the thoughtless or too daring spectators."

Shortly before this happened the Royal Infirmary had been struck by the lightning of the same storm.

" Glasgow, 5th August, Royal Infirmary."—" Sunday, near two o'clock, while the physicians were going their rounds, there was a violent thunder clap, without any perceptible interval between the flash and the stroke, which seemed to shake the Infirmary. All the chimneys were affected, but particularly the western. The lowest of the women's wards, where the writer of this was, exhibited a very awful appearance. During four or six seconds all the flame was suddenly drawn into the wards with a rustling noise, together with a dense column of soot and smoke, which instantly filled the ward. Fortunately, no person was hurt; but the patients screamed aloud, and such as could rise ran from their beds. Similar appearances, though in different degrees, took place through the whole house, which seems to have been enveloped in a thunder cloud, and which may probably have owed its preservation to the quantity of rain flowing from its roof. This occurrence, and the injury of Nelson's Monument, suggests the propriety of guarding every building much exposed, by thunder rods, which, when properly constructed, have never failed to prove a safeguard. The lightning also, a little past four o'clock, struck a house, of three storeys high, in Rottenrow Street. In the upper floor a window was shivered to pieces; in the second floor a kettle, which was on the fire, had its spout melted off; in the ground floor several children and their mother were sitting at the fire; the children's hair was much singed, and the mother was thrown a considerable distance; a hole, about an inch diameter, was made through the bottom of an oil lamp, which was standing on the chimney piece. The electric matter then went through a stone wall about nine inches thick, and struck a tin flagon on the opposite side of the room."

This storm extended throughout the whole south parts of Scotland, and north of England. At Ayr, Dumfries, Kilwinning, Carlisle, Newcastle, Whitehaven, and their respective neighbourhoods, it damaged various houses and public edifices, but, fortunately, no lives were lost, although several persons were slightly injured. At London, in the house of Mr Fraser, at Chelsea, the hailstones had fallen in such quantities into a back cellar, the door of which happened to be open, as to become a complete piece of solid ice, about eight feet in circumference and two feet in depth. In Westminster and Lambeth several houses were struck and injured; an old lady received a considerable shock, but was not severely hurt.

This was the most severe thunder-storm that has happened in Glasgow within my remembrance, and was more appalling than the great storm of the 9th of August, 1787. The Glasgow papers of the time thus commenced their reports of this great storm. "On the evening of Thursday, the 9th current, we had one of the most tremendous storms of thunder and lightning that has been known in this place." One of the strongest flashes struck a house in Finnieston; the lightning fell upon the middle chimney top, the stones of which broke through the roof of the house. It struck a woman to the floor, where she lay insensible for a considerable time. The stream appeared to have passed along the surface of her body; her skin and some of her clothes were burned. The lightning passed through her right leg, and tore her shoe to pieces. The joists were

P

split, the furniture scattered here and there; and after killing a rabbit in its passage, the fluid burst through the outer wall of the house, and sunk into the earth.

The Arns well, situated on the "brae-face" of that part of the Green which lies between the Humane Society House and Nelson's Monument, has been celebrated for ages as containing the finest spring water of any well in the city or suburbs, and its superior quality has again and again been tested by the analyzer, and proved to be one of the purest springs to be found anywhere.

In my early days the Arns well water was looked upon as a sort of dainty, and I have often heard a landlord of a feast, upon making the celebrated Glasgow cold rum punch, inform his guests, by way of commendation of his nectar, that it was made from Arns well water. In like manner, old ladies, in order to puff up the fine flavour of their tea, used to inform the company that the water had just been drawn from the Arns well.

I remember this well when it was merely an open running stream; but it afterwards was built into a neat drinking fountain, and access to it made commodious to the public, which had become necessary, as the road to it was through a spongy morass, well known to this day by the name of the "Peat-Bog."

As to the Jail and public offices, which were erected in 1810, at the western extremity of the Low Green of Glasgow, our local historians have given us so full an account of them that I have little to add to the information which they have handed down to us on the subject; but it may be here stated that these extensive buildings have been erected upon the site of the Skinners' Green (see Plan), between the Molendinar burn and the Slaughter House, a local position certainly not very favourable to the idea of our public offices resting on the land of Arabia the blessed.

Previous to the year 1744 there was no public Slaughter House in Glasgow, every butcher having a slaughter house of his own; but, in the course of the above year, the magistrates and council of the city built the Slaughter Houses on the side of the river Clyde, as shown in the two Plans herewith annexed. The stalls in these were let from time to time to the incorporation of fleshers for about ten years afterwards. It so happened, however, that at the expiry of the said ten years, some demur had taken place in the incorporation as to the expediency of continuing to rent these slaughter houses; in consequence of which the magistrates, as guardians of the public, threatened to prohibit slaughtering within burgh as a nuisance to the inhabitants. The fleshers, not choosing to slaughter without burgh, which they might have done, came into the terms of the magistrates; and upon this footing matters remained till the year 1755. The whole of this arrangement was reduced to form, and legal validity was given to it by an Act of Council, passed on the 8th December, 1755. Previous to this time the rent of the Slaughter House appears to have been £40 per annum.

"Council Records, 29th April, 1755."

"Accompt.—To rent of Slaughter House from Candlemas, 1752, "to Candlemas, 1753, £40 0s 0d."

By the arrangement of 1755, it was agreed that—"In case any " butcher or butchers shall presume to kill or slaughter their cattle " in anywhere else than their Slaughter Houses at the river side, they " shall be liable to a forfeiture of the carcases of the beast so killed " or slaughtered in any other place than the said Slaughter House " appointed for that purpose." And by another clause of the said arrangement, it was stipulated that—"The butchers and fleshers " shall pay the rents and duties therefore to the town of Glasgow " for the use of said markets and slaughter houses at the rates " following, viz.—For each head of black cattle, 6d sterling; for " every dozen of calves, sheep, or goats, 12d sterling; for every " dozen of lambs or kids, 6d sterling ; and for hogs or pigs in pro- " portion ; and that all country fleshers shall, for the use of the " market allotted to them, pay the double of the above rates ; and " ordered that the said rents be exacted and levied weekly from the " town and country butchers, viz., from the town fleshers upon " Saturday, 'weekly,' and from the country fleshers upon the " market days upon which they use and occupy the markets appointed " for them."

All questions between the magistrates and fleshers having been settled by the agreement of 1755, matters continued to go on with the utmost harmony between them until the year 1799, when the magistrates, by an Act of Council, assumed to themselves the power of augmenting the duties fixed in 1755, and this against the consent of the incorporation of fleshers. The fleshers opposed the said augmentation, in consequence of which a lengthened law suit took place between the parties before the Court of Session, which ended in their lordships of the court unanimously finding "that the " magistrates were positively barred by the agreement of 1755, " which was to be considered a definite settlement for regulating " the mutual rights of the parties."

Ever since there have been constant bickerings between the incorporation of fleshers and the magistrates of Glasgow, about some point or another, relative to the Slaughter House and stalls in the public markets, which it is unnecessary and would be tedious to discuss.

In the *Glasgow Mercury* of 11th November, 1779, the following notice from the magistrates was published.—" By the magistrates of Glasgow."—" Whereas the following regulations are necessary for the police of the town, the magistrates ordain intimation to be made in the public newspapers, and injoin all concerned to give obedience thereto as they will be answerable.—Regulations— All cattle for slaughter brought into this city must be driven agreeable to the following direction—

" The cattle that come in by the Stable Green Port must be driven down the Drygate, go from that by the old Gallowgate Toll-bar and Burnt Barns by the back of the Greendyke to the Slaughter House. Cattle coming from the eastward and by Rutherglen Bridge, to go also by the back of the Greendyke to the Slaughter House.

" Cattle coming by both bridges to be driven the shortest road to the Slaughter House.

" Cattle coming from the westward and by Cowcaddens Toll, to be driven down Jamaica Street and along Clyde Street to the Slaughter House.

" No cattle of any kind, upon any account whatever, to be driven through any part of the Town's royalty on Sunday; and if any cattle are hunted through the streets at any time, the owners as well as the drivers will be punished with the utmost rigour of law.

" No cattle of any kind, upon any account whatever, to be hung in any of the entries to the markets.

" Every master butcher must give in to the magistrates, between and Wednesday next, an exact list of the number and names of their servants, and of the exact number of dogs belonging to each of them; and they must depone to the verity of this report.

" The magistrates of this city having fitted up a market for country butchers in Bell's Wynd, the following regulations are to be observed: The market is to open on Wednesdays and Saturdays, and no other day ; and no butchers, residing in town, to be allowed to sell meat in it.

" Every person intending to have the benefit of this market, to apply for leave to the *Inspector of Police*, and subscribe the regula-tions. The market dues must be paid regularly to the tacksman.

No dogs are to be allowed in this market. Any butcher who attempts to bring bad or unwholesome meat, or to blow, or put webs on his meat, will have it confiscated, and be turned out of the market.

"No carcases of beef to be allowed in the market; and, therefore, it must be cut into quarters before it is brought there.

"All unsold meat to be removed at night, and the stalls left clean by the butchers who occupied them through the day.

"This market will be opened on Wednesday next, the 10th current, after which no butcher meat will be suffered to be sold in the Candleriggs market.

The Candleriggs market, after Tuesday next, is to be kept entirely for a potato market, after which day all potatoes are required to be carried there, as none will be allowed in the Fish market in King Street.—Glasgow, 4th November, 1779."

Previous to the notification of the above regulations, viz., on the 22d of April, 1779, the magistrates had advertised that they had appointed the old Fish market in the Candleriggs for country butchers, and ordained them to sell their meat there, and prohibited and discharged all persons from selling meat in the entry to the Wynd Church.

As the eastern portion of the Police buildings in Bell Street now occupies the site of the ancient Bell Street Flesh market, of old appropriated for the use of country fleshers, the following declaration of a witness who was examined in a process relative to the said market in 1811, may perhaps prove interesting to many of our old citizens.

"Glasgow, 9th January, 1811.—Agnes Reid, widow of John
" Haines, labourer in Glasgow, aged about 80 (say born about 1731),
" who being solemnly sworn and interrogated, depones—That she
" was born in Bell's Wynd, and her father was a butcher in Glas-
" gow, and the deponent has resided constantly there. That her
" father had a stall in the Bell's Wynd market when the rebels
" were in Glasgow. That at this period it was open every lawful
" day; but on Wednesdays, the butchers who had stalls in it sold
" their meat on stands in the Trongate. That she recollects the
" building of the King Street market (in 1744); and after they were
" built, her father removed his stall to them; and he also removed
" to a dwelling house near to them. And being interrogated,
" depones—That the Bell Street market was built at a period
" beyond her recollection. That after the King Street markets

" were built, the market in Bell Street was locked up, and made a
" repository for lumber, etc. ; and after this was again opened for
" country butchers. That before the King Street markets were
" built, it was the butchers who sold *mutton* who occupied the Bell
" Street market ; and at that time the butchers who sold *beef* had
" their stands in the Candleriggs; and when the fleshers went to
" the King Street markets, those who sold *mutton* went chiefly to
" the market on the west side of the street, and those who sold *beef*
" to the market on the east side ; and before the King Street mar-
" kets were built, there were, to the best of the deponent's know-
" ledge, no country butchers who sold meat *publicly* in Glasgow.
" That at the period before mentioned, when the Bell Street market
" came to be occupied by country butchers, it was only open to
" them on market days. And this is truth," etc.

Before Candleriggs was opened in 1724, the public markets were
probably situated in the High Street; but country fleshers seem to
have had full liberty to sell butcher meat in the town without
payment of any dues for the liberty of so doing.

" Council Records, 6th October, 1610."

" Item : It is statute and ordainit yt it sall be leisum to owt in
" towne flescheours ilk day in the ouk to mak mercate of flesche wt
" this burt, and to sell the samin in leg, bouk, and sydes, and yt na
" impediment be maid to yame, nor na nane of yame be frie men
" fleschers, and yt they bring wt yame hyde, heid, skin, and tallow,
" and yt na frie men fleschers by flesche in the land mercat, nor
" yair wyfes, bairns, or handis to sell ovir again under cullor to
" furnish nobillmen, gentile men, or countrie men, and yt under the
" payne of xty, to be tain of ilk veill, sheip, and lamb yey by, and
" xxxb. of ilk mart and   yey happen to by."

Glasgow at this time contained only 7,644 inhabitants.—*Chapman.*

During the time when Queen Mary visited her husband, Darnley,
in Glasgow, the markets and streets of the city appear to have been
usually allowed to remain in a state of great filth and nastiness,
every one using the same at his or her pleasure, as receptacles for
depositing thereon all manner of nuisances and family off-scourings.
Her Majesty never appears to have ventured during her sojourn in
Glasgow to have taken a pleasure stroll along the streets of the city,
no doubt remembering the well known cry of her capital—" *Gardez
vous !*"

" Council Records, 1st October, 1577.—Item : It is statut and

' ordanit yat yair be na middynis laid vpone ye foirgait, on ye
" greyne, nor zit on meill nor fische mercats, nor yat na fleschrs
" teyme yair vschawis vpone ye foirgate, undir ye pane of aucht
" schillings ilk falt vuforgeviu, and yat na stanes nor tymmer ly on
" ye hie gait langar nor zeir and daye, undir ye pane of escheting
" yairof."

(N.B.—Aucht schillings Scots, is about 7½d English.)

Agnes Reid, in her deposition before mentioned, stated that the
Bell Street market was for some time locked up, and made a repository for lumber, etc. I remember when it was so closed for several
years as a public market, and then again opened as the Bell Street
market. During the time that it was closed as a market, it was
occupied as a cellar by a Mr Drummond, for storing his oil casks,
he being then the contractor for lighting the city lamps, which at
this time appear to have been pretty numerous, and required a
large stock of oil to be held in reserve.

Mr Drummond became contractor in consequence of the following
advertisement :—

" *Glasgow Mercury*, 17th July, 1792.—Wanted, by the lord
" provost and magistrates of Glasgow, a person to contract for
" lighting the lamps on the streets, squares, and lanes of that city,
" for such a number of years as can be agreed upon. The number
" of lamps, including those belonging to private persons, which are
" usually lighted by the public contractor, are supposed to be about
" eight hundred. For particular information, apply to the city
" clerks."

Immediately previous to the union of the crowns in 1707, when
Glasgow, according to Chapman, contained 12,766 inhabitants,
there were no street lamps throughout the city; but it appears
that soon afterwards, about the year 1718, a few street lamps, of a
conical shape, were erected in some of the most public thoroughfares
of the city. They must, however, have been very few in number,
and not particularly conspicuous for their brilliancy, as M'Ure, who
wrote in 1736, makes no mention of street lamps then illuminating
the public places of Glasgow.

Queen Mary, on her visit to Darnley, arrived in Glasgow on the
22d of January, 1567, and remained a week there, returning to
Edinburgh with her husband by easy journeys, and arriving in the
capital on the 31st of the said month ; when the unfortunate
Darnley, just recovering from the small-pox, was, at the Queen's
desire, lodged in an outhouse of the suburbs called the "Kirk of

Field," where the well known gunpowder catastrophe took place on the 9th of February, 1567. It appears by a MS. letter in the State Paper Office, that the evening before Darnley was hurried into eternity, he repeated to those around him the following words from the fifty-fifth psalm :

" Oh Lord ! on them destruction bring,
And do their tongues divide ;
For in the city violence
And strife I have espied.
They, day and night, upon the walls
Do go about it round :
There mischief is, and sorrow there
In midst of it is found.
Abundant wickedness there is
Within her inward part,
And from her streets deceitfulness
And guile do not depart."

Many of our historians have alleged that Darnley, while in Glasgow, lodged in the Drygate, and even the site of the house where he then resided has been pointed out ; but Tytler, Vol. V., p. 372, says that Darnley, being offended, " abruptly left the Court, and " took up his residence with his father, Lennox, in Glasgow." Now, the house and garden belonging to the Earl of Lennox in Glasgow was situated in the High Street, and occupied the site of the present College Street. It no doubt was then a mansion house standing quite in the country, for we find that Queen Mary, a few years before this time, viz., in 1560, had executed a grant to the University of thirteen Scots acres of land immediately adjoining to it, which shows that the neighbourhood was then rural, although in the vicinity of the monastery of Black Friars.

As there were no such conveniences in Glasgow at the time in question as covered shores for drainage, the whole filth of the upper parts of the city of course found its way down the High Street by deep gotes and miry gutters, which seem to have been little attended to by the public authorities of the city. Even in my day, there was a deep and nauseous slough in the Candleriggs (in front of the present Bazaar), full of maggots, which was never cleaned, but was allowed to evaporate and filtrate its contents away without restraint.

It has already been stated that at this time the streets of Glasgow were permitted to remain in a condition of great filth and nastiness, every one making the street before his door his common middenstead ; but shortly after the Queen's visit, the subject seems to have been attended to by the magistrates and crafts of the city, and an assessment for causewaying the said streets was appointed to be levied on the inhabitants. This was the first assessment levied for making and repairing the public streets of Glasgow.

It may be here remarked, that the levying of an assessment on the inhabitants of the city seems to have been of so unusual an occurrence, that it was found necessary for the magistrates to obtain the concurrence of the deacons of the crafts as consenting parties to the levy. Acts of Parliament for granting such powers were not thought of in those days.

" *Burgh Records*, 19th November, 1577.—The quhilk day it
" wes condiscendit be ye prouest, baillies, and consale, witht ye
" dekynis of ye craftis, yat in respect yair is nocht to be gotten of
" comowne guddis to big ye calsayis, and yat yai halve appayntit
" witht a calsaye maker, for twa zeirs to cum. Thai, yairfoir, halve
" consentit to rais ane taxatiown of twa hundretht pundis money,
" to be tane of ye haill inhabitantis yairof, worthie yairto, and
" namit yir personis to be stentares yairto, viz., Johne Flemyng,
" Robert M'George Herbertsoun, Robert Adame, Johne Tempill,
" Matho Wilsoun, and sundry others, to be tane at twa termes, viz.,
" ye first of Januare nixt, and ye secund at Beltane nixt, and to
" convene on Furisdaye nixt, befoir none, at viij hor^s., in ye coun-
" salhous." (£200 Scots is £16 13s 4d English.)

It appears that at this time there was no person in Glasgow who possessed the skill of causewaying streets; in consequence of which it became necessary to get an accomplished pavier from Dundee to perform the work.

" *Burgh Records*, 28th October, 1578."—Item : " To Walter
" Brown, calsaye maker, for his expenss in cuming fra Dundey, and
" gang and yairto agane, quhen he wes feit, conform to rolmont,
" xl^s.—Item : To Johne Houstoun for ane owlks laubo^r.at ye calsay
" to ane compt.—xx^s. Item : To Robert Scott for leding of thre
" dosand of pulder* to ye calsay, and four dosand of sand vpone ye
" sewint, aucht, and nynt dayis of Nouember, xix^s."

" 1578, June 3d.—The quhilk daye, it is statut and ordanit, yet
" ye haill myddynis be remowit of ye hie gait, and yet nane scraip
" on ye hie gait."

" 1579, 8th October.—Item : To William Hervey, 26th Junie,
" 1578, to pass to Dundey for ye calsay maker, xx^s."

---

* " Pulder,—Powder, dust."—*Jamieson.*

"Item : To ane boy y! bro! anc vritting fra Dudley, iii ^s.

(N.B.—iii ^s. Scots is only 3d English, which payment is certainly very small for going such a journey. There was no post office establishment in Scotland till the year 1635.) *

I shall make a short digression here, and take notice of a part of Glasgow which I believe has seldom or never been visited by thousands of our west-end inhabitants, although in olden time, when the Saracen's Head inn was the fashionable inn of the city, the Dowhill was a place of some importance.

"*Mercury*, 19th October, 1780.—The lands of Dowhill for sale. " To be sold, by auction, on Friday the 27th of October next, etc., " the following subjects, lying on the east side of the Dowhill Street, " near to the Saracen's Head inn, which belonged sometime to the " deceased John Robertson, manufacturer in Glasgow, and now to " his creditors, either altogether or in the following lots, at the " upset prices after mentioned, viz. :—

" Lot 1st. The little house and two cellars possessed by Andrew
Stark, merchant, at the yearly rent of £6   0   0
And the stocking loom shop and room adjoining, possessed by
Archibald Reid, at 1 10   0
                                                             ‾‾‾‾‾‾‾‾
                                                              7 10   0
Under the burden of the roof, at the upset price of £75.

" Lot 2d. The ground storey of the large tenement possessed by
Mrs Woodrow, with the two cellars belonging to that house,
at the rent of 8 10   0
The piece of vacant ground or yard on the east of the large
house, with the dung of the whole tenement, and the dung of
Lot 1st, ...   1   0   0
                                                             ‾‾‾‾‾‾‾‾
                                                              9 10   0
At the upset price of £114.

" Lot 3d. The first storey above the ground storey of the said large
tenement, with the two cellars, possest by George Johnston,
supervisor, at the yearly rent of 10 10   0
At the upset price of £120.

" Lot 4th. The upper square storey and garrets of the said large
tenement, possest as follows : the square storey and two cellars
possest by John Muir, merchant, at   10   0   0
The garrets and two small cellars by Alexander Bandochie,
tailor, ...   4   5   0
                                                             ‾‾‾‾‾‾‾‾
                                                             14   5   0
This lot under the burden of the roof, at the upset price of £142 10s.

* In the year 1661 the postage of a single letter from Edinburgh to Glasgow was 2d beyond Glasgow, 3d; to London, 4d; to Ireland, 6d.—*Arnot's History, page* 130.

" Lot 5th. The large weavers' factory, and dwelling house above,
on the north of the large tenement, possest at the following
rents, viz. :—

A garret house and workshop by James Raeburn, at . . .	£4 12	0
A do. and do. by widow Cross, ...	4 0	0
A house and loom shop by George Mitchell, ...	3 10	0
A do. and do. by William Drysdale, ...	3 15	0
A do. and do. by William Lyon, ...	3 4	0
A garret room by Robert Nisbet, ...	0 16	0
A do. by Margaret Shaw, ...	1 0	0
A do. by Janet Lockhart, ...	0 15	0
	£21 12	0

With the whole dung of this lot, and a piece of vacant ground on the east, at
the upset price of £172 16s. Burdened with 10s of ground annual.

N.B.—Lots 2d, 3d, and 4th burdened with a proportion each of 20s of ground
annual affecting the large tenement and lot 1st.

" The articles of roup, etc., to be seen in the hands of Joseph
" Crombie, writer in Glasgow."

" *Mercury*, 23d November, 1780.—To be sold, these two acres,
" one rood, and twenty-six falls of ground lying in the Dowhill of
" Glasgow, as presently possessed by Duncan Campbell, gardener,
" with the dye-house and houses on the north side of the Gallow-
" gate, adjoining to the above grounds, as presently possessed by
" Thomas Thomson, and others. The above grounds are well
" situated for building upon, being a dry soil, and command an
" extensive prospect, and contain excellent springs of water. For
" the encouragement of purchasers or builders, the price will be
" converted into a ground rent, or ground annual, if they choose it.
" For further particulars, apply to Patrick Robertson, writer in
" Glasgow."

CHAPTER XIV.

Costume of the Lord Provost and Magistrates of Glasgow—Convener Newbigging—
Salary of the Lord Provost of Edinburgh—Scotch Episcopalians—History of and
interesting particulars regarding St Andrew's Church—Anti-Burgher intolerance—
Episcopal liberality—Union of Scotch and English Episcopalians—Articles of Union
and Act of Consecration.

FROM a very remote period it had been customary for the city of
Glasgow to pay a small annual fee to their provosts, bailies, and
certain other officials, which was continued down to the year 1756.
The following is taken from the treasurer's account for the year
1576 :—

"Item: To ye prouest for his fie, . . xx.lib. ... (£1 13s 4d.)
"Item: To Williame Conynghame, baillie, x.lib. ... (— 16s 8d.)
"Item: To Andro Baillie, baillie, for his fie, x.lib. ...   ,,
"Item: To ye clerk for his fie, . . x.lib. ...   ,,
"Item: To ye maister of work for his fie, x.lib. ...   ,,
"Item: To ye thesaurer compter for his fie, x.lib. ...   ,,
"Item: To ye herdis for their fies, . . v.lib. ... 8s 4d.

In 1720 the magistrates and town council enacted that the
provosts of Glasgow should wear a court dress on all public occasions,
and that the council should make the provost a yearly allowance of
£40 sterling. On the 9th of October, 1751, the Trades' House
resolved that the convener should wear a black velvet coat on all
public occasions, and the House ordained their collector to pay out
of the House funds the sum of £15 sterling to the convener, after his
election, to buy such habit, but "in case he do not wear the said
velvet coat he shall have no claim to the foresaid sum." On the
15th November, 1742, the House further resolved that the convener
and his successors in office shall, in all time coming, wear a gold
chain and medal as the badge of his office. In December, 1766,
the town council, the Merchants' House, and the Trades' House
resolved, that the magistrates, dean of guild, and convener, should
in future wear gold chains with medals, emblematic of their respective offices. In 1810, the town council resolved that the bailie of
the river should wear a gold chain, and in 1812 they further

resolved that the principal bailie of the Gorbals should also wear a gold chain. The court dresses and velvet coats of our city officials above mentioned appear to have become obsolete. The last exhibition of the kind that I remember was upon the occasion of a public assembly, when provost James Ewing of Strathleven appeared there dressed in full court costume, in velvet coat, dress sword, and hair tied in black silk bag, with lower habiliments, and sparkling shoe buckles of the levee days of George III. The exhibition, however, came too late for the times, and proved a failure.

Mr Archibald Newbigging, who was deacon convener in 1799, and bailie of Glasgow in 1813, was very proud of city honours, and of sporting the gold chain and medal on all public occasions.

Having occasion, while in office, to make a journey to England, he carried his gold chain and its ornaments there along with him, and, when arrived at Lancaster, he waited on the mayor of that town, and arranged with him to attend the church the ensuing Sunday along with the magistrates of the corporation. Mr Newbigging accordingly heard sermon there along with the Lancastrian officials, ostentatiously decorated with the Glasgow gold chain and its ornaments, to the no small wonderment of the natives, who could not think what great man this could be who had so honoured the town.

The wearing of gold chains and velvet coats by our Glasgow magistrates and city officials appears to have originated from a spirit of rivalry towards Edinburgh, where those dignified ensignia of office had for some time previously decorated the persons of its provosts and magistrates, and St Mungo was determined not to be thrown on the back ground by Auld Reekie, but should also see its dignitaries dressed in gold and velvet. The following notice is taken from the *Scots Magazine* of 1754, page 448 :—

" Edinburgh, September, 1754.—The wearing of velvet coats by
" the magistrates of Edinburgh being an annual expense to the city,
" a motion was made in council, the 18th of last July, by the lord
" provost, that they should be laid aside and some other distinguish-
" ing mark used. This motion having been committed, the council
" on report enacted, July 31st and August 21st, that six of the velvet
" coats should be laid aside, and that gold chains with medals should
" be " wore by the lord provost, the four bailies, the dean of guild,
" and treasurer, the medal for the lord provost to be of a larger size
" than the rest ; the expense in whole not to exceed £200 sterling.
" The device upon the medal is, on the one side, the figure of justice

" chased, and on the reverse, the arms of the city engraven. The
" lord provost is still to wear a velvet coat. By a subsequent
" Act, Sept. 18th, the council, in place of £10 sterling in use to be
" paid annually to the convener for a burgess ticket, ever since the
" £10 had been paid to each of the magistrates for their velvet
" coats, and which he usually bestowed in charity, appointed £30
" to be paid this year to the convener, to be applied for charitable
" purposes by him and his brethren, and rescinded the former Acts
" granting the said £10 annually. By Act of September of 1718,
" £10 was appointed to be paid annually to each of the four bailies,
" the dean of guild and treasurer who should wear black velvet
" coats. This £10 came in place of a burgess ticket formerly given
" to each of the gentlemen in the offices aforementioned ; or rather
" in place of £100 Scots which, at the time of passing this Act, was
" in use to be given them in place of the burgess ticket. The lord
" provost got no allowance for his velvet coat, an annual salary of
" £300 having been granted by act of council this year, 1718, in
" place of several casualties his lordship formerly enjoyed. Ever
" since Michaelmas, 1718, black velvet coats have accordingly been
" worn."

" P.S.—At this Michaelmas six of them were laid aside. The
" lord provost wears one."

In the year 1716 the city of Edinburgh first bestowed a settled
salary on the lord provost of that city, in order to enable him to
support the dignity of first magistrate. This was at first £300, but
afterwards was augmented to £500 sterling.

Dr Cleland, in his Rise and Progress of Glasgow, at page 68, thus
writes :—" Glasgow is the only town of extensive population in the
" empire whose chief magistrate does not receive an allowance for
" the support of the dignity of his office." But in a few lines afterwards the doctor adds that, in the year, 1720, our magistrates and
council enacted—" That the council should make the provost a
" yearly allowance of £40 sterling, which allowance has been con-
" tinued ever since."

This was written in 1820, and the citizens of Glasgow used to say
that it was given to his lordship to buy a pipe of wine therewith, in
order to entertain noble visitors and eminent strangers.

I now proceed to give a few gleanings regarding the early history
of the Episcopal Chapel in Glasgow ; but without any pretensions or claim of these being considered a history of this our first
Glasgow Episcopal Church.

The Scotch Episcopalians, vulgarly called Jacobites, were the first religious body, not connected with the Church of Scotland, who regularly met for worship in Glasgow, after the Revolution.

1. Bishop Alexander Duncan, formerly minister of new Kilpatrick, was the first officiating clergyman ; he was admitted in 1715. The congregation at this period met in a dwelling house in Bell Street.

2. Mr George Graham, from Perthshire ; he succeeded Bishop Duncan, in 1740. During Mr Graham's incumbency, the congregation removed to a larger dwelling house in Candleriggs Street.

3. Mr Thomas Lyon, from St Andrew's; he was admitted in 1750. About the year 1754 the congregation had so much increased that it was removed to a large hall in Stockwell Street.

4. Mr Andrew Wood, from Perthshire; he was admitted in 1778. Mr Wood was afterwards settled in America.

5. Mr Andrew M'Donald; he was admitted in 1787. Mr M'Donald was domestic chaplain to Mr Oliphant of Gask, in Perthshire, who procured him a living in London in the same year.

6. Mr Andrew Jamieson, from Marykirk, Kincardineshire; he was admitted in 1788, and officiated above thirty years. In the year 1800, the congregation was removed to a large hall in George Street, which was commodiously fitted up for worship.

There was a small Episcopal Chapel in Black Friars Wynd, Edinburgh, which was founded in the year 1722. There were also, at this time in Edinburgh, some meetings of the Episcopal Church of Scotland, who adhered to their old forms, having still their bishops and inferior clergy. For some time they were subjected to penal laws, in consequence of having refused to take the oath to Government, or to pray for the King and the Royal Family; but, subsequently conforming, their conduct came to be approved of by the crown.

The English Chapel in Edinburgh, which stands near the Cowgate Port, was founded on the 3d of April, 1771, the foundations being then laid by General Oughton.

By Act of Parliament, passed in April, 1719, it was decreed that every Episcopal minister performing divine service, in any meeting house, within Scotland, without having taken the oaths required by

Queen Anne's Toleration Act, and praying for King George *by name*, was to suffer imprisonment, and every house where nine or more persons, besides the family, should be present at Divine service, was declared to be a meeting house, within the meaning of the Act.

"*Glasgow Mercury*, 7th May, 1788.—Edinburgh, 5th May."

"On Thursday last, the 24th ult., was held at Aberdeen, a meet-
" ing of the Protestant Bishops in Scotland, who, having previously
" consulted with their clergy, took into their consideration the state
" of the church, under their inspection, and unanimously resolved
" to give an open and public proof of their allegiance to the present
" Government, by praying in express words for his Majesty King
" George, and the Royal Family. This is to take place in all their
" chapels, on Sunday the 25th of May instant, to which day it is
" deferred, that the bishops may have time to give the proper
" directions to their clergy throughout the kingdom. Thus an
" end is put to those unhappy divisions which have so long sub-
" sisted among us, and many thousands of our countrymen, sus-
" pected of disaffection to the present Government, will now be
" considered as dutiful and loyal subjects."

"May 28th, 1788.—Sunday last, the King, Queen, and Prince of
" Wales were prayed for, *by name*, and the rest of the Royal Family,
" in the usual manner, in all the nonjuring chapels."

Dr Cleland, in his Rise and Progress, page 16, informs us, that
" prior to 1806, the Scotch and English Episcopalians, in Scotland,
" were considered as distinct bodies   In the beginning of that year
" the English Episcopalian clergymen gave in their submission to
" the Scotch bishops, when a union took place, and Glasgow was
" united in a diocese with Edinburgh and Fife. The first diet of
" the examination of the English Episcopalians, in Glasgow, was on
" the 15th of May, 1806. On that occasion the Right Rev. Wm.
" Abernethy Drummond, Bishop of the United Dioceses of Edin-
" burgh, Glasgow and Fife, confirmed 90 persons."

This took place two years before the death of the Rev. Mr Falconer, minister of St Andrew's Episcopal Chapel in Glasgow, and at the time when the Rev. Mr Routledge was the junior minister of the said chapel. Dr Cleland, in his Annals, published in 1816, at page 153, further says, that the stipend of Mr Routledge, at that time, was £300 per annum, and that the sittings in the chapel then amounted to 641.

From an interesting pastoral, delivered in 1861, and from a

second article published in 1863, by the present respected minister, the Rev. Dr Gordon, regarding the rise and progress of St Andrew's Episcopal Church, in Glasgow, I have made the following extracts.

(1861) " It is now 100 years past since the first stone of this (St Andrew's Episcopal) Church was laid, and the period when it was built; the various persons and personages who in their day worshipped here, and the many vicissitudes which it has undergone, invest the old place with an interest which, excepting our Cathedral, no other church possesses. Several old people can yet recollect the powdered-headed flunkies who marched along the passages with their masters and mistresses prayer books, escorting them to their respective pews. And it was quite a sight to look down from the galleries upon the many white-wigged aristocrates who filled the body of the church. It was a usual turn out to see 25 or 30 carriages drive to the chapel gate with worshippers. From 1810, to 1825, many, now alive, had to wait for six and twelve months ere they could obtain seats for their families. It would be impossible to give a list of the good and the great who in their day attended this interesting but plain church. The following will call to mind in many memories old associations, viz. :—The Duchess of Hamilton, Lord Douglas, Lord Blantyre, Campbell of Blythswood, Oswald of Auchincruive, Sir D. K. Sandford, Lord Cathcart, Gen. Pye Douglas, Cross Buchanan, Stirlings of Glorat, Sir John Maxwell, Sir Robert Crawford of Pollok, Admiral Fleming of Cumbernauld, Sir James Stuart of Allanton, Claud Hamilton of Barns ; Spiers of Elderslie, Theodore Walrond of Calder Park, Dunn of Tannochside, T. C. Campbell of Mains, Col. Sir C. Hastings, Davidsons of Ruchill, Sir Andrew Campbell of Garscube, James Kibble of Park Place, Colquhoun of Killermont, Ambrose Dale, John Cabbell, M'Call of Daldowie, Edgar of Germiston, Sir William Hooker of Kew Gardens, Sir William Maxwell of Calderwood, John Bogle of Gilmorehill, Edward Fairlie of the Royal Bank, General Smith, Houldsworth of Cranstonhill, Haggarts of Bantaskine, Logan of Birdistone, Wilson of Benmore, &c. The pulpit is not the place for going over many reminiscences of days of yore, with great minuteness ; indeed, (said the Rev. Dr.) I could fill a thick volume from our old sederunt books with topographical details, not to be found, I believe, upon any other records; and you can easily fancy that many a particular has taken place here and hereabout, which is not even on the record of memory. I may, in brief, narrate, that St Andrew's Parish Church, in the Square, and this, our church,

Q

were being built at the same period. In consulting different histories of Glasgow, I find contrariant statements about the year when St Andrew's Parish Church was founded. What I am about to state is from the Town Council Records. The town council met and projected the building, in 1739. The first stone was laid in 1740, the year in which Lunardi ascended in a balloon from the Square, and it was 22 years ere the church was erected. The Square was a burying ground, and the grass of the church-yard was advertised to be let, by the magistrates, in 1785, and in 1786, the year after St Andrew's Square was laid out. The whole was walled in, and the only entrance to the church and the church-yard was by an iron gate on the north. The old cross of Glasgow is buried in the Square. St Andrew's Parish Church is a meagre copy of St Martin's in the Fields, London. This chapel seems to be a miniature copy of the former. At the time, church architecture was at its lowest ebb; nothing like Gothic, nor no external sacred symbol of the faith would have been allowed by the general taste, and hence was not thought of. I did what has been done in the way of raising money for alterations and repairs, for paying old debts, and for endowing the church, viz., nearly £1000. The Font was the first of correct design ever put up in Glasgow, since the Reformation, and it is well used—all and sundry being baptized who come. It is a copy of Bradley Church, Lincolnshire, and it is a memorial to Dr Campbell. I have only to characterise the former arrangements as *hideous*; what has been done is *correct*, as far as it goes, but altogether, inside and outside, St Andrew's is a poor concern, unworthy the name of a temple suitable for the worship of God. Its walls are too substantial for a good riddling fire to make any impression for final demolition, and so we must be content to let it remain, endeared for its old associations, and as being most useful for its environs. The present enamelled brazen altar cross was presented by one of the Smiths of Jordanhill, and came originally as a gift from the present Member of Parliament, Walter Buchanan, Esq. The Grecian and Elizabethan styles were, in the middle of last century, those in vogue, both for churches and private houses.

"You may perceive a close resemblance between the buildings of Charlotte Street and this church. Where we now are was called 'Willow Acre,' past which flow the Molendinar or Gallowgate burn on the west of the church, and the Camlachie burn on the south. In our records there appear long papers about the covering in and keeping up the footpaths and bridges across and around these burns, which seem to have been the occasion of incessant bargain-making between the managers and town council, each paying only their own share.

" In our early accounts I find frequent charges for 'flambeaus,' probably for lighting the roads to the church at evening services, and preventing people from falling into the burns.

" 'Willow Acre' belonged to three brothers, John, Robert, and Thomas Moodie. The two former were gardeners, and likely cultivated this spot as a garden; the latter, Thomas, was a bookbinder.

" I find no mention of 'Willow Acre' except in our own charters. The name may have been given from willows growing by the two brooks which flowed past the plot of ground. We have still 'Brook' Street, from its proximity to one of these brooks, which both meet a little way from here, opposite Mr Lynch's stables gate, and flow into the Clyde opposite the south side of the jail, and which are carried in pipes below the bed of the river. I have said that probably this 'Willow Acre,' from being the property of the two Moodies who were gardeners, was then public gardens; at all events, the ground on which Charlotte Street stands was occupied as a garden, for the sale of fruits and vegetables, at the rent of 365 merks per annum. Hence the street when first built was called 'Merkdailly.' This piece of ground consists of 1083 square ells, for which £360 sterling per square ell were paid of what is called 'dead earnest,' and £1 Scots for every ell additional. There is no burden or feu-duty, but some feudal right (a grey duck's egg, I believe) payable to the superior—the preceptor of St Ninian's Hospital—when asked, which it never has been, and I dare say never will be.

" In the original charter, registered in the Commissary Court books here, this church and church-yard are declared to be 'for the people ' of the communion of the Church of England who have seats and ' attend divine worship in the said chapel.' The first meeting of the original subscribers and contributors, called by advertisement in the *Glasgow Journal*, was held on the 15th of March, 1750, in the house of Robert Tennent, vintner, and the names of the first directors are as follows, viz. : Alexander Oswald, merchant ; Casper Claussen, sugar baker ; James Dennistoune, merchant ; Robert Parr, dyer ; David Dalyell, merchant ; David Cochran, merchant ; George Sangster, tobacconist ; Robert Tennent, vintner ; and Andrew Stalker, bookseller. Most of these are buried outside, and this latter, Andrew Stalker's gravestone, is the oldest in date, at the south corner of the chancel. 'Missives' were exchanged between the directors and the tradesmen—William Paul and Andrew Hunter, masons; and Thomas Thomson, wright.

"Excerpts from the Sederunt Book:—'Glasgow, 15th May, 1751. Which day it was reported to this meeting that Messrs Richard Oswald & Company, merchants in London (who had been solicited to procure supply for the chapel in London) had, by a letter of the 4th current, directed to Messrs Oswald of Glasgow, informed that in order to obtain a "Brief" in favour of the chapel, it would be necessary to employ a solicitor; and that in answer to this, Mr Alexander Oswald, in name of the managers, to the said Richard Oswald & Co., of London, being laid before this meeting, whereby they are empowered to employ a solicitor for the above purpose, on the expense of the managers, in case it was found proper. The managers now present unanimously approve of the said answer in their name, and agree to pay the expense debursed in prosecuting the same.—James Dennistoune; John Buchanan, jun.'

" 'Glasgow, 26th September, 1751. Which day, in consequence of an advertisement in the *Glasgow Journal* for a general meeting, this time and place, of all concerned in the English Chapel, sundry of them being now met accordingly in the house of John Burns, vintner in Glasgow, and David Dalyell, merchant in Glasgow, was elected preses of the meeting, in the absence of Mr Alex. Oswald; and it is agreed, that Dr John Brisbane, physician in Glasgow, and Alex. Speirs, merchant there, should be added to the number of the present directors, and to continue in office till next general election. And further, that immediate application be made, in name of the managers and those concerned, to the Lord Bishop of London for supply to the chapel, and for a proper clergyman to the chapel, of his Lordship's nomination. And Mr Dalyell, Dr Brisbane, Mr Stalker, Mr Speirs, and John Buchanan are appointed as a committee to draw up a proper representation to his Lordship, to be laid before a meeting of the whole, to be held in this house on Tuesday next, the 3d October, of which all present are now warned in this present meeting.'

"At the present time it is altogether ludicrous to record how high the prejudice ran against the erection of this chapel; but what I am about to state evidences with what seriousness and intolerance the project was viewed. Andrew Hunter, one of the masons, happened to be a member of what was the oldest Burgher congregation here—Dr King's, or rather now Mr Calderwood's, in North Albion Street. What we now call 'U.P.'s' were then sub-divided into Seceders, termed Relief Burgher and Anti-Burgher (so termed in reference to the Burgess oath), Old Lights, and New Lights. The United Presbyterian congregation now in Greyfriars Church was then called the 'Shuttle Street Secession Congregation,' and the following minute is copied from their records of session, 26th April, 1750 :

"'The session, understanding by the moderator and some members ' of the session, that they had conversed privately with Andrew ' Hunter, mason, a member of this congregation, who had engaged ' to build the Episcopal meeting house in this place, and have been ' at great pains in convincing him of the great sin and scandal of ' such a practice ; and the session, understanding that notwith- ' standing thereof, he has actually begun the work, they therefore ' appoint him to be cited to the session at their meeting on Thurs- ' day, after sermon.'

"Andrew Hunter did go on with the 'great sin' of building the Episcopal meeting-house, and the moderator and session having failed to open his eyes as to 'the scandal of such a practice,' he was forthwith excommunicated.

"I may mention that our registers of baptisms, marriages, and burials are regularly kept from the first. We have also those of Musselburgh and Dalkeith. The Rev. John Falconer carried his registers from these places to Glasgow ; and many of Sir John Cope's soldiers' children's baptisms are engrossed in the registers for Musselburgh. The originals are still in the possession of St Andrew's Church ; but two years ago, copies were made of the whole for the Duke of Buccleuch's private chapel records at Dalkeith Palace.

"Upwards of 100,000 children have been baptized in St Andrew's, with a corresponding number of marriages ; and even yet, every Monday's average is about twenty-five—quite a scene.

"The Rev. James Riddoch, afterwards appointed to St Paul's Church, Aberdeen, was the first clergyman, and remained one year. The Rev. John Falconer succeeded him, in 1751, and served for the long period of 57 years. The following clergy were assistants, for a shorter or longer period, viz. :—The Rev. Mr Sanderson, the Rev. William Andrews, the Rev. J. Franks, the Rev. Dr Wynne, the Rev. James Forster, the Rev. J. F. Grant, and the Rev. Wm. Routledge, who came from St Bridges, in Cumberland, in 1795, as assistant to

Mr Falconer, and who was appointed to the full charge in 1808. He served here 48 years, and I need not say in what respect his memory is held. The first stained glass window, in the church, was erected to his memory. The first stained glass window that Ballantyne of Edinburgh put in a Glasgow church—what is in it, you can behold with your own eyes. The other two are diaphaned, and contain four apostles, and our blessed Lord's Resurrection, and the adoration of the Magi. The following clergy were the Dean's assistants or curates: the Rev. H. J. Urquhart, the Rev. J. P. Lawson, the Rev. D. Aitchison, the Rev. J. E. Keane, and the Rev. Louis Page Mercier. Dean Routledge died in 1843, and was succeeded by the Rev. Wm. Norval, whom I succeeded in 1844. The following are among the distinguished clergy that have occasionally officiated here : The Rev. C. Simeon of Cambridge, the Right Rev. Bishop Sandford, the Right Hon. and Rev. Lord Douglas, whose family seat is still retained by the Earl of Home, the Rev. Leigh Richmond, who officiated often, and many other well-known clergymen. I find that before Dean Routledge's appointment, in 1794, the present Sir A. Alison's father, then curate of North Shields, was on treaty to be assistant to Mr Falconer. Many years afterwards he succeeded to St Paul's, Edinburgh, where his body rests outside the altar.

"From 1795 to 1812 the singers all wore surplices. For that period we had here a regularly surpliced choir, as is customary in all cathedrals ; and before next Christmas the same shall be once more, twenty boys being now in regular weekly training, and the surplices having been already presented by Lord Belhaven's Niece. Moreover, a great addition will be about that time made to the organ.

"Strenuous exertions are to be made to render the services as popular, correct, and simple, as possible, as the funds for that intent have recently been supplied. It cannot be that in a city like Glasgow, a well-rendered Church of England music service can be lost. If our rich Episcopalians in the west are so slow and niggard to build a befitting church, those in the east are determined to spur up and not to lose ground too. The reason why the surplices were discontinued was because they were all stolen. On the 7th of May, 1812, the vestry was broken into by James Stewart and William M'Arthur, who stole these and the clergyman's robes, and a variety of other things. These two persons were sentenced to be capitally executed on the 18th of November, the same year, but Mr Routledge and the congregation having petitioned the Prince

Regent for mercy, the sentence was commuted to transportation for
life.

"The present organ was bought from the magistrates in 1812. It
was originally built by Donaldson of York, in 1792, but has often
been added to and improved in tone. It was formerly on the rood
screen of Glasgow Cathedral, immediately behind the minister's loft,
recently erected. The first one was sold to the Unitarian congregation, and was built by the renowned Snetzler. It formerly stood in
a gallery across the mouth of the chancel, which was taken down at
the alterations made by me ten years ago, above which there was
a transparency of the transfiguration. The pulpit, reading desk,
and clerk's desk were originally to the left of the present pulpit,
near the middle of the south wall, while opposite, in the gallery, was
the Duchess of Hamilton's pew, with a rich canopy over it.

"The church and church-yard were consecrated, in 1808, by Bishop
Abernethy Drummond, who married the heiress of Hawthornden, and
took, in consequence, the name of Drummond, when forty persons
were confirmed. Before the Clyde was deepened the church was
often flooded. Boats were rowed up and down Saltmarket, Bridgegate and Stockwell Streets, and in the year 1816 the water rose inside
St Andrew's Church four or five feet above the floor. This
happened on a Christmas day, when there was a large attendance.
Some twenty or thirty carriages with families—near and distant—
drove here to keep the festival. With the exception of Mr
Jamieson's little flock, the nucleus of the present St Mary's, the
faithful remnant that stuck to the Episcopal Church, through all
her persecutions, ever since the Revolution, in 1688, when Episcopacy was disestablished in Scotland ; I say, with this exception,
this church was the only one of our communion, not only in our
neighbouring towns, but in the neighbouring counties; in fact
there were no Episcopal Churches nearer than Edinburgh. The
predicament caused by the river inundation of the church was made
known to Dr Gibb, then minister of St Andrew's Parish Church,
who most readily permitted the congregation to assemble therein,
and celebrate the Christmas of 1816. There were 290 communicants, and £28 10s 10d of offerings.

"Around these walls lie many illustrious dead, and of recent years
several memorial crosses and sculptured gravestones, of ecclesiastical
design, have been placed upon their graves. There is one very
affecting gravestone, which covers the spot where Captain Suther-
land and his wife are both interred, who were drowned in the

'Comet' steamboat, on their marriage trip down the river. Dr M'Nish, the author of the 'Philosophy of Sleep,' 'Anatomy of Drunkenness,' &c., is buried at the south-east corner. The bodies of the following Episcopal clergymen lie in their different lairs, viz.: —The Rev. John Falconer, (beside his three wives), the Rev. A. Jamieson, the Rev. D. M'Coll, the Rev. J. Murray of Forres, the Rev. Wm. Alexander Aitken, Curate of Ballantoy, Antrim, and the Very Rev. Dean Routledge.* Almost every public institution in Glasgow has been benefited from the alms-deeds of those who once worshipped here, and whose deeds do follow them, though they rest from their labours. I instance a few to show how well off in funds this church at one time was.

					£	s	d
1809.	Collection for the Lunatic Asylum,	.	.	.	£51	1	0
1813.	do.	for the Lunatic Asylum,	.	.	34	12	6
"	do.	for the Magdalene, do.,	.	.	48	0	0
1815.	do.	for the Aged Women's Society,	.	.	181	0	0
1816.	do.	for the Magdalene Asylum,	.	.	32	19	6
1818.	do.	for the Royal Infirmary,	.	.	60	0	0
1819.	do.	for the Fever Hospital,	.	.	27	0	0
1821.	do.	for the Deaf and Dumb Asylum,	.	.	20	3	0
1826.	do.	for do. do.	.	.	30	0	0

"Besides these local charities there were equally large collections for the poor and for divers missionary societies. Among miscellaneous charges, &c., in 1791, occur the following.—' For porter and ' entertainment for the managers at different meetings in the Tontine, ' £2 6s 4d. The general annual dinner, appointed to be held in ' Dowell's Inn, but next year in Hemmings, at 15s a head. Agreed ' that Janet Hutcheson, beadle, shall be allowed one guinea to ' purchase her annual cloak, to be applied at the sight of John ' Fergus. 1792, 28th Dec.—Resolved unanimously that any mem-' ber who, if in town and in health, shall not attend the chapel ' once a month, at least, shall not be entitled to vote in the chapel ' affairs. 1751, Oct. 31st—Paid two soldiers filling up chapel,

---

* Mr Salmon, in his Report on Grave-yards to the magistrates and council of Glas-gow, dated 3d December, 1863, thus writes :—" St Andrew's Episcopal Burying Ground " entirely surrounds the church with which it is connected. The space applicable to " interments extends to about 694 square yards. The outward appearance of this " grave-yard has all the disagreeable characteristics inseparable from such places, while " its locality in the immediate vicinity of a dense and sunken population renders these " characteristics all the more objectionable. The effect is repugnant to every just " conception of taste and propriety. When we observe what a trifling extent the " space is now used, it is most unfortunate that the above church, long ere now, has not " been redeemed from its present obnoxious influence."

' £3 3s. Paid by Mr Tennent for stabbs for round, £1 2s 6d. Paid
' for oak nails for the gate, 8s.'

"Many legacies have been left from time to time to St Andrew's,
but they seem all to have shared the fate of the subsequent, as not
one remains, even those left for the poor were borrowed to pay
some accumulating debts, and were never afterwards paid. The
most extraordinary thing is how not hundreds of pounds but even
thousands of pounds were frittered away upon a building of the
poorest design.

"The clergymen seem to have been kept as a cheap bargain, for
the Rev. John Falconer, for 57 years, got his £50 per annum.
Witness.—'At Glasgow, the 17th of June, 1822, and within the
' vestry of the chapel, convened, Messrs Fyfe, Pinkerton, Hussey,
' Ellis, Wilson, and Jack—Mr Fyfe in the chair. There was laid
' before the meeting a letter from Mr Spreull, city chamberlain,
' stating that the magistrates of Glasgow would not pay more than
' 4½ per cent. on their bond for £100, (formerly stated as Sangster's
' annuity in the sederunt book) after Martinmas next. The meet-
' ing having taken into consideration that as the money bequeathed
' to the chapel by Mrs Sangster is at the disposal of the managers,
' resolve and authorise the treasurer to receive the £100 from the
' magistrates, and apply the same towards extinction of the debt
' due by the chapel.' Every one of those who did so were legally
liable for being accessory to such a transaction. This legacy, like
every other one, was meant to lie at interest for specified purposes,
and no managers had any right to abuse their trust by thus seizing
on the principal. Our Scottish church, from being reduced to the
lowest ebb by political persecution, has survived the withering
influence of such a storm, and during the last fifteen years she has
doubled her congregations, and no diocese has progressed more of
recent years than the diocese of Glasgow and Galloway; but 2d a-
head is the most magnificent sum which the 40,000 Episcopalians
in Scotland annually give towards the support of their church and
clergy.

"For more than half a century St Andrew's was a 'qualified
chapel,' but not defiant of the Scotch Episcopate, although the
legal penalties necessitated its position. In 1805 terms of union
with the Scotch Episcopal Church were agreed upon, and henceforth
St Andrew's became incorporated with the diocese of Glasgow and
Galloway, and for some time it was the metropolitan church of the
diocese. The following are the articles of the union.

"ARTICLES OF UNION.

"At Glasgow, the fifth day of December, eighteen hundred and five years. Present, Messrs Charles Wilson, Joshua Senior, John Shearer, Arthur White, Thomas Laycock, Hugh Love, George Pinkerton, Septimus Ellis, Richard Lawrie, Bright Langley, and Henry Wood.

" A paper, signed by the greatest part (it is believed the whole) of the members of this chapel, having been presented to the meeting, recommending a union with the ancient Episcopal Church of Scotland, agreeable to the articles of union proposed by the reverend bishop of that church, to such clergymen as officiate in Scotland, by virtue of ordination from English or Irish bishops, the managers, after mature deliberation on the articles also produced, and after seeing the opinions of the Archbishop of Canterbury, the bishops of London, Lincoln, St Asaph's, &c., in favour of the measure, unanimously approve of the proposal, inasmuch as the entire control and management of the funds and temporalities of the chapel are understood to remain in the hands of the managers or church wardens, for the congregation, as formerly; as also the nomination of the clergyman in case of vacancy. Therefore they authorise and request the Rev. William Routledge, (the Rev. John Falconer, the senior minister, not being in such health as to undertake the journey), to wait upon the diocesan, the Right Rev. Wm. Abernethy Drummond, and to sign the articles of union proposed. And the managers further order that the aforesaid articles of union be engrossed in the minute book kept for the transactions of this chapel, and signed individually by the members approving the same, as an authority and justification of this measure in all time coming.

"ARTICLES OF UNION,

" Proposed by the Right Rev. the bishops of the Scotch Episcopal Church to those clergymen who officiate in Scotland by virtue of ordination from an English or Irish bishop.

" As a union of all those who profess to be of Episcopal persuasion in Scotland appears to be a measure extremely desirable, and calculated to promote the interest of true religion, the Right Rev. the bishops of the Scotch Episcopal Church do invite and exhort all those clergymen in Scotland who have received ordination from English or Irish bishops, and the people attending their ministrations, to become pastors and members of that pure and primitive part of the Christian church of which the bishops in Scotland are the regular governors. With a view to the attainment of which desirable end, the said bishops propose the following articles of union as the conditions on which they are ready to receive the above-mentioned clergy into a holy and Christian fellowship, and to acknowledge them as pastors, and the people who shall be committed to their charge, and duly and regularly adhere to their ministration, as members of the Scotch Episcopal Church :—

" I. Every such clergyman shall exhibit to the bishop of the diocese or district in which he is settled, or in case of a vacancy, to the primus of the Episcopal College, his letters of orders, or a duly attested copy thereof, that to their authenticity and validity being ascertained, they may be entered in the diocesan book or register kept for that purpose.

" II. Every such clergyman shall declare his hearty and unfeigned assent to the whole doctrines of the gospel as revealed and set forth in the Holy Scriptures, and shall further acknowledge that the Scotch Episcopal Church, of which the bishops are the regular governors, is a pure and orthodox part of the universal Christian church.

" III. Every such clergyman shall be at liberty to use in his own congregation the liturgy of the Church of England, as well in the administration of the Sacrament of the Lord's Supper as in all other offices of the church.

" IV. Every such clergyman, when collated to any pastoral charge, shall promise, with God's assistance, faithfully and conscientiously to perform the duties thereof, promoting and maintaining, according to his power, peace, quietness, and Christian charity, and studying in a particular manner to advance, by the example and doctrine, the spiritual welfare and comfort of that portion of the flock of Christ among which he is called to exercise his ministry.

" V. Every such clergyman shall own and acknowledge as his spiritual governor, under Christ, the bishop of the diocese or district in which he is settled, and shall pay and perform to the said bishop all such canonical obedience as is usually paid by the clergy of the Scotch Episcopal Church, or by the clergy of the United Church of England and Ireland to their respective diocesans, saving and excepting only such obedience as those clergymen who do or may hold spiritual preferments in England or Ireland owe to the bishops in whose dioceses in those parts of the United Kingdom they do or may hold such preferment.

" VI. Every such clergyman, who shall approve and accept the foregoing articles as terms of agreement and union with the Scotch Episcopal Church, shall testify his approbation and acceptance of the same in the manner following, viz :—At ————, the ———— day of ————, I ———— ————, ordained deacon by the lord bishop of ————, and priest by the lord bishop of ————, do hereby testify and declare my entire approbation and acceptance of the foregoing articles or terms of union with the Scotch Episcopal Church, and oblige myself to comply with, and fulfil the same, with all sincerity and diligence. In testimony whereof I have written and subscribed this my acceptance and obligation, to be delivered into the hands of the Right Rev. ————, bishop of ————, as my diocesan and ecclesiastical superior, before these witnesses, the Rev. ———— and the Rev. ————, both clergymen of the said diocese, specially called for that purpose.

" ACT OF CONSECRATION.

" After union with the Scottish Episcopal Church, St Andrew's was duly consecrated, as will be seen from the following entry in the minute book :—

" ' Upon the fourth of May, 1808, in the presence of the congregation assembled for divine service, the Episcopal Chapel of Glasgow, and the adjoining burying ground dedicated in honour of the holy apostle and martyr, Saint Andrew, were solemnly consecrated to the worship of the Almighty God by the Right Rev. Father in God, William Abernethy Drummond, bishop of Glasgow, before the Rev. William Routledge, the Rev. Robert Adam, the Rev. Alex. Jamieson, and the managers of the chapel.—W. Abernethy Drummond; Wm. Routledge, minister; Robert Adam, clerk; Alex. Jamieson, clerk.'

" The Rev. Mr Norval, the predecessor of the present incumbent, formerly belonged to the Scottish Established Church. ' The Church Review and Scottish Ecclesiastical Magazine,' as well as several Scotch newspapers for 1837-38, narrate at full length the Presbytery and Synod speeches which contained the novel proceedings which caused Mr Norval to seek refuge in Church of England orders. This narrative is gathered therefrom :—

" The name of *Norval*, famed in song, is likely to become a *pro clarum nomen* in our annals ecclesiastic. In Mr Norval the kirk has verily found a *frugal* swain!—one who would feed his flocks on pilfered pasturage. He came to Kirriemuir in 1836 from Glasgow, his native place. No sooner was he inducted minister of the New Kirk at Kirriemuir than the provincial press blazed away in their own proper style, dwelling on his most harmonious settlement as an edifying illustration of the results of popular election. One of the charges in the parish of Brechin soon became vacant. Again Mr Norval is the man of the people, but the sermons are found out not to be *his own*, but taken, in all their material points, out of certain volumes of sermons by the Rev. Henry Melville of Camberwell Chapel, London.

" A few of the hearers bring the imposition practised upon them before the Presbytery, who refer the case to the Synod of Angus and Mearns, who refer the case to the General Assembly.

" ' Let us hope,' says a periodical, containing the minutes of this whole case, ' that Mr Norval's brethren in the ministry will be merciful, in due recollection of the sacred maxim : "He that is without sin amongst you, let him first cast a stone." Thenceforward Mr Norval betook himself to study at Durham. By the bishop of that diocese he got ordained to the incumbency of Trimdon, which he bought with his wife's money. He was just one year in St Andrew's, and was what is termed ' very low church.' "

CHAPTER XV.

I NOW beg leave to make a few passing remarks upon the foregoing interesting details regarding the early history of St Andrew's Episcopal Church, as furnished by its most respectable pastor, the Rev. Dr Gordon. The Rev. doctor thus commences : " What I am about to state is from the Town Council Records," and then continues :—" The " first stone was laid in the year that Lunardi ascended from a " balloon in the Square in 1740." Now, if the Town Council Records thus state the date of Lunardi's ascension in Glasgow, they are wrong, for it was not till Wednesday, the 23d of November, 1785, that he first ascended from St Andrew's Square. I was present on the occasion, and witnessed the ascension from the Green, as I have mentioned in another article. The following is a notice by Lunardi.

"*Glasgow Mercury*, 17th November, 1785."—"*Aerial Excursion.*" —" On Wednesday next, about noon, Mr Lunardi will ascend with " his balloon into the atmosphere, from St Andrew's Church-yard. " Mr Lunardi is happy of having in his power to acquaint the " ladies and gentlemen that, according to their wishes, the magis- " trates have granted him the *choir of the Old Cathedral*, where, on " Monday next, the balloon will be suspended in a floating state, " with the netting over it, and the car attached to it, which will be " an exact representation of its ascent. Admittance one shilling."

I must apologise for making a digression here, by giving a copy of a curious letter from Gilbert Chisholm, Esq. of Stretches, narrating the descent of Lunardi, near Hawick, in 1785.

" Dear Sir,—Yesterday afternoon (23d November), about half an hour after three, as I was returning, with Mrs Chisholm, from a visit to Sir James Naysmith, of Posso, Bart., my servant called out to me to observe a paper kite of most surprising magnitude and height. Turning my eyes to the place where the boy pointed, I perceived a body flying among the clouds, which sometimes intercepted it from my sight. As it came near the ground, I perceived it assume an oblong oval shape, something like a sugar mould; but as I could perceive no string to hold it, nor any tail appended, I was convinced that it could be no kite—which, indeed, its extraordinary height had convinced me of before. As I knew that Lunardi was in the country, and intended a voyage from Glasgow this day, I began to suspect this must be his balloon, though I was yet unable to distinguish his car, and could scarce allow myself to think that he could be at such a distance from that city. As it still came nearer, however, I was at last convinced it could be no other; and in about a quarter of an hour after I first saw him, he was got so near, that I began to call out to him, 'Mr Lunardi, come down! come down!' This invitation I gave him the more readily, because if he had still gone on he must have alighted in a very inconvenient place, on account of the high wind. After repeated calls, I had the good fortune to hear that he answered me through his speaking trumpet, though I could not distinctly hear what he said. At five minutes before four, he alighted in a place very near the water of Ale, and so effectually screened from the wind that the balloon stood quite upright, without inclining either to one side or another.

"Two shepherds who kept their sheep on the hill side were so much astonished at the descent of the balloon, with a human creature appended to it, that it was with difficulty I could persuade them that Mr Lunardi was not some devil who would destroy them. At last, by my earnest persuasion, they ran down the hill, and, with some fears in their countenances, came up to Mr Lunardi. My horse was so frightened that I could scarce come within a gunshot; but Mrs Chisholm, who rode a more peaceable beast, was allowed to come much nearer. The shepherds at my desire conveyed the balloon, and Mr Lunardi along with it, over the water which separated us, which they effected with the greatest ease, the balloon yet rising from the ground with the slightest touch. After receiving our hearty congratulations, Mr Lunardi asked Mrs Chisholm if she would take his place in the ærial car, to which she replied by jumping into it. She willingly would have had the balloon set at liberty, but as the wind was very high, Mr Lunardi judged this to be improper; for as Mrs Chisholm is considerably lighter, she must have ascended to a great height, and been conveyed to several miles distance: the car, therefore, was held near the ground by the two shepherds. In this manner she was carried for about three miles, while the hills sheltered us from the wind; but then it became so violent, and the balloon waved so much, that she was obliged to alight. After this we assisted Mr Lunardi in emptying his balloon, which was not accomplished without great difficulty, on account of the high wind. After having the pleasure of Mr Lunardi's company for the night, I had the honour of introducing him this day to the magistrates of Hawick, who, after having entertained him at dinner, presented him with the Freedom of the Burgh. Mrs Chisholm is much pleased with her aerial journey, and still wishes that she had been set at liberty."

On Monday the 5th of December, 1785, Lunardi made a second ascent from Glasgow. On this occasion he went right over the city to the north, and alighted in the parish of Campsie, about ten miles distant, returning before eight o'clock at night.

I think that the Council Records are also wrong if they state that the lands on which St Andrew's Parish Church stand was "a *burying ground*," and that the *only* entrance to the church and church-yard was by an iron gate on the north. There is no written evidence, I believe, of the lands of St Andrew's Square ever having been a cemetery, or of any church having existed upon the said lands before the present church was built. No human remains were found when the buildings of the Square were in the course of erection. The iron gate above mentioned was not on the north of the Square, but on the west, at the opening from the Saltmarket; but there was also an opening to the said lands from the Gallowgate, but it had no iron gate.

It was in the year 1787 that the lands of St Andrew's Square were first advertised for sale, viz., 14th February. "To be sold, " sundry steadings for houses in St Andrew's Square. The plan of " the Square, and the regulations for building, are to be seen in the " hands of the town clerks of Glasgow."—*Mercury.*

Dr Gordon informs us that the first meeting of the contributors for building St Andrew's Episcopal Chapel was held upon the 15th of March, 1750, in the house of Robert Tennent, vintner, who was one of the directors. Mr Tennent, besides his business as a vintner in the White Hart inn, near the old toll in the Gallowgate, was also an extensive builder; and, along with Robert Muir and David M'Arthur, he rented from the city of Glasgow the extensive stone quarry called the "Sheep Quarry," in the eastern common. Mr Robert Tennent built the Saracen's Head inn, and the magistrates

and town council, by way of encouragement to such a great undertaking, granted him liberty to take stones from the Bishop's Palace
to build the said inn. Mr Tennent appears to have availed himself
of this liberty, by demolishing the handsome gateway of the palace,
and carrying off Bishop Dunbar's coat of arms, which stood in front
of the gate. Mr Tennent at the time being also engaged in building
a large tenement on the east side of the High Street, near the Cross,
he placed the stone having Bishop Dunbar's coat of arms deeply
sculptured thereon in the back wall of the said tenement, where it
remains to this day, and may be seen from the back court of the
tenement by those who are interested in viewing antiquarian subjects.

Mr Robert Tennent belonged to the family of the Tennents of
Wellpark ; and it is curious to see a Wellpark Tennent carefully
preserving Roman Catholic relics, and superintending, as director,
the building of an Episcopal chapel.

William Paul, one of the contractors to execute the mason work of
St Andrew's Episcopal Chapel, was deacon of the incorporation of
masons in 1745 and 1749 ; and Thomas Thomson, who contracted for
the joiner work of the said chapel, was deacon of the incorporation of
wrights in 1744. As for Andrew Hunter, the other contractor to
execute the mason work of the fabric in question, Mr Pagan, in his
Glasgow, at page 181, has given a full corroboration of what Dr
Gordon states regarding the great sin which Andrew had committed
by soiling his fingers with the mortar of such a wicked temple.

Dr Gordon informs us that the present organ of the chapel was
bought from the magistrates of Glasgow in 1812, and that it was
formerly the rood screen of the Glasgow Cathedral, immediately
behind the magistrates' loft, recently erected. In Pagan's Cathedral,
at page 70, it is stated that the great organ, or "kist of whistles,"
as it was termed, which is believed to have been placed above the
rood screen, was removed at the Reformation, and a similar instrument was not again seen in Glasgow till 1775, when an organ was
placed in the then new Episcopal chapel on the Green. The Rev.
W. M. Wade, A.M., writing in 1822, says that the Unitarian meeting house in Union Street of Glasgow contains the organ which was
formerly in St Andrew's Episcopal Chapel, situated near the Green
of the city.

Although for a number of years after its erection in 1750 there
was no organ in the chapel, nevertheless the directors appear to
have taken pains to procure a professional music master as leader of

R

the choir, so as that the want of an organ might be sufficiently supplied by experienced chanters in lieu of the said organ.

"*Glasgow Mercury*, 20th December, 1756.—John Buchanan,
" CLERK to the English Chapel, Glasgow, opens his school for teach-
" ing church music in the 2nd storey of M'Nair's land, opposite the
" Main Guard, on Tuesday the 28th inst., at six o'clock in the
" evening, and will continue to teach every day in the week, except
" Saturday, at that or any other hour most convenient for his
" scholars."

(N.B.—CLERK is the layman who reads the responses to the congregation in the church, to direct the rest.—*Johnson*.)

We are left in the dark by the foregoing advertisement whether
or not John taught his scholars upon the Sundays.

The example of cultivating and improving a taste for church
music thus first set a-going in Glasgow by the directors of St
Andrew's Episcopal Chapel was immediately followed by our civic
authorities.

"*Mercury*, 22d November, 1756.—By order of the magistrates.
" To encourage and promote the improvement of church music, the
" magistrates have directed Mr Moor to open a free school in
" Hutchesons' Hospital, on Tuesday the 22d instant, at seven
" o'clock in the evening, where the inhabitants of the city will be
" admitted and taught at the public charge, on their producing
" proper certificates of their character from the minister and elders
" of the parish where they reside."

"*Mercury*, 10th November, 1785.—The managers of the licensed
" Episcopal Chapel in the city of Glasgow having some time since
" erected the same into a *collegiate charge*, by appointing two
" clergymen jointly to perform the different parts of the public
" worship at every meeting, upon the plan of divine service estab-
" lished in the new chapel in Edinburgh; and the managers having
" also erected a new gallery for the better accommodation of the
" inhabitants of this city and neighbourhood as may not be sup-
" plied with seats—all who may be interested in this public notice
" are desired to apply, by letter, to Mr John Fergus, in Glasgow,
" mentioning the seats they wish to occupy, that the same may be
" laid before the managers, to enable them to take early measures
" for their accommodation. The chapel is now warmed by a couple
" of stoves, and the floors are covered with mattings.

" The said managers, for the greater improvement of the harmony
" of the public worship, having ordered a proper number of boys to

" be educated to music, for the purpose of accompanying the organ,
" that divine service may be performed on a plan better calculated
" to improve the knowledge and refine the taste for sacred music—
" hereby give notice, that they wish to procure a clerk or precentor
" for the Episcopal Chapel, of approved abilities and knowledge in
" music, and of an unexceptionable moral character ; and for this
" purpose, they request that all candidates for this situation may,
" as soon as possible, send a note of their names, professions, and
" places of abode to Mr John Fergus, junior, organist, or Mr William
" Goold, teacher of music in Glasgow, who will immediately inform
" such candidates when they may appear upon a comparative trial.
" The salary, exclusive of perquisites, is £10 8s per annum, besides
" the undoubted advantages which may be expected to arise from
" the establishment of an able and skilful teacher of church music
" in the city of Glasgow."

The successful candidate for the above situation was a Mr Banks,
an Englishman, who possessed a good musical voice, and was an
excellent performer on the violin. On the 18th of February, 1788,
the directors of the gentlemen's private concert gave Mr Banks a
benefit concert, in which Messrs John Fergus and William Goold
took parts, the former on the harpsichord and the latter on the
German flute. On this occasion Mr Banks sung "Ma chere Ami,"
and joined in several glees. In the second act he gave a violin
concerto, which was much admired by musical connoisseurs, there
being then no other eminent performer of Italian music in Glasgow.

"*Mercury*, 12th May, 1789."—" On Thursday, the 21st of May,
" in the English Chapel, will be performed several select pieces of
" sacred music, from the works of Handel, Marcello, Boyce, &c.,

" For the Benefit of the Chapel Band.

" The doors to be opened at six o'clock, and the performance will
" begin precisely at half an hour after six of the evening. Tickets :
" 1s each."

The above entertainment was conducted by Mr Banks for behoof
of the chapel band, but soon afterwards he gave a public concert
upon his own account, in the course of which he performed several
airs on the psaltery, an instrument much in use amongst the ancient
Hebrews, who called it " Nebel." The psaltery on which Mr Banks
performed was in shape somewhat like the modern violin, but had
strings of brass wire. I was present at this concert, and I think
that the psaltery used by Mr Banks was quite different from the

ancient instrument, which had thirteen strings and two bridges; whereas Mr Banks's psaltery had only a small number of strings and but one bridge ; besides, he made use of the violin bow to draw out the notes, when, on the contrary, the ancient Jewish musicians struck the strings with a plectrum, or slender crooked stick. The performance of Mr Banks on this instrument turned out a complete failure, and this gentleman never attempted a second time to perform publicly on the psaltery. The organist of St Andrew's Chapel at this time was Mr John Fergus. He was a teacher of music, and was greatly respected by all ranks of our citizens. His manners were mild and unassuming, and as he possessed considerable talents as a musician, he was frequently invited to private musical parties. He always attended those parties as a guest, and I never heard of his having made any professional charge when invited to attend private musical parties. Besides being an excellent performer on the organ and pianoforte, he also led the violoncello, or double bass, at all our public concerts, and likewise at the gentlemen's subscription concerts, attending the rehearsals " *gratis.*"

Mr Fergus composed several pieces of music, amongst which was " The Royal Glasgow Volunteer March," which, in the volunteer days of the French war, animated the ranks and files of our citizen soldiers on their marches to and from their parades on the Green.[*]

Dr Cleland, in his Rise and Progress, at page 16, informs us that, prior to 1806, the Scotch and English Episcopalians in Scotland were considered as distinct bodies, but in the beginning of that year a union took place. That the first diet of confirmation of Episcopalians in Glasgow took place on the 15th of May, 1806, when 90 persons were confirmed by bishop Drummond. This happened two years before the death of the Rev. Mr Falconer, and at the time when the Rev. Mr Routledge was junior minister. The doctor, in his Annals, at page 153, further says that the stipend of Mr Rout-

---

[*] " *Glasgow Mercury*, 18th October, 1781."—"Music."—"John Fergus, junior, begs " leave in this manner to acquaint the public that he teaches the harpsichord, pianoforte, " and organ upon reasonable terms. Having made music his particular study under the " best masters in Edinburgh, and since, under Mr Esden of Durham Cathedral, and " others in England, he flatters himself he will be able to give complete satisfaction to " his employers. He also teaches church music in the English Chapel here; he will " teach *gratis* the children of parents belonging to that congregation who are unable to " pay for their instruction. . . . . John Fergus returns his most grateful thanks " to those who formerly employed him, and hopes to merit their further favours, and " the favours of the public at large.

" N.B.—He tunes harpsichords, pianofortes, organs, &c."

ledge, after the death of the Rev. Mr Falconer, was £300 per annum, and that the sittings in the chapel, in 1820, amounted to 641.

Denholm, in his History of Glasgow, at page 171, says that when the English Chapel was erecting in 1751, it met with no little opposition from the fanatical spirit prevailing amongst the lower orders, who vilified it by the appellation of the *Whistling Kirk*. The spirit of these times is luckily now changed, by giving place to more enlarged and generous ideas.

Even down to my early days, the operative classes in Glasgow almost unanimously were hostile to Episcopacy, looking upon the English service as being too nearly allied to Popery, to be in accordance with the word of God ; and although Denholm says, that on this subject the spirit of the times has changed, I am afraid that there is still a little lingering of the same spirit existing amongst many of the lower orders in Glasgow.

About eighty years ago I remember of the following cutting lampoon against the English Episcopalians, having been told to me by an operative weaver who had lived during the time that St Andrew's Chapel was building.

It must first be noticed that the act of building St Andrew's Parish Church proceeded at a snail's pace, more than thirty years having been consumed in erecting that edifice, while, on the contrary, the building of the English Chapel went forward at race horse speed, the foundations of it having been laid in 1750, and the chapel opened in 1751.

My informant said that while St Andrew's Parish Church was building, in the year 1750, Mungo Naysmith, the foreman of the masons employed in its erection, happened one morning very early, before dawn of day, to be standing upon the walls of the said church inspecting the workmanship of the masons, previous to any of the operatives of the craft arriving to their daily labour, when accidentally casting his eyes towards the English Chapel, then in the course of erection, he was surprised to see a strange uncouth figure there busily employed in furthering the building, and carrying huge stones (which would have required six of Mungo's men to move) with as much ease as if they had been feathers, and placing the same in position towards the erection of the building. While Mungo was thus gazing with amazement at the spectacle, the figure raised itself to its full height, and called out to Mungo : "Mungo, Mungo, come over here and help me to build my kirk!" "Na, na," instantly quoth Mungo to the figure ; "fegs, my lad, I ken better than that. The Lord sef us, man, wha are you?" But no sooner had Mungo pronounced the word "Lord," than the figure vanished in a twinkling. Mungo, however, positively affirmed that he distinctly saw that it had horns on its head and cloven feet! My informant told me the story with the greatest glee, as a capital joke currently handed about amongst the working classes of his youth, who were delighted with the innuendo against the Episcopalians.

Although the lower orders in Glasgow were hostile to Episcopacy, it was otherwise with the magistrates of the city and higher classes of the community, who were at least tolerant, if not indifferent on the subject, as the following notice shows :—

"*Glasgow Journal*, 23d August, 1764."—"On Sunday last (19th), " the Right Rev. Dr Littleton, bishop of Carlisle, preached in the " morning to a crowded audience in the licensed Episcopal Chapel " here, and in the afternoon, he went with the Right Hon. Lord " Wentworth and his son, and attended divine service in the High " Church. They were waited on next day by the magistrates, and " had the compliments of the city." (Archibald Ingram was at this time provost of Glasgow.)

Dr Gordon informs us that Willow Acre belonged to three brothers—John, Robert, and Thomas Moodie. John was deacon of the gardeners in the years 1725-6, 1729-30, and 1734. Robert was deacon of the same incorporation in 1731-2, and 1733.

The lands of Willow Acre seem to have originally extended to both sides of the Camlachie burn, and apparently to have embraced Castle Boins, which was joined to the left bank of the burn, and was bounded by the waters of the stream itself on the north. Dr Gordon states that the grounds of the Episcopal Chapel consisted of 1083 square ells, but as a Scotch acre contains 6150½ English yards, the chapel lands could only have been about the sixth part of the Willow Acre grounds.

Doctor Gordon having stated that the ground on which the chapel was built formerly formed part of the lands called Willow Acre, he suggests that the name may have been given to it in consequence of willows growing by the two brooks which flowed past the plot of ground. But although I possess little antiquarian knowledge, I doubt the correctness of this derivation, for *willow* is an English word and *Sauchie Acre* should have been the Scotch term.

I would derive the term Willow Acre from the Scotch and Saxon word Weel, weil, or welc, which signifies an eddy or whirlpool in a stream, and it will be seen from the Plan that Willow Acre stood upon a bend of the Camlachie burn at Castle Boins, where formerly there were washings, and probably an eddy. In the same manner we see the entry from the Saltmarket to the Molendinar burn called the Weel Close, leading to a bend of the said burn where washings took place. (See Plan.) The ancient term in my opinion was the "Weel Acre" corrupted into the Willow Acre, as Sauchie Haugh has been perverted into Sauchiehall, and Shield Haugh into Shield-hall. I refer to a former part of these jottings at page 197 as to the Weel Close.

Perhaps it may be objected to my etymology, that acre is not an ancient Scotch word; but Jamieson says that Acker-dale, means divided into single acres. Aecer, an acre, and dael-en, to divide. In the Origines Parochiales, Vol. I., p. 507, we find as follows: " In a not of some informationes concerning the valour of a certane " of the personage teynds of Ranfrew, dated March, 1651, it is " stated that the towne of Ranfrew, comprehending the borrow " aikers, with the knock, Sandiefurd and Bogside is a ten pund " land." I only further add, that the Encyclopædia says, that acre signified any open ground, especially a wide champaign, and in this antique sense, it seems to be preserved in the name of places as " Castle Acre," &c. But I must leave this knotty point to some of our Glasgow antiquaries, who are more able to handle the subject, in a satisfactory manner, than me.

As there never was any street called "Brook Street" in the Bridgegate district of Glasgow, I suppose that Dr Gordon, in alluding to the said street, means "Brook Street," in the Bridgeton district of the city, at Mile-end, which there is near the Camlachie burn.

With regard to the original directors of the St Andrew's Episcopal Chapel, Alexander Oswald, the first in the list of directors, died at Scotstoun, 27th January, 1763.

Casper Claussen was a Dutchman brought from Holland by the Western or Stockwell Sugar House Company, to improve and superintend the manufacture of their sugar refining process.

James Denniston belonged to the Colgraine family, and was probably the father of the James Denniston who married Miss Mary Ramsay Oswald, fifth daughter of George Oswald of Scotstoun.

Andrew Stalker was a bookseller, and also the Editor of the *Glasgow Journal.* He lived in a house which stood across the Molendinar burn, near the Gallowgate Bridge on the south, which house is shown on the Plan annexed to these jottings.

As for the other directors I have found no particulars regarding them.

In reference to the vestry of the chapel having been broken into in 1812, by Stewart and M'Arthur, I find the following account of the trial of those persons in the *Scots Magazine* of 1812, at page 801.

"Glasgow Circuit Court of Justiciary, Wednesday, 7th October, " 1812."—"James Stewart and William M'Arthur, were accused of " breaking into the vestry of the English Chapel, on the night of " Monday the 4th, and of Wednesday the 6th of May, and feloni- " ously carrying off one minister's gown, silk, one minister's cassock, " ditto, two minister's gowns, bombazeen, three linen surplices, one " black silk scarf, one table cloth, five towels, one great coat.

" Elizabeth Menzies, otherwise Stewart, was accused resetting " these articles, knowing them to be stolen. The pannels pleaded " not guilty, and after a number of witnesses had been examined, " the diet was deserted *simpliciter* against Elizabeth Menzies. " Lord Gillies delivered an admirable charge to the jury, who " returned a verdict unanimously finding James Stewart and Wm. " M'Arthur guilty of the crime libelled, and they were both " sentenced to be hanged in Glasgow, on Wednesday the 18th of " November.

" M'Arthur asserted his innocence after the sentence, and called " God to witness that he told the truth.

Dr Gordon says, " These two persons being sentenced to be " capitally executed on the 18th November the same year; but Mr " Routledge and the congregation having petitioned the Prince " Regent for mercy, the sentence was commuted to transportation for " life." But in addition to the above mentioned petition for mercy, it may be remarked that the pannels were accused not only of theft, but also of being habit and repute thieves. They were found guilty of the first charge, but the last was not proven, and it was supposed that this circumstance tended greatly to influence the crown to listen to the petition of Mr Routledge and the congregation of St Andrew's for a commutation of the capital sentence.

The sum of £1 16s sterling, of "dead-earnest" which was paid when the ground of the chapel was bought, appears to have been given by the buyers as a symbol or mark that the bargain was per- fected, and came in lieu of the ancient Scotch mode of finishing bargains by the mutual *licking of thumbs*.

The ground for the chapel and church-yard thus purchased, according to Dr Gordon, consisted of 1083 square ells, at £1 Scots, or 1s 8d English, which amounts to £90 5s sterling of annual feu-duty, or rather less than 1s 8d per square yard, the Scots ell being 37½th inches in length, and the English square yard 36 inches. Scotch square ells are now generally reckoned in round numbers as English square yards.

Our learned antiquarian citizen, J. B., informs us that the ground, now the site of the English Episcopal Chapel, originally formed part of the ancient lands of "Eaglesholm Croft," which extended from the Saltmarket eastward to the Burnt Barns, and from the Gallowgate south to the Green. J. B. further says that the ground of the said chapel came into the possession of St Nicholas Hospital, and that although it actually lies within the territory of the burgh, it does not hold burgage of the crown, through the magistrates, and consequently the chapel lands are held of St Nicholas Hospital as the superiors. St Nicholas Hospital was sold by the magistrates of Glasgow, on the 13th July, 1798. It fronted Adelphi Street, and stood about ten yards east from the Main Street of Gorbals. The ground consisted of 551 square yards.

But to return to matters immediately regarding the chapel establishment. James Riddoch was the first minister; he was admitted in 1750. Mr Riddoch was afterwards preferred to be minister of St Paul's at Aberdeen. He remained only one year in Glasgow. Mr John Falconer was ordained by the Bishop of Carlisle at Rose Castle, and was minister of Musselburgh before he came to Glasgow. He was admitted in the year 1751, and died in 1808, having been 57 years in the ministry at Glasgow. Mr Sanderson was admitted as junior minister in 1783, and left the chapel in 1785. Mr William Andrews was admitted as junior minister in 1785. He was an American Royalist, who took refuge in this country soon after the breaking out of the American war in 1774. He left Glasgow in the year 1787, and was succeeded by Mr James Franks, who was admitted as junior minister in 1788. Mr Franks was preferred to a cure in Halifax, Yorkshire, and left Glasgow in 1791. The Rev. Dr Wynne succeeded Mr Franks, but he, most probably, was only a temporary assistant, as Mr James Foster was admitted as junior minister in 1791, being the same year that Mr Franks left Glasgow. Mr Foster was a fellow of Trinity College, Cambridge; he left Glasgow in 1794. Mr James Francis Grant was admitted as junior minister in 1794. He was the son of Sir James Grant of Monymusk. He left Glasgow in the year 1795, and was succeeded by Mr William Routledge, who was admitted as junior minister, and assistant to Mr Falconer, on the 20th of April, 1795. Mr Routledge was from St Bridges, in Cumberland. He was ordained deacon by the Bishop of Carlisle, in 1791, and priest by the Archbishop of York, in 1794. Mr Falconer having died in 1808, Mr Routledge then succeeded him as first minister. Mr Routledge died in 1843, and at that date was succeeded by the Rev. William Norval, so particularly noticed by Dr Gordon in his pastoral addresses. Mr Norval was succeeded in 1844, by the present incumbent, the Rev. J. F. S. Gordon, D.D., from whose interesting notices I have given so much valuable information as to the early history of St Andrew's Episcopal Chapel.

CHAPTER XVI.

General Wolfe in Glasgow in 1753—Wade's sketch of the Episcopal Chapel—Bishop Home's opinion of the Scotch Episcopalians—Roman Catholic Meeting House Eighty years ago—Burgess Oath—Popery Riot in Glasgow in 1779-80—Address to Lord George Gordon—Statute Labour Assessment in 1765—Sundry Regulations by Town Council—Bailie Bogle's Villa, 1712—Conclusion.

THE late Captain William Marshall of Rothesay, at his death, was the oldest Episcopalian in Scotland. In a letter which I lately received from him he says:—"My father, (Robert Marshall), who came " from England, was one of the original promoters of St Andrew's " Chapel, along with old Mr Norris, bleacher, at the head of the Green, " when the Camlachie burn was a pure stream, and they were " greatly assisted by the officers of an English regiment which then " lay in Glasgow. This was always said in our family. You are " right regarding the greater gentility of the English Chapel in " Glasgow, when there was no other Episcopal Chapel in Scotland, " excepting in Edinburgh. There were a few meeting houses of *non-* "*jurors* scattered over the country, especially in the north. With " the nobility and gentry of the west of Scotland, who had sittings " in St Andrew's Chapel, I remember the Lowndes family, of " Paisley, coming to St Andrew's Chapel in a grand coach," &c.

In reference to what Captain Marshall states of the parties who assisted in promoting the scheme of erecting an Episcopal Church in Glasgow, the old Mr Norris at the head of the Green, mentioned as above, was the father of the late Alexander Norris, born in 1751, who was so generally known in Glasgow by the familiar name of "Sandy Norris." Captain Marshall states that the promoters were greatly assisted in furthering the scheme of erecting the said chapel by the officers of an English regiment which then lay in Glasgow. Now, it is known that Wolfe's regiment lay in Glasgow when the Episcopal Chapel was building, and it is remembered that General Wolfe attended service in the said chapel, in the year 1753, when he was residing with William Orr, Esq., of Barrowfield, the father of the late John Orr, town clerk.

" *Quarterly Review*, 1848, page 350."—" We have read General

" Wolfe's letters to his father and mother, during his service in
" Scotland, under the Duke of Cumberland, in 1746, and a subse-
" quent residence in Glasgow. We remember that he attended
" various classes in the College there, a good example for young
" garrison officers; but at leaving the place, signified that there
" were only two things he should remember with tenderness, ' its
" young ladies and breakfasts,' both of which, we believe, still
" command the approbation of military connoisseurs."

The Rev. W. M. Wade, A.M., author of "Walks in Oxford," &c.,
writing in 1822, thus describes St Andrew's Episcopal Chapel of
Glasgow, at the above mentioned date :—

" The Episcopal Chapel, standing in the midst of its well-walled
" and neatly-railed burying ground, has something attractive
" in its exterior. It is built of good squared freestone ; has
" a projecting entrance porch on the west; is lighted by two
" tiers of windows, all square however, except that over the
" communion table, which is of the Venetian kind, and exhibits
" as completive decoration at top, four pediments, together with
" sundry urns. Within, although certain peculiarities spring-
" ing from a requisite economy of space, are observable, the
" chapel is handsome. As the windows, though sufficiently numer-
" ous, are not large, and the three eastern ones, that in the centre,
" partly through the organ standing before it, partly through its
" being made by painted blinds to imitate painted windows, admit
" not fully the splendours of day. The general light of the interior
" has in it a good deal of the ' dim religious character ' that Milton
" loved. The beautiful gilt lustres that once accommodated and
" adorned the interior, are vanished ; but other ornaments have
" been adopted. The great richness of effect marks the combination
" of altar, pulpit, organ, and choristers' loft, at the east end of the
" chapel. Decoration has, indeed, been too freely bestowed upon
" the organ and its appendages. For the unusual position of the
" semi-circular gallery containing the organ, namely, just over the
" communion table, the necessity of gaining seat room in the
" western gallery is a sufficient apology; but the effect produced by
" extending the wings of the organ case, so as to comprehend the
" ' door' into the organ gallery is decidedly bad. A too great pro-
" fusion of gilding also appears ; otherwise the exterior even of an
" instrument of no common merit is handsome. So is the pulpit, in
" front of which, gradually descending, are placed the reading desk,
" and clerk's pew. It is canopied by a handsome sounding board,

" sustained by a square panelled pillar, with a capital of the com-
" posite order, and capped by a gilded mitre. The hangings are
" crimson. Over the communion table are, in handsome panels
" and in gold letters, the Decalogue, Creed, and Paternoster. The
" opposite gallery—that on the west, has a semicircular projecting
" front. Like the two side galleries, it is panelled, and is, in
" common with them, sustained by bronzed pillars. Most of the
" pews are lined. Nearly 700 persons may sit in this chapel, which
" in winter is warmed by a large stove placed in the entrance porch:
" this gives out heated air, which is, by means of large perforated
" tubes carried longitudinally through the chapel, beneath the
" front of the galleries, made to diffuse itself in the interior. At
" the west end of the chapel is the vestry, in which is kept a library,
" of the kind termed in England 'Parochial Lending Libraries.' It
" was founded nearly two years ago, through the instrumentality of
" the most esteemed clergyman, Mr Routledge, and bids fair to be
" very useful.

" We had almost forgotten to remark that the subject of the great
" eastern window is the ' Transfiguration,' and that the chapel con-
" tains one monument. The latter is of white marble, to the
" memory of a contributor to the building. This chapel was
" founded in 1750, a time at which prejudice ran absurdly high
" against the Church Episcopal; so much did the organ offend, that
" for a length of time the populace were won't to term the chapel
" ' the *whistling kirk.*'

" The choral establishment is here on an exceedingly liberal
" footing, and is conducted with great taste and ability by the
" present organist, Mr John Fergus."

The largest number in any single year of communicants and of
baptisms in St Andrew's Episcopal Chapel happened in the year 1815,
when Mr Routledge was assistant to the Rev. Mr Falconer. In
1815, during the four festivals of Easter, Whitsunday, Michaelmas,
and Christmas, the communicants amounted to 904, and the
baptisms in the same year were 1016.

The Scotch Episcopal bishops of my early days were as follows :
Bishop William Falconer who, we are told by our church historians,
had been minister of a chapel at Forres, and was consecrated at Alloa
on the 10th September, 1741, was elected bishop in 1761, and died
in 1784. Bishop William Abernethy Drummond was elected bishop
in 1787, and resigned in favour of Dr Daniel Sandford in 1806. Dr
Sandford on the 17th January, 1806, was elected by the clergy of

Edinburgh to be their bishop. He was the author of several professional works.

The present bishop is the Reverend William Scott Wilson, A.M., ordained in 1827, and consecrated in 1859.

Dr Gordon informs us that, in the year 1816, the waters of the Clyde rose inside of St Andrew's Chapel four or five feet above the floor. On this occasion the river rose 17 feet above its usual level ; and Denholm says that the chapel was inundated by the Clyde to such a height as not only to cover the humble situation of the clerk, but even to bathe in its waters the footstool of the more dignified pulpit. I remember this flood very well. The Clyde then reached in Stockwell Street to the present Stockwell Place, and the sunk floors of the tenements still higher up the street were inundated from the re-gorgement of the common sewer in the centre of the street, from which the waters oozed, owing to the foundations being of sand. This flood, however, was considerably less than the great flood of 1782, before noticed, when the perpendicular rise of the river above the ordinary tide was a trifle above 20 feet, consequently, the area of the chapel must then have been submerged to the extent of upwards of seven feet.

Keith in his Bishops, on the last page of his treatise, thus concludes his work :

" Bishop Horne had such an opinion of the Scotch Episcopal
" Church as to think that if the great apostle of the Gentiles were
" upon earth, and if it were put to his choice, with what denomina-
" tion of Christians he would communicate, the preference would,
" probably, be given to the Episcopalians of Scotland, as most like
" the people he had been used to."

In the Plan annexed to the present jottings, it will be seen that Dr Woodrow's garden was enclosed by a strong wall, and was bounded on the west by the Molendinar burn, so that the passage along the left bank of the said burn was interrupted, and the only regular access to the Episcopal Chapel in 1760 was by way of Saltmarket Street ; the chapel, however, might have been approached through the long and dirty closes opposite the Bridgegate, and then across the bridge, at the corner of Dr Woodrow's garden.

I have a map of Glasgow, dated 1779, in which the ground of Dr Woodrow's garden is represented as being vacant, and free from all erections. It appears as an open space of ground, bounded by a wall on the west, and having a foot road between the said wall and the Molendinar burn. About eighty years ago, I remember the property in question in this state, and it continued so after St Andrew's Square was formed. About 1770, as before stated, there was a plan projected of forming a square on the lands of Merkdailly, but after some progress had been made, and buildings had commenced to be erected, the scheme was abandoned, and the materials sold. It is probable that the walls which surrounded Dr Woodrow's garden were at that time demolished.

I have not been able to learn anything certain regarding the history of this Dr Woodrow, but I see that the Rev. Alexander Woodrow was admitted minister to the Tron Church of Glasgow in the year 1701, and Dr Woodrow might, perhaps, have been his son. I have no evidence, however, of this being the fact. None of our Glasgow historians have taken notice of such a person as Dr Woodrow residing in Glasgow about this time ; whether he was a D.D., M.D., or LL.D., I cannot say with certainty; but I observe amongst a long list of subscribers in Glasgow to "Woodrow's Church History," published in 1721, the name of "John Woodrow, doctor of medicine," who, I suppose, is the Dr Woodrow whose garden is delineated on the Plan.

When St Andrew's Square was built in 1787, a convenient entrance was made to the foot road leading to the English Chapel, by means of a covered arch or tunnel having been formed through the tenement at the south-west corner of the Square, by which ready access to St Andrew's Chapel was obtained by way of Saltmarket, the "Weel close" (or St Andrew's Open) and the Square. At this time the footpath in question had no distinctive name, but it is now known as "Low Green Street," which leads from St Andrew's Square to Greendyke Street.

About eighty years ago there was a Roman Catholic meeting house in the first storey of a back tenement, at the foot of a long close, opposite the Bridgegate, (see the Plan). This close was bounded on the east by the Molendinar burn, and led to the bridge over the burn at the corner of Dr Woodrow's garden.

I remember in 1782 of seeing the congregation of this Roman Catholic meeting house when they were separating after having attended divine service on a Sunday, and remarked at the time that the members of this congregation appeared to be mostly operatives and labourers, and that their number apparently did not exceed from twenty to thirty persons. This was then the only Roman Catholic Chapel in Glasgow. The catholics in Glasgow are now estimated to amount to upwards of 100,000 individuals.

Mr Pagan, writing in 1851, in Glasgow, Past and Present, page 88, Vol. I., informs us that : " Near to this spot three closes have " their termination, and though much altered of late years, they " still present a curious specimen of labyrinthine city architecture. " The southmost belonged to the late Dr Rae Wilson, the eastern " traveller, who died only a few weeks ago in London, and whose " remains have since been brought down and interred in the Necro- " polis here. In this close, about seventy years ago, the few Roman " Catholics then in Glasgow would appear to have gathered " together, and heard mass for the first time since their expulsion " from the Cathedral, more than 200 years ago. They met by " stealth, as if engaged in a deed of darkness.

" Although there are still some narrow old turnpike stairs in the " upper part of the close alluded to above, the ' chapel' must have " been long since removed, possibly to make way for Low Green " Street, which, for a space, runs parallel with the Molendinar. " The house near the bottom of the close is now converted into a " byre, in which, on Friday last, we saw four-and-twenty gaucy " cows chewing the cud."

Mr Pagan further adds that, according to information furnished to him by the kindness of the Roman Catholic bishop, that, in the year 1846, there were no fewer than 3000 children baptized in the various Catholic places of worship in the city.

In my early days, Roman Catholics were shamefully persecuted in Glasgow ; and even down to the present times, there still remains a sprinkling of the same ungenerous feeling among many of our rigid clergymen towards those who profess Popery, as if it were a crime conscientiously to follow the ancient doctrine of the Christian church of their forefathers. There is scarcely a newspaper of the day in which are not to be seen numerous advertisements of sermons, lectures, and other publications inveighing against Roman Catholic principles. Protestant clergymen, however, ought to look at the excellent example of moderation which the Jewish rabbis show, by keeping themselves clear of all discord and wrangling in religious matters with those who profess different tenets from themselves ; they strictly follow the golden rule, that " Whatever you " would that men should do to you, do you even the same to them ; " for this is the law and the prophets." The Jews never send forth missionaries or distribute tracts for the purpose of making prose- lytes, although by the *lex talionis* they would be fully justified in doing so, but quietly remain in peace and amity with their brethren of all sects and opinions.

That the Roman Catholics were a persecuted body in Glasgow during last century is evident from the terms of the Burgess Oath of the city, which was as follow:

BURGESS OATH.

"Here I protest before God, that I confess and allow with my
" heart the true religion presently professed within this realm, and
" authorised by the laws thereof: I shall abide thereat, and defend
" the same to my life, and renouncing the Roman religion called
" Papistry. I shall be leal and true to our sovereign lord the
" King's Majesty, and to the provost and bailies of this burgh. I
" shall obey the officers thereof, fortify, maintain, and defend them
" in the execution of their office with my body and goods. I shall
" not colour unfreemen's goods under colour of my own. In all
" taxations, watchings, and wardings to be laid upon the burgh, I
" shall willingly bear my part thereof, as I am commanded thereto
" by the magistrates. I shall not purchase nor use exemptions to
" be free thereof, renouncing the benefit of the same for ever. I
" shall do nothing hurtful to the liberties and common well of this
" burgh. I shall not brew nor cause brew any malt, but such as is
" grinded at the town's milns; and shall grind no other corns
" except wheat, pease, rye, and beans, but at the same allenarly:
" and how oft as I shall happen to break any part of this my Oath,
" I oblige me to pay to the common affairs of this burgh the sum of
" one hundred pounds Scots money, and shall remain in ward while
" the same be paid. So help me God.
"I shall give the best counsel I can, and conceal the counsel
" shown to me. I shall not consent to dispose the common goods
" of this burgh but for ane common cause and ane common profit.
" I shall make concord where discord is, to the utmost of my power.
" In all lienations and neighbourhoods, I shall give my leal and
" true judgment, but price, prayer, or reward. So help me God."

It will be seen from the terms of the above oath that no Roman Catholic could become a burgess of Glasgow without committing perjury: a Jew or Mohammedan might safely take the above oath, and so become a burgess of the city; but it was otherwise with regard to Papists.

Further, it was common among the trades' crafts, when a petition was given in to them by a person desirous of becoming a member of one of these incorporations, for the deacon of the craft, as a preliminary, to demand the production of the applicant's burgess ticket:

S

consequently, a Roman Catholic was debarred from becoming a member of any of the crafts of Glasgow, without forswearing himself. A Catholic was thus shut out from becoming a trader in Glasgow.

By Act of Parliament, 1700, it was declared that " no persons " professing the Popish religion past the age of fifteen years shall be " capable to succeed as heirs to any person whatever, nor to brink " or enjoy any estate by disposition or other conveyance, flowing " from any person to whom the said Papists might succeed as heirs " in any manner of way, until the said heirs purge themselves of " Popery."

By this Act, a Catholic could not succeed to a lair in a kirk-yard where the bones of his ancestors were deposited, unless he took the oath renouncing the Roman religion called Papistry—thereby purging himself of Popery.

In February, 1756, Hugh M'Donald, brother of M'Donald of Morar, was tried before the Lords of Justiciary for being a Papist ; and having refused to purge himself of Popery, by taking the usual oath and formula, he was found guilty, and sentenced to be banished forth of the realm, with certification, that if ever he returned thereto, being still a Papist, he shall be punished with the pain of death. (*Scots Magazine*, page 100.)

Having given a particular account of the Popery riots in Glasgow in 1778 and 1779, in Glasgow, Past and Present, Vol. III., p. 497, I shall not repeat the article. I was at that time very young, but I remember that my parents (being Dissenters) were so afraid that the mob would look upon them as Papists, and would attack and plunder our house, that they shut all the windows, and would not permit any of the family to go out of doors. This was done in order that the mob might think the house was without a tenant, and so to pass it over. Our house was situated near to Bagnall's shop, in King Street, which was burst open, and everything in it broken and destroyed. That the fears of my parents were not without some foundation, evidently appears from the following advertisement of the time, taken from the *Glasgow Mercury* of 11th February, 1779.

" As a report has been wantonly or maliciously raised and indus- " triously spread against Andrew Philp, shopkeeper in the Gallow- " gate, that he is of the Papist profession, which is entirely false, " he earnestly desires, that if any can give such information of the " persons who have raised the report as will lay a foundation for a " legal process against them, they will communicate the same, and " they shall be handsomely rewarded.   " Andrew Philp."

"*Glasgow Mercury*, 4th March, 1779.—Just published, price 6d,
" a half-sheet emblematical print, representing the introduction of
" the Popish Bill. Among the figures in the print are The Whore,
" Beast, Pope, Devil, &c. It is to be sold by Messrs Dunlop and
" Wilson, John Smith, James Duncan, and the other booksellers."

On the 11th of May, 1781, the 85 Protestant societies of Glasgow,
by their preses, John Paterson, wrote to Lord George Gordon—" I
" have the honour to transmit to your Lordship a draft for £485
" sterling, as a token of our esteem for you as a sincere friend to
" the Protestant cause. We judged it expedient to transmit you
" this sum in the meantime, as our subscriptions are not quite
" closed. We understand there will be a subscription from Paisley,
" in connexion with some other places." To which his Lordship
answered by acknowledging the receipt of the £485, and adding—
" This instance of the affection of the societies and other friends in
" Glasgow gives me the greatest comfort and satisfaction, and I beg
" that you will take the earliest opportunity of returning them my
" most sincere thanks for so convincing a proof of their real esteem
" and approbation. You may assure the societies that it is my
" fixed determination to persevere, by the grace of God, in main-
" taining and promoting, by all lawful endeavours, the true Pro-
" testant interest in these kingdoms to the latest period of my life.

(Signed)   " George Gordon."

In 1793 an Act of Parliament was passed authorising magistrates
of royal burghs to admit Roman Catholics to be burgesses and gild
brethren of their respective burghs on the administration of an oath,
whereby the applicant is to declare, *inter alia*, that he will be faithful and bear true allegiance to his Majesty George III., and to the
Hanoverian succession; that he rejects and detests the impious position that it is lawful to murder or destroy any persons whatsoever
for, or under the pretence of their being heretics or infidels; or that
faith is not to be kept with such persons. Further, he is bound to
swear that he does not believe that the Pope of Rome has any civil
or temporal jurisdiction, power, superiority, or pre-eminence, directly
or indirectly, within the realm.

Applications by Roman Catholics, under this Act, to become
burgesses of the City of Glasgow, were first made in the year 1801.
Since which time the Roman Catholics have enjoyed the usual
freedom of their fellow-citizens, and have increased in numbers so as
now to amount to 100,000 souls, or thereby.

Although Roman Catholics are now enabled to become burgesses of Glasgow, I am not aware that any Papist ever obtained a seat at the council board of the city, while Christians of all other denominations, such as members of the Established, Free, Secession, and Sectarian Churches are freely elected to that honour, without any regard being paid to their creeds.

As Roman Catholics now constitute about one-fifth of the population of Glasgow, it would be but fair that they should have a representative at the council board, seeing that Papists are admitted to seats in the House of Commons, and that all classes should be fairly represented ; to say nothing about Catholic peers sitting in the House of Lords by descent. I am afraid, however, that a Roman Catholic candidate for city honours would have little chance of success at the poll if opposed by a Free churchman or active Sectarian.

In the Act admitting Catholics to become burgesses of royal burghs there is no clause enacting SECRECY, such as that in the early burgess oath of the city, viz., " I shall give the best counsel I can, " and conceal the counsel shown to me."

It was in consequence of this clause in the former burgess oath that the proceedings of the council board of Glasgow at that time were kept profoundly secret, the citizens of the burgh being held in complete ignorance of what their representatives were doing, until an order of council was recorded allowing publicity. Hence in all our early newspapers there is not a word to be found about what was going on at meetings of the magistrates and council of the city, and so our magnates were freely allowed to elect themselves into office at the nod of some clique. Our forefathers were thus deprived of the pleasure of seeing in print an account of the oratorical flourishes, and piquant bickerings, such as usually take place at our present council board among our councillors.

" *Glasgow Mercury*, 14th February, 1787."—" The Trades'
" House of this city having lately opened a correspondence with the
" magistrates and council relative to sundry grievances alleged to
" by members of the community, and having considered these
" grievances, and council's resolutions relative to the matters com-
" plained of, after due deliberation and reasoning at great length,
" came to the opinion that the present set of the burgh was incon-
" sistent with the liberties of the citizens, and required alteration.
" The House therefore resolved that it was necessary to apply to
" Parliament for such alterations as the internal set of this burgh

" requires, either in conjunction with the other burghs of Scotland,
" or for their own particular situation, whichever may be thought
" advisable; and that proper care should be taken that the offices of
" magistrates and council, in any set that may be judged proper to
" adopt, should be so modelled, as to preserve among them a
" respectable and proper class of citizens."

It was at this time that disputes first arose regarding Sunday
delivery of letters.

" *Mercury*, 14th Feb., 1787."—"The Postmaster-General has re-
" turned an answer to the requisition of the Chamber of Commerce,
" the ministers, and the merchants of this city, relative to the
" arrival and dispatch of a post on Sunday, in which he observes
" that he cannot, in justice to the rest of the kingdom, give up the
" measure, but that, if the gentlemen who oppose it think proper,
" the letters brought by the Sunday's post, shall neither be sorted
" nor delivered till Monday."

The following extract shows the origin of the statute labour
assessment in Glasgow :—

" *Glasgow Journal*, 4th April, 1765."—"By order of the magis-
" trates of the City of Glasgow."—"The magistrates considering
" that the trustees of the several turnpike roads leading into
" Glasgow having claimed the statute work of the city of Glasgow,
" the magistrates obtained a reasonable composition in favour of
" the inhabitants in place of the statute work, and agreed that
" every householder, within the city, who possesses a house exceed-
" ing twenty-six shillings stg., real rent, should pay three shillings
" stg. of annual composition, but to be restricted to one shilling
" and sixpence in case of punctual payment, commencing at Whit-
" sunday, 1760 ; and the magistrates named Patrick Montgomerie,
" collector of the cess, to uplift the composition money so agreed
" for. And though many of the householders have paid their com-
" position, at the rate of one shilling and sixpence per year, the
" collector informs that a great many arrears are still outstanding,
" for enforcing the speedy payment whereof, the magistrates hereby
" order and require all persons who are in arrears for said composi-
" tion, with all speed, to pay the same to Patrick Montgomerie,
" collector of the stent, at the stent office, certifying, that such
" persons who shall fail to pay upon or before the 15th of April
" current, they will be prosecuted so far as the law will admit."

From the concluding passage of the above advertisement, the
magistrates of Glasgow seem to have been sensible that they had

assumed power of levying a tax on the citizens without proper legal
authority.

"*Journal*, 17th January, 1757. By order of the magistrates.
" The magistrates have fixed the assize and weight of wheat bread
" as follows. The bakers are discharged from baking any loaves, of
" the finest kind, of any higher value than twopence, and the

	Lb.	Oz.	Dr.
" Twopenny loaf to weigh, . . .	0	14	10
" The penny loaf, ...	0	7	5
" The sixpenny loaf of the wheaten, .	4	2	0
" Ditto household, ...	5	8	0

" And so in proportion. The bakers to affix the letter F., on the
" fine, W. H. for wheaten, and H. for household."

"*Journal*, 2d January, 1766."—" The corporation of bakers, in
" Glasgow, find themselves under the necessity of abolishing the
" custom of giving New-Year's-day presents to their customers, and
" have ordered this their resolution to be insert in the *Glasgow*
" *Journal*, that neither their friends in town and country may suffer
" themselves to be disappointed."

"*Journal*, 6th November, 1766."—" On Tuesday last, Colin
" Campbell, boatman, being convicted before the magistrates of
" forestalling the fish market, was fined in forty pounds, Scots, in
" terms of law."

"*Journal*, 11th December, 1766."—" The magistrates of Glasgow
" having received information that some of the inhabitants keep in
" their shops and cellars, within the burgh, considerable quantities
" of gunpowder, from which the most fatal consequences may ensue,
" the magistrates hereby order all persons who have gunpowder in
" their shops, cellars, or other repositories within the city, imme-
" diately to carry and lodge the same in the common magazine for
" powder, at the Castle of Glasgow; with certification, that if any
" gunpowder, exceeding six pounds weight, shall be found in the
" shops, cellars, or other repositories, of any of the inhabitants with-
" in this burgh, at any time within forty-eight hours, the proprietors
" of such powder shall be fined and punished in terms of law. Any
" persons who inform shall receive a reward of ten shillings stg., from
" the magistrates, upon conviction of the offender."

"*Journal*, 2d June, 1763. By order of the magistrates and town
" council of Glasgow."—" The magistrates and council, considering
" that the selling of salt within the burgh by weight and not by mea-
" sure, is enjoined by the Convention of Royal Boroughs, and as selling

" salt by measure is attended with many frauds, resolve, that in time
" coming, salt shall be sold, within this burgh, by weight only, and
" strictly forbid and discharge all persons whatever, to sell any salt,
" within the burgh, from and after the first day of September next,
" otherwise than by weight, certifying such as shall fail, of their
" being fined in the unlaw of the burgh."

But I must return from the foregoing digressive advertisements
to the Green of Glasgow, and its environs, which have been too long
thrown in the back ground, to make room for subjects which many
of my readers may consider of no value whatever.

On the south of the three labyrinthine closes, mentioned by Mr
Pagan, there stood an ancient building, known as "Silver Craigs
Land," at one time the property of the Campbells of "Silver Craigs."
It was here that Oliver Cromwell lodged when he came to Glas-
gow. It stood back a few feet from the building line of the Salt-
market, and became the property of Mr M'Gilchrist, town-clerk of
Glasgow, whose heirs appear to have turned it into a weaving
factory.

"*Glasgow Journal*, 16th August, 1764."—" Sale of Silver Craigs
" Factory. That all and hail the houses, and utensils, and yard,
" belonging to the Silver Craigs Manufactory, lying at the foot of
" the Saltmarket of Glasgow, are, jointly or separately, to be sold, by
" public roup, within the house of Mrs Armour, at the Cross of
" Glasgow, upon the 6th of September next, between the hours of
" 12 and 2 of that day. Apply to John Wilson, writer in
" Glasgow."

These subjects were subsequently converted into a shop and stand
for the sale of old furniture; the articles of furniture being showily
displayed in the open area between the buildings and Saltmarket
Street.

On the south of Silver Craigs land, there was a piece of vacant
building ground, which is thus described in the *Mercury* of 1st
April, 1779 :—

" To be sold, about a rood of ground altogether, or a steading for
" one house, which lyes south of Silver Craigs Factory, at the foot
" of the Saltmarket, opposite to the Low Green. It is very con-
" venient for building upon, as there is not the smallest probability
" of the light being interrupted by other buildings. Apply to
" Alexander Harvey, the proprietor."

The opposite corner of the Saltmarket and Bridgegate was a villa
and garden belonging to Robert Bogle, who was bailie of Glasgow

in 1712. I remember the south portion of this property still remaining as a garden, in which there stood a summer house, or fancy tea arbour, then considered an embellishment to a rural establishment.

I shall now close these loose jottings of the Low Green of Glasgow and its environs, &c., which I am afraid many readers will think have been extended too far, and have embraced rather a superabundant proportion of advertisements, notices, and quotations, in proportion to more readable matter. To this charge I must plead guilty, only remarking, as an apology, that my object in so doing was to preserve a few of such notabilia as might tend to assist some future historian of Glasgow in elucidating any subject of our city's history, which might otherwise appear to require illustration.

I have further to apologise for having introduced so many gossiping stories, amongst these jottings, but they have been given merely as characteristic of Glasgow in olden time, when such "bletherings" passed from mouth to mouth, as the ordinary chit chat of our citizens of all ranks.

ADDITAMENTA.

PREFACE TO ADDITAMENTA.

THE following miscellaneous and desultory excerpta were published in the *Glasgow Herald*, between the years 1856 and 1863 inclusive. They are re-published, with some trifling additions, as a sequel to the article regarding the Low Green of Glasgow and its environs, &c.

As these jottings, in many cases, have reference to subjects which relate to more than one point treated of at the time, it necessarily happens that some quotations and advertisements are repeated; but the loose character of the writings must be kept in view by the reader, as the only apology for so transgressing upon his patience.

A writer of fragmenta like the following, labours under many disadvantages, when compared with the writers of History; his subjects, in general, have necessarily no regular connection with each other, and being minutely related, are apt to become irksome and tiresome; the ideas which are suggested are obliterated by the sudden appearance of an intruding article, relating altogether to a new and extraneous subject, so that the reader is tantalized with a passing glimpse of various objects, which, like flakes of snow falling on a running stream, just appear and then vanish.

History, on the contrary, has the advantage of being related in a uniform and connected series, which follow in regular order, so that the reader is not harassed by the sudden interruption of new objects, but goes pleasantly along with the historian in his narration of facts, without feeling languid and tired by sudden interruptions and intrusive passages.

I am sensible that most readers will skip over a great part of these jottings, as is usually done in long chronological tracts ; but if any part of the annexed Additamenta shall prove useful to a future Glasgow historian, my object is gained.

ADDITAMENTA.

THE GLASGOW SHOWS OF OLDEN TIME.

It is said to be as natural for an author to make an ostentatious display of his reading, by giving quotations, as it is for an old man to amuse himself by telling the stories of his early days. Now, I have to apologise to your readers on the present occasion, seeing that I am about to transgress, by indulging myself in both propensities. Whosoever implicitly follows his propensities may act very rightly; but he may err most egregiously; for he is apt to think that the road before him is easy, and as smooth and trim as it causewayed by Mr Carrick's best Furnace granite ; and therefore he very likely sets off at a loose canter, which soon increases to race-course speed, and then generally ends in a *whumble.* " Tam hoc tibi in proclivi quam imber quando pluit." So says Plautus.

It is well known that the ancient Greeks and Romans were very fond of sports and shows, and that large sums of money were frequently expended from the public purse to gratify the propensities of the populace for such amusements ; but it was quite otherwise in Scotland in former times, her rulers setting their faces against patronising even the innocent recreations of the lieges, as the following quotations show :—

" 3d Parliament, James IV., 1491.—Item : It is statute and " ordained that in na place of the Realme there be vsed fute ball, " golf, or vther sik vnprofitable sportes."

" 6th Parliament, Mary, 1555.—Item : It is statute and ordaned " that in all times cumming na maner of person be chosens Robert " Hude, nor Little John, Abbot of Un-reason, Queen of May, nor " vtherwise nouther in burgh nor to Landwart in onie time." *

This last-mentioned Act of the Scottish Parliament was probably

---

* So late as 1592, we find the General Assembly complaining of the profanation of the Sabbath by making of Robin Hood plays.—*Book of Universal Kirk,* page 414.

passed in consequence of the enthusiastic preaching of John Knox, the great champion of the Scottish Reformation, who had just returned from Geneva, where he had imbibed all the tenets and fervour of the celebrated John Calvin. In 1555, Knox travelled about from place to place throughout Scotland, enforcing, with great energy and effect, his views of the Protestant doctrine, and railing against sports and shows as vain and empty shadows, totally unworthy the regard of an evangelical disciple.

It is curious to observe how entirely the amusements of Robin Hood and Little John have disappeared from amongst us. They are even more obsolete than many of our ancient Druidical rites and practices.

The following ballad regarding Robin Hood and Little John shows one of the scenes which delighted the populace of former years, and was acted as a drama on the Sabbath-days :

"STORY OF LITTLE JOHN AND THE FOUR BEGGARS ;

OR,

A Merry Song of Robin Hood and Little John, showing how Little John went a-begging, and of his fighting with four beggars, and what a prize he took from them.

"All you that delight to spend some time,
A merry song for to sing,
Unto me draw neer, and you shall hear
How Little John went a-begging.
As Robin Hood walked the forest along,
And his yeomandree,
Says Robin, 'Some of you must a-begging go,
And, Little John, it must be thee.'
Says John, 'If I must a-begging go,
I will have a Palmer's * weed ;
With a staff and a coat, and Bags of sorts,
The better then shall I speed.'
Come, now give me a Bag for my Bread,
And another for my Cheese ;
And one for a Penny, if I get any,
That nothing I may leese.
Now Little John is a-begging gone,
Seeking for some relief,
But of all the Beggars he met on the way,
Little John was the chief.
But as he was walking all alone,
Four Beggars he chanced to spy,
Some Deaf, some Blind, and some came behind :
Says John, Here's brave company ! ! !

Palmer—a pilgrim who returned from the Holy Land carrying palm.—*Johnson*.

Good morrow, said John, my Brethren dear,
Good fortune I had you to see :
Which way do you go? Pray let me know ?
For I want some company.
OH ! What's here to do ? said Little John ;
Why ring these Bells? said he:
What dog is hanging? Come, let us be ganging,
That we the truth may see.
There is no dog hanging, one of them said,
Good Fellow, I tell unto thee ;
But here is one dead, that will give cheese and bread,
And it may be, one single penny.
We have Brethren in London. Another he said,
So have we in Coventry,
In Berwick and Dover, and all the world over,
But ne'er a crooked carle like thee :
Therefore, stand thee back ! thou crooked carle,
And tak that knock on the crown.
Nay, said Little John, I'll not yet be gone,
For a Bout I will have with you round.
Now, have at you all! then said Little John,
If you be so full of blows,
Fight on all Four, and never give o'er,
Whether you be friends or foes.
John nipp'd the dumb, and made them roar,
And the blind that could not see,
And those who had been cripples for seven years,
He made them run faster than he ;
And flinging them all against the wall,
With many a sturdy bang,
It made John to sing, to hear the gold ring,
And against the wall cry twang.
Then he got out of the Beggar's cloak
Three hundred pounds in gold.
Good fortune had I, said Little John,
Such a good sight to behold.
But what found he in the Beggars' Bags
Just three hundred pounds and three ! ! !
If I drink water while this does last,
Then an ill death may I dee ;
And my begging trade I will give o'er,
My fortune hath been so good :
Therefore, I'll not stay—I will away
To the Forest of merry Sherwood.
But when to the forest of Sherwood he came,
His master stood, bold Robin Hood,
And all his company.
What news? What news? said bold Robin Hood,
Come, Little John, tell unto me?

How hast thou sped, with thy Beggar's trade?
For that I fain would see.
No news but good, said Little John;
With begging full well have I sped:
Three hundred and three I have for thee,
In silver and gold so red.
Then Robin Hood took Little John by the hand,
And danced about the oak Tree ;
If we drink water while this doth last,
Then an ill death may we dee."

The first show that I attended took place more than eighty years
ago, and was that of a white polar bear *(Ursus maritimus)*. It
was stationed alongside of a large tin trough or tank, filled with
water, in which it had the liberty of taking a bath. It was a very
fine specimen of the species, being upwards of 12 feet in length,
with hair long, soft, and white. It had more of a placid than of a
ferocious look, but appeared extremely uneasy at being confined,
and seemed to feel that it was quite out of its natural element,
which it showed by occasionally roaring dolefully, as if in distress.
In order to silence it, the keeper used to dash a pailful of water in
its face, which it took very kindly, and so ceased its clamouring.
It was not shut up in a cage, but only confined to the floor by an
iron chain, which was of a length sufficient to enable it to climb
into the water trough or tank at its pleasure. There was no display
of any other animal at this show. A polar bear has seldom been
exhibited at any of our menageries, although no great difficulty has
been felt by our Arctic whalers in capturing that animal.

The next show that I went to see was that of the celebrated lion
tiger (as it was called). This was perhaps the finest specimen of
the Royal tiger *(Tigris, Felis)* that ever was brought to this
country, both as to its size and as to the variety and brilliancy of
its colours. From my remembrance of it, I think it must have been
upwards of 6 feet long, from the point of the muzzle to the origin of
the .tail ; it was, however, a most fierce and savage animal, and
required to be strongly confined in a cage encompassed with iron
bars. The keeper having given the company strong injunctions not
to use any freedoms with it, on account of its extreme ferocity, I
felt a little alarmed, and did not approach it very closely, but was
content to take a cautious view of it at a safe distance. Naturalists,
writing of the Royal tiger, say that it seems to have no other
instinct but a constant thirst after blood, a blind fury which knows
no bounds or distinction. Neither force, restraint, or violence can

tame the tiger; it is equally irritated with good as with bad treat-
ment; it tears the hand which nourishes it with equal fury as that
which administers blows to it. This is a just character of the
animal exhibited at this show as the lion tiger. Besides the said
tiger, there were several monkeys in this show, and some foreign
birds of rich plumage, which attracted my attention more than the
tiger. The end of this last-mentioned noble animal was rather
tragical. During the night time it broke out of its cage, and
immediately attacked one of the small monkeys, which it not only
devoured, but also swallowed the iron collar which encompassed the
monkey's neck; the consequence was, that this collar remained fast
in its bowels, and in a few days caused its death.

Although, from the novelty of the exhibitions, these two shows
afforded me much pleasure, nevertheless, my gratification was not
without some alloy, for I could not altogether divest myself of feeling
a certain kind of dread, lest these wild and powerful animals
should break loose and tear me to pieces. The next show, however,
which I attended, was one of a very different kind, as it yielded me
the most intense pleasure and delight, without any fear of being
worried and devoured. This was the celebrated puppet show of
Punch's Opera. It was, however, after all, but a paltry, itinerant
exhibition, or children's penny show, and had not even the advantage of any scenic decoration, for the performances were confined to
a small open space in a wooden structure, little larger than a
common soldier's sentry box. In the lower part of this box, the
operator of the movements remained ensconced and invisible to the
audience, while the upper part of the said box formed the exposed
theatre, where the puppets were exhibited. On this occasion there
were only four figures as *dramatis personæ*, viz., Punch, Joan (his
wife), little Judy, and the Devil. The operator certainly possessed
considerable comic powers and a great share of low humour, by
which he kept the company in a constant roar of laughter. The
imitations of the voices of Joan and of Judy were excellent, and his
buffoonery, by making the figures the vehicles of his scurril mirth
and vulgar jests, showed great talents for ridicule and burlesque.
The Devil (as usually represented) had two horns on his head, a jet-
black face, and flaming fiery eyes. If at any time he popped up his
head from a corner of the stage to take a sly peep of what was going
on, Mr Punch never failed to give him a tremendous thwack on the
crown, which sent him headlong to the lower regions, amidst the
immense cheering and loud plaudits of the audience. Our music

T

consisted of various tunes from a small barrel-organ, and of a few
humorous songs, such as the "Taylor Done Over;" also of some
infantile recitatives, as—

> " Yin-erie, twa-erie, tick-erie, seven,
> Alibi, crack-erie, ten or eleven,
> Pin, pan, muskie dan,
> Tweedle-um, twaddle-um, twenty-one,"
> &c., &c.

For nearly a month after having seen this show my leisure hours
were wholly occupied in manufacturing Mr Punch and the above-
mentioned puppets, and exhibiting them at home to my companions
and others, from a pavilion and stage got up for the purpose with
chairs and old carpets.

The following notice of a show in Glasgow took place before my
day, but the effects of this exhibition extended to my juvenile
years, as it then became quite the rage in Glasgow for young ladies,
as a piece of education, to be taught the art of constructing grottos,
shell fruits, shell flowers, and other testaceous ornaments ; some of
which were to be seen adorning the drawing room mantelpieces of
all our fashionable folks of the day ; and I daresay that many of
your readers yet see some of the beautiful foreign shells of those
bygone days still forming the ornaments of the brace-pieces of many
of our old Glasgow dowagers.

" *Glasgow Journal,* 12th February, 1759.

" Mr Perrot has just arrived here from London with the most
exact and beautiful models of the following grottos and shellwork,
viz:—

" 1st, The Royal Grotto at Marli, in France.

" 2d, Sir Nathaniel Curzon's Grotto in Derbyshire.

" 3d, A piece of Shellwork in the Grand Signor's Palace.

" 4th, A Royal Grotto at Lisbon.

" 5th, The Royal Shellwork of the Emperor of Germany.

" 6th, The Royal Shellwork at Herenhausen, in Hanover.

" 7th, Trees made of sea-weeds.

" 8th, A piece ditto in the garden of Versailles.

" Also, some fine pieces in the Chinese and Gothic tastes, which
were never before exhibited.

" The above are composed of the most curious and valuable shells,
fine red and white corals, and other materials, arranged with great

propriety and elegance, and perfectly resembling those famous works (on the models of which they are formed), whose beauty of design and rural simplicity render them the admiration of all who see them.

"The above are all to be seen with the naked eye, and may be viewed by two or more at any hour from ten in the morning till ten at night, at Mr Turnbull's, the Crown and Anchor, directly opposite the Guard—Price Sixpence.

"Mr Perrot instructs ladies and gentlemen in the art of making shellwork on reasonable terms."

Mr Perrot, however, was not permitted to monopolise the instruction of young ladies in the elegant art of making grottos and shellwork; for John Gibson advertises that he has opened a warehouse on the first storey of Buchanan's Land, opposite the Main Guard, where he teaches ladies the following works (which, he says, " have been always esteemed a necessary piece of their education"), viz., japanning upon wood, painting upon glass, making jars of glass (painted in imitation of china), shell flowers, and all sorts of shell and grotto work, in the most genteel taste, &c. The prices are a guinea per month if the ladies attend the school, and a guinea and a half if they are taught at their houses.

In my early days there was a Miss Gardiner, from Edinburgh, who came to Glasgow, and advertised to teach our young ladies the following branches of fashionable accomplishments, as a necessary part of their education, viz., to make gumflowers, shellwork, glass jars (in imitation of china), Dresden fabrics, to work watch chains and strings, fringes and net purses (in imitation of lace), &c., &c. This lady also boarded young ladies at her house in Marshall's Land, Saltmarket, and undertook to improve and polish their manners, in conformity to those of the most fashionable circles in London. I remember this lady very well. She was extremely conceited and formal, and prided herself upon being able to *nap* the King's English in the purest style. I have seen many of the productions of the scholars of this lady ; in particular one of Adam and Eve, placed in a shell grotto, surrounded with trees of seaweeds, and the celebrated tree of knowledge of good and evil in front, having clusters of tempting apples upon it, made from small red coral beads. The serpent, however, was awanting. I have further had in my possession one of the famous glass jars, made, in imitation of china, by one of Miss Gardiner's pupils. It consisted of a crystal jar, in the inside parts of which were pasted Chinese prints, richly decorated by the young artist in brilliant red, blue, and green colours; having views of tea-parties enjoying themselves in arbours, amidst willow trees, Tartar pagodas, crooked bridges, and clumsy barges floating in ponds. The inside of the jar was coated with stucco, which gave it the appearance of rich porcelain, and on the whole it formed a pretty enough toy.

The following is an advertisement from the Glasgow newspapers of the times, and shows how valuable a shell grotto was then esteemed :—

"The Raffle of the Grotto belonging to Miss M'Lean is obliged to " be postponed to Friday the 2d of January next, at the house of " James Graham, vintner (Saracen's Head). It is requested that " such ladies and gentlemen who were entrusted with subscription " papers will lodge them, with the money, in the hands of James " Graham, betwixt and said date."

At this time the principal watering places on the west coast were Gourock* and Inverkip. Largs was then considered to be rather too far distant, and difficult of access, in consequence of which only a few families from Glasgow took up their summer residence there. Rothesay, for a like reason, had still fewer Glasgow visitors as salt-water lodgers. Helensburgh might then have been said as non-existent; and in the year 1779 our family were the sole summer occupiers of lodgings at Dunoon, or upon any part of the coast of Cowal, which was at that period looked upon as altogether a wild uncultivated Highland district. The young ladies and children of the families who then visited the west coast employed their whole vacant and idle hours in search of curious shells along the shores of the Frith, and in industriously picking up all the Buccinæ, Cochleæ, Volutæ, and Tellinæ from the sands, and in particular the beautiful small shells of the orange-coloured peckten, or scallop shell, in order to form their grottos and shell works. These elegant small scallop shells were in great demand, to make purses and pin-cushions of them. There was, however, a great drawback to the use of these, our Frith shells, for fashionable shell work—viz., that they were rough and unpolished. At this time the importation into London

---

* "*Glasgow Journal*, 15th March, 1764.—GOAT WHEY QUARTERS. To be let this " present year, the mansion house of Gourock, with a large garden, and enclosure of " grass that will keep half-a-dozen of horses and a couple of cows. It will easily divide " for several families, as it has separate entries. The house is two short miles from " Greenock; and as there is a turnpike road *almost* the whole way, the communication " is equally good to Glasgow by land or water. There is also to sett, a large thatch " house, for a change house, in the south end of Gourock."

of rare and beautiful shells from India, China, the West Indies, and indeed from every quarter of the world, had become an extensive and important branch of business. These shells, on arrival in London, were subjected to a regular process of cleaning, polishing, and varnishing, so as to suit them to the taste of the market. The Dutch, in particular, excelled in the art of polishing up shells. They not only filed them down on all sides, but also subjected them to the action of the wheel, by which the very character of the species became a riddle ; nor did they stop at this, but, being determined to have beauty at any rate, they set about improving nature, and frequently added some lines and colours with a pencil, and afterwards covered them over with a fine coat of varnish, so that they seemed to be the natural lineations of the shell. It was with such like rare and finely polished shells, brought from London, that nearly all our Glasgow school grottos and shell works were constructed ; and the more uncommon the appearance of the shell seemed to be, so much the more valuable it became. I must say that many of these shells were extremely beautiful, and would have claimed the admiration of any professed conchologist. I have in my possession some of the beautiful polished shells of those bygone days, which still ornament the mantelpiece of my bed-room, and are yet much admired.

About this time a Signior Powell went about the country exhibiting very wonderful deeds of fire-eating. He swallowed red-hot coals, taken directly from a blazing pile, and gulped down large draughts of liquid fire, flaming sealing wax, and burning brimstone. He also broiled steaks upon his tongue, and washed his mouth with oil of vitriol. He likewise performed numerous other extraordinary feats of pyrotechnics, to the extreme astonishment of the beholders.

In the *Journal des Scavans*, there is the following explanation how these fire-eating performances were effected, viz. :—" The secret of fire-eating was made public by a servant to one Richardson, an Englishman, who showed it in France about the year 1667, and was the first performer of the kind that ever appeared in Europe. This secret consisted only in rubbing the hands, and thoroughly washing the mouth, lips, tongue, teeth, and other parts that are to touch the fire, with pure spirit of sulphur, or a mixture of spirits of sulphur, sal-ammoniac, and essence of rosemary. This burns and cauterises the epidermis or upper skin, until it becomes as thick leather, and every time that the experiment is tried it becomes still easier than before to perform the operation with safety. In broiling a veal cutlet in his mouth, the performer first lays on a very thin slice on his tongue, then the red-hot charcoal above that, and lastly places the cutlet about to be broiled on the said glowing materials, and so dresses it, fit to be presented at the table. The red-hot coals cannot burn him before they are extinguished by the saliva which soon insensibly fills the cavity of his mouth. After the performer has retired from the exhibition, he generally drinks a plentiful dose of warm water and oil, till he has vomited up whatever of the materials he had been obliged to swallow in the course of his fiery operations."

The hands of many blacksmiths and forgemen acquire such a degree of callosity, by often handling red-hot materials, that these men will carry a glowing bar of iron from the furnace to the anvil in their naked fists without the least hurt. Tavernier, in his voyages, says that he met with a slave who would suffer himself, for a small reward, to be hung round with heavy chains of red-hot iron, and would keep them on till they were quite cold, without the least apparent sense of pain. (This, however, appears to me to be a little hyperbolical.) The ordeal by fire was a Saxon mode of trial, in which an appeal was made to Heaven, when the accused undertook to walk blindfold between nine red-hot ploughshares, and if he or she escaped unhurt, it was looked upon as a proof of innocence. Queen Emma, a Saxon princess, successfully underwent this ordeal—no doubt previously instructed by the priesthood in what manner to guard herself against the effects of the ardent ploughshares.

The next show that I shall take notice of was certainly a very curious one; and I believe that nothing of the kind has ever since been exhibited in Europe. We have had many shows of learned horses, learned dogs, and even learned pigs; but who, now-a-days, ever saw a learned flea? The very idea of the thing appears ludicrous. Nevertheless, such was the novel spectacle exhibited to our wondering citizens of olden time, as the following advertisement fully explains:—

" *Glasgow Journal*, 4th August, 1763."
" THIS IS TO ACQUAINT THE CURIOUS,

"'That there is to be exhibited by the inventor and maker, S. Boverick, from nine in the morning till eight in the evening, at the sign of the Mason's Arms, opposite the Main Guard, Trongate, at one shilling each person, the so much admired collection of Miniature Curiosities, consisting of the following pieces:—

" 1. An ivory chaise with four wheels, and all the proper apparatus belonging to them, turning readily on their axis together, with a man sitting on the chaise, all drawn by a flea, without any seeming difficulty, the chaiseman and flea being barely equal to a single grain.

" 2. A flea chained to a chain of 200 links, with a padlock and key—all weighing less than one-third of a grain. The padlock locks and unlocks. These two pieces are mentioned, with admiration, by Mr Henry Baker, of the Royal Society, in his book called ' Microscope made Easy,' which the inventor and maker has by him, to show if required.

" 3. A landau, which opens and shuts by springs, hanging on braces, with four persons therein, two footmen behind, a coachman on the box, with a dog between his legs, six horses and a postillion, all drawn by a single flea!

" 4. A pair of steel scissors weighing but the sixteenth part of a grain, which will cut a large horse-hair.

" 5. Thirty-six dozen of well-fashioned silver spoons in a peppercorn, and still room for several dozens more.

" *N. B.*—The above curiosities have been shown to the Courts of England, France, and Holland, the Royal Society in London, the Professors of Mathematics at Leyden, who have done the maker the honour to give testimonies of their approbation under their hands, in Latin, and nether Dutch, which may be seen by any person who desires it.

" ☞ To be exhibited here no longer than the 13th inst.—August, 1763."

In speaking about the show of the lion-tiger, I stated that the death of that noble animal was rather tragical; but, on the contrary, the death of this poor flea was truly comical. It took place thus, as reported to me :—A country wife, from Pollokshaws, having come to Glasgow on a market day to sell her fowls and eggs, happened to see people going into the above-mentioned show in Buchanan's Land, and, as she had made very favourable sales that day of her stock, she resolved to see the said show; accordingly, without knowing exactly what she was about to see, she paid her admission money, and directly thereafter marched up to the table on which the flea was performing its task of drawing the ivory coach and coachman. The poor woman looked only to the flea, and instantly turning down her thumb nail upon it, cracked it in a moment, exclaiming—" Filthy beast, wha could hae brought you here?" The showman in a violent rage, seized the woman by the throat, and demanded how she dared to kill the flea. On the other hand, the astonished woman, not knowing that she had done anything wrong, exclaimed—"Losh, me, man, makin' sic a wark about a flea; gif you come wi' me to the Shaws, we'll gie you a peck o' them, and be muckle obliged to you for takin' them." As the woman was a widow, and possessed little or no property, Mr Boverick thought it most prudent to put up with his loss, in place of going into a court of law for damages. In the present times, the value of a flea would be a curious question at a jury trial. The flea (*Pulex*) has six legs; nevertheless it seldom walks, but is remarkable for its agility in leaping to a height equal to 200 times that of its own body. This bloodthirsty insect, which fattens at the expense of the human species, is said to prefer the more delicate skin of young ladies, in which, with its piercer or sucker, it first makes an entrance, and then thrusts it farther into the flesh, so as to make the blood flow from the adjacent parts, and thus occasions that round red spot, with a hole in the centre, called "a flea bite." The learned flea in question, however, was not favoured with such a delicate morsel as a mouthful from the limb of a young lady, but took its meals from the plump and juicy arms of Mr Boverick himself, who fed it carefully with his own blood, and at night kept it snugly domiciled in a little box lined with soft velvet and select silken caddis, by which attentions it came to be on friendly and intimate terms with its master.

"*Glasgow Journal*, 5th January, 1764."—"To the lovers of real curiosities.—This is to acquaint the nobility, gentry, and others, that the brother of the famous Mr Zucker, a high German (who has gained such universal applause), is just come to town, and will perform at James Buchanan's, at the White Hart, in the Gallowgate,* on Friday the 6th instant, and continue to do so every day. The door to be opened at eleven forenoon, and begin exactly half-an-hour after, and ends at one; and in the evening at half an hour after six, and ends at eight. He had the honour to perform his surprising feats of arts, with general approbation, before the Royal family, nobility, and gentry, at the great concert room in Panton Street, London, for near two years successively. He has brought with him the most amazing learned little horse from Courland,

---

* This inn then stood without the Gallowgate Port. In 1754 Robert Tennent occupied it, but having built the Saracen's Head Inn, in 1755 he removed to that large inn, and the White Hart Inn came to be occupied by James Buchanan.

whose wonderful knowledge is not to be paralleled by any animal in this kingdom, or perhaps in the whole world. He wants only speech. As a specimen of his abilities, we shall mention the following particulars, viz.:—He makes a polite and curious compliment to the company ; tells the value of anything which is shown to him; he plays at cards, and finds the place where the card is hid; shows by a watch the hour of the day, and understands arithmetic ; he distinguishes ladies from gentlemen ; he understands the almanack, and demonstrates the day of the month; he plays at dice, and is always sure to win; he drinks the company's health like a human person ; his master borrows a piece of money of one of the company, and throws it on the floor; the horse takes it up, and returns it to the person that lent it; when he is told that he is to leave the empire or go to the Grand Turk he shams lame, and walks about the room as cripple; but when he is told he shall be excused, he immediately recovers, makes his compliments on his knees, and thanks the company. The master himself will likewise entertain the company with many curiosities. He turns two dishes at once in so dexterous a manner as gives pleasure and surprise to the spectators. There will be given an entertainment on the musical glasses, and also on common drinking glasses, several tunes. Amongst others—'Tweedside,' 'Corn Riggs are Bonny,' 'Hearts of Oak,' 'Artaxerxes,' 'Voi Amanta,' &c., &c. Price, one shilling."

Of all quadrupeds subject to the rule of man, there are none so valuable as the horse; he is not only extremely docile, but is also the fleetest of all animals, and capable of running down the winged ostrich itself. The famous racehorse, Childers (commonly called the Flying Childers), ran the long course at Newmarket in 7½ minutes. This course was exactly 4 miles and 380 yards, so that he ran at the rate of more than 49 feet in a second. At every bound he covered a space of upwards of 24 feet.

The little learned horse in question, although of German breed, might have been taken for one of our small Highland shelties, and, owing to its diminutive size, seemed very suitable for exhibition in a room so contracted as the one in the White Hart, where it was shown.

Perhaps some of your elderly readers may remember that an attempt was made in the theatre, Dunlop Street, to give a representation of the Newmarket races. Part of the pit was then laid off to form a race course, and there the starting post was placed. The course itself extended to the extremity of the stage. The racehorses consisted of two diminutive Shetland ponies, which were mounted by two smart boys, in full jockey costume. The race consisted of three courses, and, to all appearance, the boys exerted their utmost abilities to be first at the goal. The course, however, was greatly too short, and too narrow for such an exhibition; and, besides, the feet of the horses made a disagreeable clattering noise in racing, in consequence of the foundations of the said course having been composed of deal boards, which yielded to the weight of the horses and the riders as they ran along: this took away all idea of a race upon the turf. On the whole, the exhibition was a failure, and has never since been repeated.

There have been several exhibitions in Glasgow of learned dogs—some of which, I have no doubt, were seen by many of your readers. All these dogs performed similar feats to those of the above-mentioned learned horse ; but there was one very intelligent dog shown in my day, which, besides telling the time by a watch, finding out hidden money, and doing the usual sagacious acts of learned animals, also spelled any common word proposed by the company. The letters of the alphabet were printed on loose slips and laid upon the floor of the room, and when any person of the company requested the dog to spell a particular word of common conversation, the show-master addressed the dog, desiring him to spell the word then named, which the dog did by drawing from the alphabet lying on the floor the letters constituting the word required to be spelt; words, however, which were uncommon or difficult to spell were excepted.

I remember of being present on one of these occasions, when a gentleman of the company asked the dog to spell the word "Antigua." The show-master said that that was rather a hard word for a dog to spell, but he would try what could be done; and accordingly he told the dog that a gentleman in the room wished the word " Antigua" to be spelled, on which the dog proceeded to the loose slips of the alphabet lying on the floor of the room, and, with his paw, drew out from amongst them the capital letters " Antigua" to the great delight of the company. This I myself saw done.

According to Bailey, the longest word in the English language is " Honorificabilitudinity," but I am afraid that the spelling of this word would be beyond the most profound canine sagacity. How droll it would sound to say that such a man is a person of the greatest "honorificabilitudinity !" or to call him by the name of " Mr Honorificabilitudinitas"—(see Bailey)—but however difficult it may appear to pronounce this jaw-breaking word, nevertheless, from the following advertisement it will be seen that a "learned pig" was exhibited in Glasgow which was capable of joining together the letters which form this polysyllable.

Although none of your readers may have seen a "learned flea," I believe that many of them have viewed with admiration the pranks of a "learned horse," for there have been more than one exhibition of this kind in Glasgow in the course of the last eighty years; few of these performances, however, were at all equal to those of the learned little pig undernoted :—

"*Glasgow Mercury*, 9th May, 1787.—Among the infinite number of curiosities hitherto offered to the inspection and attention of the public, there are none which lay so great a claim to our attention and approbation as the wonderful and astonishing performances of the 'learned pig,' now exhibiting in Mr Frazer's Dancing Hall, M'Nair's Land, King Street, from eleven o'clock, forenoon, to three in the afternoon, and from five to nine at night, where it may be seen this and every day in the ensuing week, at the expiration of which the proprietor is under engagement to set off for Edinburgh.

"This most singular phenomenon is one of the many surprising instances of the ingenuity of Mr Nicholson—a man who is possessed of an exclusive and peculiar power over the most irrational part of animated nature. Many of the first personages in the three kingdoms have been witnesses to his persevering temper and patience in the tuition of beasts, birds, etc., in a degree that has seldom fallen to the lot of human infirmity. To evince this, we need only mention his having in his lifetime taught a turtle to fetch and carry articles at his pleasure ; his overcoming the timidity of a hare, by making her beat a drum ; his perfecting six turkey-cocks in a regular country dance; his completing a small bird in the performance of many surprising feats; his having taught three cats to strike several tunes on the dulcimer with their paws, and to imitate the Italian manner of singing; but above all, his conquering the natural obstinacy and stupidity of a pig, by teaching him to unite the letters of any person's name, to tell the number of persons present in the room, and the hour and minute by any watch, &c., &c. This singular creature may justly be deemed the greatest curiosity in the kingdom, and the proprietor makes no doubt but he will give that satisfaction, and receive that approbation, from the ladies and gentlemen of this city, &c., &c., which he has done in London and Edinburgh. Admittance, 6d each."

Had Pope seen this learned pig, perhaps he would not have
written

> " How instinct varies, in the grov'lling swine,
> Compar'd, half-reasoning elephant, with thine !
> 'Twixt that and reason, what a nice barrier,
> For ever separate, yet for ever near."

I paid my sixpence and witnessed the above-mentioned performances, which I must confess were truly very extraordinary, more
especially knowing how obstinate and intractable an animal a pig is.
These performances were very similar, and quite equal to those
exhibited by the learned horse and learned dog; but still the great
drawback to the pleasure of the show was the incongruity of making
a pet of a pig in a handsome room, while the natural element of the
animal is the cloaca.   A Roman author has justly written—

> " Volutatio in luto est Suum requies, ut lavatio hominum."

Mons. Buffon has stated that the hog is the most impure and
filthy of all animals, and is naturally stupid, inactive, and drowsy ;
that all its habits are gross ; all its appetites nauseous ; all its sen-
sations confined to a furious lust and a brutal gluttony.   It devours
indiscriminately everything that comes in its way—even its own
progeny, the moment after their birth.   Who could fondle with
pleasure such an an animal, however learned ?

During the time that this learned pig was in the progress of exhibition, I was attending our Glasgow Grammar School, when the
following Latin saying used to be handed to the tyros for translation
—it admitting of a double meaning—" *Mea Mater Sus est*," which
may be translated either " My mother is a sow," or, " Run, mother,
the sow is eating."*

But from these shows of the lower class of animals I must depart,
and now advert to some exhibitions of a higher description of beings
—I mean Giants.   We are informed by the Scripture that " Giants
were produced" from the marriages of the " Sons of God " with the
" Daughters of MEN ;" but we have no account of the dimensions of
this mongrel race, nor of any valiant deeds which they performed :
I therefore leave it to our learned Hebrew commentators to explain
this mysterious passage.

* The following scrap of Latin was also another of the Grammar School puzzles of
my early days :—"Malo, malo, malo, malo, malo, malo, malo, quam dente vento
occurrere."   The translation of which is—" I would rather meet with a bad apple, with
a bad tooth, than a bad mast with a bad wind."

In the *Glasgow Mercury* of 11th January, 1781, there is the following advertisement :— -

"By Permission.

"Just arrived in this City, and to be seen at Mr Heron's, at
"the Bull, the surprising
"IRISH GIANT,

"Only twenty years old, yet measures eight feet high, who is allowed to be the most extraordinary man for size and proportion that ever appeared in Europe. Admission, 1s each. Hours of admittance, from eleven in the forenoon till three in the afternoon, and from four till nine o'clock at night. To continue one week only."

The giant seems to have been very well pleased with his reception in Glasgow, for, in the ensuing paper of the 18th of January, we find the following intimation :—

"January 17, 1781.—The Irish Giant presents his most respectful compliments to the ladies and gentlemen of Glasgow, and desires to inform them that (by permission) he intends to remain at his lodgings, at the Bull, one week from the date hereof."

I did not see this giant, and therefore cannot give any particular description of him. The exhibition, however, was pretty well attended by the public.

On the 21st October, 1784, the *Glasgow Mercury* announces as follows :—

"IRISH GIANTS.

"The most gigantic Twin Brothers are just arrived in this city, and to be seen at Mr Brown's Auction Room, head of Saltmarket, from eleven in the forenoon till three in the afternoon, and from four in the afternoon till nine at night, every day (Sunday excepted). These wonderful Irish Giants are but 24 years of age, and measure very near eight feet high. These truly amazing phenomena are indisputably the most astonishing productions of the human species ever beheld since the days of Goliah.

"Their amazing size does not more agreeably surprise the curious spectator, than their proportion. in every respect, to their stupendous height, a circumstance seldom to be found in any extraordinary production of nature. Their stay is but short.

"Admittance to ladies and gentlemen, one shilling. Servants, &c., sixpence."

Although these giants gave themselves out to be nearly eight feet high, they were in fact only about seven feet and a half in height, and were not patronised so much by the public as the giant of 1781, who was a trifle taller than they were.*

I did not attend this exhibition; but, some time afterwards, I visited the show of another giant, whose name, I think, was O'Brian, who was considerably taller than any of the above-mentioned giants. He advertised himself to be eight feet and a half high. The room in which he showed himself appeared to me to have been about ten feet high, and I saw him rest his arms *akimbo*, on the top of the door, while his head and shoulders appeared above the door. Notwithstanding of his immense height, he had not the least appearance of a giant, for his body was lank and thin; his shoulders contracted; his legs and arms, though extremely long, were slender and unmuscular; while, on the other hand, his hands and feet were out of all proportion to his body, being of most enormous dimensions. I attempted to span his *thumb* with my hand, but could not encircle it, for its circumference was nearly equal to that of my own arm at the wrist. I measured the size of his hand by my own, and found that his hand reached from the tip of my fingers to the joint of my elbow—a space of more than a foot. In short, however, this giant appeared to have been merely what we call a *lang, loupin, shachlin, spindle-shank*, suddenly overgrown, clownish in his appearance, and vulgar in his manners. While I was standing looking at him, a little miss came close to me, but seeing the gaunt giant approaching, she got alarmed and ran behind me for protection, which the giant observing, he held out his immense *paw* to her, exclaiming—" Be not afraid, miss, for I am quite tame ! ! !"

I doubt if there has ever been related, on satisfactory record, any instance of a man having been taller than this giant, supposing him to have been eight feet and a half in height, as he advertised himself. We know from history that the Emperor Maximin was a little above eight feet in stature, and Scripture tells us that Goliah's "height was six cubits and a span;" but the Jewish cubit and span, like our own palm, step, and barley-corn, were merely approximating measures. Dr Johnson says that the cubit is a measure of a foot and a half; Crabb states that it is one foot nine inches; while Baylie thus writes—"Cubit is a Scripture measure about five English feet nine inches, and 888 decimal parts." According, therefore,

---

* Big Sam, once well known on the streets of Glasgow, was only about seven feet high, but he was a perfect giant in his proportions, every part of his body being of gigantic dimensions—his shoulders, arms, and legs were truly massive, as the limbs of an ox. He became porter to the Prince of Wales, at Carlton House.

to Bailey, Goliah must have been 35 feet high. I have seen an antiquarian disquisition regarding the height of Goliah, which concluded by supposing him to have been rather above eight feet. We learn from Scripture that King David, who was a little man, took the sword of Goliah, as fitting him to a hair; for he says to the priest, regarding Goliah's sword, "There is none like that—give it me." Now, if King David could wield the sword of Goliah with ease, the inference is that Goliah was not quite a Titan.

Having thus taken notice of the shows in Glasgow where giants were exhibited, I shall now proceed to give some account of the shows of dwarfs, which took place in our city in olden time.

The Romans were passionately fond of dwarfs, insomuch that they used artificial methods to prevent the growth of boys, whom they designed for dwarfs, by enclosing them in boxes, or by the use of tight bandages, as the Chinese do to the feet of their females, for the purpose of obstructing their enlargement. Such methods, however, of distorting nature are unknown to our countrymen. I have seen various shows of dwarfs, but in almost every instance these "Manikins,"* besides their small size, were deformed in some way or other, some parts of their frame being generally out of proportion to other parts of it. The only dwarf that I ever saw, whose relative proportions were good, was the celebrated Count Borulawski. I have had the pleasure not only of seeing but also of conversing with this little mannoc, whom I found to be a gentleman of highly polished manners, possessing great conversational powers, and a ready wit, united to a sound judgment and excellent memory.

Count Borulawski was the son of a Polish nobleman, attached to the fortunes of King Stanislaus, who lost his property in consequence of that attachment, and who had six children, three dwarfs and three well grown. What is singular enough, they were born alternately, a big one and a little one, though both parents were of the common size. The little Count's sister was much less than him, but died at the age of twenty-three. The Count continued to grow till he was about thirty. When I saw him he was upwards of fifty years of age, and was then only 38 inches high. At the age of forty-one he married a lady of his own country, but of French extraction, and of the middle size. This marriage was not a happy one,

---

* In estimating the relative size of "Man," the English language has only two degrees of comparison, viz., "Man, manikin;" but in Scotland we have three degrees of comparison of the said word, viz., "Man, mannie, mannoc;" also, "Lad, laddie, laddoc; Lass, lassie, lassoc," &c.

and involved the Count in great care and perplexity, as he had to provide for a family of three children, all daughters, but none of them dwarfs. To maintain this establishment became an object of great difficulty, and required the utmost exertion of his powers and talents, of which music alone afforded any view of profit. He played extremely well upon the guitar, and pretty tolerably upon the violin. He therefore commenced giving concerts in the principal cities in Germany, and was patronised by the different princes of the empire, who admitted him to great personal familiarity, which was followed by a like familiarity on the part of the nobility at these German courts. As an instance how easy he was in his intercourse with the great, it may be stated that one day, while he was sitting in familiar chit-chat alongside of the celebrated Maria Theresa, Empress of Germany and Queen of Hungary, he happened to cast his eye upon a brilliant diamond ring upon the finger of the Empress, which her Majesty observing, she asked the Count if he was admiring her ring. " No, please your Majesty," replied the Count, " I am not admiring the ring, but I am admiring the beautiful white hand which wears the ring." The Empress laughed heartily at the Count's polite and witty reply, and, in return, said— " Well, Count, the ring is too large for your finger, but I will find one to suit ;" and so calling to her her daughter, Marie Antoinette (afterwards the unfortunate Queen of France), then a child, she took a ring from the child's finger and placed it on the finger of the Count as a souvenir.

Although Count Borulawski gave public concerts ostensibly as musical entertainments, in point of fact these concerts were merely a cover for exhibiting his person. The Count felt the greatest repugnance at making himself a public show for money, considering the same as derogatory to his dignity, and, therefore, it was not till dire necessity compelled him to expose himself to public view for gain as a spectacle that he adopted that course.

Having traversed Germany, and having given concerts at all the courts of the German princes, the Count resolved to make a similar musical tour in Russia, and accordingly set out for that country, under the impression that he would find a population there as civilised as that of Germany. And strange to say, he went to Finland, and from thence to Nova Zembla, for the purpose of giving public concerts in these wild regions, but, of course, without success. From Nova Zembla he went to Archangel, and gave a concert there with some trifling good fortune. Leaving Archangel, he travelled through the wilds of Siberia, and along the north-eastern coast of Russia, till he arrived at Kamschatka, where he astonished the natives with his concert. From thence he proceeded south till he arrived at Astracan, where he also gave a concert, and with tolerable success.

He now travelled through various parts of Asiatic Turkey, giving concerts wherever he thought he could attract an audience, but the profits of his musical entertainments were found to be very trifling, and therefore he bent his course back to Vienna, where he met his former patrons, who strongly advised him to turn his thoughts towards England, where, it was believed, that the public curiosity might, in a little time, benefit him sufficiently to enable him to live independent in so cheap a country as Poland. Accordingly his friends furnished him with recommendations to the Duchess of Devonshire, the Duchess of Rutland, and other English celebrities of the time, whose kind patronage the Count most gratefully acknowledged. Through them he was introduced to the Prince of Wales, and to other branches of the Royal family.

When in London he was strongly advised to let himself be seen as a curiosity, to which he most reluctantly consented; but he then fixed the price of admission at a guinea, which prevented his visitors being numerous. After a pretty long stay in London, he, from necessity, came to the resolution of travelling about from place to place, at a small price of admission, and, accordingly, he went to Bath and Bristol, where he met with brilliant success. From thence he visited Dublin and other parts of Ireland, and afterwards travelled to Edinburgh, Glasgow, &c., returning to London by way of Liverpool, Manchester, and Birmingham. In every place he was received with the greatest *eclat*, and made a most lucrative tour ; but on one or two occasions during the progress of this tour his profits were greatly lessened by the unfortunate arrival of the learned pig at the same towns where he was exhibiting himself, and consequently the manikin and the learned pig became competing parties. Perhaps, now-a-days, they would have *amalgamated !*

When I saw the Count, the price of admission, I think, was only 1s., and the attendance at his levees was then very numerous.

I remember very well, that when the Count was exhibiting himself at Glasgow as a show, that a report became current in the city of a quarrel having taken place between the Count and his wife, and that the latter, being overcome with passion, and forgetful of her duty as a wife, had taken up the Count in her arms, and placed him

U

on the mantelpiece of the room, and there left him, so that the little man ran the most imminent risk of falling and breaking his neck. The report went on to say, that the Count was obliged to make use of many endearing expressions, and much coaxing, before the angry wife consented to relieve him. At one of the Count's levees in Glasgow, a vulgar visitor had the rudeness to ask him if this story was true. The Count replied that it was too unpolite to require an answer, and indignantly turned his back upon the impertinent querist.

While the Count was in Glasgow, Humphrey Crombie, Esq., merchant (cousin of the late Mr Ewing, of Strathleven), invited him to dinner, which invitation was accepted. Just as the company were about to sit down to the dinner-table, the Count asked Mr Crombie for the loan of his family Bible, which request was immediately complied with. Mr Crombie, knowing that the Count was a Roman Catholic, supposed that he was going to read some passage from the Scriptures before he took his seat at table; the Count, however, instead of doing so, placed the large family Bible on the seat of his chair, jocularly remarking, that he liked to rest on a good and sure foundation. In fact, without the elevation afforded by the large Bible, the Count's face would just have been flush with the surface of the dining table.

Mr Crombie informed me that he found the Count to be a most intelligent and amusing personage, possessing much vivacity and ready wit, and quite a treat as a guest at the social board.

Besides his native language, the Count spoke the French language fluently, and the English language pretty well for a foreigner. In his person, he was pleasing and graceful; and his looks, notwithstanding of his small size, were manly and engaging. He dressed like a Frenchman, with powder and pigtail, rings and ruffles, &c. By making a show of himself for some time throughout Britain, he acquired a moderate competency; and as it had always been with the greatest reluctance that he had so exhibited himself, he now resolved to retire from public view, and to spend the remainder of his days in privacy. Accordingly, he settled in Durham, where he lived many years as a private gentleman, much respected.

I think he died there about forty years ago, upwards of seventy years of age. The following was one of the Count's advertisements:

"Glasgow, 3d May, 1789.—Count Borulawski presents his respectful compliments to the ladies and gentlemen of Glasgow and the neighbourhood, will esteem himself honoured with their company to a public breakfast, at the Assembly Room, on Friday the 8th instant, at 12 o'clock, in the course of which the Count will perform some select pieces on the guitar. Tickets to be had at the Count's lodgings, Argyll Street, opposite Stockwell, or at the Room, at 3s 6d each."

I shall now make a short digression, and take notice of a still more curious instance of an extraordinary dwarf. Jeffery Hudson, the famous English dwarf, was born in 1619, and at about the age of seven was only 18 inches high. He was retained in the service of the Duke of Buckingham, and while there (soon after the marriage of Charles I.), the King and Queen being entertained at Burlegh by the Duke, little Jeffery was served up to table in a cold pie!

> "When the pye was opened,
> The dwarf began to fling ;
> And was not this a dainty dish
> To set before the King?"—*Old Rhymes.*

It is a curious circumstance that from seven years of age till thirty, Jeffery never grew taller ; but after thirty, he shot up to three feet nine inches, and there fixed. Being provoked by the sarcasms of a Mr Crofts, a man of family, a challenge and duel with pistols ensued, when Jeffery, at the first fire, shot his antagonist dead. He was afterwards made a captain in the Royal army, and in 1644 attended the Queen to France. He returned at the Restoration, and ended his life in the 63d year of his age.

But returning from this digression, I have now to take notice of a show in Glasgow, where a dwarf was exhibited of nearly as small dimensions as Count Borulawski, though far from being so interesting as the Count was. Along with him was also exhibited a lady, born without arms, who made use of her toes with great dexterity, in place of fingers, as the following advertisement intimates :—

" *Glasgow Mercury,* 24th February, 1785.

" To all who are admirers of extraordinary productions of nature.

" Just arrived, and to be seen by any number of persons in Mr Brown's Auction Room, near the head of the Saltmarket, from eleven in the morning till nine in the evening,

" THE SURPRISING DWARF.

" He is only 23 years of age, and not 39 inches high.

" His surprising smallness makes a striking impression at first sight on the spectator's mind; his countenance and figure are extremely agreeable, and his manner and address give general satisfaction.

"*N.B.*—He is the *shortest person* that has ever been exhibited to the Public.

"ALSO,

"A YOUNG LADY (from Newfoundland),

"BORN WITHOUT ARMS.

"This curious phenomenon of nature, without hands, cuts watchpapers with her toes in the neatest manner, and presents them to gentlemen and ladies; threads the finest needle; does any part of needlework; and marks initial letters on linen to great perfection.

"*N.B.*—They will remain in this city till Wednesday the 23d current, and no longer. Admittance to Ladies and Gentlemen, One Shilling; Tradesmen and Children, Sixpence.

"Glasgow, Feb. 17, 1785."

I attended this exhibition; but after having seen Count Borulawski, I felt greatly disappointed at the sight of the dwarf mentioned in the above advertisement. He had nothing manly in his appearance; on the contrary, he seemed like a child dressed up with the habiliments of a full-grown man. His features were soft, and his manners, though good, could easily have been taught to a clever child : in short, many of the visitors doubted his age being 23, as stated by him, and suspected that he was not the one-half of that period of life, and that, in fact, he was only a smart child, possessing the countenance and manners of a grown-up person. The public, therefore, felt little interest as to this dwarf, but they showed great curiosity in regard to the lady born without arms, whose wonderful dexterity in the use of her toes caused not only great astonishment, but much merriment, to the beholders. I must confess, however, that the appearance of this lady (whose name, I think, was Morgan) was by no means pleasant, for although she was destitute of arms, nevertheless there was a fleshy protuberance or stump in lieu of them at each shoulder. These were nakedly exposed to the view of the company, and the sight of them was rather revolting than agreeable. Her countenance, however, was pretty good, and her manners lively and easy. She sat upon a cushion, with her feet bare; and it was truly surprising to see with what ease she used her toes in threading a needle, in hemming handkerchiefs, in embroidering, and in doing other feats of needlework. She was equally skilful in the management of her scissors, and the use of her pen. I had the honour of receiving a watch paper from this lady, neatly cut out by her with scissors, *praesto pollice.*

Anatomists allege that parties who are greatly deformed very seldom have a progeny; but I understood that this lady, after leaving Glasgow, got married, and had a family of children, who were all well formed and healthy.

There are several instances on record, and well authenticated, of persons having been born without arms. Francis North, son of Samuel North, born without arms, his hands growing out of his shoulders, was baptized 4th July, 1619.—*(Parish Register of Greenwich.)*

John Simmons, a native of Berkshire, born without arms or hands, could write with his mouth, thread a needle, tie a knot, shuffle, cut, and deal a pack of cards, &c. ; he was shown in public in 1653.—*(Bulwer's Changeling, p. 1168.)*

Thomas Pinnington, a native of Liverpool, born without legs or arms, was publicly exhibited in 1744. He, like Simmons, could perform various extraordinary feats with his mouth.

I believe that there are other instances on record of persons having been born without arms, but none of them appear to have made use of their toes in lieu of hands, like the lady of the foregoing advertisement.

The following notice of a show in Glasgow, of another description, attracted considerable attention amongst the youngsters of the city, who could not help comparing themselves with this hairy biped, and thanking their stars that heaven had formed them otherwise.

" Glasgow, 29th April, 1779.
" Just Arrived in this City,
" And to be seen at Mr Dick's Dancing Hall, Trongate,
" (Opposite to the head of the Old Wynd,)
" THE ETHIOPIAN SAVAGE.

" This astonishing creature, when he stands erect, is near five feet high, and is a striking resemblance of the human species. His ears are small, but have large apertures, so that he is extremely quick of hearing; his cheeks are ribbed, and of a fine blue; his nose and nostrils of a beautiful scarlet; his fore feet are like the arms and hands of a man, and grow gradually taper till they come to the wrist, and he uses his fingers with surprising facility. His body is covered with a fine long hair, perfectly smooth on the surface, and beautifully variegated from a light to a dark brown. His posteriors are amazingly tinctured with blue and scarlet, and he sits on them, in a very pleasing and majestic attitude, to receive and eat his food. His beard is extremely remarkable, for it is like that of a person in years, and of great strength. He is very affable, and obedient to the commands of his keeper, who can even sleep by his side in safety. This wonderful creature is a fine display of Nature's amazing productions, and is allowed to be the greatest curiosity in England.

> ' Here fix thy searching eye, whoe'er thou art;
> Here view th' Almighty's work in every part,
> And trace its wondrous nature.
> Mark well the skilful portrait. How divine
> Each view discovers of God's grand design
> To form a like to Man, in such a creature.' "

I did not see this Ethiopian Savage, as he arrived in Glasgow just as our family were departing to our summer quarters at Dunoon, which place then (1779) was altogether a Highland village, as thus stated by me in "Glasgow, Past and Present," Vol. II., p. 138 :—" When I now look around the shores of Dunoon, from the Holy Loch to the point of Toward, and see them studded with the splendid villas of my fellow-citizens, it appears curious to recall to my recollection the bygone days when these lands were lying in a state of nature, and when our family was the only one spending in amusement the summer months on the *whole line* of that coast."

Dunoon, in its then primitive state, appeared to me to be a sort of Paradise, and soon made me forget the Ethiopian Savage.

The following advertisement gives notice of the arrival in Glasgow of a show, where the public were to see great natural curiosities.

" *Glasgow Mercury*, 9th February, 1790.

" THE WONDERS OF NATURE.

" To the Nobility, Gentry, and the Curious, who are fond of inspecting the most extraordinary Human Beings of the wild species ever born.

" There will be seen, in a large room in Andrew Dunbar's, King's Arms, Trongate, from ten in the morning till nine at night, *Three wonderful Phenomena*, know by the name of MONSTROUS CRAWS, wild born, and of the Human Species. There are two Males and a Female, of a very small stature, being little less or more than four feet high; each with a CRAW under his throat ; containing within, some Three, some Four, and some Five Balls or Glands as large as eggs, and which play upwards and downwards in their Craws, according as incited, and forced, either by their speaking or laughing.

" These three most wonderful wild born Human Beings, whose country, language, and native customs are yet unknown to all mankind, it is supposed, started in some canoes from their native place (believed in some unknown, remote land in South America), and were picked up by a Spanish vessel, which in a violent storm was lost, when these three people, and another of the same kind, since dead, were providentially saved from perishing. At that period they were of a dark olive complexion; but which has astonishingly, by degrees, changed to the colour of that of Europeans.

" These three truly surprising Beings have attracted to themselves the most minute attention and great admiration of all the Princes, celebrated Anatomists and Naturalists to whom they have been presented in Europe, for their rare, and yet unknown species; and not less, indeed, for their most apparent and surprising happiness, and content among themselves, most endearing tractableness and respectful demeanour towards all strangers, as well as for their un- paralleled, and natural, cheerful, lively, and merry disposition, singing and dancing (in their most extraordinary way) at the will and pleasure of the company.

" The Indian Ambassadors, lately at Paris, were the personages who first inspected them there, to which place they were purposely imported, and from whence they are now arrived here in their speedy passage to a Northern Kingdom.

" Admittance—To Ladies and Gentlemen, one shilling; Servants, sixpence; Children, half-price."

These *monstrous* craws, as they were called, appeared to have been merely three poor diminutive creatures, most grievously afflicted with the disease called *cretinism*, which is a malady of tumours or swellings on the fore part of the neck, seated between the trachea and the skin, termed, in French, "*goitre*," but better known in this country by the Greek name of "*bronchocele*." Anatomists consider the disease to be a dropsical affection of the thy- roid gland. The swellings are at first soft, without pain, or any evi- dent fluctuation, and the skin retains its natural appearance; but as the tumours advance in size they become unequally hard, the skin acquires a copper colour, and the veins of the neck become varicose; the face becomes flushed, and is accompanied by stinging pains through the body of the tumours.

In the *Edinburgh Medical and Surgical Journal*, Vol. V, page 35, there is a plate of the skull of a *cretin*, who died at the age of thirty. The head is very large and the face small; it is like the skull of an adult joined to the face of a child. Dr Reeve, in his "Dissertation on Cretinism," remarks "that the head of a *cretin* is generally deformed, his stature diminutive, his complexion sickly, his countenance vacant and destitute of meaning, his lips and eyelids coarse and prominent, his skin wrinkled and pendulous, his muscles loose and flabby. The quality of his mind corresponds to the deranged state of the body which it inhabits, and *cretinism* prevails in all the intermediate degrees, from excessive stupidity to complete fatuity." Such, then, were these so-called *craws*.

The exhibition of the above-mentioned " wonders of nature " was not well attended in Glasgow, and the story about the shipwreck in South America was not believed. As the advertisement mentions that the said craws were *first* purposely imported into Paris, it is probable that they were natives of some of the valleys of the Alps, where *cretinism* is a common disease, and where it is considered to be hereditary. It is also common on the French and Italian sides of the Alps, and was observed by Sir George Staunton in the alpine parts of Chinese Tartary.

It appears by the following advertisements, that about eighty years ago, the Glasgow assemblies had got into great disrepute, the directors being obliged to tempt the fashionables of the city to attend them, by introducing a musical child to perform select pieces of music between the dances by way of interludes. This is the only instance within my remembrance of a Glasgow assembly having become the vehicle of a "*Show.*"

"*Glasgow Mercury*, 25th March, 1779.

"GLASGOW ASSEMBLY.

"The Assemblies of late have been so little frequented, that it begins to be doubted whether that kind of diversion is agreeable to the public, or whether the Gentlemen, by too intense an application to their Glass, may not have impaired their LOCOMOTIVE FACULTIES. There is, however, to be a Dancing Assembly upon Thursday the first of April; if it will be well attended they will be continued as formerly."

It may be here remarked that the dancing assemblies had hitherto commenced at five o'clock in the afternoon.

"*Glasgow Journal,* 16th January, 1777.

"Notice.

"That an Assembly, in honour of the Queen's birth-day, is to be held in the Assembly Hall of Glasgow, on Monday the 20th of Jan. current, at five in the afternoon."

On the 31st December, 1779, the hour of meeting was changed from five in the afternoon to six o'clock.

At this time the directors of the assemblies were the tobacco lords and their friends; and Glasgow plebeians, however respectable, were *tabooed* persons. A Glasgow shopkeeper, of wealth and respectability, having applied to these aristocratic directors for tickets to an assembly for his wife and daughters, was haughtily told that their rank did not entitle them to attend assemblies. The consequence of such illiberal conduct is shown by the following advertisements:—

"*Glasgow Mercury,* 27th January, 1780.

"Assemblies.

"The Dancing Assemblies are to be carried on this year by a General Subscription, it being found of late that the money taken at the door will not answer the expense. They are to be held regularly at the *Rooms* on Tuesday evenings once a fortnight during the season.

"A book is opened, where Gentlemen may subscribe, at One Guinea each for the season, and lies for that purpose at Messrs Campbell and Ingram's Insurance Office.

"The ladies are to pay nothing.

"Stranger gentlemen will be admitted on paying 2s 6d, at the door of the room. No town's gentlemen will be admitted but subscribers.

"There will be a Dancing Assembly on Tuesday the 1st of February, to begin precisely at six o'clock.

"*N.B.*—There will be Card Assemblies every alternate Tuesday evening, on the usual footing."

From the above advertisement it will be seen that the aristocratic directors of these assemblies kept the freedom of admission to the said assemblies in their own hands, in so far as concerned Glasgow gentlemen. This was done for the purpose of excluding the *shopc-*

cracy of the city from mixing in the country dances with the wives and daughters of the great Virginian merchants. But in opposition to these exclusive assemblies, others of a more liberal description, called balls, came to be established, where all distinction of ranks was thrown aside, and where the ease and freedom of a private merry meeting took place. Even the common courtesies of previous introduction of one to another were seldom required; and thus stranger gentlemen found no difficulty in getting partners at these balls. The said public dances originated with the teachers of music, who respectively, on giving a public concert, finished the entertainment by establishing a general hop or ball for the company, and by providing suitable music for the dances. The following is an advertisement for one of those balls :—

"*Glasgow Mercury*, 21st January, 1779.
" NOTICE.
" On Friday the 29th instant, will be performed, in the Assembly Hall,
" Joshua Campbell's Concert of Music.
" To begin at seven o'clock in the evening precisely. He will be assisted by the best performers in the town.
" After the Concert will be a BALL. Tickets 2s 6d each."

In the same manner, Goold, D'Asti, Fergus, Reanagle, and other teachers of music in Glasgow, gave concerts, with concluding balls, which were numerously attended, and gave great satisfaction to the public.

At this time the directors of the subscription assemblies, finding that these subscription entertainments were not generally patronised, and that they did not even pay expenses, were obliged in self-defence to institute more popular assemblies, called *Rooms*, to be held once a fortnight during the season. These assemblies or rooms were divested of many of the formalities and ceremonies of the above-mentioned subscription assemblies, and were intended to be considered in the light of free-and-easy hops, where full dress was not deemed absolutely necessary. In short, they were expected to be upon nearly as easy a footing as the balls of the music teachers. The price of admission was reduced to 2s, and for that sum tea was given to the company individually.

"*Glasgow Mercury*, 1st February, 1781.
" DANCING.
" The Rooms will be held, as usual, to-night, at the Assembly

Hall. Towards defraying the expense of painting the Hall, affording better music, and having Tea for the company, the price of admittance will be Two Shillings for each person; to open at six o'clock."

Notwithstanding the introduction of those popular assemblies or "rooms" at a reduced price of admission, with the temptation of tea to each person, the public gave a preference to the balls of the music teachers, so that the subscription assemblies and the rooms became more and more neglected, in consequence of which the aristocratic directors found it necessary to try the effect of introducing the performances of a musical child at one of their assemblies, as a lure to public patronage; but all their exertions were of no avail.

" *Glasgow Mercury*, 8th March, 1781.

" ASSEMBLY ROOM.

" The Directors of the Assembly Room, finding the late necessary advance in the price of admission to the Rooms has given offence to many Gentlemen and Ladies, and prevented their attending this amusement, as formerly, beg leave to inform the public, that in order to give them entertainment at as small an expense as possible, they have contracted with the *Musical Child* (who is just arrived in Town), to perform, for this night only, at the Rooms. The admittance to be only sixpence additional.

" The Directors respectfully hope for the countenance of a generous and candid public, and at the same time assure them they will embrace every opportunity of this kind to procure them entertainment. They flatter themselves the Gentlemen and Ladies WILL NOW SEE the Directors have nothing but the public good in view, and that the late rise in the price was owing to the painting the Room, and procuring them better Music, Tea, &c."

It appears from the above advertisement that the reduction of the price of admission to the assemblies, or rooms, to 2s, including tea, did not succeed, and that the directors found it necessary to raise the rate of admittance to 2s 6d, (as before) by adding a sixpence to the 2s, in order to defray expenses. Under these calamitous circumstances, the said directors, as a *pis-aller*, were driven to the scheme of exhibiting a musical child at an assembly by way of a public *Show*. But all their exertions to keep up the exclusive Glasgow assemblies were of no avail; for the American war at this time had crippled so many of the great city merchants that it was only the few holders of tobacco who continued to be the leading aristocracy of Glasgow.

After the peace of America, in 1783, the principal citizens of the place became West Indian merchants and manufacturers, and thus the former great distinction of ranks in Glasgow came to be relaxed, and the plebeians, daily increasing in wealth and numbers, now took the ascendancy. Perhaps no circumstance about this time tended so much to cause an intermixing of classes in the city of Glasgow, as the opening of the Tontine Reading Room, where all classes daily met upon a state of perfect equality, and where the common practice among subscribers, of bespeaking from each other an exchange of newspapers, which the parties respectively might be reading, necessarily brought about mutual acquaintanceship. The institution of the Chamber of Commerce in Glasgow at this period, also tended to cause a mixture of ranks, many of its leading members being manufacturers, who had raised themselves by their talents from the plebeian ranks. At the institution of the Chamber of Commerce of Glasgow, in 1784, between 200 and 300 individuals were enrolled as members, a great proportion of whom were cotton and linen manufacturers. The fees of admission were five guineas, and one guinea yearly, or twenty guineas in all for life. Patrick Colquhoun—the most popular of all the lord provosts of Glasgow —was the originator (in 1783) of the Chamber of Commerce and Manufactures. In 1789 he settled in London, and became Deputy-Lieutenant of Middlesex, and Chief Police Magistrate of the metropolis.

When provost of Glasgow, Mr Colquhoun resided on the first floor of an old tenement in Argyll Street, with an outside stair, which stood next to the late establishment of Wylie & Lochhead, No. 28. I remember this tenement, which was placed a little back from the general line of the street. The property belonged to my uncle, who bequeathed it to my cousin, a physician in London, giving him the option of either taking the said heritage or £400 in cash. The doctor elected to take the property, which he sold for £1500. On its site the present buildings were erected.

In my early days there was a saying attributed to Provost Colquhoun, which became quite a by-word in Glasgow. It so happened that in course of a public speech, in which the provost was apologizing for some mistake committed by an official of the city, his lordship chanced to remark, " Even I myself have made a mistake ! ! !" This *lapsus* was greedily seized upon by the wits of the city, and whenever a mistake occurred, out came the saying, "Oh, even I myself have made a mistake, as Provost Colquhoun said!!!"

But to return to the assemblies and musical child, it may be here remarked that the directors, in their advertisement of the performance of the said child, made use of a curious expression, thus—"*Gentlemen* and Ladies will *now* see the Directors have nothing but the public good in view." In the first place, it is not usual in assembly matters to place gentlemen before ladies ; and in the second place, it may be inferred from the word *now*, that the public had not hitherto seen that the directors had been studying the good of the public. But however these matters may appear, the performance of the musical child turned out quite a failure, and in consequence thereof this assembly came to be the last one held under the management and auspices of the old aristocratic directors, who seem to have resigned their authority in despair of success.

During the time that Patrick Colquhoun was lord provost of Glasgow, in 1782 and 1783, there does not appear to have been any subscription assemblies as of old held in Glasgow, but the music teachers continued to give their balls in the Assembly Hall at the conclusion of their concerts, as formerly.

The Old Assembly Hall was situated at the west end of the present Tontine Buildings. It was erected by subscription, as a joint-stock concern, by the higher class of Glasgow citizens and the neighbouring country gentry, who of course retained the management of it to themselves. It was sold to the Tontine Society, and its site now forms part of the Tontine Buildings. The directors, when concluding a sale of the old hall, stipulated that a new assembly hall should be erected in lieu of it, which accordingly was done by the Tontine Society in 1783 ; and the new hall then came to be exclusively used for public assemblies till 1796, when the Assembly Rooms in Ingram Street, now the Athenæum, were built.

The new hall, which formed part of the Tontine Buildings and Hotel, was 47 feet in length, 24 in breadth, and 24 in height. It was erected under the popular superintendence of Provost Colquhoun, to the entire satisfaction of all parties in Glasgow. In the course of its erection, his lordship ordered a door to be struck out between the Town Hall and the said New Assembly Hall, in order that access might be given from the former to the Tontine Hotel, in cases of public entertainments being held in the said Town Hall.

I may here mention (as stated in a former article), that soon after the New Assembly Hall had been erected, I appeared on its boards, at a dancing school ball, as "a Jacky Tar Figurant," dressed in the full costume of a sailor, with jacket and trousers, and a cudgel under my arm—all according to the dancing-school fashion of the time. Jacky Tar, with dress in character, was then a favourite dance for boys at the balls of Dick, Campbell, Fraser, and Sellars. Minuets were still taught at the dancing schools, but were now seldom danced at the public balls.

Just at the time (1781) when the subscription assemblies had lost the favour of the public, and had been found not to pay expenses, a scheme had been set on foot to erect a public building at the Cross, by way of Tontine, in shares of £50 each. The principal proprietors of the Old Assembly Hall took shares in this new concern, and then entered into a negotiation to sell the Old Assembly Hall to the Tontine Society, upon the condition of a New Assembly Hall being erected in lieu of the old one.

The following is an advertisement on the subject:—

"*Glasgow Mercury,* 25th October, 1781.

" NOTICE.

" The Directors of the Assembly Hall in Glasgow are desirous to meet with the Magistrates of the city in the laigh Council Chamber upon Wednesday the 31st day of October current, at one o'clock mid-day, to Treat with the Tontine Society for said Hall, and to concert upon a proper plan for building a New Assembly Hall.

" *Not to be repeated.*"

Hugh Wylie was then provost of Glasgow, but he dying within four months thereafter, viz., 20th February, 1782, Patrick Colquhoun was elected lord provost, as his successor in office, on the 26th February, 1782, being only six days after Mr Wylie's decease.

The sums subscribed to the Tontine scheme having amounted to upwards of £5000, Provost Colquhoun was elected to take a general charge of seeing a suitable public building erected at the Cross, with a handsome Assembly Room attached thereto, both of which the provost, with his usual energy and activity, very soon accomplished, to the entire satisfaction of the subscribers and of the public. By the following advertisement, the Tontine Buildings appear to have been ready for occupation at the end of the year 1782:—

" *Glasgow Journal*, 21st November, 1782.

" To be Let,

" For one or more years, as can be agreed upon,

" The following parts of the Buildings belonging to the Tontine Society :—

" A large and elegant Room, to be occupied as a Coffee-Room. The present Assembly Room, with about twenty other apartments, to be occupied as a Tavern and Lodging Rooms.

" Those who incline to rent the premises are desired, on or before the 20th of December next, to give in their proposals (sealed) to John Maxwell (Dargavel), the Society's Clerk, from whom further particulars may be learned.

" N.B.—*The whole to be Let to one Person.*"

In consequence of this advertisement, the above-mentioned parts of the Tontine Buildings, consisting of the hotel, coffee-room, and assembly room, were let to the well-remembered Mr Smart, who immediately proceeded to furnish the same, and thereafter to commence the establishment of a *daily ordinary*, an institution hitherto unknown in Glasgow.

The following is Mr Smart's announcement of this public ordinary :—

" *Glasgow Mercury*, 5th June, 1783.

" Tontine.

" Mr Smart begs leave to inform the Gentlemen of Glasgow, and the public in general, that he wishes to establish an *Ordinary*, at one shilling each person. Time of Dining, one quarter past three. To commence upon Monday next, the 9th of June, 1783."

When Mr Smart first put up his signboard of the *Tontine Hotel*, the lower ranks in Glasgow did not understand this new-fangled name to mean simply *an inn*, but supposed it to imply something much grander. They called it the *Tontine Hottle ;* and truly if it was to be considered as a *model* for a fine inn, they were not far wrong in their pronunciation.

The opening of the Tontine Coffee-room was a grand affair, and was inaugurated by the most splendid ball that had ever been seen in Glasgow, at which no distinction of ranks was regarded. On this occasion there was a complete mixture of the county nobility and gentry with the city aristocracy and shopocracy, graced by the presence of the Lords of Justiciary, Justice-Clerk, and Hailes; and the whole proceedings were most satisfactorily conducted under the able management of Mr Smart, to the great delight of all present.

The following are the only notices that I have found regarding this ball:—

"Glasgow Mercury, 6th May, 1784.

"We have the pleasure to inform the public that the new Coffee-Room in the Tontine Buildings will be opened during the Circuit for the reception of company; and it is expected there will be an Assembly there on the evening of Thursday or Friday next week. The Dome of this large apartment is finished in a style particularly elegant, and has a very pleasing effect."

"Glasgow Mercury, 13th May, 1784.

"This is to Give Notice,

"That there is to be an Assembly this evening, in the New Coffee-Room in the Tontine Buildings, to begin at seven o'clock."

The Glasgow newspapers of the time have given us no account of what took place at this grand ball; but it was spoken of, for many years afterwards, by those who were present at it, as the most brilliant assembly they had ever witnessed.

I was then too young to attend assemblies; but my brother, who was there, stated to us that the coffee-room was so densely crowded that there was scarcely room for dancing, but that everything was conducted with the greatest order and regularity.

When the coffee-room was first opened, there were boxes placed on each side of the entrance door—into which boxes parties wishing to take coffee or refreshments could retire; and I have seen English travellers taking breakfast in them, while the upper part of the room was crowded with the subscribers. In a few years afterwards, however, the boxes were removed, owing to the want of patronage.

Just about the time when the Tontine Hotel and Coffee Room were opened, a native of Prussia, named Breslaw, made his appearance in Glasgow, and there performed the most astonishing tricks of legerdemain that had ever been seen in Britain. He, undoubtedly, was the most accomplished sleight-of-hand performer of his day, and accordingly his exhibitions in Glasgow met with the greatest success. The following is his advertisement :—

"Glasgow Mercury, 15th January, 1784.

"By letters from Edinburgh, we are informed that

Mr BRESLAW

closes his Exhibition there on Saturday next : and we are to assure the Public, that those Variety of New Entertainments will be displayed at Mr Heron's great room in the Black Bull Inn, Glasgow, on Tuesday, Wednesday, and Thursday next, the 20th, 21st, and 22d instant, in the evenings, as follows :—

" 1st, Several select pieces of Music ; the First Violin by a foreign Young Lady, and Whistling the Notes by Sieur Arcalani.
" 2d, A variety of Deceptions, quite new, by Mr BRESLAW, the particulars of which are expressed in the Bills.
" 3d, A Solo on the Violin by Miss Florella, who has had the honour lately of performing before their Majesties and the Royal Family ; and several Magical Card Deceptions by Sieur Andrea.
" 4th, Several new experiments on Watches, Silver Medals, Small Chests, Gold Boxes, Caskets, Silver Machineries, &c., &c., by Mr BRESLAW.
" 5th, The imitation of various Birds, by the New Venetian Rosignole, lately arrived from Naples.
" The whole to conclude with a New Invented Silver Cup, and more than Fifty other Deceptions too numerous to insert.
" The Room will be elegantly illuminated, warm, and commodiously prepared.—To begin at Seven o'clock.—Admittance Two shillings each person.—Tickets to be had ; Places to be taken ; or any Person inclined to Learn some Deceptions, they may be taught in a few minutes, on reasonable terms, by applying to Mr BRESLAW at the Place above-mentioned.
" ☞ Their stay here will be only a few days, as they are engaged to return to Edinburgh."

It is, perhaps, needless to inform your readers that the successful performance of jugglery depends altogether upon the skill of the performer, and that it requires as much toil and labour to form an accomplished juggler, as it has done to Blondin to become the pink of rope dancers, or to Paganini to have arrived at the honour of being the Prince of Fiddlers. But besides intense application to the study of the art, a certain *natural* dexterity of hand is necessary to the juggler, as well as to the surgeon, otherwise neither of them can ever arrive at the top of their respective professions.

I presume that most of your readers have seen numerous feats of legerdemain, which it is unnecessary here to recapitulate. If they will look into the " Encyclopædia Britannica" (article Legerdemain) they will find a long account of no less than eighteen pages, and

X

plates, giving a statement of the sleight-of-hand tricks which were usually exhibited, with a full explanation of the *modus operandi*. But there was one trick that Breslaw performed, which he maintained to be the *ne plus ultra* of deceptions, and he defied any person to do the like.   It was as follows :—

1st, He desired one of the company to load a pistol, and to put a nail into it in lieu of shot.

2d, He took a pack of cards, and requested one of the company to draw a card—to tear it in half—and to retain the one half— while at a candle he burned the other half of it, and placed its ashes in the centre of the pack.   A board having been hung upon the wall of the room, Breslaw took the pistol in his hand, and then, throwing the whole pack in the air, fired off the pistol among the falling cards, when lo ! the nail was seen stuck into the board, with the half card which had been reduced to ashes transfixed to the board by the nail.   The half card being removed, and compared with the other half retained by the visitor, was found to tally exactly.

Towards the close of Breslaw's life, another celebrated sleight-of-hand performer appeared, of the name of Herman Boaz.   Breslaw was of extravagant habits, and though he made great gains, he spent them as fast as he made them ; but Boaz, on the contrary, was a prudent, thrifty man, who took care to invest his profits in valuable securities.

It happened one day that Boaz and Breslaw met at an inn, and had their glass together.   In the course of their conversation, Boaz thought, from some expressions, that Breslaw considered himself to be the superior of the two in point of jugglery, on which Boaz said to Breslaw that he could show him something in the legerdemain way quite beyond the power of Breslaw to do the like.   Breslaw immediately offered to wager a bottle of wine that Boaz could not show him any performance by legerdemain which he could not perform the very same upon the spot.   Boaz took the wager, and having asked liberty to go to his bed room for his materials, he soon returned to Breslaw, and spread upon the table bonds, bills, and stock securities for upwards of £10,000, exclaiming, " There now, Mr Breslaw. Behold ! the whole done by sleight-of-hand ! Show me if you can do the like?"   Breslaw scratched his head, and, laughing heartily, acknowledged that he had fairly lost the bottle of wine.

Boaz was an expert angler, and when in Glasgow, he used to resort to the Dalmarnock fords a trout fishing.   One day, when there, a gentleman was also present enjoying the same sport, who, seeing that Boaz was very successful, while he, on the contrary, was getting very few fish, he accosted Boaz, and politely requested a sight of the flies which Mr Boaz was using. His request was readily granted, but Boaz said that he did not think the quality of the flies of any importance, as he would show him. So, having caught a trout, Boaz requested the gentleman to cut the fins of the said fish as a mark, Boaz then threw the trout again into the river; and taking the gentleman's own rod, he, at the first throw of the line, brought back the identical marked fish, to the utter astonishment of the gentleman angler.

When attending an exhibition of Boaz, I found out the secret of one of his tricks. Boaz undertook to make every one who drew a card from a pack of cards to draw the very same card. Accordingly, having exhibited a regular pack of cards to the company with their faces exposed to view, he then shuffled the said pack, and desired any of the company to draw a card, and after it had been privily inspected, to restore it to the pack. On the occasion in question, about a score of the company drew each respectively a card from the pack, and then restored it. When Boaz presented the pack to me to draw a card, I attempted in vain to draw the lowest card of the pack, for Boaz continued shuffling the cards in so masterly a manner that I could not get hold of it, until at last I loudly said that I had fixed upon drawing the undermost card of the pack. I then obtained it, and saw it to be an honour. All the others of the company who had drawn cards found they had drawn the nine of diamonds. I then discovered that the trick consisted of changing by sleight-of-hand the original correct pack of cards, and substituting a pack consisting *wholly* of nines of diamonds, except the undermost of the pack, which being liable to be seen, had been made an honour. I, however, kept silence, and did not announce my success to the company.

Boaz was an honourable man, and generally refused to play at cards for money, saying that he could easily cheat if he pleased to do so, and, therefore, he chose to keep himself above suspicion.

Shortly after this time, there came to Glasgow an impudent, self-sufficient charlatan, called Dr Katterfelto, who pretended to be deeply skilled in all kinds of knowledge, human and Divine, and who gave what he called philosophical lectures, accompanied by a display of the wonders of the solar microscope. His lectures were

merely common-place trash, but the exhibition of his solar microscope was certainly both curious and interesting.

Katterfelto thus introduced himself to the public of Glasgow in
the newspapers :—" We are very happy to inform our readers that
the *Great Divine*, and *Moral Philosopher*, DOCTOR KATTERFELTO, is
to lecture for a few nights; and as his stay at Glasgow is only for a
few nights, we have, therefore, very great reason to believe, as the
Doctor is such a *surprising* and *wonderful Great Man*, that many
will come to see his most surprising and wonderful performances,
which surpass all description."

Again—

" Glasgow, 23d June, 1789.—Last week most of the gentlemen
clergy in this city went to Fraser's Hall,* King Street, to hear that
Great Divine, and Moral Philosopher,
Dr KATTERFELTO, lecture. They also went to see his Solar Microscope Exhibition. His performance, by all accounts, surpasses
all description, and every other exhibition which has been in Glasgow these many years past; and the ladies, in particular, are much
entertained with his wonderful performances; and he is crowded by
them almost every night; and the masters of the Masonic Societies
heard one of his lectures last Wednesday night; also, most of the
Professors of the College had the curiosity of seeing the Doctor's
wonderful exhibition, and some of his experiments last week; and
the Doctor, to-morrow night, Wednesday the 24th of June, is to
deliver another lecture for the members belonging to the different
Lodges in this city ; and as the admittance now is only one shilling
each member, we have, therefore, great reason to believe he will be
very much crowded all this week, for his Solar Microscope Exhibition, as well as the night's performance, by all ranks of persons, as
this is to be the last week, the above *Great Divine*, and *Moral
Philosopher* is to lecture in this city."

I attended Katterfelto's exhibition, and saw the wonders of the
solar microscope, which was the only part of the entertainment
that was worth the price of admission. The solar microscope consisted of a tube, mirror, and convex lens. The sun's rays were re-
flected through the tube, by means of the mirror, upon the object
to be viewed, the image or picture of which object was thrown distinctly and beautifully upon a white linen sheet, and could have
been magnified to an immense extent, so that a flea was shown upon
it as large as an elephant. A drop of water was exhibited with

* Fraser was a dancing school teacher.

myriads of animalculæ in it, swimming rapidly about in all directions; some of them long, some short, others globular, and of curious out-of-the-way shapes. In a drop of vinegar there were seen whole legions of little eels wriggling hither and thither, and chasing one another. A fine razor was exhibited, the edge of which appeared on the sheet as serrated as that of a large carpenter's saw. The wing of a fly was magnified to the size of the mainsail of a first-rate man-of-war, and a piece of the finest lace seemed as coarse as the most ragged sackcloth. Various insects, and vegetable substances, were exhibited, immensely enlarged, upon the white linen sheet, which afforded much pleasure and amusement to the company; so that, on the whole, Katterfelto, although considered in the light of a mountebank, was pretty successful in Glasgow.

Subsequent to Katterfelto's exhibition, a set of Indian jugglers came to Glasgow, who appeared dressed in their native costume, and performed various tricks by sleight-of-hand; but none of them more wonderful than those which had been exhibited by Breslaw and Boaz. They did not perform any tricks with cards or dice, but with jugs, boxes, and balls. Their chief trick was the following:—Having laid themselves down squat upon the floor of the room, they produced an empty jug for the inspection of the company, which being placed on the floor amidst the visitors they then covered it with a common handkerchief, and after muttering a few mystic words and making some antic gesticulations, they withdrew the handkerchief, when lo, the jug appeared full of rice! Again covering the jug, and going through the like ceremonies, the jug, on the withdrawal of the handkerchief, appeared brimful of water! And lastly, after a repetition of the same mystical process, the jug was restored to its original empty state. The trick was certainly curious, for the company stood on the floor of the room close beside these jugglers during the performance, and there was apparently no place from whence the rice and water could have been taken. The principal part of the exhibition, however, consisted of swallowing a naked sword; but this was no trick, for it was a deed actually done. I saw one of the jugglers take a sword and introduce its blade down his throat into the very bottom of his stomach, where it remained for some time. It was a most disgusting sight, and I was glad to see the weapon withdrawn.

I need not take notice here of the performances of Dr James Graham, in 1783, as I have given an account of the doings of that celebrated quack, at Glasgow, in "Glasgow, Past and Present," Vol.

III, page 333. Dr Graham's success appears to have stimulated another quack to attempt a degree of gullibility on Glasgow folks, which looks as if he considered them all to have been deficient in plain common sense, and too flush of guineas. But he made a sad mistake by holding forth in the Briggate—an unfortunate place, both then and now-a-days, for gathering wealthy gulls and guineas.

" *Glasgow Mercury*, 8th May, 1783."—"The famous DON PEDRO, on his way through here to Edinburgh, begs leave to acquaint the ladies and gentlemen, and others, that he has travelled over the most parts of the East, and has arrived at the greatest pitch of EASTERN LEARNING, by which he can see so far into futurity, as to be able to relate to any person who may be curious to know, the future destiny of their lives, or any other important question; if any person pleases to put his art to the proof, they may, without giving themselves any trouble, but writing a letter directed to Don Pedro, at Mr Campbell's, slater in Bridgegate Street, Glasgow, with their name, age, day and year of their birth, with any other question they may want to know, when they shall receive a full answer to all their demands the day following, as the night must intervene betwixt the questions asked and their answers, as it is by his knowledge of the heavenly constellations that he is able to give just answers; all which he binds himself to do for the consideration of ONE GUINEA, which must be inclosed in the letter. No answer will be paid to any letters but such as are post-paid. *N.B.*—His stay will only be for a few days. He intends before his departure, to give a lecture on *Astrology* and *Astronomy*, with some surprising proofs of his art, in public."

The Doctor, however, did not venture to give any lecture in Glasgow, and left the Briggate without his pockets being burdened over much with guineas. In fact, he was laughed at as a low, vulgar impostor.

About this time there came to Glasgow a ventriloquist, who performed various feats of deception, by altering the tones of his voice. He did not, however, speak from his *belly*, as the word implies; but, altogether, by a modification of his lips and voice; indeed, I hold it to be physically impossible for any person to speak from his belly.

I have forgotten the name of this ventriloquist; but I went to see his performances in Fraser's Hall, and was much amused, though by no means greatly surprised with them. He announced himself to perform as follows—'To imitate the voice of a squeaking child, and make it appear to proceed from various parts of the room, and even from the pockets of individuals of the company—in the last case, much merriment arose, when the child happened to shriek and squeal from the pockets of the young ladies. He also advertised that he would hold a conversation with a wooden doll, placed at a distance, as if it were a living child; and even when the doll was placed beneath a hat that its cries would proceed apparently from its place of confinement; that he would make the cries of the child to issue from the bottom of an inverted wine glass, or from under the foot or hand of any of the company. All these I saw performed; but the most amusing part of the exhibition was, the artist's imitation of the tones of a scolding old woman, disturbed at unseasonable hours by a person demanding admission into her house, and the shrieks and alarm of her grandchild at the cause of disturbance.

We have been told that an accomplished ventriloquist could so modify his voice as to make it appear to the auditor to proceed from any distance, and in any direction that he pleased, and this without any change of his countenance, or alteration of his features; but such was not the case with the ventriloquist in question, for I distinctly saw his lips to move, and his face to be turned hither and thither, whenever he regulated his voice, so as to make it appear as proceeding from any particular place.

It has been asserted by many learned antiquaries, that the ancient oracles and responses recorded in history were mere tricks of ventriloquism, delivered by persons thus qualified, to serve the purposes of priestcraft and delusion; and this may be true, in so far as regards the responses delivered by the Oracle of Delphos. The answers from the ancient oracles were usually given by the intervention of a priest or priestess, and generally expressed in such dark and unintelligible phrases as might be easily wrested to prove the truth of the oracle, whatever might be the event.

The following little anecdote was told of the ventriloquist whom I saw in Fraser's Hall. When in Edinburgh, he went to the Fish Market, and there, at the stall of a fishwife, inquired the price of a fine haddock; at the same time, asked the wife if she was sure that the fish was quite fresh. "Oo, aye, sir," said the wife. "I'se warrant it was catched this morning." On which, to the utter astonishment of the wife, the fish replied, "It's a blasted lie, for I have been here for more than a week!"

I shall now shift the scene, and take notice of a show of an animal which, under scientific nomenclature, comes to be called "A MONSTER," that is, a production of a living being degenerating from the proper and usual disposition of parts of the species to which it belongs.

The following advertisement describes a *cow* with two heads, which, at the time, attracted much attention in Glasgow among the medical profession:—

"*Glasgow Mercury*, 3d November, 1785."—"To the nobility, gentry, and the admirers of the wonderful productions of nature.— Just arrived, and to be seen alive, in a commodious room near the Spoutmouth, Gallowgate, the surprising Worcestershire HEIFER, six years old, being the most curious production of nature ever exhibited in this kingdom. This very surprising creature has two heads, four horns, four eyes, four ears, four nostrils, through each of which it breathes, &c., and what is more surprising, it takes its sustenance with both mouths at the same time. One of the heads, together with the horns, represents that of a bull, and the other that of a cow. This heifer has had the inspection of the Royal Society, and the principal gentlemen of the Faculty in London and Edinburgh, and is by them universally allowed to be the most astonishing phenomenon of nature. The above curiosity, with several other curious beasts, alive, may be seen by any number of persons, from ten in the morning, till eight at night. Ladies or gentlemen, 1s; tradesmen, 6d; servants, 3d."

I paid a visit to this wonderful heifer, and certainly thought the show well worthy of the attention of *virtuosi*. One of the heads of this animal appeared to me to be perfect, and as vital as that of a healthy cow; but the other head was dull and sluggish, and hung down from the neck like an excrescence, the eyes in it were glazed and inanimated, and the expression of its countenance was that of imbecility. The animal itself, however, was pleasing to look at, and appeared very mild and gentle in its nature. I patted its perfect head, which it took very kindly, and seemed pleased with my attentions. The other animals in this show consisted principally of a few monkeys, and other beasts quite common to be seen in itinerant exhibitions.

While on a visit to my uncle at Greenlaw House (now the General Terminus), in the year 1780, a *lusus naturæ* took place there, whereby a "*Monster*" of the species "*aves*" (or second class of animals, according to Linnæus) was produced. It thus happened : Several young ducks having been hatched in a barn of the house, one egg remained unhatched sometime after the rest, which, not having the usual marks of being rotten, the servant maid's curiosity prompted her to break, and in it there was found a young duck come to full maturity, having two distinct heads, equally big, and of the usual proportions, each with the proper bill and tongue, and everything that belongs to a distinct and well-formed duckling. Each of the heads had its separate neck, but united to the body at the shoulders. This "monster" was preserved for some time for the satisfaction of the curious, but I believe that it was never dissected.

Buffon informs us that two female human "*Monsters*," natives of Hungary, were exhibited as a show in France and England. They were united at the loins, and could only see one another by turning their heads. When they were nearly 22 years of age, one of them fell into a lethargy, and died, and the other immediately thereafter followed the lot of her sister. In recent times we have seen a still more remarkable specimen of "*Human Monsters*," in the case of the Siamese twins, who were lately exhibited as a show throughout the kingdom. Specimens of "Monsters," however, are not confined to the animal kingdom, for they also occur occasionally in the vegetable creation, as I dare say many of your elderly readers may remember when, in their juvenile years, they hunted the fields for twigs of "*four-leaved clover*"—a "*vegetable monster*," the possession of which was supposed to bring good luck to the finder. I have several times found *four-leaved* clover, but somehow or other I never hit on the good luck which was to follow the discovery.

I shall now take notice of an exhibition which at the time afforded me more pleasure and amusement than any public entertainment I had ever witnessed; and even at this day, after a long interval of seventy-six years, I still look back with delight to the very exhilarating shadowy scenes of the "Broken Bridge" and its comic songs. I have often wondered that the amusing exhibition of "*Les Ombres Chinoises*" has never been repeated in Glasgow since the days "o' langsyne;" for I am sure that all the youngsters of our city would find more humour and fun displayed in the different shadowy scenes in question than in the most amusing theatrical farce or pantomime. I still have in my mind's eye the rapture with which I beheld the fall of the centre of the bridge, and the comic interview between a rustic mending the gap or chasm and a traveller wishing to cross the river. The traveller calls out—"Oho, yere there, how can I get over?" The rustic, continuing to work at the gap with his pick, without glancing at the traveller, sings out—

" How do the ducks and the geese get over?
Falderal, falderal, falay.
Do like them, you Highland drover,
Falderal, falderal, falay."

But I must now give the original bill of fare:—

" *Glasgow Mercury*, 2d June, 1785.

" Glasgow, 1st June, 1785.—To be seen in the large Dancing Hall above the Weigh-house, Candleriggs,* for this and every evening for a week, the celebrated

" FEMALE WIRE DANCER,

" Who will display several Grand Equilibriums on the
" SLACK WIRE.

" She balances Swords, Pipes, Plates, and Glasses horizontally and perpendicularly, standing with one foot on the wire in full swing; tosses several oranges, quite different from what the Turk or Mr Maddox ever did; throws an orange to a great height, and catches it on a Sword or Fork, to the astonishment of all present; turns on the wire as quickly as the fly of a Jack, which she challenges any performer to do. She has performed at Saddler's Wells, and most of the capital Theatres in the Kingdom, with universal applause, and is allowed to be the best and most surprising Balancer in England upon the Slack Wire, *without* a pole.

"Likewise will be introduced,
" Quite a New and Grand Exhibition of
" LES OMBRES CHINOISES,
" Consisting of a Variety of
" SCENES AND FIGURES,
" Which will be represented in the grandest manner, as follows, viz. :—

" 1st. A Comic Scene, taken from the Public Gardens at Paris ; or, the Macaroni's Escape from a Shower of Rain. In this piece a Hornpipe will be introduced before the rain.
" 2d. The Duck Hunting ; or, the Active Fisherman.
" 3d. A Comic Scene, called ' The Disappointed Traveller.'
" THE BROKEN BRIDGE;
Or, the Peasant Rewarded for his Incivility.

* This hall was the upper flat of the public weigh-house of the city, and was situated directly opposite to the large warehouses of the Messrs Campbell, in Candleriggs Street, No. 31. The weigh-house was subsequently removed to the corner of Ingram Street and Montrose Street.

" 4th. A Humorous Scene of a Cobbler's Wife and Child ; or, ' The Cat's Escape with the Dinner out of the Pot,' &c.

" 5th. A Sea Storm, amazingly executed, with Thunder and Light-ning, Ships in Distress, Shipwreck, and Sea Monsters appearing, &c., &c., as is well known at Astley's Riding School, Westminster Bridge.

" ☞ The Doors to be open at Seven o'clock, and begin at Eight.

" Admittance—Pit, 1s ; Gallery, 6d. Places to be taken and Tickets to be had at the place of performance from eleven to two o'clock afternoon. Good music will accompany the performance, and everything be conducted with propriety and decorum.

" Private performance at any time of the day, by giving a day's notice."

The whole of the above-mentioned entertainment was exceedingly well performed, and gave very general satisfaction to crowded audiences. The Female Wire Dancer executed her part with great dexterity; and though her feats would not bear a comparison with those of Blondin, the celebrated rope dancer of the present time, nevertheless they seemed very wonderful to the company present at this exhibition. The slack wire on which the said movements were achieved, consisted of twisted brass wire, about the thickness of a person's finger, which was made to hang across the room of the hall with a gentle bend. I observed that towards the close of her performance, the lady dancer appeared much fatigued; and not-withstanding of the loud plaudits of the company, she seemed very thankful when her part of the show was concluded.

The principal rope dancers of old in Scotland were itinerant mountebanks, with their clowns. Their performances consisted of little more than vaulting on a slack rope, turning round upon it like a wheel, and hanging on it by the heels or neck. Even down to my day these itinerant mountebanks or quack doctors were common, and to be seen in all fairs.

Among the Jews of Scriptural times there appear to have been no public rope dancers; but King David seems to have had a sort of a penchant for dancing and making a show of himself to the populace as an accomplished vaulter; for we are informed that David danced before the public, leaping and figuring with all his might, at the sound of trumpets, and amidst loud shoutings, for which doings his wife, Michal, despised him.

We learn from history that the ancient Greeks and Romans had their rope dancers as well as we. These are said to have had four different ways of exercising their art. The first leaped and skipped on the rope, whirled round it like a wheel, and then hung on it by their heels or neck. The second flew or slid from above, resting on their stomach, with their legs and arms extended. The third ran along a rope stretched in a right line, cr up and down. Lastly, the fourth not only walked on the rope, but made surprising leaps and turns thereon. These performances now-a-days would be considered quite common, and were certainly surpassed by the performance of the female wire dancer above-mentioned; but the feats of Blondin, the great rope dancer of the present time, throws the skill of all other rope dancers, ancient or modern, quite in the shade.

Seneca, in his 85th epistle, mentions that elephants were taught to walk on the tight rope; but even our dancing bears have never been exhibited to the public as rope dancers, so that the ancients appear to have excelled us in shows of bestial rope dancing.

The following mechanical exhibition took place in Glasgow in June, 1786, but as it happened during the time of the Grammar School vacation, our family, and I among them, were then located at country summer quarters, so that I had no opportunity of seeing it. I therefore can do no more than give the particulars of this curious mechanical display, such as was set forth in the handbills of the day.

"Glasgow, 1st June, 1786.

"EXHIBITION OF MECHANICAL FIGURES.

"At Fraser's Hall, M'Nair's Land, King Street, Glasgow, this day will begin to be exhibited the following much admired and astonishing pieces of mechanism, viz. :—

"AUTOMATON WRITER.

"This curious and beautiful Figure, three feet in height, is placed at the end of a common table, where it writes, with pen and ink, on paper whatever is proposed to it, but as this Figure's performances have hitherto sufficiently recommended themselves, and as some of them might appear impossibilities in the description, the Proprietor thinks a more minute detail unnecessary, the Public having it so easily in their power to judge for themselves.

"SPEAKING FIGURE.

"This elegant Figure of Fame, suspended in the air by a ribbon, speaks and answers questions in different languages, and will converse on any branch of science. It speaks equally well when held in the hand. If desired, the Figure will put the question.

"MODEL OF GIBRALTAR.

"This accurate model in Wood, eight feet in length, contains the Rock, with the Fortifications, ancient and modern; the Town, the Neck with the Spanish lines and approaches during the last memorable siege, &c., &c.

"CHANGEABLE PICTURE,

"which changes from old age to youth, and the contrary, with a motion too rapid to be observed.

"MECHANICAL BIRD,

"which shows the action of wings in flying, &c., &c.

"Admittance only one shilling.

"Hours of Exhibition, every day from twelve to three, and from six to eight in the evening. *N.B.*—To prevent disappointment, the Proprietor respectfully informs the ladies and gentlemen of this city, and the public in general, that on account of his engagements in London his stay here will be very short."

The ancient Jews were poor mechanics, as we learn from Scripture. In the 28th chapter of 1st Chronicles, David gives instructions to his son Solomon how he was to build the Temple. David specifies by pattern the manner in which the upper chambers and lower parlours are to be built; also gives directions regarding the formation of the golden and silver candlesticks, the golden tables of shew bread,* flesh hooks, bowls, and cups, and lastly, for making by pattern of the chariot of the cherubims, that spread out their wings. And David adds, in conclusion (verse 19), "The Lord made me understand, in writing, by His hand upon me, even all the work of this pattern."

Notwithstanding of these ample directions, we find that Solomon, when he came to build the Temple, had not workmen capable of executing the patterns ordered by David, but was obliged to send to Tyre for skilled mechanics. Solomon sent and fetched Hiram out of Tyre ; he was a widow's son, and his father was a man of Tyre, a worker in brass, and he was filled with wisdom and understanding,

---

* Shew breads were loaves which the priests put every Sabbath day upon the Golden Table. They were covered with leaves of gold, and were twelve in number, representing the twelve tribes. They were served up hot, and the stale ones taken away, as the priest alone could eat them.

and cunning to work all works in brass, and he came to Solomon and *wrought all his work.* It also appears that the common pump was unknown to the Jews in the time of our Saviour (John iv. 7-11). When St Paul was on his voyage to Rome, and the ship, containing 276 souls, was about to founder, " They used helps, undergirding the ship." . . . " And they lightened the ship, and cast out the wheat into the sea." From these passages it is evident that the ship was water-logged, but not a word is said about using the pumps of the ship ; indeed, the mechanism of the pump at that time seems to have been unknown even to the Greeks and Romans. However common the pump is at present, nothing like it was found among the ancient Peruvians or Pacific Islanders, when they first became known to Europeans; it is even said that the pump was unknown to the Chinese, when Marco Polo visited that country.

So long ago as 400 years before Christ, Archytas of Tarentum is said to have made a wooden pigeon that could fly, and no doubt the Greeks at that time were skilful mechanics. Demosthenes had upwards of thirty slaves who were cabinet-makers, so that the great orator belonged to the wright craft.

In 1738, an automaton was exhibited, which played on the German flute; its fingers, lips, and tongue were moved by means of a steel cylinder, turned by clock work. In 1769, an automaton was constructed at Presburg, which played at chess, and was exhibited to thousands in Vienna, Paris, and London. The figure was as large as life, in a Turkish dress, and sat behind a table. It beat all the first-rate players of chess in those cities ; but it was observed that it could not play unless the inventor was near it. After excit-ing the astonishment of all Europe for upwards of fifteen years, it was at last found out that the machinery of its movements were directed by the inventor himself in a curious and occult manner, and then the wonder ceased.

I was present in December, 1789, at the following optical exhibi-tion :—

" *Glasgow Mercury,* 1st December, 1789.

" Mr Bradberry's Philosophical and Optical Exhibition.

" At the Glasgow Hotel, Tavern, and Coffee House, the corner of Candleriggs.

" All the ideas of the human mind, however extensive its capacity, or accurate its researches, are received by means of the senses ; surely then to have these ministers of information well instructed is no small advantage; and as by the eye the far greater part of our ideas are transmitted to the mind, it appears of considerable importance to improve to the utmost this medium of knowledge; for which intent the present exhibition is offered to the public. By it the inventor will prove by experiment that sight is more liable to be deceived than most people imagine, by producing the following objects to the sight where nothing really exists:—

" First, a *Nosegay* will seem within reach, but on attempting to touch it, a *Dagger* will appear, and be followed by a *Lemon*. The roundness of this, with the hand that presents it, would induce every person to believe it real; and will be succeeded by the appearance and motion of a *Living Head*, in a manner beyond what words can express. The *Handle* of a *Dagger* will appear to invite the hand to touch it, but is always out of reach. A *Bird* will then present itself; but like the rest, is only an airy vision, and will be followed by one of the finest painted *Portraits* in Europe, which cannot be known from real life.

" As soon as a sufficient number have subscribed, Mr Bradberry proposes reading a *Lecture* on *Optics*.

" Admittance from 12 till 3, and from 7 till 9 in the evening, at *One Shilling*."

I must confess that I felt rather disappointed on the occasion of my visit to this exhibition, as I expected that the dagger scene in particular would have partaken a great deal more of the reality than it did. I was prepared for seeing a dagger suddenly thrust at my heart so as to cause me to start back, but it seemed too much like a dagger flourished behind a sheet of plate-glass to cause any alarm. The exhibition, however, was curious and interesting as experiments in optics. I did not understand the manner by which the changes were effected, as the movements were concealed by being carried on in a back apartment, and the spectacles were exhibited only through an aperture resembling a window.

This exhibition did not meet with great success in Glasgow, in consequence of which Mr Bradberry gave up the attempt to read a lecture on optics. I think that no other exhibition of the kind has ever since been seen in Glasgow.

There can be no doubt that these ocular spectra have been often used by impostors for the purposes of deception, and to cause a belief of the existence of supernatural beings.

We find in the early history of every nation that a general belief in the reality of ghosts, apparitions, and spectres was common among all ranks of the people. Polished nations, even down to our own times, have given credit, more or less, to the existence and pranks of these aerial beings. This belief was common to the ancient Jews, Greeks, and Romans, as we learn from sacred and profane history. On innumerable occasions supernatural beings are said to have discovered themselves to the eyes of mortals; to have held conferences with mankind; and to have interposed their aid and assistance to those in need. It is curious to observe that all ghosts, apparitions, and spectres were honest, upright, and generous beings; and never directed mortals to commit murder, to rob, or to steal; but, on the contrary, they in a friendly way pointed out the best manner of discovering horrid murders, of finding out hidden treasures, and of showing how deceased relations had been defrauded by forged wills. As for evil spirits and devils, they were always looked upon by every person as the inveterate and cursed enemies of mankind, who took pleasure in tempting poor mortals to commit all manner of wickedness, by taking possession of both soul and body. I daresay that most of your elderly readers have perused, in their young days, " Satan's Invisible World Discovered," in which will be found a wonderful collection of the malpractices of evil spirits and demons—a book which was to be found in every book-seller's shop in the Saltmarket seventy or eighty years ago, but which is now very rare, and perhaps only to be found by applying to the College Library.

The tenement, at the corner of Trongate and Candleriggs, where Mr Bradberry exhibited his optical experiments, had been built shortly before 1789, and the first floor of it came to be occupied by Henry Hemming, an Englishman, as a hotel, conducted in the English style. This tenement was built on the site of the old Guard House by Mr M'Ilhose, who changed his name thereafter to Hozier. The Guard House jutted out on the street to the whole extent of the footpath, and formed a piazza in front for the soldiers on duty. It appears from the following notice that the Guard House in question must have been built about the year 1756, as the more ancient Guard House appears to have been situated at the Well Close, on the east side of Saltmarket.

" NOTICE.

" Glasgow, 18th October, 1756.

" That the stone, timber, lead, glass work, iron, and whole other materials of the Old Guard House, and of the old houses or lands in

Well Close, on the east side of the Saltmarket, belonging to the Town of Glasgow, are to be sold by public roup, within the Court Hall of the Tolbooth of Glasgow, upon the last Wednesday of October inst., between the hours of 12 and 2, afternoon. As also, the small yearly Feu Duties, within and belonging to the Town, under Forty Shillings Sterling, are to be sold by way of public roup the said time and place.

"Those who incline to purchase the materials of said houses, may view the same betwixt and the roup : and those who incline to purchase the Feu Duties foresaid may, betwixt and the said time, enquire at Mr William Weir, writer, or Mr Arthur Robertson, chamberlain, for any particulars thereanent."

The corner shop of the ground floor of M'Ilhose's Land, as it was called, came to be occupied by Miller & Ewing, clothiers. These gentlemen were very polite and affable in their manners to all ranks, but particularly so to military gentlemen, in consequence of which their shop came to be a kind of lounge to the officers quartered in Glasgow. This clothing establishment still exists at 79 Buchanan Street, by the name of Ewing & Wingate, and I suspect that it is the sole *remnant* of the Glasgow cloth shops of olden time.

LOOSE JOTTINGS REGARDING GLASGOW ABOUT THE YEAR 1775.

At no period of its history was Glasgow ever more prosperous than at the time immediately previous to the breaking out of the American War of Independence. The tobacco trade, the established emporium or staple of Glasgow commerce, was then at its acme, and her lordly Virginian merchants were freely distributing their wealth by the erection of princely dwellings in the favourite localities of the city, some of which remain to this day as ornaments to our ancient burgh boundaries. Denholm, p. 82, says (1775) :—

" The public works themselves sufficiently demonstrate the wealth and prosperity of Glasgow at this period. In this year Glasgow employed upwards of sixty thousand tons of shipping, having in a single article of tobacco imported from America the amazing quantity of fifty-seven thousand one hundred and forty-three hogsheads."

Y

This was more than one-half of all the tobacco imported into Great Britain in 1775.

Denholm also states—

"Great inconvenience having been found to arise to the inhabitants at large from the high price of coals, a scheme was set on foot and adopted, for cutting a navigable canal from the high grounds at the back of the Cathedral Church to the parish of Monkland, with the view of lessening the price of that article, by bringing it at once to the town in larger quantities and at a cheaper rate than formerly."

That this step was necessary sufficiently appears from the annexed advertisement:—

"*Glasgow Journal*, 1775, 20th July.—At a meeting of the following coalmasters—James Buchanan, lord provost, Colin Dunlop & Son, James & Andrew Gray, John & Matthew Orr, James M'Nair & Co., Archibald Smellie & Son, John Ferrie & Richard Cameron— it was resolved that, from and after the 15th of August next, they will sell no coals from any of the works they are respectively concerned in *but for ready-money only.*"

"1776, June 13.—As John & Matthew Orr intend for the future to lead a great part of their coals with their own horses and carts, they will be very much obliged to their customers to send their orders to the Camlachie coal office."

The following notice will show that the operatives of Glasgow were, at the period first mentioned, in full employment, and were then receiving high wages:—

"*Weekly Magazine*, Edinburgh, 1775, 14th April.—Extract of a letter from Glasgow—' Trade has not been so brisk in this place for many years bygone as it is at present—not a single hand unemployed ; weavers' wages all raised, and ten, fifteen, and twenty shillings given as a premium to engage them.'"

The money market appears likewise to have been glutted in 1775.

"*Scots Magazine*, Edinburgh, December, 1775.—Since February last our banks give only 3 per cent. on money lent them for a full year, and but 2½ per cent. if lent only for six months."

"Edinburgh, 23d July, 1776.—On Tuesday last some shares in the Royal Bank here sold at the rate of £215, which is £14 higher than ever was paid before, owing to the great plenty of money now in circle. It is estimated that there is above half a million sterling at present lent out in Edinburgh at 3 per cent., and more money

ready to be lent on land security than ever was known in Scotland
at any former period."

"*Glasgow Journal*, 30th November, 1775.—Notice. Messrs
Dunlop, Houston & Co., bankers in Glasgow, desire those who have
money lodged with them at 4 per cent. that they would call at their
office as soon as possible to receive payment."

It further appears that at this juncture oatmeal was so very
plentiful, that the sheriff of Lanarkshire prohibited any importation
of it into Glasgow.

"*Glasgow Journal*, 13th February, 1775.—By the determination
of the sheriff, the ports of this county (Lanarkshire) are shut against
the importation of oats and oatmeal."

It must not be forgotten that, in this year, 1775, the following
Act of Parliament was passed, regarding an invention which has
made a greater change in Glasgow than even Arkwright's celebrated
discovery of spinning yarn by machinery. The title is—"An Act
for investing in James Watt, engineer, his executors, administrators,
and assigns, the sole use and property of certain steam engines,
commonly called 'Fire Engines,' of his invention, described in the
said Act, throughout his Majesty's dominions, for a limited time."
At the period in question there were no cotton mills in Scotland,
the first mill there having been erected in Rothesay by an English
company in 1778. It was about two years after this that David
Dale commenced erecting the Lanark Cotton Mills. The mill
which was first built was accidentally burned to the ground a few
weeks after it had begun to produce spun yarn; but it was speedily
reconstructed, and the manufacture proceeded successfully.

In my younger days the principal cotton broker in Glasgow was
Mrs Mary Brown. Her husband was a shoemaker, in pretty extensive business. At his death, Mary was at a loss how to dispose of
his shoes and leather to advantage, and accordingly applied to David
Dale for his advice on the occasion. Mr Dale advised her to work
up the raw materials of her husband's stock, into shoes suitable for
the West India market, and then to consign the whole to a respectable West India house for sale in the West Indies. Mary,
however, said that this was too great a venture for her to engage in;
but Mr Dale told her, that if she was pleased with the proposal, he
would run *halves* in the adventure. Mary at once jumped to the
offer, and accordingly, the whole of Mr Brown's finished stock was
shipped to the West Indies, upon joint account, with instructions
that the produce of the sales should be remitted in cotton. When

the cotton arrived, Mr Dale proposed to put it into the hands of a cotton broker for sale; but Mary did not approve of this plan, saying that she would sell it herself, and thereby save the broker's commission. Mary was very successful in selling the cotton at a good price, and immediately thereafter she commenced the business of a cotton broker.

I have seen Mary bustling about, with a large leather pocket at her side, containing samples of cotton, ready to show to any spinner or speculator whom she might meet. She thought nothing of bargaining off hand for thousands of pounds. Mary did not care for the company of ladies, or to talk about flounces, tucks, bowknots, trimmings, skirts, or edgings; but preferred the company of gentlemen, and to discourse with them upon the merits of the long and short staple, of Surats, Surinams, Pernams, Sea Islands, and Bowed Georgias. Mary was really a remarkable person, and I believe that she passed more money through her hands than any woman in Scotland ever did. Had she confined herself solely to her business of a cotton broker, she would in all probability have acquired a large fortune; but she most unluckily became an extensive speculator in cotton upon her own account, and the notice below will show the result:—

1794. *Edinburgh Gazette*, 15th March.—"Sequestration.—Mary Brown, cotton dealer in Glasgow. Creditors to meet in Claud Currie's, vintner there, 27th current, at noon, to name a factor, and at same place and hour, 18th April, to chuse a trustee."

I think that the following letter will be perused with interest by all your septuagenarian readers. It was addressed to me by a very old acquaintance, Mr John Aitcheson, who died in August last, in the 90th year of his age:—

"Glasgow, 2d Feb., 1855.

"My dear Sir,—Many thanks for your kind letter, and tree of the old respectable family. I do not recollect any cotton brokers in our auld town, excepting Messrs J. & G. Buchanan & Co., that is, previous to 1792. My old friend, Mrs Mary Brown, was a direct buyer from the importers; and sometimes *we*—that is, Archd. Calder & Co., and Jo. Aitcheson & Co.—used to join with her in purchasing cotton from Messrs Leitch & Smith, and we also joined in buying cotton with my old friend, the late Mr John Bartholomew, direct from the importer. Mr Andrew Templeton, being a lodger with Mrs Brown when he was clerk with Messrs Duguid, the sugar refiners, joined Mrs Brown, and their firm was Mary Brown & Co., and afterwards Templeton, Jamieson, & Co., about the years 1798 and 1799. Archibald Sorely, for a short time, acted as broker, but *became an extensive cotton speculator and dealer* in 1799. and failed for a large sum. He afterwards joined a Mr Smith, as brokers, and the business continued under the firm of Sorely & Smith, and continued for some time afterwards under the firm of Smith and Brown, and latterly under the name of John Brown (*alias Cotton Jock*). He was unfortunate some time ago, but got settled, and for several years has a bonded store, and keeps horses and carts, and I believe he is doing well. In 1799, when Mr Owen purchased the Lanark Mills, Mr Kelly commenced cotton broker and a cotton spinner; his partner, I think, was Mr William Aitken (of Gilbert Shearer & Co.). The mill was near Blackburn, but it was a losing concern. Mr Kelly was trustee in the Rothesay Spinning Co.; he afterwards purchased the mill, but it was a bad business. Mr Kelly's son carries on as cotton broker at present, and his partner is Mr Hanna, brother-in-law to Mr James Scott of Kelly. James Donaldson was partner in the firm of Robertson & Co., extensive muslin manufacturers; he left that concern, and, along with James Kibble and Matthew Robertson, both from Paisley, purchased the mill built by Mr James Robertson (my father-in-law) at Milngavie. This was at a public sale, and my father-in-law, old Mr Robertson of Mill Bank, and my friend, Charles Bennet, of Manchester, opposed them. It was not on a large scale, and only fetched £3500. I rather think old Mr Robertson was to have had a share, as his partner, along with Charles Bennet and old Robert Thompson, grandfather to the present Mr N. Thompson of Camphill. Mr Donaldson was very unfortunate as a spinner at Milngavie, but Mr Dunn and some other friends, after his misfortune, patronised him as a cotton broker. I don't know who the company of James Donaldson are who carry on the cotton business under that firm at present. You, no doubt, recollect the extensive firm in the cotton trade of Sharp & Mackenzie, but they were regular dealers and also manufacturers. The cold is so very severe, I am afraid you can scarcely read this short note. Yours, faithfully,

(Signed)   "JOHN AITCHESON."

"*P. S.*—Pray, were you a full *Private* in the squad that met in the Session House and yard of the Chapel of Ease, along with Gavin Horn (son of Wm. Horn, who built Horn's Court and Glassford

Street), when Archy Paterson was *Fifer*, and I also acted with him in that time? We were drilled by Sergt. M'Intosh of the 42d. This was in 1793, previous to our joining the first Regiment of Volunteers. You, I recollect, joined the Cavalry about the time when Archy joined the Volunteers."

THE WATER BAILIE COURT OF GLASGOW IN OLDEN TIME.

SEEING the discussions which are now going on in the Clyde Trust regarding *Water Bailie* matters, perhaps the following notice may prove interesting to your readers :—

In 1792, a case came before the Water Bailie Court of Glasgow, in which judgment having been pronounced in favour of the pursuer, the defender afterwards presented a petition to the Court of Session, praying their Lordships to find " that the judgment pronounced by the Water Bailie of Glasgow is void, and that the question was incompetent to be tried before him, or at least before answer on that point to oblige the pursuer and the Water Bailie, as having sisted himself in the case, to condescend specially how far he was in use to exercise a *civil* jurisdiction of any kind during the subsistence of a Vice-Admiralty Court at Glasgow ; or, if he was, how far back, and to what extent, and in what kind of cause, such *civil* jurisdiction appears from the Records of the Court to have been exercised by him."

The case was a very simple one, viz. :—Thomas Ewing, a boatman, was in use to ply with a boat between Glasgow and Greenock, carrying goods and other merchandise. Donald Lamont, a small trader in Mull, placed some goods on board of Ewing's boat, which was to sail next morning from the Broomielaw for Greenock. These goods were correctly stowed along with the other goods, in the proper and usual manner, and two tarpaulins fixed over the cargo. Ewing and his assistant boatman slept on board ; but about three o'clock next morning, upon getting up to observe the state of the weather, they found the hatchway fixed down, which, with difficulty, they got opened, and then they found that the tarpaulins had been removed, and one of the chests of goods broken open, and its contents carried off. For the loss so sustained, Lamont brought an action against Ewing before the Water Bailie, founding upon the edict *Nautæ Caupones Stabularii*, in answer to which Ewing pled that the Water Bailie had no jurisdiction whatever to take cognisance of the question. The Water Bailie having given judgment sustaining his jurisdiction, found Ewing liable for the value of the goods stolen, and also for expenses of process. Ewing presented a bill of advocation for the purpose of removing the question into the Court of Session, both with respect to the point of jurisdiction and upon its merits. The Lord Ordinary, on a short view of the case, was pleased to pronounce the following interlocutor :—" Finds that the jurisdiction of the Water Bailie of Glasgow was competent, and that he had sufficient power to determine in the cause, and therefore repels the reason of advocation specially insisted on on the part of the defender ; and in respect the procurator for the defender declines stating his reasons of advocation as to the merits of the cause, repels also these reasons, and upon the whole remits the cause to the Water Bailie of Glasgow in common form ; and, lastly, finds the defender, the raiser of the advocation, liable to the pursuer in expenses, and appoints an account thereof to be given in." Upon advising a short representation, his Lordship, of date 10th March, 1792, adhered to his former interlocutor.

The case having then come before the Inner House, it was stated to their Lordships that there was, till of late, an Admiralty Court held at Glasgow, under a deputation from the Vice-Admiral of Scotland, whose jurisdiction extended originally over not only the Frith of Clyde, but a great part of the western coast of Scotland, though it came afterwards, in consequence of certain grants to the family of Argyll and others, to be limited to certain parts of the Frith of Clyde, and which Court exercised a jurisdiction civil and criminal, cumulative with the High Court of Admiralty ; and, like other inferior Courts of Admiralty, was in use also, in imitation of that Court, to take cognisance of all mercantile cases, as well as those purely maritime, till this last practice was corrected, and its jurisdiction restrained to maritime causes alone, and the Court found incompetent to judge in those which were purely mercantile, even on the acquiescence or consent of parties in the case.

The Vice-Admiralty Court, formerly held at Glasgow, together with those held in other parts of the country, being suppressed in consequence of certain arrangements adopted within these few years respecting the Court of Admiralty, the Water Bailie of Glasgow, in place of the limited jurisdiction formerly exercised by him, has begun to assume that *civil* jurisdiction formerly exercised by the Admiralty Depute for Clyde. Nor has he always, during this time,

confined himself in its exercise to those questions strictly maritime ;
but, in some late instances, taken cognisance of such as would not,
it is believed, be found to come properly within that description.

The grants to the family of Argyll before alluded to, contained
grants of an Admiralty jurisdiction, within their several bounds, in
the most general and ample terms of the nature of the commissions
granted to the Vice-Admiralty Courts, where it was in view that
they should exercise, in the first instance, the proper *civil* jurisdiction of a Court of Admiralty. An example may be found in the
commission granted by the Earl of March, as Vice-Admiral of Scotland, to Robert Barclay, constituting him Admiral-Depute for the
River and Frith of Clyde, 1768, September 12th,* which gives power
" to him and his substitutes to sit, affix, affirm, hold and continue
Admiral Courts within any part of the said bounds, over all the
limits thereof most commodious for that effect, and there to
administer and do justice in all matters and causes *civil* and *criminal*
that shall be intented and pursued before them, conform to the
laws of Scotland; acts to make decreets, and sentences to pronounce,
and the same to due and lawful cause be put ; and to call for and
require all his Majesty's lieges within the said bounds to put his, and
his said substitutes, their decreets, to due and lawful execution, and
generally with power to the said Robert Barclay to use, and exercise
bruik, and enjoy, *during our pleasure only*, the foresaid office within
the foresaid bounds; and to exact, intromit with, uplift and receive,
the whole fees, duties, casualties, and profits thereof, during the
continuance of this our commission to him ; and to act and do all
things requisite and necessary thereanent, and fully and freely as
any other Deputy Vice-Admiral and factor within the said bounds
did, or might have done in any time bygone, or may do in time
coming, reserving always to the High Court of Admiralty in Scotland
the sole power of cognoscing and determining in all prizes and
piracies, and other capital crimes, and in all other causes and actions
which shall be intented and pursued before the said High Court
of Admiralty, against any person or persons within the foresaid
bounds."

The petitioner Ewing further pled, that with respect to the Water
Bailie of Glasgow, the only authority which he could find for the
nomination of such a magistrate and for the jurisdiction exercised
by him within those parts of the river Clyde over which it extends,
is an extract produced, with the answers to the Bill of a Charter

* The former Broomielaw Bridge was then building.

from Charles I. to the City of Glasgow, dated 16th October, 1636, which grants, or rather confirms to them the privilege of naming a Water Bailie, and describes his jurisdiction in the following terms—

"Ac etiam libertatem, USUM, et possessionem, quam dic: Burgos noster de Glasgow, et Magistratus ejusdem, habuerunt elijendi unum Ballivum, qui aquæ præsit lic 'Water Bailie,' infra-dict, fluvium de Clyde, ubi mare fluit et refluit, et infra integras bondas ejusdem subtus pontem de Glasgow, ad lic Clochstane, et corrigendi omnes injurias, et enormitates super dicto fluvius commiss : infra bondas ejusdem ; in omnibus et singulis capitibus articulis, conditionibus et circumstantiis eorund : quibuscunque."

Mr Wm. M'Leod Bannatyne,* counsel for Ewing, argued that the jurisdiction given to the Water Bailie of Glasgow was conferred for the limited purpose " corrigendi omnes injurias et enormitates super dicto fluvio commissas"—viz., within the bounds of his jurisdiction as described, being from the Bridge of Glasgow to the Clochstane, a few miles below Greenock, and which is also the boundary of a similar grant to the Burgh of Rothesay, of a petty criminal jurisdiction for preserving the peace of the river, by the punishment or correction of offences committed by seafaring persons within those bounds, the greater part of whom might naturally be considered as resorting to Glasgow.

For the pursuer Lamont and the Water Bailie, it was pled that USAGE of very long continuance gave the Water Bailie power to exercise a jurisdiction to determine in this and similar causes.

Their Lordships, after parties being fully heard, refused the petition of Ewing, and affirmed the interlocutor of the Lord Ordinary, with expenses.

MUNICIPAL ELECTIONS.

"Mores populi, quantum mutaverint, vel hic dies indicio erit."

"Thou as a vesture shalt them change,
And they shall changed be."

So says the Psalmist; and truly, amongst the mighty changes which have taken place in Glasgow since the days "o' langsyne," none

* Afterwards Lord Bannatyne.

have been more remarkable than the mode of getting through with
our annual municipal elections. Even down to our own days,
everything went on in a snug quiet way at the council board, and
our citizens were left to guess in the dark who was to be lord
provost, or who were to be bailies or councillors; in fact, the ruling
provost and his party were generally the nominators of those who
were to receive civic honours; and if any of our great bushy wigs
happened to be in opposition to the leading clique of the board,
they were punished by being elected provosts, bailies, deans of guild,
or councillors, it being well known that those Virginian lords would
not condescend to play a second fiddle in corporation matters, and
of course they had to pay the fine for non-acceptance of office.
How different is the case now-a-days! At present, all is bustle,
hurry-burry, and restless activity among the candidates aspiring to
the office of city councillors; all of them are willing to give their
services to the community *scot-free*, even to the neglect of their
own business and private affairs ; the expenses of newspaper advertisements, of committee rooms, and of cab-hirings, being considered
by them as quite beneath their notice, and as trifles light as air,
while thus in pursuit of municipal dignity. It was well said by Dr
Johnson, that "*Distinction* is so pleasing to the pride of man, that
a great part of the pain and pleasure of life arises from the gratification or disappointment of an incessant wish for *superiority*." But
perhaps it is rather stale to draw invidious parallels between the
present times and the past; and your readers may say that I should
leave it to carping moralists to harp on this jarring chord, and to
please their fancies by looking continually backwards, and condemn-
ing by retrospect what is presently before them. I shall, therefore,
without more ado, proceed to state a few loose facts regarding our
former corporation affairs, commencing about the middle of the
sixteenth century.

In the disturbed period of 1559, the council of Glasgow appear to
have elected the provost and bailies of the city of Glasgow, hitherto
under the nomination of the archbishops; but both before and
immediately after the Reformation in 1560, little is known in what
manner the proceedings at the council board of Glasgow were conducted; there is, however, no doubt of their having been managed
with closed doors, in the strictest sense of these words, as the
following passages, taken from the City Records, sufficiently
show :—

"Burgh Records, 4th October, 1575.—Lord Boyd having been

named provost by the archbishop,* and a list of eight burgesses having been presented to his Grace, for the purpose of naming two of them as bailies, he selected two of them as bailies for the said year. These gentlemen having accepted of office, immediately commenced their rule by the following statute:—'*Item:* It is statut and ordanit be ye provest, baillies, and counsale, yt gif ony persone of ye counsale happins to revele ony ying spoken or tretit in counsale, as counsale, sall be removit of ye counsale, and never in tymes cuming to be admittit upon ye counsale agane, bot haldin infame, and yair freedomes callit doun.' " This statute was confirmed on the 3d October, 1577, Thomas Crawfurd of Jordanhill being provost at the time. On the 30th September, 1578, Archbishop Boyd appointed the Earl of Lennox to be lord provost of Glasgow, although the Earl was not then even a burgess of the city. The nomination, however, had the sanction of the Crown.

On the 2d October, 1578, we find the following entry in the Burgh Record, which shows that the appointment of the Earl of Lennox to be provost did not give satisfaction to the lieges of the city:—"The quhilk daye comparit Thomas Crawfurde, of Jordanhill, auld provest, and allegit yat he was put of ye counsale bot ony falt, and uncallit yairfore, and protestit for remeid of law, and yat ye namyng and chesing of ye counsale, but his or ye auld baillies' consent, preinge nocht his rycht, and yat ye libertie of ye town be nocht hurt yairby." The bailies also recorded their protest against the said election.

From the following extract, it appears that about this period there was no Dean of Guild Court in Glasgow, and that the bailies and certain members of the town council acted as liners when disputes arose between conterminous proprietors of ground regarding their mutual boundaries:—"Burgh Records, 31st May, 1574.—The quhilk day the thre baillies and ane parte of ye counsale past to visie and decyde ye questione of lyneyng and nytbourheid betwixt Thomas Crawfurd, of Jordanhill, fewar of ye persone of Glasgwis mans, on that ane part, and Maister David Conynghame, fewar of ye Subdeynes mens on yat wyer part," etc. M'Ure, at pages 50 and 51, informs us that the parsonage of Glasgow Manse was situated a little to the east of the Bishop's Castle, and that the

---

* Archbishop James Boyd, of Trochrigg, who obtained the archbishopric by the Treaty of Leith settling Episcopacy in 1572. He was the son of the Hon. Adam Boyd, the brother of Lord Boyd. The Lord Boyd whom the archbishop elected as provost was his nephew.

parsonage house of the subdean stood a little to the south, and opposite the church on the little brook called the Molendinar.

For a considerable number of years after the last-mentioned period, there appears to have been great irregularity regarding the mode of nominating the magistrates and council of the city, as the following extract shows :—"Burgh Records, 4th October, 1580.— The Court and Conventioun of ye burt. and citie of Glasgw haldin ye tolbuyt. yrof in   of ye sáymyn be honobl. men, George Elphinston and Willam. Conyngha, auld baillies, ye auld counsale for nemyng of lytis of ye baillies yis zeir to cum, ye ferde [4th] daye of October, ye zeir of God J.00.Vc. four schoir zeirs." On this occasion the magistrates and council seem in fact to have elected themselves into office, as the convention of citizens made no objection to the election; but it must be observed that in the above minute two great blanks are left, as if the court and convention of the burgh had been ashamed to place the whole of their transactions on record in black and white. At this meeting there appears to have been a general assembly of the burgesses called, to act in concert with the magistrates and council. They appointed Sir Matthew Stewart, of Minto, to be lord provost; and his partisans, Hector Stewarde and John Graham, as bailies, "for ye zeir to cum," the landed interest being then too powerful for the citizens.

In 1633 the city of Glasgow was declared by Parliament to be a Royal Free Burgh, notwithstanding of which, down to the Revolution in 1688, our municipal affairs fell into the hands of a mercantile clique, composed of Bells, Campbells, Andersons, Walkinshaws, and Hamiltons, &c., who, for the most part, were connected to each other either by blood or marriage. It was during the reign of those provosts that our splendid Eastern and Western Commons were frittered away ; of which, however, their lordships took especial care to secure a goodly share of them to themselves, such as the Cowcaddens, Bell's Parks, Blythswood Holms, Anderston Faulds, Barrowfield Lands, Hamilton Hill, Stobcross, and sundry other pickings of the like kind. Whilst they and their partisans held the rule in the city, we have little information regarding what passed at the council board, further than that those worthies were in the practice of electing themselves and their dependents into office. Dr Cleland, at page 167 of his Annals, informs us, that in consequence of the Revolution, "the magistrates and council of Glasgow were elected by a poll vote of all the burgesses on the 2d July, 1689."

From this time forward we hear no more of the Bells of Cowcaddens or the Campbells of Blythswood being in office.

I now pass over the troubled times of the rebellions of 1715 and 1745, and come to the year 1748, when a committee of the town council reported that by the constitution of the burgh the government of the city might perhaps turn out to be vested in the hands of particular persons longer than was for the *public good;* the council therefore resolved, that in future two senior councillors of the Merchants' and Trades' ranks should annually retire from the council, and should not be eligible to serve as councillors till three years had elapsed. In 1801, however, by an Act of the Convention of Royal Burghs, a Merchant and a Trades' bailie were added to the magistracy. Such continued to be the position of city matters until the Reform Bill was passed in 1833.

Mr Crawfurd, in his interesting and valuable work, "A Sketch of the Trades' House of Glasgow," says, at page 96, that, in 1748, some *sleight-of-hand* alterations were made upon the set of the burgh, and he adds, " it thus appears that of the town council, composed of thirteen of the Merchant rank and twelve of the Trades' rank, besides the magistrates and the dean of guild, deacon convener, and treasurer, two of each rank retired annually by rotation, and that those who remained elected the successors of those who retired, under a *sleight-of-hand management of the ' leets'* by the provost, who was *the Great Juggler!!!*"

Mr Crawfurd, however, does not inform us exactly in what manner this legerdemain trick of the leets was performed; and Dr Cleland, though no doubt master of the subject, has been apparently intentionally silent as to all the hocus-pocus election tricks achieved at the council board of Glasgow whilst he was in office.

During all last century it was considered as a point of honour that no magistrate, councillor, or city official should disclose what took place at the meetings of the council board, in consequence of which the citizens in general were kept in complete ignorance of every measure concocted by the provost and bailies, except in so far as it pleased those worthies to give information to the public.

I have in my possession an old Court of Session paper, dated 1765, regarding a lawsuit, in which the magistrates of Glasgow were defenders. In the course of the proceedings in this case, Archibald M'Gilchrist, depute town-clerk of Glasgow, was called as a haver,—"And the said Archibald M'Gilchrist being interrogate as to the practice and custom of the magistrates and town council of

Glasgow, relative to the town's affairs,"—it was objected that no such questions could be put to Mr M'Gilchrist, he being the confidential adviser of the magistrates; the Court, however, over-ruled the objection, and accordingly "the said Archibald M'Gilchrist, aged 57 years, being solemnly sworn, depones—'That he entered to be an extractor in the Town Clerk's Chamber in the year 1730, and ever since has been particularly acquainted with the way and manner the Acts of Council have been passed, minuted, and recorded, as to which depones—that the constant and invariable practice ever since the said year 1730, has been, that the magistrates and council first resolve and agree upon what is to be done; immediately after which a distinct minute of their resolutions is taken down in writing by the town-clerk, in presence of the magistrates and council, and afterwards is read in their hearing and approved of. That thereafter, and before the next meeting of council, the matters so minuted and approved of are recorded by the town-clerk in the Records of the Acts of Council; and at the first meeting of council after an Act is resolved and agreed on, that Act is recorded from the minutes taken when the Act passed, is publicly read over to the magistrates and council, and they subscribe the Record thereof.'"

Such, then, was the mode of proceeding at the meetings of our Council Board when the first history of Glasgow was published by John M'Ure, and which system, so far as I know, was continued down to our own times.

There is a subject regarding the election of our magistrates and councillors which seems to me to have escaped the notice of all the historians of Glasgow—at least I have searched their works in vain for some explicit information on this topic. I mean what were the penalties for our magistracy refusing to accept of office? and how came known recusants to be subjected to heavy fines for declining to serve, while scores of our most respectable citizens were panting and gaping for the honour? To the best of my recollection, the following were the penalties which in my younger days could lawfully be extorted from any citizen of Glasgow for refusing to accept of office in the burgh:—

1. For refusing to accept the office of lord provost, £50.
2.   ,,   ,,   bailie,   40.
3.   ,,   ,,   dean of guild, 40.
4.   ,,   ,,   councillor,   20.
5.   ,,   ,,   deacon-convr., nil.

The crafts here seem to have been the only sapient folks at the council board, for, though legally entitled to do so, they exacted no penalty from any of their members who might refuse to accept of the convenership. I must say, however, that I never heard of such a thing as a craftsman refusing to be made a deacon-convener.

I shall now proceed to give a few examples of the above-mentioned fines having been rapaciously extracted from the purses of recusant individuals. "*Glasgow Journal*, 15th November, 1764 :—Yesterday, Arthur Connell, merchant of this place, was chosen dean of guild, in room of Mr James Simson, who refused to accept of that office." Dr Cleland, at page 175 of his Annals, says in a note that "Peter Murdoch was elected a bailie, in 1767 ;" but his name does not appear in the list of magistrates of that year ; he, of course, must have paid the fine, as all fines for refusing to accept the bailieship were rigorously exacted. "*Glasgow Journal*, 31st October, 1776 :—Tuesday—Mr James Sommerville,* merchant, was chosen dean of guild, in place of Mr Peter Murdoch, who has declined serving that office, he having paid his fine, being £40 sterling." And the very next week, viz., 7th Nov. 1776, the said journal announces that "yesterday Mr Hugh Wyllie, merchant, was elected dean of guild, in place of Mr James Sommerville, who was elected last week, he having declined serving, and has paid his fine of £40." Here the deanship was at a sad discount, two deans in succession having refused the honour of being the head of the Merchants' House, and of a seat at the council board. Perhaps, however, after all, the exaction of those fines was only a shabby way of raising the supplies upon the part of the Merchants' House, their funds being then very low, as the following advertisement shows :—"*Glasgow Journal*, 3d October, 1757 :—Since the present set of the Merchants' House was introduced in the year 1747, the number of the matriculated members who make up that House has decreased by death and other ways about one-third part; it is therefore to be hoped that this loss will be supplied by the subscription of many of the Merchants' rank who have entered since that time, to entitle them to a share of the management of the funds of the House, which, in that case, properly belong to them, on their paying *four shillings* sterling to the poor yearly. The book

---

* James Sommerville entered the Merchants' House in 1771, and was the only entrant of that year. In 1772 there were no entrants; in 1773 there were two; in 1774 there was just one ; but in 1775 the number of entrants amounted to six; so that there appears to have been some plotting at the time of the election in question.

for subscription lyes at the shop of Messrs Scott and Brown, under the Exchange Coffee-House." (*N.B.*—The above-mentioned shop was situated in the Merchants' Land, at the north-west corner of the Saltmarket, opposite the present statue of King William. This land was taken down a few years ago, and has been replaced by the present large tenement.)

Let us now proceed in our quotations.—" *Glasgow Mercury*, 12th October, 1780.—On Tuesday, the 3d instant, the magistrates of this city were elected, when John Campbell of Clathic was elected lord provost; but Mr Campbell having declined serving in that office he was unanimously chosen dean of guild." " On Monday the 16th October, Hugh Wyllie was elected lord provost in the room of Mr John Campbell." Here the Merchants' House, seeing that Mr Campbell had declined the provostship, and paid his fine, no doubt wished to have a share of the *bakes;* and *jalousing* that Mr Campbell, having refused to accept of the higher dignity of lord provost, would certainly refuse the offer of the lower dignity of dean of guild, and thus £40 sterling would be added to the funds of the Merchants' House; but Mr Campbell, thinking the double fine rather *" saut,"* accepted of the deanship, and thereby escaped a second penalty. Hugh Wyllie seems to have been a very convenient personage, who was willing to take the leavings of either the deanship or provost-ship as his party directed. He died on the 20th February, 1782.

On the 23d October, 1783, Robert Finlay, the father of Robert Finlay, Esq. of Easterhill, was elected bailie of Glasgow, in the room of Henry Ritchie, who had declined serving the office of bailie, and had paid the fine. The following, however, is a more important case, and shows in black colours the extreme shabbiness of the town council and Merchants' House, which colours are made still darker when contrasted with the opposite conduct of the Trades' House, regarding their regulations as to the convenership. The object of the Merchants' House was evidently to pocket the fine:—

" *Glasgow Mercury*, 20th January, 1780.—On Wednesday the 12th curt., the Court of Session gave judgment in the following cause :—' At Michaelmas, 1778, Mr Thomas Hopkirk, merchant in Glasgow, having been elected dean of guild of that city, and having refused to accept of the office, the town council, who are the electors, decerned him to pay the sum of £40 sterling in name of fine. Mr John M'Call, merchant, was next elected, and having in like manner declined, was find in £40 sterling.' Both these gentlemen presented suspensions, which, being pleaded before Lord Gardenstown, his Lordship 'suspended the letters *simpliciter.*' The town council reclaimed by petition to the whole Lords. The chargers rested their plea upon an Act of Council passed in 1748, and ratified by the Convention of Royal Burghs, whereby it is enacted, 'That every person who shall be elected provost, one of the bailies, dean of guild, deacon convener, or treasurer, shall, on his refusal or declining to accept any of the said offices, be fined in the sum of £40 sterling.' The defences stated for the suspenders were—1st. That the decreets charged on were null and void, being pronounced by the town council, who have no jurisdiction. 2d, That the town council had no power, by the set, to impose fines, and the Council Act, 1748, could not legally invest them with such power. 3d, That, by a special clause in the said Act of Council, 1748, it is provided 'That every person hereafter elected a councillor shall be obliged to accept of his office under a penalty of £20 sterling, declaring always that if any person shall make payment of the above fine for not accepting to be a councillor, *he shall not again be compellable to accept of that office.*' That Mr Hopkirk was elected a councillor in 1752, and, having refused to accept, was fined in £20, which he paid accordingly; and Mr M'Call having been elected a councillor in 1769, and declining officiating, he also paid a fine of £20. That therefore the suspenders must be considered as having purchased an exemption from serving as councillors at any future period. That the dean of guild is, *ex officio,* a councillor, subjected to the whole duties of this office as much as any ordinary member: and therefore the suspenders should not be obliged to accept of the office of dean of guild, *which includes the office of councillor,* agreeably to the express terms of the Act of Council, 1748, on which the decreets of the town council were founded, which declares, 'That if any person shall pay the fine of £20 for refusing to be councillor, he shall not again be compellable to accept of that *office.*'"

" The suspenders, in order to obtain a judgment on the merits of the cause, dropt their first defence ; and, upon the second, it appeared, from the reasonings upon the bench, to be the opinion of the court that town councils have an inherent power at common law to inflict moderate fines on the burgesses refusing to accept of the offices, in the duty of exercising which all the members of the community are bound to bear a share. In considering the third point, the Lords were unanimously of opinion that the suspenders, by having formerly fined off when elected councillors, could not, upon a fair construction of the Act of Council, 1748, be again fined for

z

refusing to act in the office of dean of guild, who must, *ex officio*, act as a member of the town council, and therefore 'adhered to Lord Gardenstown's interlocutors.' "

Some further particulars of this curious case are to be found in the Faculty Collections, 13th January, 1780, and are as follows:—
"James Hill *v.* Thomas Hopkirk and John M'Call.

"By the regulations enacted in 1748 by the town council, and likewise recorded in the books of council, only four councillors are to be changed every year, according to their seniority: but the dean of guild and deacon-convener must continue for one year after the expiry of their respective offices, and ever afterwards to be removed in rotation with the other members of the council. By these regulations it was further provided that every person elected, or continued as councillor, should be obliged to accept or continue in office under a penalty of £20, to be paid to the collector for the poor of the Merchants' House. After this he could not be required to undertake that office. In the same manner, every person elected dean of guild was obliged to accept, under a penalty of £40. Soon after these regulations were made, Mr Hopkirk and Mr M'Call had been elected councillors, and paid their fines for non-acceptance. In 1778 they were, one after another, elected deans of guild, and, refusing to accept, were fined each in £40. The question chiefly agitated was the legality of the regulations of 1748, which introduced a considerable change in the set, and imposed fines on persons declining offices in the burgh. The Lords found, 'in respect of the special circumstances of the case, particularly that the suspenders formerly fined off when elected into office as councillors, and paid that fine of £20 sterling each, that they could not be of new fined for refusing to accept of or act in the office of the dean of guild, who, *ex officio*, must act likewise as a member of council, and therefore suspend the letters *simpliciter.*'"

In this action the town council of Glasgow appear as chargers; but the James Hill, mentioned in the Faculty Collections as conducting the case in court, was the law agent of the Merchants' House, and the fines, if recovered, would have gone into the coffers of the said house. Altogether the affair looks wonderfully like a conspiracy between the Merchants' House and the town council of Glasgow to filch a few pounds from the pockets of gentlemen who, they well knew beforehand, would not accept of office, while at the same time they were perfectly aware that there were scores of equally respectable citizens not only willing but most

anxious to serve the office in question, solely on account of it con-
ferring distinction and dignity. The case certainly showed a gross
abuse of power and greed of pelf. We must remark, however, from
the report of the foregoing cases, that at this time the members of
the Merchants' House did not possess, or did not exercise, the right
of electing their deans of guild. When John Campbell of Clathic
was elected Provost in 1780, and refused to serve, the town council
immediately after he had declined the said office, and at the same
sederunt, "unanimously chose him dean of guild." Again, in the
report of the case of Hopkirk and M'Call, it is expressly stated that
those gentlemen were elected deans of guild by the town council of
the city, "who are the electors." In this state of matters, it may
easily be seen that the lord provost of Glasgow of that period possessed great influence and power, not only at the council board, but
over the citizens in general, whom he and his party could either
favour or annoy, by getting them elected into office in the burgh.
Tempora mutantur.

THE GRANDFATHER OF CHARLES WILSONE BROUN, ESQ.

As the public have felt much interest in the case of Charles Wilsone
Broun and wife (late Mrs Swinfen), regarding the claim of Mrs
Swinfen's counsel for £20,000, as due to him for professional
services, it may, perhaps, be interesting to your readers to listen to
an old story which made a great sensation in Glasgow in my early
days, the principal personage concerned in it, in point of rank, being
one of the most eminent surgeons in Glasgow, viz., Charles Wilsone,
Esq., for whom our townsman, Charles Wilsone Broun, Esq., was
named. I remember Mr Wilsone very well. He was a tall, portly
man, of very engaging, easy manners, and a particular favourite
with every class of our citizens. His residence was in Stockwell
Street, near its head, on the west side of the street. Unlike most
medical gentlemen, he usually wore a light-coloured dress, and in
my time he had almost retired from practice, being in independent
circumstances.

Without further preface I shall now proceed to give an account
of the occurrence in question, as taken from the *Glasgow Mercury*
of 1787 :—

" *Mercury*, 1787, 10th January.—Late on Friday night (5th), a

gentleman (Mr Wilsone) on his way home was knocked down by two
fellows, at the west end of Argyle Street, and robbed of between six
and seven pounds in notes and silver, with a case containing a
number of surgeon's instruments and other articles. Besides robbing him, they gave him several severe blows when lying on the
ground. The case with the instruments was found in a stair-case in
the Saltmarket, on Monday night; but the robbers have not been
discovered, though diligent search has been made for them."

"*Mercury*, 7th January.—Friday last, Thomas Veitch, shoemaker, and John M'Aulay, stockingmaker, were apprehended on
suspicion of knocking down and robbing Mr Charles Wilsone,
surgeon, on the night of Friday the 5th current. After examination they were committed to prison, in order to stand trial. Mr
Wilsone's gloves were found upon one of them, and on the other,
one of his small silver cases for holding matter for inoculating for
the small-pox. Veitch is about 22 years of age, and was lately
whipped out of the 63d Regiment; M'Aulay is about 19 years old.
It is said they belong to a gang of twenty."

At the Circuit Court of Justiciary, held at Glasgow on Saturday
the 14th of April, 1787, Lord Hailes proceeded to try Thomas
Gentles, indicted for stealing a piece of cloth from a bleachfield,
when the jury having found the libel proven, Gentles was sentenced
to be hanged on Wednesday the 23d of May. On Monday the 16th,
Lords Hailes and Henderland commenced the trial of John M'Aulay
and Thomas Veitch, indicted for street robbery of Dr Wilsone.
The trial lasted till three in the afternoon, when the jury were
inclosed, and on Tuesday morning they returned a verdict unanimously finding the libel proven. The Court delayed pronouncing
sentence till Wednesday.

"*Mercury*, 18th April, 1787.—John M'Aulay and Thomas
Veitch, as mentioned in our last, are to be hanged on the 23d of
May next."

"*Mercury*, 30th May, 1787.—Wednesday, the 23d inst., were
executed in the Castle Yard here, Thomas Gentles for robbing a
bleachfield, and Thomas Veitch and John M'Aulay for street
robbery. They were taken from prison a few minutes after two
o'clock afternoon, and though it is but about half a-mile to the
place of execution, it was near three before they reached the fatal
spot, owing to the great multitude of people on the street, which
retarded the procession. They were attended by three ministers—
the Rev. Mr Alex. Pirie, Mr John M'Leod, and Mr James Steven.

When near the Bell of the Brae they appeared faint, and Gentles and Veitch got a glass of wine, and M'Aulay (about nineteen years of age) made choice of a glass of water. At the scaffold the ministers prayed, and the criminals addressed the spectators to avoid such courses as had brought them to so shameful a death. When they were left with the executioner, they behaved with becoming fortitude and resignation, and took an affectionate leave of one another, and of several of their acquaintance; after which, Gentles prayed with great fervour and devotion for himself and fellow-sufferers, when they were launched into eternity, and died without any apparent struggle, amidst a commiserating multitude of spectators. It is to be hoped that particular attention will be paid to remove those houses which they made known, and were the haunts of the unhappy men, and contributed to accelerate their ruin."

Shortly before the trial of the above-mentioned culprits a most daring attempt to break out of prison was made by Gentles, Veitch, and M'Aulay, assisted by the other prisoners, men and women, which was nearly successful, it being frustrated only by the arrival of the soldier who stood sentinel at the outer door of the jail. The following is the account given of this bold enterprise in the *Glasgow Mercury* of 4th April, 1787 :—

" Last Thursday evening the prisoners indicted to stand trial before the Circuit Court to be held here on the 14th instant, made an attempt to force their way out of prison. About seven of the evening, the turnkey went up stairs to shut the windows of the prison; when in the iron room, and closing the window boards, the prisoners, who had before disengaged themselves from their irons, seized him by the throat, tied a rope tight in his mouth, and bound his hands behind his back, and took from him the keys of the close rooms, went and let loose the prisoners under sentence of banishment, in all nineteen men and women, and came down stairs in a body. But the jailer, Mr Lawson, standing at the wicket-door, and observing more people on the stair than usual, gave the alarm. They attempted to unlock the door, and struck the jailer on the face with a large key through the hatch-hole; but the sentinel, and other assistance, coming to the outer door, and they seeing their attempt frustrated, retired to their several apartments; but those in the iron room refused to admit the jailer to secure them. A party of soldiers were brought from the guard, and admittance being obtained after threatening to fire upon them, they were all put in new irons that night, and double sentinels stationed on the prison in the night-time."

It may be here remarked, that the entry to the prison from the High Street was by a narrow winding inside stair, which commenced about fifteen feet from the outer door of the building, there being a sort of lobby or room in front occupied by the jailer. The bottom of this stair was strongly secured by a massive door, while the said lobby or room, which looked into the High Street, was secured during the day merely by a half-door, over the top of which the jailer used to amuse himself, with his arms akimbo, looking at all the novelties which were going on in the High Street, and chatting over his half-door with his acquaintances on the street. The sentinel, however, walked his rounds before the prison, and was within call of the jailer.

It was the inner massive door at the bottom of the stair which the prisoners were unable to force, the outer half-door or wicket being no defence at the time when the attempt in question was made. Prisoners condemned to be executed were placed in the iron room of the prison, and strongly fettered.

At this time there was no paid police force or night watchmen in service in Glasgow to protect the lieges. Soon afterwards, however, the duty of city constabulary came to be performed by the citizens themselves, as is shown by the following very curious advertisement, issued by our lord provost and magistrates. I suspect that the present learned sheriffs of St Mungo would scarcely have endorsed this extraordinary notice, although the then town-clerks, John Orr and John Wilson, jun., seemed to think it a light affair to inflict a fine of 5s upon defaulters :—

Glasgow Mercury, 2d December, 1790.

" NOTICE.

" *To the Citizens of Glasgow.*

" The Lord Provost and Magistrates of Glasgow, in order the more effectually to protect the persons and property of the citizens, find it necessary and expedient to establish a Night Guard and Patrol, composed of the citizens, in order to watch and guard the streets ; and, for that purpose, DO hereby ORDER and REQUIRE all male house-holders, citizens and inhabitants of Glasgow, under the age of sixty and above eighteen, whose yearly rents are £3 sterling, or above, in rotation, to the number of thirty every night, as they shall be warned by an officer, two days before mounting guard, to repair to the Laigh Council Chamber, at ten o'clock at night, and to continue on guard, and patrol till next morning, subject to such orders as shall be given by the magistrates. Such as cannot, or do not choose to attend, must send the sitting magistrate two shillings and sixpence sterling, each, *the day after being warned*, that the magistrates may provide a proper *substitute;* and, in default thereof, each absentee will be fined in *five shillings sterling.* No substitute provided by the *person warned* will be accepted of.

" As an institution of this kind has become necessary, from the great extent and populousness of the city, it is expected by the magistrates that the citizens will pay a ready obedience in discharge · of a duty and service so essential and conducive to the public safety.

" Council Chamber, 27th Dec., 1790."

PROGRESS OF LOCOMOTION.

I⋊ your paper of the 21st instant, you have given us a quotation from the *North British Review,* regarding the progress of locomotion, where it is stated, " That it was not till 1758 that a regular conveyance was established between the eastern and western capitals, occupying twelve hours on the road. Thirty years afterwards, by means of lighter coaches, better horses, and improved roads, the time was greatly reduced."

There is a mistake here, as the following quotation shows :—

" *Scots Magazine,* 1749, p. 253.—An Edinburgh and Glasgow stage coach is now set up. One of the coaches sets out from Edinburgh every Monday and Thursday, and from Glasgow every Tuesday and Friday. Every person pays 9s fare, and is allowed a stone weight of baggage. The first coach set out on the 24th of April. . And an Edinburgh and Corstorphine stage chaise is set up, which goes that stage eight or nine times every week, and *four times on Sunday.* The fare is 6d each person. This was begun on the 18th of May."

The Edinburgh folks at this time do. not seem to have made any objection to Sunday travelling, as the Edinburgh and Glasgow Railway Company now do.

As to the locomotion thirty years after the year 1758 being

improved, according to the statement of the *Review*, I cannot say that I found it so; for I travelled at that date from Glasgow to Edinburgh in the "Diligence," which left Glasgow after breakfast hour, and landed us at the Grassmarket about eight o'clock P.M., after having dined and drank tea by the road.

"*Scots Magazine*, 1749, p. 459.—About the end of July a caravan was set on foot to go between Edinburgh and Glasgow, to go and return twice every week. Each person to pay 5s fare, and to be allowed a stone weight of baggage."

On the same page of the magazine, we find the following notice :

"A Highlander was taken up on the street of Edinburgh, August 12, and carried prisoner to the Castle, for wearing a philabeg. One Stewart, another Highlander, was taken into custody at Edinburgh, for the same crime, on the 18th of September."

In the year 1758, mentioned by the *Review*, the Newcastle waggon from Glasgow to London was established. It was drawn by six horses, and set out from the Gallowgate, the manager at Glasgow being Gabriel Watson, who, I daresay, is well remembered by your octogenarian readers. I heard, in my early days, that it was by this conveyance that Mr John M'Ilquham performed his first journey to London.

"*Glasgow Journal*, 18th September, 1758.—To acquaint gentlemen, tradesmen, &c., that the Newcastle-upon-Tyne new Stage-Waggon sets out from the Swan with Two Necks, Lad Lane, London, every day; delivers goods, *passengers, &c.*, from the above place, the Thursday se'nnight following (which is sooner by two days than any other waggon), at 1s 10d per stone, and so in proportion to the towns and parts adjacent."

Here follows a list of towns where goods may be sent, in which list we find Edinburgh and Glasgow.

"1763, June 23.—There is established a good stage coach between Glasgow and Greenock, to set out from Glasgow every Monday, Wednesday, and Friday, and from Greenock every Tuesday, Thursday, and Saturday. The stage to commence on Monday the 26th of June, at six o'clock in the morning, and from Greenock on Tuesday the 27th June, at three o'clock afternoon. The time of setting out will be afterwards named, according to the season of the year, and inserted on the tickets at the time. Tickets to be had at Donald Wilson's shop, opposite the Post Office, Glasgow ; and at Greenock, at Mr George Scot's, at 5s each for inside passengers, and at 2s 6d for passengers behind. That place being commodiously fitted to hold six, secured from all weather, after the best English manner. Every passenger to be allowed ten pounds weight of baggage. No person can be admitted without a ticket. *N.B.*—The stage goes only twice a week, on Mondays and Fridays, the first fortnight."

" 1766, 27th March.—Renfrew and Scotstoun fly will set off from John Parlane's house in Gallowgate, on Monday the 24th instant, and continue every day of the week, half an hour after ten o'clock in the morning, and will proceed either to Renfrew, Scotstoun, or Yoker Bridge, as the majority of the passengers agree, and will return to town a quarter before two o'clock mid-day. Each person to pay 1s 6d. If the company halt at Renfrew, they are to pay the horses and servants' maintenance. As this is undertaken for the convenience, and at the particular desire of a number of the inhabitants, it is hoped it will meet with suitable encouragement."

" 1764, August 2d.—For the benefit of the public. A new commodious landau, that will conveniently hold six persons, sets off from Mr Graham's, at the Black Bull, Glasgow, to Mr Miller's, at the Black Bull, Paisley—

" On Tuesday evening, at 7 o'clock precisely.
" On Wednesday evening, at 6 o'clock.
" On Saturday morning, at 9 o'clock.

" *From Paisley to Glasgow.*

" On Wednesday morning, at 9 o'clock ;
" And in the evening, at 8 o'clock.
" On Saturday evening, at 6 o'clock.

" To continue weekly so long as they shall meet encouragement."

" *Glasgow Journal,* 16th February, 1764.—That upon Monday the 27th February, 1764, the Edinburgh and Glasgow stage machine sets out every day of the week, from John Paxton's, at the White Hart, in the Grass Market, in Edinburgh ; and every day in the week, from John Parlane, at the sign of the Glasgow Arms, in the Gallowgate, Glasgow, at eight o'clock in the morning, from each place, and are supplied with fresh horses at Livingston and Hollowtown. Each passenger to pay as formerly—11s, and allowed one stone of luggage.

" *N.B.*—All passengers taken up on the road to pay threepence per mile, and that money to be paid to the first landlord of the stage where they stop, or whatever miles they are carried and to be carried. And also, if one passenger, they pay the half of the toll; and if two passengers, or three, they pay the whole of the tolls among them."

"*Glasgow Journal*, 9th January, 1766.—The Glasgow fly, hung upon steel springs, for four passengers, driven by two *postillions* and four horses, sets out from George Warden's stables, in the Grass Market, Edinburgh, and James Graham's, at the Black Bull, Glasgow, on Monday the 29th instant, at six o'clock in the morning. The passengers to breakfast at Whitburn, where they will always be supplied with fresh horses, and arrive at Glasgow and Edinburgh by three in the afternoon to dinner. Each passenger to pay 12s, to be allowed 14 pounds luggage, and all above to pay at the rate of 1s per stone. Passengers taken up on the road to pay 3½d per measured mile."

"*Weekly Magazine*, January, 1774, page 62.—On Saturday last, between seven and eight at night, the mail from Paisley to Glasgow was stolen, between the turnpike on the post road near the Gorbals, and the toll-bar at the end of the New Bridge. Next day the mail was found upon the south bank of the river Clyde, betwixt the old and new bridges, quite empty; and the bags were found sometime after, all the letters opened, and the contents of some of them abstracted."

"*Weekly Magazine*, January, 1777, page 127.—On Monday, about one o'clock, the post boy carrying the mail from Glasgow to Edinburgh, in crossing a small rivulet at a place called Loanhead, west of Falkirk, by the rapidity of the current and the ice breaking, was carried down the stream. He luckily saved himself by catching hold of a wooden bridge. The horse a short time after disengaged himself from the mail, and got out. The boy immediately alarmed the neighbourhood, who, with Mr Ramsay, jun., postmaster of Falkirk, went in search of the mail, and got out, and found it about a quarter of a mile down the rivulet, thrown upon a bank. The boy with the mail arrived on Tuesday afternoon at five."

"*Glasgow Mercury*, 1779, January 7th, page 7.—The Glasgow and Paisley stage coach sets out on the following days, viz. :—

"From Glasgow—Monday, ten o'clock forenoon.
        Tuesday, ten o'clock,   do.
        Wednesday, six o'clock morning.
        Do.,   six o'clock evening.
        Thursday, ten o'clock forenoon.

" From Glasgow—Friday, ten o'clock afternoon.
  Saturday, ten o'clock   do.

" From Paisley—Monday, six o'clock evening.
  Tuesday, six o'clock   do.
  Wednesday, nine o'clock morning.
  Do.,   six o'clock evening.
  Thursday, six o'clock   do.
  Friday, six o'clock   do.
  Saturday, six o'clock   do."

" *Glasgow Mercury*, 23d March, 1780, page 96.—Edinburgh and
Glasgow Diligence by Kirkliston, Linlithgow, Falkirk, Kilsyth, and
Kirkintilloch, and from Glasgow by the same road. Sets out every
day at eight o'clock in the morning precisely (Sunday excepted),
from Duncan M'Farlane's, White Hart Inn, foot of the Pleasance,
Edinburgh; and from William Reid's, at the Union and Crown Inn,
Gallowgate, Glasgow; carries three inside passengers, each to pay
12s, and to be allowed 14 lb of luggage, and all above 1s per stone.
The passengers taken up on the road to pay 3d per mile. The proprietors not to be accountable for anything above the value of £5,
unless the value thereof be specified and paid for at the time of
delivery. *N.B.*—Fresh horses at Linlithgow and Kilsyth, and time
allowed to breakfast and dine, if passengers chuse."

It was by this conveyance, as already stated, that I first visited
Edinburgh; we not only dined on the road, but also drank tea;
I took breakfast, however, before I set out.

" *Glasgow Mercury*, 16th Nov., 1780, page 368.—Waggon
betwixt Aberdeen and Glasgow. J. Ewing & Co., merchants,
Aberdeen, have established a four-wheeled covered waggon to go
regularly every fortnight between Aberdeen and Glasgow. Sets out
from Aberdeen on Friday morning next, and arrives in Glasgow on
Thursday. Leaves Glasgow on Friday morning, and arrives in
Aberdeen on Thursday. This carriage goes by the way of Perth and
Bannockburn, and sets out regularly upon the above days, whether
loaded or not. The rate of carriage is the same as is paid to
ordinary carriers. The waggon puts up at Wm. Watson's, clerk to
the Newcastle waggons, Gallowgate, Glasgow."

Glasgow Mercury, 3d May, 1781, page 144.—" Fly betwixt
Hamilton and Glasgow.—Daniel Gray, innkeeper, Hightown, Hamilton, proposes, for the accommodation of the public, to run a fly

from Hamilton to Glasgow each Monday, Wednesday, and Saturday,
to set off at eight o'clock in the morning; and from Hugh M'Indoe's,
vintner, sign of the Glasgow Arms, at six o'clock in the evening that
same day. Each passenger from Glasgow or Hamilton to pay 1s 6d.
N.B.—Tickets to be had at Hamilton from Daniel Gray, innkeeper
there, and at Hugh M'Indoe's, Gallowgate. The fly to hold six
persons."

" *Glasgow Mercury*, 31st May, 1781, page 175.—*Pro bono
publico*. The Diligence sets out from the Saracen's Head Inn,
Glasgow, as usual, by the direct road through Moffat, Lockerbie, and
Ecclefechan, for Carlisle; and it is connected with the London and
other stages from Carlisle to the different great cities and public
places in England. The communication is very quick; the passengers go from Glasgow to London in four days, and to the other
places in proportion. Tickets to Carlisle, £1 5s each. In a few
months a coach will run from Glasgow to Carlisle daily."

" *Glasgow Mercury*, 26th July, 1781, page 240.—Glasgow and
Stirling new stage begins to set out from Andrew Dunbar's, King's
Arms, Trongate, Glasgow, and from James Wingate's, Golden Lion,
Stirling, every Monday, Wednesday, and Friday, at eleven o'clock
forenoon from each place. Each passenger to pay 7s., and to be
allowed one stone weight of luggage; all above to pay 8d per stone,
and every uptake 3d per mile. This stage to begin on Monday the
30th current."

" *Glasgow Mercury*, 6th December, 1781, page 392.—A new
caravan sets out from James M'Alpin's, innkeeper, opposite to the
Brazen Head, Trongate (the gilt Galen's Head, the sign of Mrs
Balmanno, druggist), Glasgow, to Edinburgh in one day, on Friday
the 7th day of December, 1781, and continues to run every Monday,
Wednesday, and Friday from Glasgow to Edinburgh, to Mrs Montgomerie's, innkeeper, in the Grassmarket, Edinburgh; and from
Edinburgh to Glasgow on Tuesday, Thursday, and Saturday. Sets
out at eight o'clock in the morning. Tickets, 7s each person."

" *Glasgow Mercury*, 14th August, 1783, page 265.—Genteel
travelling to Carlisle, Leeds, Sheffield, London, Birmingham, Bristol,
and Bath.—A diligence sets out on Thursday evening the 7th of
August, and will continue going every Sunday, Tuesday, and Thursday evenings, at eight o'clock, by way of Hamilton, Lesmahagow,
Douglas Mill, Elven Foot Inn, Moffat, Lockerbie, Gretna Green, to
the King's Arms, Carlisle, in one day, where three places are reserved certain in a new post coach, by way of Rippon, Harrowgate,

Leeds, Sheffield, Worksop, &c., &c., to the Belle Savage Inn, Ludgate Hill, London, and returns every Monday, Wednesday, and Friday, by the same course, to Andrew Dunbar's Glasgow. Inside passengers from Glasgow to London, £4 16s; ditto from Carlisle to London, £3 6s. The proprietors of these carriages will not be accountable for any box, parcel, truss, or anything above the value of ten pounds, unless entered as such and paid for accordingly."

" *Glasgow Mercury*, 9th October, 1783, page 327.—To merchants, grocers, agents, shipmasters, or others who have occasion to transport goods, or to be accommodated as passengers through the Forth and Clyde navigation.—The proprietors of the canal, wishing to establish a system of facility and dispatch calculated to render this conveyance as secure and certain as a stage waggon, have built and completely fitted *two stage vessels*, to ply constantly upon the canal —The burden of each is about 50 tons—and these vessels are constructed to carry both goods and passengers, and to track through in one day. Apartments are fitted up commodiously for both cabin and steerage passengers, and every species of goods excepting grain in bulk will be received and carefully shipped and unloaded by Andrew French, at the West Basin, and Alexander Carrick, at Sea Lock, Bainsford, and Camelon. For safety, care, and attention the proprietors are responsible. The track boat Glasgow will begin her first periodical trip on Monday the 20th instant, at seven o'clock in the morning. Cabin passengers will be conveyed at the moderate rate of 2s, or 1d per mile in full; steerage passengers to pay only 1s, or ½d per mile in full, and both to be allowed 40lb of luggage. *N.B.*—All passengers going to Glasgow will be landed at the West Basin, and those going east will be landed at Camelon, near Falkirk, if desired, from which, if proper encouragement is given, it is expected stage coaches, caravans, and waggons will probably be established to convey passengers, with parcels and other goods, at a low rate, by land carriage to Edinburgh."

" *Glasgow Advertiser*, 17th June, 1194, page 394.—Coach Office, Tontine.—Joseph Bain begs leave with gratitude to acknowledge the liberal share of the public favour he has experienced, and to inform his friends and the public that he continues to run from this place the following public carriages, viz :—

> The Royal Mail Coach to Carlisle, &c.
> The Royal Mail Coach to Ayr.
> The Royal Mail Coach to Paisley.

The Prince of Wales Diligence by Whitburn to Edinburgh.
The Princess of Wales Diligence by Cumbernauld to ditto.

He also continues to run several post chaises, street coaches, &c., to
provide hearses, mourning coaches, &c."
   " *Glasgow Mercury*, 14th February, 1787.—Last week, a mercer
of this city received a piece of valuable goods from London, by the
mail coach, in the short space of five days and sixteen hours, from
the time he commissioned it. The letter was sent off on Wednesday afternoon, and on Tuesday following, at eight in the morning,
the goods were delivered at his shop. This expeditious mode of
conveyance may be of use when goods are wanted in haste."
   " *Glasgow Journal*, 8th September, 1763.—A gentleman going to
London, from Edinburgh, in a post chaise, wants a companion.
Apply to the publisher."
   " *Journal*, 22d November, 1764.—As I intend for the Leeward
Islands soon, all those who have claims and objections, I hope will
be so kind as to intimate them without loss of time, and oblige,
—Thomas Hill."

COTTON.

I HAVE read with much pleasure the editorial observations upon
cotton in your paper of the 18th inst., and have little to add to your
statements ; but I think it may be interesting to many of your
readers to compare the imports of cotton into Britain of the present
time, with the imports there in my early days, when the cotton
trade had just commenced to be the staple manufacture of Glasgow.
   According to a table in the " Annual Blue Book of the Trade and
Navigation of the United Kingdom," which has lately been issued,
the total quantity of raw cotton imported in 1860 was 12,419,096
cwts., valued at £35,756,889. Of this quantity 9,963,309 cwts.
came from the United States of America, being more than three-
fourths of the whole imports. 1,822,689 cwts. came from India; the
rest was imported from the Mauritius, West Indies, Africa, Guiana,
Egypt, Brazils, Peru, and other minor sources.
   In the *Scots Magazine* of 1790, page 164, we have the following
account of cotton wool imported into Great Britain in 1789 :—

Foreign West Indies,	Libs.	239,803
Turkey,	,,	4,668,231
East Indies,	,,	2,101,101
Demerara,	,,	1,345,702
French Settlements,	,,	6,143,623
Brazil,	,,	4,755,635
Spanish West Indies,	,,	93,726
West Indies, per Ireland,	,,	52,794
Georgias,	,,	18,964
Africa,	,,	1,626
Bahamas,	,,	377,980
Bermudas,	,,	5,800
British Settlements,	,,	9,998,986
Other parts,	,,	705,921
Into Scotland from the British West Indies,	,,	1,700,000
Total Libs.,		32,209,895

It thus appears that the cotton imported in 1860 amounted to about 12½ millions of cwts., while the importations of the same article in 1789 amounted only to about 287½ thousand cwts., or a little more than one-quarter of a million of cwts.

In 1781 the total imports of cotton wool into Britain were only 5,198,778 lbs., or about 46½ thousand cwts., none of which came from America, or at least only a few bags from Georgia into London. The first importation of raw cotton into Liverpool from America was in 1784—the next year after the Treaty of Independence. The Custom House at first demurred to pass the entry, not believing the cotton to be the growth of the United States. Archibald Campbell was the first who imported American cotton into Glasgow. He imported then only a few bags by way of trial. It is not my intention to enter into cotton statistics, as the subject has been so ably handled by others. I intend merely to jot down a few loose memoranda regarding the introduction of cotton and its manufacture into Glasgow.

The first public auction of cotton in Glasgow that I have found was advertised in the *Glasgow Journal* of 24th February, 1765, as follows :—" To be sold, by public roup, upon Monday the 28th of February inst., at 12 o'clock, at the callender of Messrs Gray & Co., Bell's Wynd, of Glasgow, three bags of cotton, and forty tons of fustick, which will be shown there any time betwixt and the roup, by Mr James Anderson." It appears, however, from the following advertisement in the same paper, of date 4th December, 1758, that it was then usual to retail raw cotton in Glasgow in single bags :—

"To be sold, at Joseph Anigus's cellars, in Bell's Wynd, Leeward Island cotton by the bag, or in larger quantities ; strong Jamaica rum, by the puncheon, or lesser quantities not under two gallons ; several casks of Carolina indigo, of different qualities."

From the following quotation from the Glasgow papers of 11th September, 1766, it appears that cotton, in single bags, was regularly imported into Scotland from London, as being the principal market for the article :—" Notice.—At the Carron Warehouse, Glasgow, to be owned, seven bags of cotton; one bag marked I. E., the other six of different marks ; brought from London in the *Glasgow*, Duncan, for Carron Wharf, on the 1st inst."

The first cotton mill erected in Scotland was in Rothesay, about the year 1778, or soon afterwards. In 1792 the steam-engine for the first time came to be used in driving the machinery of a cotton mill. This mill was erected on the site of the late David Todd's lands of Springfield—now part of the harbour on the south. William Scott was the managing partner, commonly called "Swearing Wully," to distinguish him from another William Scott. David Dale commenced to build his first cotton mill at New Lanark about the year 1783 ; but it was accidentally burned to the ground a few weeks after it had begun to produce spun yarn. It, however, was speedily rebuilt, and additional mills were erected beside it.

As is well known, David Dale was originally an operative weaver in Paisley ; but I have seen no account of the manner in which he commenced his career as a yarn merchant. The following advertisement, however, from one Gavin Millar, will show the nature of the trade which first enticed Mr Dale to commence yarn merchant :

" *Glasgow Journal*, 25th December, 1766.—Gavin Millar, at his house in Gallowgate, opposite to the sign of the Red Lion, Glasgow, sells all kinds of Dutch lints, drest and undrest : yarn bought and sold, and lint given out to spin. Any person well recommended, and willing to engage to take out lint, and gather in yarn, will meet with good encouragement by applying as above ; also manufactures and sells all sorts of green and white Holland cloth at the lowest price."

Mr Dale at first tramped the country on foot, in the above trade, and purchased from farmers' wives and others in the neighbouring counties their home-spun linen yarns, which he afterwards sorted according to their GRISTS, and then sold the same in the Glasgow market for customary work. He settled in Glasgow in 1763, being in his twenty-fourth year, and took a shop on the east side of the

High Street, at £5 of rent; but he let a part of it to a watchmaker for fifty shillings of rent. Shortly after commencing this business, he obtained Mr Archibald Paterson (afterwards proprietor of Merk-dailly Lands, now Charlotte Street) as a moneyed partner. Mr Paterson, however, took no share in the management of the company, which soon extended its transactions by importing linen yarns from Flanders and Holland. Mr Dale having thus established the business, and acquired some capital of his own, wished to get quit of Mr Paterson as a sleeping partner, and accordingly we find, by the following advertisement, that a dissolution of the concern took place in 1782:—

"*Glasgow Journal*, 24th May, 1782.—The partnership between Archibald Paterson and David Dale, carried on under the firm of David Dale & Co., is dissolved. Those who have claims upon the company may have them settled when they please, by applying to David Dale; and all who are indebted to the company, either by bill or open account, to pay the same to him. David Dale continues to carry on the same business on his own account.

"ARCHD. PATERSON.
"DAVID DALE.

"Glasgow, 22d May, 1782."

Mr Paterson thought that it was rather sharp on the part of Mr Dale to dissolve the connection immediately on its being firmly established and lucrative; nevertheless, through life, he continued on the most friendly terms with Mr Dale, which were greatly strengthened by a unison of sentiment in their religious views.

The acquaintances of Mr Dale were often much surprised at his intimate knowledge of the country places and localities of the counties in the neighbourhood of Glasgow, not being aware that in early life he had again and again tramped the spots to purchase home-made yarns.

Near the close of last century, Mr Dale commenced to manufacture extensively cotton fabrics suitable for printing, and I remember that the following report was then current:—It was said that he was in use to sell these fabrics to a large amount to Messrs William Stirling & Sons at the credit of twelve-months' bills, which bills he discounted at his pleasure in the Royal Bank, being manager of the said bank in Glasgow: this, in fact, made it a CASH business for Mr Dale, and the long credit secured a valuable customer. I cannot vouch for the fact, but can vouch for the currency of the report.

2 A

About sixty years ago, I happened to be in company with Mr Gilbert Innes of Stow, then a director in Edinburgh of the Royal Bank, and the largest shareholder in it. In the course of our conversation, I asked him if the Glasgow branch of the Royal Bank at its early establishment had been in the regular practice of discounting twelve-months' bills. Mr Innes evaded my question by saying that he believed that it did discount long-dated bills.

Before parting with Mr Dale, I must here give a little amusing anecdote of him, which I believe is new to most of your readers.

During the French war, one of the homeward-bound Jamaica packets was captured by the enemy. Messrs Leitch & Smith expected large remittances by that packet, and were greatly disappointed at its loss, having considerable payments falling due; to meet which they sent a large amount of bills to the Royal Bank for discount. Mr Scott Moncrieff, however, discounted only the one-half of them, and returned the other half; upon which Mr Smith (Jordanhill) went personally to the bank to remonstrate with Mr Scott on the subject. On arrival there, he found Mr Dale and Mr Scott sitting in the front parlour of the bank at St Andrew's Square. After the usual salutations had passed, Mr Smith expressed his surprise at having so limited an amount of discounts from the bank, seeing that the loss of the Jamaica packet was so well known. Mr Scott, as usual, here put on his grimmest countenance, and in a grumbling and growling manner said, " Mr Smith, you must reduce your business; you are carrying it on upon far too great a scale; you ought greatly to lessen the scale of your dealings." Upon which Mr Smith replied, " Mr Scott, upon what scale would you have me to carry them on ?" Mr Dale here interrupted the conversation, by saying to Mr Smith, " Oh, Mr Scott thinks that they should be upon a *herring scale !!*" This reply put them all in a mighty good humour, and so Mr Smith got the whole of his bills discounted.

Mr Scott Moncrieff was naturally of a mild and gentle character, and his growlings and grumblings were all forced and simulated, which the public soon discovered.

But to return to the manufacture of cotton. At a pretty early date, webs of linen warp and cotton weft were common, but James Monteith, of Anderston, was the first who gave out a web to weave composed wholly of cotton. The yarns of it were brought from India and spun by the hand ; they were imported in globular balls, pretty similar to a bird's nest, and got the name of "Bird-Nest

Yarns." They were very soft to feel, but quite irregular as to the GRIST; in consequence of which, all muslins manufactured wholly from these bird-nest yarns were clouded, owing to the irregularity of the threads. Bird-nest yarns have long disappeared from the market, our own cotton yarns being much superior to them, both as to strength and regularity of GRIST.

Mr William Stirling was the first who brought India printed cottons to Glasgow; the printing of them, however, was executed in London, but the cloth itself was of India manufacture. The following is Mr Stirling's advertisement in the *Glasgow Journal* of the 10th of May, 1756 :—"At the warehouse of Mr Stirling, above the Cross, there is to be exposed to sale for a few days, *A neat Parcel* of printed *Cottons*, of the newest patterns, lately imported from London, at and below first cost."

It is certainly a little curious how Mr Stirling came to sell such rarities "at and below first cost!!!" but he probably had purchased them merely for the purpose of obtaining new and fashionable patterns, and not with any object of making profit by them; this appears the more likely to have been what he had in view, from the contents of the following advertisement:—

" *Glasgow Journal*, 15th March, 1764.—At Daleholme Printfield, near Glasgow, there is printed, all sorts of work upon linen and cotton cloth for gowns and furniture, by William Stirling & Co., merchants in Glasgow, who have engaged a man of character in the printing business lately in London; from which place he has this season brought a great variety of the newest and most fashionable prints; the patterns of which, and the prices of each may be seen, in a book kept at the shop of Jean M'Neil, Greenock; William Morison, Port-Glasgow; Wm. Wilson, Kilmarnock; Zachary Gemmil, Irvine; David Farrie, Ayr; James Paterson, Hamilton; David Nevary, Edinburgh; John Wilson, Falkirk; James Bredie, Perth; Michael Erskine, Paisley; and at the warehouse, Glasgow, who receive the cloth from our customers; and they may depend upon having it well printed, and returned in due time. Let the owners' name be sewed with linen thread, at full length, and the place of their abode, at one end, and the number of the print they chuse at the other end of the piece. No Green cloth taken in without charging threepence the yard bleaching, or twopence if the warp is made of bleached yarn, beside the price of printing."

It is curious to see the state of the printing business in Glasgow a century ago. The chief dependence for sales seems to have been from country customers, and the thrifty housewives and their daughters could then have got their home-made cloths for gowns, coverlets, or shawls, &c., printed in retail at their pleasure. It appears, from the above advertisement, that the warp of webs was frequently bleached before being put into the loom, in which case the weft was generally the India bird-nest cotton. These made a firm, soft, and substantial fabric, and excellently adapted to household purposes—in particular, they made very pleasant sheetings. Most families about this period were in the practice of employing customary weavers to execute the weaving of their home-spun yarns; but, as these yarns were generally unequal in the GRIST, itinerant yarn dealers (such as Mr Dale was in early life) either sold, bought, or exchanged yarns with them in order to have the said yarns properly classified and sorted for the loom. Even down to my time the spindle and distaff were sometimes to be seen in use for spinning. At the period in question most industrious families had their spinning wheels in constant use, and some sharp mistresses were accustomed to stipulate, at giving *arles** to their servants, that they should rise to their spinning wheels regularly at six o'clock in the morning. This early rising to spinning work is now expected only from the lasses at our cotton mills. I remember our family spinning wheel, long laid past in our garrets as lumber, and finally presented to one of our servants, who was emigrating to Nova Scotia.

In the *Glasgow Mercury*, of 3d April, 1783, we find the following notice :—"Among the premiums gained at the Linen Hall, Edinburgh, last March, were six pieces of striped muslins manufactured by Robert and Adam Thompson, manufacturers in this city, for which they received twenty pounds as a premium. The gentlemen who acted as judges for the Hon. Board of Trustees have declared that the above striped muslins were far superior in quality to any they had ever seen manufactured in Scotland."

The above-named gentlemen were the grandfather and granduncle of Neil Thompson, Esq. of Camphill. Mr Adam Thompson was amongst the first feuars of the lands of Hutchesons' Hospital, and he built several of the large tenements on the west side of Hutcheson Street.

---

* In Scotland a servant who has been hired, and who has received arles, is supposed to have a right to break the engagement, if the earnest, or arles, be returned within twenty-four hours. This may have no other sanction than custom.—*Jamieson's Scottish Dictionary.*

Having taken notice of Messrs William Stirling & Sons as being
one of the oldest and most eminent printing establishments of our
city, perhaps it may be interesting to many of your readers to hear
something regarding the site of their warehouse and dwelling
house, which now form Stirling Street and Stirling Square. The
following is extracted from the *Glasgow Mercury* of 6th October,
1789:—

"To be sold, by public voluntary roup, within the Tontine of Glasgow," &c., "That tenement of land, belonging to Messrs Stirlings,
partly occupied as a dwelling-house, and partly as warehouses, with a
complete sunk storey below the warehouses, having an entry from
the west side of the High Street, leading to the College, and another
from the Grammar School Wynd, with the offices thereto belonging,
and the whole adjoining ground. As also, the tenement and two
shops, with the houses on both sides of the close or entry leading
from the High Street to the tenement first mentioned. The whole
grounds, including what the buildings occupy, measure about 4400
square yards; and buildings might be erected to advantage upon
part of the vacant ground, without injuring the principal house.—
For further particulars, apply to Messrs William Stirling & Sons,
who will show a plan of the property, &c., and will conclude a private bargain with any person inclining to purchase previous to the
day of sale."

The property not having been sold, we find the following notice
in the *Glasgow Mercury* of 20th November, 1792:—

"A NEW STREET AND SQUARE.

"To be sold, by public roup, within the Tontine Tavern of Glasgow,
upon Thursday the 3d day of January, 1793, between the hours of
two and three o'clock, certain steadings or building lots in the proposed
New Square and Street on the west side of the High Street, the
property of William Stirling & Sons. The street will be opened
nearly opposite to the Black Fryars' Wynd, and run westwards into
the square, from which there will be smaller streets or entries to
Bell's Wynd, or Canon Street. It is intended that the fronts of the
houses shall be built on an uniform plan, corresponding to a set of
beautiful elevations, newly designed by Mr Adams, architect.
These, with commodious inside plans by the same architect, and a
plan of the ground, will be shown by David Scott, Bell's Wynd,"
&c., &c.

The Messrs Stirling removed their extensive warehouses first to one of the wings of the Shawfield Mansion, at Glassford Street, and afterwards to Cunningham's Great House, Ingram Street, now the Royal Exchange. On the 1st of October, 1792, Andrew Stirling of Drumpeller withdrew from the Glasgow establishment, and formed the extensive commission house of Stirling, Hunter & Co., of London. The following extract is from the *Gazette:*—

"Notice.—That from this date Andrew Stirling ceases to be a partner in the business carried on under the firm of William Stirling & Sons, and the business is continued under the same firm by John Stirling and James Stirling, the only remaining partners.

"Glasgow, 1st October, 1792.

"ANDW. STIRLING.
"JOHN STIRLING.
"JA. STIRLING.

"Andrew Fraser, witness.
"Roderick Macdonald, witness."

In your editorial article of the 18th instant, you say "It is generally believed that India cotton is naturally of inferior quality." Now, although this is the general belief at present, it was far otherwise in my early days; for yarns spun from India cotton bore an extra price in the market, it being then universally understood that muslins manufactured from India cotton approached nearer to the fabric of the muslins sold at the East India Company's sales than muslins manufactured from cotton of other growths.

We have all lately heard long discussions regarding short measures and short lengths, but in my early days there was another mode of making money, pretty much of the same description, as the following anecdote shows:—

About the year 1794, I purchased a lot of yarns from an extensive yarn merchant in Glasgow, but who was not the spinner of the yarns. The said yarns were invoiced to me as spun from India cotton, and accordingly were charged a higher rate on that account. When examining the bundles of yarn upon delivery, I felt surprised at seeing the inside tickets of each bundle MUTILATED, the word "India" having been written upon a piece of paper apparently torn; but upon one of the torn papers, I found at the torn part the letters "ch" remaining, and immediately concluded that I had been imposed upon, and that the said yarns had in reality been spun from Dutch cotton, the growth of the Dutch settlements in Surinam, Berbice, or Demerara, in Guiana, and that the word "Dutch," originally inscribed on the tickets by the spinner, had been torn off by the dealer, and " India" substituted in its place. Indignant at the deception, I called upon the dealer, and insisted upon the yarns being charged only as spun from Dutch cotton. Of course I was prepared for a denial of the deception, which was the case ; but showing him the mutilated tickets in my possession, and refusing to accept any bill for the lot as invoiced, he then altered his tone, and, speaking very graciously and softly, said, that as I was a new beginner, whom he wished to encourage, he would not make any words about the matter, and so deducted the extra charge for India growth. After this, I declined having any dealings with this gentleman, who soon afterwards purchased a landed estate, for which he paid upwards of fifty thousand pounds.

THE LANDS OF GORBALS.

So much of late has been said regarding the Gorbals feuars and the Gorbals lands, that little new on the subject can be expected. I, however, venture upon the following notices, in the belief that they are not generally known, even amongst the Gorbalonians themselves :—

Upon the 17th of November, 1641, an Act of Parliament was passed for dissolving the lands of Gorbals, Town of Bridge-end, and Wheat Mill of Kelvin from the shire of Clydesdale, regality of Glasgow, and parish of Govan, and annexing the same to the City of Glasgow.

In 1661, another Act of Parliament ratifies and approves the charter —— —— " of alienation and disposition therein contained and precept of sasine following thereupon, made and granted by Sir Robert Douglas of Blackerstoun, knight, with consent of Dame Susanna Douglas, his spouse, to the provost, baillies, dean of guild, and deacons, Craft's Hospital, and master of the hospital called Hutcheson Hospital, and to the rest of the counsellors of the burgh of Glasgow, and to their successors in office, in name, and to the proper use and utility of the council and community thereof, of certain parts and portions of lands and others, underwritten. As also to them in name of, and to the proper use of the hospital called Hutchesons' Hospital, and to the poor placed, and to be placed thereuntil, for certain parts and portions of the samen lands after

specified : And sicklike to the fore-named persons, and their successors in office, in name and to the proper use, and utility of the
hospital called the Craft's Hospital, for ane certain other part and
portion of the samen land and others aftermentioned, with the
pertinents, to witt of all and haill, the six pund land of old extent
of Gorbals and Bridge-end, with coals and coal heughes within the
bounds of thereof, and with the Tower, Fortallice, Manor Place,
houses, biggings, yeards, orchyards, tenements, tennandries, service
of free tenants of the samen, and all other parts and pendicles thereof
whatsomever, lying within the Barouny and Regality of Glasgow
and Sheriffdom of Lanerk, and with the heritable offices of bailliary
and justiceary within the said bounds, with all liberties and privileges whatever belonging thereto, and with all other right, property,
and possession, belonging to the said Sir Robert Douglas and his
said spouse, to be holden of the deceaced noble Prince Esimy, Duke
of Lennox and Earl of Richmont, superior thereof in feu farm, fee
and heritage, in manner specified in the said charter."

Thereafter the Act proceeds to ratify a charter of confirmation,
granted by the Commissioners of the Duke of Lennox as Lord of the
Lordship and Barony and Regality of Glasgow, superior of the said
lands ; and then the Act goes on to annex them to the town of
Glasgow, but to this effect only, viz. :—" Whereby the inhabitants
thereof may be parishioners for the church within the city next to
them ; and in all public musterings, levies, and outreicks, join, levy,
and randevous with the city and inhabitants thereof ; and likeways
bear an proportional part of all stent, taxation, and impositions with
the burgh."

It appears that, after the said Act of Parliament of 1661 was
obtained, it was immediately complained of by the feuars and
inhabitants of Gorbals and Bridge-end, and the result was a submission to Sir John Fletcher, his Majesty's advocate, on the part of the
town, and Mr Robert Sinclair of Longformachus, advocate, on the
part of the people of Gorbals, with William Earl of Glencairn, Lord
Chancellor of Scotland, as oversman ; and by the intervention of
these honourable persons, the dispute was amicably settled so early
as the 6th of November, 1661, only a few months after the Act of
Parliament had passed.

AGREEMENT BETWEEN THE TOWN OF GLASGOW, AND THE FEUARS OF GORBALS.

On the one part, the people of Gorbals agreed—

" That they shall not, in any time hereafter, question their dissolution frae the shire of Clydesdale, regality of Glasgow, and parochin of Givan, and union to the said city of Glasgow, to the effect following allenarly, viz. :—

" To the effect the said inhabitants of Gorballs may be parocheners, in and with the city and inhabitants thereof, and repair for the ordinances to the church within the said city ewest to them (if the said citie shall think the same convenient). And next to this effect that they may join in musterings, levies, and outrciks, proportionally with the said citie, providing always the said feuars and inhabitants be first freed and exeemed frae any mustering, levying, and outreiking with the said shire of Clydesdale or Lanerk."

On the other part, it was agreed to by the Commissioners for Glasgow, taking burden on them for the said city and magistrates thereof—

" That notwithstanding of the said ratification and union therein contained, the said feuars and inhabitants of Gorballs and Bridgeend shall not be liable to bear any part of any stents, taxations, impositions, either of Excise or assessment, or other public burden, with the citie of Glasgow, Ay and Until they be fully and wholly freed of bearing the said burdens, with the said shire of Clydesdale or Lanerk, or any other part of the regality of Glasgow, except with the said citie of Glasgow, allenarly, which the said Commissioners, taking burden on them for the said city, obliges them to procure before the said feuars and inhabitants of Gorballs be liable as said is; and in case the said city shall obtain the said feuars and inhabitants of Gorballs, altogether freed frae bearing burden with the said shire of Clydesdale and Lanerk, that then and in that case, the said feuars and inhabitants shall be no farther liable in stents, taxations, levies, outreiks, or other public impositions and burdens foresaid, with the said citie, but according to that proportion they were formerly liable to bear, while they remained unite to the said shire and regality, according to their several pieces of land they bruik, and rights whereby they bruik and enjoy the same ; and as the vassals and inhabitants of other burrowes and regalities by and to lundwart, beare, and are liable to their superiors and masters."

Also, the above-mentioned agreement between the town of Glasgow and the people of Gorbals, provided—

" That the feuars, inhabitants of Bridge-end and Gorbals, shall be judged and ordered by ane bailiff to be chosen by the magistrates and council of the said burgh of Glasgow ; and as to the place of holding courts, remits the same to the magistrates thereof."

Some time after this, the city of Glasgow having obtained the superiority of the Barony from the family of Lennox, then superiors of Gorbals, have ever since been in the practice of appointing the baron bailies of Gorbals.

It appears from the records of Hutchesons' Hospital, that in 1650, the Hospital bought from Sir Robert Douglas of Blackerston, one half of the lands of Gorbals and Bridge-end, at the price of £40,666, 13s. 4d. Scots, the town and the Trades' Hospital having purchased the other half betwixt them. The rent of the Hospital's half of these lands in bear, meal, capons, coals, multures, &c., with a very small sum of silver, produced, at that time, no more than £1604 Scots yearly, upon an average of nine years from £1650 to 1658, there being several life-rent tacks upon the lands. Interest of money was then six per cent.

This purchase was, for a time, the source of much distress to the Hospital, owing in part, no doubt, to the civil war which then raged in Scotland betwixt Charles II. and Cromwell, during which the crops upon the ground were trodden down and eaten up by the different parties, without any recompense being allowed. The patrons, in consequence thereof, were unable to pay more than £14,000 Scots of the money at the term of payment, from the difficulty of getting in the money owing them; the town of Glasgow, however, stepped forward to their relief, and by advancing the remainder, saved the funds of the Hospital from ruin.

The Gorbals lands were divided in 1789 betwixt the City, Trades' House, and Hutchesons' Hospital, according to their respective proportions.

COLLECTORS OF CUSTOMS IN OLDEN TIME.

I HAVE read with much interest the two articles in your papers of the 6th and 11th instant, regarding the Custom House of Glasgow in olden time, by your antiquarian correspondent, A. Ross, Esq., which throw considerable light upon the state of the King's customs in the ports of Clyde a century and a half ago. An eminent member of the Antiquarian Society in Edinburgh lately placed in my hands an Edinburgh newspaper, published shortly after the union of the two Crowns, from which I have taken the following curious extract.

Extract from No. 111 of the *Evening Post* or the *New Edinburgh Gazette*, from Saturday, August 18, to Saturday, August 21, 1711 :—

" NOTICE is hereby given to all Merchants, Captains, and Masters of Ships, and all others concerned, that *Mr John Hamilton*, appointed by the Commissioners of the Stampt Dutys at London, to be General or Head Distributor of Stampt Vellum, Parchment, and Paper, and Chief Collector of all Dutys and sums of money arising therefrom in Scotland, is to be spoke with, or got notice of at the Custom House in the Parliament Closs, Edinburgh, where all concerned may repair to be furnished with the said Stampt Paper, Parchment, &c. And for the greater ease and encouragement of the Lieges living at a distance from Edinburgh, the said *Mr Hamilton* has, by the power and authority committed by the said Commissioners for appointing Sub-Distributors of the said Paper, Parchment, &c., and Sub-Collectors of the said Dutys thereon, constituted and appointed the Collectors of Her Majesty's Customs at the several Sea Ports in North Britain to be his Distributors thereof. Likeas, the Publishers of Almanacks, and Makers of Cards and Dice, are hereby advertised that they are not to print or publish any Almanacks, or to make any Cards or Dice, without first acquainting the said *Mr Hamilton* therewith, under the peins and penalties contained in the Act of Parliament."

It appears that there were no stamp duties levied in Scotland before the Union, and that the first British Parliament appointed the collectors of Customs in Scotland to be also the distributors of stamps. Perhaps some of your antiquarian correspondents may be able to say when the collectors of Customs at Glasgow ceased to be distributors of stamps, and when the first independent distributor of stamps in Glasgow was apppinted to the office in question.

The first institution of stamp duties was by Statute 5 and 6 William and Mary, c. 2; and they have since, in many instances, been increased ten times. After this Act of Parliament had passed, it became difficult to forge deeds of any standing, as the officers of this branch of the revenue varied their stamps frequently by marks perceptible to none but themselves. A man that would forge a deed of King William's time must know and be able to counterfeit the stamp of that date also.

The first notice regarding the Glasgow Stamp Office that I have laid my hands upon is the following :—

"*Glasgow Mercury*, 12th May, 1785. — Stamp Office. The Stamp Office is to be removed to-morrow, from Dreghorn's land, foot of the Stockwell, to Shortridge's land, Argyle Street. Entry by Dunlop Street, and second door of the stair.—Glasgow, 12 May, 1785."

The distributor of stamps at this time was Mr Peter Blackburn, the grandfather of Peter Blackburn, Esq., M.P. Mr Blackburn resided in Shortridge's land, and the Stamp Office was in a room of his dwelling.

Shortridge's land was built in 1766, as the following advertisement shows :—

"*Glasgow Journal*, 24th April, 1766.—To be sold, by public roup, upon Tuesday the 10th of June, betwixt the hours of twelve and two, within the house of Mrs Armour, at the Cross of Glasgow, *two storeys* of that large tenement of land, newly built by John Shortridge, lying on the south side of Argyle Street, each storey consisting of a kitchen and eight fore rooms, with closets to most of the rooms, and two large cellars ; and a garret room to each storey. To be sold unfinished, that the purchasers may finish them to their liking. The rooms and passes are all well lighted ; the braces and bed places well disposed. Two rooms in each storey have private doors from the stairhead, for writing rooms or kitchens ; and each storey is laid out so as to serve two families, if needful. Several of the rooms are large, and the roof high ; and at the head of the closs there is a private well, with very fine soft water.

"*N.B.*—Any person who inclines to make a private purchase may apply to John Shortridge betwixt and the roup."

Mr John Shortridge was the father of the late James Shortridge (younger brother of Mr Shortridge, of Todd & Shortridge). Mr James Shortridge took the name of "Spreull," in consequence of succeeding to property bequeathed to him by Miss Spreull, whose death is thus recorded :—

"*Glasgow Mercury*, 12th February, 1784.—On Friday the 6th current, died, in the 84th year of her age, much and justly esteemed, Mrs Margaret Spreull, daughter of the deceased Mr John Spreull, merchant in this city."

Miss Spreull possessed an old tenement in the Trongate, which I remember very well. It stood about midway between Hutchesons' Hospital and the Shawfield mansion. Immediately after it became

the property of Mr James Spreull, he took it down, and built upon
its site the present elegant tenement, now called Spreull's Land.
This property is strictly entailed, and I believe that it is the only
burgage heritage in Glasgow subjected to the stringent fetters of an
entail.

The site of the Shortridge land, and of the large tenement on its
west side, belonged to my grandfather, who was born in 1696 and
and died in 1741. Upon these lands there stood a large range of
malt kilns and malt barns, with their pendicles, which were let by
my grandfather to Mr Miller of Westerton, for his malting establishment. Some of these malt kilns and barns existed in my day.
Miller Street was named for Mr Miller of Westerton.

John Buchanan, Esq., an eminent Glasgow antiquary, has given
us an interesting account how the entry to Dunlop Street from
Argyle Street came to be so contracted, when it could have been so
easily made as wide as the lower part of that street, by taking a
portion of the ground which had belonged to my grandfather.

Mr Ross, in his article in the *Herald* of the 11th instant, informs
us that James Loudoun, collector at Glasgow, hired a large chamber
in the coffee-house there, from Mrs Shields, for a "Custom House."
This seems to settle the question regarding Glasgow having a
regular Custom House at an early date, although it might have
been merely a pendicle of the lower ports. I think that the coffee-
house here alluded to was in the corner tenement at the Cross and
Saltmarket, and is thus alluded to by a notice in the *Glasgow
Mercury* of 11th January, 1781 :—"The newspapers belonging to
the Tontine Coffee-house are removed to Mr Thomas Durie's,
vintner, in the Trongate." This could not have reference to the
present Tontine Coffee-house, for it was not then built, as the
following notice shows :—

"*Glasgow Journal*, 13th June, 1782.—Notice. The committee
of the Tontine are now ready to contract for the wright work of the
coffee-house and other buildings at the back of the Exchange.
Those who propose to give in proposals may call on John Maxwell,
the society's clerk, who will show the articles for finishing the work.
Proposals will be received till the 1st day of July next."

I have not been able to find any written evidence that Mrs
Shields was tenant or proprietor of the *coffee-house at the Cross*, or
that the Glasgow Custom House was a room in the said coffee-house,
but I think it very likely to have been the case.

Mr Ross says that "the sale by inch of candle would astonish a modern auctioneer," but such a mode of sale in my young days was by no means uncommon, as the following advertisement shows :— " *Mercury*, 31st May, 1781.—For sale, by the candle, at Lawson's Coffee-house in Leith, on Monday the 11th day of June, betwixt the hours of twelve and one afternoon, the frigate Le Calonne, about 400 tons," &c., &c.

GLASGOW IN THE OLDEN TIME.

In that house (viz., at the north-west corner of Bell Street) Mr John Alston resided, and I believe that there George Douglas, and provost John Alston were born. James M'Kenzie, the father of provost M'Kenzie, also resided in that tenement. He is thus described by his son, the provost, in the roll of the Merchants' House, when the provost entered as a member of the said House :— " 1788.—December 26th.—James M'Kenzie, son of James M'Kenzie, teacher, Glasgow." I remember this old gentleman when he was teacher in Hutchesons' Hospital, then situated in the Trongate. He was highly respected, and associated with the wealthiest of our citizens. He was not known, however, by the name of *M'Kenzie*, but was called M'KEENGIE, for in those days there were no *M'Kenzies* in Glasgow ; they were all M'KEENGIES.

The whole of the new town from St David's Church westwards has been erected in my day. The following notice shows the com-mencement of this great change :—

" 1777.—June 5th.—*Notice.*—That the magistrates and council of Glasgow have resolved to open a street 70 feet broad, in a straight line from Queen Street through the west part of the Rams-horn ground, belonging to the city, and to sell the ground on each side of the said intended street, in steadings for erecting buildings thereon. As also to set the north-westmost plot of the said Rams-horn ground, consisting of 8129 yards, lying next to, and above the termination of the said intended street, conform to a plan in the hands of the town-clerks of Glasgow. Any person inclining to purchase the above-mentioned grounds may give in their proposals to the said clerks, who will immediately communicate them to the magistrates and council. Also, those eleven acres of ground, or thereby, belonging to the city, lying on the east side of the road belonging to Mr Peter Bell, of Cowcaddens, leading from the road to Wishart's house to BELL'S HAUGH, is to set in tack for 19 years, by public roup, within the clerk's chambers, on the 11th day of June current, the purchaser's entry to commence immediately after the roup; and the articles of roup to be seen in the hands of the town-clerks. *N.B.*—Some dung, belonging to the City of Glasgow, lying near the place where the Gallowgate Toll Bar lately stood (near the Saracen's Head Inn), is to be sold by roup, time and place as above."

" 1777.—19th June.—*Notice.*—That the roup of the north-westmost plot of Ramshorn ground being adjourned to Friday the 20th of June current, the said plot will be sold, by public roup, between the hours of twelve and two o'clock of that day, in the clerk's chambers, and will be set up at 2s 6d each square yard. A plan of the ground, with the articles of roup, may be seen in the hands of the town-clerks."—This roup took place immediately before William Cunningham began to erect his spacious house, now the Royal Exchange. When Mr Cunningham was building the said house, in 1778, I visited it, for it was a wonder and a show to all the citizens of Glasgow, the cost of it being £10,000.

No part of our city, in my day, has undergone a greater change than the Cross of Glasgow ; for, with the exception of the old steeple, it has been completely renovated. But, alas! the warblings of the music bells, and the nice promenade under the Pillars in the Tron-gate and Saltmarket, long the pride and boast of Glasgow, are now the tales of bygone times. The first great change in this part of Glas-gow was the erection of the Tontine and its reading-room, in 1781. I remember of playing in the foundation of the present reading-room while the excavations were going on by the workmen, and before a single stone of this elegant room had been laid. In the course of making these excavations, an ancient canoe was found, as more particularly alluded to by our eminent antiquary John Buchanan, Esquire. I subscribed to the coffee-room for more than sixty years, and I never come to Glasgow without paying it a visit for " auld lang syne." When I first subscribed it was really a coffee-room, nicely fitted up with boxes, where parties could adjourn and enjoy their beverage in quietness, piping hot from Mr Smart's kitchen up stairs.

A French philosopher has said—" I would not choose to see an old post pulled up with which I had been long acquainted." And Dr Goldsmith thus elegantly writes—" A mind long habituated to a certain set of objects insensibly becomes fond of seeing or speaking of them; visits them frequently from habit, and parts with them with reluctance. From whence proceeds the care of the old, in every kind of possession? They love the world, and all that it produces; they love life, and all its advantages—NOT because it gives them pleasure, BUT because they have known it LONG."

In the *Glasgow Mercury* of 29th March, 1781, we have the following

" NOTICE.

"The subscription for the Tontine Coffee-house will continue open till the 13th of May next, and no longer. Those who choose to subscribe, may apply to John Maxwell, jun., writer, who is empowered to receive the subscriptions of all who may wish to promote the scheme. In consequence of a resolution of the subscribers, at their general meeting, held on the 20th of March current, all persons interested in the Tontine scheme are requested, on or before the 15th of May next, to lodge with Mr Maxwell a note specifying the name of the person on the duration of whose life their interest in the scheme is to depend. If this is not complied with, the subscriber's own life, or the person's already named, where that is the case, will be considered as the life to be engrossed in the deeds."

The shares were £50 each, but any subscriber was at liberty to take two shares, but no more. There were 107 subscribers to this scheme, very few of whom took two shares. A very interesting list of the said subscribers, and the names of the parties on whose lives their interest in the Tontine depended, was published by me in the *Glasgow Herald* of the 8th and 15th of March, 1852, to which reference is made.

Of the 107 subscribers, and of the parties on the durability of whose lives their interest in the scheme depended, the last survivor was Miss Cecilia Douglas (sister of the late Sir Neil Douglas), afterwards Mrs Gilbert Douglas, of Orbiston. She died on the 25th of July, 1862, in the 91st year of her age. Two shares were taken on her life, viz. :—

1st Nominator—Alexander M'Caul, merchant in Glasgow, *one* share, upon the life of Cecilia Douglas, daughter of John Douglas, merchant in Glasgow.

2nd Nominator—William Douglas, merchant in Glasgow, *one* share, upon the life of Cecilia Douglas, daughter of John Douglas, merchant in Glasgow.

Before the Assembly Room in connection with the Tontine Buildings was erected, our assemblies and public concerts were

usually held in the Bridgegate Hall; and I believe that the following notice shows the date of the last dancing assembly which was
held in the Bridgegate Hall :—

"*Glasgow Mercury*, 5th October, 1780.—Assembly. There is to
be a dancing assembly on Friday first, the 6th instant, in the
Merchants' Hall, Bridgegate. Tickets for ladies and gentlemen, to
be had at Mr Aird's music shop, 2s 6d each."

Mr Aird's music shop is now occupied by Mr Campbell Blair, as
an extensive grocery establishment; but the place has been wonderfully improved since the time of Mr Aird. He was, at the date in
question, the principal music dealer in Glasgow, and his little shop
was situated at the corner of the Back Wynd.

The following notice shows us that the New Assembly Room, in
connection with the Tontine, was then in progress of erection :—

"*Glasgow Mercury*, 2d November, 1780.—Subscription Concert.
The managers of the subscription concert for the ensuing winter beg
leave to acquaint those ladies and gentlemen who have honoured
them with their subscription, that on account of the Assembly Hall
not being ready, the first concert will be held in the Merchants'
Hall, in the Bridgegate, on Wednesday next, being the 8th of
November. The concert will begin precisely at seven o'clock.
Subscriptions taken in at Messrs Dunlop & Wilson's; at the Tontine
Coffee-house; at Mr Heron's, sign of the Black Bull; at Mr
Buchanan's, Saracen's Head; and by Messrs Dasti, Wilson, and
Reinagle, at their houses."

The Tontine Coffee-house here alluded to most likely was then
situated in the tenement at the north-west corner of the Saltmarket,
as the present Tontine Coffee-house was not built till 1781. I never
could learn any particulars regarding this old Tontine Coffee-house,
which I think could not have had any dependence upon the durability of the lives of those interested, as it appears to have been sold
by public roup. With regard to the old Jail and ancient Court-
house, they have been superseded by the building erected on their
site, by Dr Cleland, about the year 1816.

I feel at a loss to say whereabouts the Tontine Coffee-house in
Argyle Street was situated which is mentioned in the following
advertisement; and I am inclined to think that the word "Tontine"
was frequently applied at that time to coffee-houses which had no
title to asume the name of "Tontine."

"*Glasgow Mercury*, 30th November, 1780.—To be exposed to
sale, by public roup, upon Wednesday the 13th of December, 1780,

2 B

within the Exchange Tavern in Glasgow, at one o'clock mid-day, the Tontine Coffee-house in Argyle Street, Glasgow, as presently possessed by Mr Matthew Pool, consisting of seven rooms, light closet, and other conveniences ; a very commodious large kitchen, larder, and cellars below stairs, and three garret rooms, and pertinents. The price to be paid, and the purchaser to enter to the premises at Whitsunday next." And again—

"21st December, 1780.—Tontine Tavern. For sale, by auction, on Thursday the 4th of January, 1781, at 11 o'clock forenoon, the whole standing furniture of the Tontine Tavern, all of elegant fashions and in good order ; likewise the stock on hand of exceeding old wines, of a fine flavour, and excellent London porter. *N.B.*—The gentlemen, subscribers to the coffee-house, are desired to meet there to-morrow, the 22d instant, at 12 o'clock, upon business."

The word "Tontine," as is well known, means a life annuity with benefit of survivorship, and was so called from the inventor, Laurence Tonti, an Italian. In 1689, the first Tontine scheme was set on foot in France, but it was executed very imperfectly, in consequence of which, another scheme of the same kind was projected about the year 1726, when the two schemes were united. All the actions of both of which schemes came to be possessed by Charlotte Bonnemay, who died at the age of 96. She had ventured about £15 in each scheme, and in the last year of her life she came into possession of £3600 a-year for her £30.

I must now take a glance at the opposite corner of the Cross—namely, the north-west corner of Saltmarket and Trongate. Here was situated of old a very handsome tenement belonging to the Merchants' House of Glasgow, as the following notice shows :—

"*Glasgow Journal*, 14th August, 1766.—That all and whole that first storie of that great tenement of land, sometime belonging to the Merchants' House in Glasgow, lying within the Burgh of Glasgow, fronting to both these streets, called the Saltmarket and Trongate Streets of Glasgow, together with two Cellars (formerly three) immediately under the first storie, next to the staircase of the said tenement, and houff under the said Turnpike, and a piece of waste ground adjoining to the houff under the said turnpike, with the shade above, together with the middenstead of the said land, and benefit of the dung or fuilzie thereof, is to be exposed to sale by voluntary public roup, upon Tuesday, the fourth day of November next to come, within a vacant apartment of the said storie.

" *N.B.*—The said first storic may be commodiously possessed as a Public House."

The articles and conditions of the roup, &c.—" Any person intending to make a private purchase of the premises may apply to Messrs Arthur Connel, Alexand. Campbell, and George Buchanan, merchants in Glasgow."

At this date Provost Connel, the father of Sir John Connel, and David and James Connel, lived in the third storey of a house situated on the south side of Bell's Wynd, which is thus described— " 1766.—The third storie is possessed by Mr Connel, dean of guild, consisting of four rooms, a kitchen, and two garret rooms." So much for primitive times. Mr Connel afterwards acquired Eroch Bank, comprising a mansion house and three and a half acres Scots of land.

The celebrated printers, the Messrs Foulis, had their place of business in the Merchants' House Land :—" November 17th, 1755. —To be set, just now, these two Rooms in the Old Coffee House which front the Saltmarket Street, the one of which is at present possessed by Messrs Glen and Peter, and the other by Messrs Foulis."

" *Journal,* 2d May, 1757.—Upon the 3d of May instant, within one of the rooms of the corner land betwixt the Saltmarket and Trongate Streets of the first storie, forming the Old Coffee House, will be sold, by way of auction, for ready money only, to the highest bidder, a large assortment of Tea and Table China, Glass, and Stone ware, &c."

There is a good view of the old Merchants' House Land in " Stuart's Views of Glasgow," page 80, with a perspective of the pillars under the houses of the south side of the Trongate, westward to the Tron Steeple. On the third and fourth floors there was a curious projection overhanging the corner of the street, in which there were two windows to each of the little closets which led off from the dining rooms of the respective floors. In my boyish days the third floor of this tenement was occupied by David Crawford, Esquire, who so long filled the honorary office of Preceptor to the Town's Hospital. This gentleman being a relation, I had free access to the little closet in question upon the great occasions—of the King's birthday; of the Lords of Justiciary walking in procession to the Court House, attended by the magistrates, and preceded by the red-coat officers with their halberts; of the whippings and hangings at the Cross; and from the said little windows I beheld M'Iver,

M'Callum, and Herdman stand in the pillory in 1784, probably the last exhibition of the kind that will ever take place in Glasgow.

Mr Crawford married a daughter of Mr William Horn, who built Glassford Street, Horn's Court, and numerous edifices in Glasgow. There were two daughters of the marriage, who died in their teens of that sad complaint consumption, and, as all Mr Horn's estates had been settled on them, these estates at their death passed to a distant relation of Mr Horn in Stirling.

The north-east corner of the Saltmarket at the Cross was occupied in my early days by the Trades' Lands, which were pretty extensive both in the Saltmarket and in the Gallowgate.

" *Journal*, 10th July, 1766.—That the little laigh fore shop or booth, lying on the north side of the close leading from the Salt-market, haill houses, cellars, garrets, middenstead, and lands in the closs, high and laigh, all commonly called the ' Trades' Land,' lying near the Market Cross of Glasgow, and a great part of which lands are very commodious for Warehouses, are to be exposed to public roup and sale, in different lots and parcels, within the house of Mrs Armour, at the Cross, &c."

" *Glasgow Journal*, 4th October, 1764.

" To be sold, by public roup, on the 7th November next, All and
" Haill that high fore shop and laigh one, lying under that great
" tenement of land belonging to the Town of Glasgow, being the
" corner land betwixt the Gallowgate, and above the Cross, and
" which fore shop is the one next the Cross, presently possessed by
" Andrew Carrick, merchant.

" The conditions of roup and progress of writs are to be seen in
" the hands of Peter Paterson, writer in Glasgow."

(*N.B.*—Purchased by David Allan, and afterwards by John M'Intyre and Company.)

The burning of the long stairs in 1792, and subsequent erections on their site, made a great change in the appearance of the city of Glasgow at the Cross, for these stairs were very curious and antique in their structure, and gave a venerable look to the place; but they were very far from being an ornament to the locality, and their destruction was lamented by none of our citizens, except by those who were directly interested in their preservation.

Thomas Buchanan, Esq., the father of the late John Buchanan, Esq., of Ardoch, had his place of business in the first floor of the Trades' land, at the north corner of it. He was the most extensive hat manufacturer in Glasgow of his day, and, from the following notice, he perhaps was also the best maker of hats in the city:—

"*Scots Magazine*, 1757, page 49.—Edinburgh, January 22, 1757. —The Edinburgh Society for Encouragement of Arts, Sciences, and Manufactures, think it their duty to acquaint the public that the premiums proposed by the society for the year 1756, have been adjudged in the following manner:—

"For the best dozen of hats, FOUR GUINEAS, to Thomas Buchanan, Junior, and Company, at Glasgow.

"*N.B.*—These gentlemen appointed the premium adjudged to them to be applied as a premium for the best dozen of felt hats for the year 1757."

Our townsman, Thomas Dunlop Douglas, Esq., commenced his mercantile career with the Messrs Buchanan, of the Trades' Land.

One of our Glasgow characters, Peter Paterson, writer, *alias* "Pawkie Pate," had his writing office in the Trades' Land. I remember him when he was a clerk with John Wilson, junior, the town-clerk of Glasgow, and he was then considered a shrewd, clever fellow, which he abundantly proved in his after life. To the best of my recollection, William Watson, Esq., the father of the Faculty of the Glasgow Procurators, was then an apprentice with Clerk Wilson, at the foot of the Saltmarket; or if he did not sit at the same desk with Pawkie Pate, he must have handled the quill there very soon after Pawkie Pate had commenced business for himself.

By far the most important change, however, which has taken place at the Cross of Glasgow was the demolition of the Trades' Land and contiguous tenements, and the opening up of London Street—an alteration of so great magnitude that the Cross of Glasgow would scarcely be known to our grandfathers, were they to come back now and take a look at the place. The cost of the ground paid for that part of London Street which opens into Saltmarket Street was no less than £50 per square yard—perhaps the highest price ever paid for ground in Glasgow. At the time when London Street was projected it was illegal to sell property by way of public lottery, but the directors of this joint stock company got over this difficulty by making it a private drawing of chances among the subscribers themselves. In Parliament this was considered an evasion of the Lottery Act, and the directors were threatened with an action for transgressing the law; but as the improvement was represented as being so beneficial, and so important for the city of Glasgow, the members of Parliament who denounced the scheme as a direct evasion of the Lottery Act were induced to withdraw their opposition, upon the express understanding that this was not in future to be considered as a precedent.

Now let us take a look at the remaining corner at the Cross of olden time. The ancient tenement at the south-east corner of the High Street and Gallowgate, which had so long withstood the ruthless hand of change, has lately undergone the fate of its fellow corners, and has been demolished to make room for a new and elegant structure. In my early days the corner shop of this old tenement was a small and dismal apartment under the pillars, and was occupied by David Allan, for the sale of duffles, flannels, blankets, linens, fustians, drugget, harns, durants, and a variety of woollen stuffs. After Mr Allan's death his widow continued the business and attended to the affairs of the shop, which throve greatly under her management. I think it was late in Mrs Allan's life before Mr John M'Intyre took the principal charge of the establishment. At the death of Mrs Allan, her daughter, Miss Betty Allan, succeeded not only to the said business, but also to a respectable competency, in consequence of which she did not attend the shop as her mother had done, but assumed Mr M'Intyre as the managing partner, under whose energetic direction the business rapidly increased. The little dark shop was extended in size, by the addition to it of the space under the pillars, and it then had a light and cheerful look. After the death of Miss Betty, Mr John M'Intyre became the sole partner of the concern, which still increased in the magnitude of its dealings, under his able exertions. He soon required more space to shew off his valuable stock of goods, which now consisted of all the costly articles of a first-rate haberdashery establishment. The first storey of the said tenement, about that time, was occupied as the printing premises of the *Glasgow Courier* newspaper, and when the *Courier* office was removed, Mr M'Intyre took this flat, and by an inside stair connected it with the ground floor. This addition to the shop, however, continued still too small for Mr M'Intyre's rapidly increasing business, so that he, from time to time, enlarged his premises, by adding one flat after another to the original tenement, until Mr M'Intyre became the sole proprietor of the corner land at the Cross of Glasgow, so well known in the city by the name of " John M'Intyre's shop in the Gallowgate." The firm of John M'Intyre & Co. have lately built new and very extensive premises in Argyll Street, nearly opposite to Queen Street, at the cost of £26,000.

Although the four corners of the Cross of Glasgow have thus been changed and renovated, we have still our old friend King William, remaining to keep us in remembrance of olden times; and on this subject I can only repeat what I said about ten years ago regarding this venerable relic of by-gone days:—"I believe that there are few of our aged citizens who do not feel a certain undefined regard for the statue of King William, and can never look up to it without the idea flashing upon their minds, that they are beholding an old and intimate friend. I must confess that I never return from a long journey without being delighted when passing the Cross to see my ancient acquaintance, with his bare toes and baton frappant, still gracing our old Exchange. What a multitude of by-gone events does this statue bring to the mind of an aged citizen!"

In the *Glasgow Mercury* of 2d February, 1781, we find the following notice regarding the statue of King William:—

"Yesterday se'ennight, a young man, disordered in his mind by intemperance, got upon the pedestal on which the equestrian statue of King William stands, and mounted the horse, when his phrenzy led him to cut off the laurel with which the statue was crowned, and otherwise maltrait it. What is surprising, he got up and down without receiving any hurt. He is since confined in the cells."

From the following extract, it appears that in 1766 there was a garden in the Trongate of Glasgow, and that the Stamp Office was situated at the Exchange:—"*Glasgow Journal*, 16th January, 1766.—The garden at the head of Mr William Anderson's tenement, and Closs of houses in Trongate, to be sold off within the Stamp Office, at the Exchange, in Glasgow, upon Tuesday the 21st inst., precisely at 12 o'clock; to be sold in whole or in parcels,—entry at Candlemass. Apply to Jas. Graham, writer."

FRIENDS OF THE PEOPLE.

THE following quotation from an Edinburgh newspaper will give some insight into the politics of our Glasgow authorities at the commencement of the French Revolution in 1789, and will show that many members of our city authorities then entertained the same political views as Thomas Muir, younger, of Huntershill; but Provost John Campbell and Bailies John Dunlop, John Alston, and Ninian Glen were strong Pittites, as well as Alexander Low, dean of guild, and John Tennant, convener of the trades. A great proportion of the deacons of the crafts, however, were energetic Foxites, and so were the generality of the operative classes of the city, who, at that time, loudly applauded all the acts of the French National Assembly, and particularly their famous "Declaration of the Rights of Men, and of Citizens," in which it was judicially proclaimed, "That the Nation is essentially the source of all Sovereignty ; nor can any individual, or any body of men, be entitled to any authority which is not expressly derived from it."

At the period of 1789, the magistrates of Glasgow elected themselves into office, and allowed no reporters to enter the Council Chamber. It is a curious circumstance that Thomas Muir did not attack this system as being contrary to the rights of men and citizens. The times which followed the outbreak of the French Revolution were certainly dangerous, and Mr Muir was, at least, incautious in his harangues to the populace of Glasgow.

"Edinburgh Advertiser, 9th January, 1789.

" On Monday last, the Trades' House of Glasgow having met to vote a letter of thanks to the Right Hon. William Pitt, for his late constitutional conduct in the House of Commons, the same was carried by a majority of five, and the Deacon Convener (John Tennant), requested to forward the letter immediately. Twenty-five members voted for the address, and twenty against it. The dissenting members entered a protest.

" The following account is sent us by some of the gentlemen who were in the minority on the above-mentioned question :—

" On the 1st January, the friends of the Minister, in the Town Council of Glasgow, attempted to get a vote of thanks also from the Trades' House of the place, being a representation of the manufacturing inhabitants; but it was carried by a majority of ONE, to delay the measure. And it was agreed that the Convener should call no meeting on the same subject, till about Thursday, the 8th current ; but the ministerialists, fearing that even this short delay might open the eyes of the people, called a meeting suddenly and unexpectedly, on the 5th current, and carried the vote of thanks by a majority of FIVE,—there being twenty against twenty-five, and a considerable number of the members absent.

" A spirited protest has been taken against the proceedings of the majority on that occasion."

"*Glasgow Mercury*, 9th October, 1792.

"Glasgow, 3d October, 1792.

"A number of Gentlemen, consisting of this City, and of several who reside in the adjoining country, having previously communicated their sentiments to each other upon the PRESENT STATE OF THE NATION, agreed to form a SOCIETY: and having this day met in the Star Inn, they constituted themselves into a permanent Society, under the name of 'THE ASSOCIATED FRIENDS OF THE CONSTITUTION AND OF THE PEOPLE.'

"Lieutenant-Colonel Dalrymple, of Fordell, was elected President.

"Thomas Muir, Esq., younger of Huntershill, Advocate, Vice-President.

"George Crawfurd, Writer in Glasgow, Secretary.

"The following Resolutions were then agreed to :—

"RESOLVED,—' To co-operate with the Association of the Friends of the People in London, in all proper measures to accomplish an equal Representation of the People in Parliament.'

"RESOLVED,—' To enter into every legal and constitutional measure to obtain a shorter duration of Parliamentary Delegation.'

"RESOLVED,—' That none shall be admitted Members of this Society who do not subscribe their concurrence to the two previous Resolutions.'

"RESOLVED,—' That these Resolutions, forming the primary objects of our Association, be printed in the Scots and English Newspapers.'

"RESOLVED,—' That the thanks of this meeting are due to the Gentlemen who have acted upon the occasion as our President and Secretary.'

"WM. DALRYMPLE, Chairman."

"*Glasgow Mercury*, 30th October, 1792.

"Star Inn, Glasgow, 17th October, 1792.

"At a meeting of the FRIENDS of the CONSTITUTION, and of the PEOPLE,—Colonel Dalrymple in the chair ;

"RESOLVED UNANIMOUSLY,—' That Charles Grey, Esq., Member for Northumberland, who announced in the House of Commons that he, at an early period of next Session, would move the House to bring in a bill for shortening the duration of Parliaments, and for a more equal Representation, deserves well of his Country, and merits the thanks of this Society.'

"RESOLVED UNANIMOUSLY,—' That the most noble the MARQUIS of

LANSDOWNE, for supporting the cause of the People, merits the approbation of his Country, and the thanks of this Society.'

"RESOLVED UNANIMOUSLY,—'That the Honourable Thomas Erskine merits the thanks of this Society, for having pledged himself to second the motion to be made by Mr Grey in the House of Commons, of a Reform Parliament.'

"RESOLVED UNANIMOUSLY,—'That the ASSOCIATED FRIENDS of the PEOPLE in London, for their exertions, merit the thanks of the People, and ought to have their constitutional support, in their endeavours to restore the constitution to its genuine principles.'

"WILLIAM DALRYMPLE, Chairman.
"THOMAS MUIR, Vice-President.
"GEORGE CRAWFURD, Secretary."

" To the MEMBERS of the ASSOCIATED SOCIETIES of the Association of the Friends of the Constitution, and of the People of GLASGOW.

" GENTLEMEN,—In following out their original plan, the Association has resolved that each affiliated Society shall send Delegates to a meeting which is to be held in Winton's Tavern, at 8 o'clock in the evening, upon Wednesday next. It is no longer necessary for the Association to hold weekly general meetings, in which all its members are personally present. The constitutional firmness, moderation, and virtue, of these general meetings, have rendered them respectable in the eyes of all good men, and of all to whom the peace and prosperity of their country is dear. In spite of the artifices of malevolence, the ASSOCIATION knows with confidence, that the Affiliated Societies will act up to their principles, and that no conduct upon their part shall ever occasion a sentiment of regret in the breast of any virtuous man who may have joined them.—I have the honour to be, Gentlemen, your most obedient Servant,

"G. CRAWFURD, Sec."
" Glasgow, Oct. 29, 1792."

THOMAS MUIR, YOUNGER OF HUNTERSHILL.

It has generally been supposed that the estate of Huntershill had been for many generations the family property of Mr Thomas Muir's ancestors, but from the following advertisement it will be seen that Huntershill appears to have been purchased by Mr Thomas Muir's father so late as 1782, being only about ten years before the first meeting of the Associated Friends of the Constitution and of the People was held in Glasgow.

" *Glasgow Journal*, 21st February, 1782.
" For Private Sale.
" To be Sold, and entered into immediately,
" The Lands of Huntershill, in the Parish of Calder, consisting of about thirty acres of arable Ground, and ten acres of Moss, or thereby, together with the new Dwelling House built thereon, by the deceased James Martin.

" For particulars, apply to James Brown, painter in Glasgow ; or Archibald Gardner, merchant in Paisley."

Mr James Brown, painter, above named, was the father of William Brown, Esq., Stockwell Street, late of Kilmardinny.

THE OLDEST HOUSE IN THE TRONGATE OF GLASGOW.

The writer of this article having been requested to throw together any information which he possessed regarding the ancient building and its pertinents, No. 142 Trongate, and also to state such anecdotes of its old proprietors, or former occupants, as might be thought worthy of recording, the writer now complies with the request.

The first object to be attended to with regard to this (now perhaps), the oldest house in the Trongate, is the small family escutcheon placed near the eastmost window of the floor immediately above the shop of Mr George Love, stationer, No. 138 Trongate, and close to the water-pipe. It bears the date of 1596; but in none of the histories of Glasgow is there any reference made with regard to the original proprietor of this building. It appears, however, from the above date, to have been erected during the time of the Reformation, about seven years before the old Tolbooth at the Cross was erected, and when Sir Matthew Stuart of Minto was lord provost of Glasgow. As for the bailies of the city, the dean of guild, deacon convener, treasurer, bailies of the river, and of Gorbals, with the officials, the town clerk, and master of works, of the above date of 1596, the names of all these parties have perished, or escaped the notice of our Glasgow historians.

It would be difficult now to trace back the names of the different proprietors of this property, for although it bears every mark of having been in former times the family mansion (with extensive offices and garden) of a wealthy Glasgow patrician, yet it seems in after times to have been parcelled out to different proprietors, down to our own days. Even in the chronicles of honest John M'Ure, it is difficult to trace this property in them; for, notwithstanding of his having given us a list of all the tenements on the north side of the Trongate in the year 1736, we nevertheless are not sure of being in the right when we fix upon his description as being applicable to the property in queston; we can merely say that it comes nearest to it, agreeably to his statement, which is as follows :—" The great tenement belonging to the heirs of Michael Coulter, late bailie; the tenement within the closs thereof belonging to William Anderson, late bailie; the tenement at the back thereof, within the closs, belonging to the heirs of Charles Crawford, merchant; the tenement at the back thereof, belonging to the heirs of John Bryson, of Craigallion; the Flesh Market, and shades within the same, belonging to the city of Glasgow." A question here occurs very fit for the Notes and Queries : Was the back court of this building our old Flesh Market, and if not, pray where was it situated? We all know where the Country, or Bell Street, Market was then situated; but there seems no existing trace of this market, which appears to have been carried from the Trongate to the Candleriggs, and ultimately from thence to King Street, in 1754, when the present markets there were erected.

By examining the map of Glasgow in Stuart's Views (dated 1783), we will see an accurate sketch of the property in question, as it stood at that time. Mr Baird of Craigton then occupied the back premises, and also the long stripe of ground (now Brunswick Street) extending to the back Cow-loan, or Ingram Street. Mr Baird kept this park or garden wholly in grass, which afforded pasture for his horses. He was a sporting gentleman; and at the south end of this said garden (now the narrow part of Brunswick Street) he erected a leaping bar, encircled with furze and thorns, about four and a half feet high, over which he trained his young hunting horses to leap. Mr Baird also, in the centre of his garden, and extending its whole length from north to south, formed a broad roadway, all laid down with tan bark, which made a pleasant soft path for giving his horses exercise upon. In these days here, daily, might have been seen Mr Baird's jockeys trying his horses in all their paces. This ground was known over the city by the name of "Baird's yard." But Mr Baird having died, and times having changed, Mr Baird's house became a tavern, and his garden Brunswick Street. At present, Mr Baird's house is occupied as the *Christian News* office.

As for the front property, in after times, the ground floor having been turned into shops, they at first were let for about five pounds of rent for each shop; but they soon rose in value, and at the beginning of the present century, Mr Robert Gray, jeweller, bought the eastmost shop, at what was then considered the enormous price of £600. James Hamilton, grocer, occupied the next to it; and John Swanston, grocer, the westmost one. Provost Mills had his writing office in the second floor above the street. The first floor above the shops, and the attics, belonged to the late Francis Reid, Esq., of Greenlaw, who was bailie of Gorbals in 1771.

"*Glasgow Mercury*, 22d September, 1789.—To be sold, by public roup, on the 20th inst., that garden, belonging to the magistrates of Glasgow and town council of the city, sometime ago acquired by them from John Clark, trustee of John Baird, merchant in Glasgow, lying on the north side of the Trongate Street, on the west side of the Candleriggs Street, and on the south side of Ingram Street, together with an entry of thirty feet wide from the Candleriggs into the said garden, with the houses and buildings erected on the said entry. Apply to the town clerks."

"*Mercury*, 29th July, 1794.—To be sold, by public roup, on the 7th of August next, a tenement of land in the fifth close west from the Candleriggs, Trongate, as possessed formerly by Mr Baird of Craigton, and last by Mr John Auchincloss, with a piece of garden ground at the back, or on the north side of it, which lies in the line of Brunswick Street, and which will come to be of consideration when the junction of that street with the Trongate is carried on. Apply to James Mathie, writer."

MUCH ADO ABOUT NOTHING.

A GLASGOW STORY OF OLDEN TIME.

"Say not unto thy neighbour 'Go, and come again, and I will give,' when thou hast it by thee."

As it has been said that there are no two human faces exactly alike, so also it has been asserted that there is no individual of any mettle who does not possess a certain odd cast of mind, some peculiar hobby, or more or less of a maggoty fancy, which distinguishes him from his neighbour. In some persons, however, the shade of difference is but weak and feeble, and so they pass through life without comment or remark; while in others the variance is so manifest and striking that they obtain the name of "eccentrics" or "originals," and amongst this latter class I must place Captain David Peter of Crossbasket,* the justice of which location will be sufficiently shown by the following narrative :—

In the year 1775 a dispute arose between Captain Peter of Crossbasket and Mr James Tennant of Annfield, regarding the possession of a sword, which the Captain had borrowed from Mr Harry Horseburgh, a merchant in Glasgow, and which sword Captain Peter alleged had been stolen from him by Mr Tennant. As in cases of this kind there are generally two ways of telling a story, I shall give the statement of both of those gentlemen, as to the manner in which the dispute arose. I begin with that of Mr Tennant of Annfield.†

In the year 1776, or thereby, Captain Peter, being about to take a trip to Lisbon on board of a ship then lying at Greenock, and bound for that port, borrowed a sword from Mr Harry Horseburgh, a merchant in Glasgow, in order that he might make a proper appearance in the capital of Portugal, where every person then wore a sword, even common labourers and mechanics. He borrowed it, however, for that specific purpose only, and merely for the time he might be absent from home. He was, therefore, bound in honour and in justice to have restored the sword to Mr Horseburgh on his arrival in Glasgow from his Continental trip. Nevertheless Captain Peter *forgot* to return the said sword, though often put in mind of it by Mr Horseburgh, who was extremely unwilling to enter into a process upon so trifling and insignificant a subject, although he began to fear that he should be obliged to do so, unless he could fall upon some more eligible way of getting it out of his hands. At length, happening to dine one day at Hamilton, in company with Mr James Tennant, the conversation over a bowl of punch

* To the best of my recollection the first wife of John Gordon, Esq., of Aitkenhead, was Miss Peter of Crossbasket. *Glasgow Mercury*, 20th February, 1788.—" Friday last died Mrs Margaret Peter, spouse of John Gordon, Esq., merchant in this city." John Gordon's father, Alexander Gordon, was bailie of Glasgow in 1772 and 1775. In 1758, Thomas Peter of Crossbasket, the father of Captain Peter, besides his mansion at Crossbasket, had a dwelling in Wilkinshaw's Close, in the Saltmarket of Glasgow. He was dean of guild in 1707 and 1708 and bailie of Glasgow in 1712.

† In 1758, Annfield belonged to Adam Tennant, tobacconist, the father of James Tennant. It then consisted of 8 acres of garden ground (let to Archibald M'Kenzie, gardener), on the north side of Camlachie Road, with a house, stable and byre, and of 4½ acres of ground on the south side of the said road, which were occupied by Mr Adam Tennant himself. He was bailie of the river and Frith of Clyde in 1741.

turned upon this same sword. Both of them knew that but a short time before Captain Peter had borrowed a ring from Mr Fleming, a merchant in Glasgow, that he had *forgotten* to restore it, and that a process had been actually brought against him, in which he had been effectually forced to make restitution, and condemned in expenses of process. Mr Horseburgh wished to recover his sword without that trouble, while Mr Tennant was willing to assist him ; and accordingly it was agreed, that as Crossbasket* was little out of the road to Glasgow, they should take it on their way, and try to get back the sword. Accordingly, having got tolerably merry, away they go to Captain Peter's, where, after drinking a little more, they observed the very identical sword, standing in an open closet off the room where they were sitting; and, in going away, Mr Tennant took up the sword, and carried it into the chaise in which he and Mr Horseburgh were returning to Glasgow.

In this manner Mr Horseburgh got possession of his own sword, and it did not once occur to him that either he or Mr Tennant had been guilty of the least impropriety, far less that they had committed an act of *theft* or of *spuilzie*, as Captain Peter alleged they had done on this occasion.

Nevertheless, three or four days after their return to Glasgow, Mr Tennant received, to his great surprise, the following very extraordinary letter from Captain Peter—" August, 1775.—Sir,—You was not gone far on Sunday last before I missed the small sword, *was given in a compliment by Mr Horseburgh.* It is no person but you that is suspected for the trick, though it is a very bad one. It may pass very well amongst acquaintances, but let me tell you, it is below the character of a gentleman to be guilty of the like." Mr Tennant immediately showed this epistle to Mr Horseburgh, and both of them were equally astonished at its contents. Mr Horseburgh, in particular, was infinitely surprised to see Captain Peter boldly asserting that the sword had been given to him in a compliment, when he knew very well that no such thing ever was done or intended, as he had only got the use of it in order to make a figure upon a single trip to Lisbon. Mr Tennant, however, did not choose to take the letter in a serious light, or to answer the abuse it contained in kind. He really could not believe that Captain Peter actually meant what he said, and therefore did all in his power for the Captain's satisfaction, by writing to him that the sword was

* In 1455, Crossbasket (along with Hamilton farm and some others) was erected into a lordship, called the Lordship of Hamilton.— *Hamilton's Lanarkshire, p.* 16.

taken away by him and Mr Horseburgh *in company*, who was the undoubted proprietor of it, and who then had it actually in his *own possession*.

Let us now look at Captain Peter's version of the story, which is as follows:—The Captain said, that having occasion to go to Lisbon upon business, at which place it is the general custom for every person to wear a sword, he found it necessary to equip himself in that article of dress; but, as the particular kind of small sword required was not necessary to him in his profession, and was a piece of dress he had no occasion to use anywhere else, he was willing to save himself the expense of purchasing one; and, with this view, he applied to Mr Harry Horseburgh, merchant in Glasgow, for a loan of his, not having at that time one of his own suitable for the occasion. Captain Peter further said that the sword had been in his possession above ten years, during which period, as Mr Horseburgh had no use for the sword himself, he had never desired it to be returned to him, from whence, the Captain said he was led to imagine that Mr Horseburgh meant to allow him to keep it altogether, and, from this idea, he never made any offer to return it. The following is Captain Peter's account of the mode in which Mr Tennant and Mr Horseburgh had abstracted the said sword from Crossbasket House:—

In the month of August, 1775, James Tennant, merchant in Glasgow, along with Mr Horseburgh, paid Captain Peter a visit on a Sunday, at his house at Crossbasket. It happened that on this occasion the Captain had other company with him, whom he entertained along with his two visitors in the best manner he could, and in the evening they took their leave. Two days after this, Captain Peter, in looking for the sword in dispute, which had been lying in a room adjoining to that in which they had been sitting, found that it was amissing. As most natural, his first suspicion fell upon his own servants. However, on examining them, he could get no light into the matter; and, therefore, he proposed to advertise the loss at the church doors and in the Glasgow newspapers, in order, if possible, to discover the offender; but he afterwards heard that, while he was entertaining his company in the dining room, Mr Tennant had gone into the next room where the sword was lying, and had privately carried it off. On receiving this information, he applied to Mr Tennant, desiring him to restore the said sword, and to acknowledge that he had acted improperly in carrying it away in the above-mentioned clandestine manner. To make this demand,

Mr Peter considered himself well entitled, as Mr Tennant was not the proprietor of the sword, seeing that he did not originally receive it from Mr Horseburgh ; and further, seeing that even Mr Horseburgh himself would not have been entitled to have recovered the said sword in any other manner than by demanding it regularly from Captain Peter himself. The Captain was therefore not a little surprised to find that Mr Tennant not only refused to return the sword, or to make any acknowledgment for abstracting it, but even to give any reason for his conduct, treating the application with ridicule and contempt. As the Captain said that he held himself bound in honour as well as in justice to preserve the sword for Mr Horseburgh himself, its right owner, and to restore it to him, if ever he should demand it, the Captain thought it incumbent on him to apply in a legal manner for redress, seeing that he was refused satisfaction in this matter by Mr Tennant. Accordingly, in the month of September, 1775, Captain Peter raised a process before the sheriff-depute of Lanark against Mr Tennant, concluding that he should be ordained to deliver to the petitioner the sword above mentioned, with the sheath thereof, or to make payment of the value of the same, with damages and expenses, &c. The following is the tenor of the summons against Mr Tennant, which was brought before the sheriff, and which set forth—

" That upon the sixth of August preceding, Mr James Tennant had, at his own hand, and without any order of law, carried away a silver-hilted small sword, and sheath thereof, which then, and for some time before, were in the possession of the pursuer, Captain David Peter, which sword and sheath the defender, James Tennant, carried away with him, without the consent or privity of the pursuer, and, though often required, refused to restore the same." It concludes—" That the said defender ought and should be deemed and ordained to restore, and deliver back to the pursuer the foresaid sword, and sheath thereof, in the like good condition the same were in when the defender dispossessed the pursuer thereof in manner foresaid, or otherwise make payment to him of the sum of £5 sterling, as the value thereof ; and for proving which value the pursuer ought to be allowed his oath *in litem.*" The summons further concluded—" That he should be deemed in £3 sterling of expenses of process, besides the expenses of extract."

Let us now hear Mr Horseburgh's version of the story.

At the very first calling of the summons, and along with Mr Tennant's defences, in which the facts were stated exactly in the

2 C

same way as above mentioned by Mr Tennant, Mr Horseburgh sisted himself as a party, and gave in a compearance in the following words :—

".That a number of years ago the pursuer, David Peter, borrowed from the compearer a silver-hilted small sword and sheath; and as the pursuer did not appear disposed to return the same, so the compearer and defender, being at Hamilton, a little way distant from Crossbasket, they went by that place, and took the sword and sheath to Glasgow with them ; that the said sword and sheath were the compearer's property, and were in his possession, and he knew no law that could take them from him ; and if the pursuer, David Peter, thought otherwise, he might bring an action against the compearer for delivery of the sword and sheath, or payment of the value thereof, *and he would defend himself.*"

Notwithstanding of Mr Horseburgh's compearance in the action, Captain Peter gave in replies to the sheriff, in which, although he admitted that the sword was Mr Horseburgh's property, and that it was only lent him for a particular purpose, now long ago answered, nevertheless that both Mr Horseburgh and Mr Tennant had been guilty of a *spuilzie*, or of a species of *theft*, and insisted that the sword and sheath should be restored to him, with expenses. After considerable litigation, the sheriff pronounced the following interlocutor :—

" Having considered the libel, answers, and replies, and compearance made for Harry Horseburgh, found it acknowledged that the sword and sheath libelled were the property of Mr Horseburgh, the said compearer, who had obtained possession thereof in manner mentioned in his compearance; wherefore dismissed the process, and found no expenses due on either side, but found the pursuer and defender and their *procurators* censurable for the illiberal strain of the debate, and fined and amerciated *each* of them in *five shillings* sterling, for behoof of the poor, and ordained execution therefor at the instance of the collector for the poor, and found them liable for the expense of the extract, in case payment was not made before extracting, and decerned for the same accordingly, as it should be certified by the clerk of the court."

The amand awarded by the sheriff having been paid by all the parties, the litigation for some time was still continued with as much obstinacy as ever before the sheriff; but on the 9th of February, 1777, this knotty question was brought by suspension before Lord Braxfield, the bill having been passed in the course of the Rolls, although the case had been previously debated before Lord Covington, Ordinary, who, after having heard parties, with their answers, replies, and duplies, had refused to pass the bill of suspension. Lord Braxfield was generally called " Old Braxy." He spoke broad Scotch, and was nearly as great an original as Captain Peter himself; but nevertheless was esteemed one of the most acute and learned judges on the bench. Whether his Lordship was diverted at the oddity of the case, or thought that Lord Covington had been in error for not passing the bill of suspension, does not exactly appear; but, at all events, " Old Braxy" passed the bill, and so the whole question came to be debated before him as Lord Ordinary, on which occasion Captain Peter employed the celebrated Henry Erskine as his advocate and counsel. On the 20th February, 1777, Lord Braxfield was pleased to pronounce the following curt interlocutor :—" Having considered the debate, suspends the letters *simpliciter*, and decerns : Finds the charger liable in expenses, and allows an account to be given in." His Lordship appeared to think that the action itself was truly "*infra observantium Judicis*," and that the Roman maxim, " *de minimis non curat Prætor* was applicable to a case of the description in question.

Against the foregoing interlocutor the petitioner offered a representation, on advising which, of date 8th March, 1777, Lord Braxfield pronounced the following interlocutor :—

" The Lord Ordinary having considered this representation and the former proceedings in the cause, in respect it is admitted that Harry Horseburgh was the owner of the sword, and that the representer, Captain Peter, had no objection against restoring the same to him when desired, and that Harry Horseburgh was in company with James Tennant, and were travelling in the same chaise together, when the sword was carried from the representer's house, and consequently it could not be unknown to Mr Horseburgh, the owner, that the sword was carried away ; and in respect that Mr Horseburgh compeared before the inferior Court, and concurred with James Tennant in defending the action that was brought for restoring the sword ; adheres to his former interlocutor, and refuses the desire of the representation; superseding extract till the 15th of June next."

Captain Peter, having been dissatisfied with this, and other interlocutors of the Lords Ordinary, gave in a petition to the Lords of the Inner House for leave to submit the same to their review, which petition, on presentation having been appointed to be answered, the

case came to be fully debated before their Lordships. Captain
Peter's petition was not a long one; he seemed to rely almost wholly
upon the following quotation from Erskine, b. 4, tit. 1, 15 :—"Thus,
spuilzie may be committed, not only by strangers, but even by the
owner of moveable goods carried off; because a right of property
itself cannot justify the proprietor in assuming a power of judging in
his own case. The pursuer, therefore, in an action of *spuilzie*, need
prove no more than that he was in the lawful possession of the subject libelled, which gives him a right to be *ante omnia* restored to
the possession; for the action is grounded on this plain principle, that
no man is to be stript of his *possession* but by the order of law."
And, accordingly, Captain Peter insisted that, whether the said
sword was carried off by Mr Tennant or by Mr Horseburgh ;
whether, if Mr Tennant took it, he had, or he had not Mr Horseburgh's authority ; and whether the sword be or be not now in Mr
Horseburgh's possession, the consequence is all the same ; in short,
either the law with regard to *spuilzies* is totally nugatory, or in the
power of judges to apply it in one case and not in another, or Mr
Tennant was guilty of a *spuilzie*.

Mr Fergusson, the counsel for Mr Tennant, in reply to the above
arguments of Captain Peter, made a short reply, seeing that Lord
Braxfield's interlocutor had already exhausted the subject : he,
however, thus addressed the bench :—" My Lords, it is not supposed
that your Lordships will incline to appoint the respondent, Mr
Tennant, to give up the sword to Captain Peter, in order that it
may in the next place be delivered to the real owner. Even supposing that the sword was in Mr Tennant's possession, it would be
rather easier to make him give it to the owner himself; but when it
is admitted that Mr Horseburgh has it *already*, Mr Tennant frankly
owns that it passes his comprehension to conceive what it is that the
petitioner, Captain Peter, would have your Lordships' order on the
respondent to do. Surely he will hardly desire that you should
appoint it to be delivered up, in order that he may keep it to himself, for he admits that it does not belong to him, neither will he
desire your Lordships to appoint it to be delivered up, in order that
it may be restored to Mr Horseburgh, for this very satisfactory
reason, *because Mr Horseburgh has it already !*"

Although the following quotation was not urged by Mr Fergusson, there can be little doubt but it was well known to their
Lordships, and tended to influence them in their decision of the
case :—

Balfour, 472—" He quha makis lauchful retributioun of the gudis may not be callit for *spuilzie.*"

" Gif ony man be persew it forspoliatioun and away-taking of ony gudis and gear, he aucht and sould be assoilzeit thairfra, gif he, or ony in his name, restorit reallie and with effect, efter the committing of the *spuilzie*, and befoir the intenting of the summoundis, the samin gudis and gear to the owner thairof, or to his wife and servandis, als gude as thay wer the time thay wer takin away. 16th Julij, 1532."

Their Lordships, after the case had been fully debated before them, affirmed Lord Braxfield's interlocutor, with expenses, and so ended this *pugna gladiatoria.*

THE DEANSIDE WELL AND THE CONVENTS OF THE FRIAR PREACHERS. .

In the year 1789 I had occasion daily to mount and descend the Deanside Brae, upon business, so that the state of the place at that date is quite familiar to me. The whole of the Deanside Brae was then vacant ground, as is shown in the old Maps of Glasgow. The Deanside or Meadow Well was situated in a meadow at the west end of Grayfriars' (or Bun's) Wynd, close to the footpath leading up to the Rottenrow; it is now on the street, at 88 George Street, opposite to the lane leading into Shuttle Street. The Deanside Well was then in a rural spot, the whole lands on the west, as far as Partick, being garden grounds and corn fields.

In Stuart's Views the lonely foot passage up the Deanside Brae, to the Rottenrow, is very distinctly shown. The well stood at the south extremity of the said footpath, about the centre of the wynd.

By the formation of George Street, Bun's Wynd became extinct, and has been replaced by St Nicholas Street, the corner house of which, in the High Street, (having corby steps), appears to have been also the corner tenement of Grayfriars' (or Bun's) Wynd. St Nicholas Hospital, from which the name of St Nicholas Street is derived, was situated in the High Street, near the Gas Works and Infirmary. Keith, in his Bishops, at page 475, says, there was the Hospital of St Nicholas in Glasgow, "Wherein there were some " waiting maids to attend the sick. It is made mention of in the " Chartulary of Paisley, p. 297, where it is said, 'unus lectus

" fundatus in hospitali, Sancti Nicholai in Glasgow, per venera-
" bilem virum Michaelem Fleming.'" Bishop Muirhead founded
the hospital in 1471, for 12 old men and a priest.

In the year 1304, Robert, bishop of Glasgow, gave the Deanside
or Meadow Well in a present to the Friar Preachers, to enable them
to lead its stream into their convent.

M'Ure, at page 66, says, "There was within the precincts of the
" city a convent of Gray Friars or Franciscans, at the foot of the
" wynd called the Gray Friars' Wynd, and by corruption is now called
" Bun's Wynd. They had some feu duties payable to them in
" town, and of several tenements which they had by the gift of
" the bishops, which at the reformation were made over to the com-
" munity of the city." There appear formerly to have been two
monastic establishments in Glasgow,—viz., the Black Friars, or
Dominicans, and the Gray Friars, or St Franciscans. I think it
was the Gray Friars who had their convent, or monastery, near the
Deanside. About the year 1820, upon digging the foundation of
Dr Dick's church, in North Albion Street, a number of human
bones were found, which by some of our Glasgow *savans* were considered the bones of the Gray Friar Preachers, and that Dr Dick's
church covers the cemetery of their convent. The exact site where
the convent itself stood is not known.

The order of Black Friars was founded in Spain in 1206, and the
Gray Friars in Italy in 1198. The Gray Friars came to England
about the year 1224, and probably came to Glasgow not long after.
There were two orders of them; the one, embracing severe discipline
and absolute poverty, were called "*Spirituals*," the other, less
austere, were denominated "*Brethren of the Community.*" The
latter resided in convents, but the former did not. I suppose that
the "Brethren of the Community" had their convent near the Grayfriars' Wynd.

M'Ure, page 59, writes as follows:—"In the city of Glasgow,
both the Black and Gray Friars had convents, the Black Friars,
Dominicans, or Friar Preachers, Fratres Predicatorum, had their
convent near to the Black Friar Church, which belonged to them."

"Keith's Bishops, page 451:—There was a convent of Gray
" Friars founded in Glasgow in 1476, by John, Bishop of Glasgow,
" and Thomas Forsyth, rector of Glasgow. Jeremy Russell, or Friar
" of that place, was burnt as an heretic in the year 1559, and the
" year thereafter (1560) the convent was demolished by the Duke
" of Chatelherault, and the Earl of Argyle." "(Page 446) The

" Black Friars' convent was founded by the Bishop and Chapter of
" the city, in the year 1220, by King Robert 1st, (Bruce), he grants
" to the monks of the city of Glasgow, 'viginti mercas sterlingorum
" pro sustentatione luminarium, anno, 1315.'"

" Keith, page 454 :—The third order of the Begging Friars was the
" 'Carmelites,' who had their beginning in Syria. They were
" divided into thirty-two provinces, of which Scotland was the
" thirteenth, where they were called White Friars, from their
" outer garment. They came into this kingdom the 11th year of
" the reign of Alexander III., and had nine convents in Scotland,
" but none of them were situated in Glasgow."

I think that there was a plot of ground to the south of Anderston
Walk which belonged to the Black Friars, and became the property
of our University at the Reformation; it is now called "College
Street," and runs from M'Alpine Street to Brown Street. It
further occurs to me that the University also acquired some old
buildings among the wynds, at the same period, which belonged to
the Dominicans.* These probably formed part of the gift of John of
Govan, who is mentioned as having been a great benefactor to the
order. From the following advertisement, it appears that the
University had acquired at the Reformation the *whole* of the north
side of Grammar School Wynd, including Barr's Land ground and
the ancient erection behind the same.

" *Glasgow Mercury*, 17th April, 1792.—To be sold, feued, or
set, entry at Whitsunday.—The back houses of Barr's Land, lying
on the west side of the High Street, opposite to the College Church,
and also the large garden behind the said houses, fronting Shuttle
Street and the Grammar School Wynd, are to be sold, feued, or set,
by private bargain. Persons inclining to be purchasers, feuars,
or tenants of the premises, may give in their proposals to Mr Hill,
College factor, or to Robert Grahame, jr., writer in Glasgow."

There was a well situated in Canon Street, nearly opposite to the
gate of St David's new burying-ground. The water of this well was
always considered of inferior quality, and was seldom used by the
public at the table, or for culinary purposes. In consequence
thereof there came to be an extra run upon the Deanside Well,
which, along with the West Port Well and Lady Well, was considered to yield the finest water of any of our city wells, and next

* I believe that the University claimed an exemption from all city taxes, upon these
properties, alleging that they were all " College Lands," and therefore exempt. This
was before the Police Act passed.

in point of quality to the Arns Well in the Green. I must confess
that I entertained a good deal of the prejudice of the public against
the water of the Canon Street Well. It was situated on a gradual
declivity immediately south of the burying-grounds, and the common people alleged that it was strongly impregnated with a flavour
of dead men's bones. It is quite possible that a portion of the
surface water of the burying-ground may have filtrated into the said
well; more particularly as the substratum of Canon Street is whinstone rock, which commences at the College, and runs through the
said street to Ingram Street. Perhaps this state of the substratum
is sufficient of itself to cause a hardness and disagreeable flavour to
the water. I think that St David's burying-grounds were not in
existence in the days of the Friars Preachers, but their own cemetery
was not far distant, and there is a descent of the whinstone rock
from the College Church burial-yard through Canon Street.

<hr />

ANSWER TO AN "OLD BURGESS."

M'URE does not say that the fair of Glasgow was *held*, in his day,
in Grayfriars' Wynd; he merely says that formerly, before opening
the fair, the city authorities were in the practice of paying a complimentary visit to the prior of the convent, and giving thanks to
the convent for having originated the fair. The fair was then
fenced. M'Ure thus concludes:—

" To this day the fair is *fenced*, within an enclosure or garden,
where the convent stood, at a place they called Craignaught."*

Jamieson thus defines the word *fence:*—

" 1st, To fence a court. This was anciently done in name of the
Sovereign, by the use of a particular form of words. 2d, To fence

---

* M'Ure says, that the fair was fenced within an enclosure or garden where the Gray
Friars' convent stood. By examining the old Maps of Glasgow, and down to Fleming's
large Map of 1807, it will be seen that there was a large garden or piece of vacant
ground at the west extremity of Bun's Wynd, being the north-west corner of Shuttle
Street and close to the Deanside Well, which answers the description given to us by
M'Ure of the place where the fair was fenced. I remember of having been in this
garden in my youth, which at the time I visited it was enclosed on the south and west
by a strong stone wall; but old houses fronted it upon the north and east sides. In
Fleming's large Map of 1807, it is there represented as wholly covered with trees,
having open grounds to the west, and Albion Street Chapel, (the late Dr Dick's) to
the south west. I must leave this matter in the hands of our antiquaries.

the Lord's Table or Tables. Addressed to those who design to communicate."

M'Ure wrote in 1736, and at that time the cattle fair was held at the West Port, which port was taken down in 1741, after which the cattle fair came to be held in Stockwell Street.

From the following quotations, we find that in 1577 the fair itself was then HELD at a place called "Craigmak," which last word is no doubt the Craignaught of M'Ure. If we could find out the exact site of this Craigmak or Craignaught, we might then be able to ascertain correctly the locality of the convent of Grayfriars.

"Burgh Records, 1577.—Curia.—The court of the burght and citie of Glasgow holdin at Craigmak, bq George Elphinstounn and Johne Wilsoun baillies thairof, ye saxt day of Julii, being ye fair ewin, the zeir of God, &c., Lxxij zeir: the court confermit: Dempstar, Rober Letterik.

"Item.—becaus the fair daye of Glasgow approcheard, fallis vpone Sondaye nixt, vpone the quhilk na mercat aucht to be kepit: Thairfor it is statute be ye baillies and counsale, yat na merchandis crame on ye gait, nor yit appin yair buithes for selling of merchandis vpone the said Sondaye nixt vnder ye pane of fywe pundis ilk persone, and ordains yis statut to be publist be appin proclam'n, at the mercat croce incontinent.

"16th July 1577.—The quhilk daye Matho Falconare, sone to Johne Falconare, tailzor, is fund in the wrang and amchiament of court, for casting of ane stane at Bessie Cochrane, spous to James Witherspwne, hitting hir, and hir barne in hir arme yairwitht, and bludit the barne, vpone Weddinsdaye the tent day of Julii instant, within the cry of the fair, and is fund in ye bludwyte: and dome gevin thairupon."

Striking a person in open court is held to be a greater crime than striking a person on the public street, because it is a contempt of court. In like manner, it appears from the last quotation that striking a person "within the cry of the fair," was held to have been a more heinous crime than a common assault elsewhere.

MY FIRST DECADE.

WHEN a Glasgow octogenarian takes a daunder along the old streets of our city, he feels surprised at the great change which has taken place in their appearance : their old and grim Flemish countenances have been transmogrified, and have now assumed the gay and smiling looks of a well-dressed beaux ; while what were open fields in their immediate neighbourhood, have become a mass of *terra incognita* masonry, in traversing which the daunderer will soon become bewildered, and lose his way amidst piles of modern sculpture. But however great those changes may now appear to the view of the ancient carl, they vanish in the misty recollection of the names of his many old acquaintances who used to perambulate those streets in high health and vigour of life. Alas! where are most of them now? How few of his old cronies have the sweep of Time and the maze of accidents left to croon over with him the tales of olden time, when the Trongate and the Westergate formed the fashionable mall for the pleasure strolls of our dashing belles, and the gossiping lounge of our idle gentlemen stravaigers.

Before the year 1777 there were no flagged pavements in Glasgow, so that there was little inducement for ladies or idlers to perambulate our streets for pleasure. Previously to this time, most of the public thoroughfares of Glasgow were allowed to remain in a state of great filth, and in many of them there were deep ruts filled with mire, and their gutters were made the receptacles of putrid accumulations. The streets were seldom swept or cleaned, except when the heavens kindly sent down a pelting shower of rain, which acted as the gratis scavenger-general of the city. Often heaps of dung were formed by individuals on the public streets, and allowed to remain there till it suited the proprietor to use it for manure, or to sell it to others for that purpose. This was particularly the case in bye streets and lanes, which seem at that time to have been little attended to by the public authorities of the city.

The following advertisement appears in the *Glasgow Mercury* of 19th May, 1785 :—

" As the magistrates of Glasgow have lately got an offer made to them for keeping the streets of the city clean, for one year, from the tenth day of June, 1785, upon condition that the person undertaking that work shall have authority from the magistrates and town council to gather and carry off the whole dung and rubbish lying upon the streets, and shall have the property of that dung : Notice is hereby given, that the magistrates are ready to make an agreement for that purpose, and that they will prefer the person who shall undertake to perform the work upon the most reasonable terms, and find security for performing his part of the agreement. For particulars, apply to the town clerks."

It is curious to look at the state of our great leading street, Queen Street, within my recollection :—

"*Mercury*, 21st October, 1779.—A Tan Yard to be sold. That tan yard in Queen Street, at present possessed by John Bengo, consisting of thirty-seven tan pits, twelve lime, bait, and water pits, and a pond, a curriers' shop, two large drying shades, a large bark house, a bark mill and kill, two cellars, and a stable. The ground upon which it stands consists of 1600 square yards, and by making a small purchase, has the prospect of fronting three streets. Entry may be had immediately."

Before flagged trottoirs were laid on the public streets of Glasgow, our ladies in wet weather were obliged to make use of pattens when they had occasion to go out of doors; and on paying visits in the evenings, they were usually attended in advance by a maid servant with a lantern, who stopped at all the dubs and gaps upon the road, and showed the way of safety. In short distances, ladies frequently made use of hand bowets, having plates of thin horn in lieu of glass, which afforded a ready light to their footsteps, and had the additional economical advantage of not being liable to breakage, like glass.

A considerable change took place on the streets of the city shortly after the year 1777, by Mr John Brown, the master of work, aided by the proprietors of the front tenements of the streets, having laid down handsome flagged trottoirs, with curb stones, from the Cross to Buchanan Street, by which this spot immediately thereafter became the fashionable mall of the city; and here daily might then have been seen our belles and beaux traversing the said range from east to west, and again returning by the same route, which tramp was repeated again and again at their pleasure. St Enoch's burn was then the west boundary of the royalty.

As the process of laying flagged trottoirs upon the streets of all our public thoroughfares came to be general throughout the city, the ladies abandoned the use of pattens, lanterns, and bowets, and trusted to the comfortable tread of the plane stanes, and the glimmering light of a few scattered conical lamps, which had been first erected by our magistrates in 1718.

The following is a correct description of the dress of our fashionable Glasgow belles during the days of my first decade, which truly bears no small resemblance to the balloon habiliments of our present fashionables, only our modern misses want the powder and pomatum, the frizzled toupet, and the high-heel shoe pegs of my early days, which added some three inches to the height of their grandmothers.

" Glasgow Mercury, 9th December, 1779.

"A NEW SONG.

"GIVE Betsey a bushel of horse-hair and wool,
 Of paste and pomatum a pound ;
Ten yards of gay ribbon to deck her sweet skull,
 And gauze to encompass it round.
Of all the bright colours the rainbow displays,
 Are those ribbons which hang from her head ;
And her flounces adapted to make the folks gaze,
 For around the whole work are they spread.
Her flaps fly behind for a yard at the least,
 And her curls meet just under her chin ;
And those curls are supported, to keep up the jest,
 With an hundred, instead of one pin.
Her gown is tucked up to the hip on each side,
 Shoes too high for to walk or to jump ;
And to deck the sweet creature complete for a bride,
 The corkcutter has made her a rump.
Thus finished in taste, while on her I gaze,
 I think I could take her for life ;
But I fear to undress her, for out of her stays,
 I should find I had lost *half* my wife.

" (To be sung to the tune of ' There was an old woman at Grinston ') "

" Glasgow Mercury, 11th March, 1779.—Notice. The magistrates of the city of Glasgow hereby intimate, that every beggar found begging in the city will be sent to the workhouse ; and as all the poor who are entitled to charity are either in the Town's Hospital, or provided with meal, it is requested the inhabitants will serve none of them at their doors.

" All persons shaking carpets or throwing any filth over windows will be severely punished.

" The inhabitants are required instantly to remove all dung and rubbish from the streets and lanes of this city.

" All dung lying within five yards of the sides of any of the highways within the Royalty will be confiscated immediately."

The following advertisement shows that the practice of making use of the public streets of the city for the deposition of all manner of filth in middens, had been an evil of long standing :—

" Glasgow Courant, June, 1755.—By the magistrates. Whereas of late advertisement was given to all concerned not to lay down any middens of dung upon the sides of the causeways, avenues, or highways leading into the city, by which the passages may be rendered uneasy for carriages, travellers, or otherwise, and to

remove all such middens of dung upon the sides aforesaid, under the pains and penalties mentioned in the former advertisement; and that nevertheless several persons do yet continue to lay down their dung, and allow the same to lie upon the sides of the causeways, highways, and entrances into the city : they are therefore hereby required immediately to remove the same, and not to lay down any more for the future, within the limits of the town, otherways they will be fined and punished by the magistrates, in terms of law."

Before the year 1777, the finest footpaths of the city were those under the pillars in the four streets leading from the Cross. As they were laid with dressed flag-stones, and protected from rain, they were much used by every class in the city ; and to add to their general popularity, they were always kept neat and clean by the shopkeepers under the piazzas. I have often with great delight taken refuge under those covered ways during a passing blast of rain, and must confess that I felt regret at seeing them (as old acquaintances) laid aside by the march of modern improvements.

At the time in question, no such machine as an umbrella had been seen in the streets of Glasgow. It was first introduced by Dr Jamieson, in 1782, on his return from Paris, and helped to console our citizens for the loss of their far-famed piazzas.

The teeming thoroughfare of the plane stanes between the Cross and the boundary of the royalty at St Enoch's burn having become the fashionable mall of the city shortly after 1777, a great change followed immediately thereafter. The Westergate now assumed the name of Argyle Street, and five new streets came to be opened, branching off from the north line of the said mall—viz., Nelson Street, Brunswick Street, Hutcheson Street, Glassford Street, and Buchanan Street.

Virginia Street was opened in 1753, and Miller Street in 1771 ; but at the commencement of my first decade, they were very partially built upon, and might then have been termed merely skeleton streets.

The following regulations, issued by the magistrates and town council of Glasgow, in the year 1776, show in a very clear manner the general outline of the state of the city at that date, in so far as regards the principal localities of business.

1776. 18th of January.—Regulations and fees for the Porters in Glasgow, as established by the magistrates and council of Glasgow, by their Act dated 19th December, 1775 :—

For a letter or parcel not exceeding seven pounds weight, carried anywhere within the city of Glasgow, not exceeding the half of the length of the city, ...	£0	0	0½
For a letter or parcel aforesaid in weight, carried anywhere from the city, not exceeding one mile from the Cross, . .	0	0	1
For a letter or parcel of the weight aforesaid, carried anywhere from the city, not exceeding two miles from the Cross, . .	0	0	2
For carriage of a back load from any wareroom to any of the calenders, or carrying a back load from the Cross to the Broomielaw, Wyndhead, Calton, or Gorbals, ...	0	0	2
For carrying a load on a wheel-barrow, not exceeding three stone weight, to any of the last-mentioned distances, . . .	0	0	3
For weighing a ton of goods, for the first ton, . . .	0	0	4
For every other ton, ...	0	0	2
For going express in the day time, for each measured mile, .	0	0	2
For going express in the night time, for each measured mile, .	0	0	3
For a day's work, to consist of ten working hours, in weighing, sorting, or packing any sort of goods, ...	0	1	6
For a night's watching, ...	0	1	0
For carriage of a letter or parcel to Anderston, or any place of the like distance from the Cross of Glasgow, . . .	0	0	2
For carrying a letter or parcel to any place not exceeding two measured miles from the Cross of Glasgow, . . .	0	0	3
For the first hour's work, ...	0	0	3
For each hour's work after the first hour, . . .	0	0	1

(*N.B.*—At this time the only stand in Glasgow for porters was at the Cross.)

Regulations and fees for the Sedan Chairmen in Glasgow, as established by the magistrates and council of Glasgow, by their Act dated December 19th, 1775 :—

Every lift of a sedan chair in town, though ever so short a distance,	£0	0	6
From the Saracen's Head to the Wyndhead or High Church, .	0	0	9
From the Saracen's Head Inn to the Playhouse and Grahamston,	0	0	9
From the Black Bull Inn to the Saracen's Head Inn, . .	0	0	6
From the Trongate Street to the Wyndhead or High Church, .	0	0	9
From the Bridgegate Street to the College, or like distance, .	0	0	6
From the Merchants' Hall to the College, or New Court thereof, .	0	0	6
From the Bridgegate Street to the Wyndhead or the High Church,	0	1	0
From the Cross of Glasgow to any place in Gorbals, . .	0	1	0
From the Stockwell to the Wyndhead, ...	0	1	0
From any place above Bell's Wynd, and below the College, to the Calton, ...	0	0	9
From any place above Bell's Wynd, and below the College, to the Gorbals, ...	0	1	0
From the Gorbals to the High Church, or like distance, . .	0	2	0

	£	s	d
For every hour a chair waits (when not engaged for forenoon or afternoon), besides ordinary dues, ...	£0	0	6
From the Cross of Glasgow, each computed mile round the same,	0	2	0
For a chair attending from three to four o'clock afternoon till eleven at night, ...	0	2	6
From Jamaica Street to Saracen's Head Inn, or like distance, .	0	0	9
From Jamaica Street to the Cross, or the like distance, . .	0	0	6
From Jamaica Street to any place above Burrel's Hall, within the Port, ...	0	1	0
From Jamaica Street to any place in the Bridgegate Street, .	0	0	6
From Jamaica Street to the Gorbals, ...	0	1	0
For each mile carried to or from the city of Glasgow, . .	0	1	6
From the Playhouse and Jamaica Street to Bun's Wynd, or the like distance, ...	0	0	9
From the Playhouse or Jamaica Street to the High Church, or the like distance, ...	0	1	0
To a chair hire for a forenoon, ...	0	2	0
To a chair hire for a whole day, ...	0	4	0
To a chair hire for a week, ...	1	1	0

(*Encyclopædia*—" Sedan chair is a covered vehicle for carrying a single person, suspended by two poles, and borne by two men, hence denominated *chairmen.* They were first introduced in London in 1634, when Sir Sardon Duncomb obtained the sole privilege to use, let, and hire a number of the said covered chairs for fourteen years.")

At this time the Theatre of Glasgow was situated at Grahamston, beyond the bounds of the royalty, to the west of Mitchell Street, then called Malt Dubs. The original promoters of the erection were William M'Dowall, William Bogle, John Baird, Robert Bogle, and James Dunlop, each of whom advanced £100 towards its construction. These gentlemen having attempted in vain to obtain a site for the theatre within the bounds of the burgh, no one being hardy enough, at any price, to accommodate them there with ground for the purpose, they therefore purchased a plot from Mr Miller of Westerton, lying immediately beyond the royalty, for which they paid him the then enormous price of 5s per square yard. The above named gentlemen having made a strong remonstrance against the immensity of the price, Mr Miller coolly replied that as it was intended to be occupied as a Temple of Satan, he was entitled to receive an extraordinary sum for the purchase.

Though the above-named gentlemen had raised the fabric, they could not lay the ferment in the minds of the lower orders of the populace ; for before the intended night of opening, the house was set on fire, and with difficulty saved from being reduced to ashes ; but the whole of the theatrical wardrobe, which lay in packages there, was destroyed. Mrs Bellamy, the celebrated actress, lost her whole paraphernalia, valued at several hundred pounds, and the total loss was stated to have been about £900.

"*Glasgow Mercury*, Thursday, 11th May, 1780."

" On Friday morning, about two o'clock, the play house here was " discovered to be on fire. The magistrates and many gentlemen of " the place immediately attended; and with the assistance of the " fire-engines and the Northern Fencible Regiment, the fire was got " under before four, but the whole inside of the theatre, clothes, " scenery, &c., were totally consumed. All the houses in the " neighbourhood were saved, though in the utmost danger."

It was alleged that the conflagration was occasioned by the intemperate oratory of a bigoted field preacher, who held forth to the multitude that he had dreamed the preceding night that he was in the infernal regions at a grand entertainment, where all the devils in hell were present, when Satan, their chief, rising up to his full height, gave for his toast, " The health of Mr Miller of Westerton, who had so nobly sold his ground to build thereon a Temple of Belial, and which was to be opened for worship the very next day, so that they might thereafter reign there in triumph."

At this time there was no stand in Glasgow for carriages, so that any person requiring to hire a chaise, was obliged to apply at the office of the chaise master.

"*Glasgow Journal*, 7th February, 1765."

" The following chaise masters hereto subscribing, in Glasgow, do " unanimously agree to furnish all ladies and gentlemen who will " please to favour them with their employment, with a neat four-" wheeled chaise, two good horses, and a complete driver, at nine-" pence per measured mile from Glasgow to Edinburgh, or from " Glasgow to Port-Glasgow or Greenock, for a set down, ditto with " four horses and a chaise to either of the above places at one " shilling and fourpence as above, and to any other place except the " above-mentioned, as usual, at one shilling and fourpence per com-" puted mile.

" As there is no chance of return-money from any other place than " the above mentioned, it always being understood that the owner

" is to pay the maintenance of man and horse, and the employer
" the ferries and tolls.

" James Grahame.	William Buchanan.
" Ninian Craig.	John Barron.
" James Blyth.	William Anderson.
" John Parlan.	Hugh Anderson.
" John Hutcheson,	Alexander Blyth.
" Malcom M'Intyre."	

(*N.B.*—No mention is made of coaches.)

In the year 1800, sedan chairs were still in use as public vehicles. In that year there were 27 sedan chairs lent out on hire by chair masters, and several wealthy individuals in Glasgow then kept their sedan chairs for their own private use.

On the 16th of August, 1780, the magistrates and council directed the master of work to put up nine lamps on the south side of the Trongate, from the Laigh Kirk Steeple to Stockwell Street, in consideration that the proprietors of houses in the said portion of the city had just laid a foot pavement, similar to that on the opposite side of the street; and they expressed their willingness to do the like, west from Stockwell Street, as soon as the proprietors in the line aforesaid had laid foot pavements similar to those on the north side of the street.

" *Glasgow Mercury*, 30th July, 1778.

" On Monday, Barbara Barber was tried before the magistrates of
" this city for keeping a bawdy-house. She was sentenced to remain
" in prison till Wednesday, the 12th of August next, and then to
" stand for the space of an hour, bareheaded, on the Tolbooth stair-
" head, with a label on her breast, having these words ' For keeping
" a notorious bawdy-house,' and afterwards to be banished the city
" and liberties for seven years, under the usual certification."

" August 13th.—Yesterday Barbara Barber stood on the Tolbooth
" stair-head, pursuant to her sentence of 30th ult."

" May 11th, 1780."—" Yesterday Barbara Barber was whipped
" through this city by the common hangman. She had formerly
" been banished by the magistrates for keeping a disorderly house,
" under the certification of the above disgraceful punishment in case
" of her returning."

" Mercury, 5th May, 1789."

" To be sold, by public roup, if not sold privately, that large and
" elegant dwelling house, offices, and area of ground wherein they
" stand, containing about 4617 square yards, situated on the west-
" side of Queen Street, and fronting Ingram Street, Glasgow,
" belonging to William Cunninghame of Lainshaw.

" If it is in the wish of the purchaser, payment of the price or any
" part will be made to answer his conveniency, upon satisfactory
" security.

" The Plans of the whole buildings are in the hands of William
" Martine, wright in Glasgow. There is a servant in waiting for
" showing the houses."

This property was generally allowed to be the most superb urban
place of residence of any in Scotland.

It became the dwelling house of John Stirling, Esq., and the wings
were then made into the extensive warehouses of William Stirling
and Sons, calico printers. It was afterwards purchased by the
Royal Bank of Scotland for the Glasgow branch of that establishment, and, after considerable alterations, it now forms the Royal
Exchange of Glasgow.

The mansion house cost Mr Cunninghame £10,000, but it was
said that Mr Stirling paid only £5000 for it, which would amount
to about 21s 8d per square yard.

I went through the house in 1778 while it was building ; indeed,
it was quite a raree show to our citizens to inspect it during the
progress of its erection. It was built on the site of two small
cottages which fronted the Cowloan. The land was rather marshy,
in consequence of which Mr Cunninghame was obliged to be at considerable expense in draining it.

THE 10TH OF OCTOBER, AND THE GLASGOW GRAMMAR
SCHOOL OF OLDEN TIME.

As the 10th of October is approaching, when the usual social meetings of the Alumni of our public Grammar School take place, and as
I am the oldest individual alive who attended the ancient Grammar
School of Glasgow, situated in Greyfriars' Wynd, I have taken upon
myself to jot down a few loose memoranda regarding that academy
and of the school-days of olden time, which perhaps may be interest-

ing to many of those who were educated at our public Grammar
School—especially to the scholars of Daniel M'Arthur, who was
teacher in the said seminary for the long period of a quarter of a
century. I am ignorant of the birth-place or parentage of
M'Arthur, but I have ascertained as follows regarding his early
history. Before Daniel M'Arthur became a teacher in the public
Grammar School of Glasgow, he was a licensed preacher of the
Gospel, and also kept a private school for teaching the Latin
language, as the following advertisements show:—*Glasgow Mercury*,
10th December, 1778,—" On Monday will be published, price 4d,
' The Church of Rome the Mother of Abominations;' a sermon
delivered in the Blackfriars' Church on Monday the 16th of November, 1778, by Daniel M'Arthur, preacher of the Gospel." In this
sermon Mr M'Arthur inveighed most violently and sarcastically
against the errors of Romanism. Shortly afterwards there appeared
a caricature print, price 6d, showing the Scarlet Whore, the Winged
Beast full of eyes, the mitred Pope, and the horned Devil with his
imps; sold by Dunlop & Wilson, John Smith and James Duncan,
booksellers. At this time Glasgow was in a state of furor against
the Roman Catholics; Lord George Gordon's Popery riots having
taken place, followed by the celebrated Bagnal's Rabble Case, so
well-known in the history of Glasgow.

Perhaps it is not generally known that Daniel M'Arthur taught
the French language, as well as the Latin, before he was elected
Grammar School teacher in 1782; this, however, is shown by the
following advertisement, taken from the *Glasgow Mercury* of 5th
October, 1780:—" Education.—Daniel M'Arthur, 2d close west
from the Exchange, continues to teach the Latin language. On
Tuesday next he will begin a class in the rudiments of that
language. At private hours he teaches the French and English
languages. Accordingly, on the first of November he will open two
classes, one for French, the other for English grammar; together
with the reading and spelling of English."

Mr M'Arthur's Latin class was pretty well attended, and many
of his scholars followed him to the public Grammar School on his
election as teacher there in 1782. At school and in common
conversation M'Arthur affected to speak the English language with
the English accent, which made him appear a stiff and formal
dominie; but he pronounced the Latin tongue in good broad Scotch
idiom. I never heard him use a French expression. It would have
been curious, however, to have listened to him when he came to

decline the relative, "Quis, Quæ, Quod, vel Quid" with French pronunciation. The Common hall of the old Grammar School, where the four classes assembled in the morning to hear prayers, is thus described in an advertisement in the *Glasgow Mercury* of 23d July, 1788:—

"A LARGE HALL.—To be let and entered immediately—That large and convenient Room, in the ground floor of the old Grammar School, which is above 20 feet in breadth, and 14 feet in height; the floor is of wood, and is surrounded by as many fixed seats as may accommodate above 400 boys. It is lighted by six large windows; has two entries and a centrical fire-place. As the hall is both elegant and convenient, it may be applied to many different purposes. Those who wish to see it may have an opportunity every forenoon by calling on any of the teachers in the upper rooms. Proposals for taking it will be received by Andrew Younger, treasurer to the General Session."

In the year 1783, being shortly after M'Arthur was elected teacher, the Grammar School was publicly examined no less than eight several times by the Magistrates of Glasgow, the clergymen of the city, and Professors of the University, when the regulations made in 1782, on the death of Bar and entrance of M'Arthur, as to the management of the school, were found to have had the best effects in improving the proficiency of the boys, and a committee was appointed to make any new regulations that they might think necessary. Accordingly, the said committee recommended that no new scholars should be admitted into a class that had made some proficiency ; and that when any class shall exceed the number of Fifty Boys, the master shall give an additional hour to a certain proportion of those who are at the bottom of the class.

The roll of Mr M'Arthur's class at this time consisted of 110 scholars, and in consequence of the foregoing regulation he adopted the plan of having a private class, which was attended more generally by the advanced students than by the dunces. In fact this private class, came in place of private tutors assisting the boys at their homes, it being a cheaper mode of furthering the scholar in his lessons than private tutorage. It certainly was a great advantage to the boys whose parents were rich, and who could afford the additional expense of education; but it was, on the other hand, exceedingly disheartening to the poor scholar, who, unassisted, had to compete for his place in the class against boys who received the advantage of the master's private teaching.

Another of the regulations now adopted was that the teachers were directed to keep a regular catalogue of the boys' attendance at school. In consequence of the death of William Bald, the magistrates of Glasgow, on the 26th of March, 1783, made choice of Mr David Allison, schoolmaster in Gorbals, and lately from Beith, to be one of the masters of the Grammar School of Glasgow, in place of the said William Bald, deceased. This class was immediately elder than M'Arthur's class.

At the period in question, among the schoolboys, the different classes in the Grammar School were distinguished by the names of Cocks, Hens, Earocks, and Chickens, according to the dates of entrance. When Allison was elected teacher, Mr Arthur's class were Chickens, and did not become Earocks till the ensuing October. I may here say that an earock, according to Jamieson, is a hen when she begins to lay eggs.

The eldest and biggest boy in our class was the late Alexander M'Gregor, Esq., writer. It now appears curious to me to look back to the days of old, when I saw the tears copiously flowing over the cheeks of Sandy M'Gregor, because he had lost a place in the class! The littlest boy of the class was the late Mr George Morrison, writer, who, by way of banter, was commonly called "Gigas." The two best scholars in our class were Alexander Brown, the brother of the present Mrs Ewing Maclae of Cathkin, and Alexander M'Aslan, afterwards of Austin & M'Aslan, nurserymen. Each of these scholars was declared dux of the class for two years—the former for the years 1783 and 1786, and the latter for the years 1784 and 1785.

In 1782, when I entered the Grammar School, the following were the four teachers:—

1st, Alexander Bradfute, as head master, taught the Cocks. He died during the session of 1788, and was succeeded by John Wilson.

2d, John Dow taught the Hens. He died in the session 1795, and was succeeded by James Gibson.

3d, William Bald taught the Earocks. He died during the session of 1783, and was succeeded by David Allison.

4th, Daniel M'Arthur taught the Chickens. He died in 1808, and was succeeded by John Dymock.

Perhaps it may be interesting to the scholars of Mr M'Arthur to state that he was buried in the Ramshorn new burying ground, and that the following inscription is placed on his tomb:—

The Burial Place
of the late
REV. DANIEL MACARTHUR,
For Twenty-five years
one of the
Masters of the Grammar School
in this City,
who departed this life February 9th,
1808,
Aged 61 years.
Also of
ELIZABETH ORR,
His Wife,
And two of their children.
There is also interred here
ALEXANDER MACARTHUR,*
late Merchant in Glasgow,
who died February 18th, 1826,
Aged 61 years.

Mr M'Arthur left no male issue, but was succeeded by two daughters.

When M'Arthur was elected as teacher in 1782, the office of rector, which had lately been held by James Bar, was discontinued, and the teacher of the oldest class became the President of the School, and had a casting vote; at the same time the quarterly wages were raised from 4s to 5s, and the teachers were directed to wear gowns. Shortly after this the wages per quarter were raised to 6s, and before I left the school they were enlarged to 7s 6d.

When the quarterly wages, some time after this, came to be raised to 10s 6d, the teachers' annual salaries were fixed at £25, independent of school fees, and the presiding teacher (viz., of the 4th class) was allowed £10 additional, in consideration of his increased charge. Each scholar paid 2s 6d for coals, and 1s was usually the fee of the janitor. The hours of attendance in summer were from 7 in the morning till 9, from 10 till 12, and from 1 till 3; but the Saturdays, in summer, were play-days. In winter, the hours of meeting were from 9 till 12, and from 1 till 3; but on the Saturdays only from 9 till 12. Our extra play-days were, during the Sacraments, on Christmas-day, and New-Year's-day, and at the Deacons' choosing. But on Wednesday the 23d of November; 1785, we got an extraordinary play-day, to see Lunardi ascend in his balloon, which favour we attributed solely to the anxious desire on the part of the teachers themselves to witness the sight.

* Younger Brother of Daniel M'Arthur.

During the whole of our course the Candlemas offering was still continued. This practice, degrading to the teacher and invidious to the scholar, has happily disappeared in our schools. I remember M'Arthur sitting in his school pulpit, with the roll of the class before him, and as each scholar in his turn came forward and presented his offering, the same was regularly marked down in M'Arthur's catalogue. I and most others generally gave three half-crowns, many gave only 5s, and some merely 2s 6d, while one or two, whose parents were of the poorer class, presented still less, to the sad humiliation of the unhappy scholar. Some of the boys, by way of ridicule, presented their gifts in coppers, and this set the whole class a-tittering, seeing that M'Arthur had to count the half-pence carefully over before entering the amount in his catalogue. There were a very few who gave a gold half-guinea, and Hugh Houston, afterwards Colonel Houston, gave a gold guinea, and accordingly was declared "king" amidst loud ruffings and cries of "*Vivat, Floriat, Gloriat.*"

Mr Alexander Houston was supposed to be the only millionaire parent of our schoolboys; but, some time after this, when the abolition of the slave trade came to be agitated in the House of Commons, Mr Houston, in anticipation of the event taking place, entered into an immense speculation of purchasing slaves. The motion for the abolition of the slave trade, however, not having been then carried in Parliament, the speculation became an entire failure, in consequence of which Mr Houston lost all his fortune, and sold Jordanhill. His slaves had to be fed and clothed, and disease spread rapidly amongst them, carrying them off by hundreds, while the price of slaves fell immensely.

In 1815, the magistrates of Glasgow enacted that there should be a fifth class added to the four others, and placed under the management of a rector, in which class the rudiments of the Greek language should be taught, as well as the usual Latin course, and that the quarterly wages should be raised to 10s 6d. Dr William Chrystal, then one of the teachers, was elected rector of the said fifth class on the 30th May, 1815.

I may here mention that it was usual for the scholars to draw lots for places in the class two or three times in the course of the session, so as to allow each boy an opportunity of finding his level. In 1807 and 1809 Mr John Glas Sandeman, having some religious scruples against "casting of lots," requested the teacher, Mr Allison, to place his son, George Glas Sandeman, at the bottom of the class, instead of drawing by lot for his place, which request was complied with, and so, for three several times during these respective sessions, George was placed at the bottom of the class; nevertheless, he worked himself up to be dux of the class in 1807 and 1809. The honour of being declared dux was thus decided :—The boy who had been upon an average the nearest to the top of the class during the different examinations of the session was declared dux.

As already stated, our class, being M'Arthur's first class, was formed in 1782, and was continued till October, 1786.

In 1782 the magistrates established a Grammar School Library, but it was of no use, except to the teachers themselves, the scholars totally neglecting it ; indeed, no catalogue of the books was ever exhibited to them by the said teachers.

Our first class meeting was held in October, 1789, when John Wilson Rae,* afterwards advocate in Edinburgh, and brother of Dr Rae Wilson, was elected preses, and I was elected secretary and croupier. The next year, 1790, I had the honour of being elected preses. We held regular annual meetings in October for many years afterwards, but Thomas Watson, brother of the Watsons, bankers, having died when he was secretary, no meetings were called after that time.

In looking back upon the history of our class-fellows of 1782, the most of them, so far as known to me, have passed through life with honour, and with a fair average share of success as to worldly matters. Two of them became knights—viz., Sir Neil Douglas and Sir James Stevenson Barns. Sir Neil's father was Mr John Douglas, insurance broker, Glasgow. Sir Neil first commenced business in Glasgow, about the close of last century, as a muslin manufacturer, under the firm of Douglas & Brown ; but, in 1800, a few years afterwards, when, in the 26th year of his age, he gave up the manufacturing business, and entered the army in the 21st Regiment. He gradually rose to be Lieut.-General, Commander of the Forces in Scotland, and was made a knight. His rapid rise in the army must be attributed to his distinguished merit and business habits, and not to family interest. Sir Neil died in 1853, aged 80. Sir James Stevenson Barns was the second son of Dr Stevenson, physician in Glasgow, and took the name of Barns on succeeding to

---

* John Wilson Rae (named for his uncle, the town-clerk, John Wilson) was a young man of splendid abilities: but he destroyed his constitution from overstraining his mental powers by intense study. He died in 1823, quite childish—a sad example of the bad effects of overtaxing the human brain.

the estate of John Barns of Barns, commonly called "Old Jacky Barns," from his eccentricity. Mr Barns resided in Miller Street. Sir James was Colonel in the army, but I have not heard how he came to be knighted.

None of our class became millionaires; but Dr Thomas Brown, Professor of Botany in our University, certainly died the wealthiest of all M'Arthur's scholars of 1782. He succeeded his elder brothers, George and Robert, in the Langside estate, and by the will of his cousin, Nicol Brown, acquired the estates of Lanfin and Water-haughs, besides the large personal estate of Nicol Brown in the concern of Carrick, Brown & Co., of the Ship Bank. Dr Brown's father was Thomas Brown, a surgeon, who went to India, where, having realised a fortune, he came to reside first in London, and then in Glasgow. He built the present Langside House about 80 years ago. Dr Brown married Miss Jeffrey, a sister of the late Lord Jeffrey. Dr Brown died in 1853, aged 79.

I only recollect one instance of any of our class having lost caste. This was a John M'Lean, who, poor fellow, died many years ago in the station of a common operative. He was the greatest dunce of our class, and was always on the dults' form. I recollect of his having attended one of our class meetings, in the course of which he got tipsy, and then set about catechising Daniel M'Arthur, who was present, saying, "Mr M'Arthur, do you remember what shocking bad names you called me at school?" "No," replied M'Arthur; "what were they?" "Why," said M'Lean, "did you not hold up your two hands and call out to me, 'Oh tu stulte?'" "Ah," answered M'Arthur, "I see, Mr M'Lean, that you have not forgotten what you were?" M'Lean took the repartee in good humour, and laughed as heartily on the occasion as any of us.

The late Dr John Burns, Professor of Surgery in the University of Glasgow, was one year in M'Arthur's first class, but, getting into bad health, he fell behind the class, and finished his Grammar School course in Bradfute's class, being the class immediately below ours. Dr Burns was unfortunately drowned in the Orion steamer, off Portpatrick, on the 18th of June, 1850.

Dr Thomas Christie, another of M'Arthur's first class, was an eminent physician. He went to India pretty early in life, and afterwards settled in the Island of Ceylon, where he became the head of the medical staff. He died there a few years ago. He was the son of Robert Christie, provost of Glasgow in 1756 and 1757. The provost was an American merchant, but lost nearly his all by the

War of Independence, and died in Maryland in June, 1780. It was during his provostship that Mr Bar was elected rector of the Grammar School, as the following advertisement shows :—*Glasgow Journal*, 12th April, 1756.—" On Friday last, the magistates and town council made choice of Mr James Bar as rector of the Grammar School, in place of Mr James Purdie, who has resigned." Mr Bar built the large tenement opposite the Blackfriars' Church, and in a niche at the centre of its front he placed a bust of Cicero, on the pedestal of which were inscribed in capitals, " M. T. CICERO." I remember of M'Arthur telling us that a countryman one day, passing along the High Street, and looking up to the inscription on the said bust, and supposing it to have been the proprietor's name, exclaimed, " I wonder who this Mr Thomas Kikero is, for I never heard of him ?" The story, of course, was received by the class with loud ruffings. The bust of Cicero had been taken down, but the niche where it was placed still remains in front of Bar's land.

I may here remark, *en passant*, that it was in the first floor of this tenement that John Stirling, Esq., took up his residence upon his marriage with Miss Bogle, and here, I believe, his eldest son, William, now of Cordale, was born. Mr Stirling afterwards purchased, for £5000, Cunninghame's Great House, now the Royal Exchange.

Of the 110 boys in our class, a great many died in early life, and a considerable number of them went abroad and were lost sight of. Among those that remained there were 6 lawyers, 6 of the medical faculty, 18 who followed mercantile pursuits, 5 officers in the army, and 1 minister of the gospel, viz., the present Rev. Dr Gardiner of Bothwell.

Amongst the officers of the army was Major Archibald Monteith, who, as the story goes, made his fortune in India by capturing a rich stray baggage elephant, belonging to a Rajah, from part of which prize, it was alleged, he purchased the large tenement at the corner of Buchanan Street, now occupied by Arthur & Fraser, and another large tenement at the corner of St Enoch Square, long the warehouse of Kevan and Buttle. The Major by his will bequeathed £1000 to raise a monument to his own memory, which is now a conspicuous object in the Necropolis.* None of our class belonged

---

* Archy Monteith was able to perform a feat which, when exhibited by him to his schoolfellows, excited their great astonishment and merriment. Archy could touch the point of his nose with the tip of his tongue ! We all endeavoured to achieve the like deed, but in vain. No one in M'Arthur's class could perform this *magnum opus* but Archy himself.

to the navy, and none of us ever reached to city honours. We had no lord provosts, lord deans of guild, deacon conveners, bailies, or treasurers amongst us, nor any lawyer who reached a seat on the bench. The last death in our class was James Milligan, house factor, who died in 1858, aged 84. His father was a reed maker in the High Street.

I am not aware of there being any scholar alive of the Grammar School classes which existed previous to 1782. Adam Watson, whose father was a linen manufacturer, was the last member of the Latin classes before M'Arthur's. He was of Dow's class of 1780. He died in 1850, aged 78. Mr Adam Watson was uncle of our townsman, William West Watson, Esq. Of M'Arthur's first class of 1782, there are still three alive, viz., the Rev. Dr Gardiner, Bothwell; Captain William Marshall, Rothesay,* and myself—Dr Gardiner and Captain Marshall, however, are a year or two younger than me. Dr Gardiner attended several of our early class meetings, and entertained us greatly with some excellent comic songs. I hope the Rev. Doctor is still able to amuse the Bothwellani with those merry ditties of Auld Lang Syne.

M'Arthur kept his class in very good order, and was by no means a harsh or austere disciplinarian; his punishments never exceeded a few "loofies." Dow, on the contrary, was most severe and rigorous as to punishing delinquents, and I remember of his inflicting a certain nameless punishment on K. F., one of our embryo lord provosts and members of Parliament, for some frolicksome trick that he had played.

On another occasion, when Dow was in the act of unbuttoning the dress of an obstinate, unruly boy, in order to inflict a similar punishment on him, the little fellow resisted with all his strength; and in the struggle he seized hold of Dow's wig, which he pulled off the Dominie's head and dashed it on the hall floor, thereby exposing poor Dow's *bare pow*, to the infinite merriment and delight of the whole class, which they expressed by a general roar of laughter.

It was usual about Candlemas for a deputation of students from the University to repair to the Grammar School, at Common Hall

* Captain William Marshall is the second son of Robert Marshall, Esq., who was partner and manager of the extensive tannery situated at the Gallowgate Bridge. M'Ure, p. 284, informs us that this concern consisted of six partners, four of whom bore the rank of bailies. Captain Marshall was second lieutenant in the Glasgow Sharp-shooters, raised in 1803. To the best of my recollection, he soon afterwards went to Canada, and was there appointed Captain of Militia. (P.S.—He died 22nd Feb., 1864.)

time, and to solicit a play-day for each of the four classes, which the teachers always readily granted; and in return for this act of kindness, four boys of the oldest class in the school resorted to the College and requested a like favour from the Principal for the University students, which, of course, was never denied. On these occasions the Latin language was only used by both parties.

I need hardly take notice of the great rejoicings which took place in the Grammar School when the "*Vacans*" came to be announced on the 4th of June, the King's Birthday. There was then nothing but tremendous ruffings and loud hurrahings; cries of " Memento Feriarum." "Bene vobis, Bene omnibus, Huzzah." In short, it was altogether a scene of unbridled joy, in which the teachers themselves participated.

In 1786, during the last session of our course, the old Grammar School having been found incommodious and unsuitable for the increasing population of the city, the magistrates and town council resolved to build a new school-house. Accordingly, on the 16th of July, 1787, the foundation stone of an elegant Glasgow " Ludus Literarius" was laid upon the north side of George Street—the cost of the building per estimate being £1950. In the *Glasgow Mercury* of the 5th of June, 1787, we have the following notice :—" Last week part of the skeleton of a human body was found in the site of the New Grammar School, in the Ramshorn grounds. It was seven feet below the surface, and supposed to have been a female. A set of amber beads and a piece of tartan cloth were found at the same time." The handsome Grammar School above mentioned was afterwards sold, and now forms the Andersonian University.

There seem to have been Grammar Schools, or Pedagogia, in Glasgow in early times. In September, 1494, the chancellor of the diocese brought a complaint before the bishop against David Dun, a priest of the diocese, for openly and publicly teaching scholars in grammar, and children in the rudiments of learning, without the allowance of the chancellor.—(*Origines Parochiales*, p. 7.) It may be further stated, that by an old deed, preserved in the charter-room of the University, dated 1525, the said " Aulde Pedagog" was situated on the south side of the Rottenrow, as the following quotation shows :—

" ——— de terris tenementi et loci nuncupati 'Aulde Pedagog' jacentibus in via Ratonum ——— ex parte australi inter tenementum Magistri Johannis Reid ex parte occidentali et terras Roberti Reid ex parte orientali."

From our family documents, it is believed that the above John Reid and Robert Reid were the ancestors of Robert Reid, bailie of Glasgow in 1726, who was shot in the Saltmarket, endeavouring to quell a riot. The bailie's lair in the High Church has descended to me. His title to the lair is in my possession.

It may here be remarked that the Pedagog being described as "Aulde," was probably of older date than our University.

I shall here drop these gossiping jottings by calling the attention of your readers to a very curious Grammar School relique, which is little known to the public, and which appears to have escaped the notice of most of our Glasgow historians. As is well known, the Grammar School of my early days was situated in the present Grayfriars' Wynd, and the said building now is No. 3. The ground floor of it (formerly the Common Hall) is now occupied by Robert Pinkerton as a cabinetmaker's workshop. In the wall of the back court of the building in question, and immediately above the entrance door, there is placed a stone tablet, having the Arms of the City of Glasgow sculptured in the centre of it, and the following Latin inscription, in capitals, engraven on the sides of the Arms :—

	The Arms	
SCHOLAGRAM	of the	MATICORASENA
TVCIVIBVSQVE		GLASGVANISBO
NARLITERARPA	City of	TRONISCONDITA
	Glasgow.*	

("Schola Grammaticor : A Senatu Civibusque Glasguanis, Bonar Literar ; Patronis Condita.")

(In English.)

"The Grammar School erected by its Patrons, the Municipal Authorities, and Citizens of Glasgow, for the Promotion of Literature."

There is no date upon the building by which the time of its erection can be ascertained ; but this school-house appears to have been built upon the site of a still older school-house, which, by the following record, was in a state of decay in the year 1577, and not even water-tight :—

* " Here's the bird that never flew ;
Here's the tree that never grew ;
Here's the bell that never rang ;
Here's the fish that never swam ;
And here's the dru'ken salmon."

"Burgh Records, 16th November, 1577.—Item : *Yai* condes-
cendit and ordanit ye maister of work to mak ye gramer scole wattir
fast, and at ye spring of ye year to mend ye east parte yairof."

Again, in October, 1578, we find by an entry in the Burgh
Records that the Grammar School was a thatched house.

"Item : For xii. threif of quheit straye to theik the gramer scole
—xlviii s."

The Grammar School of my early days appears to have been built
about twenty-four years afterwards, as we find that the presbytery
of Glasgow, on the 11th of March, 1601, ordered the scholars of the
Grammar School to meet in the High Church during the time that
the new school-house was building. It therefore may be presumed
that the late Grammar School in Grayfriars' Wynd was erected in
1601.

I may here remark that the present Grayfriars' Wynd is a mis-
nomer, the proper name of the Wynd being the "Grammar School
Wynd." This may be seen by an examination of M'Ure's History,
page 153, wherein it is stated that Grayfriars' Wynd was situated
nearly opposite to the present Havannah Street, and led to the west
of the city, where in former times there was a monastery of Gray
Friars, near to the Deanside Well, now 88 George Street. It appears
that Robert, bishop of Glasgow, made a present of the Deanside
Well to the said Gray Friars, in order to enable them to lead its
water into their convent. The charter, dated in 1304, says :—
"Noveritis Nos intuita caritatis, Dedisse fratribus Predicatoribus
de Glasgu, fontem quendam qui dicitur 'Medow Wel,' in loco
qui dicitur Denside scaturientem, in perpetuum conducendum in
claustrum dictorum fratrum, ad usus necessarios eorundem."—
(Hamilton's Lanarkshire, 190.*) M'Ure's Grayfriars' Wynd (even

---

* From the word *scaturientem* we learn that the Deanside Well was then a running
spring, and not a draw-well. (There were no pump-wells in Glasgow at that time.)
Two hundred and seventy years afterwards, the Deanside Well (now 88 George Street)
was still a running spring in the fields, as is shown by the following extract :—
"Burgh Records, 1st June, 1574.—Item: The haill passage of ye Deynside well is
stoppit throw oure casting of erd and stanes of zairdis nixt adjacent yairto."
Magna mutatio loci ! Instead of a purling spring, then meandering through verdant
meadows, and giving only a scanty supply of water for domestic use, we have now a
flowing lake in the midst of our city, sufficient, if set loose, to drown the whole population of St Mungo. I may here state that in my Grammar School days the Deanside
Well continued to be in the open fields, at the foot of the Deanside Brae ; it, however,
was no longer a purling spring, but a pump-well. It is now situated at No. 88 George
Street, opposite the lane leading to Shuttle Street ; and as it is described in the
charter of 1304 as being "scaturiens fons," or overflowing fountain, the stream could

down to my day) was afterwards called "Bun's Wynd," and now it is called "Nicholas Street." It led into Shuttle Street, which last street was a continuation of M'Ure's Grayfriars' Wynd. In the map of Glasgow, published in Glasgow in 1777 and 1778, Shuttle Street is called Grayfriars' Wynd. M'Ure does not mention Shuttle Street. But to return to our Grammar School relique. As the Arms of the City of Glasgow are sculptured upon it, and as it is therein declared to be under the patronage of our magistrates and council, I trust that these official gentlemen will take some steps to have this curious antiquarian document removed for preservation from its present hidden position, and placed in front of our modern Grammar School in John Street.

With the exception of what relates to its Cathedral, Glasgow has few ancient reliques, and therefore it is the more necessary to preserve such as remain.

Besides, it will be seen by the following extract, taken from a document in the possession of the magistrates and town council themselves, that they are not only appointed the patrons of the old Glasgow Grammar School, but are also nominated, *especially*, its *governours* and *defenders*.

"Extract from the Inventar of ye Wrytes and evidents of ye Burgh of Glasgow, A.D. J.M.VICXCVI. (1696)
G. H. Burdle, 38th.

"Donation of a house to the Mr. of the Grammar School.

"*Imprimis*, Ane Donation made be Simeon Dalgleish, precenter and officer of Glasgow, whereby he gives and dispones in free donation, All and Haill ane tenement lyand in the meikle wynd of the said Burgh, leading frae the Church to the Crosse, and upon the west side of the said wynde, betwixt the great Vennell, commonly called 'Ronald's Wynde, on the north side, otherwise bounded in manner yungpeid, with the haill pertinents yrof, in favour of Master Alexander Galbraith, Rector and Master of the Grammar School, and as master of that school, and to his successors in office, for his and his scholars performing some Papish rites, whereby the said Master Simon appoints the Magistrates and Council of the Burgh Patrons, *Governours*, and *Defenders* of the said Donation, dated 20 January, 1460 years.

easily have been led to the Gray Friars' garden at the foot of the Grammar School Wynd, there being a direct and easy descent from the well to the said garden at the south-east corner of Shuttle Street.

"Item : Ane wryte granted be Robert Huchesone, Merd., and Katherine Alstone, spouses, whereby they renounced their seisin and all title of right and possession that they had in and to ane tenement or house, with the little piece yaird adjacent thereto, sometime occupied by the said spouses, which is ane part of the tenement pertaining to the Grammar School, lyand betwixt the Grammar School on the eist, and and ane hall thorne hedge on the west, to the effect the same may be joined to the said school and augment the roome yrof, dated 27 Jany., 1577.

"Item : Ane Contract betwixt the Town and William Wallace, Schoolmaster, on the ane pairt, and William Fleming, Commissr. Clerk of Glasgow, on the other pairt, whereby the Town and the said Schoolmaster dispones to the said William the little yaird therein specified, pertaining to the Grammar School, and the said William disponed in excambion yrof that little piece of yaird called the Garden Circuit about, with a stone dyke adjacent to the back side of the school, dated 9 Feby., 1633.

"Item : Four Papers and a missive letter, containing directions and rules of the management of the Grammar School (therein specified)."

(Holograph of the town clerk of Glasgow, dated 1696.)

In Mr Pagan's "Glasgow, Past and Present," page 19, I took notice of a curious old back building, entering through Barr's Land, by No. 157 High Street (of which Mr Stewart, in his Views of Glasgow, at page 67, has given us a lithographic sketch).

In 1782, when I was at the Grammar School, the whole of the back garden, even down to Shuttle Street, was fenced in by a high stone wall. The building itself had a front to the wynd, and an ancient covered entry to it, which was about seven feet wide. On each side of the said entry there were stone seats. The tradition among the schoolboys was that those seats had been used by the friars' preachers, in Popish times, as a lounging resort of the members of their convent. Similar stone seats were placed in the gallery of the ground floor of old Hutchesons' Hospital, upon the west compartment of the inner court, for resting places to the old and decrepit inmates of the hospital. The front of the old building in question, which stood directly opposite the entry to the Grammar School, in the wynd, has been taken down, and is now replaced by a brick building, and the back court and large garden reaching to Shuttle Street have been wholly built upon. Even since the time when Mr Stewart's Views were published, nearly all the arched vaults of the old fabric have been built up and altered, so that only a small part of the said old building now remains for examination. I suggested to the late John Baird, Esq., architect, to look at this ancient tenement, as I thought that it was the remains of the convent of Franciscan or Gray Friars, where Edward I. lodged when in Glasgow. Accordingly, Mr Baird was so obliging as to examine it; but his report was unfavourable to my views. Mr Baird, who was an eminent antiquary, said that he thought the old parts of the building had been erected within the last two centuries. Notwithstanding, however, of such high authority against my conjecture, I still have my doubts of the said old parts being so modern as Mr Baird supposed them to be. I have no pretensions of being an antiquary, and therefore my opinion is of little value in a matter of this kind; but, a few weeks ago, I happened accidentally to meet with the following very interesting passage in Brown's Ecclesiastical History of Glasgow and Paisley, at page 18 :—

" George Crawfurd, in his History of Renfrewshire, says—' I have seen a mortification by Isobel, Duchess of Albany and Countess of Lennox, to the Convent of Gray Friars of Glasgow,* of the lands of Balagan, which grant she expresses to be made for the salvation of our soul and that of Murdoch, Duke of Albany, of worthy memory, our very dear husband ; and also for Duncan, Earl of Lennox, our father, and of Walter, James, and Alexander, our sons : dated at Inchmyrin, 18th May, 1451.' The house of the Earl of Lennox filled up the space of ground which the reader may remember a timber land. Tradition says it was afterwards occupied as the Bishop's prison and guard house, and in the last century was the scene of the torture inflicted on the celebrated Mr Ogilvie, the Jesuit."

This unhappy missionary, John Ogilvie, a student from the college of Gratz, after having been tortured, was tried in 1615, for endeavouring to inculcate Popish principles tending to destroy the supremacy of the king as head of the Church. He was found guilty, and executed the same day that he received his doom—a sad example of the frailty of the human mind in religious matters. The tragedy of torturing and hanging poor Ogilvie on the spot in question is quite sufficient to give a historical interest to the above-mentioned old building, independent of the tradition of its having been the lodging of Edward I. while he remained in Glasgow. But

* *N.B.*—Observe that Brown states that the mansion of the Earl of Lennox was next to the site of Barr's Land.

2 F

there is still another reason for our regarding this locality as a memorable spot in the annals of Glasgow, and well worthy of the attention of your antiquarian readers. M'Ure, at page 66, thus writes in 1736 :—

"It was at the special instance of a prior of the Convent of Gray Friars, that the fair that commences in the city here on the first day of July, and continues till the seventh, was procured ; and the community of the city was so sensible of this favour, and the advantage of that fair or concourse of the neighbourhood of all ranks coming to the city, that every last day of the fair annually, they went and paid their compliments to the prior of the Gray Friars at the convent; and to THIS DAY, the fair is fenced WITHIN the INCLOSURE or GARDEN where the convent stood, at a place they call (but on what account I cannot tell) Craignaught."

Jamieson, in his Scottish Dictionary, states that Craig signifies a rock, and that Noit means "a small rocky height"—both derived from the Gaelic. About the year 1830, a large tenement was erecting in Shuttle Street, on the garden ground in question, and in digging the foundations of it there appeared a solid rock of basalt or whinstone, apparently of great extent, for it seemed to extend from the College to Ingram Street, and it was so near the surface that part of it had to be quarried and carried away, in order to deepen the foundation of the erection. I personally inspected this basaltic rock while the building was going on, and I think that in former times a small portion of the said rock was bare, and appeared above the level of the surface of the garden, but that the friars had carefully covered it over with garden mould, so as to render it fit for raising vegetables, and to improve their garden ; farther, that the ancient name of Craignaut or Craignoit had been handed down to the days of M'Ure as the name of the protruded portion of basalt. I leave this knotty point, however, in the hands of your antiquarian readers to solve ; only observing that Nout signifies black cattle, and Craignought might have been the cattle-market.

M'Ure further informs us at page 66—"That at the Reformation, when the convent was dissolved and the friars dispersed, the rents, lands, and possessions of all that belonged to the convents of the Black and Gray Friars were given to the University of Glasgow, and these small duties paid out of the several tenements within the city that held of the Black and Gray Friars are now (1736) payable by the heritors to the College."

From the following advertisement it will be seen that the old

property in question, with the large garden, which in my day extended to Shuttle Street, was bestowed upon the College at the
Reformation :—

"*Glasgow Mercury*, 17th April, 1792."

" Houses and Ground to be sold, feued, or let, entry at Whitsunday
next.—The back houses of Barr's land, lying on the west side of the
High Street, opposite to the College Church, and also the large garden
behind the said houses fronting Shuttle Street and the Grammar
School Wynd, are to be Sold, Feued, or Let, by private bargain.
Persons inclining to be purchasers, feuars, or tenants of the premises,
may give in their proposals to Mr Hill, College Factor, or to Robert
Grahame, writer in Glasgow."

By examining Fleming's large Map, published in 1807, the state
of the above-mentioned property, including the large garden, will
be distinctly shown, and it was in the same state in 1782, when I
attended the Grammar School. At the left corner of Fleming's said
Map, there is a small Map of the city of Glasgow, dated 1779, the
same having been drawn up before Barr's land was built. This
small Map exhibits a building nearly as large as the Black Friars'
Church, which stood on the united sites of the old building fronting
the Grammar School Wynd and of the present Barr's land. I
therefore conclude that these two structures united, formed at one
time the mansion of the Earl of Lennox, the Bishop's Prison and
Guard-house, mentioned by Brown in his Ecclesiastical History of
Glasgow and Paisley, at page 18, and that in 1615 poor Ogilvie, the
Jesuit student, had been confined in the Bishop's Prison or Guard-
house, and then hanged in the public street opposite to the Black
Friars' Church.

There was formerly a flight of stair steps from the High Street,
extending across the entry to the Black Friars' Church, which entry,
rising eastwards like an amphitheatre, would then have given the
populace a fine opportunity of witnessing the sad scene of Ogilvie's
execution on the High Street.

I now close these desultory jottings by giving my fellow Alumni
one of their old Grammar School aphorisms—

" Multorum cúm facta Senex et dicta recenses,
Fac tibi succurrant, Juvenis quæ feceris ipse."

DEPRECIATION OF AMERICAN PAPER MONEY.

In the *Glasgow Herald* there is a quotation from the "World,"
regarding the present depreciation of American paper money, by
which it appears that in the States "1000 dollars, a year ago, were
equal to 1400 dollars of paper money to-day," and further, that
"the prices of merchandise of all descriptions are raised from 25 to
50 per cent. higher than they were one year ago."

There can be no doubt that, if the war continues for a few years,
that the above-mentioned depreciation will only be "the beginning
of the end" (as elsewhere remarked by you), and this may be clearly
shown from the following extracts, exhibiting the gradual depreciation of American currency which took place towards the close of the
War of Independence, and which may again happen to our American brethren before a final settlement of their disputes can be
arranged.

An inspection of the following tables will explain the cause of so
many of our Glasgow American Houses of my early days having
been ruined by the result of the War of Independence which began
in 1776, and ended with the peace of 1783. Our present American
merchants should take warning from the past, and carefully calculate
on what may again come to pass:—

"*Glasgow Mercury*, 29th March, 1781.—The province of South
Carolina, being now happily restored to Government, and peace and
tranquillity established, Lord Cornwallis, as one of the first salutary
works of the new Government, has appointed a Board of Commissioners 'to ascertain the progressive depreciation of the paper
currency, issued by the usurpers in that province, and by the Continental Congress.'

"The Commission sets forth that the debtors had taken the
advantage of this depreciation by discharging their bonds and other
pecuniary securities that were made and entered into for *gold* and
silver, or lawful currency of the province, by which their creditors
were defrauded of their just dues. To prevent disputes and litigation that may arise, touching the discharge 'of those bonds and
pecuniary obligations, this Commission is appointed.'

"The Commissioners begin with January, February, and March,
1777, when there was the first appearance of this depreciation; and,
from the average of these three months of the exchange of specie
for Congress dollars among traders, they fix the depreciation on
April 1st, 1777, at 113¼ per cent.

"The Commissioners go on taking the average of every three months in 1777, and of every two months after; and by their tables it appears that—

January 1, 1778, the depreciation was	. .	287¼ per cent.
January 1, 1779, " "	. .	1000 "
January 1, 1780, " "	. .	3833¼ "
April 1, " "	. .	11,000 "

"In May, 1780, they could find no proof of any *gold* or *silver* being bought or sold, and here they close their commission at the amazing depreciation of 11,000 per cent.

"The Commissioners also proceed to ascertain the depreciation of produce during the usurpation, and the following will show some of the most remarkable instances of their inquiries. It is extracted from the tables as published, and signed by the Commissioners at Charleston, December 19, 1780:—

	Jan. 1, 1777.		Jan. 1, 1779.		May, 1780.
Rice per cent., .	. £3 5 5	...	£5 16 5	...	£162 10 0
Flour per cent., .	. 4 5 9	...	37 10 0	...	500 0 0
Butter per lb., .	. 0 4 0	...	1 10 7	...	48 15 0
Tallow per lb., .	. 0 3 9	...	1 6 8	...	9 15 0
Cattle per head, .	. 18 18 0	...	125 0 0	...	975 0 0
Calves do, .	. 7 10 0	...	48 5 0	...	229 10 0
Sheep do., .	. 4 0 0	...	27 10 0	...	153 0 0
Hoggs do., .	. 3 0 0	...	40 0 0	...	325 0 0
Corn per bushel, .	1 1 4	...	3 10 0	...	65 0 0
Firewood per cord, .	4 15 0	...	16 0 0	...	262 10 0

"The Commissioners occasionally add some sensible and judicious remarks and explanations, and at the end of their tables are observations on Bills of Exchange, the quantity of dollars current, and other matters that were any way connected with their commission; and, upon the whole, they appear to have had a very laborious task of it, and to have spared no pains or abilities to complete it in a manner that does them great honour both as good citizens and men of business."

It appears, however, from the following quotation, that at this time the depreciation of American paper money was not so great in the State of Virginia as in the State of South Carolina, which perhaps may be accounted for by the circumstance of Virginia being then the great tobacco growing district of America, and the principal mart of our old Virginia lords, whose bills of exchange were everywhere in high repute :—

" Glasgow Mercury, 24th June, 1784.

" Scale of depreciation of the paper money in the State of Virginia.

Date,	1777	1778	1779	1780	1781
January,	1¼	4	8	42	75
February,	1½	5	10	45	80
March,	2	5	10	50	90
April,	2¼	5	16	60	100
May,	2½	5	20	60	150
June,	2¼	5	20	65	200
July,	3	5	21	65	400
August,	3	5	22	.70	500
September,	3	5	24	72	600
October,	3	5	28	73	700
November,	3	6	36	74	800
December,	4	6	40	75	1000

It may be curious to look back to the position of America at the period in question, and to see how closely the state of America at present resembles it in many other respects besides that in the matter of depreciated paper currency. The following extract is taken from a treatise called " Common Sense," published at the close of the War of Independence by the celebrated Thomas Paine, for which the Congress voted him a grant of land. Every word of this article may now be aptly applied to the present condition of America :—

" Common Sense," page 30.—" The present state of America is truly alarming to every man who is capable of reflection. Without law, without government, without any other mode of power than what is founded on and granted by courtesy, held together by an unexampled concurrence of sentiments, which is nevertheless subject to change, and which every secret enemy is endeavouring to dissolve. Our present condition is—legislation without law, wisdom without a plan, a constitution without a name, and what is strangely astonishing, perfect independence contending for dependence. The instance is without a precedent—the case never existed before, and who can tell the event ? The property of no man is secure in the present unbraced system of things ; the mind of the multitude is left at random; and, seeing no fixed object before them, they pursue such as fancy or opinion starts. Nothing is criminal ; there is no such thing as treason; wherefore every one thinks himself at liberty to act as he pleases. Notwithstanding our wisdom there is a visible feebleness in some of our proceedings which gives encouragement to dissensions; the continental belt is too loosely buckled, and if something is not done in time it will be too late to do anything, and we shall fall into a state in which neither *reconciliation nor independence* will be practicable. It is easy getting into holes and corners and talking of reconciliation, but do such men seriously consider how difficult the task is, and how dangerous it may prove should the Continent divide thereon? Do they take within their view all the various orders of men whose situations and circumstances, as well as their own, are to be considered therein? Do they put themselves in the place of the sufferer whose *all* is already *gone*, and of the soldier who hath quitted *all* for the defence of his country? If their ill-judged moderation be suited to their own private situations only, regardless of others, the event will convince them ' that they are reckoning without their host.' "

" Mercury, 13th May, 1784."

" Taxes in the State of Virginia for 1784.—10s per annum on
" each slave under 21 years; 20s on each slave above 21 years; 20s
" on each white man; 4d per head on all black cattle ; 25s on each
" horse. Each covering horse, 8d per mare; 1½d per cent. on annual
" value of lands. Each billiard table, £50 per annum. Besides
" poor rates, road money, &c., which used formerly to be paid.
" Taxes upon foreign commodities.—33s 4d on all rum and wine
" per 100 gallons; sugar of all kinds, 4s 2d per cwt. ; coffee, 8s 4d
" per cwt. ; cordage, 1s per cwt. ; snuff, 1s per lb. One per cent. on
" dry goods; 25 per cent. discount if you import the money. 1s 3d
" per ton on each foreign ship."

FIRST AMERICAN AMBASSADOR TO LONDON.

" *Glasgow Mercury,* 16th June, 1785.—Last week a circumstance
" happened, the most humiliating to this country that ever we
" beheld. Although we cannot say that this broke in upon us by
" surprise, we being sufficiently prepared to meet it; yet what true
" lover of his country is there who did not feel a speechless pang,
" when he heard that The Ambassador from the United States of
" America, had had an audience with his Britannic Majesty!
" To be resigned under this stroke is not easy. Those wretches
" whose misconduct and blunders have brought us to this pass, have

" now completed their triumph, and they may continue for the
" remainder of a life (long since forfeited to justice) to insult the
" feelings of a depressed national spirit."

"*Mercury*, 16th June, 1785."

" Mr Adams, the American Ambassador, was so embarrassed
" at his first audience as not to pronounce the compliments pre-
" scribed by etiquette.   The great person (George III.) before whom
" he stood, very good naturedly passed by the omission, and told
" him, that though it could not be a pleasing circumstance to
" receive an embassy from those who were once his subjects, yet as
" the right was insured to them by treaty, he, Mr Adams, might
" depend on being treated with every mark of regard and protec-
" tion."

N.B.—It was thought by many at the time that the omission of
court etiquette by Mr Adams, on his first introduction to his
Majesty, was a premeditated act, and had not arisen from any want
of knowledge of the usual court forms ; but that the omission of
them by the ambassador would be pleasing to the Americans, and
show off the Yankee spirit of liberty and equality.

Immediately after the commencement of the French revolutionary
war in 1793, the following proclamation was issued by the United
States of America :—

" *Scots Magazine*, 1793, page 297."—" A proclamation is issued
" by the President of the United States, April 22d, intimating that
" they were to remain strictly neutral, and to pursue a conduct
" friendly and impartial towards the belligerent powers.

" Any of the subjects of the States who shall be aiding or abetting
" hostilities against any of the powers at war, or by carrying to
" them, or any of them, those articles that are deemed contraband
" by the modern usage of nations, will not receive the protection of
" the United States.."

N.B.—This is precisely the rule which the British Government
has adopted with regard to the belligerents of North and South
America.

" *Glasgow Advertiser*, 10th February, 1794."

" The whole expenditure of the American States on all establish-
" ments, civil and military, did not amount in the last year to
" £180,000.

A FRENCH PROPHECY REGARDING AMERICA.

The following French prophecy, uttered a century ago, regarding the American New Englanders, is so characteristic of their descendants, the modern Federalists, that it appears at present to show them off quite *quasi in speculo* :—

On the 10th of February, 1763, a treaty of peace was concluded between the Kings of Great Britain, France, and Portugal, by which, *inter alia*, the King of France " cedes and guarantees to his Britannic Majesty, in full right, CANADA, with all its dependencies, as well as the Island of Cape Breton, and all the other islands and coasts in the Gulph and River of St Lawrence, and in general everything that depends on the said countries, lands, islands, and coasts, with the sovereignty, property, possession, and all rights acquired by treaty or otherwise, which the most Christian King and the Crown of France have had till now over the said countries, islands, lands, places, coasts, and their inhabitants."

In the London newspapers, of 12th July, 1775, we have the following anecdote :—

" When the last peace was negotiating at Paris (1762), the Duke de Choiseul was Minister of France ; and some of the Cabinet, who wanted to supplant him, found great fault at the facility with which he ceded the Province of Canada to the King of Great Britain. They exclaimed that it was disgraceful in the highest degree to surrender the whole Continent of America to the English, and made such a clamour on the subject that his most Christian Majesty at last spoke of it to the Duke.

" Sire," returned Choiseul, " we have now but one Province of Canada on the whole Continent of America, and the charge of maintaining it against such powerful neighbours as the English will not only exceed its value to us but will open a door of perpetual hostility with England, whereas ceding it at once to his Britannic Majesty will prevent these inconveniences, and find constant employment for the British nation; for, give me leave to tell you, Sire, that if the English Ministry had as much wisdom as they ought to have, they would almost pay your Majesty a subsidy to retain it in your hands. Their colonies are now *all flourishing*, and will speedily be *all insolent*. They want the protection of the mother country no longer than while Canada is ours. They have for several years manifested a strong inclination of independence, and will assert that independency the moment a foreign enemy is removed from their back. The provinces particularly which go by the name of *New England* are peopled by a set of hypocrites, descended from the fanatics who murdered their prince in the seventeenth century; and they retain in a peculiar manner all that abhorrence to monarchical government which characterised the Regicides, their ancestors. My advice, therefore, Sire, most humbly is that the *mastiffs* may have full liberty to worry one another; so long as Canada belongs to your Majesty, so long the British Colonies will be dutiful to their Sovereign, because they will stand in need of his protection, but remove the want of that protection, and you remove their obedience instantly. From powerful friends you turn them into the most *formidable enemies* of England, and rescue all Europe from the spirit of dictation which has rendered the English so long intolerable as a people."

There can be no doubt but Canada in possession of Great Britain has long been a thorn in the sides of the Federalists; and, accordingly, we find them, upon every petty difference with this country, loudly sounding a crusade against Canada, and threatening to seize it as an easy prey; but supposing they were to acquire it, the acquisition, according to Choiseul's prophecy, would only tend to a further secession, and to a splitting of the Union into various independent States.

FIRST TRADER BETWEEN GLASGOW AND BELFAST,

AND FIRST VESSEL THAT PASSED THROUGH THE GREAT CANAL FROM SEA TO SEA; ALSO, FIRST SPANISH PRIZE.

YOUR readers of late have received various interesting notices regarding the early steamers which plied on the river Clyde, but none of your correspondents have given us any information as to the first sea-going vessel direct from the Broomielaw to Ireland. I have looked over a long list of vessels advertised to sail from the Clyde, during my early years; and the following advertisement is the first notice of a Glasgow trader sailing direct from the Broomielaw to England or Ireland which I have found :—

"*Glasgow Mercury*, 26th February, 1784.—For Belfast. The sloop Peggy, John Mun, master, will be ready first spring tides to take in goods at Glasgow. For freight or passage, apply to John Girvin, Broomielaw."

The following notice may perhaps be interesting to many of your readers :—

"*Glasgow Mercury*, 21st September, 1790.—On the 31st ult., passed through the Great Canal the sloop Agnes, belonging to Port-Glasgow, built at Leith for the herring fishing and coasting trade, upwards of 80 tons burthen, being the first vessel that ever went from sea to sea by the canal ; and on Thursday the 9th inst., the sloop Mary M'Ewan arrived at Grangemouth from Greenock, being the first vessel that passed through the canal from Clyde since it was opened from sea to sea."

"Glasgow, 7th August, 1783.—On Saturday last, the American brigantine Fly, Captain Brown, arrived in the Clyde, from Edington, North Carolina, with tobacco, after a passage of 37 days. She is the first vessel from America which has arrived in this port since the Peace."

The first American prize was brought into Greenock in August, 1776, being the schooner Betsey, of Massachusetts, taken by the Otter sloop of war.

"*Glasgow Mercury*, 18th May, 1780.—Yesterday 60 tierces of French brandy were discharged at the Broomielaw, out of the Triton, Thomas Martindale, master, from Dublin, for which the duties were paid at the Custom House and Excise in this city, being the first importation at this place since it became a port of entry," &c.

In the spring of 1816, James Finlay & Co. dispatched the ship Earl of Buckinghamshire, 600 tons burthen, to Calcutta, being the first vessel from Scotland bound to India direct.

"*Glasgow Mercury*, 21st September, 1780.—On Saturday last, the privateer Bellona, belonging to Glasgow, brought into Port-Glasgow the Spanish packet Cologn, Juan Antonio de la Bega, master, from Buenos Ayres to Corunna, with Government despatches. She fell in with her in latitude 40 north, longitude 33 west, and took her after a running engagement of about an hour and a quarter. The Cologn mounted 12 guns and 65 men. There was one man killed on board of the Bellona, and one wounded ; on board the Cologn, one killed, and the captain and three men wounded.

"This packet was carrying accounts to Spain of a rebellion in several provinces of South America, but the public mail was thrown overboard when she struck. However, there have been several letters and papers found on board."

OLD GLASGOW CELEBRITIES.

YOUR correspondents of late have taken notice of some of our old Glasgow celebrities, but there were several others regarding whom nothing has been said, who, notwithstanding, were well-known characters of my early days, and merit a corner of your paper in conjunction with those mentioned by your correspondents.

Amongst these were "Daft Davie" and "Creeping Kate." Daft Davie was not quite crazy, nor was he altogether *compos*, but just between the *twa*. Mrs Brown, the mother of Davie, though poor, was a most industrious decent woman, who lived in a back house in the Candleriggs. She took great pride in keeping Davie neat and clean, and in finding such payable employments for him as were suitable to one of impaired intellect. She would not suffer him to beg, although her means to support him were limited to the trifle which she could earn by her industry.

There were several letters of the alphabet which Davie could not pronounce ; in particular, he could never articulate the letter R nor the dipthong TH, and this defect often caused much merriment to those who conversed with him. Mrs Brown, Davie's mother, wishing him to learn the business of a shoemaker, sent him on trial to a shoemaker in the Candleriggs, where, after a short trial, he was obliged to abandon the trade, being found unfit to perform the finer parts of the work, and only capable of doing the cobbling parts.

At this time there was a lively young lady in Glasgow named Miss Fanny Marshall, a Glasgow beauty (who afterwards married Mr James Gray, a brother of the late Robert Gray, Esq. of Orchyard, jeweller). One day Miss Marshall, having called at the shoe shop where Davie was working, said to him in her usual lively style, "Davie, I am come for you to take the measure of my foot for a pair of shoes." On this, Davie, looking up in Miss Marshall's face, said—"Ah, bonnie Fanny Mesha, me eya [rather] tak' e meashu o oo mou." Lord Chesterfield himself could not have given a more complimentary answer.

As for Creeping Kate, I never could learn the history of this poor decrepit creature. She appeared to have lost nearly all use of her lower extremities, and *hirsled* along our footpaths, by means of an old shoe in one hand and another old shoe on one foot. By means of these, serving her as a pair of oars, she trailed and shuffled along the streets upon her haunches in all weathers, her tattered petticoat being constructed so as to defy all rain, dirt, and draggling. She was really a miserable object; but although she did not beg, nevertheless she thankfully received any little pittance that happened to be presented to her. While Kate was crawling and creeping along our pavements, every person from pity gave way to her, seeing such a deplorable and defenceless piece of humanity. Kate's face was coarse, masculine, and haggard, and the stare of her eye was like that of an enraged cat. However singular the appearance of Kate was, the boys never attempted to make game of her, or to disturb her in her perambulations through the streets.

I hope that some of your octogenarian readers may be able to give a better history of this remarkable female than I can.

Your correspondents have given us an account of Dugald Graham, but none of them have quoted the following notice, by which it appears that Dugald was unhappy in his domestic establishment :—

" *Glasgow Journal*, 14th June, 1764.—Notice. Whereas, Jean Stark, spouse to Dugald Graham, ale seller, above the Cross, Glasgow, has parted from her husband, he thinks it proper to inform the public that she be inhibit by him from contracting debt in his name, or yet receiving any debt due to him, after this present day.—June 14, 1764."

About eighty years ago, by far the most dashing belle in Glasgow was Miss Sophia Ramsay, daughter of Andrew Ramsay, Esq., one of our old tobacco lords, who was lord provost of Glasgow in 1734 and 1735. Sophia was a fine sprightly girl, but was rather too fond of dress and show. She associated very little with the mercantile class of Glasgow gentlemen, giving an open and decided preference to officers of the army, with whom she delighted to parade the Trongate and Argyle Street, showing off her handsome person, and exhibiting it to the greatest advantage side by side of a red coat. When Sophia began to get rather oldish for attracting notice, our ancient dames used to say that she might have had a choice of lovers among the young men of Glasgow in business, but that she had missed her market by frittering away the most valuable time of her life in vain show and glitter, thereby deservedly becoming an old maid. The following acrostic was published in the *Glasgow*

Journal of 28th November, 1782, when Sophia was shining peerless in all her glory as first belle of Glasgow :—

"VERSES ADDRESSED TO A YOUNG LADY BY HER SINCERE, THOUGH
UNKNOWN, ADMIRER.

" Struck with your charms, so radiant, so divine,
Oh lovely maid ! I bow before your shrine ;
Pleased in my bondage, happy in my pain,
How can I wish my freedom to regain ?
In silent murmur let me vent my sighs,
And drink my poison from your killing eyes.

Resistless charms sit smiling on your face,
And blooming sweetness marks its every trace ;
Modest each look, and innocent each smile ;
Skilled in no prudish or coquettish wile.
Adoring men are slaves unto your will :
You look to conquer, and you smile to kill."

HIRSLING KATE.

To the Editor of the Glasgow Herald.

SIR,—Reading, as I always do, with great pleasure, the communications of your venerable correspondent, " Senex," I was happy to have awakened to my recollection a very juvenile reminiscence of one of the " Old Glasgow Celebrities" mentioned by him in his paper in the *Herald* of this date—I mean the poor cripple, Hirsling Kate. I am yet, happily, far from being an octogenarian ; and although it is from readers of that age that he hopes to receive additional information regarding the history of this remarkable female, yet I have a very distinct recollection of frequently seeing Kate as she painfully dragged her body past my father's house in Anderston Walk, on her way homewards from the city. I recognise " Senex's" description as minutely correct, although it is many years since a thought of Kate has passed through my mind. The only part awanting in his description is the rows of pins which she always had stuck into the breast of her dress. These pins were the gifts of juveniles like myself to Kate, in return for which she would sing a verse or verses of a song. I have often had the pleasure of giving Kate a pin, and getting in return the usual reward. One verse of Kate's song has stuck to my memory almost from childhood, and was in the following words, sung in low plaintive tones, which I can yet imitate :—

" The cuckoo sits on yonder tree,
  He sings a song that pleases me ;
  He sings a song that pleases me well,
  I wish I were where the cuckoo doth dwell."

I have frequently followed Kate from the neighbourhood of what is now Pitt Street to her own house, which was a small stone building on the western slope of Cranston Hill, placed inside the hedge that formed the boundary of that property, and situated nearly half-way down from the Dumbarton Road, in what is called Finnieston Street at the present day. Cranston Hill House was, at the time I speak of, inhabited by Lady Janet Buchanan and her husband ; and I think it likely that poor Kate owed her lodging to the kindness of that benevolent lady. With the exception of the above personal recollections, I am sorry I cannot add more to the history of the unfortunate woman, whose miserable appearance is one of the earliest of my boyish recollections, and the association, as connected with the words which I have quoted from her song, is by no means an unpleasant one.—I am, yours,

J. R. M.

Glasgow, 18th April, 1863.

P.S.—I have not noticed, either in the interesting papers read by Sheriff Strathern before the Archæological Society, or in the *Memorabilia Glasguensia* of " Senex," any reference to a character who was the terror of the boys of my day, called by the significant name of " Thunder Jack." He was a fierce and desperate fellow, within the range of whose crutch no one was willing to approach. If his stroke was luckily missed, no one who annoyed Jack escaped the profane sally of his wicked tongue. He was a man of a powerful frame, but dragged his left limb trailing on the ground. If I recollect aright, it was powerless from the hip joint. He had the use of the right leg, and by the aid of it and a short crutch he creeped along the ground. He appeared to have been a man-of-war's man, from his dress, and the liberal use of tobacco, which he constantly chewed. It is fully thirty years since I last saw him.

J. R. M.

CANDLERIGGS STREET IN 1760.

No street in Glasgow has undergone a greater change in the course of those last hundred years than Candleriggs. With the exception of an old tenement of two storeys, the whole street has been rebuilt, including the Ramshorn Church and its spire. Even the said old tenement, situated a little to the north of Wilson's Street, has been so altered and modernized that it may be said to have been renewed.

The present rough sketch of Candleriggs, as the street stood in 1760, shows the sites of the principal buildings then existing in the locality, all of which were in being in my day, and are well remembered by me, having been born and brought up in the north part of the said street.

The Guard-house at the south west corner of Candleriggs Street, has been often described by our Glasgow historians, but none of them have stated the exact date of its erection. From an advertisement in the *Glasgow Journal*, of 11th October, it appears that in 1756, the Old Guard-house of the city stood in the "Weel Close," (now St Andrew's open from Saltmarket), and that on its being then demolished, the Guard-house at the corner of Candleriggs and Trongate was built in lieu of the one so taken down.

The Guard-house of the sketch was a coarse building of two storeys, with a Piazza, supported by four Ionic columns, with their entablature. It projected about ten feet upon the line of the Trongate, and was raised about a foot above the level of the street. The soldier when on guard marched backwards and forwards within this portico, and would not suffer any citizen to trespass upon it. The ground floor consisted of one large apartment flagged with stone, having an inside stair leading to the upper storey. In this upper storey there was an apartment fitted up for the officer on duty, and also a store room; but the place altogether was kept in a dirty condition.

"*Glasgow Journal*, 21st March, 1787.—Notice.—That the Guard-
"house, old weigh house, and old fish market belonging to the city
"of Glasgow, upon the west side of the Candleriggs Street of
"Glasgow, are jointly to be exposed to public roup and sale in
"the Laigh Council Chamber of Glasgow, upon the 25th day of
"April next, between the hours of 12 and 2 of the day. The
"articles of roup are in the hands of the town-clerks."

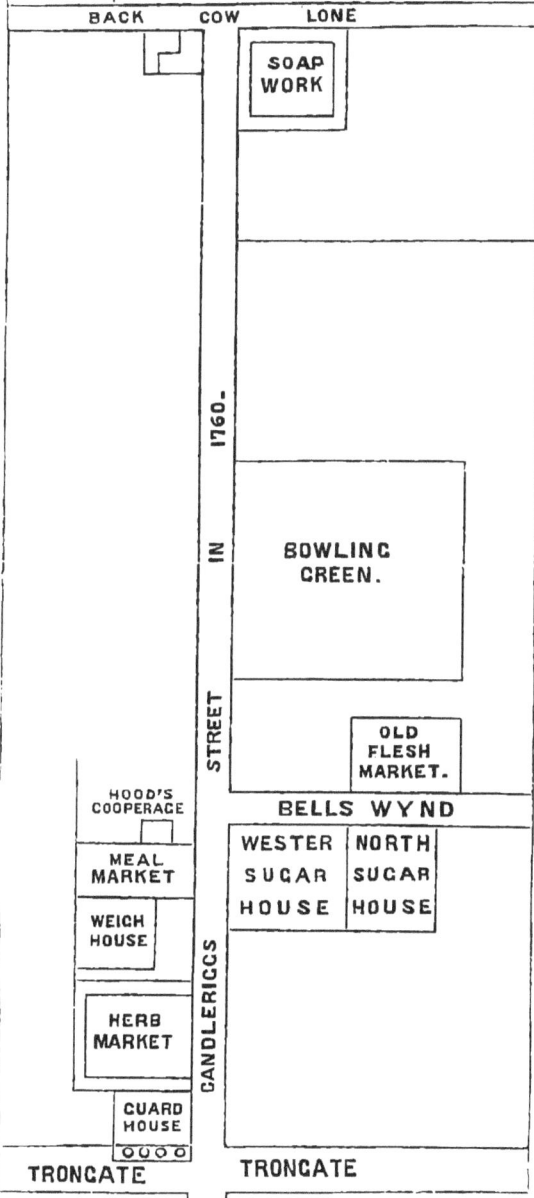

CANDLERIGGS IN 1760.

On the site of this Guard-house the present large corner tenement was erected by Mr James M'Illhose, convener in 1791-2, whose son changed the family name to "Hozier." The *Herald* newspaper establishment was removed from Bell Street, to the back premises of this new building. Its court is called "Post Office Court," from the Post Office having been there at one time. The Messrs Watson occupied part of the premises for their banking business, and another part of them was taken by a congregation of the Jewish persuasion, for a synagogue. Henry Hemming, an Englishman, rented the floors above the shops as an hotel.

To the north of the Guard-house in the Candleriggs was situated the Herb or Green Market. It was about 160 feet in length, having a course ruble wall fronting the street, with an entrance door near each extremity, and altogether was a copy of the King Street markets, but got up on cheap principles. On market days the space of the street opposite the Herb Market, was used for the sale of kail and cabbage plants, and the like.

"*Glasgow Journal*, 6th September, 1756.—Whereas, great com-
" plaints have been made to the magistrates of the oppression
" which the poor suffer, by persons buying up meal and other vivers,
" before it is brought to the market, or before market time; and
" also by buying up quantities of meal and other vivers in the
" market, in order to sell the same in their shops at a higher price;
" and also by laying up and concealing the same in cellars, and
" withholding the same from the public market, to the great oppres-
" sion of the poor, in this time of dearth. These are therefore
" advertising, That the magistrates have ordered another *public*
" market, for selling and retailing meal, in that place in Candleriggs,
" which was formerly the Fish Market, to be immediately opened,
" and requiring and inviting all victuallers and meal merchants, to
" repair and carry their meal thereto, or to the present public
" market, to be sold and retailed at the current market prices; and
" as the said market in Candleriggs is to be kept open every lawful
" day, from eight o'clock forenoon, to eight o'clock at night, for the
" retail of meal; these are requiring that all concerned do bring
" their meal and victual to the said market for sale, and not there-
" after to be carried forth thereof, but there to be left and to remain
" until it is fully retailed; and that none keep up or conceal meal
" and other victual intended for sale (accustomed in the market to
" be sold), in their own houses, cellars, or other places in their pos-
" session; with certification, That all and every person who shall be

2 F

" convicted of the same will be prosecuted by the magistrates, and
" fined and punished as forestallers and regraters, in terms of law."
N.B.—The magistrates of Glasgow who issued the above curious
notice were,

George Murdoch, lord provost.
Robert Christie, bailie, American merchant.
James Spreull,   do.,   merchant,
James Whytlaw, do.,   saddler.

Next to the Herb Market, towards the north, and standing a
little back from the line of the street, was the public Weigh-house—
a clumsy building like a large shed, with a high roof, and similar to
many of our carriers' quarters.

In 1789, the Weigh-house was removed from the Candleriggs to
the east side of Montrose Street, next Ingram Street, and on its
site was built a Guard-house, with the materials of the one shown
on the annexed sketch. This Guard-house was merely a copy of
the former one, but the Portico was placed in a line with the street,
and closed at each end.

In 1810, this last Guard-house was removed from the Candleriggs, and another erected in its place, on the east side of Montrose
Street, next to the newly built Weigh-house.

The Herb Market was removed in 1808, to the site of the Wynd
Church, off King Street, when the congregation of that church were
translated to St George's Church—and at the same time the Meal
Market was taken down. In 1812, the Weigh-house in Montrose
Street was let for £365 per annum, being 20s per diem.

" *Glasgow Journal,* 4th December, 1758.—By order of the magis-
" trates of Glasgow.—Whereas, the Gardeners in Glasgow are now
" in possession of the New Green Mercate, fitted up by the magis-
" trates, for selling of all roots, fruits, herbs, and other produce of
" garden ground; these are therefore intimating to all the inhabi-
" tants of this city and other lieges, that they repair to the said
" green mercate for buying their garden goods; and these are also
" strictly prohibiting and discharging all and every person and persons
" whomever, from selling or exposing to sale, any roots, fruits, herbs, or
" other produce of garden grounds, upon the public streets or any
" other public place within the city, but in the said green mercate,
" under all pains of law."

The cooperage to the north of the Meal Market belonged to the
old Glasgow family of " Hoods." Andrew Hood was deacon of the

coopers in 1780; John Hood, deacon in 1793, and Robert Hood, bailie of Glasgow in 1814-15. After the markets in the Candleriggs were taken down, Bailie Hood removed his cooperage to the site of the present bazaar, situated between the bowling green and soap work. This cooperage formerly belonged to Robert Young, deacon in 1773. He was the father of Archibald Young, surgeon, and grandfather of the late Archibald Young, writer.

I remember old Mr Young occupying the said premises, which, however, were not very extensive. I think that Bailie Hood, or his heirs, sold this property to the magistrates of Glasgow.

Immediately opposite to Bell Street, there was a property belonging to the heirs of James Scruton, writing master, consisting of a front and back tenement, with a court between them. When Wilson Street was first projected, Robert Smith, builder, wished to purchase this property, so as to have carried Wilson Street westward on the same line as Bell Street, but the price demanded being considered too high, Mr Smith altered his original plan, and formed the entrance from Candleriggs to Wilson Street, a little to the north of Messrs Scruton's property. This spot consisted of some old houses and an open court, fronting the Candleriggs, with a public well in its centre. There was no thoroughfare from this court to the west; but it led to the property of Robert Smith, builder, which extended as far back as the present Brunswick Street. Wilson's Charity School was situated on the north side of this court, and gave its name to the street.

The following advertisement shows the state of this property one hundred years ago, and is a notable example of the change of times in Glasgow.

"*Glasgow Journal*, 13th September, 1764.—To be sold, by " public roup, within the house of Mrs Armour, vintner, upon the " seventh day of November next, A tenement of land, consisting of " shops, dwelling house, cellar, and garrets, with a yeard, coal-cellar, " a milnhouse and ten weavers' loom shops, lying at the back of the " same. All situate immediately at the back of the Candleriggs " well. Apply to John Millar, maltman, or James Todd, mer- " chant."

From the following advertisement it appears, that previous to the erection of the markets in King Street, in the year 1754, the Fish Market was held in the Meal Market of the sketch annexed to this.

"*Mercury*, 22d November, 1781.—To be sold, by public roup, on

" the 5th of December next, &c.—That laigh house and shop in
" Candleriggs, which belonged to the deceased Robert Young, being
" the 3d above the old fish market, same side of the street. Apply
" to Th. & Rt. Graham, writers."

The most fashionable house in the Candleriggs was built by Mr
Dunlop, a partner of the Dumbarton Class Work Company. It
was a miniature copy of the "Shawfield Mansion," with a double
stair projecting into the street and occupying the foot path. It
stood opposite the north end of the bowling green, but its immediate neighbourhood was very bad, for, on the south of it there was
a common smith's shop fronting the street, daily at work, and on
the north it had for its next neighbours old decayed tenements
with wooden fronts, and thatch roofs.

After Mr Dunlop's death, about 1780, it was first occupied as a
store, and afterwards let as a dwelling house, to Mrs Brown, of
Langside. The hay loft above the stables in the back court, was
let to Mr John Lang, dean of faculty of the Glasgow Procurators,
for his writing office, and in this hay loft the late John Fleming,
Esq., writer, served his apprenticeship.

Any person standing upon the stair head of this house, at the
entrance door, had a full view, over the wall of the bowling green,
of those who were engaged at the game of bowls. This was a great
annoyance to Mrs Brown, as her stair head was daily crowded with
idle children amusing themselves upon it, and looking at the bowling gamesters when at their sport.

Between Mr Dunlop's house and the corner tenement of the
street there were a few old decayed houses, some of which had
wooden fronts, thatched roofs, and outside stairs.

The corner tenement, as shown on the Plan, was a respectable
ancient building of three storeys, having Dutch gables and corby
steps, and a double front; the principal one fronting the Candleriggs, and the other facing the Back-cowloan. The offices, with
cellars, stables, and hay-loft, &c., were situated in the back court,
to which there was an entry from the Back-cowloan.

When the Candleriggs was opened in the year 1724, this tenement appeared to have formed the north-west corner of the street,
but previously to that date, it probably was the country mansion of
one of our wealthy citizens, standing on the line of the then direct
rural highway, leading westward from the Cathedral, by way of
Bun's Wynd, Shuttle Street, and Canon Street, till it joined the
Main Cowloan in Queen Street.

On a stone in the back wall of this house, there was the following inscription:—

"BLESSIT BE YE LORD OVR GOD FOR ALL HIS GIFTS.—1597."

So that this said ancient mansion house must have existed 127 years before the Candleriggs Street was opened. This stone is preserved, and is now placed in the back wall of the present corner tenement of the street, immediately above the entrance from the Candleriggs to the back court of the building.

"*Glasgow Mercury*, 23d July, 1778.—To be sold.—That large " tenement of land with the stables, whole cellars and offices at the " back thereof, lying upon the west corner, between the Candleriggs " and the Back-cowlone Street, opposite to the north-west church, " and over-looks the Ramshorn Gardens. Also, these three shops, " situated below the corner house, betwen King's Street and Gibson's " Wynd, two whereof possessed by John Phillips, and James Aird, " and one facing Gibson's Wynd, lately possessed by Robert Wal- " lace, surgeon.* Apply to Archibald Grahame, or Joseph Crombie, " writers in Glasgow."

With regard to Canon Street, Denholm, at page 132, says:— " That this street was so called from the scite of a seminary of " canons regular, that formerly stood immediately to the north." The name, however, is of modern date, for, in my early days, it was generally known by its original name of the "Back-cowloan," it forming part of the west country road, from Shuttle Street to Queen Street. M'Ure calls it the "Grammar School Wynd," and the Candleriggs the "New Street," but says nothing about the buildings on these streets.

The North-west or Ramshorn Church, situated at the northern extremity of the Candleriggs, was erected by the town, in 1720, and opened in 1721. The Rev. John Anderson, father of Professor John Anderson, was the first minister; he was translated from Dumbarton in 1720.

Denholm, at page 167, thus writes:—"This church is well lighted " by several very large windows that run from very near the level " of the ground to the pediment, circular at the top, and divided " perpendicularly by stone pillars. It is also ornamented with "lustres, and a clock in the front of the gallery, opposite the pulpit.

---

* John Phillips, afterwards of Stobcross, was a grocer, his daughter, Polly, was Dr Rae Wilson's first wife. James Aird was the principal music dealer in Glasgow, and Robert Wallace was at the top of his profession as a medical man.

" From the front towards the south, rises a square tower with a
" balustrade, and four dial-plates. Above this the steeple contracts
" its square, and one storey from the balustrade terminates in a
" handsone ogee roof, covered with lead, and a gilt fane or weather-
" cock placed at the height of 140 feet from the ground."

M'Ure, at page 285, says, "That the stately and magnificent
structure, the North-west Church, lies at the head of the New Street,
in a pleasant valley, and is of length 27 ells, from east to west, and
in breadth, at the west end, 26 ells. It is illuminated with curious
shorn windows, and a fine roof curiously painted, and is beautified
with a stately high steeple, one hundred and forty-one feet high."

According to M'Ure (page 281) the soap work shown on the Plan,
and situated at the north-east corner of the Candleriggs, was erected
in 1667, consequently, it must have been built upon what was then
the Back-cowloan or country-road, among corn fields, for my grandmother, who was born in 1715, told us that she remembered the
Candleriggs and its neighbourhood being under the usual hus-
bandry of the plough. M'Ure further says that there were nine
partners concerned in this establishment, each of whom advanced
£1500 sterling of capital—certainly a large sum in those days.

Mr Pagan, in his Glasgow, at page 78, says:—" An advertisement
from this company appeared in the *Glasgow Courant*, on the 11th
November, 1715, being the first advertisement in the first newspaper
published in the West of Scotland, intimating, 'that any one who
wants black or speckled soap, may be served by Robert Luke,
manager of the soaperie of Glasgow at reasonable terms.' The
soaperie then stood at the head of Candleriggs."

This was an extensive building, and consisted of a large square,
having erections on each side of it, and an open court in the centre.
The north and east compartments were occupied in the manufacture
of the soap, and the south and west parts of the building were laid
out in cellars and storehouses. The manager's dwelling house was
in the first storey of the range fronting the Candleriggs, the entry
to it being from the inside court, by an outside stair. The building
was closed in upon all the four sides, and the general entry to the
works was by way of the Candleriggs, through a large arched gateway.

I went through these works about eighty years ago, and remarked
that the concern was languishing. There appeared only about half-
a-dozen of men employed, and these were clamping about the stone
floor in a very inactive manner, having heavy iron shoes upon their

feet. It was easy to be seen that they were working at days' wages.

The Commercial Buildings were erected on the site of this soaperie by William and James Carswell, builders, who also re-built a considerable portion of Candleriggs Street.

"*Glasgow Mercury*, 15th August, 1785."—"To be sold, by public roup, &c., The whole ground, buildings, and utensils, belonging to the Soap Work Company.

"This property, extending about 156 feet along the east side of the Candleriggs Street, and about 138½ feet along the south side of Canon Street, is very conveniently situated either for building, or manufacturers, being free from restrictions, to which most part of grounds, at present for sale, is subject to.

"Apply to John Maxwell of Dargavel, writer, or John Craig, merchant, Glasgow."

The Soap Work Company rented part of the ground immediately south of their works, next to which was the cooperage of Mr Young, already noticed, and then in continuation southward, there were some old buildings and vacant ground between the cooperage and the Bowling Green.

Dr Cleland, in his Annals, page 21, states—That about the year 1695, the town council of Glasgow disposed of a piece of ground in the Candleriggs to Mungo Cochran for a Bowling Green, with the express provision, that it should be kept as such in all time coming.

It was said in my early days that the family of Cochran, afterwards Earls of Dundonald, was of Glasgow origin, and that the family mansion house stood upon the south side of Canon Street, but I have seen no written evidence of this.

The Bowling Green was surrounded by a stone wall about eight feet in height, and although there was an entrance door from the Candleriggs it was always kept lock-fast, the regular entry to the Green being by a passage from Bell Street.

All along the front of the Bowling Green at Candleriggs there was a deep ditch, which was never cleaned, and consequently became a perfect nuisance pool filled with putrid "glar," and swarming with maggots.

Admission to the Green was given to any person upon payment of one penny; but, in my younger days, the smoke of the city had so injured the growth of the grass that in many parts the ground was without verdure, in consequence of which the resort of bowlers to it became so trifling that it was given up as a place of amusement, and sold. The magistrates of Glasgow having acquired right to the Bowling Green about the year 1816, have erected thereon the present Bazaar or public market.

From the following advertisement it appears that a century ago, the Bowling Green was the property of Richard and John Bell, through whose ancestors Bell Street received its name :—

"*Glasgow Journal*, 10th May, 1764."

"That all and hail that Green called the Bowling Green, lying on the north side of Bell's Wynd, with an entry thereto from the Candleriggs, and the back houses, office-houses, and others adjoining to the said Green, belonging to the proprietors thereof ; as also that tenement of land, high and laigh, back and fore, lying on the west side of the closs or entry to the said Bowling Green, all of which belonged to the deceased Richard Bell, merchant in Glasgow, and now to John Bell, his heir, are to be exposed to public roup and sale in different lots and parcels, within the house of Mrs Armour, at the Cross of Glasgow, upon the 17th of June, 1764, between the hours of twelve and two, mid-day.

"Apply to John Wardrop, writer in Glasgow."

The following notice refers to the Bowling Green Close, adjoining the present Police Buildings :—

"*Mercury*, 10th February, 1780.—To be sold, &c., A laigh back dwelling house, two cellars, and pertinents of the same, lying on the north side of Bell's Wynd, and upon the east side of the Bowling Green Close, as now possessed by William and James Watts. Apply to Jo. Wilson, jun., writer."

In my early days the corner shop of the Candleriggs and Bell Street was occupied by John Gardner, optician, who laid out the lands of Tradestown in 1790. To the east of Mr Gardner's shop there was an entry from Bell Street to a square back court, and from this court there was access to the different flats of the corner tenement by common inside stairs. The *Herald* Printing Office was in this court, also the dwelling houses of Provost M'Kenzie and of Bailie John Alston, whose sons, Douglas Alston, and Provost John Alston, were born in this tenement. The north front of the dwelling houses of the above-named gentlemen looked into the Bowling Green, there being no intervening erections between the two properties.

M'Ure, in his History of Glasgow, published in 1736, informs us at page 282, that, in his time, there were four sugar works in operation within the city, viz., 1st, The Wester, or Candleriggs Sugar Work; 2d, The Easter, or Gallowgate ditto; 3d, The South, or Stockwell ditto; 4th, The King's Street, ditto.

All these works continued to be carried on down to my day, but none of them appeared to me to be thriving concerns, and consequently they came to be abandoned, one after the other. The south, or Stockwell Sugar Work, was the last of them that was taken down, and on its site we have now " Stockwell Place."

M'Ure thus describes the Wester or Candleriggs Sugar House :—

" In the year 1667 began the Wester Sugar Work by four merchants, viz., Peter Gemmill, Frederick Hamilton, John Caldwell and Robert Cumings, merchants, who put in a joint stock for carrying on a sugar work, and having got a little apartment for boiling sugar, a Dutchman being master-boiler ; this undertaking proved effectual, and their endeavours wonderful successful, so that they left this little apartment, and built a great stone tenement, with convenient office houses for their work, within a great court, with a pleasant garden belonging thereto."

M'Ure makes no mention of the North Sugar House (exhibited on the Plan), which, on the east, adjoined the Wester Sugar House.

In my day these two works formed only one concern, and, hence, I conclude that the North Sugar House was built in the garden mentioned by M'Ure as an addition to the Wester Sugar Works.

The North Sugar House had a dead stone wall fronting Bell Street, and the entry to it was from the Candleriggs through the great back court of the Wester Sugar House. This court had a passage on the south, by which access was obtained to the court immediately behind the present warehouses of the Messrs Campbell in Candleriggs.

" *Glasgow Journal,* 7th November, 1782."—" To be sold by public roup," &c.—" The Sugar House, lying on the south side of Bell's Wynd, and fronting the same, known by the name of ' The North Sugar House,' with all the utensils belonging thereto, employed in the manufacturing raw sugars, with vacant ground or yard behind, on which is also built a new house. These buildings are all calculated in such a manner that they can be easily turned into good dwelling houses and shops at a small expense, if not continued as a sugar house, and the ground behind is of such extent as to afford sufficient room for building a regular square. There is also an entry to the Trongate through Dunbar's Closs, of singular advantage to the subject. Apply to Robert Barbour and George Household."

Mr George Household, above mentioned, had the charge of the sugar sample-room shortly after this erected behind the Tontine buildings; and upon being appointed to this charge, he appears to have sold his interest in the Sugar House to Mr Robert Barbour.

About this time, or shortly afterwards, the West or Candleriggs Sugar-house seems to have been sold to a Mr Schevis, while Mr Barbour retained the North Sugar House.

"*Mercury*, 1st August, 1787.—A Sugar House and area for building to be sold. The West Sugar House buildings, having a front of 104 feet to the Candleriggs Street, and 126 feet to Bell's Wynd Street. The grounds are well situated for building shops and warehouses on. Until sold, the business will be carried on as usual. For particulars, apply to Alex. Schevis."

"*Mercury*, 23d January, 1788.—Sugar House in Glasgow for sale. The North Sugar House, lying on the south side of Bell's Wynd, and fronting the same, with the vacant ground behind, on which is also a new house. The area is of such extent as to allow sufficient room for building upon both sides of the closs, through which there is an entry to the Trongate, by Dunbar's Closs, though the proprietors there have no right of entry through this subject to Bell's Wynd. Apply to Robert Barbour."

Dunbar's Closs, above mentioned, was the long closs in the Trongate opposite the Laigh Kirk Steeple, where the late Mr Joseph Baine kept the mail coach office.

With regard to the Bell Street Flesh Market, having given an article in "Glasgow, Past and Present," at page 88, I shall not repeat it here, but merely add one or two public notices respecting it from the Glasgow newspapers of the times.

"*Journal*, 18th April, 1757.—The Old Mutton Market, lying on the north side of Bell's Wynd Street, is to be exposed to sale, by public roup, on Thursday the 28th of April instant, within the Court Hall of the Tolbooth of Glasgow, between the hours of twelve and two o'clock mid-day. And at the same time and place, several of the trees in the New Green, as the same will be pitched out and marked by the magistrates. The terms of the roup may be seen in the town clerk's hands."

No sale of the Bell Street Market appears to have been effected at this time, as we find the magistrates again advertising as follows :—

" *Mercury*, 4th November, 1779.—The magistrates of this city having fitted up a market for country butchers in Bell's Wynd, the following regulations are to be observed:—The market is to be open on Wednesdays and Saturdays, and no other day ; and no butchers residing in town to be allowed to sell meat in it. Every person intending to have the benefit of this market to apply for leave to the inspector of police, and subscribe the regulations. The market dues must be paid regularly to the tacksman. No dogs are to be allowed in this market. Any butcher who attempts to bring bad or unwholesome meat, or to blow or put webs on his meat, will get it confiscated, and be turned out of the market. No carcases of beef to be allowed in the market, and therefore it must be cut into quarters before it is brought there. All unsold meat to be removed at night, and the stalls left clean by the butchers who occupied them through the day. This market will be opened on Wednesday next, the 10th current, after which no butcher meat will be suffered to be sold in the Candleriggs Market.—The Candleriggs Market, after Tuesday next, is to be kept entirely for a Potato Market, after which day all potatoes are required to be carried there, as none will be allowed in the Fish Market in King Street."

Shortly before this time, disputes having arisen between the magistrates and the country butchers, the magistrates had thereon shut up the Bell Street Market for the sale of butcher meat. The country butchers, in opposition thereto, appear to have carried their traffic to the entry leading to the Wynd Church in King Street. The magistrates, however, issued the following proclamation against this practice, and directed the Country Butcher Market to be held in the Candleriggs ; but the parties having come to some understanding, the Bell Street Market was again opened, in terms of the advertisement before stated.

" *Mercury*, 22d April, 1779.—By order of the magistrates of Glasgow. The magistrates having appointed the old Fish Market in Candleriggs for country butchers, ordain them after this day to sell their meat there, and discharge all persons from selling meat in the entry to the Wynd Church.—The magistrates discharge every person belonging to the market from keeping more than one dog, and that dog to have about his neck a collar, with the owner's name engraved on it."

No dogs, however, were allowed to run about in the Bell Street Mutton Market, and the butchers having stalls there were prohibited from selling beef, and confined to the sale of mutton, lamb, and veal.

Before the markets in King Street were built, in 1754, the Beef Market was held in the Candleriggs.

When the Bell Street Market was shut up, the magistrates let the place to a Mr Drummond, who was contractor for lighting the city lamps. Mr Drummond occupied it as a depository for storing his casks of train oil. On this site the Police Buildings were erected in 1810,* but since that time they have been greatly enlarged and improved, both towards the north and towards the west.

The houses in the Candleriggs, lying immediately south of the Sugar-house, consisted of common buildings of shops and houses upon the ground floors, and of houses on the upper flats. The house and shop next the Sugar-house was occupied in my time by a Mrs Miller, a dealer in meal and barley. She was generally called "Barley Miller," on account of being celebrated for keeping the best "pearl barley" in the city. Barley broth in those days formed a standing dish at the tables of all economical housewives, especially where there was a numerous family of children. Mrs Miller was quite a lady in her appearance and address, and was much respected by all ranks in Glasgow. It was then common for ladies in the best society of the city to attend to their husbands' affairs in the shop. Mrs Milller's house and shop stood upon the site of the Messrs Campbells' large establishment in the Candleriggs, and was opposite the public markets.

- Near the foot of the Candleriggs, and on the east side thereof, Mr Graham, baker, had his shop. He was the father of John Graham, commonly called "Lottery Graham," in consequence of his having fortunately obtained a prize in the Government lottery, which windfall he invested in buildings in George Street, known by the name of "Lottery Buildings." Mr Graham was well known in Glasgow as city marshal of the burgh, and acting as police master on all necessary occasions.

---

* Extract, Chapman's Glasgow, 128.—"The Guard House and Police Office—the former, erected in 1810, is a plain, convenient building, situated on the east side of the foot of Montrose Street: the latter was removed in the same year to the foot of South Albion Street, near its junction with Bell Street."

ORIGIN OF THE ROYAL BANK OF SCOTLAND.

I BELIEVE that I am the oldest customer now alive of the Glasgow Branch of the Royal Bank of Scotland, having commenced doing business there in 1793 as a manufacturer; so that I may say that I have enjoyed the benefit of the liberality of that establishment for the long space of threescore and ten years or thereby—viz., as the Psalmist says, " during the life of man."

Your very able and learned correspondent, J. B., has furnished us with some valuable and interesting articles regarding the origin of our Glasgow Banks, and, in addition thereto, I hope that the following notice of the origin of the Royal Bank of Scotland may prove acceptable to your mercantile readers. I therefore commence without further preface, by stating that, "By the Act 5, Geo. I., for settling certain yearly funds, to satisfy public debts in Scotland, and to discharge the equivalents claimed on behalf of Scotland in the terms of the treaty of Union, &c.," the King was empowered to incorporate into one body politic and corporate, by letters patent, under the great seal of Great Britain, all the proprietors of the debts due to the creditors of the public in Scotland, stated to amount to £248,550 0s. 9½d. sterling, with such powers as to his Majesty should seem meet concerning the said sum, which was to be the capital of the corporation, and concerning the sum of £10,000 sterling which the Act appointed to be paid annually from June 24th, 1719, to the proprietors of that capital, till it should be redeemed by Parliament.

Accordingly, by letters patent, dated November 21st, 1724 (11, Geo. I.), these proprietors were erected into a corporation by the name of "THE EQUIVALENT COMPANY." As some of them resided in Scotland, and some of them in England, the Company was to have one office in London, and another in Edinburgh; at either of which the proprietors, as they should respectively choose, were to book their stock, and to receive their shares of the aforementioned sum, and of the capital when redeemed, and stock was to be transferable from either to the other. The Company's affairs were to be under the management of thirteen directors.

This Company having by a petition humbly requested the King to give such of the proprietors as should subscribe their stock for that purpose a power of banking in Scotland, and to erect such subscribers into a corporation, his Majesty, by Royal warrant, dated May 31st, 1727 (13, Geo. I.), authorised the Directors of the *Equivalent Company* to receive such voluntary subscriptions as should be made at Edinburgh, on or before 29th September, 1727, by any of the proprietors of all or any part of their share of stock in that Company, and authorised those who should so subscribe, to be one body politic and corporate, with perpetual succession by the name of " THE ROYAL BANK OF SCOTLAND," to have the rights and powers of banking in Scotland ! The corporation's affairs to be under the management of a governor, a deputy-governor, and nine ordinary and nine extraordinary directors, to be chosen annually on the first Tuesday of March, out of the members of the corporation, by a majority of the votes of those present and of the proxies of the absent.

Those first in office, named by the King, were Archibald Earl of Ilay, the governor ; Sir Hugh Dalrymple, Lord-President of the Court of Session, the deputy-governor ; Andrew Fletcher, one of the Senators of the College of Justice ; George Drummond, Lord Provost of Edinburgh ; Patrick Campbell, of Monzie ; Richard Dowdeswell ; John Philip ; James Paterson, one of the Commissaries of Edinburgh ; Hugh Sommerville, Writer to the Signet ; Patrick Crawfurd, and George Irving, of Newtown, Esqrs., the nine ordinary directors ; and Matthew Lant, Chief Baron of Exchequer ; James Erskine, one of the Senators of the College of Justice, Esq. ; Sir John Clerk, one of the Barons of Exchequer ; Hew Dalrymple, one of the Senators of the College of Justice ; George Baillie, of Jerviswood ; Charles Cathcart, Receiver-General ; George Ross, one of the Commissioners of Excise ; Charles Areskine, Solicitor-General, and James Nimmo, cashier of Excise, Esqrs., the nine extraordinary directors. The corporation was empowered at any general court to be held within two years after the date of this warrant to allow the proprietors who should not have subscribed any part or the whole of their stock in the *Equivalent Company*, on or before the 29th September, 1727, to subscribe such part or the whole into the stock of the Bank upon such terms as the majority of the court should appoint, and his Majesty became engaged, on the part of the Crown, to grant such further privileges as should at any time thereafter be devised for rendering this grant more effectual.

In consequence of this Royal warrant or signature, a charter was soon passed under the great seal, the stock subscribed to the new corporation being £111,347 19s. 10 5·12d. sterling, and the Bank was opened at Edinburgh—its first notes bearing date 8th December, 1727. The remainder of the public debt unsubscribed to the Bank was the separate stock of the *Equivalent Company*, and continued under the management of the Directors of that Company at their offices in London and Edinburgh.

By a second charter, dated November 1st, 1738 (12, Geo. II.), the Royal Bank obtained further privileges and powers, and its establishment as a Bank was rendered PERPETUAL, even though its capital should be redeemed by Parliament.

GLASGOW:
PRINTED BY DUNN AND WRIGHT,
WEST NILE STREET.